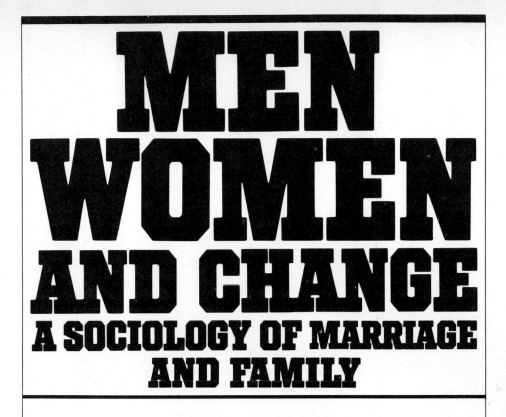

MEN WOMEN AND CHANGE
A SOCIOLOGY OF MARRIAGE AND FAMILY

LETHA SCANZONI

JOHN SCANZONI
Indiana University

McGRAW-HILL BOOK COMPANY

New York St. Louis San Francisco Auckland Düsseldorf
Johannesburg Kuala Lumpur London Mexico Montreal
New Delhi Panama Paris São Paulo Singapore
Sydney Tokyo Toronto

This book was set in Helvetica by Black Dot, Inc.
The editors were Robert A. Fry, Alison Meersschaert,
Lyle Linder, and David Dunham;
the designer was J. E. O'Connor;
the production supervisor was Sam Ratkewitch.
The photo editor was Cheryl Mehalik.
The drawings were done by Fred Haynes.
R. R. Donnelley & Sons Company was printer and binder.

Cover: Jean-Paul Darriau, "Adam and Eve." 1968 Indiana University.
Photograph by Ralph Veal.

MEN, WOMEN, AND CHANGE: A SOCIOLOGY OF MARRIAGE AND FAMILY

1 2 3 4 5 6 7 8 9 0 D O D O 7 9 8 7 6 5

Library of Congress Cataloging in Publication Data

Scanzoni, Letha.
Men, women, and change.

Bibliography: p.
Includes index.
1. Marriage. 2. Family. 3. Sex role.
4. Socialization. I. Scanzoni, John H., date,
joint author. II. Title.
HQ734.S3764 1976 301.42 75-25661
ISBN 0-07-055040-9

Picture Credits

Peter Arnold: James H. Karales, 363 Marcia Keegan, 222 Barbara Kirk, 381 Werner H. Müller, 403 Erika Stone, 50 **The Bettmann Archive, Inc:** 21, 57, 61 **Ken DeBlien:** 361 **Editorial Photocolor Archives:** Bruce Anspach, 121 Seth Beckerman, 232 Marion Bernstein, 34, 117 James Carroll, 304 Mark Chester, 14 Berne Greene, 311, 411 Joel Last, 201 Rudolph Robinson, 254 Andrew Sacks, 54 Arthur Sirdofsky, 1 Alan Winston, 139 **Feminist Art Journal:** 207 **Charles Gatewood:** 97, 158, 171 **Virginia Hamilton:** 42 **Library of Congress:** 26, 179, 215, 256 **Magnum:** Rene Burri, 72 Bruce Davidson, 370, 478 Elliot Erwitt, 105 Leonard Freed, 443 Charles Harbutt, 385 Burk Uzzle, 3 **Monkmeyer:** 129 Paul Conklin, 368 Mimi Forsyth, 199, 241, 300, 337, 350, 427, 454 Nancy Hays, 436, 441 A. Hinton, 431 Hugh Rogers, 103 **New York Public Library Picture Collection:** 108 **Temple University, Public Relations Department:** 291 **James R. Smith:** 319 **United Press International:** 29, 188

CONTENTS

PREFACE

All too often, students (and others) seem to have the impression that sociology is dull—a dry recitation of facts and numbers far removed from the concerns uppermost in their minds. In this book, we hope to correct that impression. Sociology is really a way of looking at the stuff of which everyday life is made: human beings in relationship with each other, human beings in conflict with each other. Sociology is right there where students are—asking questions and seeking understanding about such issues as gender roles, changing male-female relationships, alternatives to marriage, why persons are attracted to each other, why relationships break up, and much more.

Our hope is that *Men, Women, and Change* will appeal not only to students but to professionals as well. In recent years, a number of sociologists have pointed out that the sociology of marriage and family needs to become more integrated into the *mainstream* of sociology. Sometimes the family field has appeared to exist alongside the general field almost as a separate discipline instead of being on the cutting edge of the exciting happenings that are occurring in sociology as a whole. Our aim was to write a marriage and family textbook that would utilize the best in recent sociological theory, presented not in some abstract way but in terms of issues that students care about most. In this way, students are provided with analytical tools to help them think sociologically. Not only will they learn what various theories are, but hopefully they will grasp an understanding of how theories are built and how such theories help explain a wide range of human behavior and interaction.

The book is designed in such a way that students are likely to find themselves analyzing marriage-family patterns on their own, using information and insights gained from the course and explaining and interpreting social phenomena in terms of the conceptual frameworks presented. Building upon this interest, instructors may want to amplify and extend further the book's ideas through additional research and may wish to encourage students to undertake certain research projects as well. Since the book is not only a study of marriage and family as ends in themselves but a study of *sociology* as it applies to these areas, we've endeavored to do more than simply provide interesting data discovered through sociological research. We've tried to show how sociologists go about conducting their research in the first place. And we have pointed out the problems and advantages of various research methods, showing also how ideas are modified as new facts come to light, how concepts are measured, and so on. (The discussion of power in the family in Chapter 8 is an example of how we have tried to show something of what is involved in sociological investigation and theory building, what happens when sociologists disagree among themselves, and how further research and theory building are stimulated.)

Although this book is different from other textbooks in the field, it is not so idiosyncratic that it makes a radical break from what is familiar to most instructors. The essential materials, the most up-to-date statistics available at the time of writing, the definitions, the tables, the statistics—all these are included. But the organization is different. We felt that the book's convergence with the mainstream of modern sociological theory (social exchange, conflict, and process) called for an approach that would constantly take into account the unifying theme: men, women, and *change*. Thus, this textbook is arranged in a sense as an unfolding story, incorporating cross-national studies, historical material, demographic data, other research, and theory in a way that emphasizes the ongoing changes and exchanges occurring in male-female relationships—especially as female autonomy becomes more widespread.

CONTENTS AND ORGANIZATION

The information and theory presented is applicable to all families—not only to white middle-class families. Material on marriages and families which vary by socioeconomic status and race is interwoven throughout rather than being bunched in separate sections and treated in isolated fashion as has often been the custom. For example, while the book abounds with material on black families of both higher and lower socioeconomic status, there is no chapter on "the black family" as such. We believe that students are interested in learning about similarities and differences among racial and socioeconomic groupings with respect to each subject area treated: premarital sex, reproduction, divorce, and so on. As one illustration: Differences between blacks and whites in gender-role socialization are noted. Social and historical reasons for these differences are pointed out, with explanations and research evidence provided in our chapters on gender-role socialization, socialization of children for achievement, and in chapters on marital structure and process, among others. Or to take another example, there is no chapter on the kibbutz as such. Instead, gender-role socialization in the kibbutz is described in Chapter 2, attitudes and behavior with regard to sex before marriage in the kibbutz are discussed in Chapter 3, the kibbutz outlook on legitimacy and illegitimacy is presented in Chapter 5, and so on.

Similarly, certain subject areas are treated in terms of the overall theme of the book and are presented at points where their introduction seems most logical and likely to grab students' attention. Here, too, we found greater rationale for arranging the material this way than following the pattern that has been customary in the past. Rather than having a separate chapter on the kin, we discuss the functions of the kin in juxtaposition with communal living arrangements which serve as functional equivalents of the extended kin (Chapter 5). In addition, the part played by the kin in mate selection is discussed in Chapter 4.

Or to take another illustration, we felt that the subject of incest fitted best in the discussion of endogamy. Therefore, in the discussion on choosing a marriage partner (Chapter 4), the question is raised: If in-group marriage is so common, why is there a taboo about marrying within the group with the closest ties of all—one's family? In treating certain subjects in terms of the theme of men, women, and change, we have sometimes found that older explanations are no longer adequate and need modification. One example of this is found in Chapter 5 in the discussion on single parenthood, where we offer the "principle of status adequacy" as an updated approach replacing or modifying Malinowski's "principle of legitimacy."

In sum, although this book is organized differently from others in the family field, the instructor may be assured that essential information is included. Furthermore, students are provided not only with information in the form of facts but also with learning tools to aid them in their ongoing understanding of marriage and family in sociological perspective outside the classroom as well. Analytical tools include the theoretical approaches suggested throughout the book (especially exchange theory and conflict theory). Another tool is the extensive bibliography which will acquaint students with the latest research and enable them to pursue further those subject areas of greatest interest to them as individuals.

The book is current and gives attention to the numerous new patterns emerging (living together out of marriage, group marriage, "swinging," gay marriage, communes, singleness, voluntary childlessness, dual-career marriage, and so on), but at the same time it does not center around fads. It centers around the most significant and profound phenomenon touching upon marriage and family: the fact that female and male roles are being altered and becoming more interchangeable over time—a long-range pattern that cannot help but affect the relationships of all human beings to one another.

The book is also practical. We hope that it will equip students with the kind of accurate insight and understanding necessary to rational decision making and sound judgments, providing them with a solid basis for the kinds of choices they will be making in matters concerning themselves, their present and future families, and social policies to be supported, influenced, or opposed.

COLLEAGUESHIP

In Chapter 7, we describe the sense of colleagueship that tends to occur in equal-partner marriages and refer to a husband-wife meteorologist team who reported that their complementary skills meant that the two of them were able to create more than double the sum of their individual efforts. Perhaps the same could be said of our teamwork in writing this book. Letha Scanzoni is a professional writer who has pored over many hundreds of journal articles and books, sifting out and organizing research findings and explanations which tie in with the overall theme of the textbook. Believing that writing about sociology need not be stodgy, ponderous, and dull, she has sought to make the material come alive to students by writing in a clear and interesting style, while capturing attention and illuminating the subject material through the use of abundant stories, examples, and diagrams. Often, illustrations are used to show concepts in "real life" before labeling them. As a result, definitions, research findings, and theoretical explanations are more easily grasped, understood, and retained. (See, for example, Chapter 6 where introductory case studies are presented, followed by explanations of marital structure in four basic patterns. Or see Chapter 9 where case studies are tied into research findings to show how and why reproductive patterns vary by socioeconomic status, race, and religion.)

John Scanzoni is a sociologist who brings to the project not only many years of classroom experience in teaching the sociology of marriage and family but has also conducted many large-scale research studies bearing on the subject at hand. This book incorporates both his findings and theoretical explanations for such subjects as these (among others): the family as it relates to the economic-opportunity system, socialization for achievement, how fertility is related to gender-role norms, how expressive and instrumental duties and rights in the husband-wife relationship can hold the relationship together not as something static but in a constant and dynamic pattern of exchanges, how conflict occurs and how negotiations may be carried out, and a study of stable black families.

Working together as a team, we have tried to treat the subject in a way that is solidly scientific but at the same time in a way warmly human (because, after all, sociology is not only about numbers; it's about people).

CHANGE

Having summed up the two c's of content and colleagueship, it seems appropriate to reiterate a third point of importance to our readers. Repeatedly, we have emphasized the fact of change. Changes are occurring so rapidly in male-female roles and relationships that this book should be viewed more as a television set tuned to late-breaking news than as a photo album with frozen pictures of the way marriages and families "are." We have tried to show from the title onward that "things aren't the way they used to be" as women and men relate to each other and to the world at large. Even as we went to press, a phone call from the U.S. Bureau of the Census informed us of signs of change in marriage rates which, although too soon to label as the beginning of a trend, may indicate that the numbers of persons entering marriage are moving down from the highs reported in Chapter 5. (See notes 2 and 3 for that chapter.) After examining census figures for late 1974, demographer Paul Glick points out that "for the first time since soon after World War II the marriage total for a twelve-month period was significantly smaller (by 68,000) than it had been in the preceding year."*

However, because of the approach we've taken throughout this textbook, such incoming new information will only underscore our main thrust: Change is taking place, and the explanation has to do primarily with increasing autonomy among women. The book keeps pace with all that is happening because its emphasis is on this very dynamic—change, motion, and process. In other words, the systematic integration of material into an overall theoretical framework of rewards and costs, conflict, exchanges and interchanges means that the book should remain right on top of any new developments that take place, explaining them, organizing them, making sense of them, and generating additional predictions regarding the future.

Finally, keeping in mind our statements in Chapter 4 about the importance of gratitude in interpersonal exchanges, we would be remiss not to express our appreciation to those of the McGraw-Hill editorial staff who have so faithfully stood behind us in our efforts. Special thanks to Robert Fry, who suggested that we write this book; to Alison Meersschaert, who has not only been a fine editor encouraging us to do our best but has also proven to be a dear friend; and to Cheryl Mehalik for her tireless efforts in tracking down just the right photos to illustrate some of the main points of the text. Thanks, too, are due our friend Nancy Hardesty for her diligent work in preparing the index.

Also our appreciation goes out to those undergraduate and graduate students and colleagues with whom we have interacted over the years and whose questions, comments, challenges, and insights on male-female roles and relationships have stimulated and prodded our thinking and research all the more, making it possible for this book to come about.

Letha Scanzoni
John Scanzoni

*Paul C. Glick, *Some Recent Changes in American Families*, U.S. Bureau of the Census, *Current Population Reports*, Special Studies, Series P-23, No. 52, 1975.

FOR OUR SONS
STEVE
AND DAVE

UNIT 1
EXPLORING RELATIONSHIPS

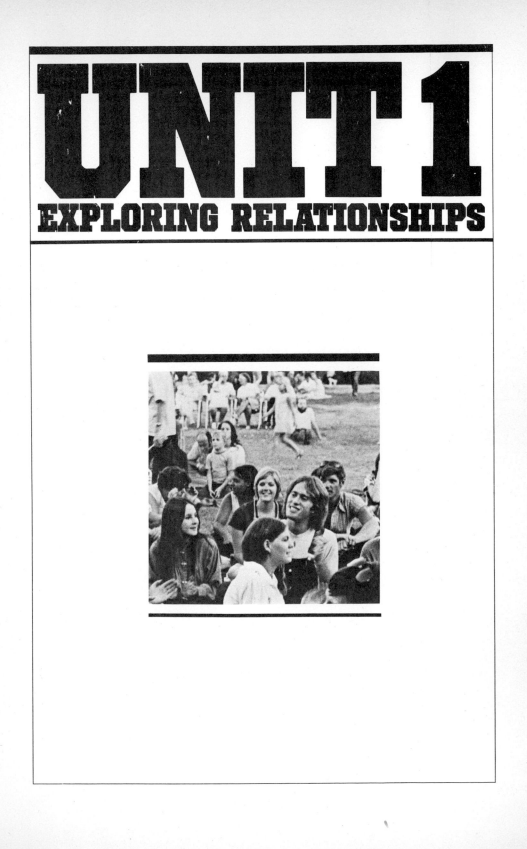

STUDYING MARRIAGE AND FAMILY

Love, sex, marriage, family, kinship, divorce. These words may mean different things to different people, but they are concepts that cannot be ignored in studying the human experience. For one thing, the family (in one form or another) represents the social arena where most people live out a large share of their lives. And beyond that, the family is interrelated with other institutions of society. It is not an entity separate and remote from the realms of politics, economics, education, and religion. If we want to understand social relationships and patterns and processes in society, we must take the family into account.

Familial isolationism is not feasible. People don't live one part of their lives in the world of work or politics and at the same time live a totally separate existence in their homes. What people do in business and industrial organizations has considerable impact on what they do in their families. For example, husbands who feel powerless in their occupations may try to compensate by exercising power over their wives and children. Wives who are employed have fewer children than wives who don't work outside the home. Persons whose education, income, and occupational status are higher behave differently in

3

their marriage and family relationships than do persons whose status is lower.

Conversely, the behavior of people in family relationships may have considerable impact on the larger society. Population growth or the lack of it may result in governmental decisions to influence families to change their reproductive behaviors in the desired direction. The family as the society's chief consumption unit affects government economic policies in such matters as saving and spending, taxes, and so on.

In short, the family is an important part of society. No society has ever existed without some kinds of social arrangements that may be labeled kinship or familial. And all evidence indicates that family patterns of some sort will continue to exist in modern and developing societies. Therefore, we need to give attention to the institution of the family, studying it just as carefully as is done in examining bureaucracies, political parties, urbanization, race relations, and all the other concerns of sociology today.

APPROACHING THE FAMILY SOCIOLOGICALLY

If the family is a subject calling for the attention of sociologists, it requires a treatment that is sociological. From the time of its origin in the nineteenth century, modern sociology has rested on the notion that the basic principles and methods of science could be applied to the study of human societies in much the same way that they are applied to the biological and physical sciences.

Science is a way of thinking, a way of discovering why things happen as they do, how things work, and what can be used for humanity's benefit as a result of such knowledge. By utilizing a sociological approach, we seek *systematic knowledge* of the social world, endeavoring to understand the what, why, and how of social arrangements, just as scientists in other fields seek systematic knowledge of the natural world.

However, many persons have the notion that to be scientific is to be both dull and impractical. They may also fear that such a study will dehumanize the family—that something which is warm and pulsating with life will be reduced to a cold corpse to be dissected or viewed as a machine with interacting parts but no human spirit. Such fears are groundless. There is nothing about the sociology of the family that requires a mechanistic approach in which the humane element is banished. Quite the contrary.

Though not intentionally, Finley Peter Dunne illustrated the point in one of his turn-of-the-century syndicated newspaper columns. Witty and often caustic social commentary was voiced through a likeable character called Mr. Dooley. Dooley was a bachelor who never hesitated to give his opinions on anything—including marriage. One day his friend Mr. Hennessy asked how this could be. How did he appear to know so much about marriage when he had never been married himself? Mr. Dooley answered that he knew about marriage "the way an astronomer knows about the stars."[1]

Although Dooley certainly did not pretend to be a sociologist, he seemed to have some notion of what we are talking about here. First, he sensed the value of standing back as an observer, watching, listening, and examining the institution of marriage. This did not strike him as strange or incongruous any more than it would be out of place for an astronomer to observe the stars in order to learn about them. Research, inquiry, close scrutiny, probing, contemplation—these were things the scientist did. Evidently Mr. Dooley felt he could approach the subject of marriage in somewhat the same way. Second, with his own simple folk wisdom, he was eager to share his observations and see them applied to life.

All this is by way of saying that a scientific approach need not crowd out the practical. The nineteenth-century founding fathers of sociology looked not only at the immense body of *knowledge* provided by the physical and natural sciences; they also saw the great *practical changes* these sciences were bringing about in everyday life. And they asked in essence, "Could not a 'science of society' have a similar function for the social concerns of mankind?"

This was the reasoning of men like Auguste Comte, known as the father of sociology. His native France was in constant political and economic turmoil. The Revolution had upset society to such an extent that it never fully recovered. Vast social problems plagued the country, and Comte was convinced that sociology could generate the knowledge to solve them. His passion was to conduct scientific investigations of human society and its institutions "to know in order to predict and predict in order to control."

His counterpart in England, Herbert Spencer, was of similar persuasion. The industrial revolution was sweeping England, and Spencer saw firsthand the human misery that Dickens describes in his novels—the slums, the workhouse system with its abuses of children, debtors' prisons, cruelties in asylums for the insane, the greed of businessmen, and injustices perpetrated on the poor. Like Comte, Spencer was motivated by humanitarian concerns. He believed that rational social change could result from sociology's contribution to the understanding of human society.

The founding fathers of American sociology shared the same conviction. Yet in the decades since, the balance between scientific research and social activism has not always been maintained. At times, sociologists have expressed most concern for basic research and little for practical application. At other times, the emphasis has been reversed. Currently, sociologists are trying hard to maintain the balance of research and application.

Keeping the history of sociology in mind, we make no apologies in pointing out that the study of the family should have practical value. Students of the sociology of marriage and family should be able to apply its information to their own lives and situations and to the larger society as well. The understanding gleaned from a sociological perspective can aid persons in making individual decisions, family-related decisions, and decisions on social policies.

Actually, the best science is often the most practical. In other words, the more we can understand and explain something, the better we can apply our knowledge and insights to obtain the objectives we think are important.

HOW THE SOCIOLOGIST STUDIES THE FAMILY

An important aspect of the scientific method is the measurement of concepts. A concept is a general idea or notion about something which is arrived at by mentally combining its various particulars into one overall picture. Education is a concept, as is fertility. When we begin using some measure, concepts are also known as *variables.* For example, counting the number of years in school is a way to measure education. Years in school could *vary* anywhere from zero to ten or twelve or more; thus we may call "number of years in school" (education) a variable. Or to take another example, the number of children born to a woman is a way to measure fertility. Again, that too could vary—anywhere from zero to six to twenty. Scientists are vitally interested in the *relationships* between variables. Therefore, they often make use of statistics to examine relationships. Here, for instance, it has been found that the more education a woman has, the fewer children she is likely to have. In other words, there is an *inverse relationship* between education and fertility. As education goes up, fertility goes down.

The procedure of selecting concepts, measuring them, and examining their interrelationships is part of theory building. We might think of theory as consisting of connected sets of verified relationships (such as the one just described) which generate hypotheses (or hunches) about relationships not yet tested. The scientist then tries to test these new hunches and subsequently either adds to or corrects the body of theory from which the hypotheses were drawn. Theory involves explanation; it is an effort to help us understand the *why* of things. For example, we might talk about a theory of fertility and try to explain why people have fewer or greater numbers of children. Or we might discuss a theory of divorce in an attempt to explain why some marriages hang together while others fall apart.

By seeking answers to "why" questions, we can better understand what marriage and family are all about. However, in doing theory building, we needn't be "theoretical" in the popular meaning of that term. In many people's minds, to be theoretical is to be far removed from the real world. A picture is conjured up of a thinker contentedly tucked away to muse in an ivory tower. Our attention to sociological theory will mean something quite different.

Drawing upon the very latest research in the areas related to the family, sociologists try to put together this vast store of information in ways that help explain the things that are happening. The understanding gleaned from this procedure often provides guidelines for predicting future trends. Such understanding may also aid us as individuals in exercising control over the various levels touching upon our lives (the personal, familial, and societal).

As part of their scientific study of the family, including theory building, sociologists have developed various *conceptual frameworks* or ways of viewing marriage and the family. Each of these perspectives brings together a particular cluster of interrelated ideas (concepts) about the family and shows how they fit together within the appropriate framework. It is as though several different family photos were cut up into jigsaw puzzles, with the parts of each whole placed in a separate box. Then each photo could be put back together again and placed in its own frame.

There are a number of such frameworks in the sociology of the family, but we shall confine ourselves to a few of the most important ones. In each frame, we shall see a different picture of the family because something different is emphasized in each one. But viewed together, we'll see that each has a unique contribution to make toward our overall understanding of what the family is and how it operates.

Developmental Framework

In the make-believe world of children's storybooks, people simply "get married and live happily ever after." However, we know that the wedding is not the end of the story but only the beginning. We can expect that the man and woman who have just recited their vows will go through various stages of life together. There will be the honeymoon period; the early months of learning to live together as husband and wife; the coming of the first child, then perhaps other children; the time when the children go to school; the period when the children depart for college or job, leaving the parents alone again as in the early period of marriage; the retirement years; and then the death of one spouse, leaving the other a widow or widower. We see a cycle in which a person has gone from being single, to being one of a pair, then one of a group, then again one of a pair or back to a single existence once again.

We might also think in terms of a related cycle in which one family leads to another. Children grow up under their parents' care in one *nuclear family* (the term sociologists use for the basic unit of father, mother, and children, since it forms the nucleus or core grouping of what is meant by the term *family*). This first nuclear family is a child's *family of orientation,* the family from which he or she originates. (The word *orientation* comes from a Latin root meaning "the east" or "sunrise.") Upon reaching adulthood, persons continue to remain members of their families of orientation; but they are also likely to marry and have children of their own. The new nuclear family thus formed is called by sociologists the *family of procreation.*

A focus on these cycles and the changes in relationships and patterns that occur to families over the passage of time is the distinguishing characteristic of the developmental framework. Sometimes the terms *life-cycle approach* or *family-career approach* are also used to describe this same perspective in the study of the family. But the key ideas of this framework, by whatever name, are always time and change.

Interactional Framework

Some sociologists zoom in for a close-up picture of the family, concentrating on the dynamics of interpersonal relationships between and among family members. How do the husband and wife, parents and children, brothers and sisters interact with one another? If *time* and *change* sum up the developmental framework, the key words for the interactional approach are *bonding* and *communication.*

By giving attention to bonding, the investigator asks: What is it that attracts certain people to each other, that brings and holds people together? How are relationships formed and maintained? Why do certain individuals marry and either stay together or dissolve the marriage? What sequence of events is associated with the loosening of family ties?

In seeking an understanding of communication processes, the sociologist asks: How do family members arrive at decisions? How do they determine ways to divide up tasks? How do they act and react toward one another? How do persons interpret one another's gestures, words, tone of voice; and what is their response? What kinds of role playing go on in families? How do families consciously and unconsciously train their children to be members of society (a process sociologists speak of as *socialization*)? How do family relationships affect a person's view of himself or herself?

While factors outside the family are not ignored entirely, the main focus of the interaction approach to the family is always on the internal dynamics within the family unit itself, in other words, on what is going on between and among the persons in relation to each other. Since human beings use symbols (such as words and gestures) in their interactions and communication, this framework or approach is sometimes called *symbolic interactionism.*

Structure-Functional Framework

Dictionaries define the word *system* as a combination of parts that work together to form a complex, unified whole. We're all familiar with terms like transportation system, heating system, system of government, reproductive system, and so on. In sociology, we hear about social systems. Fraternities and sororities are examples of social systems, as are churches, business corporations, and educational institutions.

What makes up a social system? It must have interdependent parts, with each part affecting the other parts as well as the whole in some way. It must have boundaries, so that it can be seen as a separate entity. It must have ways of adapting itself to problems that could disrupt and break down the system. And it must have a definite purpose and task-performing function that gives it a reason for being.

It isn't difficult to see how such characteristics describe systems in a general sense. For example, in the human body, we know that the respiratory system has *interdependent parts*—the nose, the trachea, bronchial tubes, lungs, the respiratory center in the brain, and so on. We know this system has certain *boundaries,* so that we can view it as separate from, say, the circulatory or excretory systems. Likewise, the respiratory system has *mechanisms for keeping the system in operation when disruptive elements are introduced.* We cough if something "goes down the wrong pipe." We can breathe through our mouths if a cold clogs the nasal passages. Last, the respiratory system certainly has a *reason for its existence.* Its task is to perform a most basic chemical activity necessary to all living things—oxidation. Without this process, no energy could be produced.

But how is it possible to view the *family* as a system? Sociologists who focus on a structure-functional framework borrow from the biological sciences and view the family as an organism with a structural arrangement of interdependent parts, each having a function to perform, just as is true in the human body. Structure functionalists also look at the family in relation to other parts of the larger social system (society)—for example, the occupational realm. This approach may be compared to the way a physiologist sees the functions of the respiratory system in relation to the nervous or circulatory systems and in relation to the body as a whole. Some of the functions the family performs in society are reproduction, socialization of children, producing and consuming goods and services, maintaining the physical and emotional well-being of its members, and performing specified tasks within the home and community.

As a social system, the family is characterized by persons in various positions (husband, wife, parent, child) whose behavior affects one another (interdependence of parts). The family can easily be distinguished from the school or church or labor union; thus, it fulfills the condition of having definite boundaries as a separate system. And when there are tensions and conflicts within the family which could cause a breakdown of the system, there are ways in which family members can adapt to each other or the situation in order to keep the system in equilibrium.

This equilibrium seeking is sometimes compared to *homeostasis* in the human body. Homeostasis is the term physiologists give to the "steady state" of the body's internal environment. For example, our bodies are equipped with mechanisms to maintain the same body temperature regardless of the heat or cold of the external environment. We shiver when we come out of a swimming pool on a cool day, and we sweat as we ride a bicycle on a hot summer day. We become thirsty so that we drink more water to replace fluids lost in perspiring. All of these are ways in which the body maintains dynamic equilibrium or homeostasis.

In the family system, a type of homeostasis takes place as family members make adjustments to one another in order to keep the system intact. Sociologists who emphasize the structure-functional approach have these things in mind when they use a specialized vocabulary about *system maintenance, equilibrium,* happenings that are either *functional* or *dysfunctional* for the system, and so on.

Conflict Theory (Engels-Marxist Framework)

In view of the revival of feminism in America, increasing attention is being paid to an approach to the family that has been largely neglected in the past. Persons active in the women's liberation movement have pointed out that society is patterned in such a way that men and women occupy different social positions both inside and outside the family. This situation can be viewed in Marxist terms in that it provides a picture of a class society with one class ruling and the other class serving in subordinate status.

Karl Marx and Friedrich Engels viewed history as a series of class struggles—conflicts between those who were exploited and those who exploited, the oppressed and the powerful. Engels charged that the family is a capitalist society's basic unit and is the chief source of female oppression. "Within the family," he wrote, "he [the husband] is the bourgeois and the wife represents the proletariat."[2]

The use of the Engels-Marxist approach, as applied to the sociology of the family, has nothing to do with Russian or Chinese communism or violent revolution. Rather, the stress is on the coercion of women and changes in current inequalities between the sexes. Besides examining conflict between men and women in general, this framework is also applied to conflicts within families—between husbands and wives, parents and children, and among members of the kin network.

Social Exchange Framework

Life is a series of exchanges. We give the store clerk a dollar, and the clerk gives us a desired item. We invite friends to dinner, and they invite us to attend a concert with them two weeks later. We do someone a favor, and that person does something special for us in return. Tit for tat. This for that. "Give and it shall be given unto you," to use the old biblical phrase.

However, when we give, it costs us something—time, energy, money or material goods, comfort and convenience, or perhaps something else, depending on the situation. And when we receive, someone else is experiencing cost, while we experience a reward or benefit. These basic notions, cost and reward, lie at the heart of a sociological approach known as *exchange theory.*

Like the interactional approach, exchange theory is concerned with a process that is going on between persons, something that is dynamic and on the move because of the constant interchanges taking place. Persons are interested in entering and continuing in relationships that are rewarding to them. At the same time, it wouldn't be fair to expect one person to do all the giving so that the other person would gain all the benefits. An exchange is involved. Each person makes investments in a relationship, but they are expected to pay off. In a relationship considered worth keeping up, persons expect that the rewards gained will equal or exceed the costs. In other words, the parties involved hope to make a profit or at least break even. These exchange processes are not necessarily conscious or deliberate; persons who are carrying them out may be only vaguely aware (or even totally unaware) of what is going on.

Sociologists may look at many areas related to the family in terms of exchange theory. For example, we can understand mate selection better by observing how persons are attracted to one another on the basis of the rewards each holds out to the other. Marital stability can also be studied in terms of the ongoing exchange of benefits taking place between the spouses. Similarly, separation and divorce may be viewed in terms of a breakdown in the exchange process and an unjust distribution of rewards. One spouse may feel that he or she is putting into the relationship much more than the other spouse is, so that a net loss is perceived. In some cases, the costs incurred may be thought of as penalties rather than as investments. One spouse might belittle, nag, or humiliate the other spouse to the point that the relationship is not only unrewarding but actually punishing. The costs might exceed the benefits to such an extent that one spouse considers the relationship a total loss and decides to get out of it by filing for divorce.

The above illustrations are only a few of the ways sociologists utilize the ideas of social exchange in attempting to understand patterns related to the family. We shall be looking at these matters in much greater detail throughout this book.

Getting the Total Picture

A sociological study of marriage and family patterns includes giving attention to what has been and is taking place in other cultures as well as in our own. Such a study also includes an examination of family forms in history and an awareness of future trends.

In approaching the family sociologically, we might want to think of our study as a journey. Perhaps the analogy of an automobile ride is appropriate. Careful drivers pay attention to the road ahead, but at the same time they don't ignore what is behind. They use the rearview mirror frequently. To get the total scene, they move their eyes constantly in order to be alert to oncoming traffic, passing cars, side roads, merging lanes, and other activity along the way that demands their awareness. Concurrently, they are interested in what is going on inside the cars they drive as their passengers interact with them and with each other.

An examination of various issues related to marriage and the family may be compared to these simultaneous occurrences of an auto trip. We'll want to look at issues such as gender roles, sex behavior, mate selection, alternate family forms, and so on by approaching subjects in a variety of ways. There will be glances into the rearview mirror of history to see what the past can teach us. Attempts will be made to get the total picture by letting our eyes sweep across the landscape and the side roads, so that we can understand what is known about a particular subject currently in the United States and also what is known in cross-cultural perspective. At the same time, much attention will be given to understanding the dynamics of interpersonal relationships (the interaction, communication, and conflict of the "passengers"). In other words, what exchange processes are going on? How do persons act and react toward one another in decisions relating to the particular issue under discussion?

A sociological understanding of the family also includes gazing at the road ahead by using past, present, and cross-national data to ask, "What set of alternative predictions can we make about this phenomenon? What are its possible futures?" Through the use of these several perspectives (*historical, national* [current United States], *cross cultural,* and *projected*), it is possible to gain a very thorough understanding of what is presently known about various issues relating to marriage and family and also an awareness of areas in which further research and theory building are needed.

Some modern sociologists think in terms of a computer rather than an automobile ride. The computer analogy also suggests movement, action, process. In a computer system, something is going on constantly as various parts of the system affect other parts and all together have an effect on the whole. Input, feedback, and interchanges suggest a picture of continual motion while at the same time not ignoring the place of structure. Sociologists who think of the family in this way blend various approaches, frameworks, and perspectives, and focus on the notions of process and movement. Terms such as *modern systems theory* or *process strategy* describe this outlook on marital and family patterns.[3]

SUMMARY

We have seen that sociologists study marriage and family forms as important parts of society, both affecting and being affected by other areas of social life such as government and politics, education, the economy, and religion. A sociological approach to the family includes an effort to seek systematic knowledge of the social world by utilizing the principles of the scientific method—asking questions and seeking verified answers through research. On the basis of this research, theories are formed which, in turn, stimulate new directions for research.

In studying the family, sociologists may work within one of several frameworks or they may seek to combine them. The developmental framework or life-cycle approach emphasizes time and change as families pass through various stages of life. The interactional framework is concerned with the interactions of family members as they relate to one another in processes of bonding and communication. The structure-functional framework emphasizes order and equilibrium in the family and society as a whole; this framework uses the analogy of the human body with all its interdependent parts having specific functions to perform in order to maintain the steady-state condition of good health. Conflict theory or the Engels-Marxist framework views the family as a class society in miniature, with one class (men) ruling and the other class (women) oppressed. As women resist, there is conflict between the sexes. The family, as viewed in this framework, is a potential battleground in which the exploiters and the exploited clash with one another. The fifth framework we examined was the social exchange framework in which family relationships are viewed in terms of costs and rewards. An exchange that is considered "profitable" may attract persons to one another and cause them to remain in a relationship, whereas an "unprofitable" exchange may have just the opposite results.

Sociologists attempt to get a total picture by looking not only upon the current happenings within their own nations but on other nations as well. In addition, attention is given to history and to emerging trends which seem to suggest what might happen in the future. Modern systems theory, a blending of approaches, with attention to the constant movement, feedback, and process taking place in human relationships is increasingly being utilized in the sociological study of the family. The workings of the computer provide a model of the complex interworkings and interchanges taking place in the family as well as between the family and the larger society.

NOTES

1 Dunne, 1969, p. 22.
2 Engels, 1884.
3 Aldous, 1970; Broderick, 1971; Hill, 1971; Straus, 1973; Buckley, 1967, 1968.

2
BECOMING MEN AND WOMEN

A baby boy survived a highway crash in which both his parents died. The baby's aunt, an unmarried middle-aged woman, took the child to rear. This was the theme of a strange and eerie television drama that unwittingly presented a lesson in *role socialization* (how people are trained to play a particular part in society).

The infant's aunt was obsessed with an intense hatred of men. Unable to bear the thought that this tiny baby would grow to be a noisy, irksome boy, she decided to rear him as a girl. She moved to a remote area where her situation would not be known, gave the boy a girl's name, kept him isolated and virtually housebound, and dressed him in frilly, feminine clothes. The child contentedly played with dolls and in other ways acted as girls are expected to act, never having the slightest idea that he was a male. Only after several years when an outsider happened upon the scene was the shocking secret discovered.

Farfetched? Perhaps. Yet John Money and Anke Ehrhardt, authorities on psychohormonal research, report the case of a baby boy who through a tragic accident lost his penis. The event occurred as circumcision was being performed by electrocautery in which the electrical current was too powerful. The distraught parents were eventually directed to the Johns Hopkins Hospital and School of Medicine where they were counseled to rear the child as a girl, which is being done quite successfully.[1] Surgery and hormonal treatment were also utilized, as is also done in cases of hermaphroditism.

Hermaphroditism is a congenital condition in which the sexual anatomy is not clearly differentiated. Thus the baby is "sexually unfinished" and not clearly distinguishable as either totally male or totally female. The word *hermaphrodite* is a composite of the names of the Greek god and goddess Hermes and Aphrodite. In cases such as the circumcision accident or where there is evidence of hermaphroditism, Money and Ehrhardt emphasize that what really matters in gender identity is the "sex of assignment." They point out that a certain hermaphrodite may in actuality be female insofar as chromosomal and hormonal makeup are concerned but can be reared as either a boy or girl, depending upon the sex *assigned* to the child by others.[2] Gender identity is more dependent upon social learning than upon genetic makeup. That a child was born with XX chromosomes (designating a female) and female sex glands (ovaries) or was born with an XY chromosomal makeup (male) and male sex glands (testes) is less important in such a case of hermaphroditism than is the "sex of rearing." "To use the Pygmalion allegory," say Money and Ehrhardt, "one may begin with the same clay and fashion a god or a goddess."[3]

Of course, for most people, the biological sexual makeup (chromosome pattern, sex glands, and internal and external sex organs) and the sex of assignment are one and the same. A male child is reared as a boy, a female child as a girl.

But what does it mean to be reared as a boy or as a girl? What does it mean to become "masculine" or "feminine"? Why are girls told, "Act like a lady," while boys are encouraged to grow up to be "a man's man"? How do persons learn to fulfill such instructions? These are the questions we want to explore in this chapter.

SEX ROLES

Freud believed that "anatomy determines destiny." Others have agreed that a person born male has an innate predisposition to act in a certain way—to be "masculine." He is expected to be strong, dominant, aggressive, competitive, rational, able to be in charge, a leader. Likewise, many people believe that to be born female is to be "feminine"—gentle, quiet, passive, romantic, dependent, nurturant, loving, understanding, a good follower. In such reasoning, it is simply assumed that once you know a person's sex you can predict how that person will behave.

However, as the opening stories suggest, the physiological differences between the sexes do not in themselves determine the dissimilarities in thinking and behavior. *Learning* makes the difference. This does not mean, of course, that biological factors play no part at all in male-female distinctions. For example, recent research has provided a certain amount of evidence of the part male and female hormones play as the fetus develops in the uterus, including some differing effects of these hormones on the fetal brain.[4] However, Money and Ehrhardt make it clear that the influence of prenatal hormones should not be overestimated, since "much that pertains to human gender-identity differentiation remains to be accomplished after birth, not in a developmental vacuum, so to speak, but like language, in interaction with the social environment."[5]

The social environment includes the significant people in a child's life—parents, siblings, other relatives, friends, teachers, and so on. It also includes the wider world to which the child is exposed through television, movies, books, magazines, radio, records, and the like. Through all of these means, children learn the sex-typed patterns they are expected to follow. Girls learn that they are expected to act one way and boys another. Often the expected behavior overlaps and in certain areas is similar for both sexes; nevertheless, very basic distinctions are expected to be maintained both in childhood and in the adult years, with each sex having a separate role to play.

By the term *role,* sociologists generally mean the totality of norms (behavior expectations) associated with a social position. In a sense, we may compare the idea to the theater where an actor takes a certain part and then speaks and conducts himself according to the script. If he is playing the role of Macbeth, he is expected to act like Macbeth and not like MacDuff.

A sex role (or gender role) is a sum of expected behaviors attached to the differing social positions of male and female. These expected behaviors are related to both temperaments and tasks assigned to each sex. However, the personality characteristics considered appropriate for each sex and the division of labor that is considered desirable are by no means matters of universal agreement. Sex roles vary considerably among different cultures.

Take the matter of temperament, for example. In Margaret Mead's widely cited anthropological study of tribes in New Guinea, she found that one group considered a gentle temperament the ideal for both sexes. But in another tribe, an aggressive temperament was the ideal for both sexes. In yet another tribe, the cultural ideal was that women should have an aggressive, dominating temperament, while the men were expected to be characterized by sensitivity, emotionality, and dependence.[6] In the familiar pattern of our own culture, we have the reverse of this third tribe.

Besides such variations in ideal *temperaments* encouraged for each sex, there are also variations in the *tasks* which are considered "men's work" or "women's work." Such variations (as illustrated by Table 2-A) again emphasize the point that human behavioral patterns do not spring from natural, biological traits or "instincts" of some sort which cause men to "act like men" and women to "act like women." Rather, gender differences are matters of cultural conditioning or socialization. We learn to be masculine or feminine according

TABLE 2-A CROSS-CULTURAL DATA FROM 224 SOCIETIES ON DIVISION OF LABOR BY SEX

Activity	Number of Societies in Which Activity is Performed by				
	Men Always	Men Usually	Either Sex	Women Usually	Women Always
Subsistence Activities					
Pursuit of sea mammals	34	1	0	0	0
Hunting	166	13	0	0	0
Trapping small animals	128	13	4	1	2
Herding	38	8	4	0	5
Fishing	98	34	19	3	4
Clearing land for agriculture	73	22	17	5	13
Dairy operations	17	4	3	1	13
Preparing and planting soil	31	23	33	20	37
Erecting and dismantling shelter	14	2	5	6	22
Tending fowl and small animals	21	4	8	1	39
Tending and harvesting crops	10	15	35	39	44
Gathering shellfish	9	4	8	7	25
Making and tending fires	18	6	25	22	62
Bearing burdens	12	6	35	20	57
Preparing drinks and narcotics	20	1	13	8	57
Gathering fruits, berries, nuts	12	3	15	13	63
Gathering fuel	22	1	10	19	89
Preservation of meat and fish	8	2	10	14	74
Gatherings herbs, roots, seeds	8	1	11	7	74
Cooking	5	1	9	28	158
Carrying water	7	0	5	7	119
Grinding grain	2	4	5	13	114
Manufacture of Objects					
Metalworking	78	0	0	0	0
Weapon making	121	1	0	0	0
Boatbuilding	91	4	4	0	1
Manufacture of musical instruments	45	2	0	0	1
Work in wood and bark	113	9	5	1	1
Work in stone	68	3	2	0	2
Work in bone, horn, shell	67	4	3	0	3
Manufacture of ceremonial objects	37	1	13	0	1
House building	86	32	25	3	14
Net making	44	6	4	2	11
Manufacture of ornaments	24	3	40	6	18
Manufacture of leather products	29	3	9	3	32
Hide preparation	31	2	4	4	49
Manufacture of nontextile fabrics	14	0	9	2	32
Manufacture of thread and cordage	23	2	11	10	73
Basket making	25	3	10	6	82
Mat making	16	2	6	4	61
Weaving	19	2	2	6	67
Pottery making	13	2	6	8	77
Manufacture and repair of clothing	12	3	8	9	95

SOURCE: D'Andrade, 1966, pp. 177–178.

to our particular society's ideas about what the respective sex roles should be.

Many persons today are saying that traditional notions of masculinity and femininity have hindered both sexes from living up to their full *human* potential.[7] At the same time, other persons are frightened at the prospect of "unisex" tendencies that seem to be emerging and are calling for rigidly segregated sex roles to make sure that traditional gender distinctions remain, one reason being to avoid confusing children as to their gender identity. Professors Money and Ehrhardt make some points that are helpful in this regard. They indicate that while it is true that a growing child needs to recognize that there are two distinguishable sexes, the distinctiveness of the sexes is not a matter of "how great or small the amount of overlap in appearance and behavior culturally prescribed or permitted in any place or period of history. . . . Nature herself supplies the basic irreducible elements of sex difference which no culture can eradicate, at least not on a large scale. . . ." These basic elements of sex difference include the differing sexual organs and the fact that women menstruate, give birth, and produce milk in their breasts for their infants, while men cannot do these things but can produce sperm and impregnate. Secondary sexual characteristics in adulthood, such as differences in voice pitch or male facial hair, are also reminders that the bodies of the two sexes differ. Money and Ehrhardt write:

> Provided that a child grows up to know that sex differences are primarily defined by the reproductive capacity of the sex organs, and to have a positive feeling of pride in his or her own genitalia and their ultimate reproductive use, then it does not much matter whether various child-care, domestic, and vocational activities are or are not interchangeable between mother and father. It does not even matter if mother is a bus driver and daddy a cook. . . .[8]

However, throughout history, societies have tended to add to the basic sexual distinctions just described and have insisted upon other kinds of differences between the sexes. Thus little boys and little girls have been treated differently and taught differently in order to assure their growing up to fill the societal roles assigned men and women respectively. Perhaps we can understand this better if we first take a backwards look to find out what it meant to grow up female or male in the era prior to the twentieth century.

HISTORICAL PERSPECTIVE ON SEX-ROLE SOCIALIZATION

Both in England and America, it was held that there were divinely ordained separate spheres for the sexes. Church, school, and family—these chief agents of a child's socialization—worked together to transmit the notion that boys should grow up to be the doers, thinkers, and movers in the world at large. Girls, on the other hand, were expected to grow up to be wives and mothers. Any involvement in the world outside the home would be indirect rather than direct. The young wife of the nineteenth century was instructed "to be distinguished in the world, not so much in her own name as by her influence on her husband and family, and through them on others."[9]

For young men, the advice was altogether different. "Young man, dig for success!" came the admonition from pulpits and pens. "Great men have always been known as men of action in some line of service," a medical book pointed out in a special chapter for boys. The author challenged boys to work hard, remembering that "God makes the trees; man must build the house. God supplies the timber; men must construct the ship. God buries iron in the earth; man must dig it, smelt it, and fashion it."[10] For a boy, life was a call to conquest and adventure. To become a true man, a boy must develop abilities for rational decision making, control, and mastery.

Contrary attitudes were drummed into girls—ideas deliberately intended to limit horizons and restrict aspirations. "There is, indeed, something unfeminine in independence. It is contrary to nature, and therefore offends," wrote Mrs. John Sandford in one of a spate of "female culture" books designed to show eighteenth and nineteenth century girls what womanhood should be.[11] Girls were told they were intended by nature to be "vines" clinging to the "sturdy oak" (the male sex). Independence and assertiveness in a woman was said not only to mean a "loss of femininity" but also allegedly caused mental breakdowns. Worst of all, the warnings and admonitions emphasized, such qualities could ruin a woman's chances for marriage and make her a failure in life.

Some persons questioned this dichotomy of roles. They were convinced that differences in the sexes stemmed from *training* rather than from something innate. Indeed, Plato had raised the same issue four centuries before the birth of Christ, pointing out that no occupation belongs exclusively to either sex, because "natural gifts are to be found here and there in both creatures alike." Therefore, said Plato, "if we are to set women to the same tasks as men, we must teach them the same things."[12]

In 1790, a sea captain's daughter, under the pen name "Constantia," wrote with passion and conviction as she criticized the diverse socialization of males and females. If men possessed superior judgment, she asked, "may we not trace its source in the difference of education and continued advantages?" Constantia pleaded for equality of education for girls, pointing out that educated women would be less apt to fill up their time with useless trifles and would be better companions upon marriage. Furthermore, she argued (evidently with a view to those who thought education for women was contrary to the divine will), a knowledge of astronomy, geography, and philosophy could improve a woman's piety and make her better appreciate the Creator's works.[13]

However, despite the pleadings of Constantia and a few others, higher education for women would not open up for nearly three-quarters of a century.

Even then, girls would be warned that college would "unsex them" and that college women would be incapable of safe and sound motherhood because "sustained brain activity" would drain away energies nature intended for maternity.[14] All the learning a woman needed, said some speakers and writers, was enough chemistry to keep the pot boiling and enough geography to find the rooms of her house. Education for boys was an altogether different matter, because they needed training for vocations.

Sex-Role Socialization in Colonial America

The Puritans were deeply concerned that children of both sexes be able to read the Scriptures for themselves. Thus, both boys and girls studied reading and, in addition, the other basics, writing and arithmetic. The girls often went to school in the summer time when there was room for them because the boys were working in the fields. Beyond the elementary level, however, educational opportunities for girls were limited. Boys, in contrast, could go on to the secondary level (grammar school) and even to college—if their parents could afford it.

Small boys and girls dressed identically in long robes, but at age six, there was a change into adult dress which had symbolic significance for children. Henceforth, according to John Demos' history of childhood in the Plymouth Colony, "the young boy appeared as a miniature of his father, and the young girl as a miniature of her mother. . . . Children learned the behavior appropriate to their sex and station by sharing in the activities of their parents."[15]

Chores were assigned according to sex. Boys helped their fathers with planting, harvesting, building barns, repairing fences, and so on. Girls learned housekeeping from their mothers and were kept busy with such tasks as cooking, spinning, cleaning, sewing, and candlemaking. Childhood was considered a time of preparation for adulthood, and the two most important aspects of adult life for both sexes were occupation and marriage. For women, these were considered to be one and the same. Sometimes girls served as apprentices in other homes to further develop their domestic skills.

For a boy, the matter was more complex. He could not train for his life's work until he knew what that work would be. Whereas his sisters had but one option open to them (homemaking), a boy knew that he had the grave responsibility of choosing from among many possibilities. Furthermore, with the guidance of his parents, he must make the choice at a relatively young age, because apprenticeship for most trades meant a seven-year training period. In order to be able to earn his living at age twenty-one, a boy couldn't delay his decision past his fourteenth birthday. If he made such a decision carelessly, it was only with extreme difficulty that he could change his mind and begin another type of work later.

For these reasons alone, the matter of vocational choice was of serious concern to young boys. But in addition, the Puritans saw great religious

In colonial America, young girls appeared as miniatures of their mothers in both dress and tasks.

significance in such a choice. The home, church, and school drilled into a boy that God had for him a "particular calling," or in other words, a special job which God expected him to find and fulfill. In Puritan thought, according to historian Edmund Morgan, "God called a man to a particular occupation by giving him talents and inclination for it."[16]

Interestingly, the limitation of girls' aspirations to that of housewifery did not mean that according to Puritan theology girls didn't receive "particular callings." Rather, the particular calling of *each* woman was assumed to be the same for *all* women. And evidently the same reasoning applied to the "talents and inclination" divinely bestowed as a means of guiding persons to their life's work. It was simply taken for granted that all women were designed for domestic tasks. Talents bestowed on boys, however, might lead them into such careers as farmers, cobblers, metalsmiths, booksellers, shopkeepers, clergymen, teachers, physicians, and so on.

Sex-Role Socialization in the Nineteenth Century

The idea that women were designed for only one kind of life's work, while men were suited to a wide variety of choices was still prevalent in 1855 when Lucy

Stone spoke up for equal rights for women. Alluding to Wendell Phillips' statement that "the best and greatest thing one is capable of doing" is that person's "sphere," Lucy Stone argued, "Leave women, then, to find their sphere. And do not tell us before we are born even, that our province is to cook dinners, darn stockings, and sew on buttons."[17]

Many persons of both sexes had trouble accepting such thinking. Nineteenth-century socialization patterns laid great stress on the expectation that boys and girls would grow up having different characteristics and different tasks in life. In the home, children watched parents fulfilling traditional sex roles. These observations were reinforced as the church lifted biblical admonitions from first-century cultural settings and taught that the traditional division of labor between the sexes (men in the world, women in the home) was "God's will."

And education played a great part in seeing to it that boys and girls were socialized differently and prepared for different adult roles. In the first place, education beyond the elementary level was for a long time open only to persons of the male sex. And in the second place, when education *was* provided for young women, it was expected to serve a different purpose than in the case of the men.

In the first half of the nineteenth century, private secondary schools opened for girls. Called "seminaries," they were intended to prepare women to be better wives and mothers, along with training young women for teaching school in case they worked for a few years before marriage. In 1824, the first public high school opened for girls; but college was still for men only.

Around the middle of the century, things began to change. Elmira Female College and Vassar opened with the intention of providing women with a college education somewhat comparable to that offered by male institutions. Oberlin went a step further, demonstrating that women could not only be educated *like* men but also *beside* men. Several other schools, including some state universities in the West and Midwest, followed Oberlin's example in becoming coeducational.

The trend upset many people. "Identical education of the two sexes is a crime before God and humanity," wrote one physician, who predicted women's constitutions would be so weakened by college life that their future child bearing would be imperiled.[18] Women's education must be kept "feminine." If education caused a woman to become discontent with her lot as housewife, then something was wrong—not with woman's lot but with her education. Dr. Alcott, in his 1837 advice book for women, expresses shock and dismay upon observing educated young women who "regard home—the kitchen especially—as the grave of all true freedom and enjoyment."[19]

Alcott and others felt that education must have particular goals. It should (1) make women better companions for their educated husbands, (2) equip them to mold the characters of their children, and (3) provide them with practical knowledge for household management. For example, Dr. Alcott recommended that women study chemistry. Why? Because it could improve their cooking and help them prevent food poisoning. Furthermore, he said, a knowledge of the chemical composition of the air would make women more diligent about ventilating and cleaning the rooms of the house.

Besides formal education, children were expected to learn gender-appropriate behavior through the role models they were encouraged to imitate. Mothers and fathers were of course the first role models children observed. We have already seen how both dress and chores were patterned after these parental examples in Colonial New England. In addition to their fathers, boys also looked up to the clergy and other esteemed male adults. Girls had their attention directed toward the loving, submissive wives of these men and toward certain biblical examples.

The contrast in role models held out to the two sexes is very obvious in writings of the 1800s. An 1899 book entitled *Helps for Ambitious Boys* includes pictures and short biographical sketches of men whom boys were encouraged to take as examples worth following. Some of them were the Spanish-American war hero Adm. George Dewey; the clergyman, Henry Ward Beecher; orator and abolitionist, Wendell Phillips; inventor Thomas A. Edison; Washington Roebling, the civil engineer who built the Brooklyn Bridge; Maj. Gen. Nelson A. Miles, who forced the surrender of Geronimo; and multimillionaire businessman Henry B. Plant.

Girls were encouraged to pattern their lives after very different role models. When girls did highly esteem nontraditional women, they were criticized for admiring "that which was not fitting to their sex." An 1859 book warns its young female readers not to admire Joan of Arc. Why not? Because "her masculine attitude casts . . . a shadow upon her more womanly qualities. . . . Her position, as a military leader and combatant, unsexes her before your feelings." In a similar vein, the writer goes on to ask, "Who can love the masculine energy of that really strong-minded woman, Queen Elizabeth?" He encourages his female readers to look up to the example of Queen Victoria instead, because in her "the woman is more prominent than the queen."[20]

Whereas the role models boys were encouraged to follow were persons known for their accomplishments, with little concern for their family relationships (unless they were scandalous!), the role models girls were expected to follow were known chiefly for their family relationships, with little concern for their accomplishments. For men, the emphasis was on doing; for women, the emphasis was on being. Role models held up to girls were women who devoted their energies to their homes and families. One writer was appalled when certain women were honored "not so much because they are excellent wives, mothers, daughters or sisters, as because they are excellent poets, moralists, or mathematicians." "These characters, however valuable to the world they may be, would be more valuable if more devoted to their appropriate sphere," he wrote.

Why should such women be complimented while "thousands in useful domestic life" were forgotten? Couldn't this be "why so many young females of the present day have such aversion to the kitchen, and gravely tell us they would almost as soon die as have their hands in dish water?"[21]

It is clear that the role models and education offered to girls and boys were intended to socialize them in such a way that each sex would display the appropriate characteristics and perform the appropriate duties expected in adult life. Boys would one day be breadwinners and heads of families. To fulfill this function, they must cultivate courage, strength, drive, ambition, leadership capabilities, and so on.

Girls, on the other hand, must cultivate sweetness, gentleness, submissiveness, religiosity, compassion, and dependency. A women's role would include at least six functions. She must be a ministering angel, a beautiful ornament, the preserver of morality, a submissive wife, a diligent housekeeper, and a trainer of children.[22]

Such were the familiar stereotypes. Not that all persons of either sex fulfilled them, but these were the cultural *ideals* of manhood and womanhood that males and females were expected to follow.

Purpose of Sex-Role Socialization

Gender-role socialization had as its purpose the preparation of persons for their adult functioning in relation to the economic-opportunity system—that network of means and ends associated with achievement and all the benefits of success.

White males were socialized for direct participation in the opportunity system. They learned the importance of hard work, competitiveness, and strivings toward achievement in order to gain the system's rewards. White females were socialized for indirect participation in the opportunity system; their rewards would be channeled to them through their husbands. Therefore women were expected to develop those nurturant qualities which would provide their husbands with a home atmosphere that would be (in the words of one nineteenth-century writer) "a blessed retreat from the turmoil of business" and which would encourage men to great achievements.

Not all persons had equal access to the economic-opportunity system, either directly or indirectly. And not all persons fitted the familiar sex-role stereotypes. Numerous men found to their disappointment that despite the rags-to-riches theme of the Horatio Alger stories, hard work did not always bring wealth and success. Educational opportunities were blocked for many. Likewise, we must keep in mind the women who worked side by side with their men in carving out the wilderness, running family farms, and laboring for long hard hours in factories. They hardly fulfilled the stereotype of the weak, passive, dependent, genteel "beautiful ornament" that was held up in the female-advice books.

History of Sex-Role Socialization among Blacks

Black persons, even when socialized to *want* the American Dream and to aspire toward it, were hindered constantly by the obstacles the dominant white society placed in their way. The door to opportunity might appear open, but as soon as blacks ran up to it, they would find it slammed in their faces. Black men and black women learned that together they had to try to take the rewards of the opportunity system in the best way they could. They had to develop strength, perseverance, and resiliency in order to survive. Cut off from the economic opportunities open to whites, black males found that socialization for mastery, achievement, and competition could count for nothing if one were judged on the basis of skin color rather than on ability.

The black male's self-concept was dealt heavy blows both under slavery and later during the period of Jim Crow (when segregation was legal and encouraged). He was told both directly and indirectly that he was inferior because he was black. However, at the same time, he was a man. And according to societal gender-role norms, one proved his manhood through achievement. A man must show his worthiness by providing his family with a good living. Yet when the black man tried to make socioeconomic gains, he found that the American Dream did not include him. The white-controlled occupational and educational systems blocked his chances for the very thing societal norms demanded of males—achievement in the economic-opportunity structure. For black men, there had first been the degradation of slavery; later there was the degradation of being given only the lowest-paid, unskilled service jobs or no jobs at all. For some black males in the agricultural South, sharecropping opportunities opened up, and in these cases, husbands, wives, and children worked together on farms under former slaveowners.

When black males couldn't find work, their families had to depend on the efforts of their wives, sometimes being forced to rely on incomes that meant bare subsistence.[23] Under slavery, black females had learned from earliest childhood that being female did not mean being docile, weak, passive, and dependent. Black women worked right alongside men—cutting wood, building fences, driving oxcarts, and working in the fields in the blazing heat for exhausting hours. Gender made no difference.

Sojourner Truth, a tall black woman with no formal education who traveled around speaking and singing for the antislavery cause, underscored the point that women are capable of doing the same kinds of work that men can do. At the second National Woman's Suffrage Convention held in Akron, Ohio, in 1852, there had been an invasion of learned clergymen who monopolized the

"I have plowed and planted and gathered into barns and no man could head me! And ain't I a woman?"—Sojourner Truth.

convention with endless discourses about woman's supposed "inferior nature" and "proper place in life." After one speaker had stressed that woman was innately helpless and dependent, Sojourner Truth rose and dramatically laid to rest such myths by referring to her days as a slave. It took strength to bear the lash. It took strength not to give up and let one's spirit be crushed and broken as one's children were taken away and sold. And it took strength to do the work required of her. What was all this talk about woman's need to be treated as a fragile object? Nobody ever helped *her* into carriages or lifted *her* over mud puddles, Sojourner Truth declared. Nobody ever gave *her* the best place. "And ain't I a woman?" she asked. Telling the audience to look at her upheld arm, she continued: "I have plowed and planted and gathered into barns, and no man could head me! And ain't I a woman?"[24] Sojourner Truth provided the delegates with a living example of the way black women refused to be confined to the sex-role stereotypes held up by white society. Circumstances had forced them to be active, assertive, and independent in spirit.

After slavery had ended, black women frequently found it easier than black men did to find employment. Why this is so is not certain, although it may be that whites looked upon black females as being somehow less threatening than black males. And black women, already accustomed to an activist role from slavery days, were not opposed to the working-wife role. They took advantage of their access to the opportunity system in order to help their families.

However, in saying black women had access to the economic structure, we must keep in mind that it was a very limited access. Racial discrimination was felt by women and men alike. Black women usually found employment in domestic and service occupations, working as maids, cooks, laundresses, seamstresses, hairdressers, parlor maids, and day laborers. These were occupations where there was little competition from whites. Factories were an altogether different matter, although there were certain notable exceptions where blacks were welcomed and given other than the lowest jobs. But in general, there were only limited opportunities in manufacturing for blacks of either sex in the South and the North from the time the Civil War ended until nearly the end of the century.[25]

In sum, the socialization patterns of the nineteenth century were designed to prepare white men to be achievers and white women to be the wives and mothers who would stand behind the men. Socialization patterns for blacks were in some ways similar and in some ways different from those of whites. Black males learned the dominant society's values with regard to achievement and success but found that they were blocked from economic opportunities in adulthood. Young black women learned that having been born female need not mean that they had to fulfill the gender-role stereotypes held up by the dominant society. By force of circumstances, black women learned that they could participate directly in the economic system and could strive to bring its rewards to their families.

SEX-ROLE SOCIALIZATION TODAY

Studies have shown that in most societies, whether preliterate or modern, boys are more likely than girls to be socialized to be active, aggressive, dominant, self-reliant, achievement-oriented, and controlled in the area of emotional and affectionate expression. Conversely, girls are more likely than boys to be socialized to be nonaggressive, emotionally expressive, affectionate, nurturant, and concerned about interpersonal relationships.[26] Sociologists use the term *instrumental* to describe the first set of characteristics (those generally associated with boys' socialization) and the term *expressive* to describe the second set of characteristics (those generally associated with girls' socialization). Instrumental behaviors are those related to getting a job done. They are behaviors concerned with work, accomplishment, mastery, achievement. Expressive behaviors have to do with human emotions and the expressions of these feelings, relating to other people, and so on. Instrumental behavior is task-oriented; expressive behavior is people-oriented.

The economic-opportunity system bestows its rewards not on those who perform expressively but on those who perform instrumentally. Autonomy, activity, creativity, individualism, drive, ambition, leadership abilities, and the like are not male qualities per se. There is nothing intrinsically "masculine" about them at all. Rather, they are simply the kinds of norms and behaviors that are essential in order to receive the rewards of the economic system. Such qualities are tools—required instruments for achievement in a modern society that offers its prizes by way of the occupational route. The word *instrumental* is derived from a Latin word meaning "equipment." An emphasis on the instrumental dimension of life, then, refers to being equipped to obtain the benefits held out by society today. Money, of course, is the most tangible and obvious of these benefits; but there are other rewards that are equally and often even more important—a sense of fulfillment, self-worth, satisfaction, enhanced self-esteem, prestige, and power.

Anthropological studies indicate that the control of economic capital in various societies is related to who does the "productive" work (as contrasted with the "care and maintenance" work). The kinds of productive work deemed important and essential may vary from culture to culture, and division of labor by sex may also vary, as we saw in Table 2-A. However, although there are noteworthy exceptions, the predominant pattern cross-culturally is one in which males do the productive work, building up and controlling the economic capital of a particular society. Therefore, males are socialized in ways that will help them develop self-reliance and achievement strivings, qualities necessary for instrumental behaviors in adult life. Females are socialized in ways that will elicit expressive behavior in adulthood, because women are expected to devote their lives to loving service for their families and others. During girlhood, such qualities as nurturance, obedience, and responsibility are stressed.[27]

But why is this sex-role socialization pattern so widespread? And how did it come about in the first place? Anthropologist Roy D'Andrade refers to the part played by physical differences but hastens to add that "most anthropological explanations of regularities in sex differences are not based on biological differences alone, but on the complex interactions of biological differences with environmental and technological factors."[28] Psychologist Jeanne Humphrey Block, referring to studies of nonliterate cultures, offers an explanation of how these factors interrelate. She writes:

> These differential socialization emphases seem to derive, in these primitive societies, from the different biological and socioeconomic functions the sexes must assume in their adult roles. Thus, when hunting or conquest is required for societal survival, the task naturally and functionally falls upon the male because of his intrinsically superior physical strength. . . . Childbearing is biologically assigned to women, and because, in marginally surviving societies, men must be out foraging for food, child rearing, with its requirement of continuous responsibility, is assigned to women.[29]

A woman who achieves is not "playing like a man."

Block points out that sex-role socialization designed to fit males and females for separate adult roles based upon biological differences might make sense in early and marginal cultures. But she wonders to what extent the socialization patterns of the past should control current patterns of socialization in complex, technological, affluent societies such as our own where "physical strength is no longer especially important and where procreation is under some control."

As we have seen, the rewards of a modern economic-opportunity system are achieved through instrumental-type behaviors. And in a technological society, instrumentality need not be related to physical strength. It should not be surprising, then, if persons who only incidentally happen to be females are aspiring to attain society's benefits by equipping themselves with the necessary means toward that end. Gender has nothing to do with those means (instrumental-type behaviors) in a modern society. Tennis champion Billie Jean King has sometimes been contrasted with other women athletes by assertions that "she plays tennis like a man." The statement is incorrect. A woman who achieves is not "playing like a man." Rather, she is adopting whatever legitimate means are necessary to win or succeed. That is not related to a person's sex.

Sex-role Socialization and Race

Just as utilizing the means to succeed is not a matter of gender, neither is it a matter of race. Earlier, we saw that sex-role differentiation was not maintained among slaves on the plantation. Following emancipation, black women were forced into employment because of the determination of whites to keep black men out of the labor force. One of the unintended results of this pattern was that black children learned to view sex roles as being less rigidly distinct than is true in the socialization of white children.[30] Young black females are likely to be more active, autonomous, and independent than are young white females with the same amount of education. And black males, accustomed to the economic role black women have played, are more likely than white men to hold sex-role norms that prescribe egalitarian behaviors.[31]

Sometimes people think of and speak of society's benefits and the means to attain them as being "white," just as they are sometimes alleged to be "male." Thus, we hear of hard work, aspiration, drive, ambition, competitiveness, and so on as being qualities of white middle-class males who are following the rainbow of "white male values," hoping to end their quest at the golden pot of success. However, again it must be stressed: the benefits of modern society and the means to them are neither white nor male; they possess neither race nor gender in themselves. Rather, they are intrinsic elements in the social system of any modern society. The evidence shows that black parents value both the means and ends, and they socialize their children to adopt both.[32] Furthermore, their daughters are socialized toward instrumental-type behaviors to a greater degree than is true of white females and thus are more likely to be characterized by strength, drive, independence, and mastery. This pattern of sex-role socialization grew up not so much because blacks had some kind of "natural" inclination toward feminist ideology, but rather because white society, by discriminating against black men and limiting their chances to achieve in the economic system, forced black women into assuming a provider role. As a result of this development, the notion of employment for black women as a right or option has become institutionalized; it is accepted and taken for granted among blacks. Socialization practices take this option into account. Black women have behind them a tradition of going after the rewards of the economic system in a direct manner instead of assuming that such rewards can only be mediated through husbands.

Sex-Role Socialization and Social Status

The theme song of television's popular "All in the Family" program contains a line of nostalgic longing for a time when sex roles were clearly distinct: "Girls were girls and men were men. . . . Those were the days!" Archie Bunker, like most blue-collar persons, is troubled by any blurring of sexual distinctions. He prefers to see males and females looking differently, acting differently, and occupying different roles in life. In contrast, persons at higher status levels tend to be less rigid about gender-based differences in temperament or activities. Studies show that social status has a great deal to do with how parents view sex-role norms and how they socialize their children to fulfill such behavioral expectations.[33]

Social stratification is an important concept to sociologists because the class position of an individual or family bears upon how that person or family will think and act. Just as a geologist examines the various layers (or *strata*) of rock that make up a cliff, aware that each layer will generally consist of a particular kind of sedimentary matter in contrast to that of another layer, so the sociologist notes the characteristics of one stratum of society in contrast to those of another stratum. The idea of speaking of people as though they were rock deposits (one layer above, another layer beneath, and so on) may unnerve some persons, because it seems to imply that certain groups of people are somehow "better" than others. Such notions are troubling in view of Western democratic ideals with their emphasis on the worth and dignity of all people and the goals of equal rights and equal opportunities for all. However, we need to keep in mind that when sociologists speak of higher and lower social statuses, they are not judging the white-collar corporation executive to be "better" as a person than the blue-collar factory worker. What they are saying is that the executive holds a "better" position in relation to the economic-opportunity system in a society that values individuals according to where they fit into that system. Persons who through their achievements hold the better positions in the economic structure are the ones who receive its choice rewards: money, prestige, and power. In speaking of social status, then, we are referring to one's placement and participation within the opportunity system.

But how can we know where someone fits in relation to the economic-opportunity structure? The United States Census Bureau measures social status by looking at three indicators—education, occupation, and income. And since occupation and income depend to a large extent upon education, many sociologists consider the level of education itself to be a good indicator of social status. Keeping this in mind and returning to the subject of sex-role socialization, we may state some of our research findings as follows: The less education parents have, the more likely they are to encourage sex-typed behaviors on the part of their children. Males in the family are treated one way, and females are treated in a very different manner. In other words, the lower the social status, the greater the gender differentiation. Or to state the converse: the higher the social status, the less the gender differentiation. Parents with more education tend to minimize differences between the way they train their sons and the way they train their daughters. They do not encourage the rigid sex typing that is common in families where the parents have lower levels of education.

Education seems to be the key in explaining the variation in sex-role norms associated with social status. Education involves questioning traditional values and ways of doing things, exposing oneself to new ideas, gaining new knowledge, and bringing about change. Persons with limited education are less likely to raise questions about traditional values and customs and tend to be less open to change. As we have seen, traditional sex-role norms probably grew up and persisted on the basis of a sexual division of labor which assigned males to the provider role (because of their strength and greater freedom to travel) and females to the homemaker role (because of their part in reproduction as childbearers and all the restrictions associated with pregnancy, giving birth, and child care). This pattern became institutionalized and came to be thought of as the "natural order of things."

However, education calls into question the notion that traditional sex-role stereotypes are "nature's plan" or "God's will." Norwegian social scientist Harriet Holter suggests that one reason for the association between egalitarian sex-role norms and a high level of education may lie in the fact that "advanced education entails the indoctrination of democratic and humanistic values, and the examination of traditional beliefs that are not supported by scientific evidence." She goes on to speak of other differences in value orientation between persons who are more educated and those who have less education, pointing out that higher education tends to deemphasize those criteria (such as physical strength in men and emotional qualities in women) which have been used to support traditional sex-typed behaviors. At the same time, education "favors qualities, such as intellectual capacities, which are more equally bestowed on men and women."[34]

Persons of limited education are not carrying on what sociologist Melvin Kohn calls "historically derived cultural traditions" just for the sake of keeping the past alive. Rather, says Kohn, the realistic conditions under which working-class persons live today explains why their historically derived class culture persists.[35] The structural conditions that affect the thinking and behavior of persons lower on the social-status ladder are at least twofold: their relative lack of education and the restrictive natures of their jobs, which permit little creative thought and independent judgment or decision making. Kohn makes the point that how persons look at life—their "views of social reality" (which would include sex-role norms)—are profoundly affected by systematically differentiated conditions of life related to social class. Kohn writes: "The essence of higher class position is the expectation that one's decisions and actions can be consequential; the essence of lower class position is the belief that one is at the mercy of forces and people beyond one's control, often, beyond one's understanding."[36]

Because of these differing expectations (related to both educational and job factors), persons of higher social status are likely to be characterized by *self-direction,* and persons of lower social status are likely to be characterized by *conformity.* In other words, according to Kohn's studies, persons in a higher class position learn to act on the basis of their own judgment. And, says Kohn, "this is possible only if the actual conditions of life allow some freedom of action, some reason to feel in control of fate." But persons at lower status levels experience "conditions of life that allow little freedom of action, little reason to feel in control of fate." Therefore, persons lower on the social-status hierarchy tend to follow the dictates of authority, emphasizing obedience and a concern with outward consequences rather than with internal processes. They tend to be less trustful of others and intolerant of nonconformity.

Conformity, rigidity, and intolerance of ambiguity (an inability to accept matters that are not clear-cut and seem uncertain and left open to question) are all characteristics of what has come to be known as the "authoritarian personality."[37] Another characteristic of authoritarianism is a rigid segregation of female and male roles.[38] In the words of behavioral scientists Daniel Levinson and Phyllis Huffman, "Masculinity and femininity are conceived of as opposites, with no overlapping traits."[39]

The authoritarian personality is much more common among lower socio-economic groups.[40] Sociologist Donald McKinley expresses the view that authoritarianism, with its emphasis on controlling and being controlled and its tendency toward strictly separated sex roles, is so much more prevalent among persons of lower social status not because of internal personality predisposi-tions but again occurs as a response to a person's position in the social structure. Such persons, having failed to attain a high *achieved* status through self-direction lay emphasis on *ascribed* status (a status assigned by others so that one fits into one's "proper" place in life). Sex roles are ascribed roles. According to McKinley, a lower-status individual's feelings "of anxious vulnera-bility" seem to be "soothed by rigidly defined social relationships."[41] In view of these factors, it is of interest to note that studies have demonstrated that, at lower status levels, marriages are characterized by more rigidly segregated roles for husbands and wives,[42] parents are likely to stress obedience to outward controls rather than autonomy and thinking for oneself,[43] and peer-group influence among adolescents is in the direction of traditional sex-role norms and stereotyped gender behavior.[44]

Earlier, we spoke of instrumental (task-oriented) behaviors and expressive (person-oriented) behaviors and pointed out that instrumentality has usually been emphasized in the socialization of boys and expressiveness in the socialization of girls. However, neither instrumentality nor expressiveness is "masculine" or "feminine" in itself. What is of interest at this point is the variation according to social class in the relative emphasis on either instrumen-tality or expressiveness in the socialization of boys and girls. Middle-class parents are interested in seeing their children develop along *both* instrumental and expressive lines to a greater degree than is true of blue-collar parents. Working-class parents, on the other hand, are more interested in seeing their sons develop instrumental qualities and their daughters expressive qualities.

Both middle-class and working-class parents socialize their sons to be active, aggressive, competitive, independent, adventuresome, and physically strong and courageous. But while instrumentality in boys is similarly stressed at both higher and lower social-status levels, there is a difference in the degree of expressiveness emphasized. Middle-class parents tend to strive for greater nurturance and tenderness (expressiveness) in their sons than do parents at lower status levels.[45] Sociologist Janet Saltzman Chafetz also points out some differences in what instrumentality means among boys at different status levels, most notable of which is a deemphasis on and even denigration of school

Parents encourage traditionally "feminine" behaviors—nurturance, tenderness—in girls. But boys are supposed to
be aggressive and tough.

success among adolescent boys at lower positions of social status.[46] In
contrast, as emphasized in homes where the parents have more education,
instrumentality involves a much greater stress on mastery, competency, aspirations for academic excellence, and working toward achievement within higher-
status occupations.

When it comes to daughters, middle-class parents encourage traditionally
"feminine" behaviors such as nurturance, support, and tenderness; but at the
same time, they want their daughters to develop a high degree of independence
and assertiveness. In other words, middle-class parents desire that their
daughters be somewhat instrumental as well as expressive. But working-class
parents and parents at lower status levels tend to consider instrumental
behaviors as "masculine" and do not encourage such behaviors in their
daughters. The lower the education of parents, the more likely they are to

socialize their girls to rank high on the expressive side of life, giving little attention to the instrumental side. Therefore, females at lower status levels are likely to be more passive and subordinate than are females at higher status levels.

Sex-Role Socialization and Religion

Just as race and social status make a difference in patterns of sex-role socialization, religion also has a part to play. Persons associated with religious groups which emphasize traditional sex roles as being divinely ordained, for example, may be expected to consider sex-typed behaviors and a high degree of gender differentiation desirable. Conversely, persons who have no religious preference or who are associated with groups that do not lay stress on sexual distinctiveness in temperament or division of labor may be expected to lean away from traditional sex-role norms and be more open to egalitarianism.

Holter refers to the belief of some religious groups that "the Bible prescribes a differentiation of religious tasks between men and women" and suggests that, despite secularization trends in Scandinavia, religious beliefs have to some extent accounted for continued traditional attitudes toward sex-role norms. She also refers to studies showing an "association between the tendency to be religious and the advocacy of traditional sex role norms" among samples of Catholics in the United States and among girls in modern Israel.[47] Sociologists Charles Westoff and Raymond Potvin have reported on the influence of religious ideology on a sample of American college women.[48] They found that among Mormons and Catholics, more than among women from other religious groups, marriage and motherhood were considered to be sacred callings. A woman's destiny and divine mission in life was to be a wife and mother. Women affiliated with groups that held such beliefs were found to want more children than women influenced by other religious ideologies or who had no religious preference. Westoff and Potvin suggest that the ideal role defined for women in Catholicism and Mormonism influences the sex-role norms of its members not only through the belief systems of these groups but also through their social systems. "There is considerable evidence that for Mormons and Catholics religious affiliation does in fact serve as a primary source of informal social relations," write Westoff and Potvin. In other words, the church body at the local level serves almost as a quasi-kin group with a certain amount of sway over those who belong to it.

Of course, Mormons and Catholics are not the only groups which may be influenced by religious ideology and church-connected social relationships in which traditional sex-role norms are emphasized. And not *all* persons within these groups may be expected to hold traditional views on gender differentiated traits and tasks. Similarly, although there is evidence that Protestants and Jews are less likely than Catholics and Mormons to view motherhood as a sacred calling and a woman's primary destiny, not *every* Protestant or Jew can be said to have a more "secular" view of woman's role. Sociologists study trends and characteristics that describe groups as a whole in order to get the large picture. Patterns, not individual persons, are the focus of research. But there may be deviations from the overall pattern. Certain individuals among Protestants and Jews may hold sex-role norms that are quite traditional and they may adhere to a religious ideology which emphasizes gender-typed behavior. This may be true not only of certain individuals but may also be true of some subgroups within Protestantism and Judaism—for example, certain conservative Protestant groups and the Orthodox branch of Judaism, both of which emphasize differentiated roles for the sexes.

The main point to keep in mind is that religion does make a difference when it comes to sex-role norms. Both personal religious beliefs and affiliation with particular groups are related to views on gender roles. This became clear in our own research among a random regional sample of 3,100 married women and men. Included were two questions designed to test the degree to which respondents attached a quality of sacredness to marital and family roles: (1) Do you believe that the institution of marriage and family was established by God? (2) Do you feel that being a mother is a special calling from God? We found that persons who held a more sacred view of the motherhood role tended to hold a more traditional view of the wife role, or in other words, more traditional sex-role norms.

In measuring the wife role, we asked questions designed to find out whether there was an emphasis on a wife's individualistic interests as being equal to those of her husband and children, or whether there was an emphasis on a wife's submerging her own interests in the belief that a woman's most important task in life should be taking care of her family and finding her greatest satisfaction through husband and children. Also included was a question designed to ascertain respondents' agreement or disagreement with beliefs about gender-linked differences in mental and emotional makeup and in household division of labor. Persons who believed that God instituted marriage and who believed that motherhood is a divine calling also tended to believe that a woman's greatest responsibility in life should be her family and that women were naturally suited to certain tasks by virtue of their emotional, mental, and biological makeup.[49]

Moving from beliefs to affiliation, we found that Catholics hold more strongly to a sacred legitimation of the mother role than do non-Catholics. But there was little difference between the Catholic group of respondents and the non-Catholic group when it came to the effect their religious beliefs had on attitudes toward sex-role norms for wives. Persons in both groups had a more traditional orientation toward the wife role if they believed strongly in the religious legitimation of motherhood.

Where the difference showed up *between* religious groups was in attitudes toward the husband role. Catholics were less willing than non-Catholics for men's behavior to change. In assessing beliefs generally associated with a patriarchal ideology with its rigid role specialization, we found that Catholics were more likely to consider the husband's individualistic interests and endeavors to be predominant in importance and the wife's interests to be secondary. To a greater extent than non-Catholics, Catholics felt a husband had the right to be bothered if the wife's job sometimes required her to be away overnight or if the wife earned more money than the husband. They did not feel that the husband should be as willing as the wife to stay home from work to care for a sick child, or that the husband should be willing to forgo the experience of having a large family so that his wife could pursue career interests. And there was less willingness among Catholics than among non-Catholics to agree with the idea that men should be open to working for women supervisors. In sum, traditional sex-role norms which authorize male interests and power on the basis of an ascribed position due to gender are held to a greater degree by Catholics than by non-Catholics (Protestants, Jews, and all others, including those with no religious preference).[50]

Sex-Role Socialization Cross-Nationally

Even though race, social status, and religion make a difference in how children are socialized with regard to gender-role norms, the *overall* pattern remains much the same: boys are trained to develop certain traits that will steer them toward independence, achievement, and a fulfilling of the provider role in marriage; and girls are trained to develop traits that will fit them for a more dependent and nurturant role in adulthood. As we have seen, this pattern is a matter of relative emphasis; and there are great variations among different social groupings in the United States as to what is considered appropriate sex-role behavior. But what about other countries?

Swedish researcher Rita Liljeström published in 1966 the results of a study of books for adolescents in Sweden. She found that boys were presented in the books as aggressive and objective, while girls were presented as passive and emotional. In boys' books, women were mentioned only rarely and then usually in negative terms.[51] The same findings emerged in a study of literature for children and adolescents in Norway. Stereotyped images and traditional roles were emphasized throughout the large sample of books, with boys presented as "active, initiating, and ready to explore the world outside the family, whereas the girls are passive, sensitive to emotions, devoted to the family, and inclined to stay home."[52]

In a study of award-winning books for preschoolers published during the years from 1967 to 1970 in the United States, similar findings came to light. For example, there were 261 pictures of males and only 23 of females in the books; and overwhelmingly, boys were described as active, assertive, and in control of their environments, while girls were described as submissive and controlled by the people and circumstances around them.[53] Books may play an important part in the socialization process, and it is of interest at this point to see the similar results of the Scandinavian and American studies. However, what is especially significant is that, in Sweden at least, the achievement of the equality of the sexes is *official government policy.*[54] Yet, in spite of the removal of all legal arrangements that might encourage sex discrimination, girls and boys continue to be exposed to traditional socialization patterns. Such patterns of inequality have not ceased to remain dominant throughout Western societies, including for example West Germany, where the constitution declares men and women to have equal rights but where studies of adolescents have shown sex-role patterns to remain traditional.[55]

At the same time, it is clear that all Western societies have demonstrated remarkable changes with regard to sex-role socialization. There has been a discernible movement away from the very rigid, constricting historical patterns described earlier in the chapter. However, although changes in legislation such as those cited (or the American Equal Rights Amendment [ERA]) may have some effect on sex-role socialization, law and policy changes are not sufficient by themselves. As long as parents and other adults are convinced that traditional sex-role socialization is rewarding both to them and to their children, they will continue to train sons and daughters in traditional patterns of masculinity and femininity. Only as they come to view less traditional sex roles more positively (seeing value in a woman's desire to achieve, for example, or accepting sensitivity and tenderness in a man) will parents alter their child-socialization patterns accordingly.

Because Marx and Engels deplored the social system in which men dominated women, the socialist and communist countries represent a special case of trying to extol and propagandize the benefits of sex-role equality.[56] For example, observers from East Germany conclude that "[sex role] emancipation over there is much further advanced than in West Germany."[57] Both in East Germany and in the Soviet Union, women are much more actively involved in occupational achievements than in the United States.[58] Many American women work for "extra money" or "to help out" or because there is nothing better to do; but in communist countries there is an attitude of *commitment.* Women in these countries are more likely to approach the occupational world as do most men both there and in the United States—with serious purpose, viewing achievement in work as a major life activity. Again they furnish young girls and boys with very different kinds of role models than has been true of many working women in the United States.

Nevertheless, studies show that Soviet women remain responsible for home activities even when they are heavily involved in occupational achievement.[59] Thus, the role models to which children in East European countries are exposed maintain certain aspects of role differentiation or specialization. Children continue to learn that, whatever else women do, they are still mainly responsible for domestic tasks. Some leaders of the Communist Party are concerned about this in view of Lenin's chidings. "So few men—even among the proletariat—realize how much effort and trouble they could save women, even quite do away with, if they were to lend a hand in 'women's work,'" he wrote. "But no. . . . They want their peace and comfort."[60] A journal of the Communist Party, U.S.A., has called attention to the problem in several articles, suggesting collective child-care arrangements and the socialization of housework as possible solutions. In the meantime, writes Alva Buxenbaum, "we have had to take into account the fact that the double burden of house and job (or in the case of housewives with young children, being tied down to the household) is a major obstacle to their consistent participation in activity. . . . A sharing of household chores by conscious Communist husbands and wives can free Communist Women for political activity."[61]

The Israeli kibbutz represents the most dramatic attempt anywhere to experiment with alternative life-styles and variations in family forms. These agricultural communes were based on Engels' notion that all social differences between the sexes should be done away with.

How can this be done? Rather elaborate steps are taken in the kibbutz to assure that children may learn undifferentiated sex roles from their earliest days. The process begins at birth by housing the infant with other infants in a crèche or "baby-house" separate from the parents. From birth to nine months, infants interact with their biological parents progressively less. At nine months, contacts are restricted to two or three hours daily after the parents complete their workday, with longer periods permitted on holidays. Until children are eighteen years old, virtually all their socialization is transmitted by a *metapelet* (the caretaker, usually female, of each group of from five to thirteen children), as well as by schoolteachers and peers.

While there are many contacts between parents and children during this period, parents reinforce what the children learn from their other role models. The entire system is designed to eliminate traditional sex-role images among kibbutz children, and it appears to work relatively well. When kibbutz and American children of ten years of age were compared, it was found that the kibbutz children were much less aware of sex differences. Also, unlike the American child who tends to identify with the same-sex parent, a child in the kibbutz identifies with persons of *both* sexes. Psychologist Albert Rabin reports no negative clinical or psychological effects of these kinds of sex-role learning patterns which are so different from the sex-role socialization found in other societies. Children, removed from parental control at infancy, do not appear to be harmed. They are learning primarily to be *persons* rather than to be "masculine" or "feminine."[62]

Mainland China is of particular interest in this regard, since up to the time of the 1949 Revolution, traditional male-female sex roles were deeply imbedded within the rigid, authoritarian norms of Confucianism. The Chinese Communist Party has determined to accomplish the same blurring of sex-role differences that has occurred in the kibbutzim.[63] However, changing socialization practices that involve over 800 million people is vastly more complex than in a situation involving only several hundred. But the task is not so overwhelming in China as one might think. The great majority of China's people live in the countryside. Most are organized into relatively small collective farms, somewhat like the kibbutzim. It is through these kinds of social systems that the Chinese government is working to alter socialization patterns in order that children will grow up not as "masculine men" or "feminine women" but as Chinese people.

A comparison of China with Japan is fascinating, because Japan too has been heavily influenced by Confucian thought regarding sex-role differentiation. Social scientists have pointed out that the Japanese emphasize achievement as much as do persons in Western society. Through various rewards and punishments, sons learn "a direct identification with the male familial role as the major goal of life."[64] Japanese girls learn just as strongly that they too must "achieve." Achieve what? Success in wifehood and motherhood! Much more than in contemporary America, girls in Japan learn that their highest mission in life is to nurture, support, and develop husband and children so that the husband and children, in turn, can behave in ways appropriate for them. Confucian teachings idealize the "listening wife," and as anthropologists George De Vos and Hiroshi Wagatsuma note, the current "implicit role expectations . . . do not differ much from the past."[65] But they also hint that things might be changing. Among those under thirty, there appears to be some slight movement away from the long-standing rigidities of traditional sex-role socialization.

The history and culture of Latin America is obviously quite different from that of Japan. The patterns of family structure and the importance attached to achievement are also vastly different. Yet, sex-role socialization is quite similar in the two settings.[66] In Latin America, tiny females learn during toilet training that they must be more modest than boys. Likewise, girls are more restrained in their temper tantrums than are boys. Bolivian boys wear only a short shirt until age seven, but girls must be fully clothed.

Throughout most Latin countries, young girls are channeled into household chores. Boys are channeled into manual skills, plus hunting, fishing, and horseback riding. During play, even small children are separated according to sex. They are also generally separated in their elementary school classes, and almost no high schools are coeducational.

Clearly, socialization patterns both in the Latin home and school contribute toward the continuation of the machismo system in which the man proves to the world and to himself that he is a "man's man" or "he-man"—virile, powerful, stereotypically "masculine." Often he demonstrates his masculinity at the expense of the passive, gentle, sweet, kind, subordinate, long-suffering woman—that is, one who is stereotypically "feminine."

SEX-ROLE SOCIALIZATION AND THEORY

Why do parents almost universally socialize their boys and girls into different gender roles? And how do parents go about their task of socialization? The various theoretical frameworks described in Chapter 1 are useful at this point because they show the ways sociologists have attempted to explain what goes on in the process of becoming men and women.

Symbolic-Interactional Approach

The symbolic-interactional approach helps us see something of the "how" of sex-role socialization. For example, social psychologist Ralph Turner refers to the way parents distinguish between baby boys and baby girls in the way they dress them, play with them, and generally treat them.[67] Parents speak to baby girls in a different tone of voice than that used for baby boys. As children grow older, sex-typed activities are encouraged through "task bonds" or being united with someone in a common project. By working in home chores with the parent of the same sex, a child learns what is considered appropriate sex-role behavior and is thereby linked to that parent with a special sense of comradeship. Because it is common for fathers to work outside the home, father-son collaboration is often more difficult than mother-daughter collaboration. Sometimes fathers and sons build strong task bonds through working together in crafts, landscaping, or traditional male jobs around the house, such as mowing, painting, or fixing things. However, boys learn that "the work that is crucial to the male identity is usually removed from the home."

Turner points out that deep comradeship between a mother and daughter is most likely to occur if "the daughter forms a somewhat traditional self-conception. The common interest in domestic activities permits a collaboration that can continue even into adulthood, so long as the daughter's self-conception does not move toward a repudiation of traditional feminine activity." Mothers who socialize their daughters through teaching them to do traditional "women's work" (sewing, decorating, cooking, making beds, doing dishes, and so on) are essentially working to build a friendship based on shared interests that will last throughout life, a friendship that mothers anticipate as being very rewarding. Thus, mothers express joy and admiration at evidence of a girl's budding "femininity"; but at the same time, according to Turner, there is a fear that the girl might still retain some of her earlier tomboy tendencies. Thus, "even as she compliments her daughter, it is difficult not to offer a suggestion concerning how she might be still more of a young woman."

With a boy, parents and teachers alike emphasize that he must have *masculine* self-respect if he is to have any self-respect at all. Turner refers to the ways a boy's masculinity is challenged if he shows signs of weakness or a desire for sympathy. Peers, too, learn that the interruptions caused by pleas for compassion are quickly quieted by dismissing such pleas as feminine. A boy

Mothers who socialize their daughters through teaching them to do traditional "women's work" are essentially working to build a friendship based on shared interests.

who is hurt during a rough game or who cries out for a fight to stop will likely hear stinging taunts. "Ah, he's a sissy. He's acting like a girl. He can't take it." Schools have disciplined boys by threatening to make them sit with the girls. Organized boys' groups, say Turner, "are regularly regarded as places where boys, and frequently the men who assist, can get away from the dominance of women, worrying less about cleanliness, intellectual and cultural matters, and gentleness." Camp leaders tell boys that they will "make men" of them and undo the damage of mothers who spoil them and make them weak.

Since society has established certain patterns of interaction based on sex roles and the behaviors associated with them, Turner points out, "it is easier for parents, peers, and others to act toward the child when his behavior is clear and sex-appropriate." Thus, at home, school, and in play groups, persons tend to interact with one another so that sex-typing is reinforced. This brings us to the functionalist approach to the question.

Structure-Functional Approach

A functional approach deals with the "why" of sex-role socialization by calling attention to the matter of *order* or equilibrium.[68] Present gender-role socialization patterns, which stress definite sex-role differences, pave the way for sex-role specialization later on in marriage. Division of labor can thus be clearly defined and complementary. Boys who learn to be brave, active, competitive, strong go-getters during childhood will likely grow up to be men who achieve in the world and who bring home to their families the material symbols of their success. Girls who learn to be sweet, kind, gentle, passive, and submissive during childhood will likely grow up to be the shadows behind great men, encouraging them in their accomplishments.

Relating this to the life-cycle approach (or developmental theory), one could say that traditional sex-role socialization at an early stage of the life cycle prepares the male or female for appropriate behavior at a later stage. There is a kind of systematic social progression from stage to stage which might be compared to the progression that occurs as a human body grows.

Talcott Parsons is very explicit in declaring ways sex-role specialization benefits the nuclear family.[69] In his thinking, such specialization is "functional" for the maintenance of that system. If the husband attends to his occupation and the wife attends to her role as "expressive hub" of the family, there is little chance for rivalry between them which might lead to marital dissolution. However, from a functionalist perspective, serious conflict and system disruption could occur if a woman chose to be as active, aggressive, autonomous, and achievement-oriented as her husband in pursuing a job or career. Therefore, the functionalist would say that parents socialize their children in traditional ways in order to avoid such disruption as much as possible. Parents may sense (consciously or otherwise) that things will "work out best" and run more smoothly if men are leaders and women are followers.

Conflict Theory

Those who hold to a conflict (or Engels-Marxist) approach would argue that the functionalist perspective is a freezing of the status quo. Such persons would instead emphasize a coercion-conflict framework for understanding sex roles. According to this approach, present socialization practices simply reflect the domination of women by men.[70]

In all the societies we looked at (including the kibbutz), men hold most of the power. They control the economic resources and the sources of prestige. In other words, the prizes their societies offer seem to be wrapped in a package marked "for men only." Why? Because men are the ones who have access to the occupational system and all its benefits. To grant equal access to women would mean sharing these benefits. Therefore, according to conflict theory, it is out of self-interest that men desire to limit the participation of women in the sphere of occupational opportunity. In this way, one-half the population can be kept from its rewards so that the other half might enjoy them totally. One method of accomplishing this is through socializing girls to behave in precisely the opposite manner than is necessary for achieving society's economic and power benefits.

But why would mothers act this way as well as fathers? Is it because of their own "false consciousness," having been so victimized by "brainwashing" that they themselves continue female subjugation by failing to question it? Yet how conscious are parents of either sex that women are being held down?

What is in view during current history is not necessarily an overt conspiracy but rather a lack of awareness of the realities involved, especially on the part of mothers. However, the conflict theorist argues that if men are confronted with the realities, they are likely to resist change because it will be costly to them. Therefore, women are urged to engage in conflict with men to whatever degree is necessary. Only then will women be able to achieve changes in socialization practices in home, school, and the larger society that will result in the removal of gender-role typing.

Social Exchange and Social Process

The idea implicit in conflict theory—that parents are not conscious of what they are doing to their children—leaves unanswered the question of why they do it. Even many mothers who have been confronted by the women's movement of recent years have continued to "feminize" their daughters and "masculinize" their sons. And fathers, too, have continued in large measure to carry on traditional gender-role socialization patterns.

Turner's symbolic interactional approach provided us with some clues that help explain why parents perpetuate gender-role socialization. Through observing the same-sex parent and forming task bonds with that parent, the child identifies with (or imitates) that parent. Parents find such identification both gratifying and reassuring. The gratification comes in knowing that the child esteems the parent as a *role model,* a living example of what it means to be a man or a woman, and that the child wants to grow up to "be like Daddy" (if the child is a boy) or "be like Mommy" (if the child is a girl). Similarly, there is a feeling of reassurance or of feeling comfortable in watching children develop in the sex-typed characteristics and behaviors which the larger society has established and maintains for the sake of order (according to the functional approach). Parents can therefore feel they are doing a "good job" in child rearing and are living up to the expectations of their *reference group* (the term sociologists use to describe those persons whom parents themselves identify with and measure themselves by—the group they feel close to in values and outlook and whose approval they desire).

What is taking place in the interactions between parents and children and between families and the larger society is a social process involving exchange theory, including such notions as rewards, costs, and sanctions (both positive and negative). Parents reward their children for certain behaviors in order to encourage or reinforce their children in such behaviors. In exchange, the parents receive rewards from their children—not only the rewards of affection, gratitude, and the like, but also the reward of sex-role identification.

It is said that imitation is the sincerest form of flattery. It means a great deal to any one of us to know that somebody looks up to us and wants to be like us. And parents especially, having had the primary task of molding their children from infancy, desire to have their task rewarded by producing human beings who admire them enough to want to identify with them. When children don't identify with their parents and reject them as role models, the parents feel punished—not only by their children's repudiation of their example but also by the disapproval of the parents' peers (their reference group). The parents then are experiencing *costs* rather than rewards in the process of social exchange, and the sense of "net profit" in the parent-child relationship is diminished.

Let's take some hypothetical examples to see how this works. Alice Grey has two daughters and a son. The son is established in a business and is happily married to a young woman who reminds Alice of herself as a young bride years ago. The daughter-in-law holds traditional sex-role norms and regards her greatest responsibility and joy in life to lie in "being a good wife and mother." This outlook on life is precisely that which Alice has always held. She and her husband feel rewarded not only in that their son followed the pattern of his father in developing qualities suited to achievement in the business world, but also in his choice of a wife who fulfills the sex-role norms his parents held up for females during his childhood socialization. Alice's younger daughter's aspirations also are rewarding to Alice and make her feel a success in having socialized her for an appropriate role in adult life. The young woman is presently working as a secretary but hopes to marry and settle down to raising a family soon.

It's the older daughter Susan who worries Alice. Susan is working on a Ph.D. in marine biology and is not at all concerned about marriage. If she does marry at some point in life, she tells Alice, the marriage will be egalitarian and there will be no sacrifice of career commitment on Susan's part. Furthermore, Susan has no desire to have children and says that if she were to marry either she or her husband would have sterilization surgery. Alice cannot understand Susan and feels she is rejecting all that Alice has lived for and held dear. Susan has no desire to be the kind of woman her mother is; in fact, Susan thinks of her mother as a *negative* role model—an example of what she doesn't want to be, a pattern of the kind of life she doesn't want to lead. By not identifying with her mother, Susan is calling into question her mother's own self-identity and the values her mother upholds. This is threatening to Alice Grey and hurts her deeply. Her daughter has failed to reward her and, in fact, is punishing her.

In another case, the hard-driving businessman who lives for money and buries himself in work may find that his son turns completely away from this way of life. The boy becomes antimaterialistic and takes his values from the legacy of the long-haired, gentle flower-children of the sixties. He joins a rural commune and settles into a pastoral life far removed from the bustling world of his father.

Of course, children may also take *non*traditional parents as negative role models and may order their behavior in more conventional societal patterns instead of following their parents' life-style. At the height of the counterculture movement, a common cartoon theme was that of a bewildered couple, in surroundings and dress clearly indicating their antiestablishment values, voicing dismay over their short-haired son in suit and tie. The caption would read something like this: "Where did we go wrong? He says he wants to study and work hard and be rich someday!"

Similarly, a mother who has emphasized intellectual excellence, independence, achievement, mastery, and career commitment for her daughter and has provided her daughter with a living example of professional accomplishment would be deeply disappointed if the daughter chooses to order her life according to traditional sex-role norms. One mother who went to medical school when her youngest daughter was four years old cannot understand why the child, now an adolescent, doesn't share in the mother's joy in opening a new clinic but instead expresses aspirations to be a full-time housewife and isn't interested in either college or career.

When children do not take their parents as role models during the socialization process, it is likely that one of two circumstances (or both) may to a great extent account for the lack of identification. Either a child's parents have failed to handle sanctions successfully or else an outside influence has provided the child with a more satisfactory role model, calling into question some of the parents' norms and values.

Sanctions   Animal trainers elicit desired behaviors by offering rewards. The porpoise learns that if he jumps through the hoop he will receive a tasty morsel of food; but if he fails to follow the trainer's instructions, the choice prize will be withheld. If he were to fully misbehave and not cooperate at all, he might be taken out of the game and set aside for awhile. He is being trained by the use of sanctions, both positive ones and negative ones.

As human beings interact with one another, sanctions also come into the picture. This is particularly true in sex-role socialization. To put it simply, a positive sanction is a reward for appropriate behavior, and a negative sanction is a punishment for inappropriate behavior. Both parents and the larger society outside the home employ sanctions during the gender-role socialization process. For example, if a little girl announces that she wants to be a nurse when she grows up, adults may pat her on the head and smile approvingly. But if the girl says she plans to be a brain surgeon, adult encouragement may not be so quickly forthcoming. Or suppose a small boy were to announce he plans not to be a doctor but a nurse when he grows up. With few exceptions, adults would voice disapproval and would tell him that his aspirations are "too low" or that nursing is "woman's work" and not at all a man's job.[71]

As another illustration of how sanctions are used in gender typing, think for a moment of a young girl who asks to join the neighborhood boys in a football team. She is likely to be negatively sanctioned not only by their refusal to admit her but also by the ridicule of both the boys themselves and the girls who are watching. Girls are expected to be cheerleaders, not football players. On the other hand, if she offered to run over to her house and bring out some lemonade to the thirsty players, she would be positively sanctioned by their expressions of gratitude.

Or we might think of a boy who enjoys designing women's fashions and outfitting miniature dolls. His parents might worry about his behavior to the point of taking him to a psychiatrist. In addition, he would feel the disapproval of his friends and face their jeers and innuendos if his hobbies were known. On the other hand, if he displayed talent for designing houses or building model planes, there would be positive sanctions. He would be praised by his parents, encouraged in his pursuits through gifts of necessary equipment, and would be further reinforced by his peers.

Sanctions are related to the power parents hold in controlling resources that a child needs or desires—both tangible resources and intangible resources. For example, the boy described above might find that his parents would not give him money to spend on his collection of dolls from around the world, but they would be more than happy to buy him a baseball glove or football. But beyond such obvious material aspects of parental power, there are intangible aspects which exert a tremendous influence. A child's desire to know that his parents approve of his conduct, feel warmly toward him, and are proud and pleased by his behavior makes him very conscious of any sanctions—whether positive or negative.

In such a social exchange process, it is as though the parents are saying through their actions: "If you give me what I want from you, I'll give you what pleases you in return. But if you don't act the way I want you to, you'll be sorry—because I'll show my displeasure. I'll withhold the rewards, or there will be penalties of some other sort. Then you'll know how important it is that you shape up to my expectations." Of course, this is never stated in such bald terms! But it provides a description of the underlying dynamics taking place between parents and children. Parental control of resources gives parents the upper hand while children are young. During the early years, children lack the kinds of resources that might cause them to question and challenge their parents' power.

Outside influences The power of one person over another is lessened as the second person finds alternative sources of rewards. Thus, as children are increasingly exposed to influences beyond those of their parents, they may not respond quite so readily to parental sanctions. Outside sources may provide the benefits once largely sought from parents alone. Pleasing one's peers may become more important than pleasing one's parents on certain issues. New ideas learned in school or through the media may cause children to challenge their parents' views on politics, religion, or social customs. Also, as children grow older, they become more aware of their own part in the exchange process between them and their parents. Children obtain more bargaining leverage as they awaken to the potential power they have through being able to give or withhold the positive reinforcement desired by their parents. If children feel they are not being rewarded for certain behaviors for which they feel they deserve to be rewarded, they may in turn not reward their parents with the approval and role-model identification that matters so much to the parents.

Adolescents in particular may identify with role models who provide benefits they consider more worthwhile than those provided by their parents. These alternative role models may markedly influence the gender-role norms the young person chooses to follow. For example, Bill's father may be a truck driver, part-time auto racer, and have little interest in the world of ideas. His hobbies may be mechanics and hunting. Bill's interests may lie in books and music. Of a gentle, sensitive temperament, he cringes at the thought of killing animals for sport and refuses to accompany his father on hunting trips. Bill prefers to attend the nature-study club sponsored by the public library. He likes to write poetry and play the piano. Bill's father worries about his son and fears he is a "sissy," not living up to the father's stereotyped notions of masculinity. But Bill has found a friend in Mr. Peterson, the English teacher at Bill's junior high school. Mr. Peterson provides Bill with books and articles to read, gives him the encouragement and approval the boy yearns for, and provides Bill with a sounding board for the discussion of his ideas and poetry. Already Bill is planning to major in literature in college and someday to be a teacher like Mr. Peterson.

Or we might think of Marilyn, an adolescent girl who takes a summer job which brings her into contact with Ms. Curtis, an advertising executive. Over time, Marilyn grows to admire the qualities that have made Ms. Curtis a success in her field. And she is impressed with the executive's exciting life. Marilyn looks up to Ms. Curtis as a role model and tells her friends and family, "I want to be like Ms. Curtis and have a career like hers." Even though the girl's parents have reinforced her in ways that would have been likely to result in her acceptance of traditional gender-role norms, she refuses to follow a pattern of passivity and dependence. Instead, she seeks to develop the more active, aggressive behaviors that will be required of her in the world of business. The rewards offered by the advertising executive appear much more compelling than the rewards offered by Marilyn's parents. Therefore, she has chosen to reject her mother's traditional life as an example of what a woman should be and has chosen Ms. Curtis as her role model instead.

Social exchange theory, then, helps to explain gender-role socialization by focusing attention on the interchange of rewards and costs experienced by those who socialize (parents in particular, but others as well) and those who are being socialized (children). In this process, the reward most sought by parents is imitation or role-model identification, and the reward especially sought by children is approval. As parents reward behavior they consider to be gender-appropriate in their children, the parents reinforce such behavior and encourage its further development. Conversely, by penalizing behavior considered to be inappropriate for the child's particular sex, parents discourage further behavior of that sort. This process is not necessarily calculated or conscious, especially when the behavior positively or negatively sanctioned is in accordance with traditional sex typing and is undergirded by the gender-role norms of the larger society. In such a case, parents may simply believe that their sanctions are part of the "natural order of things" and may carry them out without much thought or planning, believing them to be in their children's best interest—a way of fitting sons and daughters into the roles society has laid down for them.

FUTURE TRENDS

The processes we have just described are still taking place. And very likely they will continue into the future. But changes are occurring. Although most parents will go on trying to socialize their children in relatively traditional ways, they will be influenced by the revival of the women's movement and a renewed stress on the equality of the sexes. As a result, parents will be less rigid than their own parents were, and they will find this greater flexibility more rewarding. Children, for their part, will be more likely to engage in conflict with parents in order to alter any remaining rigidities which seem unreasonable. And because parents value their children's identification, they may seek to achieve it by a willingness to alter sex-role expectations, permitting less gender differentiation.

However, this will vary by social class. Middle-class parents will continue to strive for less gender differentiation than working-class parents and will be more open to negotiation and change. In general, whites should continue to move closer to blacks in this regard. The religiously traditional, while moving slowly in the direction of less differentiated sex roles, will nevertheless continue to be more rigid than others.

But don't expect an immediate, abrupt halt to sex typing by parents. Changes will not be sudden, but rather gradual, mild, and discernible only by comparison to the situation some years previous. We can see this already.[72] Compared to ten years ago, there is a growth in the handful of highly educated parents (usually urban and professional) who are self-consciously working toward the elimination of all sex typing in their own and in others' children (such as through school textbooks, for example). That's new and will continue and increase.

At the same time, reaction is quite possible. The well-organized groups that

As parents move away from rigid gender-role socialization, activities once restricted to one sex will increasingly be open to both boys and girls.

directed efforts toward defeating the Equal Rights Amendment are one example. Other examples are the discussion groups spawned by such books as *Fascinating Womanhood,* which tells women that "submission" (whether actual or pretended) and childlike mannerisms (such as pouting, crying, and sticking out one's lower lip) are ways by which women get their way with their king-of-the-home husbands.[73] Several organizations have arisen with the aim of convincing women and men that the traditional idea that "woman's place is in the home" is much better than anything feminism can come up with.

Such a backlash will likely continue. And as such interest groups urge parents to "preserve femininity and masculinity," a significant proportion of working-class and lower-middle class parents may respond by seeking to impose quite rigid sex differentiation on their children. However this could boomerang, with the result being that many such children may reject traditional sex roles more strongly than would have been the case if the parents hadn't insisted on them so firmly.

In short, the dominant trend should be toward parental socialization of children in life-styles that are less sex-specific than has been the tradition in the past. As one indication of this trend, Charles Winick points out a growing tendency for parents to give their children names which do not clearly indicate a person's sex. For example, names like Terry, Kim, Robin, Dale, Lynn, Tracy, and Leslie are popular; and they are used for both boys and girls.[74] Winick also refers to the similar ways in which boys and girls are dressed and wear their hair, so that the physical appearance of the sexes is much more alike than was once the case.

The movement toward greater role interchangeability has thus far been gradual but steady. It appears that it will continue in the same way, with some sets of parents going along with the current much more rapidly than others.

SUMMARY

In this chapter, we have seen that although persons are *born* male or female, they *become* "masculine" or "feminine" according to the norms of their particular society. Gender-role socialization is the process of training males and females for their sex-differentiated, assigned roles in adult life. These roles are primarily socially and not biologically determined (except for reproduction). Exactly what it means to "be a man" or "be a woman" has varied in different times and places throughout history, but the predominant pattern has been one in which boys have been socialized to be assertive and independent in preparation for an adult role as occupational achiever and family provider, and girls have been socialized to be less assertive and more dependent in preparation for an adult role as the nurturant support behind the husband and caretaker of the home and children.

This predominant pattern continues into the present. At the same time, we saw that in the United States there are variations in gender-role socialization by race, social status, and religion; and there are cross-national variations as well. From the standpoint of sociological theory, sex-role socialization may be explained according to several different theoretical frameworks. The symbolic-interactional approach provides insights into the interaction processes taking place between parents (and others) and the children they are socializing; this approach helps us understand certain aspects of the "how" of socialization. The structure-functional approach attempts to answer the "why" of sex-role socialization by asserting that sex-differentiated tasks and gender-determined marital roles are necessary to the smooth functioning of the societal system.

Conflict theory challenges the structure-functional approach and sees the sexes as two opposing groups. According to conflict theory, males have the greater privileges through access to the economic-opportunity system and control of capital, privileges which are jealously guarded and which are perpetuated by socializing females in qualities that hinder their gaining power and resources through achievement in the opportunity system.

Social exchange theory, while having much in common with some of the other approaches (particularly symbolic-interactional theory), draws attention to the processes of reward seeking and cost avoidance in the exchange between parents and children (the "why" of sex-role socialization) and at the same time presents a view of the part sanctions and identification play in gender typing (the "how" of sex-role socialization).

As for the future, there is already evidence of changing attitudes toward what is and is not appropriate for persons of either sex and an openness to less rigid gender differentiation during childhood socialization than has been the case in the past. Throughout this book, we will be examining evidences of this trend and what it will mean in male-female relationships as well as in the individual lives of both men and women. In the words of sociologist Janet Saltzman Chafetz, traditional sex-role socialization has meant that "from birth on we are all encouraged to assume a self-definition and certain behaviors that may or may not be congruent with our natural proclivities, and which, at any rate, expresses only half, if that, of our human potential." She points out that "this is a costly procedure for everyone involved."[75] As more and more parents and their children begin to view traditional sex-role norms as costly rather than rewarding, we may expect to see a movement away from gender typing and an emphasis on human qualities and experiences desirable for all persons regardless of sex.

NOTES

1 Money and Ehrhardt, 1972, chap. 7.
2 Money and Ehrhardt, 1972, chap. 8; Money, 1970.
3 Money and Ehrhardt, 1972, chap. 8.
4 Money and Ehrhardt, 1972; Chafetz, 1974; Bardwick, 1971.
5 Money and Ehrhardt, 1972, chap. 6.
6 Mead, 1935.
7 Block, 1973; Chafetz, 1974.
8 Money and Ehrhardt, 1972, chap. 1.
9 Alcott, 1837.
10 Shannon, 1917.
11 Sandford, 1834.
12 Plato, *The Republic.*
13 Kraditor, 1968.
14 Calhoun, 1919, vol. 3.
15 Demos, 1970.
16 Morgan, 1956.
17 Kraditor, 1968.
18 Quoted in Riegel, 1970.
19 Alcott, 1837.
20 Wise, 1859.
21 Alcott, 1837.
22 For a summary of literature extolling such qualities, see Welter, 1966.
23 Learner, 1972.
24 Brawley, 1921.
25 Learner, 1972.
26 Block, 1973.

27 D'Andrade, 1966; Block, 1973; Barry, Bacon, and Child, 1957.
28 D'Andrade, 1966.
29 Block, 1973.
30 Noble, 1966; Steinmann, Fox, and Farkas, 1968; Scanzoni, 1971.
31 Scanzoni, 1975a, 1975b.
32 Scanzoni, 1971.
33 Scanzoni, 1971, 1975a, 1975b; Holter, 1970.
34 Holter, 1970.
35 Kohn, 1969.
36 Kohn, 1969.
37 Adorno et al., 1950.
38 Holter, 1970; Schneider and Smith, 1973.
39 Levinson and Huffman, 1955.
40 McKinley, 1964; Brown, 1965.
41 McKinley, 1964.
42 Rainwater, 1965.
43 Scanzoni, 1971.
44 Chafetz, 1974.
45 Komarovsky, 1962; Balswick and Peek, 1971.
46 Chafetz, 1974.
47 Holter, 1970.
48 Westoff and Potvin, 1967.
49 Scanzoni, 1975b.
50 Scanzoni, 1975b.
51 Liljeström, 1966.
52 Cited in Holter, 1970.
53 Weitzman et al., 1972.
54 Sandlund, 1968; Liljeström, 1970.
55 Lehr and Rauh, 1970.
56 Holter, 1970.
57 Katzenstein, 1970.
58 Geiger, 1968; Field and Flynn, 1970.
59 Field and Flynn, 1970.
60 Zetkin, 1934.
61 Buxembaum, 1973.
62 Rabin, 1970.
63 Fong, 1970; Aird, 1972.
64 De Vos and Wagatsuma, 1970.
65 De Vos and Wagatsuma, 1970.
66 Williamson, 1970, pp. 188–191.
67 Turner, 1970; Kagan, 1964.
68 Holter, 1970; Seeley, Sim, and Loosley, 1956; Parsons, 1955; Pitts, 1964.
69 Parsons, 1955.
70 Engels, 1884; Rowbotham, 1972; Mitchell, 1971.
71 Etzkowitz, 1971.
72 Scanzoni, 1975c.
73 Andelin, 1965.
74 Winick, 1968.
75 Chafetz, 1974.

3

SEX BEFORE MARRIAGE

"If a virgin happens to walk by, the statue of the pioneer mother over there will rise up in surprise!" So goes the campus folklore at one university. Other colleges have similar legends. Maybe a cannon will spontaneously fire or the stone lions will roar. Of course, no one expects this to happen. After all, there aren't any virgins any more. Or are there?

Most people seem to have opinions about the incidence of premarital sexual intercourse today, but all too often such opinions are poorly informed. Yet there is no reason to rely on hearsay. There are reliable sociological studies that can help us understand what is going on today. And information from history can help us understand what went on yesterday as well. What about tomorrow? We can observe trends, formulate theories about what is happening, and then speculate about the future of sex without marriage.

The gender-role definitions discussed in the last chapter clearly carry over into sexuality. Part of traditional masculinity has been the assumption that sex has different meanings for men and women. Men have assumed that they have stronger physiological cravings than women—that they have boundless sex drives that can only be satisfied by having a woman in the way that they want her. Traditional femininity, on the other hand, has included the idea that women have milder physiological inclinations toward sex—that for them sexual desire is less compelling and overpowering.

Therefore, it is understandable that many Americans were shocked by the revelations of the 1953 Kinsey volume. Dr. Alfred Kinsey and his associates at the Institute for Sex Research at Indiana University had found that, of the married women in their sample born after 1900, nearly 50 percent had engaged in sex before marriage. Americans who were accustomed to the double standard that maintained that boys-will-be-boys-but-girls-will-be-angels found it a bit easier to accept the Kinsey findings on male sexual behavior. Data on men in Kinsey's sample indicated that 98 percent of those with only a grade school education had engaged in sexual intercourse before marriage. For men with a high school education, the figure was 85 percent; and among men who had some college, the figure dropped to 68 percent.[1]

One thing became clear. If the norms for sexual behavior decreed abstinence before marriage, they were being flouted or ignored by large numbers of people. In literature, religious teachings, marriage manuals, and popular folklore, the wedding night was portrayed as a mysterious rite in which two nervous, inexperienced virgins shyly gave themselves to one another in the marital embrace. But for over half the population, this vision was mythical. (For others, of course, the traditional ideas about the wedding night were close to reality, with one or both partners never having experienced sex relations prior to marriage.)

Although, at first, many questions were raised about the reliability of the Kinsey studies because of sampling procedures, studies by others verified his findings. Sociologist Ira Reiss points out that the studies of Terman (published in 1938), Burgess and Wallin (1953), and Kinsey (1948 and 1953) included couples from California, Chicago, and the Northeast, yet the results were strikingly similar. Each of these major studies indicated that about 50 percent of the women born in this century were not virgins at the time of marriage. "Considering the geographical and time spans that separate these studies and their respondents," says Reiss, "such findings are indicative of high validity."[2]

Another point of agreement in these studies was the finding that women tended to link sex with love and affection. Their premarital sexual activity did not necessarily indicate "promiscuity," in the sense of having engaged in sex with a variety of partners. The Terman, Burgess and Wallin, and Kinsey studies taken together showed that of the women studied who reported having had premarital intercourse, from one-half to two-thirds reported that their only partner was the man they later married.[3]

Until recently, many sociologists have maintained that premarital sexual behavior remained much as Kinsey found it, particularly with regard to rates of premarital intercourse.[4] Reiss has pointed out, for example, that there seems to be little room for change in male rates of nonvirginity, because, for generations, from 85 to 90 percent of men have experienced sexual relations before marriage.[5] And among women born in the present century, the 50-percent figure seemed to be holding steady until the late 1960s.

To be sure, many people *believed* that rates of premarital intercourse were soaring, and the popular press kept referring to a "sexual revolution." However, the word *revolution* implies an abrupt and radical change; and scholars could find no evidence that any such thing had occurred since the period around World War I. At that time, it was true that there was a sudden upsurge in rates of premarital sex, as shown in Kinsey's finding that only 25 percent of women born before 1900 entered marriage nonvirginal in contrast to 50 percent of the women born between 1900 and 1910.[6] This doubling of the rate of nonvirginity among women in just one decade could be called with some justification a sexual revolution. But since that time, any changes have been gradual and the continuation of a trend rather than something abrupt. Some scholars have suggested that it might be more accurate to speak of an evolution in sexual permissiveness rather than a revolution.

According to Reiss and other researchers, the kinds of changes that occurred after the 1920s had to do mainly with *attitudes* toward premarital sexuality rather than a lowering of the proportion of virginal males and females.[7] People began feeling more free to discuss sex openly. Regrets and guilt feelings about premarital sex—particularly in a stable, affectionate relationship—were reduced. Other changes related to both the timing of premarital sex (nearness to marriage being less important than was once the case) and the meaning of premarital sex (a move toward what Reiss calls person-centered sex rather than body-centered sex).

Another significant change that took place had to do with petting. Kinsey and associates used the term *petting* to refer to "physical contacts which involve a deliberate attempt to effect erotic arousal," that is, sexual contacts that do not involve an actual union of the male and female genitals. Petting might involve manual or oral stimulation of the breasts and genitals, or it might include the placing of the genitals close together without any effort toward penetration. Sometimes petting is a prelude to actual sexual union, but in other cases, petting (especially to the point of orgasm) is an end in itself—a substitute for sexual intercourse. Kinsey pointed out that although premarital petting certainly existed among Americans in earlier decades and centuries, the practice became more widespread among those born after 1900 and its incidence had increased steadily down to the time of his studies.[8]

Robert R. Bell speaks of this increase in premarital petting as "the greatest behavioral change in premarital sexual experience since the 1920s,"[9] a point that was also stressed by Winston Ehrmann in the late fifties.[10] In a similar vein, Reiss found in his research on sexual attitudes that among those who believed in abstinence from sexual intercourse before marriage, there was nevertheless a great increase in the number who felt petting was permissible.[11] Petting

The evolution of bathing suit styles from 1900 to 1920 reflects changes in sex attitudes and behavior during that same period.

provided a way to engage in considerable sexual intimacies while at the same time preserving one's virginity since actual *coitus* (sexual intercourse) did not occur.

The publications of Ira Reiss have added significantly to the body of sociological studies on premarital sex. One of his most important contributions has been his differentiating and labeling four main categories of premarital sexual attitudes or standards which are held in the United States today. His research showed that during the years between 1920 and 1965, "young people increasingly came to see the selection of a sexual code and sexual behavior itself as a private choice similar to that made in politics and religion."[12]

Attitudes toward premarital sex, according to Reiss, fall into these four categories: abstinence, the double standard, permissiveness with affection, and permissiveness without affection.[13] Persons who hold the *abstinence standard* believe that sexual intercourse before marriage is wrong for both males and females. The *double standard,* on the other hand, is in essence two standards—

one for males and one for females. Persons who hold the double standard believe that males have the right to engage in sexual intercourse before marriage but that premarital sexual intercourse is not permissible for females. Traditionally, the abstinence standard and the double standard have existed side by side, with abstinence being viewed as almost a kind of "official" standard while covertly the double standard was widely accepted and put into practice.

Reiss found that young men and women were no longer willing to limit their notions about premarital sex to a choice between these two standards alone. They added to abstinence and the double standard two new standards, both of which were basically equalitarian. Reiss labeled these *permissiveness with affection* and *permissiveness without affection*. Persons who hold the permissiveness with affection standard believe that a man and woman who are in a stable relationship such as engagement or who love each other or have strong affection for one another have the right to express their feelings through coitus. In other words, premarital sex is not wrong for either males or females if deep affection is present.

The remaining standard, permissiveness without affection, also makes no distinctions between male and female privileges. Those who hold this standard believe that both men and women may engage in premarital sexual intercourse regardless of how stable the relationship is or how much affection the partners feel toward each other. Physical attraction and desire are emphasized rather than love. Sex is viewed as primarily a giving and receiving of sexual pleasure, a part of the good time a man and woman may have together in going out with one another.

Sociologists are interested both in what people believe and in how people behave. Reiss concentrated on beliefs or attitudes. Although he predicted in 1960 that attitudes allowing for greater sexual freedom would eventually result in behavioral changes in the same direction, he himself remained skeptical that such a change was actually taking place until nearly ten years later, when the data from several studies by others convinced him that there was a rise in female nonvirginity rates. In 1972, he wrote, "I still feel that the evidence is not fully in, but the data that are coming in are so consistent in their findings of higher nonvirginity rates at specified ages, I am now willing to assert that the change predicted has occurred and that the actual premarital nonvirginity rate is now close to 70 percent for females."[14]

HISTORICAL BACKGROUND

It is important to note that most of the so-called sex revolution or evolution has centered around female autonomy. Autonomy has to do with self-government, independence, being free to carry out one's own will and being responsible for one's own actions, in contrast to being under the control of another. Traditionally, women have been under the control of men—first their fathers, later their husbands. This means that female sexuality has usually been subject to stricter regulations than has been true of men, who throughout history have been given freedom by parents and the larger society to "sow their wild oats" with prostitutes or women of low social position.

Sexual intercourse before marriage is not a new phenomenon. If one takes a historical perspective, it must be remembered that prior to modernization and the rise of the dominant Puritan ethic regarding sex, most Western societies consisted largely of lower-class, uneducated masses, with the remainder being upper-class aristocrats and gentry. Literature of the times indicates that premarital sex was very widespread among the masses and among much of the upper strata as well. However, with the rise of the middle classes and the influences of Lutheranism and especially Calvinism (in which both the Protestant work ethic and the Puritan sex ethic are rooted), sexual permissiveness came to be less acceptable.

Puritan theology took seriously biblical warnings against both pre- and extra-marital sex. Sanctions against sex outside of marriage were rigidly enforced, as is clearly seen both in the Puritans' own writings and in such fictionalized accounts as Hawthorne's *The Scarlet Letter.* Both men and women were expected to be chaste and to abstain from coitus until after wedding vows had been exchanged and from that time forward to be completely faithful to each other.

Rationality and self-discipline were important virtues in Puritan thinking, and they were expected to be demonstrated in sexual conduct as well as in affairs of business. Over time, rational control meant financial and occupational success as the Protestant work ethic took root and blossomed into the middle-class life-style. And to be "of good character" meant steering clear of irrational and irresponsible sexual behavior that might disgrace the family, bring about an unwise "forced" marriage, or dishonor one's reputation through the birth of an illegitimate child. Since women were the childbearers, it was they who faced greater restrictions and tighter controls.

The great eighteenth-century Wesleyan revivals in England and similar movements in America converted large numbers of the lower-class masses into lives that involved frugality, hard work, and respectability. Historians have pointed out that, although revivalism did not fully accept the Calvinistic theology of the Puritans, the movement was in thorough agreement with "the Puritan concern for a rigorous public and private moral code."[15] Any indication of sexual permissiveness was attacked in the interests of protecting the sanctity of marriage and the home. The religious groups that grew out of revivalism as well as those that descended from Puritanism greatly influenced the moral tone of the United States. One reflection of this was in the materials people read. As Joseph Gaer and Ben Siegel, authorities on religion and literature, have pointed out, "So successfully did evangelical Protestantism impose its views on literature that nineteenth-century American fiction was almost totally devoid of illicit love at a time when Europe's romantic writers were making it a central theme."[16]

If one result of the revivalistic movements was increasingly strict control over sexuality—particularly female sexuality, it remained for nineteenth-century Victorianism to attempt to desexualize women totally. Women were taught that no decent woman had sexual desires; only "loose" women enjoyed sex. Married women were expected to tolerate coitus as a wifely duty and a necessary indulgence of their husbands' "animal nature." As much as possible, respectable women were protected from all that might add to their knowledge of sex; they were to be kept innocent. Newspapers in some cases refused to publish news of births (though marriages and deaths were published), and pregnant women were ashamed to be seen publicly in what was euphemistically called "a delicate condition." Female physicians were rare, and many women delayed essential medical examinations and treatment rather than endure the embarrassment of having their bodies seen and touched by a male. Some doctors tried to help the situation by having dummies in their offices so that a woman could point to the corresponding areas that were troubling her in her own body.[17]

Women in their roles as angel-of-the-house and guardian-of-virtue were to be characterized by refined speech. References to anything related to sex or parts of the human body must be expurgated from vocabularies or spoken of in euphemisms. For example, respectable women substituted such words as *lower extremities* or *limbs* in speaking of legs—even if they were referring to table legs or the legs of a piano. The word *breast* was also taboo; in the presence of ladies, it was proper to refer to a *bosom* of chicken at the dinner table. Both the clothing styles and furniture styles of the period showed a desire to cover up any hint of nakedness, with even the "limbs" of furniture often wearing ruffles and skirts.

Censors abounded. Eager to save society, such crusaders even sought to remove all earthy or sexual references from great works of art. Noah Webster in 1833 issued a special edition of the Bible in which offensive words (such as *womb, belly,* or *teat*) were removed or changed and all sexual references were blurred and made as inexplicit as possible. For example, the testicles were referred to as "peculiar members" or "secrets." Thomas Bowdler's nineteenth-century *Family Shakespeare* was another attempt to take great writings and make them tame and decent enough for women and children. With abandonment, he mutilated the great plays of Shakespeare, cutting out all that in Bowdler's opinion was offensive and coarse.[18]

There seemed no end to prudery. The first museum in the United States endeavored to protect modesty by having separate visiting days for ladies, so that they would be spared the embarrassment of viewing nude statues and paintings in the presence of men. And in England, Lady Gough in her 1863 *Etiquette* wrote that the perfect hostess should make sure that "the works of male and female authors be properly separated on her bookshelves." It was

With large numbers of young women laboring for meager wages, factory owners took full advantage of the situation.

considered indecent for books by male and female authors to rest side by side unless the authors happened to be married to each other.[19]

However, scholars are quick to point out that the notion of Victorian prudery was nothing but a myth if one considers society *as a whole.* The congested conditions of the cities in the wake of the industrial revolution, in which working-class families were crowded together in deplorable, subhuman conditions, constantly threw persons of both sexes together in such a way that sexual relations were difficult to avoid. James Graham-Murray in his book *A History of Morals* refers to the communal dormitories of nineteenth-century England in which there was no segregation by sex. Men, women, boys, and girls who worked together in the factories also slept together at night on piles of dirty straw in hovels called "padding kens." Graham-Murray also points out that it was legal at that time to have intercourse with any girl over twelve years of age. With large numbers of young girls and women laboring for meager wages in their factories, factory owners and managers took full advantage of the situation. Prostitution flourished. "During the Victorian age the supply of prostitutes in proportion to the size of the population was greater than ever before or since," writes Graham-Murray. Pornographic materials were also widely distributed in Victorian England, especially pornography that featured bizarre acts and torture.[20]

How could all this occur in a society so obsessed with sexual morality and prudery? The Victorian middle and upper classes were concerned about one aspect of sexual morality only—female chastity. Perhaps never in history did the double standard enjoy wider acceptance. Wives tolerated their husbands' extramarital affairs and visits to prostitutes as a necessary evil in view of men's supposedly greater sexual needs and stronger passions. For unmarried men, prostitution was even considered a positive good in that it provided a means of sexual outlet. Single young men could thereby satisfy their sexual urges without degrading respectable women who were in the pool of eligible marriage prospects. At the same time, there were cases of moralists who advised men to test the virtue of young women they courted; and if a woman responded to amorous advances, she was to be spurned as unworthy.[21]

In view of this historical perspective, particularly with respect to the century prior to our own, it is easy to see that the major place for change (whether in the "sex revolution" around the 1920s or the "sex evolution" afterward) would likely be in the area of female sexuality. And this is exactly what various sociological studies have shown. We are not saying that changes have not also occurred among males; because there *are* certain changes, one illustration of which is a lowering in the percentage of males who have their first experience of sexual intercourse with a prostitute. However, the greatest changes in premarital sexual behavior have been changes among females. Sociological studies that have shown this have not been attempts to "count virgins" in an effort to show that things are getting better or worse (depending on one's personal value position), nor are such studies indicative of a biased male perspective colored by a Victorian-like obsession with female virginity or nonvirginity. Rather, sociologists are interested in studying current social phenomena, contrasting them with the past, and then trying to find out why changes occur and what they mean. If changes have been and are occurring with regard to female sexuality, we need to attempt to understand what these changes mean to both men and women before and after marriage. In other words, we must examine available studies and then utilize sociological theory to explain what is taking place and what is likely to take place in the future.

PREMARITAL SEX TODAY

Some sociologists have suggested that the term *premarital* implies premarriage sexual intercourse between two persons who will eventually be wed to one another or at least that they will marry someone eventually. They suggest that the more general notion of sexual behavior outside of marriage might be better described as "nonmarital sex." However, since most studies of the sex behavior of nonmarried persons use the term *premarital* without assuming that all such behavior is oriented toward marriage, we will use the same terminology as we examine some of these studies.

In 1971, two professors from Johns Hopkins University conducted a massive research project to learn about the sexual experience of young unmarried women in the United States. John Kantner and Melvin Zelnik are authorities on the dynamics of population growth and change, and they wanted to find information on females aged fifteen to nineteen years. Were young unmarried women having sexual intercourse? Did they understand the basic facts of conception? Of contraception? These were the kinds of questions to which the researchers wanted to find answers.

Kantner and Zelnik carefully drew a large national sample and conducted interviews with over four thousand young women who had never been married. Among the data they collected was the finding that 46 percent were no longer virgins at age nineteen.[22] In contrast, Kinsey's 1953 volume indicated that 20 percent of the women in his sample had experienced sexual intercourse by age twenty.[23]

Other sociologists also began noticing changes taking place in the mid-1960s. As we saw earlier, in the interval after World War I through the 1950s, the sexual scene remained much the same insofar as rates of premarital intercourse were concerned. But now something was beginning to happen. Why? And what did it mean?

The evidence kept coming in. Two sociologists who had conducted a study among female university students in 1958 decided to return to the same university with the same questionnaire ten years later. Robert Bell and Jay Chaskes found that not only had there been an increase in the percentage of women who reported having sexual intercourse during engagement, but even more significantly, there were indications that women in 1968 were less likely to think engagement was necessary before sexual intercourse was permissible. Over the ten-year period, nearly a doubling of rates of sexual intercourse among those going steady or in simple dating relationships had occurred.[24] (See Table 3-A.) While pointing out that this study involved only small samples (250 and 205) at one university and therefore should not lead to broad generalizations, the researchers felt nevertheless that the factor of change was noteworthy. It provided one more piece of evidence that a shift in the sexual behavior of unmarried women took place somewhere in the middle of the 1960s.

TABLE 3-A PERCENT OF COLLEGE FEMALES HAVING INTERCOURSE, BY TYPE OF RELATIONSHIP, 1958 AND 1968

	1958 %	Number of cases	1968 %	Number of cases
Dating	10	(25)	23	(48)
Going steady	15	(25)	28	(46)
Engaged	31	(20)	39	(30)

SOURCE: Bell and Chaskes, 1970, p. 83.

Two other sociologists repeated in 1968 a study of college students which they had originally conducted in 1958. Harold Christensen and Christina Gregg compared a sample of students from the Mormon culture of the Intermountain region of the Western states with a sample of students from the Midwest.[25] Male rates of premarital sexual intercourse among both groups remained roughly the same over the ten-year period. But there was a significant jump in female rates. In the Intermountain group, for example, the percentage of women who had experienced sexual intercourse more than tripled. (See Table 3-B.)

Not only was the incidence of premarital sexual intercourse increasing, but the age at which persons experienced it was decreasing. Whereas 3 percent of the women in Kinsey's sample had experienced premarital coitus by age fifteen, the figure had increased to 14 percent in the Kantner and Zelnik sample nearly two decades later.[26] A marked reduction in the age of first coitus was also found in a study of West German adolescents, with a particularly big jump in the percentage of both male and female sixteen-year-olds who experienced sexual intercourse.[27] (See Tables 3-C and 3-D.)

Especially striking to German sociologists Gunter Schmidt and Volkmar Sigusch were the parallel changes in sexual behavior in the United States and Germany during both the 1920s and the 1960s. Furthermore, there was a corresponding rise in premarital coitus during those two decades in other industrialized countries, such as England and France.[28] Were these happenings mere coincidences, or do they show us something?

A number of sociologists suggest that these kinds of patterns do indeed have something to say to us. They can help us to see that social factors are involved even in such personal matters as sexual intercourse. The times and places in which people live and the persons with whom they associate are intricately tied in with how they think about premarital sex and what they do about it. It is not simply an individual, private decision. Wider social forces and events also enter in. In this light, we might want to look at certain similarities in the two different time periods in this century when great and rapid changes in premarital sex behavior occurred.

TABLE 3-B PERCENTAGE OF COLLEGE STUDENTS WITH PREMARITAL COITAL EXPERIENCE

				Region				
		Intermountain					Midwestern	
Years	Males %	Total Number in Sample	Females %	Total Number in Sample	Males %	Total Number in Sample	Females %	Total Number in Sample
1958	39	(94)	10	(74)	51	(213)	21	(142)
1968	37	(115)	32	(105)	50	(245)	34	(238)

SOURCE: Adapted from Christensen and Gregg, 1970, p. 621.

Two Periods of Significant Change

There is some debate about the exact time when the first period of increased freedom in premarital sex began, with some sociologists saying the 1920s and others suggesting several years earlier,[29] but there is general agreement that it occurred sometime around World War I. Ira Reiss singles out the period of 1915–1920 to be compared with the years, 1965–1970. Both five-year periods were times of rapid social change.[30]

World War I marked the end of one era and the beginning of another. As Reiss points out, "Historically, this period appeared as a culmination of trends toward making the United States a modern, industrial nation," adding that the increase in female nonvirginity at this time "seemingly was part and parcel of an overall societal change occurring in all major social institutions." Similarly, in the mid-1960s, the United States was again involved in another major war, Vietnam, and in addition was undergoing another change into a different kind of society, a post industrial society. Reiss writes: "The post industrial society is usually distinguished by its concern for the equitable distribution of rights and privileges whereas the industrial society is primarily concerned with the production of goods and services." During both the 1915–1920 and the 1965–1970 periods, doubts and questions were raised about society, its values, and its

TABLE 3-C CUMULATIVE INCIDENCE: AGE AT FIRST COITUS (HIGH EDUCATIONAL LEVEL) BY YEAR OF BIRTH (West Germany)

Age (yrs.)	1966 Study				1970 Study
	Born 1936–1940	Born 1941–1942	Born 1943–1944	Born 1945–1946	Born 1953–1954
	Males (%)				
	(n = 649)	(n = 881)	(n = 838)	(n = 395)	(n = 108)
13	2	1	1	1	1
14	3	3	2	2	2
15	5	4	4	4	10
16	9	7	7	6	38
17	14	11	11	12	
18	21	18	20	21	
	Females (%)				
	(n = 92)	(n = 208)	(n = 266)	(n = 212)	(n = 108)
13	0	0	1	1	1
14	0	0	1	1	1
15	1	1	2	1	7
16	1	1	3	3	26
17	2	4	7	7	
18	4	12	11	14	

SOURCE: Schmidt and Sigusch, 1972, p. 35.

TABLE 3-D CUMULATIVE INCIDENCE: AGE AT FIRST COITUS (LOW EDUCATIONAL LEVEL) BY YEAR OF BIRTH (West Germany)

Age (yrs.)	Males (%)		Females (%)	
	1968 Study Born 1947–1948 (n = 150)	1970 Study Born 1953–1954 (n = 94)	1968 Study Born 1947–1948 (n = 150)	1970 Study Born 1953–1954 (n = 89)
13	4	3	5	0
14	9	10	5	7
15	15	18	7	16
16	25	40	19	25
17	44		33	
18	60		53	

SOURCE: Schmidt and Sigusch, 1972, p. 36.

morals. Some sociologists viewed this as a rebellion on the part of youth and a rejection of norms imposed upon them by adults, including sexual norms. It was a movement away from the traditional roles assigned to youth as "dependent and inexperienced learners," with emphasis instead on a new self-definition in which young people came to view themselves as a social and political force in their own right.[31] "The result was a radical rejection of the societal infantilization of youth and an emphasis on a new autonomy," write Schmidt and Sigusch. They suggest that, at least in West Germany, there were probably two reasons that sexuality played such a key role in this process: (1) the conflict between restrictive sexual norms and the strong sexual desires of youth, and (2) a feeling that sexual prohibitions are demonstrative and symbolic of overall "societal tendencies toward the infantilization of youth." To demand *sexual* freedom is a way of demanding the right to other freedoms as well. Schmidt and Sigusch write: "A society which denies legal sexuality to those of its members who have the strongest sexual desire creates the preconditions for making sexuality the central problem in generation conflict and for instrumentalizing sexuality as a weapon and provocative challenge in this conflict."[32]

At the same time, from the vantage point of the United States, Ira Reiss suggests that what may appear to be rebellion against adult values is in reality "an actualization of rather traditional American values . . . equalitarianism, openness, honesty, legitimation of choice, autonomy, happiness, pleasure, love, affection, and experimentation."[33] These values, including attempts to implement them in the sexual realm, have deep roots in the past. Historian William O'Neill, for example, has suggested that the late-nineteenth-century debates over divorce and the victory of the pro-divorce forces in the early years of the present century meant a triumph for an individualistic approach to marriage. This triumph was on the cutting edge of a new outlook on morality.[34]

In comparing the commonly called "sexual revolutions" of the two time periods under discussion (around the time of World War I and in the latter half of the sixties), we should keep in mind that there have been other periods with a high incidence of premarital sexual activity and there will doubtless be others, with periods of lower incidence in between. This raises the possibility of a cyclical pattern over history (with highs and lows of premarital sexual intercourse) rather than a linear pattern (a continually increasing incidence of premarital sexual intercourse over time).

Daniel Scott Smith, the social historian, provides evidence of a cyclical pattern in comparing proportions of American women who were pregnant at the time of marriage during different historical periods. (See Table 3-E.) He did not rely on this information alone, but on other data and considerations as well (such as contraceptive usage, ability to bear children, and induced abortions which could also affect premarital pregnancy rates). All the information taken together, however, presents "a coherent and plausible pattern," according to Smith. The peak period of premarital pregnancy in America prior to this century occurred in the late eighteenth century, with lows occurring in the mid-seventeenth and mid-nineteenth centuries. With certain variations, there was a similar cycle in Western European premarital pregnancy and illegitimacy data.[35]

Much more research needs to be done to explain what the probable upsurge in premarital sex meant during certain earlier periods; but for the two time periods in our century to which we have been giving attention, the desire for *autonomy*—for control over one's own sexual destiny—stands out as a major factor.

Already we have focused on the quest for autonomy among youth, both around the time of World War I and again in the 1960s, but we cannot pass over that other segment of the population which also made new demands for autonomy during these two time periods. *Women* began to insist on their right to control their own lives rather than being dependent upon and subordinate to men. The feminist movement of the early decades of the twentieth century and the women's movement which received much of its impetus from the publication of Betty Friedan's book *The Feminine Mystique* in 1963 coincide with the two periods of a greater incidence of premarital sexual intercourse. In saying this, we are not implying that feminism "causes" premarital sexual activity to increase, nor that conversely an increase in premarital sex will "cause" feminism to emerge. The link between feminism and sexual freedom is simply that cluster of values mentioned earlier, particularly the quest for autonomy (the right to individual choice and self-direction for all persons) and equalitarianism, which insists that women and men deserve equal treatment, rights, and privileges, and which therefore demolishes the arguments for the old double standard.

SEX AND SOCIALIST EXPERIMENTS

Sociologist Richard F. Tomasson has suggested that crossnational and intranational differences in premarital sex codes may be explained in terms of the following proposition: "Where females have greater equality and are subject

TABLE 3-E LONG-TERM HISTORICAL VARIATION IN WHITE AMERICAN PREMARITAL PREGNANCY

Period	Percentage of First Births within Nine Months of Marriage		Description of Sample
	Marriages	Areas	
Before 1701*	11.1%	9.9%	1,113 marriages in nine areas (8 in New England)
1701–1760*	23.3	19.4	1,311 marriages in nine areas (6 in New England)
1761–1800*	33.7	34.0	1,011 marriages in six areas (5 in New England)
1801–1840*	25.1	28.3	573 marriages in two areas (1 in New England)
1841–1880*	15.5	16.9	555 marriages in two areas (both in New England)
1960–1964†	22.5		
1964–1966‡	19.5		

*Daniel Scott Smith and Michael S. Hindus, "Premarital Pregnancy in America, 1640–1966: An Overview and Interpretation. " (Paper presented at the annual meeting of the American Historical Association, New York City, December 1971).

†Wilson H. Grabill and Maria Davidson, "Marriage, Fertility and Childspacing: June 1965," U.S. Bureau of the Census, Current Population Reports, series p-20, no. 186 (Washington, 1969), table 17, p. 39. This measure includes births from eight months and zero days to nine months and thirty days after marriage but excludes those born before marriage; the denominator includes all births after forty-eight months of marriage.

‡U.S. Department of Health, Education and Welfare, Public Health Service, "Interval between first marriage and legitimate first birth, United States, 1964–66," *Monthly Vital Statistics Report,* vol. 18, no. 12 (March 27, 1970): 2, table 2. Proportion of first births under eight months of marriage.

SOURCE: Smith, 1973, p. 323.

to less occupational and social differentiation, the premarital sex codes will be more permissive than where the female's status is completely or primarily dependent on the status of her husband."[36] As a cross-national example, he refers to Scandinavia with its emphasis on gender-role equality and also its greater acceptance of premarital sexual permissiveness. And as an intranational example, Tomasson refers to sociologist James Coleman's suggestion that differences in black and white premarital sex codes in the United States may be related to the differing degrees of female autonomy in the two groups. Coleman argues that where women are more independent and equalitarian, as is true among blacks, we can expect that "the sex codes will be less rigid."[37]

It would seem that, if Tomasson and Coleman are correct, the most likely nations to have a high degree of premarital sexual permissiveness would be socialist countries. The equality of the sexes is an important part of socialist ideology. Such an ideology leaves no room for the double standard which gives premarital sexual privileges to males but not to females. However, an equalitarian ideology could mean either that *both* males and females should be free to engage in premarital coitus or else that *neither* males nor females should be free to engage in premarital coitus. Several socialist experiments give evidence of a struggle between these two extremes—total sexual permissiveness on the one hand, and total sexual abstinence before marriage on the other. In some cases, a position between the two polar extremes has become the prevailing norm, namely, the standard that Ira Reiss has named "permissiveness with affection."

Soviet Union

Freedom in sexual matters, or discipline in sexual matters? This was the question Russia struggled with repeatedly. In the early years after the 1917 Revolution, the Communist Party followed the thinking of Marx and Engels in making it clear that sex belonged to the private sphere of individual freedom rather than to the public sphere subject to regulation by the State. At the same time, the institution of the family was devalued and expected to wither away in the years ahead, along with other social institutions considered no longer necessary. As a result of all this, Russia had its own version of the "roaring twenties." A 1920 Party journal carried an article asserting that "an unimaginable bacchanalia is going on . . . the best people are interpreting free love as free debauchery."[38]

There are many ideas about how sexual freedom fitted into the Revolution and Marxist philosophy. Sociologist H. Kent Geiger points out that the peasants in particular simply accepted the new sexual freedom as "a gift of the Revolution," a "pleasure to be enjoyed to the full."Others followed what came to be known as the "glass of water theory," a more sophisticated view in which the significance of sex was akin to swallowing a drink of water to quench physical thirst. And some suggested that "sexual property" should be held in common and shared along with all other kinds of property. Closely linked to the drink-of-water theory was what Geiger calls the "elemental nature" view. Here sex was treated merely as an instinct to be satisfied and was rationalized on the basis of writings of Marx and Engels which emphasized "natural man."[39]

Many persons viewed sexual permissiveness as a symbolic defiance of the entire old order, a patriotic means of opposing bourgeois morality. Others found still different ways to link sexual freedom with the communist cause. Some said they needed alternative outlets for sex drives because their devotion to the Revolution left no time for settling down with a family. Others said a permanent union involved too much risk, since the spouse might later turn out to be uncommitted to the cause. Still others suggested that poverty justifies promiscuity, since the poor can't maintain a family.

The notion of "free love" in the writings of Marx and Engels actually emphasized the freeing of love from economic concerns so that a man and woman could form a union based on deep feeling for one another rather than on other considerations. But the term *free* was widely misinterpreted, as was the idea of "love." Among the students, there arose the opinion that the way to enter into love was through sex. If good Marxists were to love, then they must realize that sexual attraction formed the base on which love could be built. If the sexual foundation didn't work out, the whole superstructure would topple.

Such rationalizations and the accompanying behavior troubled the older generation of Marxists. For one thing, it soon became clear that even in a social order that promised the equality of the sexes, women were the least likely to benefit from the sexual anarchism being advocated by some. Through mockery and ridicule, young communists used a new "male line" as they tried to persuade young women to grant sexual favors. They told women they were not true comrades if they still followed bourgeois prejudices about sex outside of marriage. Lunacharski indignantly remarked, "The frightened girl thinks she is acting like a marxist, like a leninist, if she denies no one."[40]

However, the old values were still strong among the majority of the population, and many persons were genuinely concerned about the sexual excesses that seemed to follow in the wake of the overturned social order. Yet how could the young be trained? It was hard to come up with convincing reasons for sexual restraint in view of the way many young theorists had begun to interpret Marxist thought. Men, even Party leaders, were engaging in sexual adventures that left helpless women pregnant and abandoned while the men went on their merry way enjoying still more of the new freedoms. As Geiger points out, this problem caused deep distress among those who took Marxist thought seriously and therefore decried the exploitation of the weak by the strong.

One female writer suggested that a possible solution might lie in freeing women from enslavement to certain ideas, such as the quest for love and identity through attachment to men. The aim of Alexandra Kollontai was to "teach women not to put all their hearts and souls into the love for a man, but into the essential thing, creative work. . . . Love must not crush the woman's individuality, not bind her wings."[41] She didn't deny that sex and love could or even should go hand in hand, but she wanted people to view them as separate feelings. In Kollontai's thought, a sexual union could be either prolonged or transient and still express love, totally apart from institutional forms. She argued that women had the right to enjoy sexual gratifications with a number of men, just as men felt they had such rights with regard to women.[42]

The new sexual freedom brought other problems besides the exploitation of women. Kollontai, drawing on Marx and Engels, looked forward to a new order in which the self-absorption of traditional romantic love where the sexual partners focused only on themselves and each other would give way to "solidarity love." This higher love would embrace the whole of the new society in "sympathetic bonds." But until that time, male-female relationships would present problems. In Kollontai's words, "Contemporary love always sins in that, absorbing the thoughts and feelings of 'the two loving hearts' it at the same time isolates, separates off the loving pair from the collective."[43]

There was also the very real problem of energies deflected from the task of building the new society. An ascetic wing of the Party had emphasized this all along. Lenin, among others, argued that the Revolution "cannot tolerate orgiastic conditions . . . no weakening, no waste, no destruction of forces. Self-control, self-discipline, is not slavery, not even in love." He argued against the glass-of-water theory of sex as being contrary to the true meaning of "free" love in communist thought which emphasized a union based on deep feeling and comradeship. His own opinion was that a normal man wouldn't drink out of a gutter nor out of a glass "with the rim greasy from many lips."[44]

Others selectively used Freudian ideas to emphasize sublimation, arguing that a common pool of energy could express itself either in sexual activity or in socially constructive activity. Energy expended on sex was considered to be stolen and diverted from uses more beneficial to society. Young people must channel their sexual drives, redirecting energies into the service of the Revolution. They were now told that preoccupation with sex was characteristic of capitalism and bourgeois society and not at all in keeping with the rigorous discipline needed to build communism. If, under capitalism, religion served as opium to deaden the sensitivities of the masses, sex served in a similar capacity and likewise produced a narcotic effect.[45]

Thus, the pendulum began to swing the other way. During the 1920s, the cry was for human liberation and noninterference in sex as a private matter. But by the end of the twenties, the emphasis was on "social usefulness," with interference and regulation justified on the basis of Lenin's contention that sexual promiscuity was not a private and personal matter at all but rather of social concern because of the possibility of pregnancy.[46]

People's Republic of China

In China, the cultural revolution seems to have skipped the early stages of total sexual freedom that at first characterized the Soviet experience. Instead, the People's Republic has from the outset nurtured a puritanism that calls for premarital sexual abstinence for both sexes, along with faithfulness after

Chinese women want to assert themselves as persons and workers, not sex objects.

marriage. Prostitution was abolished, and new jobs were provided for the prostitutes.[47] Women concerned with emancipation and equal rights were not interested in freedom to engage in premarital coitus. Quite the contrary. Chinese women wanted to escape the sexual slavery to men that had bound them for centuries. They wanted to assert themselves as persons and workers, not sex objects.[48]

The Maoists encourage late marriages for both sexes, since love affairs and family concerns are thought to divert energies from educational and career pursuits and from service to the revolution. As part of the propaganda campaign of the early 1960s, young women were warned that early marriage and childbearing would severely damage their health and that of their offspring. Young men under twenty-five were told that "unrestrained indulgence of the sexual impulse" would hinder their sleep and exercise after work, that it would dissipate bodily fluid, bring about nervous disorders, and cause such ailments as headaches, dizziness, tension, memory decline, mental and physical pain, impotence, and premature old age.[49] Such warnings are similar to those that were spread in the nineteenth-century United States through advice books addressed to young men. The emphasis was upon the supposed conservation of energy by restraining from masturbation and sexual intercourse in order to redirect energies into occupational success. One historian has called this view of sexuality "the spermatic economy."[50] It is interesting to observe its revival in China as late as the 1960s.

Israeli Kibbutzim

In the early revolutionary phase, the young pioneers of the kibbutz, like their counterparts in Russia and China, attempted to build a society free of sex-role differentiation. At the same time, this new society would discourage the bonding of women and men into small isolated family units. Part of this was in reaction to anything "bourgeois," as traditional marriage was considered.[51] For one thing, conventional marriage kept women in a lower status socially, economically, and legally. But another strain that was just as strong in the antifamilistic tendencies of these collectives was the realization that the internal ties of small family units would bind the individuals within them to one another more than to the community as a whole. "Families may easily become competing foci of emotional involvement that can infringe on loyalty to the collective," explains sociologist Yonina Talmon.[52] We saw earlier that similar concerns were voiced at one time in the Soviet Union.

Quite naturally questions began to arise about handling sexuality in the kibbutz. If conventional marriage were abolished, would it mean total sexual freedom? Could anyone have sex relations with anyone he or she desired? The kibbutz had no clear-cut ideology, so things had to work themselves out by trial and error. There were experiments with polygamy, for example, and a rejection of "bourgeois" standards such as premarital chastity and lifelong fidelity.[53] At the same time, there were efforts toward de-eroticizing the sexes, with emphasis on how alike men and women were. Women adopted male dress and discontinued concern with cosmetics and beauty care. Dormitory rooms were shared by men and women in groups in casual, nonsexual roommate arrangements. A mixed shower was instituted but was soon abandoned because the persons involved felt their previous training was too strong and inhibiting.

Sexual relations were themselves considered a personal matter, and premarital intercourse met with no disapproval on the part of the community. Promiscuity (in the sense of casual sex with a variety of partners) was discouraged, but if a man and woman both desired coitus out of love for each other and deep emotional attachment, they felt free to engage in intercourse. At the same time the exclusiveness of romantic love presented problems for the collective in the way it set couples apart. Thus, it became customary for couples to try to keep secret the special ties between them.

This secrecy and restraint in public demonstration of "coupleness," was one of several counterbalances that Talmon suggests were operative in keeping in check the liberal "emphasis on personal autonomy and erotic gratification." Other counterbalances were the sexual modesty and reticence the young people brought from their Jewish upbringing, and the rigorous way of life in the kibbutz, with its emphasis on deferred gratification, commitment to the task at hand, and strict self-discipline.[54]

As a result of the strong counterbalances to the earlier free love notions, there arose a comparatively conservative attitude toward sex in the kibbutz. Group activities are encouraged rather than couple activities, and children and adolescents are encouraged to view one another in nonsexual ways, that is, to simply see one another as persons.[55] Sexual relations during high school days have been discouraged primarily because they are considered distracting and would hinder young people in their work and studies. After high school graduation, however, young men and women are considered full-fledged members of the kibbutz and may freely engage in sexual relations. The community regards this as a private matter of concern only to the man and woman involved until a couple wishes to marry. Traditionally, at the time of marriage the couple would apply for a common room and this gesture would be the only ceremony required.[56] However, in recent years, there has been a move toward having a wedding as a meaningful and memorable event.[57]

There have been other changes in recent years. Talmon has pointed out trends away from asceticism and austerity and a working out of new compromise patterns. She sees evidence that the sense of social mission that once imbued the kibbutz community is declining. Other sociologists have shown that this "laxist tendency" has had an effect in the sexual sphere.[58] The traditional sexual code, with its stress on restraint, is still the official standard; but there is more pairing off among high school students. Sexual relations sometimes occur among these couples, and abortions have been arranged for some of the teenage pregnancies that have resulted. Some girls begin dating as early as the eighth grade, and they usually date upperclassmen. High school girls are more apt to be sexually experienced than are boys, since many girls of high school age have older boyfriends from among soldiers or young men of the kibbutz.[59] At the same time, sexual promiscuity continues to be frowned upon; and premarital sexual intercourse is most acceptable in a relationship likely to lead to marriage.

The kibbutz in recent years has been characterized by a growing differentiation of sex roles, with women being allotted more traditionally feminine tasks in the work of the collective. Women have also begun showing more concern about dress, including jewelry and makeup. Even a hairdresser may now be found in the kibbutz. Attractiveness to males and an emphasis on marriage and children seem to be taking on an importance to kibbutz women that was unknown in the early days of the movement. In this context, the permissiveness-with-affection standard appears to be widely accepted.

Socialist Democracy of Sweden

When Tomasson formulated his proposition regarding an association between female equality and greater permissiveness in premarital sex, he had in mind primarily the Scandinavian countries—particularly Sweden, which was the focus of his sociological study. He refers to research which indicates that "the majority of young Swedes have premarital intercourse and that they begin at an early age." For example, a 1968 study showed that over 95 percent of the married persons in the sample had experienced premarital coitus. A study of military draftees in 1964 indicated that 83 percent of the men had experienced sexual intercourse before marriage.[60] Studies of college students conducted in 1960 and 1965 yielded the information that within the five-year period, the percentage of boys who had experienced premarital coitus rose from 72 percent to 81 percent. For girls, the percentage rose from 40 percent to 65 percent. And in another 1965 study designed to investigate the sexual habits and knowledge of teenagers, it was found that 57 percent of the boys and 46 percent of the girls had experienced coitus by their late teens. For boys, the median age for their first experience was 16; for girls, it was 17.[61]

Birgitta Linner, a Swedish authority in family counseling, has pointed out that sex surveys were woefully few in Sweden until rather recently, since Swedish sociologists tended to rely on studies done in the United States. Because of this, we have no record of a jump in nonvirginity in the 1920s that might be compared with what was happening elsewhere in the world—such as the United States, England, France, and Germany—during that time of rapid social change.

However, an event did take place in Sweden in 1920 that laid the ground-work for vast changes in the years to follow. In that year, Sweden passed the first democratic family laws anywhere in the world.[62] Husband and wife, according to the new Marriage Code, were to have equal roles and rights and mutual responsibilities within the family—including the assumption of financial obliga-tions for one another and their children, with housework being considered as a financial contribution to the household. Other laws followed in the decades ahead—laws affecting divorce, women's rights, the care of children, benefits for unwed mothers, financial allowances, and so on. Both official government policy and the general social climate were moving in the direction of full equality for both sexes and away from the old double standard in any of its forms.

Sex education has been required in all school grades for more than a decade. This has included efforts to socialize children to look upon their roles in the family and society as being equal and interchangeable rather than linked to gender. Contraceptive information is also considered important and is dissemi-nated through sex education in the schools and through public service advertisements. Although there are moral debates over the issue, the feeling is rather strong in Sweden and other Scandinavian countries that young people should be able to act upon their sexual urges responsibly, using birth control, rather than being told they must refrain from sex until marriage with the result that unwise early marriages are entered or else unplanned pregnancies before marriage occur.

Even so, from one-third to one-half of Swedish brides are pregnant on their wedding day.[63] This does not reflect a high proportion of "forced marriages" so much as it indicates the norm of sexual intercourse during engagement. It also tells us something about the social acceptance of premaritally conceived children and their parents in Swedish society. Unmarried pregnant girls are not encouraged to marry just to "give the child a name" or protect themselves and their children from the cruel taunts of society. In Sweden, large numbers of unmarried women elect to keep their children born out of wedlock, and the laws and social policy provide generous and humane support.[64] Overall, the emphasis in Sweden is more on the permissiveness-with-affection standard rather than casual sex with a variety of partners. At the same time, there is enough "casual sex" to cause what Linner refers to as the one "pessimistic aspect of sex in Swedish society," the rising frequency of venereal disease.

It should be kept in mind that premarital sexual experience is not a new thing in the Scandinavian countries. As sociologist Harold T. Christensen points out, "In Denmark . . . sexual intercourse during engagement is a tradition at least three or four centuries old," and it was not at all unusual for couples to wait until pregnancy occurred before going ahead with the wedding.[65] Linner likewise refers to the agricultural roots and peasant culture that are part of Sweden's history; and in this setting sex relations before marriage and premaritally conceived children were not at all unusual. In fact, the number of children born out of wedlock is lower now than in the nineteenth century.[66] Nevertheless, the older generation has had some difficulty in accepting the newer attitudes toward sex in Sweden, no doubt because of greater openness in discussing the subject and the replacement of double-standard thinking with a norm of sexual equality for both sexes.

Tomasson has written that "a permissive sex ethic, which is essentially a premarital sex ethic that gives females the same rights and privileges that men tacitly enjoy in other more sexually restrictive societies, is only an aspect of the general status of women in a society." He describes the requisite "general status of women" in terms of four characteristics: a high level of equality with males, minimization of sexual differentiation in roles, relative economic independence from males, and status determined by individualistic achievements rather than by the status of husbands.[67]

These four characteristics are descriptive of Sweden, and Tomasson's proposition fits. The premarital sex ethic in Sweden is permissive. However, these four characteristics are also descriptive of Communist China, and there the premarital sex ethic is restrictive. Both countries have in common the renunciation of the double standard. But while Sweden has moved toward equality in permissiveness, the People's Republic of China has moved toward equality in abstinence. Even socialist experiments have no "one and only" answer to the question of premarital sex.

THEORETICAL PERSPECTIVE ON PREMARITAL SEX

We have seen that traditionally throughout history and in various cultures, males have been more sexually permissive before marriage than have females. Table 3-F illustrates this not only by showing higher overall male rates of nonvirginity, but also through presenting the different percentages for men and women during each year of college. The data came from a 1967 national sample of nearly 1,200 undergraduates from twelve colleges and universities in the United States and may be compared to some of the studies cited earlier in this chapter.

Not only is the percentage of males who experience premarital sexual intercourse higher than that of females, there is also evidence that more males than females engage in other forms of sexual expression outside of marriage as well. For example, sociologist Donald Carns found in this same sample of college students that 93 percent of the males had masturbated in comparison to 49 percent of the females.[68] And in an international sample of college and university students, two sociologists, Eleanore Luckey and Gilbert Nass, found that "women subjects in general reported less participation in all categories of sexual behavior than men did."[69] (See Table 3-G.)

Males and females differ in attitudes as well as behavior, with males accepting higher levels of sexual permissiveness than females do, according to

TABLE 3-F GENDER, YEAR IN COLLEGE, AND SEXUAL STATUS (VIRGIN OR NONVIRGIN)

Year in College	Sexual Status (% nonvirgin)	
	Male	Female
Freshman	36	19
Sophomore	63	30
Junior	60	37
Senior	68	44
Total from entire sample, all years of school combined	56	32
Number of students in sample (n)	(593)	(584)

SOURCE: Adapted from Simon, Berger, and Gagnon, 1972, p. 208.

TABLE 3-G   PERCENT OF FEMALES AND MALES REPORTING EXPERIENCING RESPECTIVE SEXUAL BEHAVIORS

Type of Sexual Behavior	United States	Canada	England	Germany	Norway
Females					
Light embracing or fond holding of hands	97.5	96.5	91.9	94.8	89.3
Casual goodnight kissing	96.8	91.8	93.0	74.0	75.0
Deep kissing	96.5	91.8	93.0	90.6	89.3
Horizontal embrace with some petting but not undressed	83.3	81.2	79.1	77.1	75.0
Petting of girl's breast area from outside her clothing	78.3	78.8	82.6	76.0	64.3
Petting of girl's breast area without clothes intervening	67.8	64.7	70.9	66.7	58.9
Petting below the waist of the girl under her clothing	61.2	64.7	70.9	63.5	53.6
Petting below the waist of both man and girl, under clothing	57.8	50.6	61.6	56.3	42.9
Nude embrace	49.6	47.6	64.0	62.1	51.8
Coitus	43.2	35.3	62.8	59.4	53.6
One-night affair involving coitus; didn't date person again	7.2	5.9	33.7	4.2	12.5
Whipping or spanking before petting or other intimacy	4.5	5.9	17.4	1.0	7.1
(n)	(688)	(85)	(86)	(96)	(56)

Ira Reiss.[70] His studies indicated that females are more likely to have permissive or liberal attitudes toward premarital sexual behavior if *love* is involved. Moving from attitudes to the actual experience of premarital sexual intercourse, there is evidence from the 1967 United States study of college students that "women almost universally had at least emotional ties to their first coital partner and that 59 percent planned to marry him." Sociologists William Simon, Alan Berger, and John Gagnon contrast this finding with the experience of males. Only 14 percent reported that their first coitus was with the woman they planned to marry.[71] In seeking an explanation for these male-female differences, we need

TABLE 3-G (Continued)

Type of Sexual Behavior	United States	Canada	England	Germany	Norway
Males					
Light embracing or fond holding of hands	98.6	98.9	93.5	93.8	93.7
Casual goodnight kissing	96.7	97.7	93.5	78.6	86.1
Deep kissing	96.0	97.7	91.9	91.1	96.2
Horizontal embrace with some petting but not undressed	89.9	92.0	85.4	68.8	93.6
Petting of girl's breast area from outside her clothing	89.9	93.2	87.0	80.4	83.5
Petting of girl's breast area without clothes intervening	83.4	92.0	82.8	69.6	83.5
Petting below the waist of the girl under her clothing	81.1	85.2	84.6	70.5	83.5
Petting below the waist of both man and girl, under clothing	62.9	64.8	68.3	52.7	55.1
Nude embrace	65.6	69.3	70.5	50.0	69.6
Coitus	58.2	56.8	74.8	54.5	66.7
One-night affair involving coitus; didn't date person again	29.9	21.6	43.1	17.0	32.9
Whipping or spanking before petting or other intimacy	8.2	5.7	17.1	0.9	5.1
Sex on pay-as-you-go basis	4.2	4.5	13.8	9.8	2.5
(n)	(644)	(88)	(123)	(112)	(79)

SOURCE: Luckey and Nass, 1969, pp. 374–375.

to look again at how and why males and females are socialized for different roles, and how this gender typing affects sexual attitudes and behavior.

Sexual Learning and Gender-Role Socialization

The attitudinal and behavioral differences in men and women with regard to premarital sex do not indicate that males are biologically more "highly sexed" than females. It is true that at one time people believed that men had stronger sex desires, drives, and needs than women, who were considered uninterested in sex; but modern scientific research has shown such beliefs to be in error. William H. Masters, a professor of obstetrics and gynecology, and his associate Virginia Johnson, have conducted careful scientific studies of human sexuality which show that physiologically what happens during sexual orgasm is the same for both men and women—that is, both males and females go through the same four stages of arousal and sexual climax: a time of excitement, then a "plateau" of pleasurable sensations, followed by the explosive sexual climax (orgasm), and then the phase called "resolution" (a return to the normal preexcitement state).[72] Men and women are not so different sexually as was once thought. Women are capable of sexual response and enjoyment to the same degree as men. In fact, the Masters/Johnson research showed that women have the capability for more sexual orgasms in a shorter space of time than is usually true of men.

West German sociologists Gunter Schmidt and Volkmar Sigusch also found that women can be aroused and react just as strongly as men through viewing erotic films and slides or reading sexually explicit stories.[73] Through carefully conducted, controlled, and measured laboratory experiments in which persons reported on their sexual behavior and sexual reactions in the twenty-four hours before and twenty-four hours after exposure to sexually explicit materials, Schmidt and Sigusch found that 87 percent of the men and 72 percent of the women observed some sort of physiosexual reaction (usually a full or partial erection in the men and genital sensations and vaginal lubrication in the women), and that furthermore, "psychosexual stimulation leads to an increase of masturbation to the same extent in both men and women."[74] However, although there were similarities in physical reaction, the emotional reaction of the women to the films was somewhat more pronounced than was true of men, particularly in the degree to which they reported shock, irritation, or disgust.

These findings differed greatly from the Kinsey studies two decades earlier, which had seemed to indicate that women are not generally aroused by observing portrayals of sexual action in pictures and films or by reading erotic novels and stories. Kinsey suggested the likelihood that "most females are indifferent or antagonistic to the existence of such material because it means nothing to them erotically."[75] Women, said Kinsey, indicated more interest in "more general situations, affectional relationships, and love."

Schmidt, Sigusch, and Schafer attempted to discover if sexually explicit stories in the context of affectionate expression would be more erotically stimulating to females than to males, and also whether the introduction of the affection element would cause a greater response in women than would a sexual situation separated from affection. On the basis of their research, these social scientists concluded that "the stories with and without affection do not have a significantly differing effect on men or women." They went on to say:

Affection is not a necessary precondition for women to react sexually to sexual stimuli in the same manner as men. Even for stories which describe sexual relations in detail excluding and avoiding any expressions of tenderness and affection . . . sexual arousal and sexual activation among females are as great as among males. This finding tends to refute the claim that female sexuality is basically more dependent on affection than male sexuality.[76]

Commenting on these findings, Paul Gebhard, who became director of the Institute for Sex Research upon Kinsey's death, suggests that the discrepancies with the earlier Kinsey findings may be explained by the wording of the Kinsey question (which depended upon respondents' recall of earlier feelings) and which did not take into account the different cultural conditioning males and females have received. Gebhard points out that women in our culture are trained to be cautious about sex whereas males "do not receive this defensive conditioning." Thus, when women are suddenly presented with a picture of sexual activity, they may react negatively; whereas when presented with such materials gradually, as in a motion picture, they are likely to experience sexual arousal. The Kinsey research uncovered indications of this tendency, but it was not taken into account when male and female responsiveness was compared. Gebhard reaches the same conclusion as did the West German researchers. He points out that both Masters and Johnson and the Institute for Sex Research have shown "the essential equality of males and females in response to tactile stimuli," that is, the capabilities of both sexes to react when the sense of touch is involved (as in petting, masturbation, or coitus). And he suspects that if culturally produced variables are taken into account, research will show males and females to be "very similar, if not identical, in their inherent capacity to respond sexually to visual stimuli," as well.[77]

Gebhard's reference to cultural conditioning on top of the studies that show that males and females are not *biologically* different with respect to sexual arousal and response brings us once again to the matter of *socialization,* the training that persons receive to fit them for their roles in society. In the last chapter, we saw that males and females are socialized differently from one another. These differences may be seen even in the learning and experience of sexuality.

Mary Walshok, a sociologist who has conducted research on the relationship between gender-role typing and sexuality, states that males are typically more "instrumental" in their sexual attitudes and behavior, while females tend to be more "expressive." "On the whole," writes Walshok, "male patterns are characterized by a capacity to treat sexuality as an end in itself, whereas female patterns are less directly sexual and more typically an outgrowth or expression of some more encompassing emotional or social commitment."[78] Earlier, we saw that the degree to which persons are either instrumental (task-centered and goal-oriented) or expressive (person-oriented) is a matter of social learning.

At the very beginning of sexual awareness, gender-typed differences show up. Almost twice as many males as females experience sexual orgasm through masturbation during adolescence; and among females who have experienced orgasm through masturbation, about half do so only after having first experienced orgasm through a sexual experience with a male.[79] The male peer group encourages boys to experiment with sex, talk about it, joke about it, and so on. Adolescent boys more than adolescent girls come in contact with pornographic materials and similarly are more likely to report sexual arousal through sexual fantasies and daydreams. When adolescent girls daydream, they are more likely to be thinking about a situation of romantic love rather than about sex as an end in itself. Sociologists William Simon and John Gagnon report that for females "opportunities for learning and performing sexual activity are not provided" so that "an interest in sexuality for its own sake or for the sake of pleasure" is not developed to the extent it is in males during this period of life.[80]

Even the graffiti found on the walls of public rest rooms gives evidence of gender-typed approaches to sexuality. The Kinsey researchers found that 86 percent of male toilet wall inscriptions were sexual in nature, both in words and pictures. Females were much less likely to make any sorts of inscriptions; but when they did, they tended to draw pictures of hearts or to write in lipstick phrases such as "Bill and Sue" or "Kathy loves Jeff." Kinsey and his associates viewed this comparison of the female and male inscriptions as indicative of "some of the most basic sexual differences between females and males."[81] For males, sexual interest appeared to be genital-centered, while for females it was relationship-centered.

Gagnon and Simon point out that, in the unwritten script usually followed during adolescent petting, "the description is one of male as subject (active, controlling) and female as object (passive, controlled). Males . . . do, females react or gate keep."[82] Less awakened to her sexual self, the female is concentrating on preventing too much access to her body at the same time that the more erotically aware and experienced male is attempting sexual activity which is clearly goal-directed.

Sociologist Lester Kirkendall has written of the problems of male virgins,[83] calling attention to the pressures peer groups place upon males who are relatively sexually inexperienced. If a male has not yet tried sexual intercourse, he is sometimes made to feel that something must be wrong with him and that he is not demonstrating masculinity. Such pressures toward sexual performance may be felt in high school, college, the military, or in work situations with older males who tease about sexual intercourse.

Gagnon and Simon make the observation that the adolescent male world is a *homosocial* (not to be confused with homosexual) world, with a great concern for the approval of those of the same gender. Sexual contacts with females, then, become ways of establishing and confirming social status among males.[84] Males talk together about "scoring," "how far one can get," "making bases or hitting a home run," and so on. The emphasis is on the "degree of sexual access achieved," write Gagnon and Simon, contrasting these male conversations with female conversations where girls describe relationships in terms of the "level of affection offered." Females have traditionally spoken less about sex and more about perceived or hoped-for feelings of fondness or love on the part of the male.

Sociologist Donald Carns, using data from the 1967 national sample of college students, found gender differences even in the management of the first coital experience.[85] Males tended to talk about the experience sooner and to more people and more often met with approval on the part of those to whom the event was reported than was true of females. Among males who had experienced sexual intercourse, more than half reported that five or more college friends knew about it. Among the sexually experienced females, less than one-fourth indicated that five or more college friends knew about their premarital coitus, and 27 percent had told no one at all. Twenty-nine percent of the women had talked about the event with only one or two friends. Among sexually experienced men, nearly 18 percent told no one, and only 14 percent reported the event to as few as one or two friends.

A difference also showed up in *when* persons told their friends, with 30 percent of the males reporting that they told someone immediately after the event, in contrast to 14 percent of the females. Among the sexually experienced males, 86 percent reported that the first person who was told about the event reacted approvingly. Sixty-seven percent of the females met with such approval, with the remainder meeting with mixed reactions or disapproval. Carns concluded that the evidence points to "a pattern of male 'ego-sex' [which] emerges within the context of the so-called 'male bond' (male peers as audiences for sexual prowess)." This is in sharp contrast to the female's management of the first experience of sexual intercourse.

In explaining why he focused on the first event of sexual intercourse, Carns described it as "pivotal behavior, one which creates either problems or prospects," because in our society the first coitus is "decidedly an irreversible event. One possesses one sexual status before the act—'virgin'—and another afterwards." A person's management of the event and its public presentation would therefore seem to tell us a great deal about that person's conception of his or her sexual identity.

Traditionally, males and females have conceived of their respective sexual identities differently. But why? At this point, some insights from John Gagnon and William Simon are helpful. They take issue with psychoanalytic theories that view adolescent and adult sexuality as a reenactment of sexual predispositions developed during infancy and suggest instead that sexual behavior is *learned* behavior. "The development of the sexual comes relatively late in character development," they write, "and rather than being the engine of change, it takes its meaning primarily from other sources of personality development."[86] They point out that part of the legacy of Freud is our ability to seek out a sexual ingredient in nonsexual behavior and symbolism. But it may be erroneous to begin with sex and see how other areas of life are affected by sexuality. Perhaps the order should be reversed. Perhaps this should be the question: How does sexual behavior "express and serve nonsexual motives"?[87]

In viewing sexual attitudes and behavior as resulting from social learning, Gagnon and Simon draw attention to the part played by gender-role socialization. Training for society's assigned roles, masculine and feminine, produces two different approaches to sexuality (rather than being the other way around). Whereas males learn sexuality "prior to profound linkages with the rest of life," females act out their sexuality "later and in response to the demands of males and within the framework of societal expectations." Gagnon and Simon write: "For the female, sexual activity does not occur for its own sake, but for the sake of children, family, and love. Thus sexuality for the female has less autonomy than it has for the male, and the body (either of the self or of others) is not seen by women as an instrument of self-pleasure. This vision of sexuality as a form of service to others is continuous with the rest of female socialization."[88]

How Sociological Theories Apply

In accounting for the learned differences in male and female sexuality, sociologists have taken different approaches. Some, arguing from the structure-functionalist vantage point, would say that the gender-role learning which emphasizes female sexuality in the context of love and commitment is necessary for her fulfillment of her traditional family-centered role in adulthood (wifehood, motherhood, and serving the interests of others as the expressive hub of the home).

Others would question this approach, raising the objections that males, too, could be socialized to view sex in a context of love, commitment, marriage, and family; or that females could be socialized to have more autonomy in sex and learn to appreciate it for its own sake in the way males are trained to. One sociologist has spelled out a detailed analysis of what he calls "sexual stratification" in terms of conflict theory and social exchange. Randall Collins asserts that historically and cross-culturally men have usually been the "sexual aggressors" and women the "sexual prizes for men."[89] The model is one of coercion, with a dominant group (males) having control over a subordinate group (females). In some societies, females are clearly viewed as sexual property, taken as booty in war, used by fathers in economic bargaining, considered to be owned by husbands, and so on. Collins argues that the root of male dominance has lain in the physical strength, size, and aggressiveness of the male sex, while female vulnerability stemmed not only from their generally smaller size but also from their role in bearing and caring for children. As we saw in Chapter 2, these physical differences may also lie at the root of male *economic* dominance in traditional societies.

Collins refers to the conflict model of stratification of the social theorist Max Weber and shows how it applies to the male-female sexual situation in various types of societies. The first point is that "persons struggle for as much dominance as their resources permit." Thus males by virtue of their physical strength, freedom from the biological limitations of menstruation and childbirth, and greater economic advantages gained domination over women. The main resource of a female was considered to be her sexuality, to which a man acquired exclusive rights because of his greater resources. In some societies this exchange resulted from economic bargaining with the woman's father; and in such societies, women "are closely guarded so as not to lose their market value," which has given rise to customs such as wearing a veil, strict chaperonage, and so on. In ancient Hebrew society, for example, if a man seduced and had sexual intercourse with an unbetrothed virgin, he was required to take her as his wife and pay her father the bride price. If the father refused to give his daughter to him, the man still had to pay the father the bride price, since the loss of virginity made the woman of less worth on the marriage market.[90]

Collins' second point refers to Weber's belief that ideals are used as weapons in struggles for domination (in this case, the double standard with its emphasis on *female* chastity is illustrative). The third factor is that changes in the structure of domination take place when there are shifts in resources. As certain political and economic changes occur, women gain a better bargaining position. No longer under the control of their fathers, they "become at least potentially free to negotiate their own sexual relationships," writes Collins. "But since their main resource is their sexuality, the emerging free marriage market is organized around male trades of economic and status resources for possession of a woman."[91] Along with sexuality, female capabilities in homemaking and in providing emotional support for males also came to be valued resources as the ideology of romantic love grew.

The situation described by Collins is a possible explanation for the survival of the double standard, since it helps explain the traditionally greater reticence of females to accept for themselves the sexual permissiveness that has characterized males. Collins suggests that "the most favorable female strategy, in a situation where men control the economic world, is to maximize her bargaining power by appearing both as attractive and as inaccessible as possible." Overt sexuality may not be used to attract the male but only hinted at indirectly as a sort of grand prize or ultimate reward, because "sexuality must be reserved as a bargaining resource for the male wealth and income that can only be stably acquired through a marriage contract." Since men and women are bargaining with "unequal goods," femininity and female chastity are idealized, and woman is placed on a pedestal so that "an element of sexual repression is thus built into the situation."

The greatest bargaining power of all for women comes with increasing employment opportunities. Freed from economic dependence upon males, the sexual bargains struck by women can be less concerned with marriage and more concerned about other kinds of exchanges. Collins suggests that in a situation where women have their own economic resources, "dating can go on as a form of short-run bargaining, in which both men and women trade on their own attractiveness or capacity to entertain in return for sexual favors and/or being entertained."

Collins began with a picture of coercion in which one socially dominant group oppresses or exploits the other (conflict theory), but he moved on to a situation described in terms of a "free market," "bargaining," trading sexual resources for status and security (in other words, exchange theory). Persons give and receive in sexual relationships, and the exchange may be a fair one or it may be one in which one person has a greater advantage and receives the higher profits.[92]

Referring to traditional male-female dating relationships in a society where males dominate, Gagnon and Simon point out that "the physical exchanges are surrounded by other exchanges of words and gifts that affirm the increasing accessibility of the female's body."[93] Males in particular may use as resources words (assuring females of affection so that intimacy is legitimated from the female perspective) and gifts (paying for the dinners, movies, and so on, indicating an investment that is expected to result in varying degrees of sexual payoffs).

On the other hand, in societies where gender-role differentiation is not emphasized and females and males are in a more equal position by virtue of equal opportunities in the economic system, there is not the same kind of game playing in dating relationships. In Sweden, for example, dating is more casual, with little emphasis on playing the roles of feminine charmer, using sexual attractiveness as bait, or masculine pursuer on a mission of conquest. Friendship and equality are emphasized, with females feeling free to take the initiative in establishing relationships and to pay their own way on dates. It is conventional for dating partners to meet at the place of their date rather than an arrangement whereby the boy calls for the girl. In the early stages of relationship in Sweden, there is actually less emphasis on sex than is true in the United States, where kissing and petting are often introduced very early in a dating relationship. Swedish young people tend to take time to let intimacy develop slowly; but when intimacy in other aspects of the relationship has been developed, they tend to move on to the full sexual intimacy of coitus rather than leveling off at heavy petting and "technical virginity."[94] Females in Sweden, less concerned about guarding their sexuality as their chief bargaining resource, do not feel compelled to engage in intercourse because of the insistence of their boyfriends but rather do so because they themselves want to. "It even occasionally happens that boys agree to coitus because the girls want it," writes Swedish family-life authority Birgitta Linner.[95]

The term *technical virginity* has sometimes been used to describe the widespread practice of engaging in various sexual intimacies while still maintaining technically a state of virginity. Petting to orgasm through what is sometimes called "mutual masturbation," oral-genital stimulation, and placing the genitals together without proceeding to penetration, are examples of such intimacies.[96] It is widely believed that engaging in them will not make persons "nonvirginal."

Social Meaning of Virginity

Those who write and speak of virginity as a concept tend to think of it as a "given," something with an agreed-upon meaning so that "everybody knows what it is." Two sociologists, David Berger and Morton Wenger, have raised questions about this idea. They have concluded that the concept of virginity is a "variable one, assigned different meanings in different social contexts," and that furthermore the lack of agreement on the meaning and norms surrounding virginity "is due to the long-term changes in the economic role of women in modern industrial society."

Speaking of female virginity, Berger and Wenger claim that the ideology has persisted because it has served both sexes: "[It] not only serves the interests of men as a class by giving them overall control of women as property, but it also serves women's interests as individuals in that they find society legitimizing their control (marginal though it may be) over the only scarce resource available to them, the sexual and ego-gratification of males."[97] These sociologists further suggest that support of the concept of virginity as an ideal will decline with women's economic advancement.

In an attempt to find out if their ideas were on the right track, Berger and Wenger asked sociology students at two state-related Eastern colleges to complete a questionnaire designed to find out if the concepts of male virginity and female virginity are considered valid concepts, and if so, what does virginity mean? In answer to the question, "Does it make sense to say a woman (man) has lost her (his) virginity," 43 percent of their sample rejected the concept of virginity for both sexes, while 57 percent retained a belief that the notion of virginity *as a concept* has value.

However, what is of particular interest is that even among those who grant validity to the concept of virginity, there is considerable disagreement about exactly what constitutes virginity or its loss. The researchers asked a series of questions describing various types of sexual behavior and experiences for both males and females, and the respondents were asked to state whether or not each event constituted "loss of virginity." (See Table 3-H.)

Only about one-third of the respondents viewed the rupture of the hymen as meaning a female has lost her virginity, indicating that to most respondents the concept has another meaning than a physical state of being. But 81 percent considered the full penetration of a vagina by a penis to mean the loss of virginity for a female, which the researchers point out "is somewhat consistent with conventional notions of virginity." But they raise additional questions: "How, though, is the bringing of a male to climax consistent with this notion? Or the bringing of self to climax?" With regard to male virginity, slightly over half of the respondents considered the penetration of a woman's vagina, even without ejaculation, to constitute the loss of male virginity. A majority (around two-thirds or more in most cases) did not consider a male to have "lost his virginity" if he had intimate contact but did not ejaculate, or ejaculated by a woman's manipulations, or brought a woman to climax, or reached orgasm through masturbation.

From this data, Berger and Wenger conclude that a *variable* concept of virginity exists and that such a variable concept "is in the interests of both males and females in a society wherein there is considerable social stratification (economic and otherwise) by sex." According to these sociologists, the variable concept which allows a woman a certain amount of leeway in terms of the point where she crosses the line from virgin to nonvirgin permits her to have a degree of sexual gratification while still maintaining "her sexual value as an exclusive mate." Furthermore, it puts her in a position of advertising her product so that a man is enticed to become a captive "consumer market" at the same time that

TABLE 3-H ATTITUDES TOWARD SEXUAL EVENTS AND/OR BEHAVIORS CONSTITUTING "LOSS OF VIRGINITY"

	Yes, Means Loss		No, Doesn't Mean Loss	
	%	Number	%	Number
Has a female lost her virginity if:				
She brings a male to climax?	16.3	(33)	67.8	(137)
Her vagina is penetrated other than by penis?	16.8	(34)	66.5	(135)
Her vagina is fully penetrated by a penis?	81.3	(165)	4.9	(10)
Her hymen is ruptured?	32.7	(66)	51.5	(104)
She brings herself to climax?	40.9	(83)	40.4	(82)
Her vagina is partially penetrated by other than a penis?	6.4	(13)	74.9	(152)
A male brings her to climax?	21.7	(44)	61.1	(124)
("No responses" account for missing percentages.)				
Has a male lost his virginity if:				
He has a wet dream?	0.0	(0)	76.7	(128)
Penetrates a woman's vagina, but doesn't ejaculate?	53.3	(89)	22.8	(38)
He has intimate sexual contact, but doesn't ejaculate?	6.6	(11)	69.3	(115)
He ejaculates by a woman's manipulations?	5.4	(9)	68.7	(114)
Only if he brings a woman to climax?	12.7	(21)	62.7	(104)
He ejaculates by self-manipulation?	1.8	(3)	73.0	(119)
("No responses" account for missing percentages.)				

SOURCE: Berger and Wenger, 1973, p. 672.

the woman has a socially sanctioned reason (the ideology of virginity) for not giving away the ultimate reward, thus keeping her market value high.

For males, the variable concept of female virginity also serves a purpose, claim Berger and Wenger. "It allows the buyer with low resources (poor, unattractive, powerless, etc.) to buy 'used goods' while providing the ego-maintaining illusion that he has bought a new product." They are of course using the term *used goods* from the standpoint of the traditional ideology of virginity with its emphasis on being "untouched" and reserved for the exclusive possession of one man. It was also found that persons who had already engaged in sexual intercourse were less likely to feel that there was any validity in the notion of virginity as a concept. The researchers explain this too in terms of a market analogy by saying that the coitally experienced have "lost their market value along a certain commodity dimension, and therefore may wish to maximize their status along it by denying its existence." Those who had engaged only in petting were less apt to deny that virginity is a valid concept.

One point that Berger and Wenger emphasize is that an effective ideology cannot be too specific about what constitutes its violation. Therefore certain female conduct is viewed as acceptable because it does not deprive women of their one scarce resource (total sexual access), although, as Table 3-H makes clear, there is considerable disagreement about just what conduct does cause a female to pass over the invisible line between virginity and nonvirginity.

As regards male virginity, the only response showing considerable agreement about what constitutes its loss was the item about vaginal penetration. In fact, there is some indication that male loss of virginity is not viewed as a loss at all but rather as a gain. Acts indicating physical maturity (for example, ejaculation through "wet dreams" or masturbation) are not thought to change one's sexual status. Rather, according to Berger and Wenger, "it is possession (use) of a woman's unique resource (to be blunt, her vagina) that for males constitutes movement to the status of 'sexually experienced,' i.e., 'powerful' or 'wealthy.'" Having borrowed from exchange theory and conflict theory, these sociologists reach this conclusion: "Virginity, rather than seen as a 'state of being' in society, is viewed as a social-relational concept having to do with the state of conflict between two parties contending for scarce rewards in society, and in which conflict the contenders bring to bear those resources most available to them."[98]

As we have seen repeatedly, the ideology of female virginity is particularly strong in cultures with high male dominance. When varieties of sexual activity short of actual intercourse are practiced in such settings, the unwritten rules may be stricter than in the bargaining context of cultures where women have more autonomy. Political scientist Evelyn Stevens writes of the double-standard situation in Latin America where a young woman usually engages in intimate forms of noncoital sexual activity only with her fiance and then only as a means of holding his interest in her until they are married. If he is quite certain that she has not engaged in such behavior with any other man and if she provides him with the assurance that she is not enjoying the behavior, the Latin American male "may encourage or even insist on her 'obliging' him in this way."[99]

PREMARITAL SEX IN SOCIAL CONTEXT

Sociologist Ira Reiss has demonstrated that many different sociocultural factors enter into a person's attitudes and behavior with respect to premarital sex. Just as no other behavior develops in a social vacuum, so it is with sex. A basic theory of Reiss is that "the degree of premarital sexual permissiveness which is acceptable among courting individuals varies directly with the degree of autonomy in the courtship roles and with the degree of premarital sexual permissiveness accepted in the social and cultural setting of those individuals."[100] Increased autonomy for women usually is a factor in increasing courtship autonomy (for example, by eliminating the chaperonage system, lessening or doing away with parental control of mate selection, and making possible greater individualistic bargaining power). However, the second part of Reiss's proposition also comes into play. We saw this demonstrated in our examination of premarital sex in communist countries such as the Soviet Union and the People's Republic of China. The prevailing social norms discourage premarital sexual permissiveness in spite of the emphasis on female autonomy.

Some of the social factors in the United States which are most associated with different outlooks on premarital sex are religion, socioeconomic status, and race.

Religion

Research has shown that religion does make a difference in sexual attitudes and behavior. The particular religious faith doesn't seem to matter so much as does a person's commitment to that faith. A religiously devout person is less likely to engage in premarital sexual intercourse than a person who is less devout.

But how can sociologists measure devoutness or degree of religious commitment? One way is to measure the frequency with which persons attend religious services. Admittedly, this method has its shortcomings and measures devoutness in terms of involvement in institutional religion; yet it is helpful in tapping the degree of an individual's commitment.

When Zelnik and Kantner studied the data from their national sample of fifteen-to-nineteen-year-old females, they found that the likelihood of a young woman's having engaged in premarital sexual intercourse went down as her church attendance went up. The highest rates of premarital sexual intercourse are found among those young women who report they subscribe to no religion. This is true of both blacks and whites.[101]

Traditionally, the teachings of Catholicism, Protestantism, and Judaism have emphasized that sexual intercourse should be reserved for marriage.

Donald Carns, in analyzing data from a national survey of college students, found that religiosity does act as a brake and has a powerful effect on the degree of premarital sexual involvement. Carns measured religiosity two ways: in terms of *attendance* (including not only worship services but all types of religious functions, such as Sunday school, choir rehearsals, church-sponsored youth groups, and so on) and in terms of *religious self-image.* That is, respondents were asked how religious they personally perceived themselves to be, regardless of their degree of involvement in institutional religion.

Carns found that the more religious students were (whether rated by their own self-perception or by frequency of attendance at religious functions), the less likely they were to engage in premarital sexual activities. This was true for both males and females. It was also found that the higher persons rate in terms of religiosity, the more likely they are to cite "the wrongness or immorality of premarital coitus" as the reason they abstain. In addition to moral reasons for not engaging in premarital sexual intercourse, highly religious persons also tend to cite social reasons—namely, that their reputations would likely be damaged if they were to have sex relations before marriage. They are particularly concerned about their reputations among other religious persons.[102]

Religiosity is an example of how additional elements are brought into the sexual exchange process. What the devout person is saying to the partner is this: "You may have sexual access to me only if you commit yourself to me in marriage." The religious person is interested in more than a sexual exchange alone and is seeking certain kinds of spiritual gratifications from the partner. If these are not forthcoming, that partner is not deemed satisfying enough for consideration as a marriage eligible.[103] When the dating partner is not viewed as a marriage eligible, sexual interaction becomes more limited and restrained. By broadening the scope of male-female exchange in this way to include additional factors than sexual gratification and status seeking, the religiously devout place themselves in a situation that reduces the likelihood of sexual experience with a number of different partners, lowers the frequency of coitus, and cuts down the probability of exchanges that are considered unfair (exploitation).

This driving a hard bargain occurs even though more devout persons may have more traditional sex roles. Though religiously devout women may see themselves as less autonomous and more subordinate to men in general, [104] they are not prepared to grant many sexual favors unless men provide religious gratifications that show they could be marriage eligibles. And they are prepared to grant coitus only on consummation of marriage. Carns' data on males indicate that religious values and influences similarly guide male premarital sexual attitudes and behavior.

Socioeconomic Status

The Kantner/Zelnick data from the national probability sample of fifteen-to-nineteen-year-old females showed that "the higher the socioeconomic status—whether measured by poverty status, family income or parental or guardian education—the lower, generally, are the proportions with coital experience."[105]

Other studies indicate that the *meaning* of premarital sex also seems to vary according to social class. Whereas among middle-class young people there has been a move away from the double standard toward what Reiss calls "person-centered" sex, lower-class persons continue to think in terms of the double standard. Lee Rainwater points out that this is particularly true of white males in lower-status groups. Such males take pride in their sexual conquests, boast of their ability to have sexual intercourse with a large number of girls, and categorize girls according to their accessibility for sexual relations. Highest in value are virgins, and lowest are the "easy lays," with "one-man girls" ranking somewhere in between. Rainwater points out that among blacks there are not such clear-cut differences in the amount of sexual activity viewed as permissible for males and females.[106]

Even so, a study of lower-class boys from among three ethnic groups showed that the double standard is very much alive regardless of race. Bernard Lander interviewed Puerto Ricans living in New York, Appalachian whites living in Chicago, and blacks from Washington, D.C., with regard to sex attitudes and conduct. The double standard was particularly observable in the Chicago and Washington samples.[107]

Commenting on Lander's study, Bernard Rosenberg and Joseph Bensman point out that middle-class values of personalized sex have little relevance among impoverished groups in urban ghettos. Sex and love are not viewed in terms of emotional or material responsibility, nor on the other hand is there much evidence of "pure joy in unrestrained sexuality," which is sometimes thought to characterize lower-class persons. Rather, premarital sex is often considered to be sheer physical release, "the 'friction of two membranes'— in which the female is the necessary but unequal partner." Sex is also considered a way of winning prestige in peer-group competition and thereby proving one's masculinity. Rosenberg and Bensman write, "Since [sex] is a competitive game, the boy who plays cannot expect to earn points for scoring over an easy mark, a 'pig.' Victory consists in overcoming the largest possible number of inaccessible girls. The conversion of females into trophies reduces them to nonpersons."[108]

It isn't hard to see the connection between sex-role socialization and sexual attitudes and behavior later on. In the last chapter, we talked about the greater rigidity in sex roles that characterizes persons of lower social status. Boys are taught to be "masculine"—strong, dominant over women, emotionally cool and tough. Girls are taught to be "feminine"—dependent on men and submissive to them, emotionally warm and tender. Adults and peers encourage boys in their sexual pursuits, but at the same time daughters are usually shielded from even the basic facts about sex in the hope that such guarding will keep them innocent, pure, "good girls" in contrast to those who are promiscuous.[109] Being sexually restrained, in turn, is believed to win the greater respect and admiration of boys. Thus, when one of Lander's sample of Chicago whites from Appalachia was asked if he still considered a girl "decent" if she went to bed with him, the boy replied, "It's a matter of how hard I have to work. If I have to work real hard I think a lot of them. If they give it to me right off I think they're pigs."

Before leaving the general subject of social-class differences with regard to sexual permissiveness, it might be well to mention a conclusion reached by Ira Reiss. It will be recalled that Reiss concentrated in his research on *attitudes* toward premarital sex rather than on actual behavior, but he has suggested that a change is occurring which now makes questionable the idea (though rooted in historical fact) that the lower classes are more permissive in both attitudes and behavior. Reiss refers to his national sample of 1963 which did not show the expected differences by class as far as attitudes are concerned.

"After very elaborate computer checks," he wrote, "we discovered that there were, in relation to sexual orientation at least, two radically different social class systems." He was referring to whether persons at all class levels were either *liberal* or *conservative* in views on politics, education, and religion. He found that out of a group of conservatives, lower-status persons among them were the most permissive sexually. But in a group of liberals, the most permissive sexually turn out to be those of the higher classes (college-educated people). Reiss says it is not really surprising that this new permissiveness shows up among persons with college backgrounds, pointing out that this new sexual orientation "emphasizes control of pregnancy and venereal disease and stresses person-centered sexual encounters." "In short," writes Reiss, "it differs from the older, lower-class permissiveness which had an economic base and a fatalistic philosophy."[110]

Race

Because of the lack of privacy and crowded conditions of the ghetto, children of the black underclass (below the poverty line) are exposed to sex at a very early age. In the words of one black mother, "I can't hide the facts of life from them because they can see them every day on any stairway, hall, or elevator in the project."[111] Parents may attempt to protect girls more than boys because of fears of such consequences as pregnancy, but at the same time, parents know that a great deal of sexual experimentation is likely to go on.

Although lower-class black girls are not stigmatized in quite the same way as is true of lower-class white girls who engage in premarital sex, there are still some elements of an unequal power distribution between males and females in the sexual realm. A sexually experienced eight-year-old girl told researchers, "I don't like any of the boys around here cause they 'do it' with you and then they 'do it' with somebody else and they act like yourself ain't yourself." Already, this young female seemed to long to be "special" to a male rather than serving as one of his many sexual conquests. "In the later adolescent years, however, sex for girls takes on the important function of being a form of exchange," write sociologists Boone Hammond and Joyce Ladner, "primarily for material goods and services (gifts, money, etc.). Some economically and emotionally deprived girls are able to gain access to certain necessities from boy friends through their participation in sexual activities."[112]

In Kantner and Zelnik's national sample of both black and white teenage girls at all social levels, the main differences that showed up are these: First, the percentage of black young women who had experienced coitus was higher than that for whites at all socioeconomic levels. For both races, as family income goes up, the rates of premarital sex go down. Also, as the male parent or guardian's education goes up, the rates of premarital intercourse among fifteen-to-nineteen-year-olds goes down; and the difference is especially striking in the case of blacks. Black young women whose father or male guardian had only an elementary education have 58 percent rates of nonvirginity, but only 37.4 percent are sexually experienced where the father or male guardian has had some college. Among whites, the rates are 26.1 percent and 22.4 percent respectively. Another difference between blacks and whites in the Kantner/Zelnik study had to do with the age at which sexual intercourse begins, with sexually experienced blacks having begun coitus earlier than whites.[113]

One way to account for these differences is to think in terms of social exchange and the resources that are brought into the bargaining in such an exchange. Almost inevitably, additional elements beyond sex itself enter into the sexual bargaining process. If blacks are shown to be more sexually active than whites, it has nothing to do with the old myth that blacks are more "sexy" and have higher sex drives than whites. Rather, the explanation may lie in the fact that white racism has caused blacks to have been relatively blocked in their achievement aspirations at every class level.

Since among blacks there is likely to be less optimism about future educational and job opportunities, many young black women may feel that sexual favors are the only bargaining elements they have in their relationships with men. Thus physical gratifications and the approval and attention they bring may seem to be the only kinds of rewards they can reasonably expect. Hammond and Ladner, for example, tell of girls who engage in sexual intercourse in exchange for a movie date or even a ride in a car. One fifteen-year-old from a background of deprivation told the interviewers that sex relations provided a way of escape from her feelings of poverty. "[Sexual intercourse] makes you forget that you don't have the kinds of things you need for school," she said, "the money to buy your lunch and clothes to wear and stuff like that. I play hooky sometimes because I don't have those things but then I 'do it' and have a good time and I don't have to worry about those things."[114]

It is the absence of viable alternatives, then, that makes young black women (particularly in the underclass) more likely to seek sexual gratifications. Along with this comes increased vulnerability to exploitation. This is true in spite of the observation in Chapter 2 that blacks tend to hold more egalitarian sex roles than whites. The aspiration to be autonomous rather than merely dependent must be coupled with education and economic resources that make such autonomy possible. Many young black women from economically deprived backgrounds lack the resources which would enable them to fulfill their individualistic aspirations. There is evidence that young blacks are keenly aware of the systematic deprivation of economic rewards that their parents experience and that they will later face as adults.[115] Because of this deprivation, they may therefore be more likely than whites to turn elsewhere for meaningful rewards and gratifications. The sexual arena is one such source of rewards that are attainable. Thus, the socioeconomic deprivation may be part of the explanation for their greater sexual activity.

We saw in the Kantner and Zelnik data some findings that serve to illustrate this. Among young women from black homes where the income was less than $3,000, 60 percent had engaged in premarital intercourse. But where the family income was over $15,000, the percentage dropped to about 45. However, whites at this upper economic level had a nonvirginity rate of slightly over 25 percent. Similarly, we saw the nonvirginity rate for black young women drop more than 20 percent as the father's or male guardian's education rose from the elementary to the college level. However, even in families where the father or male guardian had gone to college, 15 percent more black girls than white girls had engaged in premarital sex relations.

One explanation of these differences between black and white young women may be related to the matter of *absolute* and *relative* comparisons. Absolutely, higher educated blacks have more economic rewards than less educated blacks; therefore girls in these families have less reason to pursue alternative rewards (such as physical, social, and material rewards associated with sexual activities). The rate of premarital intercourse thus goes down among blacks as the socioeconomic status rises. Relatively, however, when blacks are compared to whites with the same education, there is deprivation. Blacks, even with college and professional training, get fewer economic rewards than their white counterparts. This relative deprivation helps explain why young persons in higher-status black families nonetheless have higher rates of premarital sex than whites at the same income level. Dollar wise, they are actually not at the same level as whites with similar training; they are blocked from the full achievement and its accompanying benefits that their education would seem to promise. Thus, alternative gratifications such as sex are apt to be sought after to a greater degree than would otherwise be the case.

However, another explanation is possible. While it is true that greater premarital sexual activity among black females below the poverty line may indicate a quest for pleasures that are open to them when they are blocked from other gratifications, there may be another explanation for greater sexual permissiveness among black females at higher status levels. Recall Coleman's thesis that greater female autonomy means less rigidity in premarital sex codes—a thesis that seems to be borne out in Sweden. Coleman reiterates a point we made in Chapter 2, namely that female autonomy among blacks is greater than among whites for both historical and occupational reasons. Where females are dependent upon males, the principal good-in-exchange of females (sexual access) must be closely guarded and carefully conserved in order to retain its value; but when female status is not so dependent upon their relationship to males, females can be less cautious. Sexual activity may then be engaged in for its own sake, as a source of pleasure, rather than as a means of bargaining to obtain status through a marriage contract. Coleman writes of the autonomous woman: "Her sexual activity is not so much a commodity by which she establishes her ultimate social position, and she need no longer withhold it for exchange purposes. She becomes more like the male in this regard, having less reason to maintain her sexual activity as a scarce good in a market, more reason to consume it for its direct enjoyment."[116]

TRENDS

The question may be raised: Will the greater autonomy that women are gaining through greater opportunities in the economic sphere inevitably mean greater premarital sexual permissiveness in attitudes and behavior? The answer is not clear-cut. Sociologist Mary Walshok has concluded from her research that women with high occupational aspirations are likely to be unconventional with regard to gender roles. Possessing a more "masculine" view of roles as segmented and distinct so that "work is work, play is play, and sex is sex," such women "can take a less contextual and romantic view of sexuality."[117]

On the other hand, psychologist Judith Bardwick points out that women are in a transitional era and that there is much pain and tension since women have internalized older values even though they may now view such values as injurious. They are not sure as yet of the sexual life-style they would like to put in place of the older view, which incorporated sex into love, commitment, marriage, and motherhood, and which provided "justification" for sexual pleasure. Sex in itself has not been able to fill an empty void of self-esteem and identity among many women who expected to find a new sense of meaning through sexual liberation, says Bardwick.[118]

Various spokeswomen for feminism have made a similar point, showing also how men have taken advantage of the so-called sexual revolution by further using women as sex objects.[119] One writer for the women's movement, Shulamith Firestone, has written: "By convincing women that the usual female games and demands were despicable, unfair, prudish, old-fashioned, puritanical, and self-destructive, a new reservoir of available females was created to expand the tight supply of goods available for traditional sexual exploitation, disarming women of even the little protection they had so painfully acquired."[120]

Sexual liberation for women has not changed male attitudes.

Perhaps at this stage of change, the problem lies in the different ways males and females view the sexual autonomy of women. Females may think of it as freedom to be consumers rather than sellers, enjoying their "scarce resource" in a direct manner rather than conserving it for bargaining purposes to obtain other kinds of benefits. Many males, on the other hand, accustomed to the traditional male outlook on sex, may find it hard to understand female desires and capacities to enjoy sex as males have done. Such males may simply consider the "scarce resource" to have become more plentiful. Furthermore, its "market value" may be seen as lower due to an increased supply, with the result that men may bargain with fewer rewards in the exchange, thus increasing the exploitation of women.

However, at the same time, there are indications of change among males. Donald Carns suggests that two trends may be occurring simultaneously and at their own pace, with males moving away from concerns about performance, conquest, the adolescent male bond, and preoccupation with sex isolated from other factors. Women, on their part, having been awakened to a new awareness and appreciation of their sexuality, may be moving toward a pleasure-centered approach. "One would hope," says Carns, "that if indeed these trends are occurring, the genders do not pass each other in the night." While women may be heading in the direction of "seeking genital expression so long denied them by a sexually repressive culture," Carns suggests, men are "looking for situations of affection and tenderness unalloyed by the performance principle forced upon them by the restrictions of hypermasculinity."[121] In a broader context than sexuality, according to sociologist Alice Rossi, male college students in recent years have begun to indicate that they expect to find major gratifications less in their occupations and more in their family relationships.[122]

Actually, it is not likely that the two sexes will "pass as ships in the night." Rather, they may very well find themselves in the same harbor. Sexual exchange isolated from other rewards is exceedingly difficult to maintain. The parties involved (male or female) are likely to find they want something more—love, attention, a meaningful relationship, a sense of belonging and "being special" to one another as total persons. This may account for the popularity of the permissiveness-with-affection standard which appears to be the most widely accepted standard today, not only in the United States but in other nations such as West Germany and Sweden as well.[123]

NOTES

1 Kinsey et al., 1953, chap. 8. There are some problems in interpreting the data on the grade school population since the Kinsey sample included males with criminal records. See Wallin, 1949.
2 Reiss, 1960a, chap. 3.
3 Terman et al., 1938; Kinsey et al., 1948, 1953; Burgess and Wallin, 1953.
4 Reiss, 1960a; Bell, 1966; Ehrmann, 1959; Gagnon and Simon, 1970.
5 Reiss, 1972, p. 179.
6 Kinsey, et al., 1953, chap. 8.
7 Reiss, 1972, p. 169.
8 Kinsey, et al., 1953, chap. 7.
9 Bell, 1966, p. 58.
10 Ehrmann, 1957.
11 Reiss, 1960a, chap. 10.

12 Reiss, 1973.
13 Reiss, 1960*a*.
14 Reiss, 1973, 1972, p. 180.
15 Gaer and Siegel, 1964, p. 190. Also see Cowing, 1968.
16 Gaer and Siegel, 1964, p. 190.
17 Graham-Murray, 1966, p. 153.
18 Rugoff, 1971, chap. 6.
19 Rugoff, 1971, pp. 61, 111.
20 Graham-Murray, 1966, pp. 149, 152.
21 Rugoff, 1971, p. 49.
22 Kantner and Zelnik, 1972.
23 Kinsey, et al., 1953.
24 Bell and Chaskes, 1970.
25 Christensen and Gregg, 1970.
26 Kinsey, et al., 1953, chap. 8; Kantner and Zelnik, 1972.
27 Schmidt and Sigusch, 1972.
28 Schmidt and Sigusch, 1972; Chesser, 1957; French Institute of Public Opinion, 1961.
29 Smith, 1973.
30 Reiss, 1973.
31 Schmidt and Sigusch, 1972.
32 Schmidt and Sigusch, 1972.
33 Reiss, 1973.
34 O'Neill, 1967.
35 Smith, 1973.
36 Tomasson, 1970, p. 180.
37 Coleman, 1966, p. 217.
38 Geiger, 1968, p. 64.
39 Geiger, 1968, pp. 66–71.
40 Quoted in Geiger, 1968, p. 70.
41 Rowbotham, 1972, chap. 6.
42 Geiger, 1968, p. 62 ff., Rowbotham, 1972, chap. 6.
43 Quoted in Geiger, 1968, p. 63.
44 Lenin, as quoted in Geiger, 1968, p. 84.
45 A statement of Zalkind, quoted in Geiger, 1968, p. 85.
46 Geiger, 1968, p. 84.
47 Sidel, 1972, chap. 3.
48 Rowbotham, 1972, chap. 7.
49 Aird, 1972.
50 Barker-Benfield, 1972.
51 Spiro, 1970, chap. 5.
52 Talmon, 1972, p. 4.
53 Spiro, 1970.
54 Talmon, 1972, pp. 8–10.
55 Spiro, 1965, p. 327.
56 Spiro, 1970, p. 113.
57 Talmon, 1972, p. 21.
58 Rabkin and Spiro, in Spiro, 1970, chap. 9.
59 Rabkin and Spiro, 1970.
60 Tomasson, 1970, chap. 6.
61 Linner, 1967, chap. 2.
62 Linner, 1967, chap. 1.
63 Linner, 1967, chap. 3; Tomasson, 1970, p. 184.

64   Linner, 1967, chap. 3; Linner, 1966.
65   Christensen, 1969.
66   Linner, 1967 and 1966.
67   Tomasson, 1970, chap. 6.
68   Carns, 1969, p. 57.
69   Luckey and Nass, 1969.
70   Reiss, 1960*a*, 1967*b*.
71   Simon, Berger, and Gagnon, 1972, pp. 216–217.
72   Masters and Johnson, 1966.
73   Schmidt and Sigusch, 1970, 1973; Schmidt, Sigusch, and Schafer, 1973.
74   Schmidt and Sigusch, 1970, 1973.
75   Kinsey, et al., 1953, chap. 16.
76   Schmidt, Sigusch and Schafer, 1973.
77   Gebhard, 1973.
78   Walshok, 1973, p. 2.
79   Gagnon and Simon, 1973, p. 181.
80   Gagnon and Simon, 1973, pp. 181–182.
81   Kinsey et al., 1953, chap. 16; on a related matter, see Kutner and Brogan, 1974.
82   Gagnon and Simon, 1973, pp. 12, 73.
83   Kirkendall, 1968.
84   Gagnon and Simon, 1973, pp. 68–81.
85   Carns, 1973.
86   Gagnon and Simon, 1973, pp. 12, 73.
87   Simon and Gagnon, 1969, pp. 736, 750.
88   Gagnon and Simon, 1973, pp. 181–182.
89   Collins, 1971.
90   Exod. 22: 16–17.
91   Collins, 1971, p. 13.
92   Libby and Carlson, 1973.
93   Gagnon and Simon, 1973, p. 76.
94   Tomasson, 1970, pp. 180–181.
95   Linner, 1967, chap. 2.
96   Reiss, 1960*a*; Bell, 1966.
97   Berger and Wenger, 1973, p. 666.
98   Berger and Wenger, p. 675.
99   Stevens, 1973, p. 97.
100 Reiss, 1967*a*; 1967*b*.
101 Kantner and Zelnik, 1972.
102 Carns, 1969.
103 Blau, 1964, p. 122.
104 Holter, 1970; Scanzoni, 1975b.
105 Kantner and Zelnik, 1972, p. 12.
106 Rainwater, 1966*a*.
107 Cited in Rosenberg and Bensman, 1968.
108 Rosenberg and Bensman, 1968.
109 Rainwater, 1966*a*.
110 Reiss, 1972, pp. 176–177.
111 Hammond and Ladner, 1969, pp. 43–44.
112 Hammond and Ladner, 1969, p. 49.
113 Kantner and Zelnik, 1972.

114 Hammond and Ladner, 1969, p. 50.
115 Lott and Lott, 1963; Scanzoni, 1971.
116 Coleman, 1966, p. 217.
117 Walshok, 1973.
118 Bardwick, 1973.
119 Mitchell, 1971; Firestone, 1970.
120 Firestone, 1970, chap. 6.
121 Carns, 1973, p. 687.
122 Rossi, 1973.
123 Tomasson, 1970; Linner, 1967; Reiss, 1960*a*, 1967*b*, 1973; Schmidt and Sigusch, 1972.

UNIT 2
DECISIONS ABOUT MARRIAGE

4
STRIKING A MARRIAGE BARGAIN

A 1968 study commission on marriage and divorce in Kenya concluded that the elimination of the custom of the bride price would be impractical. Young Africans immediately protested. How could they afford to marry if the bride price kept going up? The average price of $550 seemed exorbitant. Yet, to parents of daughters, the amount requested in the transferral of a young woman from one family to another seemed only reasonable. The increased costs of rearing daughters and paying for their schooling had to be taken into consideration since educational opportunities had opened up for females.[1]

Sometimes called the bridewealth, the bride-price may consist of money, livestock, or other goods paid by the groom (usually with the assistance of his relatives) which signify a compensation to the woman's parents for the loss of her domestic service and also symbolizes a linkage between the family of the bride and the family of the groom. In some societies, the family of the bride also contributes a dowry (money, goods, or other property) to the marriage. Such customs draw attention both to kin involvement and the extent to which economic factors may play a part in marriage.

In China, one of the first orders of business after the 1949 communist revolution was to draw up legislation changing traditional Chinese marriage customs. The 1950 law gave young people the right to choose their own mates, have full equality in marriage, and have the right to divorce. The law came about partly through the efforts of a woman lawyer who, while a political prisoner, met two women who had opposed the feudal marriage laws. One woman was serving a life sentence, and the other was sentenced to death.

These women faced such stringent penalties because they had opposed Chinese village marriages based on bargaining between two sets of parents and which often involved an intermediary who negotiated the bride price. Many of the marriages were "blind marriages," so named because the man and woman had never seen each other before the wedding. In some cases, parents arranged the marriages of their offspring while the boy and girl were yet small children, although the couple would not live together as husband and wife until they were older. The Chinese elders claimed that the old god in the moon bound together the feet of males and females destined for each other, and parents and intermediaries merely acted as instruments to carry out his will.[2]

Religious concerns likewise played an important part in marriage negotiations among the Puritans in seventeenth-century New England. Parents considered it their duty before God not only to make sure that their children found their "particular calling" with regard to a life's work, but also to make certain that their children were settled in a proper marriage. However, the wishes of the couple were not overlooked. Ministers admonished parents not to impose their wills on their children, pointing out that "we know by long Experience that forc'd Matches any way seldome do well." Historian Edmund Morgan writes that usually "the Puritan fathers must have confined the exercise of their power to haggling over the financial agreement after the children had chosen for themselves—provided of course that they had chosen within the proper economic and religious limitations."[3]

Deciding on financial agreements involved a great deal of bickering and bargaining between the two sets of parents, although the normal ratio was for the woman's parents to furnish half as much as was furnished by the man's parents. Sometimes the settlements included lands and other times money; but in any case, once the bargaining ended, a legal contract was drawn up binding the parties to the financial agreement. Only then could the marriage take place.

Japan is another country where tradition decreed that parents must participate in bargaining arrangements about the marriages of their offspring. The young people were not involved with one another or with the marriage plans until their two families had made the contract which would be sealed at the betrothal ceremony. Sociologist Robert O. Blood points out that "Concern on both sides created a bargaining situation in which each party exaggerated its assets and hid its liabilities, worrying lest the antagonist succeed in doing the same."[4] To avoid the problems and feuds this might cause, and to save face in cases where offers were rejected, families engaged the services of a match-maker who acted as a go-between to work out negotiations between the two families.

It's easy to see that bargaining in mate selection has been known through-out history all over the world. Since marriage was usually thought of in terms of linking two families rather than simply two individuals, the kin considered it a right and duty to make marital choices for young men and women. And economic factors, such as bride prices, dowries, inheritances, and so on, played a crucial part in the decisions.

However, for the most part, the right to choose one's own mate has been a freedom taken for granted throughout the history of the United States. The early immigrants often left behind parents and other relatives (the extended kin), with the result that finding a marriage partner was up to the individual rather than to his or her family. The fact that a *woman* had such free choice in finding a marriage partner seemed surprising to a French traveler who visited America in the mid-nineteenth century. "While still quite young," he wrote, "ignorant of herself, life not yet a lesson, when circumstances the most frivolous, appearanc-es the most deceptive, and errors of judgment may blind her reason—she makes the most important decision of her life."[5]

We saw that even among the Puritans free choice in mate selection was not discouraged, although parents supervised and gave advice. The bargaining between families was rooted in a concern that the newlyweds would have sufficient goods to set up housekeeping rather than springing from a concern that the families might make a profit or strike a good deal in uniting two kinship lines. "What shall these young beginners do for household stuff?" asked one worried Puritan father who had given a sum of money toward his daughter's marriage but realized the father of her future husband had given only a tract of land. On the advice of a third party, both fathers agreed to add more money so that the young couple could purchase needed supplies for their new home.[6]

Such illustrations from the past or from other cultures may strike most people as interesting; but at the same time, they seem remote from life today. After all, goes the reasoning, modern young people no longer dicker and negotiate and bargain in choosing a marriage partner; they simply fall in love. Yet the idea of marriage as a marketplace is more entrenched in our minds and vocabulary than we realize. People shake their heads in pity as they observe the sufferings of the wife of an alcoholic or compulsive gambler. "She certainly got a rotten deal in marrying him," they say. "That man deserved better," they say of another marriage. "He really struck a poor bargain when he married that woman." Of a woman recently divorced or widowed, people may remark, "I think she's in the market for another husband, but she'll probably take some time to shop around first." In another case, we hear, "He's trying to talk her into marrying him. You should hear his sales pitch!" All of these terms, of course, are

A YOUNG LADY'S DOWER HER WEIGHT IN PINE TREE SHILLINGS

Economic factors, such as dowries, were important in seventeenth-century marriage bargaining.

borrowed from the world of business and trade. In other words, we can't escape the conclusion that marriage and bargaining are very much interrelated. But how? And what does it all mean?

MARRIAGE BARGAINING TODAY

Before we can understand marriage bargaining, we first need to define marriage and then try to understand what the institution means to people and why they enter it.

What Is Marriage?

In recent years there has been a great deal of discussion about when a relationship becomes a marriage. Some have argued that the whole idea of legal marriage should be discarded because legal bonds suffocate freedom and spontaneity, causing persons to stay together because they "ought to" or "must" rather than because they want to. Such critics of conventional ideas about marriage suggest that the relationship of a man and woman should be regarded as a private matter, concerning only the individuals involved. They see no need for the regulations and forms set up by society. "How can a piece of paper or reciting some words make us married?" some have asked. "We feel we're already married in our own hearts—perhaps even in the eyes of God. We can't see why some sort of ceremony is necessary."

But even though such persons may feel married, are they really? What *does* make people married? Is it sex? Are two persons married who have coitus with each other twice a week? What if, in addition, each has sexual intercourse with another person? Does a group marriage then exist? Few people would be willing to define marriage on the basis of sex relations alone. Could it be the license then that makes a marriage? No, not really. However, there have been cases of poorly informed and often illiterate persons who have mistakenly thought that obtaining the license was all that was required of them, only to find out after many years of living together that they were never legally married.

If it isn't sex and it isn't a license that makes a couple married, then it must be the wedding ceremony—right? Not really. There isn't anything magic in the words themselves that transports two people from one state (singleness) into another state (marriage). Furthermore, there is a wide variation in wedding ceremonies in various cultures. In ancient biblical times, Isaac and Rebekah's wedding ceremony consisted of nothing more than an exchange of gifts and entering a tent together; but in our culture, a man and woman who entered a house together after a gift exchange could hardly argue that these acts made them married.

Or to take another example, anthropologists have written of the marriage ritual practiced by the Kwoma of New Guinea. A prospective bride is brought to live with a young man's family for a time of observation by his mother. If the mother feels the young woman is a suitable future daughter-in-law, she asks her to cook some food for the young man. Unsuspectingly, he eats it, without realizing it has been cooked by his future wife. At that moment, the mother announces that the young man is now married, because he is eating food prepared by his betrothed. Upon hearing this announcement, the new husband is supposed to rush out shouting that the food tastes awful. This is the public declaration to the tribe that the couple is now considered to be married.[7] Needless to say, no one in our society could consider himself married because he ate dinner at his girl friend's apartment and then told his friends that she is a terrible cook. It is not the ceremony itself that makes a marriage but rather what it signifies in a particular culture.

What we need is a definition of marriage that is applicable historically and cross-culturally, but yet is able to fit new varieties of marriage patterns that are emerging. Anthropologist George Murdock provides us with the basis of just such a definition. From his studies, he concludes that there are two essential dimensions to marriage—the economic and the sexual. When a man and woman are interdependent both economically and sexually, they may be said to be married.[8]

We can broaden the scope of the definition and say that marriage exists when two (or more) persons maintain ongoing instrumental and expressive exchanges. The *expressive* or person-oriented dimension includes sexual gratification, but it may also include other elements such as companionship (someone to do things with, joint participation in leisure activities) and empathy (someone to listen and talk to, someone who understands and cares). The *instrumental* or task-oriented dimension of marriage includes economic behaviors (earning and spending income) and the performance of necessary household tasks. Furthermore, for marriage to be valid from a societal point of view, there must be some sort of public disclosure. Therefore, societies require rituals, ceremonies, licenses, and the like, to symbolize that a legal bond between a particular man and woman exists, a bond recognized by the society in which they live. The arrangement of mutual sexual access and economic sharing between the two persons is of concern not only to the individuals but to others as well (parents and other relatives, friends, and society as a whole).

If we ask *why* people get married, the answer now becomes clear. People enter marriage because they believe it to be a rewarding situation both in terms of the instrumental and expressive sides of life. And that's where bargaining comes in. Before marriage and afterward as well, the processes of social exchange go on as each partner endeavors to find ways of giving and receiving both expressively and instrumentally to the satisfaction of each one and for the overall benefit of the relationship.

People often think of a wedding as a distinct event somehow separated from all that has gone before and all that follows after the exchange of vows. This is probably because of the pomp and unique character of most marriage ceremonies—celebrations that set them off markedly from the daily routines of life. Yet, if we think in terms of actual social processes, we see that men and women engage in a great deal of reward seeking and bargaining with each other prior to the wedding day. It is out of a feeling that each has something to offer the other that the two persons are attracted to one another in the first place. And a considerable amount of decision making and give-and-take (bargaining) goes into entering and maintaining an ongoing relationship. In fact, the marriage itself is a decision that has emerged out of this bargaining process. Most important, after that decision has been enacted, these exchanges keep right on flowing just as they did beforehand.

In this chapter, we'll be focusing on processes leading up to decisions about marriage. The questions are familiar ones: Should I marry at all? If so, whom? When? What type of marriage bargain is most advantageous?

Kin Influence and Marital Choice

Throughout history, as we have seen, persons eligible for marriage were not given the opportunity to ask and answer the kinds of questions just mentioned.

Figure 4-1 Party A has high degree of power because of the resources A is able to hold out to party B.

The decisions were made *for* them rather than *by* them, because mate selection was in the hands of parents. Kin control over marital choice simply reflects the high level of power that the kin had over its young. Power is the capability to affect the behavior of others, and power derives its strength and potency from resources.[9]

Figure 4-1 illustrates the relationship between resources and power. When A gives more benefits to B than B gives to A, A has the greater power. B needs the resources of A more than A needs the resources that B has to offer. In the past, parents obviously had more resources to hold out to their offspring than vice versa, and thus parents could choose or else strongly influence the selection of mates. Parents could offer to pass on farms, lands, and family businesses to those offspring who conformed to their wishes with regard to marriage and could threaten to withhold such benefits from children who refused to comply.

However, A's power is limited to the degree that B has alternative sources of benefits. (See Figure 4-2.) As societies modernize and business and industrial enterprises develop, young persons have opportunities to obtain both tangible and intangible benefits apart from their parents. Thus the power of parents over their children is diminished, with subsequent loss of influence in mate selection.

Figure 4-2 Party A has limited power because party B has alternative source of rewards.

Another way that A's power can be limited occurs if B renounces the rewards that A can give. (See Figure 4-3.) Even in premodern times, if a young person decided to become a priest or nun, for example, both the material benefits offered by parents and the prospect of marriage benefits became meaningless. Church power totally replaced parental power. Or to take another example of renouncing rewards, a young person might be willing to finance his or her own college education rather than accept parental money known to have ''strings attached'' as to college choice and career and/or marriage decisions. Similarly, persons have been known to renounce family inheritances in order to marry someone parents disapprove, and with the renunciation of these financial rewards comes a freedom from the parents' control.

Finally, power is limited on the part of parents if their children have the capability to persuade them to change their minds about marital choice. The process of persuasion can take the form of discussion, a bargaining session, blackmail, or various types of coercion, including actual physical force. Young people might threaten to elope if their parents withhold consent to marry, or they might use a premarital pregnancy to force their parents to go along with their wishes. There has been speculation that such may have been the case with Lord and Lady Randolph Churchill, the parents of Winston. Both families had opposed the marriage, and there had been interminable negotiations about financial arrangements and legal matters. Yet, rather suddenly, a surprisingly small, simple wedding took place; and Randolph's parents did not even attend. These factors, combined with the birth of Winston Churchill seven months later, raised in some people's minds a question about whether the marriage may have been forced by the young couple.[10]

The ability to persuade or bargain with one's parents so that they will accept one's own choice of a mate depends in great measure on the outside resources a young person has *as compared to the parents' resources.* On this basis, for

Figure 4-3 Party A has limited power if party B renounces the kind of rewards party A can give.

example, upper-class youth would have least power or freedom in mate selection, middle-class youth more, working class still more, and lower-class most freedom of all. (See Figure 4-4.) Overall, however, in the United States and in Western society generally, young persons have considerable power and autonomy in selecting whom they wish to marry.

Even though the source of power has shifted from parents to youth, the goal still remains the same; the aim is to strike the best bargain possible. In family-controlled mate selection, members of kin X wanted to get as many rewards as possible from kin Y for themselves and for their son or daughter. A marriage contract was drawn up in an attempt to meet the best interests of each party. Similarly, individual men and women have continued this same process of reward seeking. They go with, become engaged to, and marry persons whom they believe will provide them with the most satisfactory range of rewards open to them.

The influence of parents is not completely diminished in all of this, though as we saw, it varies by class. But modern parents, just as was true of parents in other times and cultures, are concerned about their children's marriages and do everything they can do to make sure that their young people don't strike a poor bargain on the marriage market. Parents like to be able to boast, "Our daughter married well. We're so proud of her and her husband," or "Our son has made a really good marriage. He married a wonderful girl from a fine family." Parents influence their children's marriage choices by the way they socialize them in their growing up years and by the neighborhoods to which they move, the people with whom they associate, the schools to which the children are sent, and so on. In the past, one function of sororities and fraternities was to serve in the parents' stead, making sure that young men and women away from home supervision would mix with the "right" persons on the university campus so that marriages outside one's social class, race, or religious group would be less likely to occur.[11]

Figure 4-4

WHO MARRIES WHOM?

Anthropologists and sociologists use the term *endogamy* to describe marriages between persons within the same social group. When a person marries someone outside his or her own social group, the practice is called *exogamy*. (The terms are easily remembered by thinking of their roots. The ending comes from the Greek *gamia*, meaning "act of marrying." *Endo* means "within," and *ex* means "out of.") Thus, endogamy occurs when blacks marry blacks. Exogamy occurs when blacks marry whites. Jews who marry fellow Jews are marrying endogamously, whereas exogamy occurs when Jews marry Gentiles.

Another commonly used term is *homogamy* (from the Greek term *homos*, meaning "the same."), which refers to the tendency of persons to marry persons with characteristics similar to their own—particularly in terms of age, intelligence, education, and social background. The physician's daughter marries the lawyer's son. The college graduate marries a fellow college graduate. The waitress marries the factory worker—and so on.

However, if a woman marries someone of quite different educational and social background, she is said to have married either up or down. The physician's daughter who completes four years of college and then marries the factory worker who is a high school dropout illustrates the principle of *hypogamy* or marrying down. On the other hand, if a waitress (with only a high school education or less) were to marry a lawyer or physician, she would serve as an example of *hypergamy* or marrying up. (Again, you can avoid confusing these terms by recalling their roots. *Hypo* derives from the Greek for "under" or "below" and is used in such words as hypodermic needle, a needle which injects material under the skin. *Hyper* means "over" or "above" and is familiar to us from such terms as hyperacidity or references to a child's hyperactivity.) In speaking of hypogamy and hypergamy, it is customary for social scientists to take the woman as the reference point. That is, it is the *wife* who is considered to have married either beneath or above her social status, no doubt because in traditional social-class measurements women have been considered to take on the social status of their husbands rather than having an independent status of their own.

Education

One area where the principle of homogamy is clearly at work is education. Most people marry those whose amount of education is similar to their own. "Similar" may be defined as the same educational level or one level removed. (See Table 4-A.)

In terms of exchange theory, education is a resource persons may offer in marriage bargaining and it is also an indication of social status. Persons with the same or similar education levels are more likely to perceive the marriage bargain to be a just and fair one than would usually be true of spouses having vast differences in education (where there would be an imbalance in resources brought to the marriage). And of course, it goes without saying that persons with similar education are likely to hold similar values, goals, and outlooks on life, and thus have more in common with one another than is generally true where there are wide gaps in educational background.

TABLE 4-A   MARRIAGES BY LEVELS OF EDUCATION

In 1970, Out of Every 100 Married Couples (All Races Combined):

39 husbands and wives were at the same educational level;*
19 husbands were one level* higher than their wives;
18 wives were one level* higher than their husbands;
12 husbands were two or more levels* higher than their wives;
12 wives were two or more levels* higher than their husbands.

*Educational levels:

0–4 years elementary school
5–7 years elementary school
8 years elementary school
1–3 years high school
4 years high school
1–3 years college
4 years college
5 or more years college

SOURCE: Based on data from the 1970 census. U.S. Bureau of the Census, 1972, PC(2)-4C, p. 269.

Religion

Data on religious intermarriage is not as complete as social scientists would like it to be—one reason being that questions on religious identification are not included in the census or on many other public registrations. However, the limited data on trends in interfaith marriages seem to indicate an increase in such marriages.[12] Particularly among Catholics and Protestants, a great deal of exogamy occurs. The religious climate of greater openness, tolerance, and cooperation between Catholics and Protestants since Vatican II may be one explanation for more persons' feeling free to marry outside their particular church group.[13]

Exogamy is rarest of all among the third major religious grouping, Jews, where persons are strongly encouraged to select mates from within their own group. Loyal Jews are expected by parents and religious leaders alike to marry endogamously. Such a stance has been taken by the Jewish community throughout their history. The popular musical *Fiddler on the Roof* made clear the agony that Jewish parents have traditionally undergone when one of their offspring marries a Gentile. The Hebrew Scriptures provide warnings against marriages between Jews and non-Jews. The prophet Ezra, for example, counseled his people to divorce their foreign wives. On the other hand, the two Old Testament books named after women both contain stories of Jewish-Gentile marriages. Esther, a Jew, by her influence as the wife of a Persian king, saved her people from destruction. And the Gentile Ruth had Jewish husbands in both her first and second marriages. Ruth, however, was willing to say, "Thy people shall be my people, and thy God my God." Such conversion to Judaism by a

The ritual of smashing a glass, symbolizing the destruction of Jerusalem, cements group loyalty by reminding the couple of Jewish history and traditions.

non-Jew has traditionally been the one way in which he or she becomes acceptable as a potential marriage partner for a Jew.[14]

However, despite the long traditions and negative sanctions relating to marriages between Jews and non-Jews, several studies indicate that there has been an upsurge in such marriages in recent years, particularly among third- and fourth-generation Jews in certain areas of the United States.[15] This has caused considerable concern among many rabbis. As Rabbi Albert I. Gordon, a social anthropologist, reports, "Intermarriage is generally regarded by American Jewish leaders as a symptom of the weakening of Jewish religious ties and the lack of the empathy for their own people that has characterized Jews in the past."[16] On the other hand, among Gentiles there seems to be a growing acceptance of Gentile-Jewish marriage unions. An analysis of public opinion poll data showed that in 1950, 57 percent of those who classified themselves as Christians responded that they "definitely would not" marry a Jew. But by 1962, that figure had fallen to 37 percent.[17]

Race

With rare exceptions, people tend to marry within their own racial grouping. In other words, racial endogamy seems to be the strongest of all. Official government statistics have shown for example that less than 1 percent of marriages that took place between 1963 and 1967 were between blacks and whites, whites and other races, or blacks and other races. (In reporting data, the term "other races" is used in reference to those whose national origin is Japanese, Chinese, Filipino, American Indian, and so on.) In white other-marriages, the white partner was more often the groom. In white-black marriages, the white partner was more often the bride. The Bureau of the Census reports that in 1970, 98.1 percent of married couples with at least one black spouse were marriages in which *both* spouses were black, again indicating that racial endogamy is widespread.[18]

Some states had laws against interracial marriage up until the 1967 United States Supreme Court decision which declared such laws unconstitutional. According to census information based upon a 5 percent sample of the total population, there is evidence that black-white marriages have been increasing in recent years. (See Table 4-B.) But although such marriages have increased 26 percent in the United States as a whole, they have decreased in the South by about 35 percent. The greatest increase of black-white marriages has occurred in the North and West.

A number of sociologists have pointed out that much more research needs to be done in the area of interracial marriage before we can clearly ascertain trends and understand their meaning.[19] Past explanations for the low incidence of white-black marriages have focused on evidence that in a color-caste society the dominant group rates the characteristics of the less-dominant group as

TABLE 4-B NUMBER OF BLACK-WHITE MARRIAGES BY TYPE AND REGION, UNITED STATES, 1960 AND 1970

	1960	1970	Percentage Change Since 1960
United States:			
Total	51,409	64,789	+ 26.0
Husband black, wife white	25,496	41,223	+ 61.7
Husband white, wife black	25,913	23,566	− 9.1
North and West:			
Total	30,977	51,420	+ 66.0
Husband black, wife white	16,872	34,937	+107.1
Husband white, wife black	14,105	16,483	+ 16.9
South:			
Total	20,432	13,369	− 34.6
Husband black, wife white	8,624	6,286	− 27.1
Husband white, wife black	11,808	7,083	− 40.0

SOURCE: David M. Heer, 1974, p. 247.

being of less worth than the characteristics of the dominant group.[20] Thus, in a white-dominated society, whites have defined blackness as of less value than whiteness and therefore have tended not to strike a marriage bargain that seemed unfavorable. Not only did the exchange of rewards in interracial marriage seem unequal according to this line of reasoning, but there were also costs to consider. Whites who marry blacks have traditionally suffered severe disapproval from other whites, with especially negative sanctions from relatives and close friends.

Blacks, too, may negatively sanction those of their number who marry outside their race. Many feel strongly against such marriages for reasons similar to the traditional views of Jews cited earlier. Pride in one's own group and loyalty to that group are expected to be reinforced by endogamy. Convinced that black is beautiful, many blacks look upon marriage to a white person as not only undesirable but almost as an act of treason against the black race and black culture. To enter such a marriage is viewed by some as acquiescence to a society that has held blacks down, an alliance with the oppressor.

One way sociologists have attempted to explain what happens in black-white marriages has been in terms of a theory of *racial*-caste hypogamy coupled with *social*-class hypergamy. First suggested in 1941 by sociologists Kingsley Davis and Robert Merton, the theory states that a woman from a higher racial caste is willing to marry a man from a lower racial caste in a situation where to do so will raise her from a lower social class to one of higher status.[21] What is "marrying down" on the one hand (hypogamy) is "marrying up" on the other (hypergamy). David Heer, a sociologist who has given much attention to the study of black-white marriages, suggests caution with regard to such an explanation, although he points out that the theory may have some validity if other considerations are taken into account.[22]

The Merton-Davis theory has been widely accepted because of evidence from government studies which show a tendency for black men who marry white women to have a higher level of education than is true of black men who marry black women. White women who marry black men have tended to have a lower level of education than white women who marry white men.[23] Sociologist Zick Rubin sums up what has sometimes been called the "compensation principle" in terms of exchange theory. He writes: "These interracial marriages can be seen as exchanges on the interpersonal marketplace, in which the higher educational status of the black husband (and the earning power that may go along with it) is exchanged for the higher social status of the white wife (which accrues to her simply by virtue of her skin color.)"[24]

However, Jessie Bernard, another sociologist, has taken issue with this notion. Bernard's analysis of the 1960 census data did not show a tendency for wives of black men to have relatively lower education if white rather than black.[25] The idea that interracial marriage involves an exchange of status based on skin color for status based on educational and occupational achievement may be increasingly questionable.[26]

Perhaps what may be occurring is a tendency for marriages between blacks and whites to involve other kinds of exchanges, with persons being attracted to one another on the basis of rewards which make the consideration of racial differences less important than was once the case. Education, exposure to persons of other races in travel, work, and school, and ideological concerns based on humanistic and religious values may all play a part in de-emphasizing skin color as a basis for evaluating persons.

Among highly educated persons with a common universe of values, for example, partners in *cross-national* marriages have been known to consider themselves as belonging to a kind of international community or life-style that transcends national boundaries. In one study of Western nationals who married persons from India, it was found that spouses considered the culture they shared in common (for example, the scientific community) to be far more important than the cultures of their countries of origin. As one Indian respondent summed it up: "I would have so little in common with a parochial Indian." Sociologist Ann Baker Cottrell concludes that such Indian-Western mar-

Mutual values and concerns may make the consideration of racial differences less important in contemporary relationships.

riages are inaccurately called "mixed marriages."[27] Perhaps a similar statement might be made about many black-white marriages as well.

The Incest Taboo

The question may arise: If persons tend to marry within their own group (e.g., the same race or religion), why don't persons marry within the most basic group of all—their own family? Wouldn't that be endogamy of the purest type? This brings us to the matter of *incest* or sexual intercourse between persons who are closely related. The incest taboo is an institutionalized norm found almost universally which prohibits sex relations between parents and their children, between brothers and sisters, and (with some variations about the degree of kinship) between members of the nuclear family and relatives outside the nuclear family (for example, with in-laws, aunts and uncles, cousins, etc.).

There have been many attempts to explain the existence of the incest taboo, and the usual rationale for its existence today is related to genetics, namely, a concern that marriages between closely related persons might increase the likelihood of defective offspring (since both spouses might be carriers of the same inherited genetic weakness). However, although this rationale has provided support for the incest taboo, it does not explain its origin, since there is no evidence that a concern about genetic abnormalities guided the ancients in forming their prohibitions. Nor does the genetic explanation always seem logical even today (for example, in cases where elderly first cousins, long past the age of child-bearing, are forbidden to marry by certain state laws).

One way we might attempt to explain the prohibitions against incest, as well as exceptions such as the brother-sister marriages in ancient Egypt, is to think again in terms of exchange theory.

Anthropologist Claude Lévi-Strauss has written of the way the incest taboo reinforces the interdependency of families. "For incest-prohibition simply states that families (however they should be defined) can only marry between each other and that they cannot marry inside themselves."[28] Furthermore, "the prohibition of incest is a rule of reciprocity. It means: I will only give up my daughter or my sister if my neighbor will give up his also. . . . The fact that I can obtain a wife is, in the last analysis, the consequence of the fact that a brother or a father has given up a woman."[29]

The emphasis in these statements is upon an exchange of women, and we are again reminded of the customs surrounding the bridewealth or bride-price in many cultures and of the economic gains and social linkages which are associated with marriage. Building upon the ideas of Lévi-Strauss, we might suggest that the incest prohibition originally served as a means of ensuring an institutionalized pattern of gains through exchanges. Couples who married within their own families would only be sharing what they already possessed; it would be a closed arrangement with no bride-prices, dowries, greater social linkages, and so on. But to marry *outside* one's family opened the way to bring other resources in.

Exceptions to the keeping of the incest taboo may be similarly explained. If persons married outside their families in order to bring in additional resources, there might also be cases where persons married inside their families in order to keep resources. Marrying out of the family could bring gains; but marrying in the family could prevent loss. This is likely the reason for the father-daughter and brother-sister marriages during the time of the Pharaohs. In fact, Egyptologists have uncovered evidence of brother-sister marriages in many periods of Egypt's history, not only within the royalty but also among the commoners. Russell Middleton, a sociologist, suggests that the most plausible explanation is that such unions "served to maintain the property of the family intact and to prevent the splintering of the estate through the operation of the laws of inheritance. Since daughters usually inherited a share of the estate, the device of brother-sister marriage would have served to preserve intact the material resources of the family as a unit." Often these were "marriages of convenience" so that property could be transmitted which would otherwise have fallen to the state.[30]

WHY DO PEOPLE CHOOSE PARTICULAR MATES?

"I can't for the life of me figure out how those two got together!" "I wonder what she sees in *him*?" "That guy could have married any girl he pleased, and yet he picked her. I can't understand it."

We've all heard statements like these, and perhaps we've made similar remarks ourselves. Most people are interested in how particular persons got together and decided to form a marriage partnership. All sorts of questions arise: Why do persons tend to choose mates with similar social characteristics? How can we explain mate selection in terms of our earlier discussion about male-female exchanges prior to marriage? And what is the place of love in all of this?

Field of Potential Mates

Men and women view each other through an initial screening or filtering process which 's represented by a potential "field of eligibles." Screened out are persons not defined as eligible, perhaps because they are not within the same race, religion, or educational grouping. We have seen, for example, that the percentage of black-white marriages is small. Or to take another illustration, a devout Catholic is unlikely to consider an atheist as a potential marriage partner. A woman with a Ph.D. in psychology is not likely to marry the auto mechanic who services her car—no matter what movies and soap operas may say. Often *age* is also involved in the screening process. The thirty-year-old single woman who is introduced to her friend's seventy-year-old bachelor uncle will in all probability think of him as only an acquaintance and not as a possible marriage partner. There are, of course, exceptions to all of these patterns; but in general, as we have seen from the statistics, they hold true.

Narrowing the Choice

When persons have passed through the filtering process and have been defined as belonging to a category that makes a marriage bargain seem equitable, there still remains the question of which one to marry.[31] Obviously, no one can marry all of them; he or she is faced with the task of selecting just one potential mate out of the total field of eligibles. How is that selection made? And why do some people cross these lines to marry persons from somewhat different backgrounds?

Again we see the part that exchange and bargaining play in the mate-selection process. Clearly, there are numerous kinds of resources that men and women can offer each other in addition to those benefits represented by the broad categories of race, religion, and educational groupings. Particularly important are those resources that cluster around sex-role definitions.

The traditional form of marriage places the husband in the role of breadwinner and the wife in the role of nurturant sustainer of the home. Persons who want this form of marriage will gravitate toward those who hold similar views, and again it is a matter of reward seeking. Women who hold traditional gender-role patterns will be attracted to men who appear able to provide them with the kinds of economic security, status, and material comfort they define as acceptable. Sociologist Willard Waller had this in mind when he wrote in 1938: "There is this difference between the man and the woman in the pattern of bourgeois family life; a man, when he marries, chooses a companion and perhaps a helpmate, but a woman chooses a companion and at the same time a standard of living. It is necessary for a woman to be mercenary."[32]

At the same time, men who hold traditional views of sex roles are attracted to women who likewise hold such views. Such men desire wives who will provide the nurturance, comfort, support, encouragement, and respect that husbands have traditionally sought and deemed essential in a good wife, homemaker, and mother. They are looking for women who will center their lives around husbands and children and for whom all other interests are secondary.

Persons who hold modern, egalitarian notions of marriage also seek out like-minded partners. Women who are persuaded that they have the right to self-determination and an individual identity are certainly not interested in joining themselves in marriage to men who believe that females should be passive, dependent, and subordinate to male leadership. Instead such women are attracted to men who give promise of granting them the rewards of acceptance, recognition, free choice, affirmation of talents, and encouragement to achieve.

Some men, for their part, are driven away by any hint of what they consider female aggressiveness, whereas other men highly value and admire achievement-oriented women and are drawn toward them. An example of an achievement-oriented woman married to a man with similar views of female autonomy is Patricia Roberts Harris, a black woman who has won recognition as a lawyer in a prominent Washington firm, as a member of the board of directors of IBM, and as Ambassador to Luxembourg. Regarding female role definitions, she has said, "I hate to hear people say a woman is charming. I don't want to be loved. I want to be esteemed." Her lawyer husband, who does not at all find her achievements threatening and was willing to give up his own law practice to accompany her to Luxembourg, comments: "Nothing surpasses being married to a really intelligent woman. They always know how to treat their men."[33]

Sex-role patterns and the rewards they provide are important parts of the exchange process prior to marriage because they set the stage for what will occur in marriage. The partners are either implicitly or explicitly anticipating the roles they will subsequently play. To be sure, the couples may be unaware of the process. Most men and women have not in the past consciously bargained about sex-role patterns and their accompanying rewards. Generally, because of their earlier gender-role learning in the home and its reinforcement in school and elsewhere, they have acted in traditional masculine and feminine ways, accepting the role specialization that sees the man as the unique provider and the woman as the expressive hub. Indeed, the whole thrust of romantic love is to obscure what really goes on between the sexes prior to marriage. The old adage that declares "love is blind" may contain a great deal of truth.

What Part Does Love Play?

We say that persons "marry for love," but already we have seen that love isn't some mysterious force that strikes indiscriminately. Rather, love seems to be sparked among persons of similar social characteristics and resources. Whatever love is, it is clear that persons do not "fall in love" with just anybody; only certain ones will do.

Love has many meanings, but one of the first meanings that comes to mind in connection with man-woman relationships is the notion of romantic love. Such love has its roots in the Greek idea of *eros* or what the ancient Greeks saw as "diseased hysteria," an overwhelming force that irresistibly draws two persons together and makes them helpless under its power. All that matters is that the two are together, and all other considerations become secondary. Smitten, overcome, engulfed, the star-crossed lovers try to explain what has happened to them and conclude that it must have been moonglow or fate or the season or a magic potion of the gods or some other strange power which brought them straight to one another.

The idea is as recent as current love songs, and as ancient as the dramas of Euripides, whose Phaedra "groans in bitterness of heart and the goads of love prick her cruelly, and she is like to die." The goddess Aphrodite had stricken Phaedra with an uncontrollable seizure of desire for the chaste young man, Hippolytus, Phaedra's husband's illegitimate son. Aphrodite did this out of spite, desiring to punish Hippolytus for ignoring her, the goddess of love, and worshiping another goddess instead. Poor Phaedra in her suffering tries to fight off the lovesickness, believing she can conquer love "with discretion and good sense," but when that fails, she concludes that death is the only answer. Her faithful nurse provides comfort, telling Phaedra that it is futile to think that her puny swimming could provide an escape from the great sea of love into which she had fallen. "Give up your railing," counsels the old woman. "It's only insolent pride to wish to be superior to the gods. Endure your love. The gods have willed it so. You are sick."[34]

The ballads of the twelfth-century troubadours with their themes of knights who pledged undying devotion to their ladies went a step further and exalted romantic love as the noblest emotion of which the human heart is capable. This courtly love of which the troubadours sang reinforces traditional male-female images. The man is the aggressive pursuer, and the woman is the pure, beautiful prize to be pursued. The gentleman is to *serve* his lady—to perform significant deeds for her that will make her justly proud of him. Now she is in his debt, and to repay him dances off to bed with him. Eight centuries later, though the dragons have all been slain, the pattern remains. The gentleman serves his lady by providing economic benefits for her both before and especially after marriage. She thus is in his debt, and he gains authority over her.

This is not to say that the "diseased hysteria" and courtly "Amor" notions of romantic love exhaust the meanings of the word *love* as it applies to men and women. Denis de Rougemont, for example, makes a distinction between "an obsession which is undergone and a destiny that we shoulder." He writes: "*To be in love* is not necessarily *to love.* To be in love is a state; to love, an act. A state is suffered or undergone; but an act has to be decided upon."[35] Even when mates were selected by parents, there were expectations that the mates would develop a love or at least a deep affection.[36] The Bible speaks of Isaac who watched the camel caravan which brought the bride whom he had never seen before but who was chosen by his father's servant. "Then Isaac brought her into the tent, and took Rebekah, and she became his wife; and he loved her." (Gen. 24:67). In these situations, of course, love was not the *basis* for marriage as it is supposed to be in modern societies. Nor was it the criterion for marital stability that some believe it to be ("Since we don't love each other any more, why not get a divorce?").

If we think of love as "an act to be decided upon," to use de Rougemont's description, rather than "a state to be suffered or undergone" (romantic love), there still is the question of why one certain person is drawn to a particular other person. Again, we shall see that the matter of exchanging rewards enters the picture.

Attractions between persons may be thought of as either extrinsic or intrinsic. In an *extrinsic* relationship, the emphasis is on something outward and tangible. A milkman courteously introduces himself to a housewife and presents her with a free sample of cottage cheese, hoping that she will decide to become a regular customer. Some firms advertise very bluntly: "We want your business." But in an *intrinsic* relationship, the emphasis is on the inward and intangible. It is not a case of "wanting someone's business," but rather of wanting someone—and wanting that person for his or her own sake. (The military may, of course, say, "We want *you!*" in their recruiting advertisements; but there the emphasis is on something extrinsic—the service a person can give.)

In an extrinsic relationship, one person treats the other as a means to some end. We might think of philosopher Martin Buber's description of an "I-it" relationship in which a subject is relating to an object.[37] Thus, a salesman takes a client out to dinner, hoping to make a sale. Their being together has only this end in view. In contrast, the intrinsic relationship corresponds to Buber's notion of an "I-Thou" encounter, where the relationship is one of subject to subject rather than of subject to object. The two persons are attracted because of each other and because of the relationship itself. Friends or lovers go out for dinner simply because they enjoy each other and like to be together. There is an exchange of listening and speaking in which each person's self is revealed to the other. There are inputs on both sides which shape and mold the relationship itself. The two persons are associating with one another for their own sakes and not for the sake of some expected external benefit.

This does not mean, however, that no benefits are desired or expected at all. Throughout this book, we have observed the general sociological principle of reward-exchange in the formation and maintenance of associations. Love does not mean that a relationship is exempted from this principle. As sociologist Peter Blau has pointed out, "Exchange processes occur in love relations as well as in social associations of only extrinsic significance," but different dynamics are at work in a love relationship.[38] In an extrinsic relationship (the salesman and his client), the exchange of specific rewards is the very reason that the association exists; and the rewards themselves are the aim. But in an intrinsic association, the supreme value is the association in and of itself, with the mutual exchange of rewards taking place in order to sustain the relationship.

While we usually think of love in altruistic terms, Blau makes the point that "selfless devotion generally rests on an interest in maintaining the other's love." Persons in love furnish rewards and benefits to each other—not necessarily to receive benefits in return, but to show commitment to the partner and to their relationship and to induce the partner to enlarge his commitment and inputs as well. Love, therefore, is the extreme example of a deep, strong, intrinsic attraction between persons; but it is based on the norm of reciprocity. To love is to expect love in return. Love unrequited becomes love unkindled.

Rewards of Love

The question quite naturally arises at this point: what rewards do men and women seek from one another in love relationships? In discussing the nature of the social bond, some sociologists point out that a crucial force in bringing and holding persons together is *gratitude*.[39] When persons do something for others, they expect to receive in return some recognition for their deed or gift and are deeply disappointed if there is no indication of appreciation. The student who observes a fellow student drop an armload of books and papers and stops to help pick them up might perform his good deed without any conscious desire for recognition or reward. But if he meets with only a cold indifference that refuses even a simple "thank you" or is told to go away and mind his own business, a potential bond between the two persons will be slashed. If this element of gratitude is so important in social bonding in general, it is especially important in the interactions associated with love. Such a point is being made by the wife who complains, "You just take me for granted. I never hear a word of thanks for all the things I do for you." Or the husband who laments, "Nag, nag,

nag. That's all you ever do! Does it occur to you that a man would like to hear a word of appreciation once in a while?'' Interactions that call forth admiration, recognition, and gratitude go on before marriage as well—whether in the exchange of tangible gifts or of intangible benefits, such as compliments and loving gestures.

Of course, the development of love as an exchange involves more than gratefulness. Social psychologists have in recent years given much attention to what they call the ''social-penetration process'' or how persons get into one another so that interpersonal relationships can grow and develop.[40] It is clear that if true intimacy is to develop, the interaction between persons must involve self-disclosure. A person reveals information about himself (his feelings, ambitions, fears, attitudes, anxieties, incidents from his past, and so on) which would otherwise not be known by another person. This intentional self-disclosure is perceived by the second person as a social reward because it shows him that the discloser likes him, trusts him, and is also freeing him to make similar disclosures about himself.[41] At the same time, there is always an element of risk in self-disclosure. The person to whom one reveals himself might react negatively to the information revealed and may lower his regard for the one who has thus shared himself or may even use the information to take advantage of him. This is one reason that self-disclosure is difficult for many people.[42]

However, in a relationship involving commitment and love, a high degree of self-disclosure comes to be expected as an element of reward in the social exchange process. Being loved by someone means that person accepts you as you are—even when the secrets of your heart are laid bare. Thus you have a confidant to whom you can unload your heartaches and expose your innermost feelings. And loving someone in return means that likewise you are rewarded by that person's trust and confidence through self-disclosure on his or her part.

Sociologist Ira Reiss sees this as a crucial second step in his ''wheel theory'' of love and its development. Reiss conceptualizes love as an ongoing cycle that begins with a sense of rapport between two individuals. This rapport then turns toward mutual self-revelation; and as the ''wheel'' turns further, the persons develop a mutual dependency on one another. Reiss notes that the more technical term for such mutual dependencies is ''interdependent habit systems.'' He explains: ''One becomes dependent on the other person to fulfill one's own habits: e.g., one needs the other person to tell one's ideas or feelings; . . . to joke with; . . . to fulfill one's sexual desires. When such habitual expectations are not fulfilled, loneliness and frustration are experienced. Thus, such habits tend to perpetuate a relationship.''[43] From mutual dependencies, the wheel turns to personality need fulfillment. The harmonious connection between the persons (rapport) is increased, the self-revelation continues, and so on, as the wheel keeps turning. (See Figure 4-5.)

At the same time, says Reiss, the wheel could hit a snare at some point and the relationship could begin to ''unwind.'' An argument or competing interest

Being loved by someone means you have a confidant to whom you can expose your innermost feelings.

might lessen rapport between the persons, which in turn would block the self-disclosure, disturb the "interdependent habit systems" of mutual dependency, and frustrate fulfillment of the personality needs of the individuals concerned.

Akin to this notion of mutual dependency is the emphasis of two psychologists on the part reinforcement plays in building a sense of self-worth in persons who are loved. "Through reinforcement, lovers mutually enhance each other's self-concept," write Howard Miller and Paul Siegel. Pointing out that in an ongoing love relationship, reinforcement efforts often need to be *intentional,* they write: "By 'conscious and deliberate' we mean that each partner can deliberately choose to help satisfy the other's needs, to bolster the other's feelings of self-worth and attractiveness. The fading of the original thrill of mutual discovery and infatuation can be replaced by consciously learning how to make the other person feel attractive, adequate, and simply good, about himself. This can be as obvious as praise, or as subtle as paying attention at appropriate moments."[44] However, unless this reinforcement springs from honesty, it has little value. When compliments and expressed interest are not genuine, "that person will lose his power to reward you."

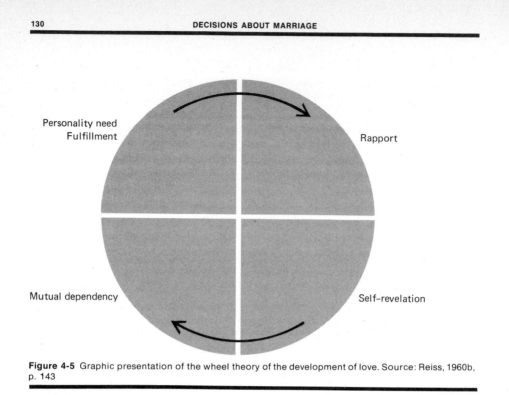

Figure 4-5 Graphic presentation of the wheel theory of the development of love. Source: Reiss, 1960b, p. 143

This brings us back to the matter of social exchange and our emphasis on bargaining and costs and rewards. All of the foregoing attempts to analyze and describe the dynamics of love make it clear that benefit seeking and reward exchanges are very much involved in the entire process. As we have seen, both the giving and receiving of personal disclosures are perceived as social rewards. Likewise, the benefits described by Reiss as "interdependent habit systems" are very much related to reward seeking and reward granting in social exchange. This is also true of the Miller and Siegel emphasis on reinforcement as a sought-after prize in human relationships.

Many people are reluctant to admit that an exchange of rewards occurs in love. They feel that such a notion somehow devalues the ideal of love as intrinsically selfless and sacrificial, without any expectation of anything in return. However, a little reflection on the kinds of rewards sought in a love relationship might make the notions of exchange, bargaining, and benefits a bit more easy to accept. After all, why else would persons enter into love relationships and marriage than out of an expectation that they would gain something from such relationships?

Earlier, we talked about two parts of marriage, the instrumental side being concerned with economic factors and task performance, and the expressive side having to do with the affectionate-companionate dimension. To speak of love is to speak of the expressive rewards persons seek from a marriage partner—rewards such as *companionship* (someone to do things with, go places with, spend leisure hours with), *empathy* (someone to talk things over with, someone to bring reinforcement of one's self-concept, someone to understand and care), and *physical affection* (hugging, kissing, the squeeze of a hand, caressing, sexual gratifications). Prior to marriage, these same three elements in one degree or another are sought after as valued rewards in a developing relationship. Though it is often unconscious, a type of bargaining is going on between the partners as they reach out to receive these benefits from one another. The decision to continue the relationship and later to enter into marriage hinges in large part on this reward exchange.

RATIONALITY AND LOVE

For years, critics have charged that it is the nature of romantic love to hamper and inhibit rational discussion of elements extrinsic to the couple's relationship itself—elements such as finances, status, education, occupation, and life-style. The point becomes clear in a popular song of recent years which emphasized that it doesn't matter "if we don't have money" because "I'm still in love with you, honey." Critics of romantic love would be quick to say, "They'll find out! When the honeymoon is over and the bills have to be paid, they'll find how little they have to hold them together. Those ecstatic feelings are going to fade away fast when the rent is due and groceries have to be bought and all the rest."

Added to these older criticisms are the new challenges to romantic love that are beginning to emerge on several fronts. Essentially, the goal is to make the mate-selection process more rational so that persons become more aware of the realities (actual costs and rewards) involved. The new emphasis on a consideration of gender roles before marriage is one way that marriage eligibles are being encouraged to develop more deliberate consciousness of the extrinsic (as well as intrinsic) elements involved in male-female relationships.

Sex

According to the romantic-love notion, sex "just happens" because two people are swept off their feet and helplessly carried away by their passions. That costs may be involved has often been overlooked until later. We saw in the last chapter that feminists have begun to point out some of these costs in advance, particularly for women, and have stressed a need for negotiating a fair bargain in order to avoid exploitation. Such a consideration of costs is another way of bringing rationality into the male-female relationship, this time specifically in the area of sex.

Similarly, the introduction of contraceptive usage in premarital sexual relations is based upon rational considerations. Through the efforts of organizations such as Planned Parenthood, sexually active unmarried men and women are urged to take precautions against conceiving children. Even some religious groups and spokespersons have suggested that, despite traditional teachings on the wrongness of sex outside marriage, a realistic approach needs to take into account that many persons do engage in premarital sex and need guidance in avoiding undesirable consequences such as pregnancy and venereal disease. One minister has suggested that an unmarried couple who are engaging in sexual intercourse should have a "deep-think" discussion, considering every angle of what they are doing, and if they feel they cannot quit, they should determine to use contraceptives. "Since you can't be as good as you wish," he writes, "will you at least be as smart as you can?"[45] The essence of the advice is rationality.

There is some evidence that in the past young women have resisted the idea of using contraception before marriage.[46] They tended to feel that if coitus occurred it "just happened," spontaneously emerging out of the romantic love that had engulfed them and their partners. In such situations, being ready with contraceptives would indicate preplanning and an intentional focus on sex. This would never do. Romantic love emphasizes being overcome by the emotions of the moment, falling under a magic spell as Cupid's arrow strikes.

Furthermore, the old double standard played a part. "Nice" girls weren't supposed to be interested in sex; and if a young woman did engage in intercourse before marriage, it was much more forgivable if she had been caught off guard and overtaken by sudden irresistible impulses in her lover's embrace. A girl, conditioned by the double standard, would be reluctant to admit she had a diaphragm in her purse or was on the pill or had brought some contraceptive foam with her. Nor would she be likely to ask her boyfriend if he had brought a condom. Her interest in such preparations might cheapen her in his eyes and mark her as an easy woman. Consequently, the use of contraceptives before marriage was often disregarded.

However, if contraception is not used, the odds of conceiving a child are obviously high. In many societies, premarital pregnancy has often served as a mechanism for confronting a man with his obligation to a particular woman. He has had his sexual gratification; now in exchange he must take on the responsibilities of caring for the woman and the child he has fathered. The so-called forced marriage or shotgun wedding is an example of a marriage bargain involving something very different from the romantic-love ideal. One is a "have to" marriage, while the other is a "want to" marriage. Of course, in certain instances, the sexually active couple may have planned to marry prior to the pregnancy, and thus coercion is somewhat less of a factor—except perhaps to speed up the date of the wedding.

In the mid-1960s, 22 percent of all legitimate first births in the United States occurred eight months or less after marriage. Where the mother was fifteen-to-nineteen years old, the figure was 42 percent.[47] Clearly, therefore, a substantial number of marriage bargains are struck with coercion present to at least some degree. This is especially true among younger girls.

The kind of situation occurs most often at lower socioeconomic levels. (See

TABLE 4-C ANNUAL AVERAGE NUMBER OF LEGITIMATE FIRST BIRTHS TO WOMEN AGED 15 TO 44 TAKING PLACE UNDER EIGHT MONTHS AFTER FIRST MARRIAGE, ACCORDING TO FAMILY INCOME

| | Total | Family Income | | | | |
		Under $3,000	$3,000–$4,999	$5,000–$6,999	$7,000–$9,999	$10,000 and Over
Number of mothers (in thousands)	1,008	248	230	228	184	118
Percentage of mothers giving birth under eight months after first marriage	22%	38%	24%	18%	12%	8%

SOURCE: Based upon the United States 1964–66 National Natality Survey. U.S. Department of Health, Education and Welfare, *Monthly Vital Statistics Report 18*, no. 12, 1970, p. 3.

Table 4-C.) Females with few resources are the ones least able to bargain effectively for justice in their dealings with males. Such young women have few alternative rewards besides sex and motherhood.

The percentages mentioned in Table 4-C do not tell us how many premarital *conceptions* take place, since not all such conceptions result in live births. And of those that do result in live births, not all take place within marriage. Often a man cannot be coerced into marrying the woman he impregnated, and often a woman doesn't want to marry the man involved with her in the conception.

With the increasing availability of abortion, many premarital pregnancies are being terminated. Persons who take this alternative avoid striking a marriage bargain based upon coercion, and it is therefore no coincidence that feminist groups have supported liberal abortion laws. The option to abort increases a woman's freedom by giving her power to refrain from entering a marriage she doesn't want. This is another example of the introduction of rationality into the mate-selection process, emphasizing control over one's destiny rather than surrender to circumstances.

By the same token, contraception increases a woman's power by freeing her from being confronted with decisions about managing a premarital pregnancy and its potential for disrupting her life. Yet research shows that among sexually active, young, unmarried women (ages fifteen-to-nineteen), contraceptive usage is a sometimes thing, with only one-fifth of the women reporting that they *always* protected themselves.[48] Socioeconomic status has a great deal to do with a young woman's use or nonuse of contraception in premarital sexual intercourse. Women with a greater range of status advantages (including higher education of their parents and higher education for themselves) are more likely to use contraceptives than are women of lower status.

Since young women from higher-status homes tend to have the most modern views of sex roles, they do not see themselves as being limited to the traditional rewards of wifehood and motherhood. It stands to reason that such women would be more motivated to avoid unwanted pregnancies than would be true of lower-status women who hold more traditional gender-role norms. Women with more egalitarian ideals, being concerned with individualistic achievement and autonomy, would tend to define a premarital pregnancy as an unacceptable and unnecessary cost blocking them from other sought-after rewards. Thus, they are more likely to attempt to avoid such costs through more extensive and rigorous contraception.[49]

Age at First Marriage

As we have seen, rationality in mate selection involves many things—deciding about sex roles (particularly as they affect women who opt for nontraditional roles), having some idea about future aspirations, determining how the question of sexual gratification shall be handled, making choices with regard to contraception if premarital sex is engaged in, and so on. Closely related to all of these is the matter of a person's age at the time of marriage.

It isn't difficult to see that there are important connections among sex roles, contraception, pregnancy, and the age at first marriage. A teenager who expects only to be a wife and mother some day, and who begins dating early, engages in premarital sex, does not use contraceptives, and who becomes pregnant before she finishes high school, quite likely will marry young. Moreover, age at marriage has important consequences for the future. The adolescent girl in the example above has a high chance of becoming divorced. If she and her husband remain married, they are likely to have a higher number of children than if they had married later. And their income can be expected to be lower than that of persons who marry later.

The longer one delays marriage, the longer one is deferring the kinds of gratifications that marriage supplies. But for a woman to be able to delay marital rewards, there have to be alternatives to take their place. The 1970 census shows that the more education that persons have, the older they are when they marry.[50] We have already seen the association between education and gender roles. The more a woman seeks individualistic rewards for herself, the greater her autonomy and independence as a person, the later she is likely to marry. Men who favor such female reward seeking are also likely to marry later, choosing women who have taken time to complete their education and perhaps already embarked on careers.

Women who are less educated marry younger because there are fewer alternative rewards open to them. When such women become pregnant out of wedlock, their marriage age is often lowered still further. Regardless of class background, however, premarital conceptions tend to have a lowering effect on age at marriage.

Nationally, the median age at first marriage in the United States had been dropping from about 1890 to 1956. (See Table 4-D.) During that same period, the gap between the sexes at the age of first marriage began to narrow. In 1890, there was a four-year difference between the age at which women married and the age at which men married; but by 1956, that difference had shrunk to two and a half years.

Beginning in 1957, one of the trends began to reverse. While the ages of marital partners continued to move closer together, there was a new trend for both sexes to wait longer to marry. By 1974, the median age for males at first marriage was 23.1 years. For females, it had risen to 21.1. Explanations for the phenomenon of later marriage today may be related to changes in gender-role norms and shifts in life-styles—a topic to be discussed more fully in the next chapter.

SUMMARY AND FUTURES

So far we have described deciding on marriage as a process of reward seeking in which the objective is to strike the best bargain possible. This process is related to a variety of factors, such as romantic love, premarital conceptions, social-background characteristics, age at marriage, and sex roles.

TABLE 4-D MEDIAN AGE AT FIRST MARRIAGE, BY SEX, FOR THE UNITED STATES, 1960 TO 1974 AND FOR CONTERMINOUS UNITED STATES, 1890 TO 1959

Year	Male	Female	Year	Male	Female
1974	23.1	21.1	1956	22.5	20.1
1973	23.2	21.0	1955	22.6	20.2
1972	23.3	20.9	1954	23.0	20.3
1971	23.1	20.9	1953	22.8	20.2
1970	23.2	20.8	1952	23.0	20.2
1969	23.2	20.8	1951	22.9	20.4
1968	23.1	20.8	1950	22.8	20.3
1967	23.1	20.6	1949	22.7	20.3
1966	22.8	20.5			
1965	22.8	20.6			
1964	23.1	20.5	1948	23.3	20.4
1963	22.8	20.5	1947	23.7	20.5
1962	22.7	20.3	1940	24.3	21.5
1961	22.8	20.3	1930	24.3	21.3
1960	22.8	20.3	1920	24.6	21.2
1959	22.5	20.2	1910	25.1	21.6
1958	22.6	20.2	1900	25.9	21.9
1957	22.6	20.3	1890	26.1	22.0

SOURCE: U.S. Bureau of the Census, 1974, *Current Population Reports*, P-20, no. 271, p. 1.

A crucial part of the process relates to the gender-role norms held by women and men. Persons holding modern, egalitarian gender-role norms seek different kinds of rewards from marriage than do persons who hold traditional gender-role norms.

While the whole thrust of romantic love is to make persons nonquestioning and nonrational (with regard to standing back and counting present and anticipated costs and rewards), women with more education and more modern gender-role norms tend to introduce elements of rationality into the mate-selection process. Such women question more and try to make sure they are striking equitable bargains. They are less likely, for instance, to allow themselves to be sexually exploited or to be coerced (through pregnancy) into marriages they do not want.

Nevertheless, the great majority of marriages up to now have started out on a traditional footing. Owing to earlier sex-role socialization and to the basic nature of predominant dating and courtship patterns in most modern societies, the husband is designated as the *unique provider,* and the marriage centers around his job demands and its rewards. Decisions about such matters as where to live, the wife's job or educational plans, the family's life-style, and the number and spacing of children are largely determined by the husband and his occupational role.

The woman, in this traditional pattern, is designated as the warm, nurturant, supportive companion—an adjunct to her husband who orders her life in terms of his. Sociologist Shirley Angrist, speaks of the "contingency orientation" that is part of a young girl's socialization.[51] Women grow up having learned to be flexible and malleable so that they can be prepared to adapt to whatever contingencies life may bring their way. Long-range goals, mastery, and self-determination cannot hold a high place in the lives of persons who know that plans may be disrupted at any point. The first contingency is marriage, but at the same time, a young woman knows she must be prepared for an occupation—just in case she doesn't marry, or in case the marriage ends through divorce or the husband's death. Within the marriage, pregnancy and childcare are further contingencies for which she must be prepared to adjust. And likewise, women who hold traditional gender roles are constantly prepared to adapt to their husbands. ("If he does this, I'll do that." "If he works there, perhaps I can find new friends and interests there." "If it fits in with my husband's plans, maybe I can do thus and so.") As to the immediate future (the next decade or two), we may expect that for a large proportion of persons (especially the noncollege population), the processes of dating, courtship, and marriage formation will continue to follow these traditional patterns.

Yet, a major theme of this book is change; and certainly changes are occurring in the area of mate selection. Marriage patterns have not stood still for the past 200 years, and they are not standing still today. As never before, they are coming under close scrutiny, and frank questions are being asked. Upturns in the age at first marriage may in part be a reflection of this new posture. The basis of the scrutiny is a very simple one: What good is marriage? In other words, how rewarding is it?

Not so many years ago, it was virtually unthinkable that marriage should be scrutinized. Marriage was considered too sacred, too mysterious, too mind-boggling to be rationally analyzed. After all, wasn't marriage supposed to be based on love? And who could ever hope to understand the love of a man and woman? But such notions are evaporating. Patterns surrounding the institution of marriage are being examined and reevaluated. We have already seen ways that women are being encouraged to be more rational—more conscious of their own interests—in terms of sexual and contraceptive behavior. As we turn to the remaining chapters, we shall begin to see that this attempt to make women more conscious of their own interests is at the core of the most significant and fundamental changes in marriage patterns taking place today.

NOTES

1   Lord, 1970, p. 57.
2   Macciocchi, 1972, pp. 356–357.
3   Morgan, 1956, pp. 41–43.
4   Blood, 1967, p. 5.
5   Carlier, 1867, pp. 33–34.
6   Morgan, 1956, p. 41.
7   Stephens, 1963, pp. 221–222.
8   Murdock, 1949.
9   Emerson, 1962.
10 Martin, 1969, chap. 4.
11 Rubin, 1973, pp. 201–203; Scott, 1965.
12 Barron, 1972; Mueller, 1971.
13 Mueller, 1971, p. 21; Besanceney, 1970, pp. 162–167.
14 Gordon, 1964.
15 Mueller, 1971; Gordon, 1964.
16 Gordon, 1964, p. 213.
17 Stember, 1966, pp. 104–107.
18 National Center for Health Statistics, 21, no. 21, 1971, pp. 19-20; *Current Population Reports*, P-23, no. 48, 1974, p. 77.
19 Monahan, 1973; Aldridge, 1973; Heer, 1974.
20 Washington, 1970; Sickels, 1972; Barron, 1972; Gordon, 1964.
21 Davis, 1941; Merton, 1941.
22 Heer, 1974.
23 Carter and Glick, 1970, pp. 126–129.
24 Rubin, 1973, p. 196.
25 Bernard, 1966.
26 Monahan, 1973.
27 Cottrell, 1973.
28 Lévi-Strauss, 1956.
29 Lévi-Strauss, 1949.
30 Middleton, 1962.
31 Becker, 1973.

32   Waller, 1938, p. 243, as quoted in Rubin, 1973, p. 205.
33   Yette, 1971.
34   Euripides, *Hippolytus,* Prologue, lines 395–400, 470–475.
35   De Rougemont, 1940.
36   Goode, 1959; Rubin, 1973.
37   Buber, 1958.
38   Blau, 1964, p. 76; see also p. 36.
39   Nisbet, 1970.
40   Taylor, 1968.
41   Worthy, Gary, and Kahn, 1969; Taylor, Altman, and Sorrentino, 1969.
42   Rubin, 1973, pp. 160–162.
43   Reiss, 1960*b*.
44   Miller and Siegel, 1972, pp. 14–22.
45   Shedd, 1968, p. 78.
46   Walshok, 1969; Reiss, 1971, p. 343.
47   *Monthly Vital Statistics Report* 18, no. 12, 1970, p. 1.
48   Kantner and Zelnik, 1973.
49   Walshok, 1969.
50   U.S. Bureau of the Census, 1973, PC(2)-4D, p. 266.
51   Angrist, 1969.

5
ALTERNATIVES TO MARRIAGE

At a California church, a couple lovingly gaze into one another's eyes as they exchange their vows to love, honor, and cherish one another in sickness and in health. The marriage service ends, they kiss, and then march hand-in-hand to the reception where they will hear the congratulations and good wishes of their friends. Everyone gathers around to watch the newlyweds cut the wedding cake, and little attention is paid to the fact that it differs in one respect from other wedding cakes. This particular cake is not topped with the customary figurines which represent the bride in her long white gown and the groom in his dark suit. Instead, it is adorned with two male figurines. The partners have just been united in a gay marriage.

In another section of the country, a leading feminist is being interviewed on a talk show. She is asked why she never married and how she feels about marriage as an institution. She replies that marriage as it presently exists is stifling to wives and prevents a woman from fulfilling her total potential. She announces that she has no interest in marrying unless present arrangements of marriage and the family are drastically changed. Until such a time, singleness is preferable.

On another TV talk show, a young unmarried couple tell why they have chosen to live together. The man speaks of the unhappiness of his own childhood and the heartbreak of his parents' divorce, and how this soured him on the institution of marriage. As he speaks, he cuddles the squirming infant on his lap. The woman tells of her concern for their child's well-being. She maintains that she and the baby's father are together because they want to be, not because they *have* to be, adding that their relationship is not dependent upon a contract signed in accordance with society's decrees. Like many other unmarried couples who have chosen to live together, this man and woman feel that marriage can be a trap, forcing people into roles and destroying the freedom and spontaneity they enjoy in their present arrangement.

Because such examples are given wide coverage in the mass media, there is much talk about the "death of the family" in modern society. Spokespersons for certain groups of youth, women's liberation, homosexual organizations, and even some religious groups have alleged that traditional marriage is indeed a dying institution. The nuclear family of mother, father, and children seems obsolete, a relic of the nineteenth century, as outmoded as the bustle.

In order to cope with the basic question of whether or not the institution of marriage really is an outdated concept, we need first to ask: To what extent are women and men legally marrying one another? If rates of legal marriage are dropping substantially, then there are grounds for believing in the collapse of marriage as an institution. But if people continue to apply for licenses to wed, the matter is not so simple.

At the same time, it is clear that some persons are interested in life-styles different from traditional concepts of marriage. We'll want to examine some of these alternatives as this chapter progresses, giving attention to unmarried living together and trial marriage, singleness, parenthood apart from marriage, communal living, group marriage, and homosexual marriage.

IS LEGAL MARRIAGE BEING REJECTED?

Demographers are social scientists who study the statistics of populations and can tell us all sorts of interesting facts and trends about births, deaths, marriages, divorces, and other matters of vital concern. In 1974, demographers pointed out that in the United States there had been an uninterrupted fifteen-year period of increases in both the number of marriages and in marriage rates.[1] This finding tells us something: namely, that there hasn't been a trend to reject marriage as is so often asserted. From 1959 through the end of 1973, persons were still entering legal marriage each year in larger numbers than the year before.

One might argue that the fact of more marriages could be explained by the fact of more young people—that is, large numbers of persons from the baby boom of the late 1940s and early 1950s were reaching marriageable age during the fifteen-year period of marriage increases. However, we would still expect to find a downward trend in numbers of marriages performed if persons (even if there were more of them) really were abandoning the institution. No evidence of such abandonment showed up. Demographers do not only look at the raw figures of how many men and women exchange wedding vows; they also take note of *percentages*. In 1968, there was a steep increase of 7 percent more marriages than the year before; after that year, the average yearly increase in numbers of marriages per year slowed down to less than 2 percent a year. However, it has still been a matter of increases and not decreases.[2]

Another way demographers study marriage trends is to compare the number of marriages in a given year with the total population in that same year. That way they can show how many marriage events take place for every thousand people. The number of marriages per thousand is called the *marriage rate*. Since it rests on a constant base, the marriage rate makes meaningful comparisons possible. In 1972 and 1973, there were 10.9 marriages for every thousand Americans. This was the highest rate since 1950 (at 11.1) which was the tail end of the post–World War II marriage boom.

However, merely looking at overall marriage rates masks the difference between persons who are being married for the first time and those who are remarrying. Actually, since the mid-1950s, trends in remarriages and in first marriages have been going in opposite directions. Remarriage rates are rising sharply in the United States, at the same time that first-marriage rates are gradually declining.[3] (See Table 5-A.) Apparently, persons who have lived in the structural situation of legal monogamy are eager to reenter it. This includes not only persons who have lost a spouse through death, but also persons whose marriages have been broken by divorce. They were evidently not disillusioned by the institution of marriage per se but rather were disenchanted by the level of rewards and costs in a particular relationship. Thus, they are eager to try again

TABLE 5-A RATE OF FIRST MARRIAGES, DIVORCES, AND REMARRIAGES FOR SELECTED YEARS IN THE UNITED STATES

Period	Marriages per 1,000 Single Women Ages 14–44	Divorces per 1,000 Married Women Ages 14–44	Remarriages per 1,000 Widowed and Divorced Women 14–54 Years of Age
1945–47	143	24	163
1954–56	120	15	129
1960–62	116	16	133
1969–71	107	26	168

SOURCE: Adapted from Glick and Norton, 1973, Table 1, p. 302.

in a new marital relationship where a new exchange of costs and rewards can be worked out. These are the persons most responsible for pushing American marriage rates to new heights.

On the other hand, persons who have never entered marriage are increasingly cautious about doing so. This is particularly true of younger persons. As we saw in the preceding chapter, the trend among young women and men to postpone marriage longer than they have in the recent past may be one indication of increased rationality in the mate-selection process. Notions of romantic love are being pushed into a different perspective; and of prime concern are such matters as self-determination, manipulating circumstances rather than being crushed by them, and calculating in advance the costs and rewards likely to be the outcome of any particular decision—especially decisions about marriage.

TRIAL MARRIAGE AND AD HOC ARRANGEMENTS

Before purchasing a new car, it's only rational to take it out for a test-drive first. Some people have suggested that marriage should follow a similar pattern, allowing a test period of living together before making the final commitment. Such an arrangement usually goes by the name *trial marriage.* Some proponents suggest a structured form, others an unstructured.

Structured Trial Marriage

Structured trial marriages would be institutionalized in some way, with regulations by society to legitimate the union. The idea in itself is not new, although new variations continue to be suggested from time to time. Maurice of Saxony was already suggesting trial marriage in the eighteenth century because he considered marriage for life "a betrayal of the self, an unnatural compulsion." His proposed solution was the formation of temporary marriages, with contracts acknowledged as being for a limited period of time.[4]

A similar idea was proposed by one Judge Ben B. Lindsey. He called his concept "companionate marriage" and wrote up his ideas for *Redbook* magazine in 1926, only to meet with ostracism and severe criticism after the article's appearance. Shortly afterward, Bertrand Russell proposed a similar idea, suggesting it would be especially applicable to university students as a better way of channeling sexual desires than was the case with the "excitement of parties and drunken orgies" during the Prohibition Era. Russell was rewarded for his efforts by scandal, slander, and the loss of his teaching position at the City College of New York. Americans made it clear that they were not ready for a revision of marriage customs.[5]

Forty years after its publication of Judge Lindsey's article, *Redbook* published another much-discussed article on trial marriage—this time by anthropologist Margaret Mead. Mead proposed a two-step marriage arrangement, each step differing in commitments and responsibilities. The first (or trial) part would be called *individual marriage.* It would be entered by a simple ceremony, carry limited economic responsibilities, would not allow children, and would be easy to end. The second (or permanent) step would be called *parental marriage.* It would be entered only by those couples who, after the first step of individual marriage, desired to form a lifetime relationship and undertake the obligations of parenthood.[6]

Responses to Dr. Mead's proposal varied from praise for its emphasis on responsible parenthood to criticism for suggesting the temporary arrangement of the "individual" marriage form. One woman wrote: "I still prefer God's one-step plan, which is *only* for mature couples, united for life, who *are* prepared for responsible parenthood." Other persons suggested that many couples already follow a similar plan through existing channels: they enter legal marriage, responsibly use contraceptives for a few years of getting to know one another sexually and socially, then embark on parenthood when they feel the time is right. If the marriage doesn't seem to be working, there is divorce. In view of this, they wondered, what would be the need for such a two-step plan? Students especially seemed to reject the idea. They couldn't see any reason to go through a marriage ceremony in order to live together and have sex relations if no children were desired. Why have new laws for what many were already doing anyway? One student flatly accused Dr. Mead of wanting "to bottle up freedom, to hedge it with ceremony and publicly acknowledged responsibility." In the end, Margaret Mead concluded, "It now seems clear to me that neither elders nor young people want to make a change to two forms of marriage. They want to reserve the word 'marriage' for a commitment that they can feel is permanent and final, no matter how often the actual marriages may fail."[7]

There have been other attempts to add a new dimension of rationality to marriage through structured trial unions, all of which would of course require changes in present marriage laws.[8] One example was Virginia Satir's proposal at the 1967 convention of the American Psychological Association which suggested that marriage be made a statutory, five-year, renewable contract. This would provide a built-in mechanism for periodic review of the marriage so that a decision could be made either to go on with the relationship or to let it be terminated.[9]

Unstructured Trial Marriage

The proposals for structured trial marriages just examined would involve licensing and regulation by society. Many couples see no need for such involvement by the state, preferring to view the man-woman relationship as a private matter.[10] They see the rationality in the trial-marriage idea but prefer an unstructured form. They simply live together. If they get along well and want the relationship to continue on a permanent basis, they can become legally married. On the other hand, if their living together convinces them they're unsuited for each other, the man and woman can go their separate ways.

Unstructured trial marriages go by various names—nonlegal voluntary associations, "the arrangement," "unmarried living together," "unlawful union," or just plain "shacking up." One sociologist coined his own term for such associations—*Unmalias,* which was a word formed from the words *unmarried liaisons.*[11] If there is no consensus on a name for the *arrangement* in which an unmarried couple lives together, there seems to be even more of a problem in knowing what to call the *person* with whom one sets up housekeeping. In this pattern, one can't introduce the other as "my husband," "my wife," or "my spouse." Some persons simply say, "my man," "my woman," or "my old man," or "my old woman." A few might say, "my friend" or "my roommate." Sometimes terms derived from the word *cohabitation* are used, for example, "my cohab," or "cohabitant."

Again, it must be stressed that the basic idea behind trial marriages is the notion that the selection of a marriage partner should involve rationality. Persons in such arrangements do not hold to the idealism of folklore (such as, "They fell in love, got married, and lived happily ever after—because love conquers all"). A trial marriage is entered in the expectation that rewards and especially the costs of a particular male-female exchange will become apparent before a permanent decision about the relationship is made.

Earlier, we saw that mate selection is essentially a process of seeking to strike the best bargain possible. Sociologist George Homans uses the term *profit* to describe the ratio of rewards to costs as experienced by persons in social exchange.[12] In a trial marriage, if the ratio is perceived as unfavorable (too many punishments, not enough rewards), the partners are not encumbered by legal requirements to stay together. A "low profit" situation can easily be terminated. This does not mean that decisions to break up will be painless. Just as in actual divorce, if one partner perceives the reward/cost ratio to be favorable and wishes to continue the arrangement, he or she is the one likely to feel the more hurt and deprived when the relationship ends.

But what if both partners consider the profits acceptable? They could either enter into a legal marriage or else just go on living together without legal sanctions. There are no reliable statistics on the incidence of trial marriage in America. We simply don't know how many persons choose that particular life-style. But whatever their numbers, the data on marriages and marriage rates cited earlier indicate that most persons who are satisfied with a living-together arrangement evidently seek a marriage license eventually. In other words, trial marriage at the present time seems to be defined as a prelude to legal marriage, and not as a substitute for it. For those who engage in it, it is a kind of experiment to determine whether or not to seek legal marriage with this particular partner or some other partner (the person may have a long series of trials) or never with anyone.

Ad Hoc Arrangements

The Latin expression *ad hoc* means "for this [special purpose]." Some couples who choose to live together unmarried view their arrangement as simply an ad hoc situation, existing for its own sake. For them, living together is not viewed as an experiment, and the persons concerned do not think of it as a trial marriage (structured or unstructured) or any other kind of *marital* arrangement. They are not interested in entering legal marriage through licensing and ceremonies, nor are they interested in having their relationship become a common-law marriage through default. They simply want to live together totally apart from the institution of marriage, and they don't want others to consider them "married" in any sense.[13] Research on unmarried couples living together has thus far been scanty, but two small-scale studies have shown that females are more likely than males to think of their living together arrangement as a prelude to marriage rather than as a substitute for it.[14]

Concealed Arrangements and Open Arrangements

Marriage, sociologically defined, consists of a relationship in which two or more persons maintain ongoing expressive (including sexual) and instrumental (including economic) exchanges. This definition is broad enough to encompass marriage in many forms—trial, legal, group, gay, traditional, modern, and so on. An important adjunct to this way of viewing marriage has to do with the public nature of the arrangement.

It is not likely that anyone would call an "affair" a marriage. Affairs are romantic attachments and regularized sexual liaisons usually carried out secretly and often considered to be of brief duration. While there are certain expressive interchanges and quite possibly a giving and receiving of material gifts, there is no expectation of the ongoing sexual and economic interdependency that characterizes marital arrangements. What is more, persons involved in affairs try to keep their relationship hidden. Public revelation is the last thing such lovers would want!

However, suppose two persons move in together and carry on both expressive and economic exchanges in much the same way as married persons. Yet, they carry on their relationship covertly, even though it is often difficult. Parents, peers, the postal service, telephone company, insurance companies, the Internal Revenue Service, employers, and others who have interest in them have no idea that this man and woman are sharing the same apartment. Even though their arrangement is a step closer to marriage than an affair would be, it still cannot be called a marriage—even in the sociological sense. Why? Because their relationship is clandestine and there is a deliberate avoidance of any public disclosure and social recognition.

If persons are secretive about their living together—covert instead of overt—it probably means that they fear punishments that could be imposed upon them by people they consider important in their lives, those whom sociologists call "significant others." Such people might apply negative sanctions so severe that they could disrupt the relationship entirely. If the relationship is that uncertain, tentative, and fragile, it cannot be called a marriage, since a marriage by definition is an *ongoing* exchange.

Two hypothetical couples serve as illustrations of the difference between covert and overt arrangements. Natalie and Kurt decide during college days to share a small apartment together. They don't hide the fact that they are living together, and their friends continue to accept them, visit them, and include them in invitations to various events and activities. Fran and Ed, on the other hand, don't want people to know about their similar living arrangement. They make it a point not to tell their friends out of fear that their friends would shun them if they knew. They are not prepared to accept such a cost, because they know it might undermine their attraction for each other. How? Because the cost of rejection by friends might prove to be more significant than the rewards Fran and Ed currently furnish each other. Their arrangement might not seem worth the suffering of social ostracism.

Natalie and Kurt seem to have much more going for them than is true of Fran and Ed. For one thing, the parents of both Natalie and Kurt know about their relationship and do not punish through the withholding of benefits. The parents continue to help with college expenses and also help pay for travel when the couple visits them. Both the financial aid and the willingness to visit with the couple, desiring to be with them rather than shunning them are important rewards that the parents are not withholding. Their approval of the relationship helps sustain it.

Conversely, Fran and Ed perceive that their parents would cut off all financial assistance if they knew how they were living. Furthermore, the parents would probably be icy cold to them and perhaps even refuse to see them. This lack of approval plus the loss of economic benefits could also prove of greater significance than their own mutual benefits and thus threaten the ongoingness of their relationship.

Let's assume that several years pass. Natalie and Kurt have completed college and each enters a livelihood where their living-together arrangement is not likely to incur punishments from people who provide them money (and thus exercise a certain degree of control over them). One may become a novelist, and the other may find a place in the anonymity of the civil service. By now, of course, it no longer seems reasonable to apply the term *trial* to their long-standing arrangement. Too many years have passed. All this time, Kurt and Natalie have simply continued to live together without legal sanctions, and they plan to continue their arrangement into the future. Can we say they are married? Yes and no. Sociologically speaking, they would appear to be clearly married; they are in an ongoing relationship, publicly declared, in which there is both full expressive and instrumental interdependency. If we look at Table 5-B, we can see that their situation is different from trial marriage but yet not quite the same as a legal union. Their arrangement might be called an "ongoing consensual union" (a situation of living together simply by mutual consent); and in some states, their relationship might be considered a common-law marriage.

COMMON-LAW MARRIAGE

A man and woman who have lived together for a certain period of time are considered by the courts in certain states to have a valid marriage, even though they entered their union without a marriage license or ceremony. Where common-law marriage is recognized, the children of the couple are considered legitimate; but where such marriage is not considered valid, the children are considered illegitimate. Less than one-third of the states retain the institution of common-law marriage at present, and there seems to be a growing trend toward abolishing it.[15] Many legal complications have arisen over it, particularly with regard to questions about the legitimacy of offspring and about estate settlements. Sociologist William Kephart refers to the costly court battles that are often necessary for a common-law wife after her husband dies. "Unless she can prove that a common-law marriage existed—seldom an easy task—neither she nor her children are entitled to the property rights or inheritance that normally are theirs."[16] Sometimes upon the death of a wealthy bachelor, women who claim to have been common-law wives step forth hoping to gain an inheritance. And sometimes such claims are made even with regard to a married man. For example, after a 1974 air crash in which a honeymooning couple was killed, a woman filed suit with the airlines claiming she had lived as the groom's common-law wife and had several children by him. Second spouses of persons who have been in common-law marriages often run into particular difficulties with regard to estate settlements, because a common-law husband or wife may have had the mistaken notion that getting out of such a marriage is just as

TABLE 5-B CONTINUUM OF RELATIONSHIPS BETWEEN THE SINGLE STATE AND MARRIED STATE

Premarriage		Marriage			
		Sociological Definition		Legal Definition	
The affair	Living together covertly	Living together overtly		Common law marriage	Legitimized union
(Regularized sexual liaisons)	Ad hoc arrange- ment	Trial marriage	Ongoing consensual union (not legally recognized)	(In states where legally recog- nized)	(Fulfilling state require- ments for licensing and solem- nization

simple as getting into it, not knowing that certain state laws may require a formal divorce decree. The subsequent spouse in such cases may have entered in good faith what he or she thought was a legal marriage only to find that the courts consider it to have been an illicit cohabitation because of a former common-law marriage which was never formally ended.[17]

For reasons such as these, some legal experts and social scientists believe that the institution of common-law marriage should be abolished and that the only unions considered valid should be those in which the man and woman have secured a license from the state, had a wedding ceremony of some sort, and have obtained a properly signed marriage certificate. Other authorities disagree, pointing out that this would condemn many children "to bastardy" and increase injustice and suffering in the world rather than alleviating it. "This is particularly true among those social and economic classes who have not accepted middle class standards of marriage," says one professor of law. "Certainly American marriage law should tolerate this much cultural diversity."[18]

Common-law marriage is not easy to define, since various states and even various courts tend to interpret it differently. For one thing, whether or not a union has been a valid marriage according to common law is something that is determined *after* the union has been entered. In the words of H. Clark, a law professor: "As a doctrine [common-law marriage] has little or no effect at the outset of the parties' relationship. It comes into play after the relationship has existed for some time, for the purpose of vindicating the parties' marital expectations."[19] Harry Krause, another professor of law, refers to one threefold test for such a marriage. The union is regarded as a valid marriage "if the intending spouses have presently consented to be husband and wife, if the marriage has been consummated, and if the spouses have publicly held out each other as such." He explains that "the requirement of 'present consent' to marriage distinguishes the resulting relationship from an engagement to be married at a future time."[20]

Legalization and Marriage

As we saw earlier, whatever the proportion of persons in trial marriages or consensual unions (living together simply by mutual consent), there have been steady increases in the proportions of persons who eventually seek the legal route. Why? In a modern society, the idea of formalizing or legalizing something indicates, first, serious *commitment* and, second, *protection.* There is important *symbolic significance* in this as well, both for the persons themselves and for society.

This is not to say that serious commitment is absent apart from a contract—whether we're thinking in terms of an informal agreement to buy a car from a friend or in terms of a living-together arrangement as in the case of Natalie and Kurt. Nevertheless, legal formalization of any transaction is a meaningful social symbol of commitment. In the prior chapter, we referred to de

Rougemont's description of love as "an act to be decided upon" rather than "a state to be suffered or undergone." Apparently, such a concept of love has a high rating in the minds of the great majority of Americans; they still eventually prefer the formalization of marriage as a symbol of serious commitment to a personal relationship.

To be sure, the commitment on the part of some who seek such formalization may actually be taken less seriously by the persons involved than is true of some who do not seek formalization of their relationship. Nevertheless, preferences for this symbol of "meaning business," "total commitment," and resoluteness are still quite strong. The evident continued acceptance of the challenge "If you really love me, you'll marry me" shows that the notion of legal marriage as a test of love remains widespread.

Licensing and formal solemnization are related to both the expressive and instrumental dimensions of marriage. On the expressive side, legalization of marriage signifies commitment. On the instrumental side, legalization signifies protection.

Traditionally, when the woman brought a dowry or inheritance to the marriage, she needed guarantees that these resources would not be exploited. And she needed guarantees that she and any children would share in the husband's estate if marital dissolution occurred for any reason. This last element is also an important consideration today. For example, if the courts rule that a man and woman were living in "illicit cohabitation," the woman has no valid economic claims on the man—although, as we have seen, she has a better chance if it can be proved that their association was an actual common-law marriage. Today, of course, a well-trained woman may be able to support herself and any children apart from the economic inputs of a man; but the fact remains that legalization-as-protection is not something to be passed over lightly in any examination of what marriage is all about.

The longer a man and woman have lived together—legally or not—the greater the chances are that their economic resources have become intermixed. This is so whether or not the woman is employed, because the performance of domestic duties gives the traditional housewife the right to share in her husband's economic assets. An interesting sidelight: Given some indications of male dominance in nonmarital living-together arrangements, and given traditional attitudes toward housework, couples even in these situations may find they have drifted into the familiar pattern in which the female partner performs most of the housework, just as the wife has traditionally done in a legal union.[21]

If the wife (or female partner) works outside the home, there may be pooled checking and savings accounts. And regardless of the woman's employment or nonemployment, the couple are likely to share such "consumption items" as furniture, appliances, household goods, a car, and so on—items to which both have legitimate claims of ownership. Should they decide to stop living together, how are these dollars and goods to be divided between them fairly? A legal arrangement tends to protect both partners from injustice in what often turn out to be very complicated situations. In fact, even in nonlegal arrangements, the courts may be called upon to arbitrate. One municipal judge, who handles many cases where unmarried couples seek settlements of property rights, reports that a number of couples have come to court "fighting over who gets the waterbed."[22]

In summary, perhaps it will help to clarify what constitutes the state of marriage by looking again at the continuum in Table 5-B. There is on the one side, a state of nonmarriage which gradually fades into a *sociological* definition of marriage. However, to be legitimate in terms of a *legal* definition, the relationship must be socially sanctioned by a fulfilling of state requirements for licensing and solemnization. In between the stage in which a couple may be considered to be married in a sociological sense and the stage in which there is a marriage in the legal sense, there is an intermediate stage considered legal in some states, namely common-law marriage.

Another way to think of it is this: a trial *arrangement* becomes a trial *marriage* when there is an overt ongoing exchange of instrumental and expressive benefits. The key word here is *overt*; the relationship is publicly known. A trial marriage that continues over a period of time may then go on to become either a legal marriage or a common-law or consensual union (if the couple does not choose to go through legal channels). One characteristic of both trial arrangements and trial marriages seems to be a firm disallowance of parenthood. The introduction of children into such a trial situation is usually considered a cost acceptable to neither partner. In common-law marriages, however, any children born to the couple are considered legitimate if the particular state recognizes common-law unions.

The considerable significance of the trial association lies not so much in its probable increase, since most persons eventually seek legal ties. Rather, its significance lies in its consequences for making *rationality* regarding marriage more widespread. Whether they actually engage in a trial or not, growing numbers of persons may be motivated to avoid the folk ideology of romantic love, instead weighing carefully the actual and anticipated rewards and costs of marriage.

SINGLENESS

In 1970, Roberta Hornig wrote an article for the *Washington Evening Star* entitled "See Aunt Debbie . . . First-Grade Symbol of Swinging Single," which presented the suggestion that grade school children not only needed to see women in roles other than that of homemaker; they needed also to gain a strong image of the unmarried career woman. To aid in this, first-grade reading books could introduce attractive, active, happy, fulfilled "Aunt Debbie," who could show Dick and Jane through her example that alternative life-styles exist for women. Not all women are wives and mothers. Children could learn that single women can lead interesting, exciting lives and work in occupations that bring great enjoyment.[23]

Singleness in Historical Perspective

Children in early America heard an altogether different message than that suggested by Hornig's proposal for a positive presentation of singleness. A North Carolina physician wrote in 1731: "[Girls] marry generally very young, some at thirteen or fourteen, and she that continues unmarried until twenty, is reckoned a stale maid, which is a very indifferent character in that country." In Puritan society, women were called "ancient maids" if they had not married by the time they reached their twenty-fifth birthday.[24] There were no sparkling, vivacious, ambitious, industrious Aunt Debbies around then. The single state received no encouragement whatsoever. In fact, it was positively discouraged.

Both social and economic sanctions were used to push people into marriage. Older single women were ridiculed, often despised, treated as life's failures, and assigned to unpaid drudge-work in the homes of married brothers and sisters. It is no wonder that many became bitter, joyless, and dissatisfied with their lot in life; with the result that no doubt some fulfilled the stereotype of the neurotic spinster, the meddling busybody, the sour, prim, and proper "old maid" of the children's card game.

Bachelors were mocked and treated with harsh disapproval, too. Early American society found it difficult to tolerate unattached persons of either sex. Arthur Calhoun, a social historian, points out that bachelors virtually found themselves "in the class of suspected criminals." Rarely were single men permitted to live alone or even to decide *where* they should live; the courts decided that for them. Many of the colonies had a "bachelor tax" as a further incentive to enter the married state. In Connecticut, Hartford taxed unmarried men twenty shillings a week, and New Haven enacted a law requiring unmarried persons of either sex to live with "licensed" families. Single men and women not living with relatives or in service as apprentices "are forbidden to diet or lodge alone," said the law. The city officials declared that such a law fulfilled the intent of the biblical commandment to obey parents by providing substitute parents for bachelors and spinsters (who were evidently suspected of acting in a. wayward manner if they lacked the supervision and restraints of a family). The heads of the specially selected licensed families that took single persons under their care were ordered "to observe the course, carriage, and behavior of every such single person, whether he or she walk diligently in a constant lawful employment, attending both family duties and the public worship of God, and keeping good order day and night or otherwise."[25]

Bachelors were especially under continual surveillance in the New England colonies, being watched by the constable, the watchman, and the tithingman.

Whereas today a person might choose singlehood in order to be free, it was marriage that freed a man in Puritan society. Only upon taking a wife could he escape the restrictions mentioned above. Furthermore, many New England towns provided building lots when a man exchanged his bachelor existence for the role of husband. In a society that placed a high value on family life and which needed to grow in population, pressures and incentives toward marriage were in abundance.

The main incentives to encourage persons to marry were economic. The bachelor tax drained off part of the single man's income, and in addition he was without the benefits of a wife and children to care for household needs and help him with farm chores or in the shop. Benjamin Franklin's advice about marriage was that "a single man has not nearly the value he would have in that state of union. He is an incomplete animal. He resembles the odd half of a pair of scissors."[26]

Women, too, were constantly reminded that marriage was expected of them. Almost no other way of securing financial support was open to them. Even so, an early Maryland law was designed to make sure they got the message. A woman who had inherited land was required to marry within seven years. Otherwise, the land would be forfeited to the next of kin or else she would have to dispose of it. The reason for the law was clearly spelled out: "That it may be prevented that noe woman here vow chastity in the world." She was to realize that her land "is gonne unless she git a husband."[27] Despite certain laws and informal pressures, some women did choose to remain single. The Plymouth Church records of 1667 list the death of Governor Bradford's ninety-one-year-old sister-in-law, describing her as "a godly old maid never married." Other records indicate that Taunton, Massachusetts, was founded by "an ancient maid of forty-eight."[28]

The old song about the married man who wished he were single so that his pockets would jingle gets to the root of an attitude held by many bachelors—especially in the eighteenth-century South. This was true despite the costs involved (Maryland's part in the French and Indian War was financed by taxes on light wines, billiard tables, and bachelors, for example), because many men felt the responsibility of providing for a wife and children would be an even higher price to pay. In addition, there were men who felt that a free-swinging sex life with a variety of women was to be preferred over the restraints of settled domesticity with one spouse and attention-demanding children.[29]

Some men remained single not by choice but by circumstance. With the movement Westward, there arose a situation in which the supply of women did not match the supply of men. Miners, traders, trappers, loggers, and cowboys often remained single even though many of them might have preferred marriage. Yet both the nature of their work and the scarcity of available women placed obstacles in the way. Newspapers in the 1830s suggested that "the excess of spinsters in our large cities" could be alleviated by transporting them to the new settlements. Such women came to be spoken of in terms of some commodity to be shipped. An 1837 newspaper, for example, reported that "a wagon load of girls for the western market lately past through Northhampton, Mass."[30]

Singleness as a Life-Style Today

In 1973 a new magazine was launched. Its title? Simply one word—*Single*. That a special-interest magazine would come on the scene devoted solely to the concerns of unattached persons might have seemed strange in other periods of United States history. But at the present time, the single life-style is being chosen by growing numbers of persons—in some cases temporarily (but for a longer period as we saw in our earlier discussion of rises in age at marriage) and in other cases permanently. Increases in percentages of singles indicates that persons are becoming more cautious about when (and even *if*) they eventually will enter a legal union—another indication of trends toward rationality in choices about marriage. In terms of exchange theory, we may say that as more persons begin to calculate the utilities of marriage, the greater the likelihood that some of them will assess a pattern of ongoing singleness to be basically more rewarding than legal marriage.

At various times the single person may or may not share an apartment with someone of the same or opposite sex, live in a commune, or have a trial marriage. But the significant point is that the traditional notion in our society that persons *must* marry for maximum happiness and well-being is increasingly being questioned. The terms *spinster* and *bachelor* may not necessarily call forth the pity they once did.

Census data show that singleness among both males and females under thirty-five years of age increased between 1960 and 1974. (See Table 5-C.) At the same time, singleness decreased for persons over thirty-five years. Demographers point out that the increase in the percent single occurs in age groups where persons have traditionally entered marriage, adding that it is not yet clear

TABLE 5-C PERCENT SINGLE (NEVER MARRIED) BY AGE AND SEX: 1974 AND 1960

	Male			Female		
Age	1974	1960	Change	1974	1960	Change
Total, 14 years and over	29.0	25.0	4.0	22.5	19.0	3.5
Under 35 years	54.8	50.7	4.1	44.5	37.6	6.9
35 years and over	6.3	7.8	−1.5	5.2	7.2	−2.0

SOURCE: *Current Population Reports*, 1974, P-20, no. 271, p. 3.

TABLE 5-D PROPORTIONS OF SINGLE
(NEVER-MARRIED) PERSONS OUT OF TOTAL
EIGHTEEN TO TWENTY-FOUR-YEAR-OLD
POPULATION

	Females		Males	
Year	White	Black	White	Black
1960	40%	46%	64%	68%
1974	49%	58%	66%	75%

SOURCE: *Current Population Reports*, 1975, P-23, no. 51, p. 16.

whether this means younger persons are simply waiting longer to marry or whether there is a trend toward lifelong singleness.[31]

Table 5-D shows how singleness increased among young black and white females and males during the period between 1960 and 1974. Trends toward refraining from marriage are especially significant among women, no doubt because of the pervasiveness of feminism and changes in women's roles in recent years. Full-time homemaking is no longer considered the only vocation open to women. Enough examples of successful single women in business, education, government, the professions, and the arts serve to invalidate old notions about a woman's being a failure if she doesn't marry. Many voices in the women's liberation movement have been raised to assure women that singleness is a worthy alternative to marriage, pointing out that the single life-style can in many cases expand a woman's opportunities for self-fulfillment and development in a way that would be impossible were she to assume the traditional wife role.[32] Apparently, women are heeding such advice and are much less likely to rush into marriage than was the case in the immediate past. Government statistics show that in 1974 nearly one-quarter (23.4 percent) of women aged twenty-four years were still single. This figure may be compared to 1960 when slightly less than 16 percent of women were unmarried at age twenty-four.[33]

If there are continued trends toward increasing singleness and later age at marriage among women under thirty-five, we may expect such trends to expand most rapidly among women who have access to rewarding socioeconomic alternatives to traditional marriage. Highly educated women are those with most to gain from greater female autonomy and individualism since they are best prepared to enter occupations that offer the greatest benefits in terms of prestige and income.

Sociological studies in recent years have shown that higher levels of intelligence, education, and occupation are associated with singleness among women.[34] In the past, this association has sometimes been explained by the suggestion that women of high education and achievement are "marital rejects" or "pathetic misfits," persons who are "unfeminine" and "undesirable" to males and who therefore remain unchosen. However, the explanation may very well lie in the opposite direction. The active choosing may be on the part of the *women.* One sociologist, after a study of census data which showed a direct relation between female economic attainment and unmarried status, concluded that high-achieving women may consider marriage confining and therefore reject the institution, which is an altogether different matter than saying such women are unwanted by potential husbands.[35]

Among whites, high education makes much less difference in the chances for male singleness. (See Table 5-E.) Highly educated men have not faced the dilemma faced by highly educated women. For well-educated women, the situation has generally been one of *either/or*—either major attention to occupation and a life of singleness on the one hand, or marriage on the other (with occupational interests secondary or put aside). But for highly educated men, it has been a matter of *both/and.* No one would think of telling a man upon marriage that he should now seriously consider giving up his career. If anything, marriage may be considered as an aid to his career aspirations, since having a wife in the traditional sense is expected to relieve him of concerns about everyday household matters (laundry, meals, good order), increase his opportunities for entertaining important guests and clients, and in general to provide him with the emotional support and encouragement that can be so helpful in advancing his career. This is partly what sociologist Jessie Bernard has in mind in speaking of the contrast between the "his" marriage (marriage from the male's perspective) and the "her" marriage (marriage as traditionally defined for females).[36]

It will be noticed in Table 5-E that there are no sex differences between the percentages of singleness among blacks. Eleven percent of thirty-five-to-forty-four-year-old black males and black females with five years of college or more are single. Also of interest is the fact that singleness is much less common among highly trained black women (11 percent) than is the case among highly trained white women (20 percent).

For reasons noted earlier, blacks tend to be more responsive to individualistic rights for women than are whites. Thus, it may be that the educated black

TABLE 5-E PERCENTAGE OF SINGLE (NEVER-MARRIED) PERSONS IN 1970 AGED THIRTY-FIVE TO FORTY-FOUR YEARS WITH FIVE OR MORE YEARS OF COLLEGE

Race	Females	Males
White	20%	8%
Black	11%	11%

SOURCE: U.S. Bureau of the Census, *1970 Census of Population*, PC (2) 4C, 1972, pp. 107–116.

woman has faced less of a dilemma than her white counterpart. It has been less "either/or" and more "both/and." Apparently such black women have been able to negotiate marriage arrangements that they consider fair and just with black men who are probably willing to concede more autonomy than are white men. It thus becomes more "profitable" for highly trained black women to marry than is true of highly trained white women who may perceive greater costs to pay in marriage. Therefore, fewer of these black women remain single.

Incidentally, for both sexes of both races, it is the *least* educated (less than five years of any kind of schooling) who are least likely ever to marry.[37] Demographers Hugh Carter and Paul Glick indicate that such persons may be "functionally illiterate" and "uneducable" and thus constitute a "hard core of unmarriageable" persons.[38] In short, such persons simply possess few if any assets that would make other persons desire to enter into marriage bargains with them.

Persons who remain single not because they are "unmarriageable" but because they have voluntarily chosen this life-style do so because they perceive the costs of traditional marriage to be greater than its rewards. This is particularly true in the case of women because of the greater autonomy they can have apart from the wife-mother role. The single woman can devote as much time as she wishes to her occupation, feel free to change jobs and move across the country or even across the world, and spend her income as she pleases, without having to take into account the wishes and needs of a husband and children.

This feeling of independence makes singleness attractive to some men, too. "I like the freedom of being able to do whatever I want to whenever I please," says one man commenting on the advantages of the single status. Others have emphasized their enjoyment of freedom of movement (including changing jobs, taking trips, working as many hours as they please) and the freedom of making their own financial decisions.[39]

To be sure, there are costs as well as rewards attached to the single state, just as there are both costs and rewards in marriage. The greatest costs usually mentioned by single persons are loneliness and the lack of a regularized sex life. However, when these costs are compared to the cost of giving up autonomy, they are viewed by many unmarried persons as not too high a price to pay. For those women and men who have rationally calculated in this manner, the rewards of independence are considered to more than compensate, so that singleness appears more profitable than marriage.

SINGLE PARENTHOOD

The "First Baby of the Year" contest in Iowa City had always been a happy event. As in many other American cities and towns, a local newspaper sponsored the project and the business community joined in with enthusiasm, offering a variety of prizes to the new year's first arrival. But 1974's first baby was different.

His mother wasn't married. The newspaper refused to award the prizes, giving them to the second child born instead. Baby number two had married parents.[40]

That same year, an elementary school teacher wrote to the Washington State Human Rights Commission for advice on a course of action she was considering. Divorced and the mother of a young son, she wanted to have another child but said she had not met anyone with whom she would be compatible in marriage. "I don't think I should marry for the sole purpose of reproduction," she wrote. Her plan? She wanted to remain unwed but to conceive a child by artificial insemination. Her question for the Commission centered around whether or not she could be fired from her job if she gave birth out of wedlock.[41]

And again in that same year, a national women's magazine featured a story of an unwed mother who told of why she kept her child rather than having an abortion or giving him up for adoption. She was not a young teenager, poorly educated, or from a deprived background. Rather she had a master's degree and was working on a doctorate at the time the conception occurred. The baby's father was a Ph.D. She had chosen the life-style of single parenthood as a better alternative than entering an unsatisfactory marriage.[42]

Persons seem to fall into four categories when it comes to the matter of children. Traditionally, men and women have considered children as a major reward of marriage and thus have contemplated marriage with the "joys of parenthood" in mind. But in contrast to such couples, there are others who feel that the costs of children outnumber the rewards and thus remain voluntarily childless after marriage. A third category consists of single persons who have no desire for either marriage or children since they perceive the benefits of both to be outweighed by the disadvantages and costs. However, there is a fourth group which we want to consider at this point—single persons who want children but who don't want marriage.

In recent years, many states have begun permitting unmarried persons to adopt children. This practice is upsetting to some unwed mothers who years ago were persuaded to give up their children for adoption because social workers advised them that children need to grow up in two-parent homes.[43] However, data from available studies do not seem to provide support for the old fears about a child's being emotionally harmed by growing up in a one-parent situation.[44] Unmarried persons of both sexes have proven to be excellent parents of adopted children. A Roman Catholic priest, for example, has adopted four over the years, bringing home each child during early infancy. A physician adopted two boys after she was well established in her practice and enough years had gone by to make her feel that marriage was unlikely. A bachelor in his thirties adopted a tiny boy who had been abandoned. A writer, whose engagement was broken when her fiance found she couldn't have children, later adopted children as a single woman.

The other way to become an unmarried parent is, of course, through the normal processes of conception and birth. Some single women in recent years,

A woman may choose the life-style of single parenthood by adoption or by continuing an out-of-marriage pregnancy and rearing the child herself.

including some active in the feminist movement, have chosen to continue out-of-marriage pregnancies, giving birth and rearing their children themselves rather than giving them up for adoption or having abortions. Historically, there have always been unmarried women who bore children. When these born-out-of-wedlock children were adopted by married couples, they did not have to grow up bearing the stigma "illegitimate." But if their mothers kept them, they were labeled "illegitimate" or "bastards." The baby was of course the same person in either case at the time of birth, but it was the situation into which he or she would be placed that would determine "legitimacy." This labeling would in turn have a profound effect on the child's entire life. But why does such categorization of children take place? What does it mean?

PRINCIPLE OF LEGITIMACY

According to the anthropologist Bronislaw Malinowski, there is a universal rule that "no child should be brought into the world without a man—and one man at that—assuming the role of sociological father, that is, guardian and protector, the male link between the child and the rest of the community." Malinowski calls this rule "the principle of legitimacy." He claims that throughout cultural variations, "there runs the rule that the father is indispensable for the full sociological status of the child as well as of its mother, that the group consisting of a woman and her offspring is sociologically incomplete and illegitimate. The father, in other words, is necessary for the full legal status of the family."[45]

The principle of legitimacy stems from a functionalist view of marriage and parenthood. You'll recall that in the structure-functionalist framework the family is seen as an organism with interdependent parts, each having a particular function to perform, as in the human body. Under the principle of legitimacy, the focus is on the function of the economic provider, a role assigned to the father. Thus a child is said to require a social father in order that the child can receive the status and material benefits that are rightfully his. Sociologists Lewis Coser and Rose Laub Coser report that in the French and Russian revolutions, there was an attempt to declare all children as legitimate, whether they were born in or out of wedlock. Consequently, each child born to a particular man had some legal claim on the property, name, and social standing of that man. They were his children whether born to his legal wife (if he had one) or to any other woman he had impregnated.[46]

Coser and Coser go on to point out, however, that after several years passed and both revolutionary governments had become routinized, the passions of the revolution subsided and both societies reverted to the "principle of legitimacy." The authors claim that as men began to accumulate status and wealth, they began (even in Russia) to resent having to disperse these benefits among all children they may have fathered. They wished to restrict benefits solely to their "legal" children. Consequently, both regimes reinstituted laws making some children legitimate and others not.

Coser and Coser claim that the experience of France and Russia verifies the universality of the principle of legitimacy. They also predict that China and Cuba, which during their revolutions took similar steps to abolish illegitimacy, will follow the example of Russia and France in reverting back to former patterns. However, what these authors overlook is yet another example of a revolutionary socialist experiment that also abolished illegitimacy—the kibbutz.

Legitimacy and the Kibbutzim

No notion exists in the kibbutz that some children are bastards while others are not. Sociologist Melford Spiro reports that where paternity is unknown, "there is no prejudice or ill-will felt toward either the mother or the child. Both are treated precisely as are other mothers and children."[47]

Yet there is a problem in that the kibbutzim exist within the larger social structure of the modern state of Israel, and Israeli law affirms that bastards have no civil rights. Therefore, couples in the kibbutz generally become legally married to ensure such rights. This has been more true of the sabras (second generation) than of the original settlers. The point to note is that although inside the kibbutz the principle of legitimacy is meaningless, it does have meaning in the milieu immediately outside. The result of this situation is that constraints are imposed on the kibbutz that otherwise would not exist.

But why is illegitimacy a meaningless notion within the kibbutz? Chiefly because no married man accumulates any wealth or capital that he calls his own, nor any status advantages that are uniquely his. Since all resources are owned in common, each child of the kibbutz shares equally in these resources. Both in postrevolutionary France and in Russia, whatever collective ownership there once was has given way to traditional varieties of status transmission and ownership. Accumulation and control of wealth by individual married couples creates situations in which it is in the interest of families to restrict distribution of their limited assets. One way to do this is to exclude persons not born of the same father and mother, that is, children born apart from the marriage union.

Trends Relating to the Legitimacy Issue

So far, no modern industrial society—whether capitalist, socialist, or communist—has been able to escape rewarding individual workers on the basis of their achievements. The result of this is that some workers (and in turn, their families) will receive more benefits than others and will want to keep these benefits for themselves, restricting them as much as possible. Thus, in an industrial society (in contrast to the truly collective kibbutz), it is quite likely that, in spite of widespread abortion, many children could be born who face the threat of exclusion from any meaningful pipeline to the status and economic rewards of society.

In premodern societies, it may have made sense to talk about the necessity of a social father to serve as such a pipeline. But in modern times, such a requirement is not essential and inevitable for at least two reasons. One has to do with legal redefinitions of legitimacy, and the other relates to the changing roles and status of women.

Legal redefinitions of legitimacy   It is possible for societies simply to abolish the legal distinction between legitimate and nonlegitimate. Sweden, for instance, has done precisely that.[48] A child born out of wedlock has full inheritance rights from its father as well as its mother. Thus, if a man sires two children in marriage and one outside the marriage, all three would share equally in their claims on his support, his status, and his estate. This assumes, of course, that paternity can be proven and that the father has any status and assets to transmit to the child. If either or both of these conditions cannot be met, the Swedish state is committed to provide for the child. According to government policy in Sweden, every child without a father is granted the same kinds of social and economic benefits enjoyed by other children. In that sense, the situation there is analogous to that of the kibbutz.

Recent Supreme Court decisions indicate that the United States is moving in precisely the same direction as Sweden with regard to eventual abolishment of the legal distinctions between legitimate and nonlegitimate, especially in matters of support and inheritance.[49] However, there is no indication as yet that the United States is prepared to undertake the kinds of programs necessary to equalize opportunities for children who have no male pipeline to the status system.

Legitimacy and changing female roles   The question arises: Why not a female pipeline to the status system? Why couldn't a woman provide for a child the resources that have traditionally come from a man? Increasingly, women are becoming better educated and are gaining access to jobs with levels of income and prestige formerly restricted to white men. Many such women are highly individualistic and extremely achievement-oriented. Among those who have never married, there may be some who choose to legally adopt a child. There may be others who conceive and bear a child out of wedlock and who choose to rear the child alone. Given their high level of resources, there is no reason to suspect that they could not be as adequate a pipeline for conveying society's benefits to a child as any man could be. They can provide adequate objective benefits, and they can socialize the child into achievement-type behaviors.

Thus, we see a second reason why a social father may not be requisite in modern society. From the studies of Blau and Duncan, we already know that children who have lost their fathers through death or divorce achieve in later life as well as children from husband-wife households *from the same social class.*[50] Apparently it is not the presence or absence of the father per se that affects the child's later attainments; rather, it is the benefits that the father provided while he was alive and in his estate, or else that he presently provides through child support. It therefore seems reasonable that a well-trained woman who opts for a life-style in which she raises a child alone can do at least as well as women who have been thrust into a status they did not choose nor necessarily want, namely that of provider and solo parent.

Principle of Status Adequacy

For the kinds of reasons just discussed, Malinowski's functionalist principle of legitimacy becomes dubious indeed. It needs to be changed and restated to fit the complexities of modern society. Perhaps instead of a "principle of legitimacy," we could think in terms of a *principle of status adequacy.* Very simply, a principle of status adequacy means that every child requires some sociological parent (father and/or mother) or the equivalent in a communal, kin, or political arrangement that can provide the child with adequate socialization and access to the opportunity system.

For some time, demographers have been collecting figures on the incidence of illegitimate births. If, on the birth registration form, the mother fails to name someone as the legal father of the newborn, the child is classed as illegitimate. Such data are available from nearly forty states and the District of Columbia.[51] However, such statistics may be unreliable for two reasons, although no one is sure. First, in recent years, hospitals and county clerks have been much more careful than ever before in recording all births. Thus births that are illegitimate may be recorded today as such but may have been completely missed years ago. Second, it is quite likely that some women succeed in reporting their children as legitimate when in fact they are not. Keeping these weaknesses in mind, and being aware that court decisions may soon render the legitimacy status obsolete, it may be useful nevertheless to look at some of the statistics.

Between 1955 and 1968, the illegitimacy rate (number of illegitimate births per 1,000 unmarried women) increased 53 percent for whites but decreased 8 percent among blacks.[52] Nonetheless, the actual white illegitimacy rate in 1968 was 13; for blacks it was 87. This means that 13 illegitimate births occurred per every 1,000 unmarried white women in that year, and 87 illegitimate births occurred per every 1,000 unmarried black women. Five years later, there were 12 illegitimate births per 1,000 unmarried white women and 90 per 1,000 unmarried black women. Or to look at it *another* way: Out of every 1,000 *live births* in 1973, 130 were illegitimate. Among whites, the ratio was 64 illegitimate births per 1,000 live births; among blacks, the ratio was 458. The figures were highest among women still in their teens. Among those fifteen to nineteen years of age, nearly 2 births out of 10 were classed as illegitimate among whites, and nearly 7 out of 10 were so categorized among blacks.[53] Even more significant, as Cutright points out, "Some 60 percent of white and 80 percent of nonwhite illegitimate births are to women below the near-poor poverty line."[54]

We saw in earlier chapters that women of lower social status tend to be more sexually active, to be more naive with regard to contraceptive use, and to conceive more frequently prior to marriage. Here we find that they are also more likely to bear children out of wedlock. And not only do mothers of illegitimate children tend to come from working and lower-class backgrounds, they also tend to be very young.[55]

To disadvantaged young women with few alternative rewards, it may appear as if children—even illegitimate ones—provide one of their few sources of major life gratifications. Hence there may be little motivation to resist unmarried motherhood, perhaps even to the extent of experiencing several illegitimate births. And that is precisely where the principle of status adequacy has relevance. Households headed by poor women tend to be large. Consequently, the children are exceedingly disadvantaged and simply do not receive the kinds of benefits they need to adequately compete in modern society. It is a life-style very different from the one described above in which the unmarried, well-educated woman *chooses* both singleness and a child. Women with high levels of resources choose such a life-style from a variety of alternatives, are well-equipped to provide the child with substantial benefits, and are likely to limit the number of children they will rear to only one or two. In contrast, the unmarried woman who lacks educational and economic resources may find that single motherhood is something thrust on her rather than freely chosen. She becomes an unwed mother because few other viable options appear open to her. For her, the rewards of being a solo parent are few and costs high. She is poorly equipped to provide for her child and is quite likely to have more than one illegitimate offspring. In terms of the principle of status adequacy, her child requires an *outside* source to serve as the pipeline to the economic and opportunity system.

In sum, there seem to be trends in the direction of increased single parenthood, partly due to liberalized adoption procedures which permit unmarried persons to adopt children and partly due to a desire on the part of many unmarried mothers to retain their children rather than electing abortion or giving their children up for adoption.

Where parenthood is voluntarily chosen by a single person equipped to provide the child with necessary resources, the experience can be beneficial to both parent and child. But where parenthood is forced upon a young unmarried woman poorly equipped to handle the situation, the situation may be paradoxically entrapping (cutting her and her child off from educational and economic opportunities, for example) at the same time that it may seem somewhat rewarding (providing a certain sense of gratification in the midst of an impoverished life). The basic issue in such a case is not so much a matter of "illegitimacy" as it is of "status *inadequacy.*"

KINSHIP AND COMMUNES

A wall plaque carries this message:

> We need to have people
>   who mean something to us;
> People to whom
>   we can turn,
> Knowing that being with them is
>   coming home.
> —R. Cooke

Traditionally, those people "who mean something," to whom one can turn in time of need, and who provide a sense of "coming home" have been the kin, those persons to whom one has become related either through blood or through marriage. At the same time, there may be other persons who serve as a kind of "substitute kin" even though they are unrelated to one another. In recent years, there has been much talk about building community. There have been experiments with communal living as well as efforts to create a kind of chosen family of friends with whom joys, sorrows, problems, and so on can be shared even though there are separate dwelling units, an arrangement one sociologist calls an "intimate family network."

In this section, we want to give attention to some of these "functional equivalents" of the extended family. But first we need to look at the actual extended family itself. Then we can better understand the purposes it has traditionally fulfilled and can make comparisons with communal and other arrangements which attempt to serve as substitute kin networks.

Who Are the Extended Kin?

Anthropologists and sociologists use the term *consanguinity* (derived from the Latin word for blood and blood relations) to refer to those persons whose relationship is based upon their common descent from a particular ancestor— for example, sisters and brothers, parents, cousins, aunts and uncles, grandparents. The word *affinity* is used to describe a relationship based on marital ties. "Affines" (from the Latin *adfinis,* meaning "one who is connected by marriage") are such persons as stepparents, stepbrothers and stepsisters, in-laws, and spouses of aunts and uncles. Both affines and blood relations are usually included under the term "extended kin." Both groups would be invited to an old-fashioned family reunion.

Another way to think of relatives is in terms of degree of closeness. One sociologist, for example, speaks of "the kin of orientation" (those from the same family of origin, that is, one's parents and brothers and sisters) in contrast to "secondary kin" (aunts, uncles, cousins, grandparents, and so on).[56] Another sociologist divides kin into the categories of "noneffective kin" and "effective kin."[57] Noneffective kin are persons genealogically related to an individual but with whom social relationships are not maintained.

Effective kin may be subdivided into two more categories, according to sociologist Ralph Piddington. There are the *priority kin* (members of one's nuclear family and those kinsfolk most closely related to it, particularly the parents of each spouse, where there is a certain degree "of recognized moral obligation to enter into appropriate social relationships"). And there are the *chosen kin* (more remote kin with whom one is not duty-bound to enter social relationships but with whom such relationships are entered just the same out of free choice). Most of us can think of relatives in our own lives who fit into these various categories.

Earlier in this book we saw the important part played by the kin in various times and cultures, particularly in such matters as mate selection, inheritance rights, and economic sanctions. In modern industrial societies of the Western world, however, the kin network does not have power to influence persons to the extent that was once the case (and which remains the case in some cultures). The reason is that the kin no longer control economic resources; therefore they lack the authority that would accompany such control. Industrialization makes it possible for persons to achieve on their own. They are no longer dependent on kinship connections for lands, houses, farms, and businesses; and they are no longer tied to where relatives are—either geographically or occupationally.

Aware of such changes, many persons have concluded that something worthwhile and beneficial has disappeared from modern life. They speak of the isolation of the nuclear family, the depersonalization of urban and suburban living, the evaporation of a sense of belonging, sharing, and community in contemporary society. Such reasons are often cited as a rationale for communal living, for example.

But is it really true that the modern nuclear family is isolated from the wider kin network? Has urbanization weakened kinship ties, or do such ties persist despite residential and social mobility? Sociologists have given a great deal of study to these questions and have been forced to do some rethinking over the years.

Isolation of the Kin—Fact or Fiction?

During the 1930s and 1940s, a great deal was written about what came to be known as "classical urban theory," one aspect of which concerned the kin. Certain influential sociologists suggested that people in urban society are characterized more by "secondary" (impersonal) contacts than by "primary" (more intimate) relationships with family and close friends as in rural societies. Health needs, help in trouble, education, recreation—these were things no longer provided by the kin but rather by other institutions and agencies set up for such purposes as part of urbanization. At marriage, it was assumed that couples broke away to form families which served as independent units of social life entirely separated from the extended kin.[58]

However, in the 1950s sociologists began taking another look at the widely held view that urban dwellers lived isolated lives and had few primary relationships. Studies of kinship and friendship patterns among city residents showed that such persons were *not* cut off from intimate, meaningful social contacts in general, nor were they cut off from the kin in particular. What was discovered was simply that urban dwellers have more secondary, impersonal, or segmental contacts than rural persons do. But these secondary relationships are not replacements for primary relationships; they exist right alongside them.[59]

The question of *why* kinship ties persist in modern society is discussed by sociologist Marvin Sussman, who bases his explanation on exchange theory.[60] Persons perceive that they receive valued rewards from kinfolk, and the kinfolk likewise perceive that they, too, receive as well as give valued rewards. Thus reciprocity goes on, with closest ties being maintained with those relatives who are viewed as having the greatest rewards to offer. These rewards may be tangible (for instance, gifts of money or material goods) or intangible (simple enjoyment of one another's company, grandparents' affection and attention to small children, and the like). Sometimes the rewards are in the form of mutual aid and service, such as baby-sitting or looking after the house while the nuclear family is on vacation. Just keeping in touch is in itself perceived as rewarding, whether such communication and contact is maintained through visits, letters, or phone calls. The notion of reciprocity in kin relationships also includes some sense of duty and moral obligation—particularly with regard to one's aging parents.

Intimate Network as a Kin Substitute

An anonymous writer in *Ms.* magazine told of how sentimentality over "family solidarity" repeatedly drove her to plan elaborate holiday get-togethers with relatives only to be disappointed again and again. "Generally, the family for which I have sweated so generously ruins my evening," she wrote, adding that this didn't happen when she invited her friends. "My friends, I choose myself. They were not a gift from God." This woman eventually solved her problem by a formula of inviting "eight friends per biological family member."[61]

Some persons find kin relationships more costly than rewarding and seek other relationships to serve as substitutes. There are also persons who look for substitutes because they have no "effective kin" with whom significant contacts can be maintained on a regular basis. Relatives may live at great geographical distances, or they may no longer be living at all.

One behavioral scientist, Frederick Stoller, has introduced in family workshops an idea he calls the "intimate family network." Such a plan could serve to alleviate any impoverishment some modern families may feel by being denied the richly varied experiences and emotional support traditionally associated with kin relationships. According to Stoller, "an intimate network of families could be described as a circle of three or four families who meet together regularly and frequently, share in reciprocal fashion any of their intimate secrets, offer one another a variety of services, and do not hesitate to influence one another in terms of values and attitudes."[62]

Stoller suggests that the number of families should be more than two (to provide richness, varied role models for children, and more problem-solving resources) but usually not more than four, since too large a group would be hard to manage and might also cut down intimacy. Regular and frequent get-togethers would be important in order for the families to come to know one another deeply and develop the capacity to be honest and open with each other even in painful situations.

Reciprocal sharing would mean opening up to one another about how each family lives, its concerns, problems, and so on. Stoller is aware of the value the American family system places on privacy but points out that human life is enriched if *both* privacy and connectedness are experienced. The intimate network idea would not force a surrender of the right to privacy but rather would provide an opportunity for a "voluntary movement back and forth between open sharing and self-contained areas of living."

The intimate network of families could also provide an exchange of services in the manner that the extended kin has traditionally done—not only through aid in times of crisis, but also in exchanges of advice, helping one another in special projects (such as painting a house), or providing such benefits as child care so that a husband and wife are free to take a trip together. Stoller also emphasizes the influence intimate-network families could have on one another's values and attitudes, helping one another to grow and develop in new directions.

Although the intimate-family-network concept emphasizes relationships between and among families, there is no reason why such networks could not be formed among any combination of unrelated individuals—single persons, widowed persons, divorced persons, couples with or without children, and so on. Many such informal networks already exist, particularly in urban areas where many persons live at great distances from kinfolk. A close network of friends (some of whom may be work colleagues) forms and meets together for dinners, picnics, trips, holiday celebrations, and so on. Thanksgiving, for example, may become not so much a matter of going "over the river and through the woods to Grandmother's house" as it is a situation of going across the streets and through the halls to someone's apartment opened up to friends.

Commune as a Kin Substitute

Communes are intentional communities. Like intimate networks, they bring together biologically unrelated persons in order to build a kind of large *chosen* family. The purpose of this chosen family is to fulfill many of the functions traditionally fulfilled by the extended kin. Communes differ from intimate networks in several ways, most notable of which are the living arrangements (persons in communes maintain a common dwelling place) and economic sharing. The word *commune* itself is a wide umbrella, covering several different types of living patterns and philosophies. Yet, communes have much in common in their endeavors to serve as the functional equivalent of the kin. Let's examine some ways they do this.

Affection Traditionally, the extended kin have provided a main source of primary relationships. A person could derive a sense of belonging by saying, "I'm a member of such-and-such family clan." A similar sense of togetherness is experienced by those in communal arrangements. They use family terminology, such as brotherhood and sisterhood, to express their deep feelings for one another and their commitment to the life they share. Common-unity or *community* based not on genealogy but on ideology (shared goals and values) holds them together in an affectionate bond.

Interdependence   The sense of togetherness experienced promotes among group members the feeling that they need one another and need the group as a whole. Again, there is a resemblance to the "we can count on each other" feelings characterizing the extended kin. Commune members expect to give and receive mutual aid. Though the vows may be unspoken, there is a commitment to care for one another "for richer, for poorer, in sickness, and in health."

Rituals   Group solidarity is reinforced by bringing group members together for regular participation in activities, ceremonies, and recurring events that symbolize commitment to the group as a whole. It might be so simple a matter as joining hands around a common table to recite a prayer or sing a song before eating. Or there might be a celebration in honor of a member's birthday or a couple's engagement or regular community songfests, holiday celebrations, and the like. Family rituals and traditions, whether they involve actual extended kin or the adopted chosen kin of a commune, can enhance what various writers call a sense of "communion . . . the mingling of self with the group," "we-feelings," and "we-consciousness."[63]

Migration   An additional way in which communal arrangements function like that of the kin relates to the bringing of new members into the commune. Sociologist Bert Adams points out the part played by the extended kin in residential migration. One unit of the kin (whether a nuclear family or an individual) may move to a new location and establish "an economic and residential 'foothold' in a community, to be followed there later by other kin."[64] Similarly, individuals or families that join a commune may then invite other persons of their acquaintance from "back home" (such as single persons, lonely or troubled persons, individuals who have been widowed or divorced, and so on), suggesting that joining the commune might provide a solution to their problems and sense of aloneness. This may be compared to the Appalachian family which, after settling in Chicago, writes to relatives with the suggestion that they, too, should migrate.

Influence and control   Communal relationships also may resemble traditional kinship arrangements in the control they exercise over the lives of group members. Jay and Heather Ogilvy, an academic couple who live in an urban commune, point out one aspect of this in their statement: "If a single person feels ill at ease bringing a prospective mate home to meet the parents, imagine the possibilities for tension bringing a prospective mate home to meet the commune."[65] Their comment fits in with our discussion on mate selection where we saw that the degree of family control is associated with the degree of economic dependence.

Economic Side of Commune Life

Economic arrangements vary greatly in communal living. In some cases, two or three families might own a house jointly and share household tasks and meals but might otherwise be economically independent of one another. In another case, a large number of persons might give up all personal ownership and pool resources so that all possessions are held in common. This is true of certain urban communes where earnings from outside jobs are handed over to a committee in charge of finances, just as it is true of various rural communes which try to earn a living off the land as each member pitches in and works, or in arrangements in which commune members run their own industries—such as the Bruderhof, with colonies in New York, Pennsylvania, and Connecticut, supporting themselves through the manufacture of wooden toys, sold under the name "Community Playthings."

Bruderhof Notions of private property and individualism have no place in those communal arrangements that are built around group ownership and group control. Individuals and families surrender all they have to the commune. Among the Bruderhof, for example, individuals have no money of their own and correspondingly no autonomy or power. They accept the community's decisions as to what work they shall do and must ask even for the simplest necessities of life, such as shampoo and toothpaste. In taking vows to become members of the brotherhood, they pledged to put themselves completely at the disposal of the community, including their entire property—everything they possessed at the time they joined the group and all that they might later inherit or earn.[66]

Kibbutzim The Israeli kibbutz, primarily agricultural but with some small industries added in recent years, is similar to the Bruderhof in its economic policy. Psychologist Bruno Bettelheim, who has studied the kibbutz extensively, points out that "all property belongs to the community except for some small personal belongings, and even the latter is a recent development."[67] At one time, a person did not even own his own clothes but took them from a common supply—a practice that still applies to children. Also it was decided only in recent years that each member would receive a small allowance of about thirty dollars a year to spend as he pleased. Since everything is provided by the kibbutz, it is the kibbutz (through its general assembly) that decides exactly what should be provided. Bettelheim cites such examples as decisions about whether or not each member should be given a radio, or decisions regarding the amount of money that can be taken from community funds for trips to cultural events in a nearby city. Persons who decide to sever connections with the kibbutz are not entitled to receive back any of the private possessions which they turned over to the community. Likewise, they are not given any share of the communal property to take with them.

Types of Communes

Although there are no hard and fast rules when it comes to classifying communes, it is helpful to make some basic distinctions. Rosabeth Moss Kanter, a sociologist who has written a number of books and articles based on her studies of communes, says that a simple way to describe communes is in terms of three basic themes: the land, the spirit, and the home.[68] Rural communes emphasize the land, getting back to nature; religious communes emphasize spiritual values and goals; and urban communes seem to place major stress on the shared home. Sometimes communes may be many things all at once—"a domestic unit (a large household), a production unit (a farm and/or a series of businesses), a political order (a village or town), and a religious order."[69]

Urban communes and rural communes   Sociologist Bennett Berger and his colleagues suggest that a basic distinction between communes has to do with whether they are located in the city or in the country. They point out that urban communes are easier to start ("all it takes is a rented house and a group of willing people") but that they are harder to sustain and have a more fluid membership. Rural communes, on the other hand, seem to call forth a more thorough commitment from their members; and this commitment is no doubt related to the profound consequences involved in choosing to work and live in the collective life of a communal farm. In a sense, one takes on a new identity by being isolated from one's former environment, having one's daily life structured in radically different ways than before, and engaging in unfamiliar tasks which present the constant challenge of developing new skills.[70] In urban communes, persons usually continue with their occupations in the "outside world," but come together for meals, sharing household tasks and child care, recreation, meetings and so on in their common dwelling, which is often enhanced with the "extras" made possible by their collective incomes (appliances, well-equipped music rooms, saunas, gym equipment, and the like).[71]

Creedal and noncreedal communes   Berger and his associates point out that communes may be categorized by ideology as well as by geographical location. In a *creedal* commune, whether built around religious doctrines, philosophical teachings, or utopian visions, there are clearly spelled-out beliefs and rules of conduct. These may be centered in a strong leader (such as a guru) and his closest disciples or they might be written out in formal statements, pamphlets, and books. Creedal communes usually have firmer authority structures and may in some cases be extremely authoritarian. Often they display a missionary zeal and thus are quite open toward the idea of taking outsiders "into the fold."

Members of urban communes usually work in the outside world, but share meals, recreation, and tasks in a common household.

Noncreedal communes, in contrast, tend to have a somewhat more restricted membership policy. Rather than actively seeking recruits for a cause, they tend to rely on friendship networks as sources for molding together a family of persons who know one another extremely well. As their name implies, noncreedal communes do not have the formal, clearly spelled-out ideologies and collective beliefs that characterize creedal communes, nor are they as rigid in regard to authority structures, rules and related concerns. At the same time, "there does tend to be a taken-for-granted set of beliefs which is assumed to be widely known and shared by the members, even though constitutional precepts or other written documents are absent."[72]

Monistic and pluralistic communes   Jay and Heather Ogilvy suggest another way of categorizing communes. *Monistic* communes (not necessarily religious and thus not to be confused with the word *monastic*) are those which emphasize a central core of shared values. The Greek term *monos* means "alone, single, one." Such communes stress single-mindedness. *Pluralistic* communes, on the other hand, emphasize diversity and individualism.

At first glance, the distinction between these types of communes might seem to correspond to Berger's creedal and noncreedal categories; yet, it is somewhat less clear-cut. For one thing, the Ogilvy classification doesn't only apply to differences *between* communes but also to differences *within*. These authors feel that both monists and pluralists may be found in many communes, often standing out distinctly as two separate camps with vastly different outlooks. This can lead to conflict of a sort that is not easily solved by a "live and let live" philosophy of tolerating one another's differences. The Ogilvys write: "The pluralists see a rich communal life in terms of all 'doing their own thing.' Their tolerance and pluralism may even extend to the point of telling the monists that it's fine for monists to do their monistic thing. But of course that answer cannot satisfy the monistic demand for having not just the monists but all the rest locating themselves around the common core."[73]

Problem of Individualism Versus Group Interests

The contrast in the monistic and pluralistic viewpoints illustrates a recurrent problem in the history of communes—the issue of community versus personal freedom. Berger and associates found the problem even in "hip communes" where spontaneity and unbounded freedom and impulse are highly valued. Sociologist Benjamin Zablocki discovered the problem even among the Bruderhof, despite the emphasis on authority, structure, rigidity, and rules designed to subordinate individual interests to group interests.[74]

One way to look at it is this: In communes that stress individualism and personal freedom, questions of preserving group solidarity and unity must be faced; but in communes which give primary emphasis to group unity, there arise questions of where individual freedom fits in. In other words, monists must deal with the issue of pluralism; and pluralists must come to grips with the monists' concern about a central, shared core around which the group unites and through which it derives a sense of oneness. Inevitably, communal movements must face the question: Can the many be one at the same time that the one can be many?

Zablocki reports that for the Bruderhof the answer lies in how the word *freedom* is defined. "We must consider the possibility that the problem stems from confusing individualism with freedom," he writes. Bruderhof members firmly believe that they possess freedom—even though they possess nothing of their own, must ask for the simple necessities of life, must do the work chosen for them, and are required to attend communal functions and meals at set times throughout the day, no matter how greatly personal schedules might seem interrupted. Emphatically, then, the members of the Bruderhof do not possess the freedom of individualism.

However, individualism has been the form in which Western peoples have looked for freedom, Zablocki points out, asking if this might not be why the issue of community then becomes difficult. "It seems undeniable," he writes "that community, which means bonds, obligations, and mutual interdependence, is fundamentally incompatible with individualism." Zablocki suggests that freedom can be discussed in two dimensions: "(1) the ability to decide to do something and then go ahead and do it; (2) the ability to change one's mind at any moment as to one's goal, and to act effectively to implement that change."

In the sense of the first dimension, the Bruderhof provides freedom for its members by giving them a structure for their lives, freeing them to get on with the life-goals they have chosen, and insulating them from the distractions of the outside world as well as from individual tendencies to swerve from the path they have chosen for themselves, much as a secretary might protect a busy executive from callers and unnecessary interruptions.

The second dimension of freedom mentioned by Zablocki is virtually unknown in the Bruderhof community. Psychically, economically, and socially, it is extremely difficult to change one's mind and leave the group once such a total commitment has been made; and those who do manage to break their ties are quick to admit that in their hearts they have never completely left. The way that the Bruderhof has dealt with the problem of freedom versus community is no doubt one of the most important reasons it has been such a long-lasting communal movement (it was founded in Germany in 1920 and later migrated to the United States and elsewhere), in contrast to the vast number of communes that fail after very short lives.

Continuance and Cohesiveness: Some Historical Background

The related questions of *continuance* (why some communes last for a long period while others do not) and *cohesiveness* (what causes the feelings of sticking together in some communes while others rather quickly become "unglued") are intriguing ones. Rosabeth Moss Kanter's study of thirty nineteenth-century American communes (from among the nearly one hundred such utopian communities that sprang up between the Revolutionary and Civil wars), showed that nine could be rated successful (lasting thirty-three years or more), while twenty-one were unsuccessful (lasting less than sixteen years, with an average existence of four years). Included in her study were such well-known historical intentional communities as the Shakers (successful, 180 years), Harmony (successful, 100 years), the Oneida Community (successful, 33 years, with its name still familiar through the silverware industry it began), Brook Farm (in which Nathaniel Hawthorne participated, but unsuccessful as a commune, lasting only six years), New Harmony (unsuccessful, two years), and Yellow Springs (which lasted only six months).[75]

Successful nineteenth-century communes, according to Kanter, built strong group commitment in at least four ways: (1) through the investments and sacrifices required of members, (2) through developing a strong in-group or family feeling which discouraged ties outside the group, (3) through identity-change processes so that the thinking and behavior of the individual was brought into conformity to the group, and (4) "through ideological systems and authority structures which gave meaning and direction to the community."[76]

Investments and sacrifices If participants "meant business," they were expected to show it. Investments are what members *give to* the community (for example, money and property, also such intangibles as time and energy), so that they now have a stake in the organization's fate. Sacrifices are what members *give up* for the community and which symbolize to the group "the lengths to which members are willing to go in order to belong."[77] Kanter found that successful utopian communities tended to require sacrifices in terms of *abstinence* (in some cases, sexual; in other cases, abstinence from such things as alcohol, tobacco, meat, personal adornment, and indulgences in pleasures such as dancing or reading) and *austerity* (primitive living conditions, a rugged life with much physical labor, the requirement that the group build its own buildings, and the like).

Strong ingroup feelings Lasting communes tended to be those which developed a sense of being a family through a renunciation of the outside world. If the commune is to become for the individual the functional equivalent of the extended kin, the actual extended kin may not be permitted to be a competing interest. Extreme examples of this phenomenon have occurred in recent years in connection with various religious cults which have influenced young commune members to break off relationships with parents. The parents, in turn, have resorted to various forms of "kidnapping," sometimes hiring a "deprogrammer" who spirits their sons or daughters away and tries to destroy the impact of the group's teaching. Court cases have resulted from such situations.

Kanter refers to an old Shaker hymn which emphasizes hatred for biological relatives, while "gospel relations" were to be considered "dearer . . . than all the flesh kindred." Feelings of ingroup versus outgroup in some historical communal experiments were reinforced both by geographical isolation and insulation from the outside world even by avoiding newspapers and travel. In some cases, rituals of cleansing from contamination were required of those who did venture out on a trip beyond the community. In the Oneida Community, interaction with visitors was controlled, and after they left there was a ritualistic "scrubbing bee" to purify the community.[78]

Strong husband-wife and parent-child ties were also thought to weaken the community's cohesion by deflecting devotion from the total group. Those communities that did not permit families to share dwelling units and which separated parents and children were more apt to be lasting.

Successful groups diffused affection throughout the collective by discouraging two-person exclusive relationships as well as biological family ties, and there were two chief mechanisms by which they accomplished this. Although they seem like opposites, both free love and celibacy minimized individual ties and emphasized group ties. "With free love," Kanter points out, "each member is expected to have intimate relations with *all* others; celibacy permits *no* member to have relations with *any* other." The Oneida Community provides an example of a commune in which regulated free love was practiced; the Shakers are an illustration of a celibacy-practicing group.

This is not to say, of course, that communes can be successful and lasting *only* if either celibacy or free love is practiced. The Bruderhof, now in its third generation, provides ample proof that monogamous marriage can survive in a commune, and the commune itself can survive even though it permits such marriage.

Identity changes   The third mechanism Kanter found which characterized successful communal experiments involved exchanging one's private identity for a new identity molded by and subject to the control of the community. Encounter groups and mutual-criticism sessions kept members alert to the importance of commitment to group standards. Deviance was censured and conformity rewarded. Pressures to think and act according to group norms were both subtle and not-so-subtle. In addition, there arose stratification systems in which the most-conforming members were rewarded with special privileges and esteem.

It is interesting to compare this emphasis on an identity-change process with Jay and Heather Ogilvy's observation that the entrance into a commune involves a "drastic shift" which may be compared to what happens in marriage. The Ogilvys drew upon an article by two sociologists who showed that one's sense of reality "is sustained through conversation with significant others," and that the everyday ongoing conversation between marriage partners especially colors the way they come to view something.

A commune functions similarly in "reconstructing reality" for those who enter it. The "drastic shift" of seeing oneself, one's relationship with others, and the world at large through a new "set of eyes" often comes as a shock to persons experiencing it. At marriage, the partners expect everything will be as before—except that it will now be shared with the mate. And as persons enter a commune, they likewise expect the only change to be a replacement of the "I" by the "we" in looking out upon others and looking in upon oneself. What happens, however, is that the "we" takes on its own personality, so to speak, and reconstructs reality so that it is seen in a new way, with the "I" being changed in the process.[79] Often this can be extremely unsettling because it is so unanticipated. However, such an identity change and reconstruction of reality play a crucial part in group unity and solidarity.

Belief systems and structural arrangements   Kanter's fourth social mechanism affecting group commitment and cohesion had to do with the ideological systems and authority structures. Whether built around religious beliefs or ideals of utopian socialism, the successful nineteenth-century communes were those with "*elaborate ideologies* providing purpose and meaning for community life and an ultimate guide and justification for decisions. There tended to be strong central figures, charismatic leaders, who symbolized the community's values and who made the final decisions for the community and set structural guidelines."[80] In addition, these long-lived communes usually had fixed daily routines, task guidelines, and personal-conduct rules based on the ideology which informed individuals of what was expected of them. Usually it was required that individuals be converted to the particular belief system before being admitted.

Communal living is by no means a new phenomenon. The practice stretches far back into history, long before the nineteenth-century's utopian experiments. The discovery of the Dead Sea Scrolls in 1947 provided a new understanding of the Essenes, a Jewish sect which lived communally about two thousand years ago. And the Bible records the life of the early Christians who "were together and had all things in common; and they sold their possessions and goods and distributed them to all as any had need" (Acts 2:44–45).

Problems Communes Face

Communes face difficulties from both without and within. How successful they are in meeting such difficulties has much to do with how lasting the commune will be.

Problems with the outside world   One of the most basic practical considerations in forming an intentional community is finding a suitable place to live. The zoning laws of many communities make it hard for a group of unrelated individuals to set up a household in a residential area. Even though the commune members consider themselves a family, their neighbors may think differently. In some communities, there is intense hostility toward the commune. Sociologist Frank Cox refers to the many instances of harassment by neighbors, civil authorities, and the police. The persecution may even be violent. He suggests that much of the anger probably stems from some notion (conscious or unconscious) that the existing family structure is being threatened by the commune's presence.[81]

While the outside world may give evidence of hostility toward the commune, the commune may often just as strongly reject the outside world. In modern communes, just as in historical ones, the question of "we" versus "they" is still a very big issue. This comes to light first of all with regard to entrance procedures. Though often with some reluctance, many modern communes have begun to follow the nineteenth-century pattern of setting up selective procedures for membership. Others have a more open policy; to them, anyone who comes automatically belongs. But where member–nonmember distinctions are nonexistent, group cohesion is often weakened, and the group is demoralized as it tries to define itself.

Other difficulties of relating to the outside world may come up with regard to members who hold outside jobs and thus have contacts away from the commune all day long. Then there is the matter of friends and visitors. Strong communes are those which believe their way of life is superior. The old way of life is renounced, sometimes with great bitterness being felt toward it and the people in it (even parents in some cases). Relating to persons who still belong to that despised and "inferior" way of life may prove difficult, and the commune itself may want to ensure insulation by putting controls on such contacts. The Shakers' hymn renouncing the old kin was one example, as was the Oneida scrubbing bee after visitors left. Some communes today try to find ways for outside relationships to "enhance rather than detract from the commune's cohesiveness," Kanter points out, one example being a policy in which each visitor must be regarded "as the property of the group, no matter whom they have come to visit." In other cases, visitors are separated from the regular commune members. A special visitors' dome was built by the Drop City commune in New Mexico, "in a sense putting [visitors] in their place."[82] Jay and Heather Ogilvy also refer to the difficulties they faced in trying to maintain outside connections after they moved into a commune. They point out that the structural situation of a commune not only makes it hard to keep up old friendships but even harder to enter into new ones outside the commune.[83]

Problems within the commune   Communal experiments not only face problems from without but also from within the group itself. One of the biggest issues is the matter of authority. Kanter's study of nineteenth-century communes indicated that authority structures and strong leaders were characteristic of those communities that endured over a long period of time. Group members were willing to obey and submit to the persons in charge, believing that these leaders had a right to rule over them and that they did so with the members' best interests in mind. Thus the group that formed the Putney Perfectionists in Vermont (forerunner of New York's Oneida Community) was willing to sign a statement in 1846 which declared: "John H. Noyes is the father and overseer whom the Holy Ghost has set over the family thus constituted. To John H. Noyes as such we submit ourselves in all things spiritual and temporal, appealing from his decisions only to the spirit of God, and that without disputing."[84]

Many communes today attempt to be democratic and stress pluralism rather than monism. However, a reluctance to make formal rules and a stress on minimal organization often means that tasks go undone and that group solidarity is not built. Eventually such communes are apt to break up. Indeed,

Jay and Heather Ogilvy go so far as to suggest that "unlike either marriage or the monistic commune, the pluralistic commune has a half-life built into its very nature." These authors do not consider this necessarily undesirable but suggest that the pluralistic commune might be a type of institution that, after fulfilling its purpose, should simply dissolve itself. When this occurs, members should not blame themselves for a failure but should anticipate the dissolution in advance, knowing that "when most of its members have met their challenges or made their discoveries, it has no real reason for further existence."[85] On the other hand, communes that have as their goal a more stable, permanent alternative life-style may find it necessary to draw lessons from the successful structured communes of the past.

Problem of sex roles and division of labor   Often communes begin with high ideals about the equality of the sexes. Here is one place on earth, it is thought, where the "brothers" and "sisters" can relate to one another free of stereotypes and role assignments of the larger society. Yet, the ideals are often hard to implement. The group begins to find that men are speaking up more in the meetings and making the decisions, while the women are relatively silent. Work begins to be divided along traditional lines—women in the kitchen, men in the fields.

Even in the kibbutz there has been a tendency in recent years for women to be allotted the more traditionally feminine tasks of the collective—cooking, laundry service, child care, nursing, teaching, and the like. Taking time off from work in the fields in order to give birth and breast-feed infants meant that women often left productive work to take jobs in the service institutions near the children houses. The births of more children increased the need for such service workers. Furthermore, reports sociologist Yonina Talmon, utilitarian considerations entered in so that, in spite of the ideology of sex equality, considerable gender differentiation entered into job allocations. "Since women cannot replace men fully in hard productive labor, it seems a waste to allow them to work in agriculture and at the same time to assign able-bodied men to services."[86]

Sometimes male dominance in communal living is supported by ideology. A group of researchers who studied a rural commune of persons popularly called "Jesus people" found that the group had a clearly spelled-out "theology of sex roles" based on selected Bible verses, so that the women "knew their place." This meant a male-female hierarchy that prevented women from being included in the decision-making processes of the group. Even the one woman with the title of "deaconness" had authority only over other women, primarily with regard to their kitchen chores. All women were expected to bow to male authority.[87] Psychiatrist Joseph Downing, in his observation of urban-based "hippie tribal" communes of the 1960s, notes that male dominance was "held desirable by both sexes," adding that the clothing worn was usually "in a semirural or western style" that emphasized sexual differences.[88]

Grouped by sex, Shakers danced in a ritual designed to shake out sin through the fingertips.

Sometimes the explanation given for sex-role differentiation in communes is that such differentiation is "natural"—that women are simply better suited for some tasks and men for others. Berger and his colleagues, for example, concluded from their study of twenty subsistence-type rural communes in northern California that such communes are not "likely to be praised by serious women's liberationists, since women seem to fall naturally into doing most of the traditional 'women's work.' But this is less a matter of traditionalism than of natural functionality and available skill."[89]

Interestingly, this type of explanation was even used among the Shakers, a group founded by a woman and which included an equal number of male elders and female eldresses in its governing bodies. In the early days of the movement, before the various profitable Shaker industries had begun, the elders maintained that "every commune . . . must be founded . . . on agriculture. Only the simple labors and manners of a farming people can hold a community together." In this agricultural stage, the men did the clearing and cultivation of the soil, planting, and harvesting. The women occupied their time with household tasks such as cooking, cleaning, spinning and weaving, doing the laundry, tending the garden and dairy, and sewing. But in addition, notes one historian, "Some feminine instinct was probably satisfied by the custom of assigning each brother to a sister who became responsible for the care of his clothes and his laundry and for general oversight of his habits and appearance."[90]

In agricultural communes, the more physically demanding tasks tend to be considered the province of men, simply because of male strength and the fact that males are unhindered by pregnancy, childbirth, and child-care responsibilities. (This latter fact does not, of course, apply to the celibate Shakers.) In any social system, certain tasks come to be defined as being more crucial, more important, for the maintenance of that system. Thus, from a structure-functionalist perspective, the chores connected with *producing* the food came to be regarded as more significant than the chores associated with *cooking* the food. The food must be produced before it can be cooked.

Since men control the production of the food, it follows that they have more power. Furthermore, since it is a matter of physical strength that is involved, they have greater options than women. It would be possible for a man to do *either* the more demanding task (food production) or the less demanding one (food preparation), whereas woman's only option is the less demanding one (kitchen duty).

Some communes are attempting to break this pattern, both in ideals and in practice. Kathleen Kinkade, a commune member who tells of the "Walden Two experiment" at Twin Oaks Community (a rural commune in Virginia) writes: "We have no sex roles in our work. Both men and women cook and clean and wash dishes; both women and men drive trucks and tractors, repair fences, load hay, slaughter cattle. Managerial responsibility is divided almost exactly equally—this in spite of the fact that our women are on the average two or three years younger than our men."[91] On a similar note, Rosabeth Moss Kanter tells not only of communes where men share household and child-care tasks equally with women but also of situations where the traditional gender-role division of labor was *challenged* by women who realized their collective strength and confronted the men with what they felt were injustices. In one New Mexico commune, the women ran the men off and told them not to return until they were asked! Meanwhile, "the animals were being tended, the garden harvested, the children nurtured—all without the men."[92]

There is also some evidence that certain urban communes may be moving away from traditional sex-role differentiation toward a more equal sharing of both tasks and power.[93] By jointly sharing the breadwinner role with the men, rather than living as dependents or as household servants, urban commune women tend to be regarded as equals to a greater extent than has been true of rural communes.

Other problems faced by communes   In addition to the various kinds of problems already discussed, commune members face the multitudinous daily problems involved in living together and trying to become molded into a family. This means there may be "family fights," conflicts of interest, personality clashes, and other difficulties of interpersonal relationships. There may be problems with members who shirk their duties and refuse to share in the work of keeping the community going. There is the issue of sheer economic survival which can place considerable pressure on the group. There are decisions to be made about household chores and other practical matters.

Then there is the issue of sex. How will the group handle it? Will there be experimentation with free love or group marriages? Or will monogamy and the nuclear family unit be the ideal family form so that the commune will be one "big family" made up of many little families? Will parents have chief responsibility for the children, or will the children be considered to belong to the entire group? Who will be responsible for their socialization and how will this be carried out? These are only a few of the questions that arise in connection with communal arrangements. It becomes clear that, as an alternative to the family, the commune finds itself heir to many of the same issues that confront the traditional family—plus many more besides.

GROUP MARRIAGE

One much-discussed alternative to conventional marriage is group marriage. Its current incidence is unknown, although from available evidence it appears to be practiced by only a very small minority.[94] Anthropological research indicates that it has also been extremely rare in other cultures.[95] A group marriage differs from a commune, although the two are often confused. However, most intentional communities (communes) have as their goal the formation of a family of brotherlike and sisterlike relationships, whereas group marriages emphasize spouse relationships between members. The sparse information presently available seems to show that group marriages are seldom found within communes,[96] and efforts to press for such arrangements have even caused the disruption of some intentional communities.[97]

Most persons in our society think of marriage in terms of *monogamy*—a marital relationship between one husband and one wife. Another form of marriage practiced in many cultures throughout the world has been *polygamy* (one person with two or more spouses). Polygamy may occur either in the form of polygyny (one husband with two or more wives) or polyandry (one wife with two or more husbands). The terms are easily remembered by thinking of their Greek roots; for example, the *gyn* in polygyny is the same root found in the familiar term *gynecologist. Poly* plus *gyny* means "many females." *Poly* plus *andry* means "many males."

According to anthropological evidence, monogamy is the prevailing marital form in all societies. However, some permit polygamy in some form as well. A study of 238 societies by the anthropologist George Murdock showed that in 81 percent a male was allowed to marry more than one female (polygyny) but in only 1 percent of the societies could a wife have more than one husband (polyandry).[98] Societies that recognize polygamous unions consider them to be nothing less than *marriages,* even though more than two persons are involved.

This means that such arrangements entail all the responsibilities of marriage, including publicly declared commitment to the relationship and economic and sexual interdependence.

Group marriage is not the same as polygyny and polyandry but has been traditionally defined as consisting of two or more males married to two or more females.[99] Two writers who have given much attention to group marriage, Larry and Joan Constantine, raise the objection that the traditional definition leaves no allowance for a three-person group situation in which all partners are equal in rank (in contrast to traditional polygamous situations). They suggest the term *multilateral* (or many-sided) marriage, which they define as an arrangement "in which all participants are married to at least two other participants; usually all participants are married to all others."[100] James Ramey of the Center for the Study of Innovative Life Styles prefers to retain the familiar term *group marriage* while utilizing the Constantines' definition, substituting the word *pair-bonded* for the word *married* (since persons may be pair-bonded without being legally married). Ramey makes the following distinctions: The commitment in a dyadic (two-person) marriage is to the individual. The commitment in a commune is to the group as a whole. The commitment in a group marriage is to both the group as a whole and to each individual. His conclusion is that "group marriage, which combines commitment to the group with multiple pair-bonding among the members of the group, is the most complex form of marriage."[101]

Who Enters Group Marriages and Why?

Finding persons in group marriages who are willing to be interviewed about their life-style is not easy. The Constantines were able to identify only 101 groups in the United States which could be confirmed as multilateral marriages, 66 of which had already dissolved by the time they came to the interviewers' attention. Twenty-six groups were willing to become informants or respondents for the Constantines' survey. Less than half of the groups were still together at the end of one year, while 17 percent of the groups were still intact at the end of a three-year period.[102]

It is commonly believed that only the very young are interested in multiperson marriages, but the limited information available suggests otherwise. In the Constantine project, the median age for female participants in group marriages was found to be twenty-eight, for males thirty-one. James Ramey's report on persons interested in alternate forms of marriage showed that couples who had participated in group marriages or in communes (with nearly three-quarters of the latter reporting they had been sexually involved with other couples at some time) had a median age of thirty (females) and thirty-five (males). Thus, while it is true that those wishing to try group arrangements are often young, frequently they are over thirty and sometimes considerably older. In fact, some behavioral scientists have discussed *polygyny* as a possible solution to the loneliness of old age (where widows outnumber widowers) and as a means of alleviating some of the problems of household care and financial needs among the elderly.[103]

Ramey's information was gleaned from eighty couples who were either interested in group marriages or communes or else had already participated in such arrangements. Of these, over 90 percent of husbands and wives, if employed, held academic, managerial, or professional positions. Nine out of ten men and four out of every ten women had a college education or more.[104]

In the group marriages examined by the Constantines, a wide variety of occupations were represented, including college professors, students, sales-persons, farmers, carpenters, mechanics, engineers, psychologists, social workers, nurses, a physician, a minister, and a theologian. The reasons they gave for forming group marriages related to love, personal fulfillment and growth, the desire for community and for a richer family life for children, intellectual stimulation, and interest in sexual variety. According to the Constantines, "Most of them are *not* rebelling, seeking escape, acting on religious principles, or improving what they consider to be unsatisfactory marriages."[105] In many respects, the reasons cited for forming group marriages appear to be similar to reasons persons might give for forming intimate family networks or joining communes, with the added desire (in group marriages) for freedom to experience sexual intimacy as part of emotional closeness to more than one person.

Sex in Group Marriage

Although it is popularly believed that sex is the central focus in group marriages, participants in such arrangements disagree and tend to emphasize the overall relationships of caring and sharing. Sexual intercourse usually occurs in what psychiatrist Albert Ellis calls a "round-robin" fashion, with different persons pairing off day by day (or every few days) so that each man and each woman in the marriage regularly copulate together.[106] Some group marriages have a fixed rotation pattern which is planned and structured by group consensus.

The term *group marriage* is not synonymous with *group sex,* which may be defined as sexual activity engaged in by three or more persons simultaneously. Usually group-married persons pair off privately as couples, although on rare occasions several or all of the partners may climb into bed together.[107]

Larry and Joan Constantine found that, with few exceptions, sexual activity between persons of the same sex occurred only in such group sexual encounters. The persons involved made a distinction between ambisexuality ("the capacity to relate sexually to either sex as appropriate to the circumstances") and homosexuality, pointing out that they considered "the interaction *among* several partners (hence in part between members of the same sex) as different from sex *between* two members of the same sex." Although the co-wives are considered to be "marriage partners" in the sense of commitment to each other, and the co-husbands similarly, all were much more certain about warm physical demonstrations of affection between same-sex partners than about actual sexual relationships. While every observed group made provision for heterosexual pairs to sleep together, no group provided sleeping arrangements for same-sex pairs.[108]

Problems in Group Marriages

As in most marriages and communes, difficulties may arise as persons endeavor to relate to one another deeply. In a group marriage, the problems are especially complex because of the number of persons involved. Thus, such marriages tend to last from only a few months to a few years. The problems only rarely relate to sex (jealousy, for example). Usually, the breakups occur for other reasons— incombatibility of personalities, inability to communicate and work out problems of decision making about the multitudinous details of everyday living together, conflicts about childrearing, and so on. Some couples perceive the costs to exceed the rewards and choose to end the arrangements. Although there is no formal document, a couple or a single person may in a sense "divorce" another couple.

Forming a group marriage in the first place can be problematic. In entering conventional two-partner marriages, we have seen that the selection of one person by another involves a great deal of evaluating costs and rewards. However, the process of mate selection becomes extremely complex in forming a group marriage because it means two people must find a compatible third partner who can relate satisfactorily to each of them or else another couple who can be co-spouses. The Constantines report that many people are surprised to learn that couples often carry on a courtship with other couples in much the same way that individuals do before forming traditional dyadic marriages. There may be love letters, frequent phone calls, dinner dates, and the like. In some cases, the couples begin cross-couple sexual intimacies only after deciding upon a commitment to each other, a kind of engagement to be group-married.[109]

One of the biggest problems facing group marriages is the fact that they are not recognized as legal marriages in any state at present. The group arrangement is characterized by ongoing sexual and economic interdependence, which fits with the sociological definition of marriage provided earlier, but there is often a reluctance to disclose the arrangement publicly because of the costs involved.

Although the Constantines are of the opinion that "group marriage has the signal and unique advantage of providing for sexual variety for *both* men and women *within* a stable marital configuration," they predict that it will be practiced by only a minority of families because of the complexities involved.[110]

GAY MARRIAGE

Nearly two thousand years ago, the Roman poet Ovid wrote of a man who informed his pregnant wife that family financial conditions were such that only a boy could be afforded. Tearfully, he said that if a female were born, the baby must immediately be put to death. When the mother gave birth to a girl, she followed the counsel of a goddess in not telling the father, who thought he had a son. Only the mother and a faithful nurse knew the truth. The baby was dressed in male attire and given the name Iphis, a name used for both boys and girls.

When Iphis was thirteen, the father arranged a marriage between his handsome offspring and a beautiful girl named Ianthe. The two were the same age and had been educated together, so that a deep bond of love had grown between them. Ianthe's passion for Iphis grew and she longed for the wedding day, whereas Iphis, though equally in love, kept postponing it. Her desperate mother invented excuses of illnesses or visions interpreted as bad omens. Ovid describes the sense of hopelessness:

> Iphis loved a girl whom she despaired of ever being able to enjoy, and this very frustration increased her ardour. A girl herself, she was in love with one of her own kind, and could scarcely keep back her tears, as she said: "What is to be the end of this for me, caught as I am in the snare of a strange and unnatural kind of love, which none has known before? Cows do not burn with love for cows, nor mares for mares. It is the ram which excites the ewe, the hind follows the stag, birds too mate in the same way, and never among all the animals does one female fall in love with another. How I wish I had never been born!"[111]

Iphis tried to talk herself out of her feelings. "Pull yourself together, Iphis, be firm, and shake off this foolish, useless emotion. . . . It is hope that conceives and nourishes desire: and your case denies you hope." Rebelliously, she reasoned that none of the usual obstacles kept her from her beloved's embrace; there was no guardian forbidding the marriage, no husband to whom she was bound, no stern father standing in the way of her happiness. It was all the fault of nature. She bemoaned: "My wedding day is at hand, and now Ianthe will be mine: yet she will not be. I shall thirst in the midst of waters." Crying out to the god and goddess of marriage, Iphis asked why they should even bother to "come to this ceremony, at which there is no bridegroom, where two brides are being wed."

The problem was solved through the intervention of the same goddess who had advised the girl's mother while awaiting Iphis' birth. A miracle was performed within the temple, and Iphis was changed into a young man—a suitable bridegroom for the happy Ianthe.

In mythology, such a gods-to-the-rescue ending might seem a reasonable device for solving the problems of the characters involved. But the solution is not so simple in real life. Persons interested in a same-sex marriage today would be quite unlikely to welcome the intervention of Iphis' goddess. Only a minority of homosexuals wish to identify with the opposite sex, persuaded that they are men in women's bodies or women in men's bodies.[112] It is true, of course, that some transexual homosexuals even undergo a sex reassignment operation in order to function in society as members of the opposite sex, for as Money notes, "the male transexual, being the extreme form of homosexual that he is, is able to live, work, think, and make love as a woman."[113] But, in general, persons interested in "gay marriage" are not at all thinking about undergoing a sex change. They want to be what they are and yet be able to marry the persons they love—even though they are not of the opposite sex.

What Is Homosexuality?

Paul Gebhard of the Institute for Sex Research at Indiana University defines homosexual behavior as "physical contact between two individuals of the same gender which both recognize as being sexual in nature and which ordinarily results in sexual arousal." He defines psychological homosexual response as "the desire for such physical contact and/or conscious sexual arousal from thinking of or seeing persons of the same gender."[114] The term *homosexual* is derived from the Greek *homos*, meaning "one and the same," and it may be applied to either males or females who are sexually attracted to members of their own sex. Usually, however, homosexual women are referred to as *lesbians*, a word derived from Lesbos, a Greek island where in ancient times a woman named Sappho directed a girls' school and addressed sensuous poems to her students.

In recent years, the word *gay* has come into wide usage by homosexual persons of both sexes. Once serving as a sort of secret code word among homosexuals who wanted to avoid discovery, it has now become a term of pride. "Gay is good." "Gay is power." "Gay is angry; gay is proud." Psychiatrist George Weinberg distinguishes between being homosexual (having "erotic preferences for members of one's own sex") and being gay, which he defines as being free of the need for ongoing self-inquisition, and ridding oneself of guilt, shame, and regret over being a homosexual. "To be gay," writes Weinberg, "is to view one's sexuality as the healthy heterosexual views his."[115]

Persons who regard themselves as gay are not apt to be terrified in the way Iphis was by their attraction to members of the same sex. They do not view such attraction as loathsome or unnatural. Indeed, they would even call into question Iphis' observation about the animal world by pointing out that research has indicated that animals *do* sometimes engage in homosexual behavior—including the ram, which Iphis especially cited in her lament.[116] Unlike Iphis, the gay person does not wish to be changed in order to be able to marry the loved one of the same sex, but proposes instead that society do the changing by permitting such marriages to take place.

Gay Marriage and the Law

We have pointed out that marriage exists when two (or more) persons maintain ongoing instrumental and expressive exchanges, that is, when they are both economically and sexually interdependent. Thus, from a sociological point of view, an ongoing relationship of two economically and sexually interdependent men, or of two economically and sexually interdependent women, could be called a marriage. In such cases, the persons involved share bed and board and regard themselves as spouses or lovers rather than as friends or roommates.

But although a gay marriage might be considered an actual marital union according to a *sociological* definition of marriage, it is not considered a valid marriage from a *legal* standpoint. A test case occurred when two men appealed to the Minnesota Supreme Court in 1971 after a lower court ruled in favor of a county clerk who had refused to grant the men a marriage license. The homosexual couple contended that since there was no state law specifically prohibiting same-sex marriages, there was no reason to assume such marriages would be illegal.

Their case further relied on arguments based upon the United States Constitution, in particular the Fourteenth Amendment's guarantee that no state shall "deprive any person of life, liberty, or property, without due process of law; nor deny to any person within its jurisdiction the equal protection of the laws." The petitioners argued that the "due process" clause lay at the root of the United States Supreme Court's ruling on the unconstitutionality of a Connecticut law prohibiting the use of contraceptives by married couples, because such a law was in violation of the *privacy* inherent in the marital relationship.

Furthermore, according to the homosexual couple, the state was violating the "equal protection" clause by discriminating against them as a same-sex couple. Such patent discrimination could be compared to the racial discrimination in marriage laws which the United States Supreme Court had ruled unconstitutional. The case of *Loving v. Virginia* showed that it is in violation of the Fourteenth Amendment for states to make laws against interracial marriage. In that ruling, Chief Justice Warren had written:

> Marriage is one of the "basic civil rights of man," fundamental to our very existence and survival. To deny this fundamental freedom on so unsupportable a basis as the racial classifications embodied in these [antimiscegenation] statutes, classifications so directly subversive of the principle of equality at the heart of the Fourteenth Amendment, is surely to deprive all the State's citizens of liberty without due process of law. The Fourteenth Amendment requires that the freedom of choice to marry not be restricted by invidious racial discriminations.[117]

The Supreme Court of Minnesota ruled against the homosexual couple, however, stating that these arguments did not apply to their case. While it was

The 1971 wedding of Mike McConnell and Jack Baker took place in Minneapolis, despite a court ruling against the legality of homosexual marriage.

true that the state's statute with regard to marriage did not expressly forbid same-sex marriages, the wording was such, said the court, that heterosexual marriage was clearly the intent. Terms such as *husband and wife* and *bride and groom* were used, and the word *marriage* was employed "as one of common usage, meaning the state of union between persons of the opposite sex."

The court referred to definitions found in *Webster's Dictionary* and *Black's Law Dictionary,* each of which refers to distinctions of sex, and declared that it is unlikely that the original draftsmen of the marriage statutes had anything other than this in mind. The court went on to say that "the institution of marriage as a union of man and woman, uniquely involving the procreation and rearing of children within a family, is as old as the book of Genesis." Disregarded as not applicable was the argument of the homosexual couple that "the state does not impose upon heterosexual married couples a condition that they have a proved capacity or declared willingness to procreate."

The court further declared that the ruling that struck down the Connecticut law regarding contraceptive usage by married couples could not be relied on as a basis for arguing against *all* state interference in marriage. "The basic premise of that decision . . . was that the state, having authorized marriage, was without power to intrude upon the right of privacy inherent in the marital relationship," said the Minnesota Supreme Court justices, pointing out that the state's classification of persons authorized to marry does not violate the Fourteenth Amendment.

However, the court admitted that state restrictions on the right to marry are not entirely beyond the reach of that Amendment, as was shown in the United States Supreme Court's decision which struck down state laws forbidding interracial marriages. "But in commonsense and in a constitutional sense, there is a clear distinction between a marital restriction based merely upon race and one based upon the fundamental difference in sex." It was decided by the court that the two men did not have the right to marry one another.[118]

Homosexual Marriage as an Alternative Life-style

Despite the fact that gay marriages are not recognized as legal, many lesbians and male homosexuals do form lasting same-sex unions which they may think of and speak of as marriages. The ideals of permanence, faithfulness, and a shared life (both sexually and economically) are often held up, just as in the case of heterosexual marriages. Speaking from the standpoint of the homosexual, Del Martin and Paul Mariah ask how a limiting value can be placed upon the sexual expression of love, whether heterosexual or homosexual. "Is it polarity, the joining of male-female and penis-vagina that makes a 'marriage' whole and therefore 'holy'?" they ask. "Isn't it rather the mutual respect and the mutual love for one another, each to and for the other as a human being, that makes the difference? And isn't love 'socially desirable'?"[119] Some persons enter gay unions repeatedly, each time hoping that the ideal lover has been found. Others have a relationship that has endured for a very long time. Martin and Mariah refer to two men who are now in their seventies and have lived together in a homosexual marriage for more than fifty years, at the same time consenting to one another's occasional seeking of extra sexual gratification outside their own relationship. Del Martin and Phyllis Lyon, founders of a lesbian organization, have written a book which describes their many years together in a gay marriage and provides examples of other lesbian unions that have also lasted for long periods.[120]

Many homosexual persons argue that there would be more long-lasting "gay marriages" if society would lend its support and approval. They attribute the high number of failures to society's pressures and the disdain they are subjected to rather than to any inherent weakness in the homosexual relationship itself. Recognizing the need for emotional support among gay persons, various gay organizations have sprung up in recent years, including religious ones. The Metropolitan Community Churches, a denomination founded by the Rev. Troy Perry who is himself "married" to another male, has wedding ceremonies so that homosexual couples and lesbian couples can enter into what the group speaks of as "Holy Union," thereby giving the two persons some sense of a public declaration and formalization of their relationship.[121]

The question may arise as to why homosexual persons can't simply live together without worrying about the question of a legal marriage. They reply by citing both practical reasons and a sense of need for psychic support. On the practical side, there is the matter of finding housing, because they are likely to encounter discrimination if they wish to let their relationship be known openly. Problems with regard to employment also cause difficulty. "Try telling your boss you can't move to a new job because of your lover," writes Dennis Altman, a problem that would be understood if a heterosexual person were speaking of his or her spouse. Other practical problems cluster around inheritance rights (the homosexual "spouse" is not likely to receive a share of the estate of a partner who left no will, no matter how long the couple has lived together nor how estranged the deceased had been from his or her biological family) and around some tax laws. Even something so simple as a hospital visit can become a problem. Altman refers to a report in the London *Times* which told of a dying lesbian who was permitted only visits by her immediate family and denied the privilege of seeing her partner of twenty years.[122] Some spokespersons for gay liberation argue that such problems could be solved by the legalization of gay marriage.

The matter of children is another problem encountered by homosexual persons who regard themselves as married while the state does not. Some courts have refused to permit lesbian mothers, divorced after heterosexual marriages, to have custody of their own children. Other courts have ruled differently, and some lesbian women are bringing up children along with lesbian partners who also have children, thereby creating a combined family with two mothers.[123] In some cases, a lesbian couple has considered their marriage relationship incomplete apart from the experience of parenthood together; therefore one of them becomes pregnant with the help of some willing male, and the two women then rear the baby together. There are also instances in which lesbian motherhood comes about when an unwed mother enters a gay relationship, as in the case of a single woman who brought her two-year-old child with her when she became the lover of an older woman, a pediatrician who is now regarded as the child's other parent. For males, the problem of parenthood is much more difficult, since known homosexuals would not likely be favored by agencies as adoptive parents.[124]

Some homosexuals speak of the psychic cost of being involved in a same-sex union in a society that does not recognize such a relationship as valid. Altman points out that all the world loves a lover—as long as it's not a homosexual one. He decries the fact that homosexuals do not have the right to publicly express their love without encountering severe ridicule and disapproval. "It is impossible to know to what extent love is strengthened by being public," he writes, "yet . . . I suspect that after a time lovers have a real psychological need for the support that comes from being recognized as such."[125]

Similar anguish was expressed in a letter to a San Francisco newspaper in which a young college-educated male, working his way up in a large corporation, said he could not really expect his career to progress beyond the lower end of middle management without marriage to a woman. The problem was that he already *was* "married"—but to another male who had come with him when he transferred from another city. His roommate's accompanying him in itself was difficult to explain; but beyond that, the letter writer was mentally tortured by having to pretend constantly that he was single, an eligible bachelor expected to flirt with the women at the office, take them out, and even to give his male colleagues the impression that he was having an affair with some female friend. He said he felt "trapped in a cage of pretending." "I am married!" he stated repeatedly. "I do not look one bit different from other respectable, aggressive, married young men." Yet society does not recognize his marriage, because it is a gay marriage.[126] Altman writes of the gay commune movement that has sprung up to provide emotional support and a sense of family life to homosexual persons, one way of combating the feelings of loneliness and alienation many feel.[127]

However, apart from the commune movement, the informal network known as the gay community or "gay world" may itself sometimes fail to provide a setting conducive to strong, lasting homosexual relationships—particularly in cases of males.[128] Richard Hauser, who has written on homosexuality in Great Britain, points out that "married" homosexual couples eager for their relationships to endure "do not normally mix with other homosexuals," and that for such partnerships to last, there must be common interests apart from sex.[129] An urban anthropologist, David Sonenschein, also reports that the more stable relationships are those where there is "a more conscious attempt by the individuals involved to aim at a congruence of values and interests."

In Sonenschein's study, mateships that were regarded as more personal matters, involving nothing more than setting up a household together or exchanging rings (which Sonenschein labels "cohabitation" rather than "marriage" because of the lack of ceremony), were found to be more lasting in the homosexual community than those with public imitations of heterosexual marriage. Often, a public "marriage" ritual *within* the homosexual community served more as a group affair, reaffirming group values, "particularly those that mock the heterosexual world," so that the couple's union came to be viewed almost a group property and as an antiestablishment protest rather than a wedding showing the personal commitment of two individuals.

Sonenschein's study of a homosexual community in the Southwestern United States indicated that two persons hopeful of entering a lasting sociosexual relationship "rapidly withdrew from the activity of the community and decreased participation in group affairs," with particular avoidance of those institutions conducive to sexual interaction and which could mean competition for the attention of the two trying to establish a permanent commitment to each other.[130] Two other researchers, however, found that male homosexuals who lived with homosexual roommates (presumably including those in gay marriages) were more integrated with the homosexual community than were homosexual men who lived alone, with parents, or with wives, and reflected greater psychological well-being as well.[131] It should be kept in mind that the homosexual community (as an aggregate of persons, places, and activities) exists as a support mechanism for those who are forced into a kind of segregation by societal attitudes and laws.[132] Were the larger society to recognize gay marriage, public ceremonies would likely mean something different than in the kind of situations Sonenschein describes.

In addition, the different socialization of males and females may even carry over into homosexual activity, with males having learned to view sexuality in a more detached manner while females learn to view it in a more "expressive" sense, that is, in the context of a loving relationship. Kinsey reported that among persons who reported having homosexual contact, only 29 percent of the women had experienced sexual contact with more than one or two partners, whereas 49 percent of the men reported such a pattern, with many having had "scores or hundreds of sexual partners."[133]

Social scientists Maureen Mileski and Donald Black, however, doubt the assumption that the fewer "one-night stands" among lesbians as compared to male homosexuals can be explained by presumed greater female interest in love and enduring relationships. Many male homosexuals also dream of such love relationships. Mileski and Black suggest that the key to male-female differences in promiscuity may lie in the social organization of the gay community which furnishes males with opportunities for meeting strangers and initiating casual sexual contacts in a way that is not true for lesbians. "Where lesbians do have access to bars peopled by relative strangers," say these sociologists, " . . . it appears that they are quite as likely to carry on numerous ephemeral relationships, just as many males do."[134]

According to sociologist Mehri Jensen's research, while "married" lesbian couples are not visible at gay bars, they do find support for their quasi-marital unions from other homosexual women—both from couples like themselves with whom they gather for private parties and also from "single" lesbians who watch these partnerships with envy, hoping that such an enduring relationship will one day be their own experience, too. After one gay marriage in her sample broke up, reports Jensen, all of the other lesbians in the community endeavored to comfort the partner who was considered mistreated; but at the same time, they voiced fears "that dreams of a lasting homosexual union may only be illusory."[135]

Why Gay Marriage Is a Current Issue

The issue of gay marriage has come up in recent years for at least two reasons. One is the self-conscious effort on the part of homosexual persons to assert themselves, develop a sense of dignity and self-esteem, and to demand rights long denied them. The other reason relates to the women's movement. A minority of women's liberation writers have suggested that "lesbianism is one road to freedom—freedom from oppression by men." Martha Shelly writes: "The Lesbian, through her ability to obtain love and sexual satisfaction from other women, is freed of dependence on men for love, sex, and money. She does not have to do menial chores for them (at least at home), nor cater to their egos, nor submit to hasty and inept sexual encounters. She is freed from fear of unwanted pregnancy and the pains of childbirth, and from the drudgery of child raising."[136]

In a similar vein, Jill Johnston has written, "The liberation of women is for women, not for men. We don't have to have anything to do with the men at all." She suggests that women are oppressed by the heterosexual institution and are fugitives, and "it is the banding together of fugitives which constitutes the phenomenon of revolutionary opposition."[137] She refers to Ti-Grace Atkinson's statements on the political significance of lesbianism, which means total commitment of women to women. "Can you imagine a Frenchman serving in the French army from 9 to 5, then trotting 'home' to Germany for supper and overnight?" said Atkinson. "That's called game-playing, or collaboration, not political commitment."[138]

There is some evidence that, at least in the past, lesbian marriages tended to fall into patterns similar to the traditional gender roles of heterosexual marriages, with one woman being the more dominant, functioning as the chief breadwinner, and so on. However, sociologist Mehri Jensen reports this may be changing with the influence of feminism.[139] For some women, lesbianism seems to promise a way of breaking down differentiation, thereby avoiding being locked into stereotyped roles. They think of female homosexuality in terms of finding their own identity and individuality instead of being regarded as appendages to a male.

It is likely that more test cases similar to that described earlier will come to the courts, perhaps eventually reaching the United States Supreme Court for a final decision on the validity of same-sex unions and on the legality of gay marriage. With growing assertiveness among the homosexual community and the cries for gay power and gay rights, demands for marriage privileges seem inevitable.

OTHER ALTERNATIVE LIFE-STYLES

In this chapter, we have looked at some of the alternatives to conventional marriage that are sometimes chosen by persons today. Trial marriage, common-law marriage, singleness, single parenthood, communes, group marriage, and gay marriage have been discussed. But there are other alternatives to traditional marriage which will be discussed in later chapters. Some of these are the dual-career equal-partner marriage, the voluntarily childless marriage, and consensual adultery (mate swapping or "swinging").

NOTES

1   *Monthly Vital Statistics Report,* 1974, vol. 22, no. 13, p. 8.

2   Carter and Glick, 1970, p. 41. Provisional statistics for 1974 and early 1975 became available as this book went to press. There is some indication that for the first time since 1958 a decline in both the number of marriages and the marriage rate has occurred. There is no way of knowing at this time whether this is the beginning of a downward trend or merely a temporary fluctuation in the pattern which held from 1959 onward. *Monthly Vital Statistics Report 23,* no. 12, 1975; 24, no. 3, 1975.

3   Glick and Norton, 1973. As this book went to press, we learned through a phone conversation with Arthur Norton of the U.S. Census Bureau that very recent remarriage rates show some indication of decline. At this time, it is still too early to determine whether this decline is only temporary or whether it will continue for a period of several years.

4   M. Berger, 1971.

5   Lindsey, 1926, 1927; Russell, 1929; Skolnick, 1973, p. 248.

6   Mead, 1966.

7   Mead, 1968.

8   M. Berger, 1971.

9   Satir, 1967.

10   Greenwald, 1970.

11   Whitehurst, 1969a.

12   Homans, 1961.

13   White and Wells, 1973.

14   Arafat and Yorburg, 1973; Lyness, Lipetz, and Davis, 1972.

15   Krause, 1971.

16   Kephart, 1964.

17   Sussman, Cates, and Smith, 1970, p. 270.

18   Clark, 1968, as quoted in Krause, 1971, p. 18.

19   Clark, 1968, p. 58.

20   Krause, 1971, pp. 17–18.

21   Mainardi, 1970; Whitehurst 1969b. However, one researcher recently found that 59 percent of unmarried couples in her university sample reported sharing housework equally. See Clatworthy, 1975.

22   U.P.I., "The $4 Divorce: You Need Not Be Married to Get One," Bloomington (Ind.) Herald-Telephone, Nov. 12, 1974. But see Weitzman, 1974.

23   Bernard, 1972, Chap. 10.

24   Calhoun, 1919, vol. 1, pp. 245, 67.

25   Calhoun, 1919, vol. 1, pp. 67–68.

26   B. Franklin, 1745, in Labare and Bell, 1961.

27   Quoted in Calhoun, 1919, vol. 1, p. 247.

28 Calhoun, 1919, vol. 1, p. 69.
29 Calhoun, 1919, vol. 1, p. 246; vol. 2, p. 208.
30 Calhoun, 1919, vol. 2, p. 104.
31 *Current Population Reports*, 1974, P-20, no. 271, p. 2.
32 Bernard, 1972.
33 *Current Population Reports*, 1974, P-20, no. 271, p. 3.
34 Spreitzer and Riley, 1974.
35 Havens, 1973, p. 980.
36 Bernard, 1972.
37 U.S. Bureau of the Census, 1970, PC(2)-4C.
38 Carter and Glick, 1970, p. 311.
39 Carolyn Tufford, "Being Single Not Equated with Being Lonely," in Bloomington-
    Bedford (Ind.) Sunday Herald-Times, July 8, 1973.
40 "No Scarlet Letter?" National Observer, Jan. 19, 1974, p. 4.
41 National Observer, Feb. 2, 1974, p. 6.
42 Redbook, Feb., 1974.
43 Klein, 1973.
44 Kadushin, 1970.
45 Malinowski, 1930.
46 Coser and Coser, 1972.
47 Spiro, 1965, pp. 100, 349.
48 Linner, 1967, p. 36.
49 Krause, 1971.
50 Blau and Duncan, 1967.
51 *Current Population Reports*, P-23, no. 36, 1971, p. 41. *Monthly Vital Statistics Report*,
    23, no. 11, 1975.
52 *Current Population Reports*, P-23, no. 36, 1971, p. 41.
53 *Monthly Vital Statistics Report 23*, no. 11, 1975, p. 11. The effects of the liberalization
    of abortion laws are just beginning to show up in illegitimacy statistics. See our
    Chapter 9.
54 Cutright, 1972, p. 382.
55 National Center for Health Statistics, 21, no. 23, 1973.
56 Adams, 1968, p. 12.
57 Piddington, 1965.
58 Wirth, 1938; Parsons, 1943; see also summaries in Adams, 1968, and in Sussman and
    Burchinal, 1962.
59 Adams, 1968, p. 3.
60 Sussman, 1966.
61 "The Gift of Honesty," Ms., II (Dec., 1973), p. 46.
62 Stoller, 1970.
63 Kanter, 1968, pp. 509–510.
64 Adams, 1968, p. 3.
65 Ogilvy and Ogilvy, 1972.
66 Zablocki, 1971, pp. 237, 250.
67 Bettelheim, 1969, pp. 331–332.
68 Kanter, 1974.
69 Kanter, 1973, p. xii.
70 Berger, Hackett, and Millar, 1972.
71 Kanter, 1974.
72 Berger, Hackett, and Millar, 1972.
73 Ogilvy and Ogilvy, 1972, p. 90.
74 Zablocki, 1971, pp. 250, 280–288.
75 Kanter, 1968.
76 Kanter, 1972, p. 313.
77 Kanter, 1968, p. 505.
78 Kanter, 1968, p. 508.
79 Ogilvy and Ogilvy, 1972; Berger and Kellner, 1964.

80   Kanter, 1972, p. 314.
81   Cox, 1972; see also Weitzman, 1974, p. 1231.
82   Kanter, 1972, p. 320.
83   Ogilvy and Ogilvy, 1972, pp. 88–89.
84   Robertson, 1970, p. 10.
85   Ogilvy and Ogilvy, 1972, p. 98.
86   Talmon, 1972, p. 19.
87   Harder, Richardson, and Simmonds, 1972.
88   Downing, 1970.
89   Berger, Hackett, and Millar, 1972.
90   Tyler, 1944, p. 161.
91   Kinkade, 1973, p. 171.
92   Kanter, 1974, p. 64.
93   Polk, Stein, and Polk, 1973.
94   Ellis, 1970; Constantine and Constantine, 1971, 1973a.
95   Murdock, 1949.
96   Constantine and Constantine, 1973a, pp. 68–69.
97   Ellis, 1970.
98   Murdock, 1949.
99   Nimkoff, 1965.
100 Constantine and Constantine, 1971.
101 Ramey, 1972a; 1972b.
102 Constantine and Constantine, 1973a.
103 Duberman, 1974, pp. 12–13; Kassel, 1970.
104 Ramey, 1972a.
105 Constantine and Constantine, 1973a, pp. 73, 109; Ramey, 1972a, p. 651.
106 Ellis, 1970.
107 Constantine and Constantine, 1973a, chap. 15; also 1973b.
108 Constantine and Constantine, 1973a, pp. 166–168.
109 Constantine and Constantine, 1973a, chap. 8.
110 Constantine and Constantine, 1973a, pp. 13, 235.
111 Ovid's *Metamorphoses,* p. 223, Penguin edition.
112 West, 1968, pp. 62–65.
113 Money, 1970.
114 Gebhard, 1972.
115 Weinberg, 1972, pp. 70–71; also Altman, 1971.
116 Money and Ehrhardt, 1972, p. 228.
117 Kanowitz, 1973, pp. 645–648.
118 Kanowitz, 1973, pp. 647–648.
119 Martin and Mariah, 1972, p. 126.
120 Martin and Lyon, 1972; see also Jensen, 1974.
121 Enroth and Jamison, 1973.
122 Altman, 1971, pp. 29, 49–50, Avon edition.
123 "The Uphill Custody Battles," Human Behavior, vol. 4 (Feb., 1975), pp. 46–47.
124 Klein, 1973, pp. 79, 87–88.
125 Altman, 1971, p. 66, Avon edition.
126 Quoted in Feldman and Thielbar, 1972, pp. 338–339.
127 Altman, 1971, pp. 136–137, Avon edition.
128 Hooker, 1965; Hoffman, 1968, pp. 44–63.
129 Hauser, 1962.
130 Sonenschein, 1973.
131 Weinberg and Williams, 1974, pp. 234–236.
132 Gagnon and Simon, 1967b; Hooker, 1965, 1968; Hoffman, 1968; Jensen, 1974.
133 Kinsey et al., 1953, p. 475; Gagnon and Simon, 1967a, 1973; Mileski and Black, 1972.
134 Mileski and Black, 1972.
135 Jensen, 1974.
136 Shelly, 1969, pp. 306–307; also see Kelly, 1972.

137 Johnston, 1973, pp. 91, 276.
138 Quoted in Johnston, 1973, p. 277.
139 Jensen, 1974. Also see "Lesbian Matrimony" in Human Behavior 4 (Jan., 1975), p. 51.

UNIT 3

STRUCTURE AND PROCESS IN MARRIAGE

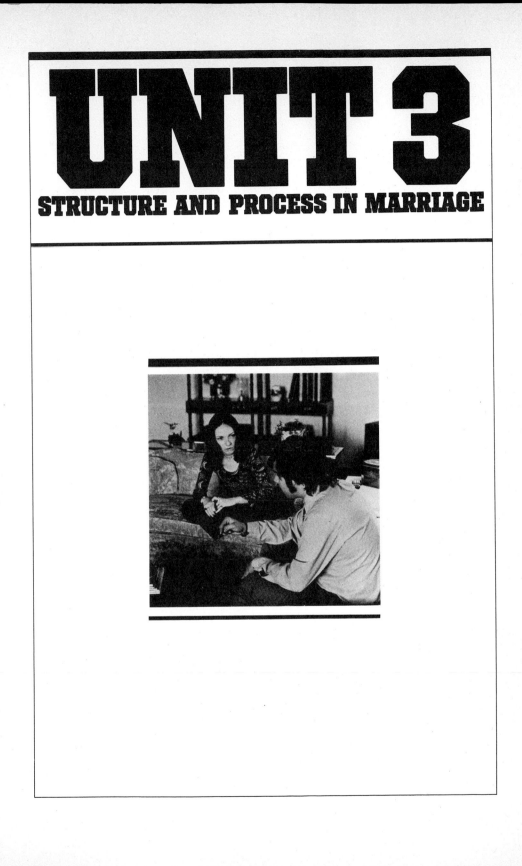

6

THE STRUCTURE OF MARRIAGE

Entering the state of marriage could be compared to entering a building. However, not all buildings are structured alike, and neither are all marriages. The following cases illustrate four basic blueprints or models. This doesn't mean that every marriage must fall neatly and totally into one or another of the patterns described (there are frameworks in between the categories, blurring into one another), but the case descriptions help us see some basic structural distinctions.

CASE ONE

During the first half of the nineteenth century, when physical punishment was sometimes used to enforce husband supremacy, a writer recalled a man in her neighborhood. This respected church and community leader regularly beat his wife with a horse-whip, claiming that such behavior was necessary "in order to keep her in subjection" and to stop her from scolding. Emily Collins commented on her neighbors: "Now this wife, surrounded by six or seven little children . . . was obliged to spin and weave cloth for all the garments of the family ... to milk ... to make butter and cheese, and do all the cooking, washing, making, and mending ... and, with the pains of maternity forced upon her every eighteen months, was whipped by her pious husband, 'because she scolded.'"[1]

CASE TWO

Cindy and Tom have been married for seven years. They have a five-year-old son and a daughter, age two. They consider their marriage and family life ideal and say they can't understand what all the shouting about "women's liberation" means. "What is there to be liberated from?" asks Tom. "Women never had it better. Look how nice Cindy has it—just being able to stay at home, be her own boss, have her own hours, while I go out and earn the living! She wouldn't have it any other way, and neither would I. We both like knowing that she's here when the kids need her, and I enjoy coming home to a neat, orderly house and a delicious dinner. Oh don't get me wrong! She isn't my slave or anything. We work together on a lot of household projects on weekends, and I'm always glad to pitch in and help her when she needs me—like helping out with the dishes some evenings when I don't have meetings to attend, or helping put the children to bed."

Cindy agrees that she enjoys her role as full-time homemaker. "I like to sew, and I like to have time to chat with friends on the phone or down at the park while the kids play in the playground. I don't feel at all trapped. Tom gives me an allowance every week in addition to the household money, so I always have spending money that I don't have to account for him for. Really, I like my life and feel I'm fulfilling woman's true role—to love, encourage, and serve my family. And I feel I can help Tom advance in his career best by being just what I am, a loving, devoted wife who supports and backs him up, believes in him, and tries to make life smooth at home. They say that behind every great man is a woman; I want to be that woman in Tom's life."

CASE THREE

Marilyn is an elementary school teacher. Her husband, Al, is the manager of a local department store which is part of a large national chain. Married eighteen years, they have three children, ranging in age from nine to fifteen. When her youngest child reached school age, Marilyn returned to teaching after not having taught for several years, except for serving occasionally as a substitute teacher.

Now back at full-time teaching, Marilyn still does not consider it her primary career. "If Al and I feel the children are being harmed in any way and that they need me at home, I'll not hesitate a moment to give up teaching," she says. "I enjoy my work and it's nice having my income for extra things, but it's not absolutely essential. Al and I believe that the husband should be the main breadwinner. He's the captain and I'm second mate. That means his work takes precedence over mine. For example, if the company asks him to move (and that's happened many times already during our marriage), my teaching position is no reason to insist we stay here. I'm sure I could always find a similar position at our new location; and if not, I'll just stay home and be a good wife and mother. Or I can always put my name on a list for substitute teaching."

CASE FOUR

Janet and Roger both have demanding careers to which they are highly committed. Arriving at a suitable lifestyle for them and their four-year-old daughter has not been easy, but they have determined to work out an equalitarian marriage in the fullest sense of that term. This means that each takes seriously the responsibility of being a parent and giving time and loving attention to Gretchen. They have not assumed that the task of arranging for child care is Janet's task, nor have the necessary funds come from Janet's salary—as though she were the parent holding major responsibility for their child. Rather, both Roger and Janet feel they must *share* the responsibility for Gretchen's needs as well as sharing the responsibility for household chores.

Janet and Roger also feel that they should have equal power in family decision making and that neither one's career is more important than that of the other. Thus, if Janet (a psychology professor) decides to accept an offer from a university in another state, her lawyer husband is willing to leave his lucrative law practice and set up a new practice in the new location (following his wife, in contrast to the traditional custom of a wife following her husband). At the same time, if Roger wanted to pursue some new opportunity (perhaps in politics or as a corporation attorney), Janet is willing to seek employment at some school in the area where Roger's new plans would take him.

UNDERSTANDING THE STRUCTURE OF MARRIAGE

The story of the nineteenth-century authoritarian husband and the modern hypothetical case studies serve to illustrate clearly that people may structure their marriages quite differently.

In defining marriage earlier, we saw that there are two sides to marriage, two main parts of the structure—the practical or instrumental side (earning family income, performing household tasks) and the personal or expressive side (love, sex, empathy, companionship). What goes on in these two areas of marriage is affected by the positions and roles of men and women. The opening four stories showed that marriage may be structured as a relationship between an owner and his property (the nineteenth-century husband who beat his wife to keep her in subjection), or between a head and its complement (Tom and

Cindy), or between a senior partner and junior partner (Al and Marilyn), or between two equal partners (Janet and Roger). Let's examine the basic setup of each of these marital situations.

OWNER-PROPERTY

The story cited in Case 1 was not unusual in the nineteenth century. The husband who used a horsewhip on his wife to keep her in subjection was held by the New York courts to be within his rights. If what was termed "a reasonable instrument" was used, wife beating was legal in almost all states as late as 1850. As social historian Alice Felt Tyler points out, "Women were legally considered perpetual minors; if unmarried, the wards of male relatives; if married, a part of their husband's chattels. . . . In legal status servile and incompetent, by social canon revered and closely guarded, in cold fact a vitally necessary part of a dynamic economic and social system."[2] A married woman and all she possessed (including any earnings she might make) were legally considered to belong to her husband. Her very being was considered to be merged into his; the two were one, and the one was the husband.

Writer Eva Figes speaks of such a concept of marriage as "basically the purchase of sexual favour in return for board and lodging."[3] The limited alternatives for women meant that the bargain was harshly one-sided. From a Marxist perspective, it could be said that men historically have been the ruling or dominant group, the bourgeoisie; women have been the ruled or subordinate group, the proletariat. Helen Campbell, the writer of an 1893 publication on women wage earners, began with "a look backward," to show how "physical facts worked with man's will . . . and early rendered women subordinate physically and dependent economically." She quotes other writers of the period to the effect that "woman at once became property. . . . Marriage . . . became the symbol of transfer of ownership," just as a formal deed signifies a purchaser's right to possess his land. It is *economic dependence on the oppressor,* argues Campbell, that is the basis of all oppression.[4]

Positions and Roles

In the picture of marriage just described, the position of the man is that of owner, and the position of the woman is that of property. This position or status indicates how the two persons stand in relationship to one another. But within this status, each has a distinct part to play—a role.

Under the owner-property arrangement, the woman's major role was that of wife-mother. It was a hyphenated role in more than word only. A woman who was a wife was expected to be a mother as well; there was no notion that wife and mother could be two separate roles. For a married man, the role of husband-father was likewise not separated. If a man were a husband, he was supposed to be a father as well. That his wife should provide him with children was considered furthermore to be one of his basic marital *rights.*

The marriage contract implies both rights and duties for both partners. The rights of one partner may involve having certain duties performed on the part of the other partner. And the duties a spouse carries out may be done in order to assure that the rights of the other spouse are met. For example, in a traditional marriage, a husband might arrive home from work (his *duty* to provide for his family) and expect to find dinner ready (his *right* to have household needs cared for by his wife). His wife on her part has prepared the meal (her *duty* to cook and do other household tasks for her family) because her husband has put in a hard day's work (fulfilling her *right* to be financially supported).

Wife's Duties and Husband's Rights

Under the owner-property arrangement of marriage, the role of wife-mother carried with it certain duties in both the practical and personal sides of marriage. Looking first at her duties within the instrumental or task-oriented dimension (the practical side), we find the following *norms* or expectations of how she was to behave:

1 Her chief task in life was to please her husband and care for his needs and those of the household.
2 She was to obey her husband in all things.
3 She was to bear children that could carry on her husband's name.
4 She was to train the children so that they would reflect credit on her husband.
5 She was to seek no independent existence of her own but rather was to order her life so as to reflect credit on her husband.

From the husband's standpoint, the fulfillment of these norms by his wife was a matter of rights—*his* rights. He considered himself to possess the right to have his wife please him, obey him, care for his household needs, bear him children, and so on. Such rights were inherent in the position of owner.

Two points stand out and summarize the role duties of the wife-mother within the position of property. One, the woman has no existence independent from that of her husband; legally she is considered a nonperson. By definition, she is merely an extension of him—of his interests, desires, needs, wants, ambitions, goals, and so on. Two, the power question is settled and beyond dispute. The husband is boss and the wife must be subject to him. Whenever there is a disagreement or clash of wills, the wife as his property merely submits to her husband's will. By this means, order and stability are maintained. Embedding the authority question in a fixed way within the normative structure of the wife's role duties is considerably different from what we shall observe in other marriage arrangements.

Campbell's classic economic history of women details the scope of household tasks performed by the woman of the preindustrial era. Not only did she have all the childrearing and household maintenance tasks that women have usually done and many still do, she also "had to spin, weave, and bleach; to make all the linen and clothes, to boil soap, to make candles and brew beer. . . . She frequently had to work in the field or garden and to attend to the poultry or cattle."[5]

The question naturally arises: Did women feel oppressed? Most Marxists would probably admit that they did not but would label this as "false consciousness"; that is, women *believed* they were as content as they could reasonably expect to be, but this was a false or inaccurate picture. Further, the Marxist might say that had wives realized just how bad their condition actually was, they simply would have revolted en masse and sought liberation from husband oppression long ago.

It is difficult to know how most wives felt historically in the position of property. A few put their feelings into writing so that we know there was discontent on the part of some. However, not many alternative roles were open to women besides that of wife-mother. Likewise, it is hard to think of alternative images other than the wife-mother role that little girls could observe as they grew up. Recall from Chapter 2 the extensive kinds of sex-role socialization that occurred during that era. It seems likely that most men and women strongly believed in the appropriateness of the marital arrangement as they knew it, the owner-property model with its respective rights and duties for husbands and wives.

Campbell's 1893 study goes to the very heart of the matter as she describes the situation in which women found themselves. "For ages, [the woman's] identity had been merged in that of the man by whose side she worked with no thought of recompense," wrote Campbell. All the traits that were considered "feminine" were expected to be cultivated (submissiveness, clinging affection, humility), while stronger traits such as assertiveness were suppressed. These combined factors stood in the way of any resistance to injustice and mistreatment. Campbell makes her point forcefully: "The mass of women had neither power nor wish to protest; and thus the few traces we find of their earliest connection with labor show us that they accepted bare subsistence as all to which they were entitled, and were grateful if they escaped the beating which the lower order of Englishman still regards as his right to give."[6]

In short, prior to the twentieth century, most women defined the rules of exchange between the sexes to be much more favorable to men than to themselves. In such a setting, wives apparently did not consider the possibility of bargaining or engaging in conflict with their husbands out of a sense of injustice. There is no evidence of attempts to change the obligations and rights of the wife's position and role. Any wives who would have seriously considered deviating from the owner-property arrangement would have found virtually no

In the owner-property arrangement, societal norms sanctioned wife-beating, and there was little women could do about it.

social support. Strong negative sanctions would have been applied by relatives, friends, civil authorities, religious institutions, and of course by their husbands. Thus it mattered little whether or not wives *believed* they were being treated unfairly; there was actually little they could do to alter their situation.

Husband's Duties and Wife's Rights

Having seen the wife's duties (which are also the husband's rights), we might wonder about the husband's duties (and correspondingly, the wife's rights). It is at this point that we discover the most important reason that the owner-property arrangement could be maintained. The husband's chief duty was to provide economic resources for the family's survival and well-being. Because the wife depended on her husband for these essential resources, he had considerable power over her. In other words, her deference was exchanged for his benefits. His power was therefore *doubly* reinforced since it rested both on the norms which prescribed wifely obedience and on the needed benefits with which he supplied his wife.

In exchange, for performing her duties, the wife received her rewards and the fulfillment of her marital rights by being provided for. She also shared in whatever prestige her husband was able to attain. She received acclaim from kin and peers based on her husband's achievements and social status. In addition, she received esteem, support, and approval from others (including her husband) because she performed her own apportioned duties so well. ("What an excellent wife and mother she is!" "She certainly keeps a neat house, and she can bake the tastiest pies in the world!" "She makes sure her children are well-behaved and mannerly, too.")

These exchanges of husband-wife rights and duties constituted an ongoing cycle. The husband's duty to provide fulfilled the wife's right to be provided for. This provision in turn motivated her to continue performing her wife-mother duties, which meant that the husband's rights were thereby fulfilled. Because of this, he continued to feel motivated to keep on providing for her, with the result that there was an uninterrupted fulfillment of role duties in the prescribed fashion. The basis for these role exchanges lay with the husband as owner and the wife as property, with the man's having exclusive access to economic resources and possessing power that men and women believed to be legitimate and right.

Expressive Dimension

All that has been said thus far has concerned the instrumental dimension of marriage with its emphasis on economic provision and task performance. What about the person-oriented side of marriage? Again, thinking in terms of rights and duties, the wife's chief duty in the expressive dimension apparently was to provide sexual gratification for her husband. And it was his right to receive that benefit or resource from her. In exchange, it was likewise his duty to provide sexual benefits to his wife. However, although provision of sex was incumbent on both partners, the quality of sexual performance was probably far less crucial. The husband was not obligated to sexually gratify his wife at a very high level. And the wife was not expected to be particularly sensuous toward her husband; all that mattered was that she be available and "not refuse him his pleasure." Moreover, it is not clear that the spouses were expected to provide one another with a very high degree of other expressive rewards such as companionship and empathy.

Finally, the husband's ultimate power meant that if there were any disagreements over sexual or other expressive matters, the wife simply had to give in to his will and judgment. If she wanted to visit relatives or neighbors and he wanted her to spend the evening at home with him, she did as he said. If he wanted to have sexual intercourse when she was not so inclined, she submitted to his will. Her own degree of expressive satisfaction had little significance for much of anything. The double standard was widely practiced by men; they could get whatever kinds and degrees of sexual satisfactions they desired through prostitutes. Mary Wollstonecraft complained about this as early as 1792 when she published her *Vindication of the Rights of Woman*. She wrote: "Their husbands acknowledge that they are good managers, and chaste wives; but leave home to seek for more agreeable . . . society; and the patient drudge, who fulfills her task, like a blind horse in a mill, is defrauded of her just reward; for the wages due to her are the caresses of her husband."[7] Undoubtedly many wives under the owner-property arrangement felt such deprivation, but there was little they could do except suffer in silence.

HEAD-COMPLEMENT

The positions of husband-as-owner and wife-as-property gradually evolved into those of husband-as-head and wife-as-complement. The kind of marriage Tom and Cindy have in Case 2 is a head-complement arrangement. Here both the wife's rights and the husband's duties increase. No longer is it a one-sided system in which the wife has little more than survival rights (food, shelter, clothing), while the husband reaps countless benefits from her services. In marriages where wives are viewed as complements or counterparts to husbands, the husband is expected to meet his wife's love and affection needs, her desires for sexual pleasure, her yearnings for warm emotional support, companionship, understanding, and open communication. Take Cindy and Tom, for example. Cindy's responsibilities may at first seem similar to those of wives in the "property" arrangement, but an altogether different marital compact is in effect. Tom is *not* considered Cindy's owner or master. In the head-complement bargain, two persons who have chosen to join their lives together decide to organize their living arrangements in a particular, convenient way. The husband fulfills his end of the bargain by going out into the world to earn the family income; the wife fulfills her end by remaining home to care for the house and children.

Freed from the necessity of earning a living, Cindy can give her time and attention to her role as family coordinator, keeper of the hearth, and emotional hub. At the same time, she is often able to arrange time for voluntary activities, thus representing the family in the community through participation in charitable work, religious service, political activities, scouting, and parent-teacher organizations.

Tom, on the other hand, is freed from many responsibilities and encumbrances related to the ordinary demands of daily life (such as meal planning, shopping, cooking, cleaning, washing clothes, sewing on buttons, answering social invitations, writing letters and birthday cards to relatives, and the myriad of other tasks that usually fall to wives). Thus, Tom is enabled to devote more time, attention, and energy to his occupation. He has a helpful, supportive, encouraging wife behind him, making it possible for him to achieve much more than if he had to be on his own. He has someone who fills up something that would be missing from his life otherwise, someone who completes him, rounds out his life—in other words a *complement*. He may fondly speak of Cindy as his "other half."

The marital arrangement in which the husband is the head and the wife is his complement is actually a biological analogy. Just as a human body requires coordination and direction from the head, so the wife needs the guidance of her husband. And just as a head needs a body to carry out its directions and function as a whole body, so the husband needs the support of his wife. This analogy fits the structure-functionalist approach to marriage described in Chapter 1. According to this approach, if the head functions as it is supposed to, and the body functions as complement to the head as it should, then all will be well.

Rights and Duties in the Head-Complement Arrangement

As in the owner-property marriage arrangement, couples who follow the head-complement pattern are expected to fulfill both rights and duties with respect to one another. These rights and duties are associated with the husband-father role and the wife-mother role, and again the *duties* of each spouse serve the *rights* of the other spouse. The norms associated with the spouse roles spell out what the respective duties of the husband and wife are.

Instrumental side of marriage   Looking first at the practical or instrumental side of marriage, we find that most of the norms associated with the wife-mother role under the earlier owner-property marriage arrangement have not changed much. The woman's chief task is still to please her husband and care for the needs of the household. She is still expected to bear and rear children who will carry on the husband's name and be a source of pride and gratification. And she is still expected to find her meaning by living through her husband and children rather than seeking a life of her own. Likewise, she is to make sure that she orders her life so that credit is reflected on her husband. Good complements are expected to bring good compliments!

Yet change has occurred in one of the expected areas of behavior—the issue of obedience. No longer is power rigidly fixed within the established norms as it was under the owner-property arrangement ("Wives must obey their husbands"). Now it becomes somewhat more problematic. The marital power issue is less settled. Gone are the days when the wife was expected to submit to the husband without question.

Instead, as her husband's counterpart, the wife is expected to give final deference. That is, she yields to her husband's will in the end and gives in to his wishes, but before that time she is free to discuss her own opinions on the particular issue. Under the owner-property arrangement, the husband could say, "Do this!" and the wife did it. Now he says, "Let's do this." The wife may reply, "Why?" or "No, I don't think so." The husband in turn asks why his wife feels as she does and then he decides, "We'll do this anyway!" or else, "You're right; maybe we shouldn't."

The final decision is still the husband's. But it differs from his rulership as exercised under the owner-property arrangement because, as head, the husband now takes into consideration the wishes of the wife as complement. To borrow from computer language, we may say that the husband permits the wife to make "inputs" into the husband's decision making. Of course, she may or may not counsel in a particular matter, and he may or may not consult on certain issues. In some cases, the husband may "allow" his wife to make the decisions.

In certain other cases, the two may decide on a course of action jointly. But always the final options are in the husband's hands; he is like a supreme court beyond which no further appeals are possible.

These shifts are subtle but meaningful in that they represent some increase in the wife's participation in power. At the same time, there are corresponding shifts in the husband's *rights.* He has now lost the right to be the absolute ruler. In terms of exchange theory, with its emphasis on costs, rewards, profit, and loss, we may say that the loss of absolute rulership rights has been a cost to the husband. Although he still retains final authority and control, his role is now that of a president in a democracy rather than that of a totalitarian dictator. This loss by no means deprives him of all profit in the marital exchange. He still receives ample rewards from his wife within the instrumental dimension of marriage and retains the rights to receive from her the fulfillment of her duties associated with the wife-mother role as described earlier.

But what about the husband's duties in the instrumental realm? Here again nothing much has changed insofar as his unique obligation to provide for his wife and children is concerned. This access to economic resources continues to be the basis for his still possessing considerable marital power. The wife's rights and rewards associated with her husband's provision for her also remain much the same as before—except for one important shift. In the head-complement pattern, the wife has the right to work—whether or not she exercises that option. With her husband's consent, she may become a wage earner under certain conditions (usually serious economic needs within the family). The existence of the work option elevates her power potential, as we shall see.

Expressive side of marriage   Moving to the expressive or person-oriented dimension of marriage, we see once more the effects of the wife's improved negotiating position. Under the owner-property arrangement, sex was exchanged between the spouses on a duties-rights basis; but the degree of satisfaction was not terribly significant, nor were other aspects of expressiveness, such as companionship and empathy. However, throughout the nineteenth and into the twentieth century, there gradually arose the notion of companionship marriage, with emphasis on the centrality of the "affectionate function." Little by little, it was becoming normative for husbands and wives to be friends and lovers. They were expected to be much more to one another than merely sources of income, status, housekeeping, sexual exchanges, and children. They were expected to enjoy one another as persons, to find pleasure in one another's company, to take one another into confidence and share problems and triumphs, to go places together and do things together.

Couples also came to expect something beyond the old just-go-through-the-motions kind of sex. They wanted sexual intercourse to be gratifying in a new way—an experience more special and delightful than it once was. Husbands and wives were expected to provide for each other's sexual rights in a reciprocal-duty fashion. If the wife did her best to make sure that the sexual expression of love was pleasurable to her husband (thereby performing her duty and fulfilling his right), she expected in turn that her husband would do his best to provide her with sexual pleasure as well (thereby performing his duty and fulfilling her right).

The same was true in serving as sounding boards for one another's problems, or in being open to each other's needs for self-disclosure regarding inmost thoughts and feelings, or in being companions to one another during leisure time. Each had rights and duties in all these areas. All of this was quite different from the former arrangement of owner-property where the emphasis was more on the wife's duties and the husband's rights with regard to sex, with little importance at all attached to companionship, empathy, and being a "best friend" to one's spouse.

One reason that these alterations occurred stemmed from women's sense of expressive inequities. (Recall Mary Wollstonecraft's complaint about wives who felt cheated when deprived of their husbands' caresses. And this was as early as the eighteenth century.) With improved negotiating power derived from economic opportunities and the option to become wage earners, women began pressing for greater rights within the expressive or personal side of marriage, desiring to make the rights-duties exchange more fair and reciprocal. Warm expressive exchanges surely must have been much more difficult to carry out between an "owner" and his "property" under the old system. The status and power differences were just too wide for the spouses to be deep friends very often or very long. But as power differences began to decline with wives in a better bargaining position, changes were gradually brought about in the personal side of marriage, making it more rewarding for both wives and husbands. In exchange terms, the cost (husband's loss of some power) was offset by gains in the expressive dimension.

What brought about the evolution of the owner-property status so that it has changed into the head-complement arrangement? To answer that question, we must look at the increasing economic opportunities afforded women beginning as early as the Colonial period.

Women in the Labor Force up to 1900

As women gained independent access to economic resources, they inevitably improved their bargaining within marriage. Though changes were slight and gradual, women began to realize the inherent contradiction in being able to gain resources on their own while still being considered property of their husbands. In 1848, the first Woman's Rights Convention called attention to numerous grievances, pointing out wrongs perpetrated by men and reinforced by laws men had drawn up. Among the complaints were these: "[Man] has made [the woman], if married, in the eye of the law, civilly dead. He has taken from her all right in property, even to the wages she earns."[8] There were many injustices under such a system. Some husbands even hired out their wives and then appropriated their wages. Such unfair practices gave rise to agitation for new legislation on property rights for married women, and various states began to enact laws that were more equitable.

Even prior to the modern era, some women did have certain limited occupational opportunities. Often such women were single or widowed, and they were involved in the guild system. During the Middle Ages, women worked as cobblers, belt and sweater makers, leather dressers, purse makers, furriers, bakers, saddlers, tanners, goldsmiths, lace makers, and embroiderers of such items as church vestments, hangings for religious display, and coats of arms. In some areas of Europe, guild records indicate that over 200 occupations were open to women.[9] But when the guild system ended, women lost the few opportunities they had begun to possess.

During the Colonial period in America (from 1620 to 1776), there were almost no female wage earners, except for those employed in domestic service. A few women did engage in home-based spinning and weaving and other types of work associated with textiles and clothing production. A woman named Betsy Metcalf discovered that meadow grass could be bleached and braided into straw goods, and this process led to a large and lucrative industry. And the American Revolution, like all wars, saw wives step into positions of heading family businesses and farms temporarily vacated by their husbands.

It should be kept in mind that this historical description refers chiefly to white women. The great majority of black women were laboring as slaves on Southern plantations. And just as it was cotton that kept black women in slavery past the 1790s, so it was cotton that at that time altered economic opportunities for white women. According to Campbell, "It is with the birth of the cotton industry that the work and wages of women begin to take coherent shape." For the first time in history, large and ever-increasing numbers of women began to get out from under their own domestic roofs to work under commercial roofs (spinning mills), earning sums of money hitherto unknown. In this version of the factory system, women from the beginning took a larger part than men. For example, in the first federal count of spinning-industry employees in 1816, there were 66,000 women and female children. There were 24,000 boys under seventeen years of age, and 10,000 males seventeen years and older.[10]

The women who worked in those New England factories throughout the first half of the nineteenth century were mostly young, single, and poorly educated. Their wages were about half or a third of those paid to men. Nevertheless, the numbers of women engaged in a variety of occupations continued to increase throughout the nineteenth century. The mechanization necessary to carry on the Civil War created a whole new series of trade-type occupations, and the reduced numbers of available men made it possible for many women to enter these newly emerging trades.

Exactly how many women were working is hard to answer accurately because the Census Bureau had difficulty getting families to admit that they contained employed females. This hesitancy was due to fear of disapproval, since many persons considered female employment undesirable and frowned on women who dared to deviate from tradition. The 1870 census recorded the number of women workers as 1,836,288. But it seems evident that there were additional women workers who were not enumerated. By 1880, the figure had risen to 2,647,157; but again there was concern about underreporting. The 1890 census showed a 10 percent increase in women wage earners over the 1880 figure. By 1900, 21 percent of all women over fourteen years of age were employed, although only 6 percent of all married women were working.[11]

That 6-percent figure for married working women is probably higher than anything that occurred in the prior century, and the record in this century has been one of dramatic change upward in the actual numbers and proportion of working wives. By 1940, the proportion had doubled to 14 percent and by 1960 doubled again to 31 percent. That the trend for married women to work outside the home has continued may be seen in the 1970 census figures, which showed that 38 percent of all white married women and half of all black married women were in the labor force.[12]

This steady increase in access to and control of economic resources by *married* women is perhaps the most significant point about the 200-year upward trend in female employment. The availability of work opportunities and the chance to gain resources on their own caused wives to question the existing marital-role structures. They began demanding more rights, more of a voice in decision making, more control over their own property, and so on. During the nineteenth and twentieth centuries, numerous legal changes gradually took place which played a large part in removing the wife from the position of property and recognizing her as more of a person in her own right.[13] When women were permitted to inherit, earn, control, and dispose of their own property to a greater measure than before, the traditional marriage arrangement was profoundly affected. The changes brought about in marital-role structures (increased rights and power for women) in turn would affect still further labor-force participation by women (with more women feeling they had the right to work outside the home); and again in feedback fashion, this would affect marriages still further (with increased power for wives because of their increased economic resources).

What we see at work here is the principle of alternative rewards described in Chapter 4. A person's power over another person depends on the resources he or she holds out to that person, how dependent that second person is on these resources, and whether or not that second person can find alternate sources for such benefits elsewhere. At the beginning of the nineteenth century, a woman had few options open to her besides marriage. If she wanted to be provided for, she needed a husband. This gave men a tremendous amount of power over

220   HARPER'S WEEKLY.   [MAY 16, 1868.

HOW IT WOULD BE, IF SOME LADIES HAD THEIR OWN WAY.

Various economic and legal changes meant a gradual recognition of women as persons in their own right, causing profound changes in the marital balance of power.

women. Utterly dependent upon her husband for economic resources, the wife became his property and he held rights of ownership over her. However, as employment opportunities increased for women, a woman could provide for her own needs. She was no longer dependent on a man. Why sit idly by waiting to get married when one could engage in the numerous occupational pursuits opening up to women? As the nineteenth century ended, almost half (46 percent) of all single women were employed.

Although it was true that only 6 percent of married women worked outside the home and their rates of employment increased more slowly than those of single women, the *availability* of employment had a considerable impact on even those wives who didn't choose to enter the labor force. As the nineteenth century progressed, there opened up the possibility of choosing another set of rewards than those held out by husbands, and the existence of that option weakened the power of husbands—whether or not their wives actually worked. The *possibility* of a wife's becoming a wage earner gradually became part of the role rights of the wife-mother, thereby putting married women in a position where they had the capability of bargaining instead of merely yielding to their husbands' wishes. Women were no longer bound to unquestioning obedience out of a sense of helpless dependence on male economic support. Instead, wives could offer suggestions, disagree, counsel and advise, even try to insist on a particular course of action.

In moving from her status as property, the married woman could go in one of two directions. (See Figure 6-1.) The existence of the option to work meant she could stay at home to look after the household and be her husband's counterpart or *complement,* or she could work outside the home and thereby take on what we shall call the *junior-partner* status in marriage. In either case, the fact that the option to work was always there meant that her negotiating power in marriage was increased.

SENIOR PARTNER AND JUNIOR PARTNER

When a wife is employed, her position as complement is changed to that of junior partner; and correspondingly, the husband's position as head is changed to that of senior partner in the relationship. This shift results from the economic inputs the wife now brings to the marriage. Her income means that she is no longer totally dependent on her husband for survival; and furthermore, at least part of the family's living standard is attributable to her resources.

She also is likely to have more power in marital decision making because, as various studies have shown, working wives tend to use their resources as a way of obtaining more bargaining leverage.[14] For some employed wives, this leverage may not be used often or at all; but the potential is always there. The wife is bringing money into the home just as the husband is, and she can always use that fact to gain what she feels is right in a particular decision. For example, since she has helped earn the money, she wants to have a voice in how it is used. She may point out the unfairness of her husband's insistence on making huge expenditures without consulting her, particularly when she knows such expenditures would be impossible without her contributions to the family income. Or on the other hand, she might object to her husband's nagging about the price of her new dress even though it was purchased out of her own earnings rather than out of some "allowance" from him as in the days when she was a complement. She might suggest ways they can negotiate about financial arrangements, perhaps coming to the conclusion that they should have separate bank accounts. Or they may decide on a plan in which each puts so much into family support and household needs and keeps another amount set aside for personal use, and so on.

The point to be stressed is that the actual or potential power stemming from a wife's employment removes her from the position of being an adjunct to a benevolent head whose ultimate jurisdiction is undisputed. As a junior partner, the wife has a greater share in the power and the husband a lesser share than in the other marital arrangements discussed. In the terminology of economics that lies behind exchange theory, we might say that the wife's *gain* in power (stepping up into partnership) becomes the husband's *loss* in power (stepping down from headship). This does not mean of course that there are not gains for him also—such as in the greater monetary resources now available to the family.

It must be kept in mind that power, in economics terminology, is a "scarce good." It is something that is limited in supply. How this commodity is divided up depends upon the respective resources of the bargainers. With the wife's

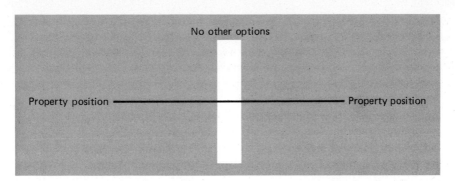

Where no alternatives existed for women, the property status continued in an ongoing line, as though a ray of light were passing through a plain sheet of glass, remaining unchanged.

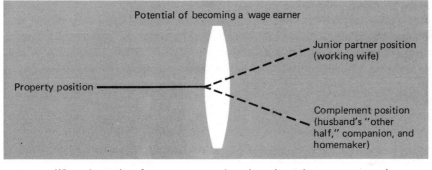

When alternatives for women opened up through employment opportunities and options, the property position "line" was bent like a ray of light passing through a special lens, bending it in two directions.

Figure 6-1 The movement away from the wife's position as property.

greater access to the opportunity system, her resources for bargaining are increased, and so is her power. However, the husband still commands more power than his wife; because, although he is a partner rather than a head, he is the *senior* partner in the relationship. He continues to be viewed as the family's chief provider and is the one through whom the family derives its social status. But now the distance between the positions held by him and his wife is narrowed, and his power is not quite so final and definitive as in the head-complement arrangement.

Al and Marilyn, the department-store manager and schoolteacher in Case 3 at the beginning of this chapter, illustrate the senior partner–junior partner arrangement. Their marriage displays several characteristics that are common in this structural form. First, there is Marilyn's moving in and out of the labor force. She worked in the early years of marriage, then dropped out until the youngest entered school, then returned to work again. Second, there is a lack of commitment to her career. If she feels she is needed at home, Marilyn says she won't hesitate to give up teaching. If her husband's company wants to transfer him, she is ready to move and take her chances at finding another teaching position in the new location. If she can't find a suitable job, she is willing simply to be a homemaker.

Third, the priority of the husband's career is emphasized. "Al and I believe that the husband should be the main breadwinner," Marilyn says. "That means his work takes precedence over mine." Al earns considerably more than Marilyn does, and with this higher income comes a higher degree of power in family decision making. "He's the captain and I'm second mate," reports Marilyn. Furthermore, the family's social status derives primarily from Al and his position in the company rather than from Marilyn's schoolteaching.

The rights-duties exchange in a marriage where the spouses follow the senior partner–junior partner pattern is quite similar to that of the head-complement pattern. The main difference is in the wife's increased power and the husband's lessened power in marital decision making. Her working and bringing in income means greater influence in both instrumental and expressive matters. However, it is still considered her duty to fulfill her wife-mother role in caring for the children and looking after household matters—although the husband might (when it is convenient) be more willing to help with such tasks than is the case under the head-complement arrangement where the wife is considered a fulltime homemaker. But it is still considered the husband's right to have these domestic duties performed by his wife.

Likewise, the *primary* responsibility for providing for the family is still assigned to the husband. It is still the wife's right to have the husband support her (even though she might contribute to that support), and it is the husband's duty to be the main breadwinner (thereby freeing his junior partner to go in and out of the job market in a way that he cannot). In the expressive or person-oriented side of marriage, the rights-duties exchange is identical to that of the head-complement arrangement (except again for increased power on the part of the wife). Each partner has the right to receive and the duty to give marital rewards in the form of sex, empathy, and companionship.

Movement between Positions

The example of Al and Marilyn shows clearly that there is not some kind of chronological progression between the positions of head-complement and those of senior partner–junior partner. Rather, many wives (such as Marilyn) move back and forth between the junior partner and complement statuses, with their husbands correspondingly moving from senior partner to head and vice versa. Young wives often work at the beginning of marriage and are thus classified as junior partners. Many of them subsequently drop out of the labor force (usually to have their first child) and are thus reclassified as complements. After a period of time, they may return to work in order to help meet expenses, particularly the increased expense of rearing a child, and once again these women are junior partners. But they may go back to the complement status a year or two later—often because they wish to give personal care to the child or else because of the birth of a second child.

This type of shifting in and out of the labor force continues to occur among women past their twenties. And since most American women have by age thirty borne all the children they will ever bear, it appears that such shifting is not due chiefly to childbearing, though of course this is an important factor. However, the off-and-on labor-force participation by junior-partner wives beyond the childbearing age may simply indicate that these women do not share the same kind of work commitment that is true of their husbands. Except under certain circumstances (injuries, illnesses, work layoffs, etc.), men do not start and stop repeatedly their participation in the labor force. Yet, when a national sample of married women aged thirty to forty-four was surveyed twice in the period from 1967 to 1969, it was found that among white women, 37 percent worked consistently, 40 percent did not work at all, and 23 percent fluctuated.[15] In other words, out of 60 percent of white women who were in the labor force sometime during the three-year period, more than one-third of them participated in the labor force in an off-and-on manner. Among black married women in the sample, more than half were employed consistently during that time (51 percent), only 22 percent did not work at all, and 27 percent worked off and on. Since more black married women than white women work (more than three-quarters of the black married women in this sample, including the group that fluctuated during the three years), it means that at any given time we may expect to find more junior partners among married blacks than among married whites.

Even so, a substantial proportion of women within both color groups are not employed, still another proportion get a job, quit, get another job, quit again, and so on. The lesser commitment to work on the part of many women as compared to men is due to many factors. Social pressures and sex-role stereotypes have meant that females are not socialized to be committed to careers. Since men still have the major responsibility to be family breadwinners, there is not the same compulsion for women to work. By the same token, males are not given the option of *not* working. Their work commitment is reinforced by necessity and is not only a matter choice.

Furthermore, since the major responsibility for child care and domestic chores has traditionally fallen on wives, some women may begin to wonder if the physical and psychological drain of two jobs (homemaking and employment) is worth it. Thus, they quit for awhile until restlessness or a desire to earn some extra money drives them temporarily back into the labor force once again.

As we have seen, moving in and out of the labor force means marital statuses shift back and forth as well. It is quite likely that the negotiating advantages of junior partnership increase the longer and more consistently the wife works. A wife who has worked steadily for five years may be expected to have greater marital power than a wife who has been in and out of several jobs during that same period. Why? Because between jobs the latter wife repeatedly shifted into the complement position and thereby moved her husband into the position of head, while the wife with a steady employment pattern remained in the junior-partner position.

Factors Associated with Wives' Employment

Viewing a subject from the standpoint of demography (the study of population characteristics) helps us get an overall picture. By examining national census data, we can discover some of the factors associated with the employment of married women. Race, for example, is one such demographic factor.

Race   Black wives are more likely to work than are white wives.[16] This reflects the combined effects of historical and current patterns discussed earlier—the long-standing economic discrimination against black males which forced black females into the labor force and the resultant norms which grew up among blacks so that female employment came to be accepted and respected.

Many black wives work because they have to rather than because they necessarily want to. Sociologist Ivan Nye has pointed out that "for minority families, those without an employed wife are moderately deprived with respect to other minority families and extremely deprived compared to whites."[17] (The term *minority* is used to designate the census category "blacks and other races," which is made up of 90 percent blacks.) In 1971, the average income for all minority families was $8,157; but if the wife was employed at some time during the year, the average income was $10,339. Among minority families where the wife worked full-time, the average income was $13,259, an amount higher than the average family income for all white families that year ($11,551).[18] It is clear that the wife's income makes a significant difference among those groups who otherwise would be granted fewer rewards from the economic-opportunity system.

On the other hand, black wives work not only because they have to but because in many cases they want to. Since among blacks it is normative for women to work, black females grow up expecting to work. A study undertaken by the United States Department of Labor indicated that black women more than white women were committed to the idea of paid employment even if their financial situation made it unnecessary. In an attempt to measure attitudes toward work, women in the age range of thirty to forty-four years were asked: "If by some chance you (and your husband) were to get enough money to live

TABLE 6-A PROPORTION OF EMPLOYED RESPON-
DENTS WHO WOULD WORK IF THEY RECEIVED ENOUGH
MONEY TO LIVE ON WITHOUT WORKING, BY OCCUPA-
TION AND COLOR (PERCENT)

Occupation	White	Nonwhite
Professional and managerial	74	76
Clerical and sales	60	62
Blue collar	45	59
Domestic service	40	66
Nondomestic	56	74
Farm	57	84
Total or average	59	67

Source: U.S. Department of Labor, 1970, *Dual Careers,*
Vol. I, No. 21, p. 174.

comfortably without working, do you think you would work anyway?" In such a
hypothetical situation, black women at all socioeconomic levels were interested
in continuing to work to a greater extent than was true of white women, with the
exception of those white women in higher-level occupations, who also indicated high work commitment. (See Table 6-A.)

The commitment to work that is generally found among highly educated
women regardless of race is especially pronounced among blacks. Black
women with four years or more of college are represented in the labor force "in
the highest proportions of any female group," reports Nye.[19]

Work, women, and children   In analyzing census data on the participation of
women in the labor force, demographer Malcolm S. Cohen concluded that of all
demographic factors associated with a married woman's working, it is the
number of children she has and how young they are that most influence her
employment behavior.[20]

One fact that emerges from census data is that employed women tend to
have fewer children than women who are not employed. This finding could be
explained by either assuming that women who want to work choose to limit their
family size so that employment is possible or easier, or one could argue that
women who have larger numbers of children are not in the labor force (even if
they would like to be) because child-care responsibilities at home act as barriers
to employment. In other words, does having children keep women from
employment, or does employment keep women from having as many children?
These questions will be discussed more fully in a later chapter on reproduction.

Of course, many women with children *do* work—even women whose
children are quite young. In 1950, some 12 percent of mothers with children
under six years of age were working. By 1960, the figure had jumped to 19
percent; and by the end of that decade, it had increased another third to 30

Staying home to care for young children is not an option for migrant workers.

percent. Table 6-B shows the changes in labor force participation by married women which have taken place since 1950. Notice that half of those mothers with children between the ages of six and seventeen are employed—an even higher percentage than among those with no children under eighteen years of age and where home responsibilities would be less.

Women who have no children or whose children are grown may find that their husbands' income is adequate for the standard of living they wish to maintain. But for others, the presence of children brings economic burdens. In order to make possible a certain desired standard of living, the family may find that two incomes will be necessary. Thus, the wife goes to work full or part-time in order to buy that new freezer or color television or to help with the house or car payments. In addition, there are of course the direct costs of childrearing— providing for food, clothing, medical and dental needs, savings for college, and so on. Families with preschoolers face childrearing expenses also, of course; but in these cases the woman considering employment is hindered by the problem of finding a mother-substitute to look after her children while she is gone. Mothers of school-age children simply find it much easier to enter the labor force.

TABLE 6-B LABOR-FORCE PARTICIPATION RATES* OF MARRIED WOMEN, HUSBAND PRESENT, BY PRESENCE AND AGE OF CHILDREN FOR SELECTED YEARS BETWEEN 1950 AND 1972

Date	No Children under 18 Years	Children 6 to 17 Years Only	Children under 6 Years
March 1950	30.3	28.3	11.9
April 1955	32.7	34.7	16.2
March 1960	34.7	39.0	18.6
March 1965	38.3	42.7	23.3
March 1970	42.2	49.2	30.3
March 1972	42.7	50.2	30.1

*Percent of civilian noninstitutional population in the labor force.

Source: From Department of Labor, *Manpower Report of the President,* 1973, p. 168.

The presence of preschoolers in the family does not affect the work status of black women as much as is true of white women. (See Table 6-C.) Again, this finding relates to economic need and the higher proportion of family income that is provided by these wives. It is also related to the tradition and norms supporting female employment among blacks.

One of the most fascinating ways of observing trends and changes is to study the same group or panel of persons over a period of time. Sociologists call such studies *panel studies* or *longitudinal studies* (since the study takes place for some years and is in that sense a ''lengthwise'' study in contrast to ''crosswise'' surveys where a sample is drawn and information is obtained from a one-time interview only). In one longitudinal study, a large national sample of both black and white thirty-to-forty-four-year-old women were interviewed over the three-year period between 1967 and 1969 in an effort to learn how

TABLE 6-C LABOR-FORCE STATUS OF EVER MARRIED WOMEN, 15 TO 49 YEARS OLD BY RACE AND PRESENCE OF YOUNG CHILDREN, 1973

Ever Married Women Aged 15 to 49 Years	Percent in Labor Force	
	Black	White
With own children under 5 years old	49%	32%
Without own children under 5 years old	66	58

Source: Adapted from U.S. Bureau of the Census, 1974, *Current Population Reports,* P-23, no. 48, p. 95.

labor-market participation is influenced by changes in marital status, age composition of children, and so on. In 1969, the researchers found significant increases in employment among women who in 1967 had reported having children under six years of age at home but who did not have children in this age range by 1969. In other words, when the children went to school, the mothers went to work. On the other hand, there was a decrease in employment among those wives who had reported no children under six in 1967 but who had preschoolers in the home by 1969.[21]

Maternal employment and effects on children   A question often arises at this point: How are children likely to be affected by their mother's employment? Until rather recently, the belief was widely held that children of working mothers would suffer emotional damage and be hindered in their development because of the long, daily physical separation from their mothers. However, in the 1960s, behavioral-science research brought to light findings that go a long way toward dispelling such beliefs. In various studies, as children of working and nonworking mothers were tested and compared, no important differences showed up. The evidence did not suggest that a mother's employment in itself has detrimental effects on her children. Psychological testing was used in order to compare the anxiety scores and personality-adjustment scores of children whose mothers were in the labor force and of children whose mothers were full-time housewives. In addition, social scientists compared children's school grades, observed their social and emotional development, and so on. Some studies focused on preschoolers and others on school-age children. But all in all, the findings did not support the old notion that a woman's working will somehow harm her children.[22]

But what about adolescents? Sociologist Ivan Nye, after a questionnaire survey of 2,350 high school students in the state of Washington, concluded from the evidence that if the familiar "concept of the neglected, maladjusted child of the employed mother has any validity, the effects involved are small." He concluded: "School performance, psychosomatic symptoms, and affectional relationship to the mother appear unrelated to employment status of the mother. A small association appears to be present between employment status and delinquent behavior."[23] The one negative finding in this sample, somewhat higher delinquency among teenage children of employed mothers, involved such things as truancy, ungovernability, petty theft, vandalism, driving without a license, and offenses involving sex and alcohol. Although there was more delinquent behavior among children of employed mothers than among children of unemployed mothers, the differences were not large. In rural areas, the delinquent behavior of adolescents whose mothers were employed was higher than in urban areas.

In a separate analysis of children from broken homes only, Nye found no significant differences between those whose mothers were employed and those whose mothers were not employed with respect to school grades, psychosomatic symptoms, delinquent behavior, and affectional relationship to the mother. In this sample, it will be noted, "no association was found between delinquent behavior and employment status of the mother."[24]

Nye's findings were reported in a 1963 book coauthored with Lois Wladis Hoffman. Entitled *The Employed Mother in America,* it attempted to gather together all available relevant research on the subject of maternal employment conducted between 1957 and 1962. Ten years after the book was published, Hoffman wrote: "The working mother had been considered quite a devil, and a great deal of the research reported in the book had originally been undertaken in the hope of documenting the ill effects of maternal employment. But the data simply would not cooperate."[25]

She points out that it really shouldn't have been surprising that "examined as a general phenomenon, the standard study with adequate controls yielded no significant differences between the children of working and nonworking women," because maternal employment in itself is too wide a variable to study. All kinds of women work at all kinds of different jobs, under various conditions, with children of different ages, and so on. Such things as these would have to be considered. Hoffman points out that we may expect differences in effects of a mother's working according to whether the woman is a member of the working class or the middle class, whether she works out of necessity or out of choice, whether her children are younger or older, boys or girls. Other important considerations are the hours the woman works, the plans she makes for her household, child-care arrangements, her attitudes about her role, and so on. "But even those studies which introduced such breakdowns found few negative effects and several positive ones," Hoffman reports.

She does however, refer to one study that "suggested a bit of caution." In a study she conducted of working mothers of elementary school children, she found that children whose mothers feel *guilty* about working may be negatively affected. It is not the mother's employment in itself that seems to cause the problem, but rather the mother's attitude toward it and how she responds.

Hoffman found that some women who enjoyed working felt guilty about this and evidently tried to compensate by overindulging their children. For example, children of these mothers helped less around the house than children of nonworking mothers and were indulged in other ways as well. The results of this showed up in their interactions with other children and in their school performances. The children of mothers who worked and felt guilty about it "played more with younger children than with their age mates; they were less likely to initiate interaction with their classmates; their academic performance was not up to par." It is important to note that "the women who liked their work were more typically—though not exclusively—the middle class, and better educated." Thus, Hoffman's conclusions are significant: "These are almost the only negative effects of maternal employment found in the middle class to date, and they appear to result not from employment *per se* but from guilt about employment."[26]

On the other hand, writes Hoffman, there is considerable support for the idea that maternal employment can have a positive effect, particularly on girls. The daughters of high-achieving women are also likely to be high-achieving and to have less restrictive self-concepts because of the role models their mothers provide. Such girls are less apt to limit their career horizons because of gender-role stereotypes.[27]

With regard to the effects of a mother's working on sons, there is little data available except for a few very limited studies. Hoffman refers, for example, to a study of a small sample of gifted boys. The low achievers in the group had more employed mothers, but the high achievers had more mothers who were *professionally* employed—that is, they were women who did not merely hold a job but were committed to a career in a profession.[28]

Working wives and education   Education is another important demographic variable associated with female employment. In general, it may be stated that the higher a woman's education, the greater the likelihood that she will be in the labor force. (See Table 6-D.)

At first, it might seem surprising to note that better-educated wives are employed in higher percentages than are those with lower education, where family financial needs may seem greater. Again, it is a matter of rewards and costs. The more years of schooling a woman has, the more her market value is increased and the greater the earnings available to her. Furthermore, the better educated she is, the more likely she is to find employment in jobs that are professional-technical, managerial, or clerical—jobs that economists William Bowen and T. Aldrich Finegan refer to as "more desirable" in that they "offer more psychic income" than do other kinds of jobs.[29] In other words, highly trained women are attracted to the labor force because of both the tangible and intangible rewards it offers them.

Many such women point out that the rewards outweigh the costs— particularly the costs of leaving children and arranging for child care when there are preschoolers at home. One professor, who in 1974 hired a professional nurse for eighty-five dollars a week to care for her two-week-old infant, explained: "I could feel my mind deteriorating with all that baby talk when I was at home. When you've invested so much time in your schooling, it goes counter to everything not to handle both worlds at once. I felt a responsibility to my students and my career." And an operations officer for Bankers Trust cut short the six months' maternity leave offered her, saying that staying home made her feel she was never doing anything and caused her to feel drained of energy. "The four months I spent at home seemed like four years," she reported.[30] To these women the psychic costs of not being in the labor force are greater than the financial costs of baby-sitting arrangements.

However, the opportunity system does not offer lower-educated women the prized rewards it offers the highly educated. In the first place, jobs for those with little schooling are scarce, and even when they can be found, they are low

TABLE 6-D LABOR-FORCE PARTICIPATION RATES FOR WOMEN 18 YEARS OF AGE AND OVER BY EDUCATIONAL ATTAINMENT, MARCH 1972

Years of School Completed	Black and Other Races*	White
Total percentage of women employed	50.4	43.5
Elementary: 8 years or less	33.2	24.2
High school: 1 to 3 years	47.8	38.9
4 years	62.0	49.4
College: 1 to 3 years	59.9	48.0
4 years or more	78.0	59.1

*Persons of all other races than white. Ninety percent of this category is black.

Source: U.S. Bureau of the Census 1973, *Current Population Reports,* P-23, no. 46, p. 45.

paying. Furthermore, jobs open to women without skills and training do not offer "psychic income" in the form of prestige, power, enhanced self-esteem, opportunities for creative expression, and the enjoyment of interesting work. To such women, the costs of working may seem to outweigh the limited rewards—particularly the costs involved in leaving their children. Among whites especially, gender-role socialization in blue-collar families and underclass homes prepares females to think of motherhood and homemaking as being the major sources of gratification in a woman's life. Being a junior partner may seem less rewarding to these women than being a complement. Hence the kind of statement sometimes made by women with fewer years of education who cannot understand some of the goals of feminism: "I can't for the life of me see why those women want to get out and get a job when they have husbands who can support them! I've *had* to work for many years and believe me, I'd give anything just to be able to stay home with my kids all day. That's what liberation would be to me."

Working wives and husbands' income   For some decades, government studies have shown a clear relationship between a married woman's employment behaviors and her husband's income. The more income a husband has had, the less has been the likelihood that his wife would be employed.[31] However, the trend seems to be changing; many working wives do not come from marriages in which the husband is financially less advantaged but rather from marriages where the husband may be relatively well-off. In recent years, the greatest gains in wife employment have been among higher-income families. Between 1951 and 1969, the percent of families with working wives in which the family income was in the $10,000–$14,999 bracket increased from 38 to 47 percent. In the $15,000-and-over family-income bracket, the percent of families in which the wife was working (and whose earnings were a part of that income) more than doubled—from 22 percent in 1951 to 52 percent in 1969.[32] Another way of stating this is to say that, out of all families with an annual income in 1969 of $15,000 or more, there were employed wives contributing to that amount in more than half of these families.

But *how much* does the wife contribute to the family income? Half? A third? Or what? Again, it is helpful to look at some government figures, particularly some based on studies in the decade between 1958 and 1968. Immediately, we notice that the contribution of the working wife (as junior partner) to the family income remains considerably below that of the husband. In 1958, the median percent of family income accounted for by the wife's earnings was 20 percent. Ten years later, it had risen to 27 percent.[33]

Table 6-E illustrates the way in which the *percentage* of the family income contributed by the wife changes according to the amount the husband earns. The greater the husband's earnings, the smaller is the proportion of the family income provided by the wife's earnings. For example, if a husband's income in 1967 was $25,000 or more, the wife's median income was 10 percent of what her

TABLE 6-E　HUSBAND-WIFE FAMILIES BY SELECTED EARNINGS CHARACTERISTICS OF WIFE, BY TOTAL MONEY EARNINGS IN 1967 OF HUSBAND

Earnings of Husband	Number of Husband-Wife Families (thousands)	Percent of Husband-Wife Families with Wife Having Earnings	Median Earnings of Wife with Earnings	Ratio of Wife's Median Earnings to Husband's Estimated Median Earnings*
Total with earnings	38,955	48%	$2,600	0.37
$1 to $999 or loss	1,537	45	1,700	3.33
$1,000 to $1,999	1,516	48	1,900	1.28
$2,000 to $2,999	1,651	55	1,900	0.77
$3,000 to $3,999	2,490	56	2,100	0.59
$4,000 to $4,999	3,205	56	2,500	0.55
$5,000 to $5,999	4,303	54	2,700	0.49
$6,000 to $6,999	4,819	55	2,700	0.41
$7,000 to $7,999	4,672	50	2,900	0.38
$8,000 to $9,999	6,222	48	2,800	0.31
$10,000 to $14,999	5,907	39	2,800	0.23
$15,000 to $24,999	2,009	31	3,100	0.16
$25,000 and over	624	25	3,600	0.10

*Husband's earnings estimated at midpoint of income interval shown in col. 1. Husband's median earnings for the $25,000-and-over class were estimated at $36,000.

Source: U.S. Bureau of the Census, 1969, *Current Population Reports,* P-60, no. 64, p. 2.

husband earned. If he earned $25,000, she earned $2,500; and the combined family income was $27,500. But if the husband's income was $8,000, the wife's earnings were 31 percent of the amount he earned, bringing the total family income up to $10,480.

The actual amount in dollars is not really that different among the wives in the various income categories (the median income for all working wives in 1967 was $2,600), but such an amount would account for a larger share of earnings in a family with total income of $5,000 than in one where total earnings add up to $30,000. In speaking of median income, it must be kept in mind that as many women earned above $2,600 as earned under that amount. Some women at the higher status levels earn much higher incomes because of their educational background and skills, whereas other women at this same level earn very little—often because they work only part-time and not out of necessity. On the other hand, women at lower status levels who do not have educational advantages may work full-time out of necessity and yet bring home similar earnings to those of more advantaged wives who are in and out of the job market or working only part-time.

Another way of looking at the working wife's contribution to total family income is shown in Table 6-F, where the average 1972 earnings of both blacks and whites are compared, as well as the overall percentages of family income provided by wives.

Working wives and husbands' attitudes   In the longitudinal study of thirty-to-forty-four-year-old women referred to earlier, it became clear that whether or not a married woman is employed is strongly related to how her husband feels about the matter. At the time of the first interview during the three-year study,

TABLE 6-F   EARNINGS IN 1972 OF HUSBAND AND WIFE FOR FAMILIES IN WHICH BOTH HUSBAND AND WIFE HAD EARNINGS

Earnings of Husband and Wife and Work Experience of Wife	Black	White
Mean family income	$12,387	$15,432
Mean earnings of husband	7,349	9,996
Mean earnings of wife	4,014	3,932
Earnings as a percent of family income	32%	26%
Wife worked 50 to 52 weeks	$5,299	$5,601
Earnings as a percent of family income	43%	36%

Source: U.S. Bureau of the Census, 1974, *Current Population Reports,* P-23, no. 48, p. 27.

wives who thought their husbands were positive or at least neutral toward the idea of working wives were more likely to be employed than wives who perceived their husbands' attitudes on the subject to be negative.

The influence of the husband's attitude becomes even more clear in the fact that by 1969 there were substantial increases in the proportion of employed women from among the group who in 1967 had indicated that their husbands approved of a wife's working. Evidently the knowledge that their husbands would not object to their seeking a job encouraged them to take steps toward that end. In contrast, among those wives who in 1967 reported husbands' disapproval of a married woman's working, there was a decrease in the percentage of labor-force participation by 1969.[34]

Another study found that among households where wives worked, the greater the husband's education the more likely he was to feel positively about the wife's working, and the more likely the wife was to *think* that her husband felt positively.[35] Less-educated men are more likely to hold negative views about wife employment, probably because they feel that a wife's holding a job could be interpreted as a failure on the husband's part.

Since the income of less-educated men is lower than that of men with more education, their wives' income makes up a higher proportion of total family income. These earnings and the wife's participation in the labor force may be viewed as threatening to the husband's self-esteem. Such men may believe that wife employment casts aspersions on their attainments as men. "After all," they may reason, "what kind of man is it who can't support his own family? A real man should be able to make ends meet without having to send his wife out to work!" If a man has negative feelings toward employment for married women (no matter what his own education level happens to be), he is likely to voice his displeasure and try to influence his wife not to work.

But why should we expect some husbands to feel threatened and resentful about wife employment? Why can't they be glad for the added income or take pride in a wife's accomplishments or rejoice in the newfound satisfaction she is experiencing in her job? Recall that in terms of conflict theory men may be viewed as a dominant group and women as a subordinate group. A dominant group that feels it is losing power may seek to put a stop to such erosion. Thus, the issue of a married woman's working comes to be viewed as a challenge to male dominance. A negative reaction sets in because many men are reluctant to give up the power and privilege that have been associated with the traditional male role of sole provider.

Psychologist Daniel Yankelovich suggests that "for the approximately one out of five men who say that their work fills their psychological as well as their economic need (primarily in the professional and managerial categories), a working wife is no threat, especially when her economic contribution is not needed." However, for the noncollege majority, claims Yankelovich, a wage-earning wife could appear threatening by making the husband's work seem less valuable. For a man whose "job is just a job," providing few psychological rewards, daily labor is made worthwhile through priding himself on all the hard work and personal sacrifices entailed in taking care of his family's material needs. "Accepting these hardships reaffirms his role as the family provider and hence as a true man." For such a man, a wife's working deprives him of the unique breadwinning function that is so bound up in his concept of masculinity.[36]

In research among low-income Puerto Rican families in New York City, social scientist Oscar Lewis found that notions of *machismo* or manliness characteristic of Latin cultures make it especially difficult for husbands to accept the idea of a wife's employment even though such income may be sorely needed. "The new-found independence of the working wife was probably the greatest source of domestic conflict among the sample families in New York," reports Lewis, adding that the conflict often was so intense that violence erupted and wife beating was quite common. The Puerto Rican husbands in the study were accustomed to being in control of both the family in general and the family finances in particular. Wives who worked no longer found it necessary to rely on their husbands for household and personal expenses. In addition, these wives had a new freedom to do as they wished and go where they pleased. Husbands resented such independence for wives, while wives for their part demanded more equal rights in the household. "The strains on family relationships were often severe," Lewis writes, "and almost every informant commented upon this problem."[37] A psychologist who has given attention to Mexican-American families also refers to strains in family relationships that are occurring in male-dominant Chicano society as more and more women are unwilling to accept the traditional roles assigned them.[38]

Our own research indicates that husbands who hold more egalitarian sex-role norms are more favorable to wives' employment than are husbands who hold more traditional ideas about gender roles.[39] Traditionalism and egalitarianism were measured according to how much respondents agreed or disagreed with various statements about a wife's role. The more strongly that husbands believe a married woman's most important task in life is caring for her husband and children, that her greatest satisfaction should be through her family, and that if a wife does work she should not try to achieve as a man does nor expect to be paid as much as a man who must support his family, the less likely they are to favor wives' working.

On the other hand, husbands who favor wives' working do not accept beliefs such as those just mentioned which restrict a woman's options and emphasize a home-centered role. Men with more egalitarian gender-role norms disagreed with the notion that wives shouldn't have equal decision-making power with husbands, nor did they agree with the idea that women are somehow mentally and emotionally unsuited to certain tasks. More modern or egalitarian gender-role norms were also related to disagreement with such statements as

The more strongly that husbands believe that a woman's most important task is family care, the less likely they are to favor wife employment.

these: "A wife should give up her job whenever it inconveniences her husband and children." And, "If a mother of young children works, it should be only while the family needs the money."

Husbands who are better educated tend to be more egalitarian in sex-role norms, believing that males and females should have equal opportunities to do whatever their abilities and training have suited them to do, without being restricted by roles based on gender. Such men are also less likely to feel threatened by wife employment. To wrap it up by a summary statement, we may say that where education is greater and sex-role norms are more egalitarian, husbands are less negative toward wives' working and are less likely to discourage or prevent wives' participation in the labor force.

Wives' attitudes toward working The longitudinal study of thirty-to-forty-four-year-old women mentioned earlier included a question on how the women felt about work outside the home, under certain conditions, for mothers of children between six and twelve years of age. Women who favored the idea of mothers' working were classified by the researchers as "permissive" and those who were not in favor of such employment were classified as "opposed." In between was a group who expressed uncertainty about the desirability of a mother's working, and this group was labeled "ambivalent."[40] The researchers found that the more "permissive" a wife was, the more likely she was to be working.

The study also showed that the women's personal beliefs about working affected their future behavior as well. By interviewing the same married women in 1969, the researchers were able to conclude that norms held by these women when interviewed two years earlier predicted what they would actually *do* about working. Working wives whose feelings were opposed or ambivalent toward working at the time of the first interview were less likely than the other working wives to still be employed by 1969. Similarly, wives who were not employed when interviewed in 1967 were more likely to be working by 1969 if their earlier attitudes had indicated approval of employment.

As we have seen, a variety of demographic and sociological factors are involved in a wife's working and thereby taking on the status of junior partner in the marriage. The age of a woman's children, her education, her race, her husband's income, the attitude of her husband toward wife employment, a woman's own attitudes toward working mothers—all of these issues enter into a woman's decision about taking a job. However, the question still arises: *Why* do some women choose to work?

Work motivation It is significant that questions are raised about why wives work and not about why husbands work. But the reason is simple. Up until this point in time at least, men haven't had the option *not* to work. Women, on the other hand, haven't had the option to work—except to a limited degree. Now that the option to work is open to them, women are increasingly exercising it; and many of them are expecting much more from their jobs than the income provided. According to the statistics we looked at earlier in this chapter, the greatest increases in wife employment are among those who are already relatively well-off. In exchange-theory terms, the explanation lies in comparative levels of rewards. Bowen and Finegan make the point that "women with considerable formal education are likely to attach a high value to the social interactions and sense of professional accomplishment which market work can offer, as compared with the psychic rewards of staying at home."[41]

If we ask working women if they work mainly because their family needs the money or because they enjoy working, about half say "money" and half say "enjoyment."[42] Those figures come from research conducted in 1971, whereas in a 1960 study only 30 percent of wives who had worked said that they worked because they "liked to."[43] The remaining 70 percent worked for "other reasons"—mostly money. Thus, over a decade, the proportion of wives who say they work to supplement the family income seems to have decreased; and the proportion who work because they enjoy working has increased.

Our research also produced the finding that the more education wives had and the more egalitarian the gender-role norms they held, the more likely they were to work for enjoyment. Similarly, the more egalitarian were husbands' gender-role norms, the more likely were husbands to report that their wives worked for enjoyment.[44]

Meaning of work   A wife's reason for working is an important consideration in examining the status of junior partner. For example, a woman who doesn't enjoy working and who never feels that her family needs her earnings is not likely to become a junior partner. But another woman may enjoy working regardless of family financial need, thereby becoming a junior partner by choice. A third woman may not want to work, yet becomes a junior partner out of necessity.

The significance of a woman's working for enjoyment is the fact that such employment behavior is based on individualistic interests; she is going after personal benefits. Her taking a job indicates a move toward autonomy. The woman who works to supplement family income, on the other hand, bases her employment behavior on group needs and interests—those of her husband and children. *Reaching for rewards* motivates the woman who works for enjoyment. In contrast, *avoiding costs* motivates the woman who works from necessity. The costs and punishments of having insufficient resources can only be avoided by additional income. Thus, in such a case, a married woman works out of coercion—because she has to, not because she wants to.

However, the evidence indicates that increasingly women are interested in working out of choice rather than being forced into employment by circumstances and need. Thus, their employment behaviors are becoming more and more like those of men. Although it is true that the option not to work has been closed to men, studies show that few men would care to exercise such an option even if it were available. This is true of both white-collar and blue-collar workers. From his studies in the sociology of occupations, Walter Slocum concludes that "no substantial group of able-bodied males between the ages of 25 and 65 in America is willingly without work."[45] And, as we shall see later, one of the most traumatic consequences of retirement for older males is being forced to give up their jobs and the sense of meaning those jobs provided for them.

There are numerous reasons why work is so central, not only in America but in every industrialized society. Besides the obvious function of work in providing subsistence (and evidence continues to show that wages *do* matter), work is the means to individualistic achievement, the way of attaining highly valued rewards—a sense of self-worth, prestige, social status, fulfillment, enriching life experiences, satisfaction in service to others, power and influence, and so on. Women and men alike value these prizes offered by an industrial society, and thus we may expect work to have an attraction for both sexes.

Wives who move into the position of junior partner in the marriage relationship are often seeking occupational rewards similar to those of their husbands. However, in the senior partner–junior partner arrangement, the husband continues to be defined as the *chief* family provider, and his occupation is regarded as more important than his wife's. Although this marriage pattern means more power for the wife than is true of the owner-property and head-complement arrangements, there is not total equality. Senior-partner husbands are expected to be more committed to their occupations than are junior-partner wives. The norms attached to the provider role do not permit husbands to move in and out of the labor force.

Related to the significance attached to the husband's occupation are certain norms which help structure the roles of husband-father and wife-mother. In all three marital arrangements looked at so far, there is a basic assumption of parenthood. To enter marriage automatically assumes that an attempt will be made at some point to form a family. However, when the family is formed, the norms prescribe that the mother is ultimately responsible for child care, just as the father is ultimately responsible for economic provision.

The fact that the wife as junior partner is expected to have children and to be responsible for them tends to reinforce the subordinate nature of any occupation she might pursue. Household cares and family needs must predominate over her work goals, and therefore she is prevented from pursuing the direct-line, orderly sequence of occupational and achievement endeavors which characterizes her husband's life.

EQUAL PARTNER–EQUAL PARTNER

The vast majority of marriages in America and in other industrial societies are represented by the head-complement and senior partner–junior partner models. Few (if any) of us can think of contemporary examples comparable to the nineteenth-century illustration of the husband who insisted on his wife's subordination and whipped her to ensure the owner-property arrangement. Yet, most of us could name many couples who remind us of Tom and Cindy (head-complement) or Al and Marilyn (senior partner–junior partner) as described in the hypothetical case studies at the beginning of this chapter.

However, there is a fourth way that marriage may be structured, and an increasing minority of marriages may fit this pattern. We are speaking of an equal-partner arrangement. In other words, if we compare Figure 6-2 with Figure 6-1, we'll see that the option to work which removes a wife from the status of property, not only opens up the possibility that she may become a complement or a junior partner. There is also a step beyond the junior-partner status; a wife may be an equal partner.

In an equal-partner marriage, both spouses are equally committed to their respective careers, and each one's occupation is considered as important as that of the other. Furthermore, there is role interchangeability with respect to the breadwinner and domestic roles. Either spouse may fill either role; both may share in both roles. Another characteristic of an equal-partner marriage is the equal power shared by husband and wife in decision making. Lastly, this marriage form differs from the other forms in that there is no longer the automatic assumption of the hyphenated wife-mother and husband-father

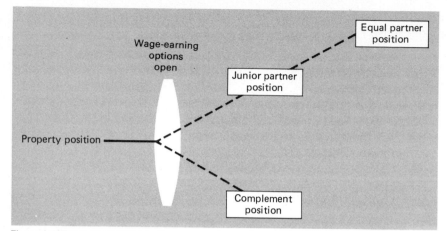

Figure 6-2 Three possibilities in the movement away from a wife's position as property.

roles. The basic marital roles are simply wife and husband, and marriage is not considered automatically to require parenthood. In our opening case studies, the equal-partner marriage is represented by Janet, the psychology professor, and her lawyer husband, Roger.

Equal Career Commitment

Based on research in England, a team of social scientists state that the "crucial element in distinguishing the dual-career family from other forms of family structure is the high commitment of both husband and wife to work on an egalitarian basis and a life-plan which involves a relatively full participation and advancement in work."[46] Importantly, the term *dual-job family* is not used; these researchers use the word *career* deliberately. A career involves continuity and commitment. And in the dual-career setting, both the husband and the wife have high aspirations to achieve in the world of work, desiring to exercise to the full their individual competencies in their respective occupations, with both spouses performing tasks that are highly productive or that carry great responsibility.[47]

A major feature, therefore, that marks off the equal-partner position from such positions as head, complement, senior partner, or junior partner are the norms endorsing the dual-achiever pattern. Speaking in terms of the rights of marriage, both partners have the *right* to careers (not merely jobs), and one career is not necessarily more significant than the other. That, of course, represents a radical departure from the other three ways in which marriages have been structured. In fact, some sociologists (arguing from the functionalist viewpoint) have suggested that such a marriage arrangement can't work.

Talcott Parsons, for example, argues that sex-role segregation and specialization are necessary to the equilibrium or stability of a marriage.[48] If the husband is chief breadwinner and the wife centers her life in home and family, a sense of competition is not likely to develop between the spouses as might be the case if both were achievers in the occupational realm. The development of such rivalries, according to Parsons, tends to disrupt the marriage. At the same time, even he has admitted that "it is, of course, possible for the adult woman to follow the masculine pattern and seek a career in fields of occupational achievement in direct competition with men of her own class." However, such departure from the traditional domestic pattern was rather rare at the time he was writing, leading him to conclude that "its generalization would only be possible with profound alterations in the structure of the family."[49]

The equal-partner marriage *is* an attempt to alter the structure of the family. The goal of such an arrangement is not to destroy marriage but rather to change marriage so that the partners can fulfill individual aspirations unhindered by gender-role stereotypes and traditional ideas about the division of labor. Although, at the present time, the dual-career marriage has been called "a statistically minor variant,"[50] it is an emerging form—a life-style that may very well represent the wave of the future. In other words, out of all the new varieties of marital arrangements (trial marriage, group marriage, gay marriage, communal living, and so on), this is the one most likely some day to replace traditional marriage as we have known it.

Travel and living arrangements   Occupations are major factors in determining where persons live and where they travel. Traditionally, a married couple has lived together in one household, with the location of that household being determined by the husband's place of employment. If the husband's job meant settling in Michigan, the couple moved to Michigan—even if the wife's preferences might be to remain in Oregon.

Furthermore, if extensive travel was required in the husband's work, few questions were raised about his right to make such business trips or about the wife's duty to stay home and attend to the household while he was gone. In some cases, the husband's occupation might even mean long periods of actually living apart from his wife—such as in the case of a merchant seaman or fisherman, or if a man was in politics, the military, or fields of science which require extensive fieldwork. Such travel and living arrangements have been optional for men but rarely for women.

However, in the equal-partner arrangement, the wife gains these options as well. Her career may require her to travel a great deal, especially if she is in the professions, or in sports, journalism, the performing arts, business, and so on. In a very small sample of dual-career marriages in which the wives held positions in universities, research laboratories, hospitals, and business, sociologist Lynda Lytle Holmstrom explored attitudes and behaviors related to the issue of the wife's travel. She found in her sample that "most husbands in the professional couples were very supportive of their wives traveling without them and felt they should have this opportunity." Some couples "accepted very easily both the idea of being apart from each other and the fact that during the wife's absence additional domestic responsibilities would fall on the husband." Other couples emphasized the difficulties, particularly in cases where the wife was gone for a long time (such as a month) and there were children left under the husband's care; but even so, the wife's travel was viewed as a necessary part of her career. In one interview, after the husband had mentioned the hardships of having the full responsibility of the household fall to him while his wife was away, he was asked if he would prefer that his wife would not take such trips. His reply was, "No, no. It's just hard." He laughed and added, "I mean, if I feel that she shouldn't go away, then I feel that I shouldn't go away. . . . It's just part of the game."[51]

Not only do dual-career couples face the issue of the wife's traveling in connection with her career just as the husband travels in his work; there is also the possibility that the spouses' separate occupations may require them to work in different geographical locations. The wife's career may require her working in Buffalo, New York, while the husband's career may require him to work in Chicago. Then what happens? Some couples may decide to spend their weekdays at their place of work and their weekends together in alternate locations or at some spot in between.

One of the most famous examples of such long-distance commuting over many years was the pattern worked out by Martha and Hicks Griffiths of Michigan. The couple met as college students, married, and went to law school together. Later they were partners in a Detroit law firm. When Martha Griffiths was elected to the state legislature, it became necessary for her to spend much of her time in Lansing, while her husband remained in Detroit. Later, when she won a seat in the House of Representatives, the couple no longer had the distance between Lansing and Detroit to consider but rather the much greater distance between Washington, D.C., and Detroit. The Griffiths solved the problem by living and working apart all week when Congress was in session, while making sure they were together from Friday through Sunday. Sometimes Martha Griffiths commuted to Detroit; other times Hicks Griffiths traveled to Washington. Apart from the high expenditure on air fares, they were said to be pleased with the arrangement since it made possible their giving attention both to their demanding jobs and to each other.[52]

Some couples reject the idea of long-distance commuting, except perhaps on a temporary basis, although they say they might be open to the possibility if no other solution were available. In some marriages, career-related moves may be decided on a husband's turn–wife's turn basis. If a husband has an occupational opportunity open to him that would require moving to another location, the wife may follow and seek to pursue her career in the new location also—even though it might mean sacrifices on her part. But then the next move will be determined by the wife's career. If better opportunities open to her elsewhere, it will be her husband's turn to follow.

Other couples might negotiate in other ways. In some cases, *neither* will accept a position elsewhere unless something really worthwhile is open to *both;* and no moves will be undertaken until such an arrangement is found. The point to be stressed here is that the traditional norm of a married couple's moving and living in conjunction with the husband's career interests is for dual-career couples no longer automatically assumed. In equal-partner marriages, the issues of residence and travel are likely to become increasingly problematic.

Role Interchangeability

The role of the wife in an equal-partner marriage is a radical departure from her role in the other positions discussed. The norms now prescribe that she has the duty to provide for her husband. At the same time, norms attached to the husband role also maintain that it is a husband's duty to provide for his wife—just as has always been the case. Since both the husband role and the wife role involve breadwinning, we have a case of *role interchangeability.* This is in contrast to the rigid *role specialization* that occurs under other marital positions. In situations of owner-property, head-complement, and senior partner-junior partner, each partner has a particular sphere according to his or her sex—for the male the occupational, for the female primarily the domestic.

Since there is role interchangeability in the equal-partner marital pattern and both sexes can fulfill breadwinner behaviors, there not only exists the norm that the wife as well as the husband has the right to a career; there also exists the norm that the husband as well as the wife has the right to be provided for. In other patterns of structuring marriage, it has been the husband's duty to provide and the wife's right to be provided for. But in the equal-partner situation, each spouse has both the duty to provide and the right to be provided for.

While it may be mind-boggling to some persons over thirty to conceive of the wife's having to provide, it may be even more unsettling to comprehend the healthy husband's having the right to be supported by his wife. The traditional work ethic, which assumed that one proved his self-worth and masculinity through occupational achievements, centered around a man's obligations to provide economic benefits, status, and prestige to his wife. But with the roles of both partners defined as interchangeable achievers, the husband can expect to share in the wife's status and bask in the prestige resulting from her accomplishments just as she has always done and will continue to do in his.

Option not to work   Although the provider-achiever role is interchangeable in an equal-partner marriage, such an arrangement does not necessarily require that both partners work full-time all the time. Either partner has the option not to work as well as the right to a career and the duty to provide. It may seem contradictory simultaneously to hold norms in which the husband or wife has the option not to work and yet at the same time has the duty to provide. However, while all the marriage structures we have examined are in constant process, the equal-partner pattern is especially in motion. It is continually being negotiated and renegotiated so that at one point a partner may be exercising his or her achievement rights, while at another time for various reasons the option *not* to work (the right to be provided for) is being exercised.

The question raised earlier now becomes very real: will males, who have traditionally been work-oriented, be likely to exercise their option not to work? Occasionally, one hears reports of couples who trade off "house-spouse" and provider roles; that is, one year the husband stays home to look after the household and children while the wife works and supports the family, and the next year the pattern is reversed. However, at the present time few occupations allow for such flexibility. Even more than that, because of the way society's reward system is related to occupational achievement, it is not likely that many men for very long would find it rewarding not to work.

There might, however, be exceptions in certain types of work. A writer who works full-time for a newspaper, for example, might find it very rewarding to absent himself from his employment for a period of months in order to write a novel to which only evenings and weekends could be devoted were it not for his wife's financial support. A similar situation could arise in other creative arts as well—music, painting, sculpturing, and the like.

It should be noted that in exercising the option not to work at a regular income-producing occupation, such men are not actually giving up work. They are changing the kind of work they do and are finding freedom for some pursuit that requires much time but is not always immediately income-producing. However, because of the reward system in an industrial society, they are seldom likely to be full-time "househusbands" in the tradition of the housewife role, although there are occasional exceptions. One man in Sweden, for example, wrote a regular feature for a magazine in which he described his life as a *hemmaman* or househusband. His wife worked as an art director, while he stayed home to cook, clean, make beds, do the laundry, and care for their six-year-old child. He had previously worked in advertising but found his job boring, whereas he said he enjoyed child care, didn't mind housework, and thought a reversal of the traditional roles made sense in order to make it easier for his wife to pursue her career, since she made more money than he anyway.[53]

Division of labor In traditional marriage arrangements, the husband has had the duty to provide for his wife and the right to have his wife take care of household tasks. In the equal-partner pattern, role interchangeability means that both the husband and wife have the reciprocal duty to be breadwinners and the reciprocal right to be supported. But what about household tasks? Does the wife as coprovider have the *right* to have these tasks performed by the

In the equal partner arrangement, couples share household tasks as well as responsibility for breadwinning.

husband? And does the husband, having the right to be provided for, have the *duty* to perform such household tasks? The answer is yes, if the exchange is to be fair. How this will be carried out will likely vary with the individual couple, but the mutual responsibility is there. Sharing household duties is a part of the equal-partner marriage pattern just as is the sharing of occupational duties.

Equal Power in Decision Making

As Figure 6-3 shows, the increasing power of the wife is perhaps the most prominent feature to be observed in moving through the four basic ways marriages may be structured. In the equal-partner position, it becomes standard or normative for both husband and wife to acknowledge that the balance of power is equal; neither spouse has more power than the other. The husband relinquishes any vestige of traditional ideas of masculine superiority, dominance, and the right to have the wife defer to her husband.

The basis for this normative egalitarianism lies in the equal career commitments of the husband and wife. A century ago, philosopher-economist John Stuart Mill argued that if two persons invest equally in a business, both partners will want equal power in order to protect their own and their mutual interests.[54] Likewise, two spouses with equal investments in their marriage (because of the

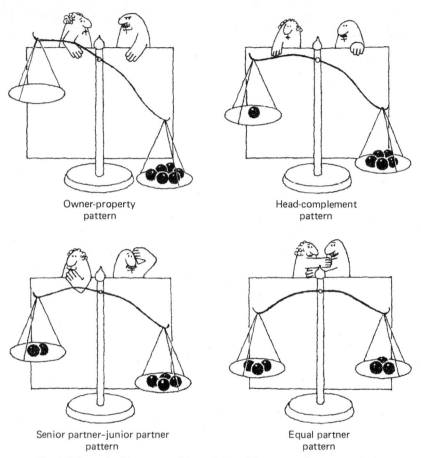

Owner-property
pattern

Head-complement
pattern

Senior partner–junior partner
pattern

Equal partner
pattern

The wife's power has more weight as her position moves from property to
complement to junior partner, until in the equal partner pattern the balance
of power between husband and wife is equal.

Figure 6-3 How the balance of power changes according to the four marriage patterns.

tangible and intangible resources contributed through their respective career
commitments) will want equal marital power. Without this equal power, the
career interests of one or the other could be threatened.

Anthropologists have studied tribes which illustrate the point of Mill's
business analogy. Among the Igbo-speaking peoples of West Africa, for example, women own lands, farm, and trade, and as a result hold positions of
economic power in their society. Wives therefore have independence and
bargaining power in their marriages, and they have equal power to that of their

husbands.[55] Similarly, the Bamenda women of West Africa have had a high degree of economic power because of their ownership of the crops on which the tribe is dependent for its existence. The men own the lands, but the women own what grows on those lands and are responsible for planting, cultivating, and harvesting. At the same time that wives control production, husbands trade and sell small goods, earning income in this fashion. Thus, both women and men bring to marriage equal resources, and because of this there is equality of power in the husband-wife relationship.[56]

Option of Parenthood

In marriages structured around the positions of owner-property, head-complement, and senior partner–junior partner, major rewards were defined as coming from children—especially for wives. There were also certain costs involved—again especially for wives since they were mainly responsible for child care. Because of this responsibility, women tended to forgo serious career commitment and its rewards. In fact, women who did choose to pursue a career over children were generally considered selfish or neurotic.

In recent years increasing numbers of young women have rejected the notion that it is selfish to want a life of their own. They refuse to subordinate individualistic interests and rewards to the interests of husbands and children. Indeed, the argument can be turned around to say that husbands may be selfish to insist that wives have a certain number of children (or any at all) and then be responsible for them. Some persons are raising the question: If individualistic occupational rewards are so valuable, why should only white men have access to them? And if children are so important, why shouldn't husbands be responsible for taking care of them as much as wives are?

Therefore, in equal-partner marriages, the roles of husband and wife are not attached to father and mother roles as they are in the other marriage patterns. The norms for both the husband role and the wife role make having or not having children a matter of choice. And if the choice is made to have children, both parents are equally responsible for their care.

MARITAL PATTERNS IN MOVEMENT

It should be clear by now that the positions of owner-property, head-complement, senior partner–junior partner, and equal partner–equal partner are not rigid, distinct categories in the sense that each marriage fits *exactly* into one of these "boxes." In the first place there may be movement between the categories. A wife may be a complement, take a job and become a junior partner, quit six months later and become a complement once again, and so on. Second, few marriages would fit exactly and indisputably on all dimensions into any one of the categories. There is room for indefiniteness, a blurring and blending rather than clear-cut lines separating the statuses. It might be helpful to think of a continuum, a thermometer-like arrangement in which marriages attain degrees of equal-partner status, degrees of senior partner–junior partner status, degrees of head-complement status, perhaps even (though much less likely today) degrees of the owner-property status. In other words, couples may be more or less in or near one of the statuses.

It should also be kept in mind that while certain marriages may be found at particular points on the continuum today, they may be at a different point than they were two years ago; and they may be at another point two years from now. For example, a couple might be described as having a head-complement arrangement in their marriage. When the wife decides to take on a part-time job selling cosmetics door to door, pursuing it very casually as somewhat of a hobby in her spare time, she may move up to being slightly more than complement. As she begins devoting more time to her occupational interests, earning more money although still only on a part-time basis, she might become almost but not quite a full junior partner. A year later, she might move to a full-time job and take on wholly the junior-partner position in her marriage. If she were to save up money for special training and then were to embark on some career with equal commitment to that of her husband, she might take on an equal-partner status at some point.

In trying to conceptualize the structure of marriage in these ways, we must be careful not to think in terms of a clear-cut linear progression, so that marriages are seen to evolve automatically from one stage to the next in some sort of upward fashion with the passage of time. Again it must be emphasized that there is change, flux, and movement between the categories. It is not so simple a matter as "ever upward and onward" from owner-property through a head-complement stage and on to the senior partner–junior partner position, with the ultimate goal of equal-partner status at the apex. Something else to guard against is the assumption that these descriptions of marital statuses automatically imply a value position (the idea that one or another status is somehow "better" than the others for each and every couple).

Changes in Distribution of Power

In one sense, theoretically speaking, there *is* a progression between the various categories, however. This must not be overlooked, because in a sense it draws together all that has been discussed in this chapter so far. As role specialization decreases and moves toward role interchangeability, husband power decreases and moves toward egalitarianism. In other words, when the breadwinner role is filled not only by the husband (whose exclusive role it was once considered to be) but is also filled by the wife in increasing degrees (rather than limiting her

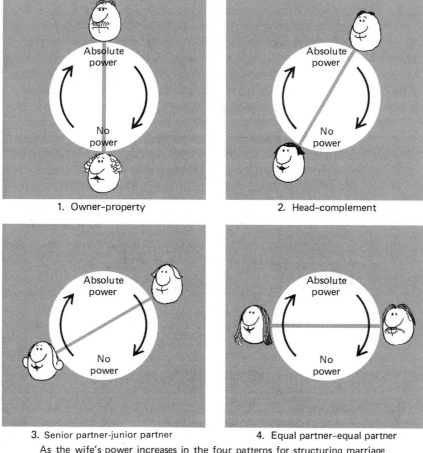

1. Owner–property

2. Head–complement

3. Senior partner–junior partner

4. Equal partner–equal partner

As the wife's power increases in the four patterns for structuring marriage, the husband's power correspondingly decreases. It is as though the positions of husband and wife are on opposite ends of a moving rod.

Figure 6-4 Marital power in the four types of marriage.

role to domestic concerns), the couple moves toward a sharing of equal power in the marriage, as we saw in Figure 6-3.

Still another way to view the distribution of marital power is seen in Figure 6-4. Picture a rod with the husband role on one end and the wife-role on the other. As the rod moves around a circle representing degrees of marital power, it becomes clear that as the husband's share of power diminishes, the wife's share of power increases. We have already seen *why* this change in power occurs in each of the marital patterns. At one extreme would be a case where a husband has absolute power and the wife none at all. This is represented by the husband at the top of the rod and the wife at the bottom. In the equal-partner marriage, the rod is on an even plane, parallel to the horizon. In the other marital structures, the power is somewhere in between but with the husband having more power than the wife.

The question may arise at this point: Could the rod continue to move in a clockwise direction so that the wife would have more power than the husband, perhaps reaching the point where the rod is completely turned around and is perpendicular once again—only this time with the husband at the bottom and the wife at the top? In other words, could the wife become the head and the husband the complement, or the wife the senior partner while the husband is in the position of junior partner?

WIFE AS SENIOR PARTNER OR SOLO PARENT BY DEFAULT

In spite of jokes and humorous greeting cards which speak of a husband's "ruling the roost" while the wife "rules the rooster," many persons view wife dominance as unnatural and undesirable. However, in expressing fears about the goals of feminism they tend to assume that women want to be senior partners just as they want to be equal partners. And they also assume that large numbers of women could move into the senior-partner status vis-à-vis their husbands, thereby forcing husbands into junior-partner status. Both assumptions lack foundation. Such fears may be compared to the anxieties some whites expressed in discussions on civil rights for blacks: "They'll try to take over and run everything. They'll force us out of our jobs and positions. Giving *them* rights means taking away *our* rights. If you give them a little, they'll keep wanting more and never stop. We're going to lose a lot of our privileges because of them." Actually, such assertions—whether voiced in connection with race or sex— reflect the anxieties of a dominant group that is not quite so dominant as it once was. The pressing for rights by a minority group becomes extremely threatening and is perceived as an attempt to seize power such as the dominant group itself has held over the minority group.

However, not only is there no evidence that women want to dominate; it is also clear that at the present time few women have access to the resources and power necessary to attain dominance over males—even if they did desire to do so. Gender-role socialization, ideology, and the way the economic-opportunity system has been structured have combined to limit female access to the resources that lead to prestige and power—at least to the extent that men have had access to these resources.

Nevertheless, there are situations where American wives are thrust into the position of senior partner—not necessarily because they seek it, but because they have no choice. It falls to them by default. They assume responsibility for the family simply because the husband has failed to fulfill his obligations.

Matrifocal Situations

Anthropologist Helen Safa has written of a common pattern in cultures of poverty: the family becomes *matrifocal* or "mother-centered." The strong mother-child bond takes precedence over the husband-wife bond; the role of the husband (if he is present) is peripheral, almost as though the man is "excess baggage" in the family, without an important part to play.

Safa points out that this form of family life has arisen among lower-income families as a way of coping under conditions of poverty. The primary function of the family is viewed as child rearing, and "marriage is not expected to provide the intense emotional intimacy sought in the middle-class nuclear family." Both husband and wife have strong ties outside the family, either with kin or same-sex friends, and they tend to rely on these relationships rather than on each other for emotional support and assistance. "Lower-class women cannot invest the conjugal [marital or husband-wife] relationship with the heavy responsibilities it carries in the middle class," writes Safa. Why? Because such wives "cannot be sure that men will be adequate providers, or will not have to leave to find work elsewhere, or may not abandon them for another woman."[57]

Another researcher who has studied lower-class family life-styles is sociologist Lee Rainwater. He points out that the matrifocal family is common among lower-class families in general and not only among blacks, as is sometimes thought. According to Rainwater, lower-class families "are matrifocal in the sense that the wife makes most of the decisions that keep the family going and has the greatest sense of responsibility to the family." Women in these families get advice from female relatives and tend to consider their husbands to be unconcerned about day-to-day problems of family life. Rainwater adds that since these tendencies are intensified among lower-class black families, "matrifocality is much clearer than in white lower-class families."[58]

Safa makes the point that socioeconomic forces "have systematically robbed the man of any basis of authority in the black ghetto family; they have curtailed his role as economic provider, as leader in his own community, and as spokesman for his family in dealing with the outside world. As a result, the woman has been forced to take over many traditionally male roles. . . ." Safa argues that wife dominance is further reinforced by welfare programs: "Because men are temporarily or permanently absent from many black homes, or cannot be reached during working hours, social workers and other government officials dealing with these families often direct most of their attention to the women. In effect, they treat her as head of the household, whether she has a husband or not."[59]

Female-Headed Households

Safa and others who study the culture of poverty refer not only to matrifocal families but also to *female-based* families, a more restrictive term "referring only to those families actually headed by females."[60] A lower-class woman might not only find herself in the position of senior partner in a marriage; she might also at some point find herself without a husband and in the position of solo parent. In Chapter 5, we looked at singleness as a life-style and also spoke of voluntarily chosen single parenthood—usually through adoption and most often among the well educated. Here we are thinking of situations where women are poor, have large numbers of children, and hold no particular commitment to the idea of solo parenthood. Yet, they find themselves forced into this role by circumstances.

In 1973, females headed 12 percent of families in the United States. About one-half of these women became heads of families either through divorce or marital discord leading to separation, and another 37 percent were widowed. The remaining 13 percent were single.[61]

Many people think of female-headed households as more likely to be black than white. However, since whites are in the majority in the United States, perhaps it will come as no surprise to learn that government figures indicate that in 1973 white women made up 71 percent of all female heads, whereas black women made up only 28 percent.[62]

However, looking at it another way, there was a much smaller proportion of all white families which were headed by females than was true of the proportion of all black families. Table 6-G compares various groupings and supplies the information that in 1973 about 1 out of every 10 white families had a female head, and about 1 out of every 6 families of Spanish origin also was headed by a female. Among blacks, the percentage was higher than among the other two major groupings, with 1 out of every 3 black families having a female head.

Impoverishment is a fact of life for more than half the black female-headed families. Exactly what the line is between being "poor" and "not poor" may at first seem difficult to say, but again government figures are helpful. In 1972, the Census Bureau set $4,275 as the dividing line. A nonfarm family of four with an income below this figure was considered to be "low income" or "below the poverty line." During that year, 53 percent of black female-headed families had incomes below that line. However, among black families where the husband was present, that figure dropped to 16 percent.[63] To intensify their poverty even

TABLE 6-G FEMALE FAMILY HEADS BY RACE AND SPANISH ORIGIN

Female-headed Families	White 1973	Black 1973	Spanish Origin 1974			
			Total	Mexican	Puerto Rican	Other Spanish*
Percentage in each category	9.6	34.6	17.4	14.4	33.2	14.1

*Comprises families with head of Cuban, Central or South American, or other Spanish origin.

Source: U.S. Bureau of the Census, 1974, *Current Population Reports,* P-23, no. 50, p.6; P-20, no. 267, p. 4.

further, female heads of black families below the poverty line during 1971 had a mean of 2.84 children living with them,[64] necessitating the stretching of meager resources for a relatively large number of persons. In 1972, about 70 percent of black children from female-headed homes were living below the low-income level, although this was a decline from 87 percent in 1959.[65]

At this point, perhaps a word of caution is in order. Hearing figures such as these has sometimes given whites the impression that such statistics describe the majority of black families. This is not true at all. Actually only about one-third of all black persons lived below the 1971 poverty line of $4,137 as compared with about one-fourth of Latinos and one-tenth of whites.[66]

Female Headship among Blacks

Thus far in this book, while we have contrasted information on blacks and whites, the underlying premise has been that their family patterns are basically similar. Any differences are not the result of conscious planning but rather stem from the way society has been structured. Those blacks who have been most vocal about family life-styles, however, have not made an effort to set up a unique and distinct family form (for example, a black matriarchy) but rather have moved toward the dominant form of the larger society in which the male has traditionally held the unique or chief provider role. The Black Muslims and other groups seeking to enhance black identity have placed great emphasis on male authority and female subordination, with the goal for marriage being the head-complement pattern.[67]

This emphasis is apparently in reaction to decades of economic discrimination practiced against black males by the white society. Black women who were forced to work in order to survive came to possess economic resources that resulted in their gaining power in the family. Black males, deprived of access to economic rewards, were also deprived of power within the household. It was this situation which gave rise to considerable folklore about the so-called black matriarchy. The most unfounded assertion in this regard is the notion that there is something within black cultural values, traceable to plantation days or even to Africa, that predisposes blacks to favor female-dominant households.

All available evidence is to the contrary. Even among blacks who may not espouse the Muslim emphasis on female subordination, it is clear that the overwhelming majority do not prefer female-headed households but rather want the husband-wife form of family life-style.[68] At the same time, although it is not preferred, the female-headed household is often accepted as an unavoidable means of economic survival.

It must be remembered that two-thirds of black society live above the poverty line. These households consist mostly of husband-wife units where sex-role equality is a pertinent issue. Here we are concerned only with that one-third of black society which is a genuine American lower class or under-class. These persons are different from poor whites and poor Spanish-speaking people in that they encounter much more severe economic discrimination due to their race. Paths to mobility out of the lower class are exceedingly limited; poverty is cyclical, generation after generation. Black males in this situation have been held back from fulfilling the provider role and have been forced into other kinds of behaviors in relation to women and to economic survival.

From his studies of black ghetto life, sociologist David Schulz describes several categories of such male behaviors. Some lower-class black men play the role of *pimp,* not only in the usual sense of living off the labors of several prostitutes but also in situations where they live off women who earn their income legitimately in domestic service or as clerks or welfare recipients. Often these are younger men who demand that their women provide them with a high standard of living (by ghetto standards), including the means to "dress like a dandy," while they reward the women with their capacity as lovers.[69]

Another category listed by Schulz is the *supportive companion* who meets a woman regularly on weekends and gives her spending money and a good time but wishes to avoid the responsibilities of marriage and parenthood. Then there is the category of the *supportive biological father* who senses some responsibility for children he has fathered, even though he may be married to someone else. To the children's mother, he plays only the role of boyfriend but at the same time does not run away from certain economic duties.

One step beyond this category is that of the *indiscreet free man* who has a legitimate family plus one or more illegitimate families and who spends much of his time, income, and energies on the "other woman" and any children he has fathered by her. He does not hide his behavior from his legal wife and often compares her to his girl friend, causing much family conflict. The legal wife often feels trapped in the situation because she has numerous children and needs his support. With no alternative sources of rewards, she is forced to "make do" with the limited rewards her husband offers. In contrast, a fifth category, the *discreet free man,* keeps his extramarital activities covert or else has an understanding with his wife. He too showers large outlays of money and attention on his "illegitimate" family but doesn't flaunt these outside interests in such a way as to antagonize his legal family.

Schulz points out that the sixth category, *the traditional monogamous type of father,* is (although rare) considered the most desirable among underclass blacks. Such men are faithful to their wives and children and consider their homes and families to be their major concerns. "Typically such a father will have good relationships with his children and high status in the family regardless of his ability to earn a living."[70]

The first five of these six patterns cast some light on why there are so many female-headed households in lower-class black society. Black women have had to interact with men who have largely been excluded from economic opportunity. These men have simply not been able to provide the kinds of socioeconomic rewards that members of modern societies (both black and white) have expected males to supply. Consequently, alternative strategies have evolved in which lower-class black men and women attempt to exchange economic and expressive benefits in ways that differ from the dominant societal pattern.

At the same time, black women are aware of exploitation by men who act out roles ranging from pimp to discreet free man. If actually married to such men, the sense of exploitation may lead some women to deep resentment. Thus, the high rates of black lower-class separation and divorce are more readily understood. The sense of exploitation may also explain why many black women are willing to remain *unmarried* female heads as well. Schulz explains that some black women "are very much afraid of marriage because no matter how good a man might seem before marriage, after he 'has papers' on you he might well change."[71]

In short, many lower-class black women find themselves thrust into roles they did not seek, nor do they necessarily prefer, but which have been forced upon them as a result of economic discrimination against black men. When these women remain married, they often find themselves having considerably more power than their husbands who have difficulty functioning as providers. On the other hand, lower-class black women who live apart from their husbands may find themselves in situations made punishing through a combination of meager resources and numerous children.

Wrap-Up

Female leadership by default is something quite different from female headship intentionally sought as a step beyond equality. Most feminists have not expressed a desire to be dominant over men, which would just be the old system in reverse. Rather they are interested in principles of egalitarianism.

Given the way work, achievement, and its rewards are valued in industrial societies, it is unlikely that many males will be interested in a complete reversal of traditional sex roles so that the wife becomes the sole breadwinner and leader and the husband enjoys being supported and led. There are exceptions to this, of course. A common example is the situation in which a married male college student is financially supported by his wife.

There are other instances where personality factors play a part; in a particular husband-wife unit the wife may be stronger, more forceful, and seem to exercise greater decision-making power than her husband. The husband's psychological makeup may be such that he prefers his wife to be dominant and finds security in her strength. However, such cases are the exception. Because of the occupational-opportunity system, most marriages at present are structured in the ways that have been described, with husbands as heads and wives as complements, or husbands as senior partners and wives as junior partners, although there is movement in the direction of increasing numbers of equal-partner marriages. In the equal-partner arrangement, either spouse may take the leader-achiever-provider role, thereby allowing greater role flexibility for both. This pattern seems far more likely to be the wave of the future than a pattern that would totally reverse roles, placing woman at the top and man at the bottom.

NOTES

1   Calhoun, 1919, vol. 2, pp. 92–93.
2   Tyler, 1944, p. 426.
3   Figes, 1970.
4   Campbell, 1893, pp. 26–27.
5   Campbell, 1893, p. 50.
6   Campbell, 1893, pp. 51–52.
7   Wollstonecraft, 1792, p. 113.
8   See historical documents section, Hole and Levine, 1971.
9   Campbell, 1893, pp. 46–49, Lasch, 1973; Oakley, 1974, chaps. 2–3.
10 Campbell, 1893, pp. 68–72.
11 Cain, 1966, p. 2.
12 U.S. Bureau of the Census, 1973, *We, the American Women*, p. 6.
13 Calhoun, 1919, vol. 2, pp. 126–129.
14 Scanzoni, 1970; Blood and Wolfe, 1960.
15 U.S. Department of Labor, 1973, *Dual Careers*, vol. 2, p. 14.
16 Nye, 1974a; Kreps, 1971; Sobol, 1974; *Current Population Reports*, 1974, P-23, no. 48.
17 Nye, 1974a, p. 28.
18 Nye, 1974a, pp. 28–29; *Current Population Reports*, 1973, P-23, no. 46, p. 23.
19 Nye, 1974a, p. 19; see also *Current Population Reports*, 1973, P-23, no. 46, p. 45.
20 Cohen, 1969; Ferriss, 1971.
21 U.S. Department of Labor, 1973, *Dual Careers*, vol. 2, pp. 22–24.
22 See Ferriss, 1971, p. 106 for brief summary of these studies. Also Hoffman, 1974.
23 Nye and Hoffman, 1963, p. 140.
24 Nye and Hoffman, 1963, pp. 139–140.
25 Hoffman, 1973, p. 212.
26 Hoffman, 1973, pp. 212–213; Nye and Hoffman, 1963, pp. 95–105.
27 Hoffman, 1973, p. 213; also see Hoffman and Nye, 1974.
28 Hoffman, 1973, p. 214 n; also see Hoffman, 1974.
29 Bowen and Finegan, 1969, pp. 114–132.
30 Jurate Kazickas, "It's Business as Usual for These Mothers," *Chicago Daily News*, Dec. 19, 1974, p. 28.
31 *Current Population Reports*, 1969, P-60, no. 64, p. 2.
32 *Current Population Reports*, 1970, P-60, no. 75, p. 3.
33 *Current Population Reports*, 1970, P-60, no. 75.
34 U.S. Department of Labor, 1973, *Dual Careers*, vol. 2, p. 43.
35 Scanzoni, 1975b.
36 Yankelovich, 1974, pp. 44–45.
37 Lewis, 1968.
38 Murillo, 1971.
39 Scanzoni, 1975b.
40 U.S. Department of Labor, 1973, vol. 2, *Dual Careers*, pp. 39–40.
41 Bowen and Finegan, 1969, p. 22.
42 Scanzoni, 1975b.
43 Whelpton, Campbell, and Patterson, 1966, p. 109.
44 Scanzoni, 1975b.

45 Slocum, 1966, p. 14; also see Form, 1974.
46 Fogarty, Rapoport, and Rapoport, 1971, pp. 334–335.
47 Fogarty, Rapoport, and Rapoport, 1971, p. 334.
48 Parsons, 1955.
49 Parsons, 1942.
50 Fogarty, Rapoport, and Rapoport, 1971, p. 337.
51 Holmstrom, 1972.
52 Lamson, 1968.
53 "The Happy 'Hemmaman,'" *Life* 67 (Aug. 15, 1969), p. 46.
54 Mill, 1869.
55 LaFree, 1974.
56 Kaberry, 1953.
57 Safa, 1971, pp. 36–38.
58 Rainwater, 1966 b, pp. 190–191.
59 Safa, 1971, pp. 39, 46.
60 Safa, 1971, p. 36.
61 *Current Population Reports*, 1974, P-23, no. 50, pp. 7, 10.
62 *Current Population Reports*, 1974, P-23, no. 50, p. 6.
63 *Current Population Reports*, 1973, P-23, no. 46, pp. 28–29.
64 *Current Population Reports*, 1972, P-60, no. 86, p. 87.
65 *Current Population Reports*, P-23, no. 50, 1974, p. 20.
66 *Current Population Reports*, 1972, P-60, no 86, p. 1.
67 Malcolm X, 1964, chap. 13.
68 Rainwater, 1966 b; Liebow, 1967; Schulz, 1969; Scanzoni, 1971.
69 Schulz, 1969, pp. 82–85.
70 Schulz, 1969, p. 128.
71 Schulz, 1969, p. 136.

7
PROCESS IN MARRIAGE: EXPRESSIVENESS

An incident a few years ago caused a publisher considerable embarrassment. The company had issued some full-color posters to illustrate a series of religious-education materials. But through some oversight, two picture captions were reversed and not noticed before the orders were shipped. A picture designed to illustrate marriage was labeled "John the Baptist in Chains." And the picture of the fettered prophet was entitled "Marriage."

No doubt the mix-up seems fitting to many people. Men have been known to speak of marriage as a kind of bondage, with freedom traded for the "chains of wedlock" (emphasis on the word *lock*). In recent years, large numbers of women have complained—perhaps even more than men—that marriage is a trap, shackling them into confining roles which prevent full development as persons and as achievers.

Such ideas about marriage come from traditional notions of wedded life as something rigidly fixed and static. Small wonder that the question has been raised: "Is there life after marriage?"[1] The word *life* suggests energy, vitality, process—just the opposite of that which is motionless, inert, or dead. Actually, to picture marriage as a state of inaction fits neither with the realities of the

husband-wife relationship nor with the exchange theory that has been emphasized throughout this book. In the preceding chapter, we examined marriage as
a structure; now we want to see marriage as a process. The word *process*
implies something dynamic, on the move; it derives from the Latin *procedere,*
"to go forward." A process suggests continuous action taking place in a
systematic fashion. Being in process means that ongoing changes and exchanges are occurring all the time. In this sense, the answer to the question, "Is
there life after marriage?" is yes.

WHAT HOLDS MARRIAGE TOGETHER?

If marriage is constantly in process, what keeps the moving parts from spinning
off in separate directions? In other words, what is the "glue" that holds a
marriage together?

The question is similar to one posed in connection with communal living.
Cohesiveness involves an effort to resolve the recurrent problem of group
solidarity versus individual freedom. As marriage has been understood traditionally, a man and woman are said to become "one flesh." According to the
biblical phrase used in many wedding ceremonies, they are "no longer two but
one." In the minds of some persons, this merger into a new social unit must
erase all traces of the two individuals as separate entities, somewhat in the
manner of the juncture of the Allegheny and Monongahela rivers which lose
their distinct identities at Pittsburgh, Pennsylvania, when they unite to become
the Ohio River.

Yet many persons today reject the idea of a total submersion of individuality
for the sake of group solidarity. To rephrase a question from our section on
communes, they are asking, "Why can't the one be two at the same time that the
two are one?" In one way of thinking, autonomy is considered to dissolve the
glue that holds marriage together. But in another way of thinking, autonomy can
be one of the basic ingredients cementing the relationship.

Marital-Adjustment School of Thought

One of the earliest attempts to explore the glue of marriage was made by
proponents of the "adjustment to marriage" school. The marital-adjustment
idea fitted nicely with the notions of functionalism and its emphasis on an
organism's need for smooth-working parts working together to preserve the
structure.

According to the marital-adjustment school of thought, the glue of marriage
is *consensus.* This consensus is manufactured by submerging individual interests for the greater good of group solidarity. The major emphasis is on harmony
and stability, the sustaining of "the commitment of husband and wife to their
marriage."[2] The goal, in other words, is group preservation rather than individu-

al development. Sociologist Harvey Locke spoke of marital adjustment as "the process of adaptation of the husband and the wife in such a way as to avoid or resolve conflicts sufficiently so that the mates feel satisfied with the marriage and with each other."[3] Similarly, sociologist Ernest Burgess and his colleagues wrote: "A well-adjusted marriage may be defined as a union in which the husband and wife are in agreement on the chief issues of marriage, such as handling finances and dealing with in-laws; in which they have come to an adjustment on interests, objectives, and values; in which they are in harmony on demonstrations of affection and sharing confidences; and in which they have few or no complaints about their marriage."[4] The emphasis was always on "adjustment," "adapting," "harmonious relations," "agreement," and avoiding or minimizing conflict.

In describing how group standards may be designed to prevent disruptions based on individual interests, social psychologist Philip Brickman makes a comment that fits well with the basic premise of the marital-adjustment school:

"In normative relationships [relationships with behavioral expectations clearly spelled out in advance], although conflicts of interest may exist, individuals are not supposed to be engaged in maximizing their own self interests. Instead they are supposed to be doing what is right or moral or normative, even if this is not in their self interest."[5]

In recent years, there has been a reaction to the marital-adjustment school of thinking. Robert Seidenberg, a psychiatrist, writes: "No marriage should ever be held of more importance than one of its participants. Persons, not marriages, are worth saving."[6] In a similar vein, anthropologists George O'Neill and Nena O'Neill have given wide dissemination to the idea of "open marriage."[7] What proponents of the marital-adjustment school call "successful marriage" corresponds to the O'Neills' definition of "closed marriage." In the closed-marriage contract, there is said to be a sense of belonging to the mate, denying one's self, maintaining a couple-front, behaving according to rigid gender-role stereotyping, and emphasizing total exclusivity. According to the O'Neills, the closed-marriage contract makes a couple slaves of their marriage because the expectations that surround such a marital pattern stifle individual wishes and potentials, while encouraging only those desires and interests the two find mutually acceptable. An alternative pattern is *open marriage,* which stresses "undependent living, personal growth, individual freedom, flexible roles, mutual trust, and expansion through openness."[8]

One reason for such critical reactions to the marital-adjustment school lies in a basic fact that champions of adjustment largely ignored, namely, that wives were doing more of the submerging of individual interests than was true of husbands.[9] The model of marriage that marriage-adjustment proponents worked with (and the pattern to which spouses were supposed to adjust) was what we have called the head-complement structure. At the same time, basic male-female inequalities were glossed over by mere assertions that modern marriage was now egalitarian. Such assertions may have been based on wishful thinking, but more likely they derived from observations that marriage was no longer an owner-property arrangement. It was assumed that if a wife wasn't owned by her husband, she must then automatically be his equal.

In its most sophisticated form, the argument that spouses are equal because they are *declared* to be such goes like this: Husbands and wives are specialists—the husband in his occupation, the wife in her household. There-fore, they complement one another; and because they complement one another, they are equal. They have differences in tasks, but no difference in rank.[10] One assumption made in this argument is that the rewards for doing household tasks are somehow comparable to rewards obtained for performing tasks in the occupational realm. Another assumption is that husbands are as depen-dent on wives as wives are on husbands. We have seen that neither assumption is valid. Women have been assigned the tasks that bring fewer rewards, lower rank, and greater dependence. It is difficult to see how this can be called "equality."

Reward Exchanges and Marital Cohesiveness

Another way of thinking of the glue that holds marriage together is to think in terms of exchange theory. A man and woman choose one another and remain together, sharing their lives, because they perceive this situation to be rewarding. It is profitable; they gain something from it. The benefits of the relationship outweigh the costs. If the relationship should cease to be rewarding to one or the other spouse, efforts can be directed toward altering whatever situation seems costly and punishing. If no solution can be found, perhaps the relationship will be dissolved—although in some cases, the anticipated costs of dissolution may seem greater than the costs of remaining in an unsatisfactory situation.

In other words, the process of marriage involves getting and giving. Each person wants to "get his money's worth" out of the relationship—not necessarily in some crassly calculating way involving dollars and cents, but in terms of all sorts of rewards, both tangible and intangible. Gaining rewards involves costs and investments, which means there is going on in marriage a constant assessment of the reward/cost ratio to make sure that the individual and the marital unit are experiencing profit.

In thinking of the reward/cost ratio as being the glue of marriage, the emphasis may seem to be on the individual rather than on group unity. However, self-interest and group interest are not necessarily incompatible. What is best for the individual may also be best for the marital unit and vice versa. Most social scientists concur with a point made by Sidney Siegel and Lawrence Fouraker in their research on economic bargaining, namely that "the two parties, if they behave rationally and in their respective self-interests, will be forced inexorably to [an exchange] which maximizes their joint benefit."[11] In other words, the most solid and cohesive social system is one in which all parties concerned experience what has been labeled *maximum joint profit* or MJP.[12] There is no reason to think that this should hold less for a marriage than for a business partnership.

According to marital-adjustment notions, marital stability is thought to be achieved through long-suffering endurance and making the best of one's fate, with efforts being directed toward adapting to the marriage no matter how unsatisfactory it is. In contrast, the social-exchange model focuses on bargaining, change, and the rewards the spouses offer each other. Rather than being a process of adjustment, marriage becomes a continual process of negotiation and profit seeking. To some persons, this way of thinking may at first seem selfish and crass. Wouldn't it be simpler to say that *love* is the glue that holds marriage together?

Love and Reciprocity

A song in the country-music tradition bears the title "The Cost of Real Love is 'No Charge.'" The lyrics tell of a child who compiles a list of all the things he does around the house and then demands payment from his mother. His mother in turn speaks of all she has done for the child, beginning with the nine months she carried him in her womb, the days of child care, the nights of sitting up while he was ill, the money put aside for his college education, and so on. However, in contrast to the child's list with specific monetary value attached to each task, the mother's list carries no price tags. After each item is a statement saying that the cost to the child is "no charge."

There is a prevailing sentiment that love—especially family love—should be freely given with no expectation of return, "no charge." However, the song itself describes reciprocity. The child wants payment, but the mother tells him he has already been paid and will continue to benefit from all that his parents do for him. At the same time, although she claims there is "no charge," the mother expects something from the child—affection, gratitude, respect, and the fulfilling of responsibilities assigned to him as a member of the family.

What is true of the parent-child relationship is also true of the husband-wife relationship. While popular sentiment would have us believe that this, too, is a situation of "no charge," the dynamics of married living suggest otherwise. In Chapter 6, we examined the exchange of rights and duties in the practical (instrumental) side of marriage, and now we want to see how such exchanges also take place in the personal (expressive) side of marriage as well. We'll also see that such exchanges take place *between* as well as *within* these two realms of marriage.

Perhaps it might be useful to think in terms of a two-story house. One story is the instrumental realm of marriage, and various changes go on between husband and wife on this level. The other floor of the house, the expressive realm, is also the site of husband-wife exchanges. But there is in addition a considerable amount of running up and down the stairs between the two stories, with exchanges of rights and duties going on between the instrumental and expressive realms.

Figure 7-1 illustrates the way in which marriage, as explained by exchange theory, means continual reciprocity. There is an ongoing chain of obligations and repayments based upon a system of roles. Each role carries with it both rights and duties.

Marriage by definition means both instrumental and expressive interdependencies. We begin in Figure 7-1 with the husband's provider role, built around his duties to supply his wife (and any children) with economic and status rewards. As the husband fulfills these duties, the wife is having her rights to be provided for met. On one level, this motivates her to perform her instrumental role as homemaker, caring for the children and attending to domestic tasks. The husband, having his rights to a smooth-running household met by his wife's performance of her duties, is then further motivated to perform his own instrumental duties in the economic realm.

However, on another level, since the wife's rights to be rewarded by her

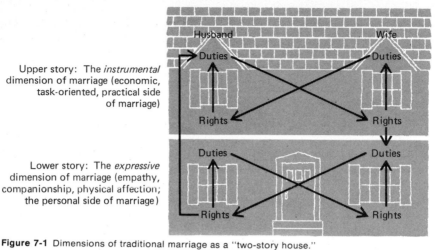

Upper story: The *instrumental* dimension of marriage (economic, task-oriented, practical side of marriage)

Lower story: The *expressive* dimension of marriage (empathy, companionship, physical affection; the personal side of marriage)

Figure 7-1 Dimensions of traditional marriage as a "two-story house."

husband in terms of economic and status benefits are met, she is also motivated to perform her expressive duties. Thus in Figure 7-1, the arrow moves down to the ground floor of the house. The wife's supportive, nurturant, affectionate behaviors (not only sexually, but including that) fulfill the husband's expressive rights. This in turn motivates him out of rectitude and gratitude to perform his expressive duties, thereby fulfilling his wife's expressive rights. It also motivates him further to perform his instrumental (breadwinning) duties.

It should be kept in mind that this entire process may not be at all conscious. Also, the marriage described is in *traditional* terms—the pattern for marriage that has been most familiar until now. Later, we'll examine how exchanges take place in an *equal-partner* marriage. But first, we want to focus on one particular dimension of process in marriage—expressiveness.

Expressive Dimension

What sociologists speak of as the "expressive" dimension of marriage is often that which first comes to mind when people think of the husband-wife relationship. Expressiveness includes three basic elements: companionship (someone to be with and do things with), empathy (someone who listens, understands, and cares), and physical affection (someone with whom love can be expressed through touch, caresses, and sexual intercourse).

At first it may seem strange to think of companionship, empathy, and physical affection as being somehow tied in with the instrumental side of marriage; but research has shown there are very real interconnections. These interconnections—particularly with respect to the economic system—are fascinating to explore.

HUSBAND'S OCCUPATION AND EXPRESSIVE SATISFACTIONS

Sociologists have found a relationship between social status and the degree to which couples are satisfied with the expressive dimension of their marriages. Couples with higher status (as measured by the husband's occupation, education, and income) are more likely than lower-status couples to feel that their marital companionship, empathy, and physical affection are satisfactory.

In order to understand what are indeed complex relationships, it helps to think of the family and the economic-opportunity structure as two separate systems, each very much involved with the other. Figure 7-2 provides some idea of how the relationship of these two social structures affects what goes on in a marriage.

The economic-opportunity structure may be thought of as a network of ways and means through which success and achievement may be attained in American society. It may also be thought of as a reward system, offering both tangible and intangible benefits. These benefits not only include money, prestige, and status; there are other significant rewards which may not seem so obvious without further reflection. For example, the degree to which a family is incorporated into the economic system is associated with such things as mental and physical health, educational, job, and cultural opportunities, and so on.

Families on the fringes of the economic-opportunity system have more problems with physical health, have more mental illness, have higher death rates and a lower life expectancy, and face problems of overcrowding, poor nutrition, excessive drinking, violence, lack of privacy, burdensome debts, and low educational and verbal skills—to mention only a few handicaps associated with poverty.[13] The rewards associated with fitting into the economic-opportunity system come to the poor in only meager packages, and the dissatisfaction felt in receiving such scanty benefits carries over into marital dissatisfaction.

We have seen that marriage involves reward seeking. But the level of rewards that may be obtained depends upon the couple's socioeconomic status. In traditional marriages (where the husband is considered the unique or chief provider, whether it is a head-complement arrangement or in the senior partner-junior partner pattern) this socioeconomic status depends upon the husband's standing in relation to the economic-opportunity structure. This standing may be looked at both in objective terms (the actual *fact* of the husband's income) and in subjective terms (how the spouses *feel* about the level of rewards the husband is able to obtain from the opportunity system).

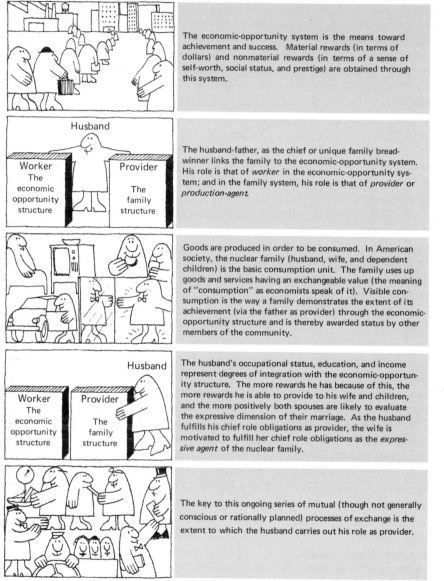

The economic-opportunity system is the means toward achievement and success. Material rewards (in terms of dollars) and nonmaterial rewards (in terms of a sense of self-worth, social status, and prestige) are obtained through this system.

The husband-father, as the chief or unique family bread-winner links the family to the economic-opportunity system. His role is that of *worker* in the economic-opportunity system; and in the family system, his role is that of *provider* or *production-agent.*

Goods are produced in order to be consumed. In American society, the nuclear family (husband, wife, and dependent children) is the basic consumption unit. The family uses up goods and services having an exchangeable value (the meaning of "consumption" as economists speak of it). Visible consumption is the way a family demonstrates the extent of its achievement (via the father as provider) through the economic-opportunity structure and is thereby awarded status by other members of the community.

The husband's occupational status, education, and income represent degrees of integration with the economic-opportunity structure. The more rewards he has because of this, the more rewards he is able to provide to his wife and children, and the more positively both spouses are likely to evaluate the expressive dimension of their marriage. As the husband fulfills his chief role obligations as provider, the wife is motivated to fulfill her chief role obligations as the *expressive agent* of the nuclear family.

The key to this ongoing series of mutual (though not generally conscious or rationally planned) processes of exchange is the extent to which the husband carries out his role as provider.

Figure 7-2 The family and the economic-opportunity system (traditional marriage). Source: Partially adapted from Scanzoni, 1971, pp. 199–200.

Research has shown that for both blacks and whites, there are positive relationships between economic factors and satisfactions within the marriage.[14] Furthermore, economic satisfactions are strongly related to the family's actual economic position.[15] The flow of causes seems to go like this: The husband's education influences his job status, which in turn influences his income. The income in turn influences his wife's economic satisfaction, which in turn influences the expressive satisfaction of both partners.[16]

Actual Income: The Objective Factor

A word of caution may be in order at this point. It is an oversimplification to try to formulate a neat, unqualified equation: more money equals more marital satisfaction. We would be telling only half the story if we were to say that the objective fact of income (the actual number of dollars the husband earns) is in itself the determining factor of expressive satisfactions. Such a simple summary of the situation applies mainly to those near or below the poverty line, where the strains of barely making ends meet do take their toll on the marital relationship and there is little doubt that expressive satisfactions would increase if income increased. One respondent from a black ghetto put it this way: "The men don't have jobs. The woman, she starts nagging. He don't have the money so he leaves. She ADC's it. If he had a job the family unit could come back together."[17]

A wife in such a situation feels an emotional estrangement from her husband because of his poor provision. Because of him, the family is not integrated into the economic-opportunity system with all its promises of success, money, and esteem. Since the objective rewards furnished by the husband are so few, both husband and wife feel a sense of alienation not only from the opportunity structure but also from each other.

This point becomes clear in sociologist Mira Komarovsky's study of blue-collar marriages. She found that when husbands are inadequate providers, wives tend to be overly sensitive to various faults in their husbands and may blame their failure on these factors. In reaction to such faultfinding, a husband may become more anxious about economic inadequacy and may take out his frustrations in drinking, angry outbursts, violence, or emotional withdrawal. The couple tends to avoid topics that matter most (bills, fears about illness, the uncertain future) because they are painful, with the result that a certain remoteness develops between the spouses.[18]

In another study, sociologists found that in nine cases out of ten, wives who ranked the economic aspect as "the most valuable aspect of marriage" were women married to men whose income was less than the median or men who were downwardly mobile (defined as having "failed to achieve the occupational level of their fathers").[19] Money evidently takes on much greater importance to those couples who have the least.

Feelings about Income: The Subjective Factor

A standard of living that is considered satisfying to one person might not seem so at all to someone else. Economic satisfaction is, after all, a subjective matter. For example, suppose that Ann Jones and Barbara Smith both have husbands who earn $10,000. Ann is content with her family's standard of living. She and her husband work together on careful budgeting, own their own home, drive an economy car, and feel they are doing well. Their economic satisfaction extends over into satisfaction with the expressive aspects of marriage as well.

In contrast, Barbara is dissatisfied with the standard of living a $10,000 annual income forces her to maintain. "How can any family get along decently on that paltry amount in these days of rising prices?" she complains. She nags her husband to look for a better job or even to "moonlight" in order to bring in more money. Barbara would like a better home in a more prestigious neighborhood, more expensive furniture, nicer clothing, more luxury items, travel opportunities, more money to spend on the children, and so on. Her lack of economic satisfaction (despite the objective fact of her husband's income, which is exactly the same as that of Ann's husband) causes Barbara to be less satisfied with the expressive elements in her marriage also. She finds it hard to show empathy and affection to a husband who is not rewarding her as she feels she deserves to be rewarded.

The contrast between the hypothetical Ann and Barbara demonstrates the point of Figure 7-3. Marital satisfactions are related to both objective and subjective economic factors. For couples considerably below the national median income, the line between the objective factor (actual dollars) is likely to be direct. But as husbands' earnings increase toward the median income level and then beyond, the line becomes more and more indirect as subjective factors (*feelings* about economic rewards) increasingly influence expressive satisfactions.

The interrelationships between economic satisfaction and the expressive dimension of marriage showed up clearly in our study of more than three thousand married persons.[20] The aspect of expressiveness found to be especially important was *empathy,* because according to the research findings it is empathy that affects the other areas of expressiveness—companionship and physical affection.

Empathy

Empathy means sharing another's thoughts, feelings, and experiences. We are empathizing with other persons when mentally and emotionally we enter into their sufferings, worries, triumphs, or joys. Empathy from others can banish feelings of aloneness and can bring a sense of affirmation, support, and encouragement. Psychotherapists of the transactional analysis school (made

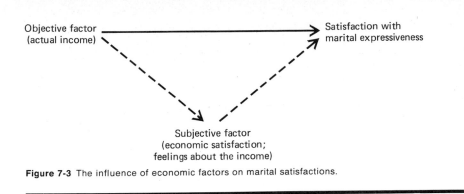

Figure 7-3 The influence of economic factors on marital satisfactions.

' popular through such books as *I'm OK—You're OK* and *Games People Play*) have emphasized that there is a need for "strokIng" in human relationships. People desire to be listened to, taken seriously, given recognition and approval. Psychiatrist Thomas Harris refers to this need as "the psychological version of the early physical stroking" which is so crucial during infancy.[21]

When people enter marriage, empathy is a sought-after reward. Spouses are expected to be able to confide in each other, talk things over, and find understanding and reinforcement. When such empathy isn't forthcoming from one's spouse, persons may seek alternate sources of rewards. A woman may phone her mother or a friend and pour out her heartaches. Or a man may proposition a female acquaintance with the familiar line, "My wife just doesn't understand me."

Sociological studies have attempted to measure the degree to which persons arc satisfied with the empathy they receive in their marriages. Empathy can be looked upon as having two major components—communication and understanding. In three separate large-scale studies, satisfaction with *communication* was measured by asking each respondent how he or she felt about the way he or she could confide in the spouse and discuss anything that comes up. Was such communication perceived to be very good, OK, or not so good? The degree of satisfaction with *understanding* was measured by asking: "How do you feel about the way your wife (husband) understands your problems and feelings? Do you feel her (his) understanding is: Very Good, OK, Not so good?"[22] In general, our findings from all these studies combined may be summed up in the form of five generalizations, each of which will be examined in turn.

First, *among both black and white women, the main positive influence on satisfaction with marital empathy is economic satisfaction.* Out of all the variables measured, economic satisfaction is the one that most influences, explains, or predicts how wives feel about the communication and understanding they receive in their relationships with their husbands.

However, as we have seen, feeling materially rewarded is a subjective matter. How then can a sociologist assume to predict that wives who are economically satisfied will also be satisfied with the expressiveness in their marriages? Might not the degree of satisfaction in either realm simply reflect personality differences?

It is important to keep in mind that explanations and predictions in sociology are based upon research showing what is true of *most* people in a given situation. But this is not to deny that there may be exceptions. In this case, for example, while it is true that most wives' economic satisfaction relates to their husbands' actual income, there are some wives who are satisfied with a lower income and more simple life-style. One illustration might be that of a married couple who choose to carry out humanitarian or religious ideals by identifying with the poor in an urban ghetto or a rural depressed area. Perhaps the husband is a doctor or minister. The wife knows he could be earning a much larger income elsewhere, but she shares his vision and is content with a much lower standard of living than his education and profession would normally imply. However, we must keep in mind that such exceptional cases spring from free choice and are quite different from those cases where persons from birth onward are trapped in a cycle of poverty and forced to endure a life-style deprived of the rewards they yearn for. Such people are *not* economically satisfied.

Sociological research looks at random samples which are representative of a total population and draws conclusions based on *probability* or likelihood. It cannot tell us what will be true of each individual case, but it can show us what is likely. We may expect and predict therefore that the empathy a lawyer's wife receives will seem more satisfactory to her than does the empathy a janitor's wife receives. Such conclusions are based on statistics showing what is true of the vast majority, but any one case might not fit the overall picture. The lawyer and his wife might be on the verge of divorce, for example, while the janitor and his wife might have a warm, loving relationship that has spanned nearly half a century.

It is interesting at this point to notice a slight difference between black wives and white wives with regard to what accounts for economic satisfaction. Among white wives, the biggest indicator is clearly the objective fact of the husband's actual income. Among men, both black and white, feelings of economic satisfaction or dissatisfaction are also linked to the actual amount of money they earn. But among black wives, although their husbands' income and education are important, the research shows these items to be secondary to something else in importance. That "something else" is the wives' own "task-capability ranking." Black wives who rated themselves positively on such matters as intellectual ability, ability to organize things, ability to handle a number of responsibilities, knowledge and experience necessary to hold a job now or later, and abilities in such areas as budgeting, home management, cooking, and child care were also wives who were more apt to be content economically—in spite of the fact that their husbands earned less than the husbands of comparable white women.[23]

Women who view themselves as more capable in skills and tasks may feel that they can therefore stretch limited income further. Economic deprivation has forced them to develop abilities that serve them well in coping with such deprivation. Apparently, the greater this coping ability, the less painful the deprivation is perceived to be; and this in turn means greater economic satisfaction.

The only exception to this pattern is among black wives whose husbands have high education. Then the pattern shifts so that it resembles that of whites; the husband's income becomes the strongest influence on economic satisfaction. It seems that where actual resources are greater (higher income is linked with higher education), there is less need to rely on a coping mechanism in order to feel a sense of economic satisfaction. Instead economic satisfaction is more directly related to one's actual economic situation.[24]

Second, *among both black and white men, satisfaction with empathy received in marriage is related to satisfaction with wives' capabilities in performing tasks.* There is no denying that economic satisfaction plays an important part in how satisfied a person feels about the communication and understanding received in marriage. This is true for men no less than for women. However, the research findings indicated that white husbands ranked economic satisfaction only in second place as an influence on satisfaction with empathy. And black husbands ranked economic satisfaction third, just after "expressive self-concept" (the degree to which the men considered themselves to be nurturant, supportive, and person-oriented). Placed at the top of the list as the major positive influence on satisfaction with marital empathy for both races was satisfaction with their wives' abilities and skills. Husbands who considered their wives to be doing a good job of carrying out mental, social, and practical tasks were likely to be husbands who reported they were satisfied with their wives' communication skills and understanding as well.[25]

One explanation for this finding may be that women who are competent in general are also women who are competent in handling the demanding processes of talking things over and working things through in a marriage relationship. Such wives may have mastered empathy skills just as they have mastered other kinds of skills.

Another explanation, particularly applicable to traditional marriages, relates to exchange theory. Just as wives feel gratitude toward their husbands because of the status and material benefits the husbands provide, husbands may feel gratitude toward their wives because of the wives' competencies and the various benefits that spring from these abilities. Although it is not necessarily conscious, a sense of obligation may be felt by both spouses so that they respond to one another with open communication and warm understanding—in other words, with empathy. The wife responds because of her husband's role as breadwinner, his role outside the home. The husband's response to his wife, according to our research, is based on her competencies both inside the home (cooking, household management, child care, entertaining) and outside the home (knowledge and appreciation of literature, music, and art; intellectual ability, ability to organize things; knowledge and experience necessary to hold a job, and so on).

To try to pinpoint one exact explanation of the relationship between the husband's empathy satisfaction and the wife's task-capability rating is difficult because no doubt more than one explanation is involved. Again we must think in terms of process, perhaps in terms of a computer system with many feedback loops intertwined and affecting one another. If the wife is empathic toward the husband, he is likely to respond with empathy toward her. At the same time, his income enters in, as does her task-performance ability.

However, one finding did emerge which again gets us back to the matter of social status. There is no way of escaping its influence on marital satisfactions. The research data indicated that better-educated wives are the ones likely to be ranked as more competent and skillful. Better-educated wives are also likely to be married to better-educated husbands, and better-educated husbands are those most likely to confer the benefits of higher social status and income. These wives are therefore more likely to be economically satisfied and hence more responsive toward their husbands with empathy for this reason in addition to their possession of skills in communication and understanding. Again it becomes clear that many different interrelated factors feed into the marital exchange process.

Third, *husbands are more likely than wives to be satisfied with the empathy received in marriage*. An "empathy gap" showed up in all three major studies— in the 1967 sample of over 900 white Indianapolis husbands and wives, again in the 1968 sample of 400 black Indianapolis husbands and wives, and once again in our 1971 five-state probability sample of 3,100 black and white respondents from metropolitan areas of Illinois, Ohio, Indiana, Michigan, and Wisconsin.[26]

The finding that husbands are more satisfied than wives with marital empathy could mean either that wives actually receive *less* empathy than husbands do, or else that wives desire *more* empathy than husbands do and therefore cannot be satisfied so easily as husbands.

Perhaps at first glance, the explanation for the empathy gap may appear to lie in the alleged loneliness and isolation of wives in the traditional housewife role. While their husbands are gone all day interacting with colleagues who understand them and discuss subjects of mutual interest, wives have only fragmentary conversations with the postal carrier, supermarket cashier, and children's pediatrician, plus answering endless questions and settling squabbles of preschoolers. While the husband may feel content with empathy received both on the job and at home, the wife may look to her husband alone for empathy. Yet not only is he not there to give it all day long, but he may also tend to expect *her* to give *him* empathy when he does arrive home and be unwilling to listen to the wife's problems. "I've had a hard day at work, honey. I want to relax and forget troubles for awhile." He expects her to reward his economic efforts by soothing and bolstering his spirits.

One problem with the "isolated housewife" explanation for wives' lesser satisfaction with marital empathy shows up in the statistics which indicate that the level of satisfaction is directly associated with level of social status. Higher satisfaction with marital empathy is more likely to be found among wives of higher social status; yet these are the very wives who are more likely to fit the popular picture of the isolated suburban housewife.

Conversely, blue-collar wives are not nearly so isolated. They have relationships that provide intimacy and empathy. Studies have shown that many blue-collar wives have female confidants who serve as the "functional equivalents" of their husbands' workmates. Being less geographically mobile, such wives stay in neighborhoods longer and have time to develop and maintain close friendships. Furthermore, blue-collar wives are more likely to have kin living nearby.[27] Yet, they are discontent with the level of empathy found in their marriages. It is not that such wives lack communication and understanding per se; it is rather a case of not receiving empathy from their *husbands.*

Perhaps rather than looking for an explanation in terms of supposed isolation, we might better turn our attention to the matter of socialization. There are two sides to this: Females more than males are socialized to expect a high level of empathic gratifications from marriage. Males, on the other hand, not only may be satisfied with a lower level of empathy, but they are also not socialized to be able to give empathy to the extent that is expected of females.[28]

Families, schools, churches, the media, and other influences join in getting across the message that girls are to think of marriage as their absorbing life interest. From the cradle onward, females hear nursery tales about the poor girl or princess who is awakened to life's meaning by the kiss of Prince Charming and whisked off to Blissful Castle to live out her days basking in the warmth of an adoring husband who devotes his life to catering to her every wish. To prepare for that day, little girls learn that females are to develop traits of kindness, tenderness, nurturance, understanding, and emotional expression. They enter marriage expecting to take on (and being granted) the role of "socioemotional hub" or "expressive leader" in the family.[29] And they likewise expect expressive gratifications in return. Thus if less empathy than anticipated is received, they feel cheated of a greatly desired reward of marriage.

Males, on the other hand, are socialized to think of the world of work as their central life-interest. Marriage is looked upon as an important part of life, but not the be-all-end-all of life as many women see it. Thus men tend not to be so totally absorbed in family affairs as are their wives. Being less absorbed, they are satisfied with what they feel are "reasonable" amounts of communication and understanding from their wives.

In the very same marriage, the husband and wife may view the situation quite differently from one another. Sociologists speak of this as the "definition of the situation," referring to how something *appears* to a person or is defined subjectively by him or her. One person may define the situation as favorable while the other may define the same situation as unfavorable. A husband might feel that the communication and understanding that takes place in a marriage is very good, but the wife might feel this area of marriage is very weak. Persons act and react according to their personal definition of the situation.

Another possible explanation for the differences in empathy satisfaction as perceived by husbands and wives also relates to gender-role socialization. Whereas girls are socialized to give empathy (and take for granted that they will receive it as well), boys are socialized to receive empathy far more than to give it. As children, they watch Mother kissing their bumps and bruises, relieving both physical and psychological hurts, and reassuring them in their fears and discouragements. And they see her do the same for Father. When they grow up, they expect to have wives who will perform the same function, because that's what women are "supposed" to do. Men may be satisfied with marital empathy to a greater degree than wives simply because husbands are *getting from* their wives more empathy than they are *giving to* their wives.

A familiar theme of cartoons and television situation comedies is that of the wife who tries to get her husband to listen and talk with her, only to be met by a series of grunts, "Yes, dears," or requests for a can of beer or a cup of coffee so that he can go on reading the newspaper or watching television in peace. Such scenes are far more likely to occur in lower-status homes than in higher-status homes because sex-role socialization is so much more rigid in lower-status families. Boys are taught to be tough, strong, nonintrospective, and to appear "manly" by keeping their feelings to themselves. The only kinds of emotions that may be expressed are those that fit with the masculine image—particularly anger and jealousy. Emotions of tenderness, compassion, and sorrow (especially when tears are involved) are considered to be the domain of the female sex; such behavior in males is looked upon with disdain as being "sissy."

Komarovsky speaks of the extreme difficulty which many lower-status men have when it comes to engaging in reciprocal exchanges of communication and understanding with their wives. The more disadvantaged a husband is (in terms of education, income, and occupational status), the harder he finds it to share feelings with his wife—even if he would like very much to do so.[30]

However, our research showed that wives were less satisfied than husbands with empathy received in marriage *not only* at lower-status levels but at higher status levels as well. Could it be that the gender-role socialization that emphasizes less expressiveness in males is also somewhat operative among higher-status husbands? Sociologists Jack Balswick and Charles Peek suggest that such may be the case. They point out that "American society is ironically shortchanging males" in terms of their ability to fulfill marital role expectations. "Society inconsistently teaches the male that to be masculine is to be inexpressive, while at the same time expectations in the marital role are defined in terms of sharing affection and companionship which involves the ability to communicate and express feelings."[31]

Balswick and Peek describe the socialization process in which parents brag about a child's being "all boy." "All boy" is used in reference to behavior that is aggressive or "getting into mischief, getting dirty, etc., but never . . . to denote behavior which is an expression of affection, tenderness, or emotion." As a result of this socialization process, two basic types may emerge: the emotionally reserved "cowboy" who tries to convey a tough, he-man image and who does not express his feelings toward women even though he has such feelings, and the "playboy" who doesn't even have emotional feelings toward women but views women as expendable commodities to be manipulated and used.

Sex-role stereotypes may cause problems not only with respect to sex-role socialization in childhood but also in the way they separate men and women into virtually two distinct worlds during adulthood. At the middle-class cocktail party the men gather in assorted groups to talk business, politics, or sports while the women gather in other assorted groups to talk about children, recipes, schools, and problems of finding household help. In blue-collar settings, the men meet together at the corner bar or enjoy spending evenings "out with the boys" playing poker or bowling, while the women gather with female relatives and friends to share their problems and advice on babies, cooking, sewing, house care, and husbands. Husbands and wives whose interests are so different from one another may find open communication and understanding extremely difficult.

Wives, having been socialized to be nurturant, might be able to give empathy to their husbands in spite of the "different worlds" they live in; but for men it may seem much harder. Not only have they grown up with the idea that inexpressiveness is associated with masculinity, they have also learned to consider women's interests trivial. Yet empathy involves entering into the emotions of another and seeing and feeling something as that person sees it. If a husband has difficulty entering into his wife's experiences because he feels a certain disdain for "woman's world" and at the same time is convinced that his wife wouldn't be able to understand and share in the most vital concerns of "man's world," it is not surprising that his wife will not be satisfied with the empathy her marriage offers.

Perhaps empathy would increase if sex roles were less rigid and husbands and wives had more in common. This point was made in a special television drama of recent years. A middle-aged, working-class wife, feeling bored and unfulfilled now that the children were grown and having had her "consciousness raised" through a women's group, tried to describe her deepest feelings to her cabdriver husband. But he refused to empathize and reacted to her communication efforts by falling asleep, turning away to watch television football broadcasts, or postponing discussion.

He *did* hear her and respond when she asked if she could get a job. The answer was clearly no. The idea threatened his masculine image. However, the wife went looking for a job anyway, and the husband had no idea where she was or if she'd ever come back. That night she phoned and asked him to meet her at a restaurant. Suddenly he didn't care about her job idea. He listened with genuine empathy as she told of waiting in employment offices, and then he said that he knew what that was like, for he too had often pounded the pavement looking for a job and had stood in lines of job applicants. A bond of comradeship and shared experience seemed to grow between the husband and the wife, and suddenly the strong, tough husband began to cry. His wife was moved. Reaching for his hand across the restaurant table, she said she had never felt closer to him. She was receiving the empathy she had longed for.

One reason that empathy satisfaction is greater at higher status levels may be that such couples live in less rigidly distinct male and female spheres and therefore have more in common. Another research finding indicates that husbands at higher levels are more likely to share information and news about their occupations with their wives, thereby giving wives a greater sense of participation in the totality of their husbands' lives than is true at lower levels. Husbands at lower income levels may feel less successful and prefer not to have their employment performances come under their wives' scrutiny any more than necessary.[32]

Fourth, *whites are more likely than blacks to be satisfied with the empathy they receive in marriage.* This fourth generalization from our research has nothing to do with inherent racial characteristics of either blacks or whites but rather may be explained by the relationship of each racial grouping to the economic-opportunity system.[33]

Because of the limited opportunities afforded blacks in a white-dominated society, the blacks in our sample as a whole were found to have significantly less education and income and lower job status as compared to whites. Even when education levels are held constant, black men earn less money than white men. According to figures from the 1970 census, the earnings of black male workers employed the year round continue to be lower than those of the comparable age groupings for whites, although there are some signs of change, most notably among college-educated younger men.[34] (See Table 7-A.)

Furthermore, although there are exceptions in certain occupations, black men generally receive lower earnings than white men, even when they hold the same jobs. Black carpenters and construction workers, for example, have an income that is slightly less than two-thirds that of comparable whites. Black farmers earn slightly over one-third the amount white farmers earn. Black physicians and dentists earn between 82 and 85 percent of what comparable whites in these professions earn.[35]

These inequities have an effect on black marriages. In discussing the exchanges that go on between a husband and wife, we saw how important economic satisfaction is for exchanges of empathy. However, economic satisfaction among blacks is lower than among whites for the simple reason that the economic situation among blacks is less favorable. It is a matter of *relative deprivation.* Relative to whites, blacks earn less and have lower status.

TABLE 7-A MEDIAN EARNINGS IN 1969 OF MALES WHO WORKED YEAR ROUND, 1970 CENSUS

Education	Age 25 to 34 Years		Age 35 to 54 Years	
	Black	White	Black	White
Total	$6,346	$8,839	$6,403	$9,736
Elementary: 8 years or less	4,743	6,618	5,200	7,422
High school: 1 to 3 years	5,749	7,910	6,462	8,775
4 years	6,789	8,613	7,400	9,651
College: 1 to 3 years	7,699	9,190	8,193	11,500
4 years	8,715	11,212	9,327	14,591
5 years or more	9,955	11,808	12,277	16,763

Source: *Current Population Reports*, 1973, P-23, no. 46, pp. 25–26.

The sociological concept of *reference group* sheds some light on the situation. A reference group is the group to which individuals or other groups compare themselves; it becomes a kind of measurement standard for assessing how well one is doing. While blacks have made considerable gains in social position as compared to the past, these gains have been accompanied by "psychological losses," according to social psychologist Thomas Pettigrew, because many blacks have shifted their frame of reference in recent decades. Whereas formerly blacks tended to judge how well off they were by comparing present conditions with their previous situation, Pettigrew points out, "the rising expectations of the present are increasingly framed in terms of the wider white society."[36]

Pettigrew and others claim that blacks at all status levels feel an intense strain resulting from relative deprivation. In fact, there is some evidence that the higher the status of blacks, the greater are the feelings of relative deprivation.[37] This may explain our finding that blacks with higher occupational status were no more satisfied with expressiveness in marriage than are blacks of less status—a finding that is not true of whites, where marital expressive satisfaction increases with higher social status.

Although these feelings of relative deprivation influence empathy satisfaction and processes of social exchange within the marriage relationship, they are not deliberate, conscious, and rational. Rather, they result from what sociologists speak of as a *socially structured* situation. Social forces rather than personal preferences and individual characteristics are influencing behavior in such cases. As white society denies equal benefits to blacks who have achieved the same educational and occupational position as whites, a sense of relative deprivation becomes very real to blacks. Since higher-status white wives take other white wives as their reference group, they can feel relatively satisfied with the objective rewards of money, prestige, and social status provided by their husbands. But black wives also take white wives as a reference group, and the comparison means relative dissatisfaction or deprivation.[38]

It is not that black wives respond with less empathy toward their husbands because they "blame" the husbands for not providing the material and immaterial rewards that white wives receive. Black wives know that their deprivation stems from the white-controlled economic-opportunity system. Yet, in traditional marriages where the husband is the link between the economic structure and the family, the wives are apt to react toward the husband simply because they can't react directly toward the reward-denying system itself. The process is subtle and usually not conscious. And even at higher status levels, since the husband represents the economic system, he meets with a response on the wife's part that because of *relative* deprivation is no more positive than that of black wives of lesser status who experience fewer *absolute* rewards.

And fifth, *satisfaction with empathy in marriage influences satisfaction with the other expressive elements: companionship and physical affection.* This fifth generalization from our research is true of both blacks and whites. Empathy is in itself a coveted reward in marriage. But in addition to its own intrinsic benefits to the spouses, empathy evidently serves as a mechanism affecting other aspects of the couple's relationship as well. The more effectively husbands and wives can empathize or communicate and understand one another, the more likely they are to be able to handle satisfactorily decisions and disagreements about spending time together, leisure pursuits, sex relations, contraception, and so on. Thus they are likely to evaluate companionship and physical affection positively.[39]

Companionship

Several years ago, a women's magazine published a letter from a widow urging wives to take care of their husbands. She wrote: "There is, truly, no relationship like marriage. Someone chose you . . . gave you the gift of status . . . and the only attempt at understanding that will again come your way. Half a man's life on a platter. A built-in best friend. Someone to play with, walk in the first snow, wrap Christmas presents. *With.* Someone who remembers the same people and places and times . . . and your own young selves."[40]

This woman's letter sums up marriage in the way Americans idealize it, particularly from the standpoint of the role of the wife in a traditional marriage where the husband is the unique or chief provider. There is an awareness of the economic-achievement aspect ("gave you the gift of status") and an appreciation of the importance of empathy ("the only attempt at understanding"). But there is also much value placed upon a third expected characteristic of marriage—*companionship* ("A built-in best friend." "Someone to [do things] with.").

In other times and places, companionship in marriage has not been emphasized or expected. Ancient Greek men kept their wives secluded to assure the legitimacy of offspring but found companionship with highly cultured mistresses called *hetairai.*[41] And in the early days of the Israeli kibbutz, the husband and wife who were often seen in one another's company were scorned by the community because such spouse companionship was viewed as disloyalty to the larger collective life.[42]

Only recently has husband-wife companionship come to be a sought-after reward among some young married couples in Japan. Traditionally, social life has not been couple-centered but sex-segregated, with husbands finding companionship with work colleagues and "bar girls," while wives interact with relatives, children, and female friends. During research on Japanese life between 1958 and 1960, sociologist Ezra Vogel found that Japanese wives were both curious and envious of American husbands and wives who went out together. Vogel writes: "One wife, upon hearing about a husband and wife going on a trip for a few days responded, 'how nice,' but after a moment's reflection added, 'but what would they talk about for so long?' "[43]

In the United States, however, the companionship ideal of marriage is held up as a major goal toward which every couple is expected to aim. Husbands and wives are expected to accompany each other to most social occasions, to devote their leisure to mutual activities, and to enjoy simply being together as best friends. But how do American couples feel about the companionship they receive in marriage? Our research uncovered some findings that are similar to the findings related to empathy satisfaction.

First of all, *the higher the level of rewards provided by the husband (especially in terms of education and prestige), the more positively both spouses evaluate companionship.*[44] Several factors appear to be at work here. First, there is the familiar pattern of the exchange model in which the husband as the chief provider fulfills his instrumental role (financial support) which motivates the wife to fulfill her expressive role (emotional support). The better he fulfills his role, the more she reciprocates with greater expressiveness, calling forth more expressiveness on his part in turn. Companionship, as an important aspect of expressiveness, is thus rated as more satisfactory for higher-status couples.

Also not to be overlooked is that chain of events in which economic satisfaction (subjective), often stemming from economic success (objective), influences satisfaction with marital empathy. If a spouse evaluates positively the *empathy* received in marriage, he or she is likely to consider the marital partner to be a good *companion* as well. Someone with whom one can talk things over and find understanding is probably someone whose company is enjoyable in leisure pursuits, too.

Life-style factors may also enter in. Lower-status couples are accustomed to greater gender-role differentiation and sex-segregated leisure activities.

Higher-status couples, on the other hand, are more likely to emphasize husband-wife togetherness in leisure pursuits. As a result, they rank the companionship aspect of marriage as more satisfactory than is true of lower-status couples.

The simple fact of money itself no doubt plays some part, too, in accounting for the relationship between higher social status and a positive evaluation of marital companionship. Leisure activities can require a considerable financial outlay. Camping and sporting equipment, travel, vacation cottages, theater tickets, dining out, entertaining friends, to name but a few of the leisure activities to which many contemporary Americans aspire, all cost money. Higher-status couples possess greater resources and thus have greater access to these means of fostering marital companionship.

Secondly, *husbands are more satisfied than wives with the companionship received in marriage.* This second research finding is again similar to the finding with regard to empathy satisfaction. Husbands were more likely than wives to evaluate the companionship they received in marriage as "very good." Wives were more likely than husbands to evaluate marital companionship as either "OK" or "not so good."[45] Why the difference? It appears that in both black and white marriages, husbands may feel they spend enough time in leisure activities with their wives, whereas wives may expect and desire more. Again, the explanation probably lies in the different socialization of males and females so that wives tend to invest the companionship element in marriage with greater meaning and importance than husbands do.

And thirdly, *whites are more likely than blacks to be satisfied with the companionship received in marriage.* Even though as we have seen there are similarities in evaluations of companionship regardless of race, there are also differences clearly associated with race. When black couples and white couples are compared, the satisfaction with marital companionship is found to be less among blacks than among whites. Again, as we saw in the evaluation of empathy, the principle of relative deprivation appears to be operative.

Physical Affection

Along with empathy and companionship, physical affection completes the trio called "expressiveness in marriage." Physical affection may include a wide range of behaviors—the squeeze of a hand, a kiss, a hug, resting one's head on the spouse's shoulder, stroking the spouse's hair, a tender caress on the back of the neck, a playful pat on the behind, snuggling up together on a couch, sitting on the partner's lap, petting, sexual intercourse.

In popular thinking, sex is considered the most important aspect of marriage; and when a divorce occurs, people often whisper that the couple must have had a sex problem. However, the causes of divorce are much too complex to pin all the blame on sexual dissatisfaction. In fact, marriage counselors can tell of cases where couples were quite happy with the sexual side of their relationship and continued to have intercourse up until the day of the divorce and even afterwards. "Good sex" doesn't necessarily result in overall marital satisfaction. On the other hand, satisfaction with other areas of marriage (economic satisfaction, empathy, companionship) is likely to show up in satisfaction with physical affection as well.

Sex and sociological inquiry   Aware that sexuality is usually considered a personal and private matter, sociologist James Henslin has endeavored to answer the question, "What does sociology have to do with sex?" He writes: "The sociological point of view . . . is that while it is individuals who engage in any given sexual behavior, it is their group membership that shapes, directs, and influences the forms or patterns that their sexual behaviors take. . . . Although sexual behaviors have a biological base, it is membership in groups which shapes or gives direction to the expression of this sexual drive."[46]

Psychotherapist Wardell Pomeroy, formerly an associate of Alfred Kinsey at the Institute for Sex Research at Indiana University, has illustrated how a person's group classification is related to that person's sexual attitudes and behavior. Pomeroy put forth the rather dramatic suggestion that one could be able to tell which of two adolescent boys would be the more likely to attend college simply by looking at their respective sex histories. How? By comparing the boys' sex histories with the Kinsey findings on different categories of people (based upon racial-cultural grouping, educational level, occupation, parents' occupation, rural-urban background, religious group, and so on).

The sex history of one boy, for example, might indicate that he has had intercourse with a number of girls, doesn't take his clothes off for sex relations, cares more about the act than about emotional involvement with the girl, disapproves of mouth-genital contact, masturbates less than he did in his earlier teens, and has infrequent "wet dreams." The sex history of the other boy may indicate that he masturbates actively but has little or no sexual intercourse, reacts strongly to erotic stimuli, engages in petting a great deal and may try oral-genital contact, and considers sex more enjoyable in the nude. The first boy, says Pomeroy, is displaying a sexual pattern that stamps him as being from a lower social-status background, and few boys in this category would be likely to go on to college. It is the second boy who is likely to further his education past high school, because his pattern of sexual behavior shows that in all probability he is from a higher social-status background.[47]

Pomeroy's way of drawing attention to the association between sex and status-level differences may seem a bit sensational but it helps make the point. His picture of the two hypothetical unmarried young men is based upon actual findings that emerged in the Kinsey studies of the 1940s and 1950s. Just as clearly, the data showed that social status affects the sexual behavior of married couples. For example, it was found that wives with higher educational backgrounds were more likely to reach orgasm during marital coitus and to achieve orgasm more frequently than wives with lower levels of education. Couples of higher educational background were also found to spend longer time in sexual foreplay before intercourse.[48]

Marital sex at lower status levels   Couples with lower levels of education and socioeconomic status differ from higher-level couples in both sexual attitudes and practices. At the same time, researchers into sex behavior have found evidence that lower-level couples have much in common *with each other* in the same culture, in other cultures, and in other periods of history.[49]

Rainwater, in comparing his own studies of American lower-status marriages with similar marriages in Mexico, Puerto Rico, and England, found several common characteristics.[50] In all four "cultures of poverty," there was a central norm that "sex is a man's pleasure and a woman's duty." Second, a double standard was practiced both with regard to childhood sex education and later sexual behavior. Girls were shielded from sex information and expected to be sexually innocent until marriage; boys were left to their own devices and expected to experiment.

A third characteristic sexual pattern among these poverty groups in all four countries was the tendency for males to separate women into categories of "good women" and "bad or loose women." "Bad women" were defined as those who were sexually active and enjoyed sex—for example, prostitutes. Wives were expected to be "good women" who were disinterested in sex. In studies of a Mexican village, anthropologist Oscar Lewis found that men generally felt that sexual play was for the seduction of other women and deliberately refrained from arousing their own wives sexually because they didn't want their wives to "get to like it too much."[51] The fear is sometimes expressed that female sexual enjoyment may lead to affairs with men other than their husbands.

What do marriages at lower status levels have in common that accounts for these attitudes toward sexuality? As Rainwater pondered that question, he came up with the hypothesis that *rigidly segregated gender roles* may be the key. Couples whose roles are widely separated are unlikely to have close sexual relations, and wives especially are unlikely to find marital sex gratifying.[52]

Several years before Rainwater suggested his hypothesis, the British social anthropologist Elizabeth Bott had come to a similar conclusion in research on urban families in England. As representative of couples with segregated sex roles, Bott referred to a semiskilled factory worker and his wife who placed little importance on shared interests and joint activities, preferring instead a "harmonious division of labor." The wife's comments indicated that "she felt physical sexuality was an intrusion on a peaceful domestic relationship rather than an expression of such a relationship." In contrast, couples in Bott's study who stressed joint activities and male-female equality were couples in which the husbands held professional, semiprofessional, and clerical occupations. For these couples, a mutual enjoyment of sex was considered an important part of shared interests in general.[53]

Sexual satisfaction and social status At this point, it becomes clear that socioeconomic status affects sexual satisfaction in marriage both indirectly and directly. *Indirectly,* social status affects marital sexual satisfaction through the degree of gender-role segregation that is characteristic of different social levels. The lower a couple's socioeconomic status, the greater is likely to be the degree of sex-role segregation (with fewer shared interests between husband and wife), and the lesser is likely to be the sexual satisfaction in marriage. The higher a couple's social status, the lesser the likelihood of highly segregated sex roles (thus more shared interests between husband and wife), and the higher the sexual satisfaction in marriage is likely to be.

On the other hand, socioeconomic status affects marital sexual satisfaction *directly* through principles of exchange theory. The husband who is more deeply assimilated into the economic-opportunity structure (and is therefore higher on the social-status continuum because of his higher education, income, and occupational status) rewards his wife with benefits of money and prestige that call forth her feelings of gratitude and affection which are then expressed to him in the physical aspects of expressiveness, including enjoyment of sexual relations. And the husband responds to her in kind.

Rainwater's studies of American marriages at different class levels are applicable here. In researching degrees of sexual interest, enjoyment, and commitment he found "a continuum from strong positive involvement with marital sexuality to strong rejection."[54] Social status plays an important part in one's position on the continuum, as Table 7-B shows. Among middle-class wives, 86 percent indicated very positive or positive feelings about marital sex, as did 69 percent of working-class wives. But among working-class wives there was an increase in the percentage reporting negative and rejecting attitudes— more than double that of middle-class wives who reported such feelings. Moving to lower-class wives, less than half reported positive or very positive evaluations of sex in marriage, and 54 percent expressed negative feelings to some degree.

Similarities between the middle class and working class in husband-wife enjoyment of sex are seen also in Table 7-C. It is the lower class that is most set off from the rest; here is seen the greatest degree of difference between how husbands and wives feel about sex. Both the more rigid gender-role segregation and the fewer economic rewards at this level are no doubt operating in the wife's lower satisfaction.

Blood and Wolfe's study of Detroit marriages also indicated that wives' satisfaction with marital expressiveness decreased as social status decreased.[55] Our own findings concur with those of Blood and Wolfe and Rainwater. While

TABLE 7-B   WIFE'S GRATIFICATION IN SEXUAL RELATIONS (PERCENT)

Social Status	Very Positive	Positive	Slightly Negative	Rejecting
Middle class*	50%	36%	11%	3%
Working class†	53	16	27	4
Lower class‡	20	26	34	20

*Includes upper middle class (professionals, executives, and certain business proprietors) and lower middle class (accountants, engineers, supervisors of clerical workers, certain skilled workers and foremen who have similar education and life-style to the white-collar persons in this category).

†Semiskilled and medium-skilled workers in manual jobs and certain service occupations such as policemen, firemen, bus and cab drivers, etc. (Rainwater speaks of this group as the upper lower class, but the term *working class* seems more appropriate for our purposes).

‡Rainwater refers to this as the lower lower class. It includes persons who consider themselves at the "bottom of the heap." Many work only intermittently or are chronically unemployed. When they do work, it is at unskilled jobs. Education is low, with few persons in this category having finished high school and many having no more than a grade school education. Their life-style is one of poverty, with substandard housing, usually in slum neighborhoods. Some sociologists call this the "underclass."

Source: adapted from Rainwater, 1965, Table 3-1 on p. 64, with category explanations from pp. 21–24.

there is no denying that personality factors play a part in physical expressiveness in marriage, social factors also play a significant role. In an achievement-oriented society where a sense of self-worth and personal excellence is linked with one's success within the economic-opportunity structure and yet there is the realization that one is only on the fringes of that structure, it is easy to feel cut off from society's benefits, blocked from the rewards of prestige and material resources, alienated, dissatisfied. This dissatisfaction affects husband-wife empathy and in turn affects how the couple feels about physical affection.[56]

Komarovsky observed this phenomenon in her study of blue-collar marriages. One twenty-nine-year-old woman said that sex was "wearing off" after ten years of marriage and five children. The wife indicated dissatisfaction with her economic situation and remarked that she might have more interest in sex if her husband were "getting along better."[57] In Rainwater's interviews, a blue-collar wife complained of her husband's irresponsibility in money matters and his failure to be mobile into the middle class and indicated that these negative feelings about her husband negatively affected her feelings about their sexual relationship. And in another case, the couple was lower class, and the husband was unemployed. Because he had no interest in finding work and the rent was past due, the wife commented that she had lost all desire for sexual intercourse, saying that now she just tolerated it.[58]

TABLE 7-C   COMPARATIVE ENJOYMENT OF SEX BY HUSBAND AND WIFE (PERCENT)

Social Status	Husband Enjoys Sex More	Equal Enjoyment	Wife Enjoys Sex More
Middle class	33%	59%	8%
Working class	47	51	2
Lower class	67	26	7

Note: More than half the couples in middle-class and working-class marriages report equal enjoyment of sex by husband and wife. This is only true of a quarter of those couples in lower-class marriages.

Source: Adapted from Rainwater, 1965, p. 68, Table 3-5.

Different views of sexuality   In the seventeenth century, an English clergyman, Jeremy Taylor, suggested these reasons for marital sex relations: "a desire for children, or to avoid fornication, or to lighten and ease the cares and sadnesses of household affairs, or to endear each other."[59] Taylor's list suggests that persons may think of sexual intercourse in terms of various functions. Some persons may consider the main purpose of sex to be procreation, while others may emphasize recreation or mention the function of sex as communication. Or perhaps they think of it in terms of sheer physical release.

Lower-educated couples tend to have more children and to find birth control more problematic than is true of couples at higher status levels. Hence, sex-as-procreation no doubt looms high in the thinking of couples at lower levels, along with views of sex-as-release. Lower-status wives in Rainwater's studies made remarks like these: "It's just getting the sexual urge out of him." "He needs it like a starving man needs food." A husband reported that "a guy gets heated up and after he has it he feels good," adding that his wife felt better and slept better after intercourse, too.[60]

As education increases, couples may emphasize other kinds of gratifications associated with sexual intercourse.[61] Sex-as-communication ("endearing each other," to use Taylor's quaint seventeenth-century expression) is considered an important part of the overall communication and empathy in general that characterizes higher-status marriages. In addition, such husbands and wives appear to give more attention to sex-as-recreation. Sexual intercourse may be considered part of the companionship side of marriage, a pleasant leisure activity or fun time in which the spouses can delight together. Kinsey reported that couples who spent a half hour or an hour in sexual foreplay were likely to be couples from the better-educated groups in his sample.[62] And Gebhard's data correlating marital satisfaction and wives' orgasmic experience showed that a couple's *spending time* in sexual activity was the key factor in enabling the wife to experience orgasm.[63] As we have seen, the Kinsey studies showed that higher female orgasm rates occurred among higher-educated couples. Such couples are also more willing to experiment with different coital positions and techniques. Gebhard points out, for example, that oral-genital techniques are quite common in the married upper-socioeconomic stratum but less frequent at lower socioeconomic levels where disapproval of such practices may be strong.[64] It may be that with higher education comes a greater acceptance and appreciation of the human body and all that sexuality has to offer in human experience. Also, higher-status couples have a greater sense of mastery with regard to birth control, and they may tend to have less fear that recreational sex will accidentally turn into procreational sex.

Frequency of sexual intercourse   One area of marital sexuality where there has seemed to be little difference by social status has been the matter of how often a husband and wife have sexual intercourse. Studies have shown weekly frequency to depend more on age and on the number of years married than upon social status. In Kinsey's sample, women who married in their late teens reported an average of nearly three times a week during the early years of marriage. By age thirty, the average was slightly more than twice a week. By age forty, the average had dropped to one and a half times weekly; and by age fifty, it was once a week. For sixty-year-old women, coitus was reported to take place about once every twelve days.[65]

In the 1965 National Fertility Study, it was also found that social status was associated with little variation in coital frequency. Similarly, race was found to make almost no difference. White husbands and wives engaged in sexual intercourse an average of 6.8 times a month, while for nonwhites the average was 6.5. As far as religion is concerned, non-Catholics had a slightly higher average monthly frequency (7.1) than did Catholics (6.3).[66] Couples as a whole who were married less than a year had sexual relations an average of ten or eleven times a month, whereas for couples married twenty-five years the average was about five times monthly.[67]

When demographers began comparing data from the 1965 and 1970 National Fertility Studies, an interesting finding emerged. The evidence suggested that a real increase in frequency of sexual intercourse had taken place among married couples during the five-year interval. (See Table 7-D.)

The first explanation for increased coital frequency that might suggest itself is that contraceptive technology has improved and better methods are now available. Therefore, couples can have intercourse more often without worrying about the risk of pregnancy. This explanation seems plausible and may have some validity; the highest (age-standardized) frequencies of intercourse take place among couples where the contraceptive method employed is the pill, IUD, or vasectomy. However, the increase in frequency has also occurred among couples using all the other contraceptive methods as well—and even among couples not using contraception at all. (See Table 7-E.)

TABLE 7-D MEAN COITAL FREQUENCY IN FOUR WEEKS PRIOR TO INTERVIEW, BY AGE, 1965 AND 1970, NATIONAL FERTILITY STUDIES

Age	Mean		Number of Women	
	1965	*1970*	*1965*	*1970*
All women	6.8	8.2	4,603	5,432
20	10.7	11.0	203	223
20–24	8.4	10.1	835	1,127
25–29	7.4	9.0	828	1,223
30–34	6.8	8.0	913	1,017
35–39	5.9	6.8	878	947
40–44	5.1	5.9	946	895

Source: Westoff, 1974*a*, p. 137.

Demographer Charles F. Westoff has suggested several possible reasons for these findings. Anxieties about unwanted pregnancies may have been reduced not only by modern contraceptive technology but also through the availability of legal abortion. And an increasingly open climate regarding sexual matters also took place during the second half of the 1960s, with sex coming to be viewed more and more as something natural rather than as something taboo. "More fundamentally," reports Westoff, "there has been a developing emphasis on a woman's right to personal fulfillment. . . . Part of this growing ideology is that woman's traditional passive sexual role may be giving way to more assertive sexual behavior." The data showed that the more education a wife had, the more frequently the couple had intercourse. Furthermore, the more modern or egalitarian were her attitudes on gender roles, the higher was coital frequency. The researchers also found that wives who worked for reasons other than money had sexual intercourse more often than wives who were not employed or who worked chiefly for financial reasons. And wives who were seriously engaged in *careers* had sexual intercourse more frequently than all other wives.[68] This brings us to our next topic.

WIFE'S OCCUPATION AND EXPRESSIVE SATISFACTIONS

In discussing the effect of socioeconomic status on each area of marital expressiveness, we have concentrated on the husband's education, occupation, and income as the chief indicators of a family's social status. Until recently, few questions have been raised about the measurement of a woman's social status in terms of her relationship to a male.[69] A 1966 book on college students, for example, asserted that "a woman's socially defined success is typically dependent not on her own occupational and job mobility but on her husband's," and that a female has but "one departure and arrival in her life cycle: her exchange

TABLE 7-E OBSERVED AND AGE-STANDARDIZED MEAN COITAL FREQUENCY IN FOUR WEEKS PRIOR TO INTERVIEW, BY TYPE OF EXPOSURE TO THE RISK OF CONCEPTION, 1965 AND 1970, NATIONAL FERTILITY STUDIES

Type of Exposure	Mean Observed		Mean Age-Standardized[a]		Number of Women	
	1965	1970	1965	1970	1965	1970
All women	6.8	8.2	7.0	8.2	4,603	5,432
Noncontraceptive total	**5.9**	**7.2**	**6.0**	**7.2**	**1,681**	**1,907**
Pregnant	6.0	6.4	4.9	5.4	367	380
Postpartum	0.1	0.9	0.0	1.0	70	65
Trying to get pregnant	8.0	10.2	7.3	9.2	239	356
Sterile[b]	5.5	6.5	6.1	8.0	436	433
Subfecund[c]	6.0	7.3	7.0	8.4	201	265
Other nonuse	6.1	7.0	6.2	7.2	368	408
Contraceptive total	**7.3**	**8.8**	**7.5**	**8.8**	**2,922**	**3,525**
Wife sterilized[d]	6.5	7.0	7.1	7.6	234	322
Husband sterilized[d]	7.8	8.8	8.2	9.6	127	264
Pill[e]	9.2	10.0	8.4	9.2	690	1,211
IUD[f]	9.9	9.4	9.6	8.9	41	267
Diaphragm[g]	7.2	8.2	7.9	8.8	271	189
Condom[h]	6.6	8.1	6.9	8.5	629	490
Withdrawal	5.8	8.5	7.5	8.6	112	74
Foam	7.8	9.2	6.2	8.5	108	216
Rhythm	5.6	7.1	5.9	7.6	285	206
Douche	7.0	7.1	7.1	7.6	196	126
Other[i]	6.5	7.3	6.8	7.5	229	160

[a]The 1970 age distribution of the total sample has been used as the standard distribution throughout, thereby simultaneously eliminating both the effects of different age distributions associated with different exposure categories and the changes in age distribution from 1965 to 1970.

[b]Includes women who have had sterilizing operations for noncontraceptive reasons or who report that conception is impossible because of menopause or that they or their doctor are certain they cannot have another child.

[c]Includes women who believe they cannot have another child, but who are less certain than women classified as "sterile."

[d]Surgical procedures undertaken at least partly for contraceptive reasons.

[e]Includes combination with any other method.

[f]Includes combination with any method except pill.

[g]Includes combination with any method except pill or IUD.

[h]Includes combination with any method except pill, IUD, or diaphragm.

[i]Includes other multiple as well as single methods and a small percentage of unreported methods.

Source: Westoff, 1974a, p. 138.

of a father-determined social status for a husband-determined one."[70] Sociologist Joan Acker calls into question the assumption that a woman must be viewed as an appendage to a male, with the woman's status determined by his, because this assumption implies that women have no resources of their own. Yet if women have such status-determining resources as education, occupation, and income, why don't these resources count as they do for men? Furthermore, asks Acker, why do we assume that such resources "are inoperative if the woman is married?"[71]

Another sociologist, Marie R. Haug, says that the practice of measuring a family's social status in terms of the husband-father alone might have seemed justified half a century ago when social scientists were beginning to introduce social-stratification measures. The proportion of employed married women was low at that time. "But there is no rational basis for persisting in outmoded practices in the face of changed realities in the work world," writes Haug.[72]

Haug's criticisms of traditional measurement practices spring from an awareness that increasing numbers of women have occupational roles, that a woman's income added to her husband's can make a significant impact on a family's life-style (making possible a move to the suburbs or the sending of the children to college, for example), and that furthermore there are cases in which the wife's education and occupational status may be higher than her husband's (for example, where the husband has only a high school education and works as a door-to-door salesman, while his wife has a college degree and teaches school). Why should the family's social status be assigned according to his job rather than hers? Could their occupational rankings somehow both be taken into account? Or should social status be based upon the occupation or income of the one who would be given the higher ranking on the usual scales? These are questions to which some sociologists are giving attention.

Meanwhile, most studies in existence have used one or all of the occupation-income-education factors in relation to the husband as the basis of determining a family's social position in the class structure. The explanation lies in the fact that most families up till now have followed the traditional pattern in which the husband is considered the chief provider. If his wife works (as in the senior partner–junior partner arrangement), his work is considered the more important. His commitment to his work is greater than hers, and it is his job rather than hers that determines where the family moves. For all these reasons, the husband has been viewed as being more closely interwoven into the economic-opportunity system than has been the wife. And since social status is related to one's position in that economic-opportunity structure, it has seemed logical to give attention to where the *husband* stands in relation to it.

But this may change in the future as more and more women show a commitment to careers that equals that of men. A woman may be able to claim social status in her own right based on her own educational and occupational

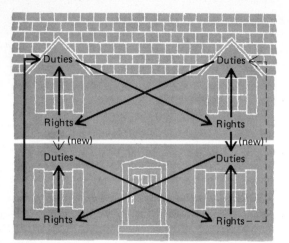

Upper story: The *instrumental* dimension of marriage (economic, task-oriented, practical side of marriage)

Lower story: The *expressive* dimension of marriage (empathy, companionship, physical affection, the personal side of marriage)

Figure 7-4 The equal partner marriage as a "two-story house" (to be compared with Figure 7-1). Source: Partially adapted from Scanzoni, 1972, p. 141.

accomplishments. We may speculate that women with higher status will be able to bestow the benefits of that status on their husbands just as husbands presently reward wives with the fruits of the opportunity system. The roles and rewards will be equal and interchangeable. But what will this do to the husband-wife relationship? In what way, if any, does a wife's employment affect marital expressiveness?

Expressive Interaction and Wives with Careers

If we think in terms of equal commitment to careers by husband and wife (an equal-partner arrangement rather than a senior partner-junior partner marriage), it is possible to theorize in terms of the model in Figure 7-4 and to suggest that expressiveness could be enhanced and strengthened rather than weakened by a wife's full participation in the economic-opportunity system. In the exchange model depicting traditional marriages in Figure 7-1, the movement of the arrows showed that the husband's fulfillment of his instrumental duties (breadwinning) called forth his wife's response in the expressive realm so that she fulfilled her duties of nurturance and affection. In Figure 7-4, we have *two* persons doing each of these things. Thus there is a reinforcement or doubling of the processes involved in the expressive side of marriage.

The model works like this: Where both partners are equally committed to careers and involved *directly* in the economic-opportunity system (rather than the wife's indirect involvement through her husband as in traditional marriage arrangements), the situation becomes one of husband-wife role reciprocity based upon equal-partner status and provider-role interchangeability. The process of fulfilling rights and duties changes from the process we examined in the traditional marriage model. No longer do the wife's instrumental duties include chief responsibility for household tasks; they are shared equally with the husband, for they are now included as part of his instrumental duties. But the wife's duties now also include equal responsibility with the husband for supplying the couple with economic and status rewards from the opportunity system. The rights of both husband and wife are met by these exchanges which in turn motivate them further to perform these instrumental duties (upper story of the house) as well as expressive duties (ground floor of the diagram). Their respective expressive rights are thereby fulfilled, further motivating each spouse in both expressive duties and instrumental duties.

As Figure 7-4 shows, what is new here is that now as the husband perceives that his economic and status rights are being met through his wife's provision, he has an *added* incentive for performing his expressive duties toward her (enhanced empathy, companionship, and physical affection). Another new feature is the way the husband's performance of expressive duties meets the wife's *rights* in the expressive realm in such a way that she is motivated to maintain ongoing occupational achievement. The husband-wife reciprocities that take place in equal-partner marriages are exactly the same for each spouse—which contrasts with the description of traditional marriages in Figure 7-1.

But isn't it rather crass to speak in terms of such reciprocities—the exchange of material benefits for expressiveness and vice versa? Actually, the idea isn't new in a *one*-sided way. Most persons have heard or read the laments of rejected suitors who complain, "She said she wouldn't marry me because I have nothing to offer her." It's the *two*-sidedness of what we're saying that may seem somewhat startling. The point being made isn't that love is something one buys. Nor do couples necessarily consciously think in terms of *rights* and *duties* in thinking of expressiveness in marriage. But what the model shows is that a process does occur in which the couple's relationship with the economic-opportunity structure has an impact on the spouses' relationship with each other as well; and that furthermore, their expressive interactions provide added motivation for achievement in the opportunity system so that they are able to provide one another with that system's rewards.

At present, there is not much actual data on how a wife's working affects the relationship between her and her husband. Much more research needs to be done as increasing numbers of women are taking seriously their option to seek employment outside the home, including strong commitment to demanding careers. However, let's examine what research is available at present and build upon that in order to speculate what future marital interaction might be like in the expressive realm, considering once again the three areas of empathy, companionship, and physical affection.

Empathy

In the past, the large-scale studies which have given attention to working wives and marital satisfaction have concentrated for the most part on marriages of the senior partner–junior partner variety. Equal-partner marriages have constituted such a small percentage of marriages until now that they have largely been ignored. Therefore, in trying to ascertain the effects of wife employment on marital expressiveness, we must keep in mind that we are speaking chiefly of marriages where the wife is in the junior-partner role; she has a job, but is not committed to a career with the same seriousness that characterizes her husband.

Even limiting our focus to junior-partner wives, we still do not come up with easy, clear-cut answers by examining the sociological literature on the subject. Occasionally, researchers even reach opposite conclusions. For example, after the Blood and Wolfe study of Detroit households, Blood concluded that a wife's employment was likely to lead to a more positive evaluation of the marriage if the couple were lower status than if they were higher status, presumably because of the tangible rewards provided by the wife in a situation where money is most needed.[73] The findings of other sociologists suggest just the opposite. Marital dissatisfaction appears to be associated with the wife's employment at lower status levels much more than is likely in marriages where education, income, and job prestige are higher.[74]

Two researchers who studied a sample of 1,325 poverty-level families found employed wives indicating less marital satisfaction than nonemployed wives. Employed wives also felt their husbands were less satisfied as well. The working wives perceived their husbands to be less satisfied with the time the couple spent together, the meals served, and just the fact of the wife's working. Actually, the wife's work was one of the two main areas in which conflict among lower-status couples with employed wives was greater than among comparable couples where the wives were not working. The other conflict area was sex.[75]

These findings fit with Goode's observation that lower-status husbands tend to view their wives' working as a usurping of the husband's provider role. From his study of divorced women, Goode concluded that if a husband feels threatened in his traditional male role it can negatively affect expressiveness in the marriage.[76] Harold Sheppard and Neal Herrick, who specialize in employment research, also found that blue-collar-worker dissatisfaction was higher among those men whose wives worked. The researchers reported that these findings were "completely unexpected," because they had assumed that the higher family income would mean *less* discontentment. They surmised that perhaps at the blue-collar level "machismo" might be a factor. "It may be that such men don't feel that they've really succeeded if, *all by themselves,* they can't provide their families with the necessary income to pay for the level of living to which they aspire."[77]

In some of our earlier research, we found that although empathy satisfaction was higher in general among higher-status couples than among lower-status couples, a wife's employment did make a difference *within* these respective categories.[78] A higher-status husband whose wife was employed was less likely to be satisfied with marital empathy than a comparable husband whose wife was not employed. In contrast, an employed wife in a higher-status marriage was likely to be more satisfied with marital empathy than was true of a nonemployed wife. It may be that the higher the status of the husband, the more he may have defined his wife's employment activities as a drain on time and energy that could have been better invested in empathy and attention to their life together. On the other hand, the wife in such a marriage may have felt satisfied that her rights were being granted her by being able to carry out her option to work; therefore in exchange she responded to her husband with what she considered to be a satisfactory level of empathy and defined his empathic responses as positive as well. Again, this may be a case of spouses' "reading" an identical situation quite differently.

Such a husband-wife difference in the definition of the situation also characterized lower-status couples. Husbands in this category were more satisfied with marital empathy if their wives worked, but employed wives at lower-status levels were less satisfied with empathy than nonemployed wives. It is possible that husbands placed such positive value on the money supplied by working wives that they were also able to empathize with them as persons who shared the burden of breadwinning. However, lower-status working wives, aware of the societal norms about the husband's primary role of provider, may have projected onto their husbands their fears that the men might feel threatened and "emasculated" by the wives' earnings. These fears and projections in turn might have caused wives to feel that processes of communication and understanding were less satisfactory than would have been the case in marriages where wives were not working.

In a study of employed wives and marital happiness, sociologists Susan Orden and Norman Bradburn found that *free choice* about working is highly important. They found that "marriages at all levels of the social structure are affected adversely when the woman is in the labor market only out of necessity," while on the other hand, a woman's working out of free choice has a positive effect on marital happiness. At only one point did these researchers find that the marriage relationship was strained by a wife's working out of free choice, and that was when there were preschoolers at home. "At other stages in the life cycle," report Orden and Bradburn, "the choice between the labor market and the home market makes little difference in an individual's assessment of his own marriage happiness."[79]

Evidence from a recent large-scale study of our own also seems to indicate that a wife's working may not be as important in evaluating marital expressive satisfaction as has been assumed in the past. Satisfaction with empathy, companionship, and physical affection was shown to be no different for either husbands or wives regardless of whether or not wives were employed.[80] And after a study of Swedish working wives, Murray Gendell reported similarly: "On the basis of these data . . . we must conclude that working wives are neither more or less satisfied with their marriages than housewives."[81] Fogarty and his associates came to a similar conclusion with regard to husbands after studying marriges with employed wives in England. "Taking all families together," they wrote, "it cannot be said that in the social group investigated 'wife working' has any clear-cut effect, whether positive or negative, on husband's estimate of happiness of the marriage."[82]

Perhaps all we can say then with regard to marital-empathy satisfaction as it relates to wives' occupational achievement is simply that more research needs to be done—particularly with respect to equal-partner marriages. On the basis of very small samples and limited case studies, we might propose that empathy could conceivably be strengthened and increased in the dual-career marriage. Each spouse is rewarding the other with both economic-status benefits and expressive benefits. Since each is involved in a career, each can understand and empathize with the other's career concerns. There is a very real sense of putting oneself in the other's position and entering into that person's feelings and experiences because they are so comparable to one's own and thus can be understood. Reciprocal advice and counsel can be exchanged between the husband and wife, since there is likely to be a feeling of colleagueship and equality that calls forth empathy. Such couples do not live in the separate worlds labeled "his" and "hers" which traditional sex roles have fostered.[83]

Colleagueship in equal-partner marriages   In traditional marriages, a husband's colleagues are usually his work associates and not the members of his conjugal family. But in Holmstrom's study contrasting more traditional marriages with those that follow the dual-career pattern, she found that "when both marital partners have careers, the possibility exists that they will also be colleagues. If so, it adds a new dimension to the marriage."[84] Holstrom found that a sense of professional colleagueship between married partners may take the form of working together jointly on the same projects (where their fields of specialty are similar or complementary) or in exchanging advice, making suggestions, and in general discussing one another's work. Sometimes, their influence on one another's careers takes more subtle forms, often in processes they may be unaware of at the time—such as in the books and magazines they bring into the home, the professional contacts each makes, the people to whom they may introduce one another, and so on.

In contrast, Holmstrom found that women who had given up their careers to devote full time to their marriages responded quite differently when asked about their influence on their husbands' work. They often replied "as a wife" rather than "as a colleague." They tended to see their roles as buffers between the

In an equal partner marriage, greater empathy satisfaction may derive from a sense of colleagueship.

husband and the pressures and demands of his work or as promoting the husband's career by playing various subordinate helping roles "rather than by collaborating or commenting as a colleague might."

Examples from dual-career marriages suggest a sharply contrasting pattern. An academic couple refers to the intellectual stimulation each provides the other with regard to their respective university careers: "Our collaboration now takes the form of long talkathons in which we discuss the subject, develop new points, downgrade old ones, and sharpen our wits on each other's thought."[85] Joanne Simpson, a meteorologist, provides another example as she tells of meeting her husband in a professional association and developing even before marriage into "a terrific research team with complementary skills." Where one was weak the other was strong, so that the two of them were able to create more than double the sum of their individual efforts. Even when federal Civil Service nepotism rules prevented their continuing to work together so that their work interests were brought into conflict, the sense of colleagueship continued. Simpson reports, "The conflict is compensated for in part by the common language, the associates, and the intellectual interests which we share."[86]

The empathy that can spring from colleagueship in an equal-partner marriage does not necessarily require that the husband and wife be doing the same work. The mere fact of their both being active in the economic-opportunity system can result in the kind of sharing mentioned above—common intellectual interests, associates, and so on, plus the exchange of counsel, advice, criticism, and suggestions in the empathic spirit that can occur between persons equally involved in career achievement goals.

Companionship

Because of the sheer demands of time and energy required by an occupation, we might expect to find that husband-wife companionship suffers when the wife takes on outside employment. We did not find this to be true in our most recent research,[87] although there was some indication of a negative effect of wife employment on companionship in the 1967 study of Indianapolis marriages.[88] In that particular sample at that particular time, there were indications that companionship satisfaction was greater if the wife was not working. But if the wife *was* working, once again there were variations by social status. In households where the wife held a higher-status job, both husbands and wives were much more satisfied with marital companionship than was the case in households where the wife held a lower-status job. Women with higher-status jobs are usually married to men with higher education and higher-status jobs as well, men who have achieved and who are secure enough in their provider role not to feel threatened by their wives' working.

Earlier, Blood and Wolfe had found that wives most satisfied with marital companionship were those who concentrated on entertaining their husbands' business associates and clients, and who devoted themselves to understanding their husbands' business problems and helping their husbands get ahead rather than concentrating on careers for themselves. Those next most satisfied were wives who worked as collaborators with their husbands in joint enterprises. Working wives were the least satisfied with companionship out of these three categories (because "her work partly separates her from her husband"), but such wives were more satisfied than were the traditional stay-at-home housewives. In the words of Blood and Wolfe, "Lowest of all [in companionship satisfaction] is the wife who 'sticks to her knitting' while the husband is absorbed in his own business. This traditional-type marriage involves relatively little companionship."[89]

One of the findings that surprised Orden and Bradburn in their study of wife employment and marital happiness was that husbands whose wives worked part-time ranked companionship satisfaction higher than did all other husbands—including those whose wives were employed full-time and those whose wives were not employed at all. It was also found in this same study that the wives who freely chose part-time work were more happy than women who had freely chosen either to work full-time or to be full-time homemakers.[90]

Gendell's study of Swedish working wives likewise led him to conclude that part-time workers were slightly more satisfied in their marriages than either full-time housewives or full-time employed wives—though the differences were really too small to be considered significant.[91] And Fogarty and his associates also found some indication of greater satisfaction with part-time wife employment in England.[92]

Companionship in career-oriented, equal-partner marriages seems to require planning and effort. On the one hand, companionship in such marriages could be enhanced by the spirit of colleagueship and the common interests that are discussed and mutually engaged in (such as travel together relating to one or the other's career where possible, or reading the same books and journals). On the other hand, companionship by definition means doing things together in leisure time; and where both husband and wife are fully committed to career interests, leisure time is likely to be at a premium and may at times seem nonexistent.

Part of the problem stems from what Fogarty and his associates call "overload"—the double job that is usually faced by a working woman because of the traditional assumption that the management of the home is her responsibility in addition to her outside work. Trying to do two jobs might easily tax her energies and time so greatly that companionship is considerably reduced— something that her husband might resent. Perhaps this is why some of the studies indicated that there was greater satisfaction on the part of both husbands and wives if the wife chose part-time employment. Yet, this way of dealing with the problem is not satisfactory for many highly educated women. For one thing, suitable part-time employment is not easy to find; and for another, part-time employment does not bring with it the economic and prestige rewards that full-time work commitment does. Furthermore, some women simply prefer a continuous, highly committed work pattern. They are more apt to feel the solution to the time and energy problem lies in persuading husbands to share more of the overload, perhaps even finding companionship through jointly performing household tasks while also making more time available for leisure-time activities.

Dual-career families also need to make adjustments more than other families in ordering their social life. Fogarty and his colleagues concluded from their studies that dual-career families have special difficulties "in finding time for contacts with relatives and neighbours."[93] And Bernard quotes an academic wife who said, "I must confess that entertaining for me is more of a chore than a pleasure because I keep thinking of all the time that its preparation takes away from my own work."[94] Holmstrom tells of one two-career couple who solved the problem through the husband's suggestion that they entertain friends by using some of their increased income to take them out to restaurants rather than serving a meal at home.[95]

In marriages where husbands and wives can agree on priorities, the quality of their time together can make up for the lack of quantity. An art professor who says "there's a lot to be said for companionship in marriage" has remarked that her career could not have progressed as it has if she had been married to "a nine-to-five man with weekends off who expected attention" during his leisure time. The man she did marry is a highly respected photographer, photojournalist, and teacher who shares his wife's creative interests and who says, "The nice thing is we talk to each other. We always seem to have something to talk about."[96] In such marriages, the empathy of colleagueship seems to result in companionship that is considered highly satisfactory despite busy schedules necessitated by the spouses' equal involvement in the economic-opportunity structure.

Physical Affection

Persons who think in stereotyped sex roles often express worries that a couple's sexual relationship will be harmed if the wife shares the breadwinner role. Fogarty and his associates described these fears: "The assumption here is that women who want to enter the male world of competition would be highly motivated by competitiveness with men and, as a consequence, would tend to emasculate their husbands. The assumption follows that these couples' sex lives would be characterized by impotence and frigidity."[97] However, while acknowledging that such a pattern might occur in certain cases, these researchers did not find evidence from their data that working wives are characterized by desires to lord it over men. Rather, the women in their sample indicated that they worked for reasons of financial security, the need to be creative, and "the desire to be effective as an individual person." As far as the sex lives of the couples in the Fogarty study were concerned, "the impression is one of a 'normal' range of sexual experience."

In our 1967 Indianapolis study, we found that husbands whose wives did not work were more satisfied with the love and physical affection received in their marriages than were husbands whose wives worked. This was true at all status levels. By the same token, wives who were employed were more satisfied with the love and physical affection in their marriages than were wives who did not work. Again, this was found at all status levels.

These husband-wife differences might relate to sex-role stereotypes and traditional notions of masculinity as it is tied into both the sexual realm and the provider role (especially at lower status levels) and a sense of resentment that the time and energy wives devote to their jobs may seem to be "stolen" from loving attention and affection that could have been given to husbands instead (particularly at higher status levels where wives are likely to have more education and higher-level jobs which make greater demands). For the wives' part, the sense of self-worth experienced through direct access to the economic-opportunity system and the sense of contributing financially to the family, plus the belief that their working meant their husbands had granted them something wives increasingly define as not only an option but a right—freedom to work—may have meant that the wives experienced a sense of contentment which carried over to their perception of the physical affection in marriage as well.[98]

Much more research needs to be done to determine the impact that wives' employment actually makes on the physical expression of love in marriage. Our most recent study indicated that a woman's working outside the home made no significant difference at all in husbands and wives' evaluation of satisfaction in this dimension of marriage.[99] Indeed, some social scientists have suggested that, rather than hurting a couple's sex life, a wife's working might enhance it. The husband and wife can relate as two separate individuals who have developed their personal identities in the occupational world; thus each has more to bring to the other in the overall marital relationship, including the sexual aspects of that relationship.[100]

Sociologist Alice Rossi has argued this point in countering charges made by defenders of traditional sex roles who claim that equality of the sexes would upset the male-female sexual relationship. While acknowledging that full sex equality would no doubt be the death knell of the traditional arrangement in which "the sex act presupposes a dominant male actor and a passive female subject," Rossi suggests that husbands and wives who participate equally in parental, occupational, and social roles "will complement each other sexually in the same way, as essentially equal partners, and not as an ascendant male and a submissive female." Rather than detract from the sexual experience, equality can enhance it since the "enlarged base of shared experience" in other realms can heighten satisfaction with the sexual experience as well.[101]

Rossi's argument fits with an exchange-theory approach to the equal-partner marriage. If there are equal exchanges of rights and duties occurring in both the instrumental and expressive dimensions of marriage in general, might we not expect equal exchanges to go on in the sexual relationship as well?

Likewise, role interchangeability in the equal-partner marriage might be expected to extend to the realm of physical affection. Psychologist A. H. Maslow has alluded to such role interchangeability in sexual relations. Maslow devoted his attention to studying characteristics of persons with a strong sense of self-esteem and self-realization, persons "who have developed or are developing to the full stature of which they are capable." He termed such persons "self-actualizing" and found that one of their characteristics was that "they made no really sharp differentiation between the roles and personalities of the two sexes." Maslow explains:

> That is, they did not assume that the female was passive and the male active, whether in sex or love or anything else. These people were all so certain of their maleness or femaleness that they did not mind taking on some of the cultural aspects of the opposite sex role. It was especially noteworthy that they could be both active and passive lovers and this was

the clearest in the sexual act and in physical love-making. Kissing and being kissed, being above or below in the sexual act, taking the initiative, being quiet and receiving love, teasing and being teased—these were all found in both sexes. The reports indicated that both were enjoyed at different times. It was considered to be a shortcoming to be limited to just active love-making or passive love-making. Both have their particular pleasures for self-actualizing people.[102]

As opportunities for women to exercise their full potentialities in the economic-opportunity system present themselves, the number of "self-actualizing" wives may be expected to increase. Thus the likelihood of growing numbers of couples in equal-partner marriages fitting the pattern Maslow describes may also increase.

Changes over time In studying human sexuality, sociologists look for patterns, trends, and indications of what is happening among groups of people, rather than focusing on individual cases. We have already seen how social status can make a difference in the sexual attitudes and behavior of people. Similarly, a changing social climate over a period of time can also mean alterations in how people view sexual matters. Kinsey and his associates for example took into account changes in sexual practices which occurred over a period of forty years. Their sample of women was divided into categories according to decade of birth, beginning with women born before 1900, then those whose birth dates fell during the periods 1900–1909, 1910–1919, and 1920–1929. There were certain areas of sexual behavior where the decade of a woman's birth made much more difference than did her social class in how she had behaved sexually over the years.

Practices such as engaging in sexual intercourse in the nude or utilizing certain petting techniques in marital foreplay (for example, manipulating the husband's genitals or participating in oral-genital sex) were much less common among the older generation in Kinsey's sample than among the younger generation. Kinsey also found that a jump in the percentages of married women who had experienced orgasm had occurred over the four decades. He attributed these changes to a freer climate and more frankness about sexual matters, along with increased scientific understanding. "There were wives and husbands in the older generation who did not even know that orgasm was possible for a female," wrote the Kinsey researchers, adding that even if persons did think female orgasm was possible they couldn't conceive of it as being either pleasurable or proper.[103]

In recent years, one of the biggest changes in attitudes toward marital sex has been with regard to the sexual needs, desires, and behavior of women. The laboratory research of Masters and Johnson has clearly demonstrated the high capacity women have for sexual enjoyment, including the capability of experiencing multiple orgasms within a short space of time. These researchers have also shown similarities in male and female orgasms, with both men and women going through the same four phases.[104] In other words, the response cycles of men and women in building up to and experiencing sexual climax are really very much alike. Such findings would no doubt have shocked the sex lecturer who wrote in the early part of this century: "The best mothers [and] wives . . . know little or nothing of the sexual pleasure. Love of home, children, and domestic duties are the only passions they feel. As a rule, the modest woman submits to her husband, but only to please him."[105] Such lecturers and writers failed to realize that the lack of sexual interest in many married women was not a sign of the "natural order of things" or the "innate goodness of the female sex," but rather stemmed from the way females were socialized in a society that emphasized both sexual repression and the double standard. Such books helped perpetuate further the view that women were sexually disinterested and unresponsive.

Marriage manuals One way to get some idea of changing sexual attitudes over time is to examine marriage manuals from different historical periods. In an examination of American marital-education literature from the period of 1830 to 1940, sociologist Michael Gordon found a profound change in conceptions of the role of sex in marriage, a change he sums up in the title of his article on the subject, "From an Unfortunate Necessity to a Cult of Mutual Orgasm."[106]

Many of the nineteenth-century books made it clear that sex should be viewed as a means to an end (procreation) rather than as an end in itself (pleasure). Warnings were sounded on the supposed dangers of excessive sex in marriage, and couples were alerted to the physical exhaustion and damage that might be incurred through overindulgence in sexual intercourse. Some books took pains to spell out exactly what "overindulgence" was, with the advice varying from calls for sexual abstinence except when a child was desired to suggestions that intercourse be limited to certain time periods. "Few should exceed the limit of once a week; while many cannot safely indulge oftener than once a month," instructed one sex manual written in 1866.

The emphasis on rationality, self-control, and moderation in marital sex was nothing new, but could be seen in writings from 200 years before. For example, the context of the comments of Jeremy Taylor, the seventeenth-century English divine quoted earlier, make it clear that he was just as concerned about misuses of sex in marriage as about its "proper" exercise. Avoiding fornication, seeking to have children, and desiring to find comfort from cares and to express endearment—these were legitimate ends; but "he is an ill husband that uses his wife as a man treats a harlot, having no other end but pleasure. The pleasure should always be joined to one or another of these ends . . . but never with a purpose, either in act or desire, to separate the sensuality from these ends which hallow it. Married people must never force themselves into high and violent lusts with arts and misbecoming devices, but be restrained and temperate in the use of their lawful pleasures." This statement was still being quoted as advice to couples in a 1917 sex-education manual.[107]

Toward the end of the nineteenth century and in the early decades of the twentieth, the winds of change began to blow—first a slight breeze and then a full-force gale. Sex took on a more important role in the marriage relationship, and pleasure for both partners began to be emphasized. Writers talked about "satisfactory sexual adjustment" and by the 1930s were giving instructions on how to achieve such adjustment. Learning and practicing such techniques was seen as an art, the goal of which was to be perfectly timed, simultaneous orgasm for husband and wife.

In almost paradoxical fashion, sex came to be viewed as *work* at the same time it came to be viewed as play. The growing societal approach to marital sexuality moved from the nineteenth-century emphasis on procreation to the twentieth-century emphasis on recreation, but as Gordon points out, it was recreation "at which one must work hard." "Work at sex because it's fun!" became the prevalent idea.[108]

One of the first sociologists to point this out was Nelson Foote, who responded to the 1953 publication of the Kinsey findings on female sexual behavior by writing an article called "Sex as Play."[109] Referring to insights from the social psychology of play, Foote wrote that "play—any kind of play—generates its own morality and values. And the enforcement of the rules of play becomes the concern of every player, because without their observance, the play cannot continue."

An examination of fifteen currently popular marriage manuals illustrates his point. Sociologists Lionel Lewis and Dennis Brissett found in these manuals an abundance of rules, duties, and do's and don'ts that husbands and wives are instructed to follow rigorously in their sexual relationship. Sex was presented almost as a chore, involving technical competence, skill development, a quest for mastery, a drive for success, and a fear of failure (defined mainly in terms of having or not having an orgasm). Deferred gratifications, self-denial, scheduling the various parts of the sexual act carefully, striving, performance, deliberation, management—these were the matters with which husbands and wives were to be concerned as they enjoyed themselves in recreational sex. Lewis and Brissett offered the thesis that "the American must justify his play . . . he has done this by transforming his play into work . . . work is felt to carry with it a certain inherent dignity." Lewis and Brissett speak of sex counselors and writers as "avocational counselors" in the same sense as teachers of other avocational interests (such as how to play tennis better, how to dance, ski, etc.).[110]

Sex researchers William Masters and Virginia Johnson also have written of "the influence of the work ethic on sexual attitudes in contemporary society" which convinces couples that "work is productive and he who works is virtuous, whereas play is wasteful and he who plays is sinful." Such a view, they emphasize, becomes goal-oriented and concerned with instant gratification rather than a mutual expression of affection between the partners in a context of overall communication and enjoyment of one another.[111]

In Gordon's study of marriage manuals from 1830 to 1940, he noticed other patterns besides the swing from sex-as-procreation to sex-as-recreation to sex-as-work. For one thing, there occurred a change in attitudes toward birth control. Early writers were very negative about limiting family size, but some signs of change began to occur in the 1920s. In the 1930s (partially due to some legal changes), contraception came to be seen in a much more favorable light. Earlier, even writers who emphasized sex for pleasure tended to be reluctant to endorse birth-control practices—except periods of sexual abstinence.

The other most noticeable trend observed by Gordon in his study was the growing emphasis on female sexuality. Early books gave the impression that a woman could be expected to show little interest in coital relations with her husband. Later books still emphasized a woman's alleged lesser desire, but it was now suggested that a dormant sensuality lay within her, waiting to be awakened and called forth by her husband's skillful techniques of love. Full participation in *marital* sexual relations came to be viewed as a woman's right, and the husband's responsibility was to make sure she could exercise this right. As part of the trend toward recreational sex, some books began telling wives to seek to make sex pleasurable for their husbands as well.

What does any of this have to do with the subject at hand, namely the effect of a wife's working on the physical aspects of marital expressiveness? Gordon suggests, in view of trends he observed in his study of marriage manuals, that research is needed to find out "to what extent was the acceptance of female sexuality linked to the increasing number of women in the work force."[112] As we have seen, the common owner-property arrangement of marriage began to change as the option to work opened to women. The wife's rights were increasing, as were her husband's duties toward her in the marital exchange— particularly with regard to fulfilling the wife's expressive rights. It is not surprising then that sexual satisfaction for wives began to receive increasing attention along with the rise in head-complement and senior partner–junior partner marriage patterns.

Yet, later research on female sexuality in more recent marriage manuals has caused Gordon and his coauthor Penelope Shankweiler to wonder if women have come as far as is sometimes thought. "Women in this century have been granted the right to experience sexual desire and have this desire satisfied," they write, "but always with the man calling the tune."[113] They suggest that this is "a manifestation of the minority group status of women," since "if women have been encouraged to take more initiative it is in order that they might give more pleasure to their husbands rather than achieve more autonomy in the sexual realm." Gordon and Shankweiler refer to James Coleman's remark that

With role interchangeability, expressive satisfaction in marriage may be enhanced.

female enjoyment of sexuality for its own sake can only come about "when [a woman's] status and ultimate position do not depend greatly on her husband."[114]

Although the need continues for more research, evidence from the 1970 National Fertility Study may indicate that many wives are already experiencing a greater degree of sexual autonomy and at least partially for the reason Coleman suggests. It could be argued that the increased frequency of sexual intercourse on the part of wives holding egalitarian gender-role norms, higher education, and career aspirations[115] would seem to indicate more of a desire for sexual pleasure for its own sake than a desire to please husbands who "call the tune" on sexual matters because wives are economically dependent upon them.

But a wife's sexual autonomy need not rule out her desire to give sexual pleasure to her husband as well. In fact, in terms of exchange theory as illustrated in Figure 7-4, the wife in an equal-partner marriage has added reasons to provide such rewards to her partner just as he provides them to her. Some husbands may find that they are experiencing increased sexual enjoyment as egalitarian gender-role norms bring freedom from assuming the major responsibility for marital sex, and they may also find it rewarding to be released from pressures to perform and to view sex as a conquest. They may find that they like being able to receive as well as achieve. One man reported, after his wife became a feminist: "Our sex life has undergone a tremendous change, because I was no longer prepared for her to just lie back and look at the ceiling. . . . I deserve a little bit of looking at the ceiling too."[116]

The equal-partner marriage emphasizes role interchangeability. In such an arrangement, the responsibilities double in both the instrumental and expressive dimensions of marriage. But the rewards double as well. Thus, it is possible to postulate that as more and more marriages are built on the equal-partner pattern, marital expressiveness will be enhanced because of the broader base of joint interests and the increased and strengthened circuits of the marital exchange process.

NOTES

1 Bernard, 1972, chap. 10.
2 Dizard, 1968, p. 4.
3 Locke, 1968, p. 45.
4 Burgess, Locke, and Thomes, 1963, p. 294.
5 Brickman, 1974, p. 269.
6 Seidenberg, 1970, pp. 304–305.
7 O'Neill and O'Neill, 1972.
8 O'Neill and O'Neill, 1972, pp. 53, 64, 71.
9 Bernard, 1972.
10 Miller and Swanson, 1958.
11 Siegel and Fouraker, 1960.
12 Kelley and Schenitzki, 1972, p. 307.
13 Herzog, 1967.
14 Blood and Wolfe, 1960.
15 Scanzoni, 1971.
16 Scanzoni, 1975a.
17 Rainwater, 1970, p. 169.
18 Komarovsky, 1962, pp. 291–292.
19 Blood and Wolfe, 1960, p. 81.
20 Scanzoni, 1975a.
21 Harris, 1967; Berne, 1964.
22 Scanzoni, 1970, 1971, 1975a; also see Blood and Wolfe, 1960.
23 Scanzoni, 1975a.
24 Scanzoni, 1975a.
25 Scanzoni, 1975a.
26 Scanzoni, 1970, 1971, 1975a.
27 Komarovsky, 1962.
28 Fasteau, 1974; Balswick and Peek, 1971; Pleck and Sawyer, 1974.
29 Seeley, Sim, and Loosley, 1956, p. 178.
30 Komarovsky, 1962, p. 156.
31 Balswick and Peek, 1971.
32 Scanzoni, 1970; Komarovsky, 1962, p. 152 ff.
33 Scanzoni, 1971, pp. 204–210; 1975a.
34 *Current Population Reports* 1973, P-23, no. 46, p. 2.
35 *Current Population Reports* 1973, P-23, no. 46, p. 52.
36 Pettigrew, 1964, p. 187.
37 Blau and Duncan, 1967.
38 Scanzoni, 1971, p. 208.

39   Scanzoni, 1975a.
40   Ladies Home Journal, circa late 1950s.
41   Seltman, 1956.
42   Talmon, 1972, p. 12.
43   Vogel, 1963; also see De Vos and Wagatsuma, 1970; Blood, 1967.
44   Scanzoni, 1970, p. 78.
45   Scanzoni, 1971, p. 201.
46   Henslin, 1971, pp. 1–3.
47   Pomeroy, 1972, p. 469.
48   Kinsey et. al., 1953, chap. 9.
49   Pomeroy, 1972, p. 470.
50   Rainwater, 1964.
51   Lewis, 1951, p. 326.
52   Rainwater, 1964.
53   Bott, 1957.
54   Rainwater, 1965, p. 63; see also Bell, 1974.
55   Blood and Wolfe, 1960, pp. 224–229.
56   Scanzoni, 1970, pp. 79–107; 1975a.
57   Komarovsky, 1962, p. 93.
58   Rainwater, 1965, pp. 90–97.
59   Taylor, 1650, chap. 2, sec. 3-2.
60   Rainwater, 1965, p. 113; 1960, p. 135.
61   See Rainwater, 1965, p. 111, Table 3-15.
62   Kinsey et. al., 1953, chap. 9.
63   Gebhard, 1966.
64   Gebhard, 1971, p. 209.
65   Kinsey et. al., 1953, chap. 9.
66   Ryder and Westoff, 1971, p. 174.
67   Westoff and Westoff, 1971, pp. 23–24.
68   Westoff, 1974a.
69   Haug, 1973; Acker, 1973.
70   Quoted in Haug, 1973.
71   Acker, 1973, p. 938.
72   Haug, 1973, p. 88.
73   Blood, 1963, p. 304; Blood and Wolfe, 1960, pp. 101–102.
74   Nye, 1963; Nye, 1974b.
75   Feldman and Feldman, 1973.
76   Goode, 1956.
77   Sheppard and Herrick, 1972, pp. 27–28.
78   Scanzoni, 1970, p. 129.
79   Orden and Bradburn, 1969, pp. 405, 392.
80   Scanzoni, 1975b.
81   Gendell, 1963, pp. 132–133.
82   Fogarty, Rapoport, and Rapoport, 1971, p. 475.
83   Fogarty, Rapoport, and Rapoport, 1971, pp. 477–478.
84   Holmstrom, 1972, p. 121.
85   Bernard, 1964, p. 234.
86   Simpson, 1973.
87   Scanzoni, 1975b.
88   Scanzoni, 1970, pp. 38–41.
89   Blood and Wolfe, 1960, p. 167.
90   Orden and Bradburn, 1969.
91   Gendell, 1963, p. 133.
92   Fogarty, Rapoport, and Rapoport, 1971, p. 478.
93   Fogarty, Rapoport, and Rapoport, 1971, p. 477.
94   Bernard, 1964, p. 240.

95 Holmstrom, 1972, p. 98.
96 Patricia Moore, interview with Art and Irene Siegle, *Chicago Daily News,* May 26, 1974, p. 15.
97 Fogarty, Rapoport, and Rapoport, 1971, p. 356.
98 Scanzoni, 1970.
99 Scanzoni, 1975b.
100 Fogarty, Rapoport, and Rapoport, 1971, p. 356.
101 Rossi, 1964, p. 139.
102 Maslow, 1954.
103 Kinsey et. al., 1953, chap. 9.
104 Masters and Johnson, 1966.
105 Shannon, 1917, p. 162.
106 Gordon, 1971.
107 Shannon, 1917, p. 162.
108 Gordon, 1971, p. 73.
109 Foote, 1954.
110 Lewis and Brissett, 1967.
111 Masters and Johnson, 1973.
112 Gordon, 1971, p. 77.
113 Gordon and Shankweiler, 1971.
114 Coleman. 1966.
115 Westoff, 1974a.
116 Quoted in Fasteau, 1974, p. 34.

8
PROCESS IN MARRIAGE: POWER, NEGOTIATION, AND CONFLICT

An experienced secretary and bookkeeper saw no reason that she shouldn't go back to work now that her children were in school. Her husband said no. Explaining the problem to a newspaper advice columnist, the woman wrote: "My husband said if I want to work outside the home I should work for him. (He owns a small retail business.) I don't want to work for him because he refuses to pay me. He says: 'You don't need any money of your own. If you want something, ask me and I'll give you the money for it.' (In the past when I've asked for money he has had to know where every dime is going.) He enjoys having me ask him for money. It makes him feel important."[1]

Persons who assert that marriage can stand on love alone are suggesting an imbalanced precarious posture. Marriage requires two legs—love and justice. Aristotle defined justice as simply "the good of others."[2] And Robert Seidenberg, a psychiatrist, points out: "Love without justice is a yoke, which more often than not, not only enslaves but strangulates the human spirit."[3] The wife in the letter quoted feels that she is being treated unfairly by her husband; she defines her situation as one of injustice, no matter what her husband may say about feelings of love for her.

However, if this wife presses for her rights and insists on furthering her own interests even though they are in opposition to her husband's interests, she is aware that a situation of conflict will develop. Negotiation will be necessary so that a satisfactory settlement can be reached and the relationship continued.

The issue of *power* also comes into play. The wife's power is limited by her dependence on her husband for resources. Aware of this, the husband refuses to allow her any discretionary income of her own even if she were to earn it in his place of business ("he refuses to pay me"). Instead he wants her to ask for any small amount as she needs it, thus keeping both himself and his wife alert to her dependence upon him and his power over her ("He enjoys having me ask him for money. It makes him feel important."). Further evidence of his power is the husband's demand for an accounting of how each dime is spent when he does give his wife money; there is a very real tie between his total control of the resources and his power in the marriage in general.

The wife senses that as long as she is utterly dependent upon her husband for material resources, his power over her will be great and she will find it necessary to go along with his wishes while submerging her own interests. Yet she seems to realize that if she can obtain resources of her own (the principle of alternate rewards as discussed in Chapter 4), her power will be increased and her husband's decreased.

POWER IN THE HUSBAND-WIFE RELATIONSHIP

Many persons have the mistaken notion that issues such as justice, negotiation, conflict and power have no place in discussions of marriage. Such issues are thought to be appropriate when it comes to discussing political affairs or labor-management disputes but not when it comes to discussing the husband-wife relationship. Yet marriage is a social system and involves social processes no less than is true of the relationships between two parties negotiating business interests or two nations trying to work out a trade agreement.

What Is Power?

The word *power* derives from the Latin *potere,* which means "to be able." Power includes the ideas of ability and control. In this sense, "I can" is the essence of power. I can do something rather than being at the mercy of other forces. I can produce an effect on something or someone else. Thus, we speak of how science has increased the ability of humans to control the environment, to have power over nature, and so on.

As psychologist David Winter points out, the behavioral scientist is concerned specifically with social power, that is, "when one or more persons have an effect on the behavior or emotions of another *person* or persons. . . . Power over things is of interest in this context only insofar as it leads to social power."[4] Furthermore, says Winter, such power means that there is intention behind it, that one's effect on others is not merely accidental. "To say that someone has the ability or can produce an effect strongly suggests that he can do something when, how, and in the way that he wants to do it." This is true even if such intentions are unconscious or denied. Winter's definition sums up the usual meaning of power as it is spoken of by psychologists, sociologists, and political scientists: "Social power is the ability or capacity of [one person or group] to produce (consciously or unconsciously) intended effects on the behavior or emotions of another person [or group] . . ."[5]

How Sociologists Measure Marital Power

We saw in Chapter 1 that selecting concepts, measuring them, and examining their interrelationships are all involved in sociological theory building. To explain the why of social behavior, we must first understand something of the what and the how. *Concepts* are notions or ideas; and in order to find out how concepts are operating in social relationships, sociologists devise ways of measuring them. For example, we have seen that the *sociological measurements* of social class (a concept) usually involve education, income, and occupational status. Each of these three items is also a concept in itself, which in turn must be measured. Education is measured by years of formal schooling, and income is measured in terms of dollars. One way that occupational status has been measured has involved the devising of a scale or index which takes into account the evaluations of large numbers of people who have been asked to rate various occupations as to their relative prestige. For instance, most people have rated a surgeon higher than a truckdriver, a schoolteacher higher than a supermarket clerk, and so on.

The concept of marital power has posed problems for sociologists, both in terms of defining it and measuring it. In fact, a great deal of controversy has raged over this subject in recent years as various sociologists who study the family have disagreed among themselves.[6] The problem in defining marital power has occurred because some sociologists use the term synonymously with other terms, such as authority, decision making, or influence, while other sociologists make distinctions between the various terms.

Sociologist Constantina Safilios-Rothschild makes the criticism that too many studies have examined only husband-wife *decision making* in measuring marital power while failing to pay enough attention to what goes on behind the scenes, such as "the patterns of tension and conflict management, or the type of prevailing division of labor." She suggests that the total configuration of these behavioral patterns must be examined and not one aspect alone if power is to be understood. In Safilios-Rothschild's thinking, family power structure should be thought of in terms of three components: *authority* (who is considered to have the legitimate right to have the most say, according to prevailing cultural and social norms), *decision-making* (who makes the decisions, how often, and so on), and *influence* (less obvious maneuvering; the degree to which a spouse is able to impose his or her point of view through various subtle or not-so-subtle pressures even though the other spouse initially opposed that point of view.)[7]

Another problem pointed out by some sociologists is that there may be various levels to familial power structure. Which level is being explored? Are we concerned with who makes particular decisions, or who decides that this person may make those decisions, or even beyond that, who determines who will decide which spouse will make the decision?[8] The picture begins to look like the proverbial "house that Jack built"! In other words, suppose a husband and wife reach an impasse on a certain decision. Finally, just to get the matter settled so that the couple can go on with other things, one of them says to the other, "*You* decide. Since we can't make up our minds, I'll turn the matter over to you and I'll abide by your decision." The spouse who gets to make the decision may seem at first glance to be the one with the greater power; after all it is his or her wishes that will be carried out. However, as Safilios-Rothschild points out, "the one spouse may relegate one or more decisions to the other spouse because he finds these decisions relatively unimportant and very time-consuming." The "relegating" spouse in such cases has considerably more power than the one who might appear to make the decisions, because the relegating spouse "can orchestrate the power structure in the family according to his preferences and wishes."[9]

Survey method of studying power   Sociologists study power in marriage by using two basic methods: *asking* or *watching and listening.* The "asking" method is sometimes called the survey method or the reputational method. A sample of husbands or wives (or both) is drawn, and questions are asked about the balance of power in their marriage. Sometimes a sample of children is drawn to find out which parent the children think has the greater power in the family. Variables such as social status, stage of the life cycle, and other factors are also introduced in an effort to find patterns that may aid in understanding marital power better. Questions used in the survey method may have to do with decision making or with the handling of conflicts. Or a key question might be as direct as this: "Who is the real boss in your marriage?" A question used in several studies including our own research is this one: "When you disagree about [particular items the respondent has listed as areas of disagreement in his or her marriage], who usually gets his way, you or your spouse?" The spouse with the higher score of "winning out" in disagreements is considered to have the greater power.

One frequently used method of measuring marital power has been to ask respondents who makes the final decisions in each of a number of areas. The list might include matters like the choice of work for either spouse, vacation decisions, what kind of car to buy, and so on. Blood and Wolfe utilized this method in their pioneering Detroit study of husband-wife relationships.[10] Yet, their approach to the issue of power has been criticized because each of the eight items they listed was given equal weight. In other words, when they tabulated the final results to find out a person's power score, decisions about the weekly food budget were treated as being just as important as the choice of the husband's job or the purchase of a house.

The problem of measuring power is further complicated by a lack of consistency in the kinds of questions asked even when marital power is thought of only in terms of decision making. Blood and Wolfe singled out eight areas of household decision making; and while some studies have duplicated these, other studies have utilized lists containing other items. Thus, it is difficult to compare studies.[11]

Another problem in connection with the survey approach relates to the respondents who are being queried. Some studies have focused on wives only, whereas other studies have sought to find out husbands' perception of decision-making power. There are also studies in which *both* husbands and wives are asked their perceptions of power within their marriages, and in addition there are studies in which children are asked to tell whom they perceive to have the greater power in their respective families. Comparison of various studies again becomes a problem, because it has been amply demonstrated that different members of the family may perceive the power structure differently.[12]

In addition to the problems clustering around the kinds of questions that are asked and the persons who are asked them, there remains the more basic problem of limiting measurements of power to the matter of decision making alone. Some sociologists suggest that rather than focusing on the *outcome* of decision making, it might prove more fruitful to concentrate on the *process* by which decisions are arrived at.[13] But how can sociologists study the processes of decision making that go on within family units? This brings us to the second commonly used method for investigating marital power.

Observational-experimental method of studying power Whereas the survey method is built around asking, the observational-experimental method is built around watching and listening. Laboratory situations are set up so that couples may be observed while they settle disagreements and make decisions. The sessions are usually tape-recorded and later evaluated by a panel of judges who code the observed behavior according to a specified rating scale. (For example, they might keep a record of who made the most interruptions in a family discussion, who made the greater number of suggestions in a husband-wife dialogue about some disagreement, and so on.)

Game techniques may also be utilized so that a couple is faced with decision making in simulated situations.[14] Sometimes a series of short stories are used as stimuli so that the husband and wife must come to an agreement about hypothetical problem situations and find ways to resolve conflicts. Their interactions are observed in an effort to see who exercises the greater power, who is most persuasive, or who gets his or her way.[15]

There are, of course, problems with the observational-experimental method just as there are with the survey method. Some critics point out that couples or families who know they are being watched may not act naturally and may present a picture somewhat different than they would in actual decision-making situations in their day-to-day living, thus creating an "onstage" effect. But other researchers have answered such criticisms with evidence that much accurate information about family interaction has been gained from observational methods. Two sociologists attempted to compare the two methods by using both on the same random sample of 211 families in metropolitan Toronto. One interesting finding was that "the questionnaire measures showed husband dominance to prevail, while the observational measures showed a balance between the spouses."[16]

Sociologist David Heer draws attention to a crucial problem common to both methods of researching marital power, namely, the fact that a person who has the greater power in one area of marital decision making may have a much smaller degree of power in another area. It is not easy to find ways to ascertain and measure power since "power is not unidimensional."[17] Heer's statement is but one more indication of the difficulties surrounding research on power in marriage. Sociologists speak of these as *methodological* problems, since they relate to methods of conceptualizing, gathering necessary data, and measuring findings. But an awareness of these problems should not mean that we despair of any understanding at all of marital power. While there are many things that sociologists do not know about this concept, there are many other things they do know. And it is on the basis of information already in that we can proceed to build theory and seek explanations about the part power plays in the marital process.

How Power Is Obtained and Maintained

A basic principle in sociology links power with resources. That is, the more resources a person, group, or nation possesses, the greater is the power held with relation to others who desire such resources. For example, suppose a country we'll call "Plentyland" has resources which another country ("Scarceland") lacks and desperately needs (oil, wheat, certain raw materials necessary for manufacturing, or other goods). Plentyland will then have a considerable amount of power over Scarceland and can force Scarceland to act in certain ways, either through threats of withholding the needed materials or through promises to increase such goods, provide better economic deals, and so on. If Scarceland's resources offered in exchange are not so essential to Plentyland as Plentyland's resources are to Scarceland, it follows that Scarceland is much more dependent upon Plentyland than is Plentyland on Scarceland. Therefore, Plentyland has the greater power and may be expected to exercise considerable influence and control over Scarceland.

But can resource theory be applied to *marital* power? Once again a certain amount of controversy has raged among sociologists.[18] Safilios-Rothschild questions limiting the concept of resources to assets that will almost without question be found in greater abundance among *husbands* in traditional marriages (for example, education, income, occupational status), while other kinds of resources are ignored. "Does not the wife have at her disposal other 'resources' tangible and intangible which she can (and does) contribute or withdraw at will and thus 'control' even the most occupationally successful husband?" asks Safilios-Rothschild. As examples of such control of resources, she names food preparation (poorly prepared or the husband's favorite dish), sloppy versus neat housekeeping, sexual enthusiasm or frigidity, the control of the home atmosphere and hospitality (or the lack of it) through pleasant or sour moods, and so on.[19]

In spite of her criticisms of resource theory, Safilios-Rothschild is herself speaking in terms of rewards, costs, and punishments. She does not appear to deny the basic sociological principle linking power with the ability to grant or withhold valued resources. Rather, her hesitancy seems to be associated with a reluctance to limit resources to an economic base.

However, in modern industrial societies, it is productive work in the marketplace that counts in terms of social worth. The work of women in the home is not assigned the same value as the work of men which is converted into dollars. "In a society in which money determines value, women are a group who work outside the money economy," writes Margaret Benston. She goes on to point out that household work when performed by a wife is not considered to be worth money, and since it isn't, society considers it valueless and not even real work at all. This in turn leads to the conclusion that "women themselves, who do this valueless work, can hardly be expected to be worth as much as men, who work for money."[20]

In commenting upon Benston's statement, sociologist Dair Gillespie emphasizes a point we have made throughout this book: Power is linked with one's degree of involvement in the economic-opportunity system. She writes: "Thus it is clear that for a wife to gain even a modicum of power in the marital relationship, she must gain it from external sources, i.e., she must participate in the work force, her education must be superior to that of her husband, and her participation in organizations must excel his."[21]

Blood and Wolfe utilized the personal-resource theory to explain their findings on marital power in the Detroit study. After seeing that a husband's degree of decision-making power was related to his education, income, and occupational status, these researchers concluded that "the higher the hus-

The work of women in the home is not assigned the same value as the work of men which is converted into dollars.

band's social status, the greater his power." In other words, as the husband brings increasing amounts of resources into the marriage, his wife is increasingly willing to defer to his wishes and consider him to have the right to have his way in decisions. There was also evidence that the wife who brings educational and occupational achievements to the marriage has a greater share in the marital balance of power because of these resources.[22]

A number of sociologists have criticized the interpretations of Blood and Wolfe, pointing out that even the findings of the Detroit study did not consistently fit with resource theory, because low blue-collar husbands had more power than high blue-collar husbands—just the opposite of the relationship between resources and power at other status levels. Also, when different areas of decision making were measured by other sociologists, the findings did not always fit so neatly with the Blood and Wolfe explanation.[23]

Three sociologists who conducted a large study among husbands and wives in Los Angeles found that some of their findings clearly supported the resource theory of marital power as set forth by Blood and Wolfe, but other of their findings did not.[24] Nevertheless, Centers, Raven, and Rodrigues do not toss out the notion that control of valued resources plays an important part in husband-wife power relations. They feel it is but one factor among several others. They call attention to personality factors, cultural factors (especially the influence of norms in the couple's culture or subculture about how much power husband or wife should have), and "role patterning" (the way the domain of authority varies by prevailing societal sex roles; in both their study and the Detroit study, wives had more to say about the choice of food for example, and husbands had more power in choices about the husband's job).

They also agree with Heer's suggestion that the *relative competence* and *relative involvement* of the spouses in specific decision-making areas must also be taken into account in examining family power. Certain decisions might require skills which one spouse possesses to a greater degree than the other. For example, in a particular marriage, the wife might decide on the color to paint the living room and the furnishings to buy because of her interest and abilities in interior decorating; the husband might make the decision about when to purchase new tires for the car since he may be the more knowledgeable in auto maintenance. Also, the spouse who is more involved in or concerned with a specific matter might be expected to be the one to make the final decision on that matter.

Modifications of resource theory Several sociologists who see merit in resource theory as an explanation of marital power and yet are aware of certain weaknesses have suggested revisions or modifications. Heer suggests a theory of exchange which takes into account *alternatives* to resources provided by one's spouse.[25] In Blood and Wolfe's interpretation, the emphasis had been on a comparison of the respective resources brought by each spouse into the marriage; and the conclusion had been that the more resources either one has in comparison to those of the other, the greater will be his or her power. Heer adds another comparison: What is the value of the resources provided by the spouse in comparison to resources available to that person outside the marriage? In other words, would the man or woman be better off married to someone else or not married at all? For example, if a wife thought the alternatives were better elsewhere, she might be less willing to defer to a dominating husband, thereby diminishing his power. The wife in such a case may be willing to risk terminating the relationship because she considers the cost of losing the husband less punishing than submitting to his control.

Heer's modification of resource theory fits with a point we have made repeatedly: a person's power over another diminishes as the second person finds that other sources of rewards are available. Sociologist Willard Waller's "principle of least interest" is also relevant.[26] According to this principle, the person who is the less interested in keeping a relationship going has the greater power. The one to whom a relationship matters the most and who feels the greater need is more willing to defer to the other in order to preserve the relationship. When preservation of the relationship ceases to matter so much, the other party loses power.

In comparing cross-cultural studies, sociologist Hyman Rodman also found some difficulties in explaining marital power solely in resource terms and therefore suggested another modification.[27] Rodman found that in France and in the United States it was true that the higher the husband's education, income, and occupational status, the greater his power in marriage; but just the opposite was found to be true in Greece and Yugoslavia. Husbands with the highest educational levels in these countries had the lowest marital-power scores. How can this be explained?

Rodman proposes a "theory of resources in cultural context" in which he sees the distribution of power in marriage as resulting from the interaction of two factors. One is the comparative resources of the husband and wife, and the other is the prevailing social norm about marital power in a particular culture or subculture. In other words, if a culture expects husbands to have the greater power in marriage, this norm can have a profound effect upon marital power in spite of the comparative resources of the husband and wife. On the other hand, if a culture favors a more equalitarian view of marriage, power is not automatically assumed and taken for granted as an inherent right of the male. Rather, any power one has must be earned, and this is where resources come in.

Rodman views the United States and France as being more flexible with regard to the distribution of power in marriage and more favorable to equalitarian ideology; therefore power is not something that is already "there" for males. Power comes instead from resources; it must be earned. Thus the higher power of higher-status husbands in advanced, industrialized countries is not surprising. On the other hand, in developing nations with strong patriarchal traditions where social norms support the husband's right to dominate, the social classes more likely to embrace modern, egalitarian marriage ideals are those who have had opportunities for advanced education. Thus, in Greece and Yugoslavia, more highly educated, higher-status husbands have been more willing than lower-status husbands to grant wives more power, with a resulting decrease in power for themselves.

In looking at this cross-national data and Rodman's explanations, we are not by any means suggesting that higher-status Yugoslavian and Greek marriages within a strongly patriarchal society are somehow more equalitarian than higher-status marriages in the United States or other advanced, industrialized nations. Rather, the comparisons were concerned with degrees of authority *within* the respective countries under study in an effort to see how social status and power were linked in a particular cultural setting.

We have already seen how the option to work (especially when it is exercised) increases a wife's marital power. And we may recall the example of West African tribes in which wives exercised high degrees of power because of their economic holdings. Similarly, women in Iran with high education and professional skills are treated and paid equally to men and have a high degree of power in their marriages. It may be that in rapidly developing countries, even if there has been a patriarchal tradition in the past, the need for competent leaders and workers is so great that discriminatory employment practices based upon sex are not given the chance to develop.

All of this brings us back to the resource theory once more. Elements of it are there even when we examine Yugoslavian and Greek data. In a 1966 study, two Yugoslavian sociologists found that in their country women who are employed gain in marital power.[28] And Safilios-Rothschild also found this to be true in her study of wives in Athens. In spite of her misgivings about resource theory, she has written that there is some evidence for its holding true for Greek women more than Greek men. When a wife is employed and especially when her occupational accomplishments are higher than those of her husband, her power in the family tends to be increased, "because the possessed resources prove her abilities in such a way that even the traditional-minded males have to accept her competence."[29]

A recognition of the part that beliefs and cultural norms play in marital power, as in Rodman's modification of resource theory, need not be seen as contradicting resource theory but rather as something that interacts with it and aids in an understanding of how power is distributed. Norms lend legitimacy to power; they do not create power.

It cannot be overstressed that power springs from resources. "Haves" possess more power than "have-nots" in a society. Norms are created to lend support to the possession of power and to show that it is "right" for those who hold power to do so. Thus, the norm that husbands should be more dominant in marriage than wives ultimately goes back to the fact that males have traditionally had greater access to the economic-opportunity system and therefore have had greater resources. Husbands *have* had greater power in marriage, and therefore behavioral expectations (or norms) have developed to support their right to this greater power. In turn, one's degree of acceptance of these norms can have an effect on marital power, along with one's resources as compared to those of the spouse. As women gain greater resources, and with these resources greater marital power, we may expect norms to develop sanctioning wives' rights to such power just as they have supported husbands' rights in the past.

Power: Legitimate and Nonlegitimate

If the following two hypothetical statements by wives were heard, the observer would immediately be struck by both a similarity and a difference with respect to their comments on their husbands.

Joyce: My husband and I make most decisions together. We talk things over and then decide what to do. But he decides the really important things—particularly if we disagree. For example, he wanted to take a trip to Florida for our vacation and I wanted to visit relatives instead. Needless to say, he won! And I feel he had a right to. After all, he works hard all year to provide our family with a good standard of living. He deserves to decide how to use his time off work and what kind of vacation to take. I feel the same about major expenditures. He earns the money after all! Why shouldn't he be the one to decide how it's spent?

Martha: My husband bought this house trailer we're living in. He didn't even ask what I thought about it—just got it and moved us in. And now he can't even keep up the payments. He's never earned a decent living in all the years we've been married. You can tell that by just looking around our shabby place! But he sure acts like a king around here. "Get me a beer, Martha!" "I need clean socks. You'd better make sure you get to the Laundromat more often. What kind of a wife are you?" Yet he won't buy me a washing machine, and he takes the car every day so that I have to try to find neighbors who'll drive me to the Laundromat. And Pete is always telling me what I can't do, always bossing me around. Like the other night, my friend Judy called and wanted me to go to one of those parties in someone's house where they sell kitchen things, but Pete said, "No, you're not going! I don't want you to." And that was that. But it doesn't seem fair.

In comparing the two statements, we notice first of all that both wives indicate that their husbands hold greater power in marriage than they themselves do. But second, we notice that one wife feels this is right and fair while the other does not. The key factor here is involvement in the economic-opportunity system.

Joyce's husband has rewarded his family with status and material benefits; thus she feels he has the right to the greater power in the marriage. Martha's husband, on the other hand, has not provided such resources and therefore she resents the way he seizes power in the marriage and tries to control her life. Unconsciously, she is acknowledging that he hasn't earned the right to have authority over her. He has failed in what sociologist George Homans has called "the most important single factor in making a man a leader," namely, "the ability to provide rare and valued rewards for his followers."[30]

Joyce feels that her husband's power in their marriage is legitimate. Martha feels that the power her husband exercises is not legitimate. This distinction is an important one which turned up in our Indianapolis study of marriages, and it throws light on many of the problems that have emerged in studies of marital power.

Some sociologists have sought to clarify the two kinds of influence and control over others by distinguishing between the terms *authority* and *power*. Authority is viewed as legitimate, power as nonlegitimate. Sociologist Walter

Buckley, for example, defines *authority* as "the direction or control of the behavior of others for the promotion of collective goals, based on some ascertainable form of their knowledgeable consent. Authority thus implies informed, voluntary compliance."[31]

In contrast, *power,* according to Buckley, is "control or influence over the actions of others to promote one's goals without their consent, against their 'will,' or without their knowledge or understanding." He points out that by the term *consent* he means something deeper than "mere acquiescence or overt compliance." Persons may give in to the wishes of another person who holds sway over them, but their submission need not mean they are actually consenting to such an exercise of power ("He has no right to tell me to do this, but I'd better do it anyway!").

Other sociologists used the terms *authority* and *power* somewhat interchangeably as in ordinary, everyday speech. Thus, they may speak of "authority relations in marriage" or "the balance of power in marriage" as being synonymous. Or what one sociologist calls the "mean power score" of a marriage partner might be termed the "mean authority score" by another sociologist. Goode has even spoken of "negative authority," which he defines as "the right to prevent others from doing what they want."[32] Since lack of consent is involved, such a definition comes close to Buckley's definition of power.

There appears to be a problem in terminology, because in normal usage the word *authority* includes the notion of power. It therefore becomes awkward to perch "power" and "authority" on two ends of a pole as opposites. Yet, the concepts involved are valid. There is a difference between control or influence over others that is deemed legitimate and involves knowledgeable consent and, on the other hand, control or influence that is not considered legitimate and which is exercised apart from the consent of the governed. But both cases involve power as defined earlier. In both instances, there is demonstrated an ability or capacity to produce intended effects on another person's (or group's) behavior or emotions. Thus, we suggest Figure 8-1 as an attempt to clarify the distinction.

Power may be exercised in a way that is legitimate (by being earned and consented to) or in a way that is nonlegitimate (by being seized and not consented to). Legitimate power, as a process involving bargaining and negotiation, moves toward *authority*—an institutionalized state. A position of authority involves a recognition of the right of a person or group to be in charge, to rule, to have control, to make decisions, to influence and direct the behavior of others. Conversely, nonlegitimate power moves in an opposite direction toward *domination*. Domination includes the idea of lording it over others against their will (the word derives from the Latin *dominus,* meaning "master, lord, owner, despot").

From the standpoint of exchange theory, we might say that nonlegitimate power is viewed by those under it as being undeserved because it was taken without having been earned and without providing sufficient rewards for the

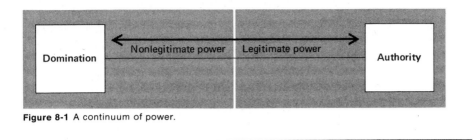

Figure 8-1 A continuum of power.

leader's followers. It is thus seen in terms of net loss (giving up one's own desires against one's will for the sake of giving in to the desires of another). In contrast, legitimate power is viewed by those who submit to it as having been earned and deserved by the one who holds the power. Therefore it is seen in terms of net profit (the rewards provided outweigh the costs of submitting to the will of another).

Nonlegitimate power tends to rely on coercion, threats, and punishment; whereas legitimate power relies on "friendly persuasion" and the provision of benefits. We might compare the distinction to the old problem of motivating the peddler's .horse. The peddler might get his wagon moving again by either applying a stick to the animal from behind or by holding a carrot on a string out front to lure the animal onward. Legitimate power tends to emphasize the "carrot approach," while nonlegitimate power puts the emphasis upon the stick.

In the Indianapolis study, we found that it is an oversimplification merely to state without qualification that with greater status comes greater husband power—unless we take into account the *kind* of power. Actually, the study showed that lower-status husbands tended to exercise more power in their marriages than did higher-status husbands. Men with less education, income, and occupational prestige tended to resolve conflicts unilaterally, carrying out their own wishes rather than paying attention to their wives' desires. Furthermore, they were less interested in working with their wives in making decisions about matters of spouse disagreement. In the processes of conflict resolution, wives were permitted little participation as compared to the situation in upper-status homes.

We saw earlier that Blood and Wolfe had also found that husbands in the lowest status group had more power than husbands in the next category (high-blue-collar) which broke the consistency of the pattern that had otherwise shown that husband power rises with social status.[33] Their only attempt at an explanation was to comment that the group of lowest-status men with high power scores were presumably older men who were carrying on a pre–World War I patriarchal ideology which held that a husband should be the boss.

Komarovsky, too, found in her sample of fifty-eight blue-collar marriages

should be enough to assure their greater power in the marriage. The hypothetical Martha in our illustration demonstrated such a marital situation. The husband feels the wife should defer to him simply because he is a man; the wife feels he doesn't deserve such deference since he has been so unsuccessful in the economic-opportunity system. Any power he takes is considered by her to be nonlegitimate and therefore *domination*. The higher-status wife, in contrast, sees her husband's greater power as legitimate and thus *authority*.

The same distinction between domination and authority emerged in our research as we focused on actual practice as well as on beliefs. The method of measurement used was based upon conflict resolution rather than routinized household decision making (which, as we have seen, poses many problems in drawing conclusions from the data). We reasoned that a more realistic picture of marital power emerges if we examine matters considered important by a couple and over which there is disagreement, and then endeavor to find out which spouse has the final say in resolving the conflict.

In a nutshell, our findings were these: The lower the social status of the husband, the more frequent is his settling of issues unilaterally ("We will do what I say! And that's that!"), and the less he tends to share decisions with his wife ("Let's talk it over and try to find an answer that suits us both"). Conversely, the higher the status of the husband, the less unilateral is his power, and the more he is likely to share decisions with his wife. Rather than saying, "I have the last word by virtue of tradition and economic success," the higher-status husband is more likely to display an attitude that says, "Maybe we can come to a compromise," or "I don't want to make the final decision by myself; let's work on it together."

Thus, although as social status increases both husbands and wives believe the husband should have the greater power in marriage, in actual conflict resolution there is greater participation by both spouses than in lower-status marriages. Less frustrated in the occupational realm and more secure in the power they hold (because it is earned and thus considered legitimate in the eyes of their wives), higher-status husbands are willing to act in a way that is more or less equalitarian, even when contested issues are being discussed. Lower-status husbands, on the other hand, may hang on tightly to every shred of marital power that tradition has granted them since they have no power elsewhere, not having achieved in the economic system and thus lacking the resources that bring power. They therefore *take* power even though in their wives' eyes they have not earned it. In such marriages, in spite of the equalitarian ideals of the wives, husbands tend to make unilateral decisions in areas of disagreement. They are less apt to permit or encourage the participation of their wives in making such decisions, and this lack of shared power is resented by the wives.

In both cases (higher status and lower status), husbands hold the power.

But how wives see that power is different. Higher-status wives tend to see it as right and proper; lower-status wives do not. Higher-status wives get to share in husbands' power; lower-status wives do not. In a certain sense, we might see here a distinction in types of power that has been made in psychoanalytic theory. Freud, Adler, and Horney all took pains to show a difference in *positive power* which originates in strength and *negative power* which originates in weakness.[36] As viewed by lower-status wives, the domination of their husbands is negative power.

It must be kept in mind that we are speaking here of marriages in the traditional sense in which the husband is the chief provider or only provider. Research on equal-partner marriages in which each spouse is equally committed to a career and equally a provider of economic resources might be expected to show a considerable change in the marital power picture. Hints of this were found in the Indianapolis data with regard to wife employment. We found, as have other researchers, that a wife's employment is associated with greater power in her marriage—both in terms of her beliefs (more favorable to equality than to patriarchy) and her actual behavior (she tends to make more decisions alone rather than sharing them jointly with her husband).[37]

NEGOTIATION

In marriage, as in any relationship between intimates (friends, lovers, parents and children, siblings), there is an ongoing give-and-take.[38] The power structure plays an important part in this exchange, but simply knowing who has the greater influence does not totally explain the exchange itself. Who gives what, and why? Who takes what, and why? Who gains? Who loses? What kinds of processes occur in making decisions, solving problems, resolving disagreements, working out compromises, developing plans, and so on?

Probably the best word to describe these kinds of social exchanges is *negotiation.* Negotiation may be defined as arranging the terms of a contract, transaction, or agreement through talking matters over and working things out. The word has its roots in the Latin *negotior* which refers to doing business or trading. The husband-wife relationship involves negotiation in that there generally is mutual discussion and an arrangement of terms of agreement concerning areas of married life. How will the spouses divide up household chores? How will they make decisions about whether or not to have children? How will they decide on leisure, friends, visits to relatives, and other aspects of social life? What kind of house or car should they buy? How can they arrange their sex life so that it will be satisfactory to both of them?

In arriving at terms of agreement, the husband and wife do not necessarily settle a particular issue once and for all. As circumstances change or as desires of one or the other change, various matters may need to be renegotiated. Again, the idea of process enters the picture. Marriage involves an *ongoing* series of exchanges—in other words, continuous negotiation and renegotiation. Even a relationship that over the years seems to have settled into very routinized ways of doing things often is caught unawares by new circumstances and faces the issue of renegotiation. Time brings changes. The children grow into different stages and require new kinds of guidance or have different needs than earlier. One spouse's health may fail, necessitating a renegotiation on how the household will be run or how the income will be produced. The retirement period of life may jolt a couple into seeing areas of their marriage needing reexamination and calling for efforts toward change.

The Latin origin of the term *negotiation* fits well with what goes on in such husband-wife interchanges. In a very real sense, it is a matter of "doing business" through a series of trade-offs. The tit-for-tat might not be conscious in every case. Nevertheless, an exchange is taking place that entails both rewards and costs. "I did that for him, so he should do that for me." "If I gave up a big chunk of my day off to help her out, I don't see why she can't give up some time to bake pies for the guys coming over to play cards tonight—even if she doesn't like my friends!" "Of course, I'm going to hear my wife's speech at the PTA tonight. She always cheers me on when I do things like that; why shouldn't I encourage her, too?" "George got a big raise! Now we can take that trip we've been dreaming about! I'm going to do something special tonight. I asked my mother to take the children overnight, and George and I can have a special evening together making plans—and making love. I'll cook his favorite meal and maybe we'll even eat by candlelight!" "Well, it seems to me that if a wife works at a job all day, she shouldn't have to come home and do all the housework, too. That's why I try to help Sue with the dishes and cleaning and stuff."

Statements such as these illustrate how rewards and costs shape everyday marital life. The husband who gave up much of his day off to help his wife (costs) expects her to likewise give up time for him (costs again) in order to reward him as he rewarded her. The husband who has been rewarded with his wife's encouragement and approval is willing to take the time (costs, the extent of which depends on how else he might have used that particular block of time) in order to provide her likewise with encouragement and approval by listening to her speech. The wife who is delighted by the increased rewards of her husband's raise tries to find a way to reward him in turn; she chooses to go the "expressive" route by planning a romantic evening. The husband who is rewarded by his wife's monetary earnings accepts the costs of added participation in household chores to reward his wife with more free time.

Case Study

A hypothetical couple named Bob and Julie illustrate how marital negotiation works. Their case seems particularly apt because it combines elements of both traditional marriage (in that Bob is the chief provider) and modern, equalitarian ideals (in that Julie has a job which gives her a greater degree of power than would be likely otherwise). In terms of the four main kinds of marital structures, we would say that Bob and Julie come closest to the senior partner–junior partner arrangement.

Let's assume that Bob and Julie have been married about six months. Without necessarily thinking in terms of bargaining, the two have negotiated with one another as to how their marriage should be structured in terms of rights, duties, and options. Bob was already established as a real estate agent at the time of their marriage, and they have mutually agreed that Julie will teach elementary school for two or three years before they think about having children. Household chores are divided between them. Bob straightens up the apartment and does the laundry. Julie takes care of the meal planning, shopping, and cooking. Additional arrangements have been worked out for other areas of marriage, both in the expressive and instrumental realms. Birth-control methods, use of leisure time, budgeting, visiting relatives, personal habits—these and more have all been subjects of negotiation.

Implicit in such a set of marital negotiations is the question of legitimate power or authority. Bob and Julie have agreed to pattern their marriage so that Bob is the chief provider, which means that he has certain fixed, fully structured rights and duties which are inherent in the breadwinner role. Julie shares in breadwinning, but her commitment to work is less than Bob's. It is understood and agreed upon by both husband and wife that the main support of the family will be Bob's responsibility. He is the senior partner.

Bob's position gives him the stronger leverage in decision-making processes and conflict resolution within the marriage. Thus, when Julie suggested Bob's doing the cooking several evenings a week, since her own schedule seemed pressured with commuting and extracurricular school activities, Bob rejected the suggestion. "Sure, my hours are more flexible than yours," he said, "but still my work requires me to be on call constantly. If a prospective customer wants to look at a house, I've got to be free at *their* convenience, not mine. I can't be tied down with cooking! But I'll tell you what I will do. I can help you out by doing the shopping, and that will give you some extra free time on Saturdays. You'll still have to plan the meals and make out the list so I'll know what to buy; but I'm willing to save you the time and energy that you'd have to spend on picking up the stuff. How's that for a compromise?"

As we have seen, the person in an exchange relationship who has the greater resources to offer tends to have more legitimate authority. Therefore, that person tends to shape or influence decision making in his or her favor. If, for example, Julie were the full-time support of her husband while he completed college, she might have considerably more authority than in her present situation. Or if she were not employed at all, she would have less.

As matters now stand, however, Bob has more legitimate power than Julie does. This is true not only because of his greater financial resources, but also because of the chief provider role he fills. His job is looked upon by both him and his wife as being more important than hers. He can always argue that whatever might interfere with his career will be punishing or costly to both of them. Sociologist William Goode has pointed out that upper-status men obtain many rights and have a high degree of power because they can always claim that family demands must not interfere with their work. Such a man, writes Goode, "takes preference as a professional, not as a family head or as a male; nevertheless, the precedence is his. By contrast, lower-class men demand deference as *men,* as heads of families."[39]

So long as Julie accepts the senior partner–junior partner structural arrangement and values the rewards Bob supplies her, she will tend to recognize as legitimate Bob's authority. "After all," she says, "*someone* has to have the final say if we can't agree on something. Somebody has to be the last court of appeals. We feel it's only right that it should be Bob. Even though we like to think of each other as equals, and we certainly talk everything over, there's still a sense in which Bob is sort of 'in charge' of the marriage. He has the main responsibility to provide for us. My income comes in handy, but it's his that we always depend on. Mine might stop someday because we'll probably have children and I'll quit work. But Bob can't do that. He has to shoulder the greater load, so I guess he deserves to have the greater power."

Bob and Julie are maintaining a relationship in which each considers the exchange to be profitable. They are providing benefits to one another (at cost to each individually), but in return they are receiving certain rewards. They are maintaining an ongoing situation of *maximum joint profit,* to use the term from economics. The situation is comparable to that in which a single buyer of a certain commodity and a single seller of that commodity enter into bargaining. Maximum profit for each is the goal. Psychologist Sidney Siegel and economist Lawrence Fouraker have pointed out that such a situation "appeals to the mutual interests of the participants, and would seem to call for harmonious cooperation between them." But at the same time, "the interests of the participants are exactly in opposition, and acrimonious competition would seem to be the behavior norm." If these two opposing factors (cooperation and competition) can be made to work together in the decision-making process, it becomes possible for the two parties in the negotiations to be forced into a contract which is in their *mutual* interest.[40] Each individual and the relationship as a whole benefit. Both buyer and seller are satisfied that profit has been maximum for each. At the same time, the transaction sets up a bond between the bargainers and a climate conducive to doing further business together.

In the ongoing exchanges of Bob and Julie, the greater authority of Bob as senior partner and chief provider has been acceptable to Julie. The "costs" of her deferring to him in certain decisions and stalemates are considered to be fewer than the rewards she receives from him; therefore she is satisfied with her margin of profit in the relationship. Bob too feels that his rewards from the marriage are high. The offers and counteroffers of their various negotiations have resulted in a situation of maximum joint profit.

However, at any point in these exchanges, one or the other partner may come to define the distribution of rewards and costs as being unfair. Homans calls such a perception of inequity "the problem of *distributive justice*."[41] In other words, has the distribution of rewards and costs between the persons been just and equitable? Rewards should be comparable to investments for person A relative to person B if the bargain they have struck is to be considered fair by each.

To illustrate, let's assume that there comes a time when Bob's sales have fallen off and his commissions are down. Julie's salary has remained constant and her income is now higher than Bob's. Yet, she is continuing to do the cooking and finds it a real hardship in view of her tight schedule—especially now that she is helping the fifth graders put out a school newspaper and is staying an extra hour after school. Bob, in contrast, has more free time on his hands than ever and is almost always back at their apartment long before she arrives home. Julie has begun to resent his unwillingness to prepare the evening meal. She feels that she is providing many rewards to him at the same time that she is incurring costs which she considers unacceptable (the necessity of rushing home to cook after an exhausting day of teaching), while in her opinion, Bob isn't bearing sufficient costs. She feels he "has it a lot easier" than she. Her schedule is fixed while his is flexible, he is home more hours than she is, he is providing less income now than she does. In view of all this, his refusal to cook seems unjust. Julie begins to negotiate, making clear her feelings about the matter. Since there has been a shift in the relative resources of this husband and wife over time, the gap in their relative authority is much less.

In order for the situation to change and the problem to be resolved, Julie and Bob will have to have some honest discussions. Earlier, we saw the important role that empathy plays in marriage. Being able to listen to, understand, share with, and enter into the feelings of the other person is important in any close relationship—and particularly so in the daily interaction of a husband and wife. Thus, social psychologist Philip Brickman makes the important point that in the process of bargaining over a particular issue so that a situation will be changed, "a prerequisite . . . is the ability of the parties in the situation to communicate with one another about their various alternatives and intentions." At the same time, he stresses that problems of communication should not be considered the *cause* of the need for renegotiation or the cause of conflict.[42] The prime cause of a bargainer's desire to change situational profits is a sense of inequity rather than a lack of communication. But communication is essential if renegotiation is to take place. An inability to communicate could only worsen the difficulties and delay the solution.

Going back to Bob and Julie, we find that as soon as the sense of unfairness crystallizes in her own mind, Julie brings up the matter again to Bob. She makes a suggestion to alleviate the unfairness (Bob should cook), and in view of their changed circumstances and her better bargaining situation, Bob is more open to her proposal than previously. Julie has not let her resentment smolder but has acted immediately. After time spent in negotiation, the couple arrive at a new exchange in which Bob agrees to do the cooking—with certain qualifications. He will cook for a three-month trial period to find out how costly it will be to him and also to find out how things go with his job situation. But for the time being at least, Julie has persuaded him that it is only fair for him to take on this household duty. Bob accepts the legitimacy of Julie's request, and both persons begin to maintain their new, renegotiated sets of costs and rewards. Both have established what has been variously called "balance" or "equilibrium,"[43] and there is a sense of "distributive justice." Once again, both parties feel that current exchanges are operating for maximum joint profit and mutual gain.

The process of negotiating and renegotiating exchanges in marriage is illustrated as a series of steps in Figure 8-2. Bob and Julie's story focuses on just one area of renegotiation, but such renegotiations may take place in many other areas as well—often concurrently. For example, in the area of sex relations, one spouse might suggest having intercourse more frequently or trying new positions and techniques, and this matter could be renegotiated. For another couple, leisure time and companionship might be issues requiring renegotiation as one spouse complains of the other's absorption in occupational interests.

Written contracts All of the ongoing exchanges between a husband and wife are interconnected. And altering one exchange is bound to have certain effects on other exchanges as well. These complex webs, plus changing conditions both internal and external to a marriage relationship, point up the difficulty of written marriage contracts. While it is sometimes proposed that spelling out negotiated bargains about who does what and when can serve to make the bargaining process explicit, written contracts have a major drawback. That drawback is the complexity that would be required in order for an agreement to be drawn up which adequately covered all the possibilities that might emerge in a marriage. A contract would have to be complex because marriage itself is complex. To spell out all projected negotiations and renegotiations at the beginning of marriage would likely mean writing something as intricate and detailed as any meticulous legal document. Even then as new situations would arise, there would have to be constant amendments (and negotiations about making the amendments!). A couple might find such a contract cumbersome to implement and burdensome to alter.

A major theorist in sociology, Emile Durkheim noted decades ago that much of the force even of legal contracts lies with the noncontractual rules that surround them.[44] It simply isn't possible to write everything into a contract. In social exchange, trust is essential[45]—just as "good faith" is highly important in ongoing exchanges between buyers and sellers in the business world.[46] Persons must *believe* that others will fulfill their obligations—that they will do what is fair and just by them. And in a dyad (two-person relationship) such as marriage, many behaviors must be left relatively unspecified with the understanding—implicit or explicit—that each person is seeking the best interests of both (maximum joint profit).

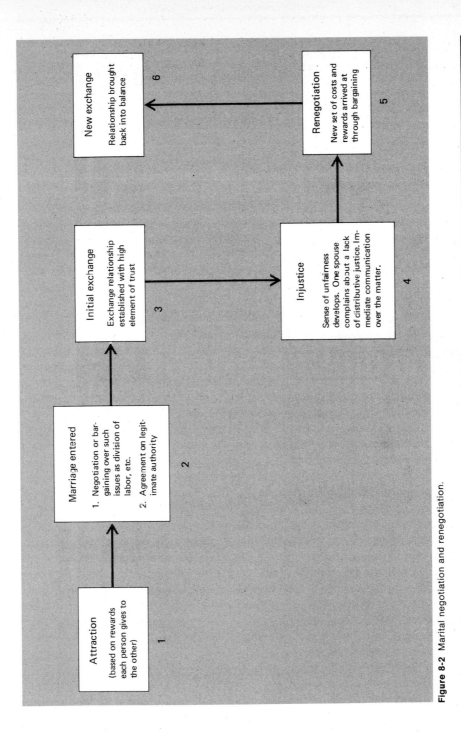

Figure 8-2 Marital negotiation and renegotiation.

Attraction	**Marriage entered**	**Initial exchange**
(based on rewards each person gives to the other)	1. Negotiation or bargaining over such issues as division of labor, etc. 2. Agreement on legitimate authority	Exchange relationship established with high element of trust
1	2	3

New exchange	**Renegotiation**	**Injustice**
Relationship brought back into balance	New set of costs and rewards arrived at through bargaining	Sense of unfairness develops. One spouse complains about a lack of distributive justice. Immediate communication over the matter.
6	5	4

Apart from such confidence that others will reciprocate, it is exceedingly difficult for stable, ongoing social relations to exist.[47] However, trust cannot be written into a contract. It develops because two parties strongly value the rewards that each supplies to the other. These rewards may be tangible or intangible, extrinsic or intrinsic, but in either case they mean much to the parties involved. Neither person wants to risk losing them, and therefore, each puts forth an effort to act toward the other in good faith.

CONFLICT AND ITS MANAGEMENT

Let's move back to Bob and Julie. Something new is happening in their ongoing exchanges as we rejoin them. Their situation is no longer one of negotiation, but rather one of *conflict*. It started when Bob decided they should buy a new car. Julie insisted they couldn't afford it and there was no use even thinking about it. Bob now feels a sense of "distributive injustice." He feels that his investment in the relationship is not producing desired payoffs.

Bob seeks to renegotiate the matter, and communication is established quickly; but in the bargaining that follows, it becomes clear that Bob's authority in this particular matter is less than his wife's. Real estate sales have continued to be low and Bob's earnings have remained less than Julie's for several months. There is no assurance that matters will change in the near future. If the couple were to buy a new car, Julie's larger income would be the main resource to make the monthly payments.

At a certain point in the negotiations between Bob and Julie, conflict emerges. Social conflict may be defined as *a struggle over limited resources and/or incompatible goals so that it appears that the more one party gets, the less the other party can have.*[48]

The struggle concerns *limited* resources, because if the resources were infinite there would not be the problem of dividing them up so that all parties would feel they had enough. Farmers in an area with abundant rainfall are unlikely to engage in conflict over water supplies. But in an area where water is scarce, two farmers are likely to engage in conflict when one finds the other has dammed the creek to hoard the scanty water supply for his own farm needs. Two children who race for the one remaining swing in the playground are also likely to engage in conflict because the resources are limited ("I got here first!" "No, I did! It's mine!"); but on another day when all the swings are empty, they will each take one and play together amiably.

Similarly, *incompatible goals* may be the basis of conflict. If one person wants to go one way and the other person wants to go in the opposite direction, they cannot walk together and simultaneously reach both goals. One can yield to the other so that they pursue one of the goals, or they might take a third goal as a compromise. Or they might go their separate ways with each pursuing his or her own goal. In a marriage, for example, one spouse might desire a large family while the other desires maximum freedom from anything that would tie them down. One person sees marriage in terms of child-centeredness and wants at least four children; the other person sees marriage in terms of couple-centeredness and wants no children. Their goals are clearly incompatible. Another illustration might be that of a spouse who is deeply involved in social issues and wants a simple life-style with much of their income given to humanitarian causes, but the other spouse wishes to live lavishly. Again, the two goals are incompatible, and conflict is likely to emerge.

The key word in the definition, however, is *struggle*. Whenever one party *resists* the claims of another, they are then engaged in conflict.[49] Resistance, contention, or struggle occurs when counteroffers are refused outright or no modifications are suggested. The negotiations have reached a seeming dead end; they can evidently proceed no further. However, one or both parties continue to press their claims, and one or both keep resisting because they believe that it is *not* in their best interests to accept the claims of the other. Each perceives that it would be too costly to do so. In the case of Bob and Julie, Julie feels the financial cost. Their material resources are limited at this particular time. Her aim is to put as much money as possible into regular savings rather than spending it. Bob's goal, on the other hand, is to have a new car. He not only feels that the reward of the car is being denied him but that his status and authority are being undercut as well—a loss that is costly to him.

During the process of conflict, communication may continue in the sense that both parties press their claims and each completely understands and accurately perceives what the other wants. Clear communication in itself, however, is no guarantee that conflict will cease. Henry Kissinger is quoted as saying that "a diplomat believes that an international conflict derives from misunderstanding. Therefore he seeks a verbal formula to overcome it. The statesman believes that conflict derives from a difference of interest and confrontation positions. Therefore he tries to change the realities on the ground."[50]

Since, as psychologist Morton Deutsch notes, the same principles that apply to international and intergroup conflict may also apply to interpersonal conflict as well,[51] they are applicable to the marital situation. Here the point is that marital "diplomacy" (seeking to resolve the conflict through talking things over and clearing up alleged misunderstandings) is neither as significant nor as important to conflict resolution as is "statesmanship" (changing the situation so that grievances and inequities are removed in a manner satisfactory to both sides).

This is not to say that communication plays no part in situations of conflict. Conflict often tends to be associated with garbled communication or with a breakdown of communication. There is a variety of data from the laboratory and from investigations of wars showing that misperceptions, miscalculations, and misinterpretations can seriously affect conflict.[52] Many Americans became deeply concerned about the seriousness of the cold war between the United States and the Soviet Union when Premier Khrushchev made the statement:

"We will bury you." They interpreted it to mean that the Soviets planned to destroy the United States. However, Khrushchev was simply using a Russian phrase that means, "We will outlive you."[53] In other words, the thought was something like, "Our nation will outlast yours. We'll be around long after you."

Misperceptions especially can affect the resolution of conflict. In the case of Bob and Julie, Bob might be saying that he wants *any* new car, whereas Julie may be understanding him to insist on a luxury car—since this is what he has always spoken of in the past. Bob might be understanding Julie to say she wouldn't even consider *any* new car under *any* circumstances, whereas Julie's resistance has mainly been buttressed against the idea of an expensive, luxury car that she is persuaded lies beyond their means. Somehow these two persons have failed to convey their own feelings and to hear what the other is saying. By attributing to one another motives and intentions that are not there at all, they have hindered effective communication.

Sometimes communication is simply broken off at some point during the conflict process. The parties concerned may decide they have nothing more to say to one another, and attempts to negotiate are given up. However, silence itself may become a form of communication. Social scientists T. C. Schelling and M. H. Halperin note that "failure to deny rumors, refusal to answer questions, attempts to take emphasis away from certain issues, all tend to communicate something."[54]

Whether or not verbal communication exists, and whether or not it is garbled, one or both parties may move toward trying to settle the conflict. In the case of our hypothetical couple, Julie seeks to resolve it by fiat—by giving an order or issuing a directive. Her pronouncement is, "No, we're not going to get a new car for you at this particular time." By using her authority based on their relative incomes, she attempts to end the conflict by simply refusing Bob's wishes outright.

However, at any point in the conflict process, legitimate authority can be transformed into nonlegitimate power. When one person or group makes demands on the other that seem excessive, the party on whom the demands are being made tends to develop a sense of exploitation.[55] Demands become "excessive" when they are not justified by sufficient levels of rewards. In our illustration, the wife makes a demand ("Forget about the car"), but the husband considers it excessive. Bob doesn't feel that Julie is offering any reward that would justify her demand or that would somehow "make up" for the sacrifice that would be required on his part by giving up his wishes for the new car. Second, Bob still thinks of himself as chief provider deserving to exercise the greater power in the marriage. He considers his current financial setbacks to be merely temporary, and he doesn't feel that his wife has the right to be as arbitrary as he feels she is.

When demands become excessive in the eyes of persons who are neverthe-less forced to comply with them, such persons feel they are being coerced into situations they would not choose for themselves. These situations are regarded as painful, punishing, and costly. The power being exercised over them is no longer viewed as right or legitimate authority; rather it is seen as raw, nonlegitimate power. An example of such a conflict situation occurred in the 1974 feud between members of the National Football League Players Association (NFLPA) and the team owners. Players demanded numerous changes in the way summer training camps and exhibition schedules were being conducted. Life in the training camps was austere and uncomfortable. Rigid restrictions governed virtually every aspect of the men's lives. Curfews kept the players confined to the camp after a certain hour. Lights-out rules and bed checks demanded that they be in bed when they were ordered to be, and guards made regular rounds to make sure everyone was asleep. There were rules against using alcohol, wearing mod clothes, and dating local women (with heavy fines for those who failed to comply). Not surprisingly, the football players began to call such regulations "leash laws" and insisted that they be eliminated. Some men, resentful of being told how to run their lives and of being penned up in what they regarded as a kind of detention camp, were willing to give up football. Others engaged in all-out conflict in the form of a strike. They felt the power of the owners was nonlegitimate because of demands the players considered excessive. "It's the owners' way of showing their power and maintaining their monopoly of all decision making," the NFLPA executive director was quoted as saying. He went on to say that whereas that kind of control had worked in the past, it would not work any longer.[56] On the other side, the team owners felt that their power was legitimate, and that since they paid the bills they had every right to tell the players what they may or may not do.

One consequence of nonlegitimate power is that the trust we spoke of earlier can become corroded. Parties who feel exploited may begin to doubt that the other party is really concerned for their best interests. Instead, the other person appears to be unduly selfish and more concerned with profit for himself than with maximum joint profit. This became a common gripe among the football players. They felt underpaid and complained that the owners had worked out a system in which the men were working almost for nothing during the preseason months of practice and exhibition games. The owners appeared to care only about lining their own pockets. Similarly, this breakdown of trust was beginning to occur between Bob and Julie. Bob resented her telling him they could not purchase the car, and he began to wonder if she was hoarding her earnings selfishly toward her own goals rather than caring about him.

By trying to settle the conflict through simply giving an order, Julie was seeking to reestablish the kind of exchange relationship that existed prior to the conflict. She wanted the conflict to "be over with." Thus, she took advantage of her present position of power based on control of the resources. But to Bob, that power seemed nonlegitimate. He is unwilling to let the conflict end in such a manner. He wants the conflict to be *resolved*, not merely *regulated*.

Any relationship based on nonlegitimate power is potentially unstable and can easily become unbalanced or even unglued. Persons who feel exploited want to change the status quo and thus are apt to resist and struggle in the face of what they consider unfair demands and insufficient rewards. Therefore, Bob simply refuses to accept his wife's decision and persuades her to reopen communication. "The conflict is *not* settled," Bob declares, convincing Julie that they should engage in renegotiation. This time he is able to strike a bargain with her. While it is true that originally he had set his heart on a particular luxury model, he had begun thinking matters over and became increasingly willing to settle for a less expensive car—even a sub-compact. Julie concedes that with careful budgeting they can try to afford a car of this kind. They decide to visit various automobile showrooms and will choose a car together.

The conflict has been resolved satisfactorily in the sense that the original injustice has been removed along with the sense that nonlegitimate power is being exercised. Feelings of exploitation are also gone, and the sense of trust is restored. The struggle over authority and allocation of material resources is ended in that each party feels not only that his (her) own aims have been achieved, but also perceives that the other feels the same way. The renegotiation has led to a new exchange relationship in which the relative authority of each party is deemed legitimate, and the costs and rewards experienced by each are considered fair. In other words, a new balance of genuine mutual profit has been accomplished. (See Figure 8-3.)

Something else has likely been taking place in the relationship of Bob and Julie—though not necessarily in a rational manner or consciously. Persons or groups in any social situation are continually making "comparison levels for alternatives."[57] Comparisons are made between the current profit level (rewards minus costs) and what profit levels might exist in other potentially available situations. Persons are more likely to remain in their present situation if they define the rewards offered there as being greater than those elsewhere. In the case of Bob and Julie, their renegotiation and conflict resolution have reinforced their sense of overall profit so that the situation in which they find themselves seems more desirable than any alternative one. They have no desire to end the relationship.

Inevitability of Conflict

Up until recently, sociologists tended to view social conflict as "bad." In terms of the structure-functionalist approach, conflict was thought to disrupt and tear apart social systems. Conflict within the institution of marriage was thought to have only negative consequences and was to be avoided at all costs.

Currently, the overwhelming weight of evidence suggests that conflict is an inevitable part of any ongoing social relationship—including marriage. Given the processes of social exchange and given the likelihood that all parties involved are seeking to maximize rewards and minimize costs, a certain amount

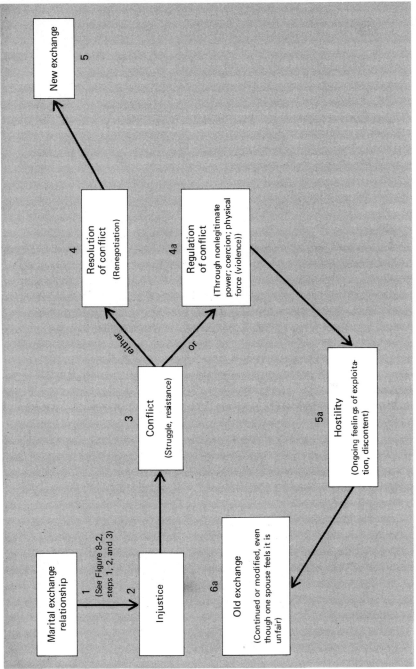

Figure 8-3 Directions in which marital conflict may move resolution or regulation.

of conflict on occasion is to be expected. There are bound to be occasions of struggling over incompatible goals or resisting the profit seeking of others because of the costs to oneself.

Given its inevitability, the issue becomes not how to avoid conflict but how to resolve it. Increasingly, social scientists agree that conflict may often strengthen the bonds of a social relationship and make it more rewarding.[58] Conflict, when satisfactorily resolved, removes injustice and punishments. The end result of conflict can be such that maximum joint profit is greater than it was before. "Opposition," says sociologist Peter Blau, "is a regenerative force that introjects new vitality into a social structure. . . ."[59] The new bargains that grow out of the conflict mean that numerous aspects of the total relationship can be revised, altered, and made more rewarding than if resistance and struggle had not occurred.

This "regenerative" process can be viewed not only from the micro perspective, such as the husband-wife unit; it can also be viewed on the macro level, where nations contend with one another or groups within society dispute with one another (for example, labor and management). Historically, the feminist movement has meant social conflict between women and men. Females have sought to increase their share of scarce resources (material rewards, education, prestige, power) inevitably at the expense of male dominance and control. The struggle of blacks against whites has been of the same type. When a minority group presses for a greater share of rewards disproportionately enjoyed by a majority group, there is conflict. During the conflict, there is likely to be suffering (costs) on both sides; but when the conflict is resolved satisfactorily, both sides are likely to benefit and experience maximum joint profit.

Looking back over the past two centuries, virtually all social scientists would conclude that the conflicts between blacks and whites and between males and females have indeed been "regenerative" or "healthy" for Western societies. American society is probably stronger and more stable than it would have been had not resistances occurred. And it is not only that these minority groups are becoming better off. It may be assumed that men and whites in general are also better off as a result of gains made by women and blacks. Although it has been costly to males and whites in terms of traditional rewards (privileged position, unchallenged economic advantages, greater power, and so on), new rewards have been emerging as compensation. For example, society benefits through a greater utilization of talents when certain persons aren't blocked from achievement because of race or sex. Freedom from racial or sex-role stereotypes may enable persons to be themselves and relate as human beings with much in common to unite them rather than stressing differences that separate. Husbands might find that they are emancipated from many pressures as wives come to share the economic load. And wives may prove to be more interesting companions as well.

However, Coser raises the question: "If conflict unites, what tears apart?"[60]

In saying that conflict has the potential of being cohesive (holding social groups together and bringing benefits), we are not denying that conflict also has the potential of being divisive (tearing groups apart, breaking up relationships). Conflicts can bring about the dissolution of business partnerships, entertainment teams, alliances between nations, friendships, and marriages. If a husband and wife, for example, try to resolve conflicts by continually resorting to nonlegitimate power, feelings of exploitation, discontent, and distrust may be generated. The partner who feels exploited might eventually leave the relationship. As we saw earlier, there is some indication that working-class husbands try to resolve conflicts through exercising power that their wives do not recognize as legitimate, since the husbands have fewer resources and give their wives fewer economic-status benefits than is true of middle-class husbands. This may be one reason why divorce rates are higher among working-class marriages than among middle-class marriages. Conflicts tend not to be resolved in ways that are regenerative but rather in ways that are disruptive.

Areas of Conflict in Marriage

What kinds of issues are involved in conflicts between husbands and wives? In our study of Indianapolis marriages, we asked each respondent to name in rank order the four things the respondent and spouse disagreed about most often. The question was open ended; that is, there was no list read of areas of potential conflict in marriages. Thirty-eight percent of the respondents said that the major area of contention in their marriages was money (producing it and spending it); 19 percent cited issues connected with children, 10 percent indicated problems over friends, and 3 percent said problems over kin. Twenty-one percent were placed in a category called "miscellaneous" since they indicated problems common only to a few families, problems too individualized to warrant a special category for each one; and 9 percent of the respondents reported nothing.[61]

Among areas of disagreement placed in the miscellaneous category were issues sometimes called "tremendous trifles" (matters pertaining to personal habits, preferences, and manners of conducting day-to-day living). Slightly more than one-fifth of our respondents cited some such issue as the major area of disagreement. Examples were decisions about colors to paint the home interior, concerns about punctuality, disagreements over the thermostat setting, and so on. Such matters can become highly significant in a husband-wife conflict, particularly when one feels the other is exercising nonlegitimate power and taking unfair advantage.

Although many people think that sexual problems are the major cause of husband-wife disagreements, the number of respondents who mentioned sex as their number one contention area was too few to warrant listing sex as a separate category. The seven-tenths of 1 percent who did name sex were included under "miscellaneous." Blood and Wolfe, in their Detroit study, also found that only a very small percentage of their respondents (less than one-half of 1 percent) specified sexual conflict as their major trouble area.[62] Perhaps folklore, movies, the popular press, and reports of case studies by marriage counselors and sex counselors have combined to present an exaggerated picture of the part sexual disagreements play in marital conflict and dissolution.

On the other hand, Blood and Wolfe may have a point in saying that there may be an *underreporting* of sex problems as the major area of disagreement. These researchers suggest that persons might be shy and hesitant to name this area of marriage, since sex is generally considered to be a personal and private matter. Yet, the social climate regarding sexual matters has become increasingly open. More than a decade has passed since the Blood and Wolfe findings; and while it is possible that the shyness-privacy explanation may have been a factor in the low reporting of sexual conflict in their study, it would seem to be less valid as an explanation of the low percentage in more recent research. For example, our own latest study indicates that only 1.4 percent of husbands and wives consider sex to be their major area of disagreement.[63] While there is no denying serious conflicts over sex in some marriages, the weight of evidence shows that among marriages in general there are disagreement areas of far more concern to the couples involved. Money and children continue to be the main issues over which there is husband-wife conflict.

Table 8-A compares the findings of Blood and Wolfe with those of our Indianapolis study and also with our more recent study in which 3,096 husbands and wives in ten major northern metropolitan areas were interviewed.[64] In this latest research effort, nearly 33 percent reported money matters as the major area of marital disagreement, and 18.6 percent specified child-related matters. Each remaining category shows a lower percentage than either of these.

Economic matters Given the interrelationship of the family with the economic-opportunity system, it is not surprising that issues relating to money and jobs are so important to husband and wives. Self-worth is intricately bound up with achievement and acquisitiveness in a modern industrial society, and husbands and wives are apt to have great concern about whether or not they are living up to personal and societal expectations. Their concern might sometimes take the form of disagreements over occupational matters (the *production* aspect of the economic side of marriage) or over matters of expenditure (the *consumption* aspect). The couple might disagree about the wife's career aspirations or about the husband's working overtime or moonlighting on a second job, or about changing jobs. They might have conflicts about how much they should pay for new furniture, about how far to go into debt, about a spouse's extravagance (or conversely, a spouse's miserliness and hoarding), about having a joint checking account, about savings, investments, credit cards, and a myriad of other matters.

Disagreements over children Since children require a considerable investment on the part of parents, they constitute another area of great importance

TABLE 8-A MAJOR CONFLICT AREAS IN MARRIAGE (PERCENT OF RESPONDENTS REPORTING EACH AREA)

Chief Disagreement	Blood and Wolfe, 1960	Scanzoni, 1970	Scanzoni, 1975
Money-related matters (producing and spending)	24%	38%	33%
Child-related matters (e.g., discipline and number)	16	19	19
Friend-related matters		10	1
Kin-related matters	6	3	3
Companionship, leisure, recreation (kind, quality, and quantity)	16		8
Activities disapproved by spouse (problem drinking, gambling, extramarital affairs, etc.)	14		3
Roles, household division of labor	4		3
Miscellaneous (all else, including religion, politics, sex, communication in marriage, "tremendous trifles," etc.)	3	21	13
"Nothing" reported, "Nothing specific," not ascertained	17	9	17
Total	100%	100%	100%
Number	(731)	(916)	(3,096)

Source: Adapted from Blood and Wolfe, 1960, p. 241; Scanzoni, 1970, p. 157; Scanzoni, unpublished data from the study described in 1975b.

and potential husband-wife disagreement. Emotionally and financially, as well as in terms of time and energy, parents are spending a great deal on children. In spite of these costs, parents also may view children as sources of rewards. Husbands and wives may disagree about the best way to ensure that the rewards of children will exceed the costs. To one spouse, the very idea of having children in the first place might appear to be too costly; while to the other spouse, "starting a family" may be a cherished goal. Similarly, there may be conflict about the spacing of children or the number desired. In one situation, a father continued to pressure his wife to "try one more time for a boy" after they had eight daughters. The wife balked at the suggestion.

Child-related marital conflicts are not only centered around having children

Money continues to be a major issue in husband-wife conflict.

(if, when, and how many) but also about how to rear them. One spouse might be strict, while the other is lenient; the result is often severe disagreement about matters of nurture and discipline. Clashes about techniques of securing obedience from small children, or about how much allowance to give the elementary schoolchild, or about how much freedom to grant adolescents are not uncommon as husbands and wives share the task of parenting.

Conflicts in marriage, whether about money or children or anything else, may be settled amiably through negotiation, or they may lead to a breakup of the marital relationship. Sometimes, however, they explode into actual violence—a possibility that has often been overlooked by researchers, perhaps because of the "touchiness" and unpleasantness of the subject and the common belief that violence only occurs on occasion in "abnormal" families.[65]

Violence in Marriage

One June day in 1974, an Indiana minister and his wife went for a drive. The trip ended tragically. When their bodies were found one week apart floating in the Wabash River, law officers theorized that an assailant must have slain the couple and stolen their car. Later, however, the automobile was found submerged at the point where it had been driven 200 feet into a stream. After an extensive investigation, a coroner's jury concluded that the plunge into the water had been deliberate and that the minister planned to kill his wife and possibly himself. The charge of homicide was definite, although there was some doubt about the suicide attempt in view of evidence that the minister had tried to escape but had been trapped when his shoe caught on something in the car. In its study, the jury learned that the couple, both in their mid-thirties and married only six months, had been having severe marital difficulties.

This case may seem as bizarre as it is tragic. Yet, according to the National Commission on the Causes and Prevention of Violence, what appear to be automobile "accidents" have not infrequently been found to have been intentional acts of murder and suicide.[66] Not only is the family car sometimes the murder weapon itself; it also serves as the setting for many murders in which other weapons are used—such as in the case of a woman depressed over her forty-fifth birthday who asked her husband to go for a drive with her and then, as he slid behind the steering wheel, shot him and then herself. Other common settings for family murders are the kitchen (a central location for interaction between family members and often the site of arguments) and the bedroom (where husband and wife are closed off in privacy with one another at the end of the day, providing an occasion where built-up tensions and hostilities may suddenly erupt).[67]

According to official FBI statistics, murders within the family accounted for about one-fourth of all murder offenses during 1972. In over half of these family killings, one spouse killed the other spouse. The victims in these husband-wife murders were almost evenly divided with regard to sex and race. Wives were victims in 52 percent of the incidents, and husbands were victims in 48 percent. Blacks were victims in 52 percent of spouse killings, whites in 47 percent, and other races accounted for the remaining 1 percent.

Spouse killings in 1972 accounted for 12.5 percent of all murders. In nearly 3 percent of all homicide offenses, parents killed their children. And 9 percent of murder incidents involved other kinds of in-family killings.[68] Family homicide is a gruesome reality in which husbands kill wives, wives kill husbands, parents kill children, children kill parents, brothers and sisters kill one another, people kill in-laws and grandparents, and so on. Viewed this way, the family looks more like a bloodstained battlefield than a peaceful haven of love and tenderness.

Most families, of course, are not broken up by the murder of one family member by another family member. Yet, many other kinds of violence may be far more common than is generally realized. Until recently, sociologists have given little attention to family violence, and research has been scanty. We simply do not know the actual incidence of physical force or the threat of physical force between spouses. Similarly, even though the problem of the "battered child syndrome" has been more publicized, there are no statistics on the actual number of children who are physically abused by their parents—although officially reported cases run between six and ten thousand per year.[69] Furthermore, exactly what constitutes *abuse* in the case of children is somewhat more difficult to determine, since societal norms permit parents to use physical force (such as spankings) in disciplining their offspring. No laws exist against employing such means of correction.

Up until late in the last century, the situation was similar in the case of wives. Wife beating was considered to be a husband's right, supported by laws affirming such chastisement as a means of enforcing "domestic discipline." Although husbands have lost the right to beat their wives, social scientists who have examined legal history conclude that the change came about not because of new laws but rather because of socioeconomic changes in the population.[70] As educational and occupational opportunities opened for women, and as women took greater steps toward equality (by pressing for the vote, for example), the owner-property pattern of marriage which permitted husbands to use physical force came to be viewed as less desirable. Legislation against wife beating reflected these structural changes.

This is not to say that wife beating (or husband beating, for that matter) no longer occurs. According to a national sample survey conducted for the Violence Commission, more than one-fifth of the respondents said they approved of spouse slapping under certain conditions.[71] How many husbands and wives actually do resort to hitting each other is not known with certainty. One legal researcher has pointed out that more police calls are made for family fights than for any other kind of criminal incident.[72] Calls for police intervention in domestic disturbances are not popular with policemen because such work can be very dangerous. Irate husbands and wives sometimes turn and vent their rage on the police, throwing bottles or furniture or even using knives and guns. In 1972, more policemen were assaulted while responding to the category of "disturbance calls" (primarily family quarrels, man with a gun, and the like) than in responding to any other kind of calls. Twenty-seven percent of assaults on police officers occurred under such circumstances. In that same year, of the 112 policemen killed, 15 (or 13.5 percent) died as a result of responding to disturbance calls.[73]

The exact amount of husband-wife violence is not known with certainty because so little research has focused on the subject. Some researchers have endeavored to find some answers through interviews with applicants for divorce. In one such study, 17 percent of those interviewed spontaneously mentioned physical abuse as a reason for the deterioration of their marriage and a major factor in initiating divorce action.[74]

In another study, George Levinger examined records of 600 applicants for divorce in the greater Cleveland area, where, by order of the court, divorce applicants with children under fourteen years of age were required to meet with experienced marriage counselors. In analyzing the counselors' interview records, Levinger found that physical abuse was a complaint in more than one-third of the cases, with wives complaining far more than husbands of being physically hurt by the spouse. Nearly 37 percent of the women applying for divorce voiced such a complaint, compared to 3.3 percent of husbands.

Social-class differences were also found. Among middle-class couples in Levinger's sample, 22.8 percent of wives and 2.9 percent of husbands complained of being physically abused by the marital partner. Among working-class and lower-class couples, 40.1 percent of wives reported that their husbands hurt them physically, and 3.5 percent of husbands complained of physical abuse by their wives.[75] While such figures may provide some rough idea of the extent of physical violence in marriages that end in divorce, they do not furnish us with data on marriages in general. Thus, generalizations from these figures should be avoided.

Since violence has often been regarded as almost exclusively a phenomenon of the lower socioeconomic strata of society, the extent to which it occurs in middle-class marriages may strike many as surprising. While it is true that more violence occurs in lower-class marriages than occurs at higher levels, there is nevertheless evidence that a considerable amount of physical abuse does occur among middle-class couples. Slightly more than one out of five middle-class wives in Levinger's study of divorce applicants reported violence, as compared to two out of five working-class and lower-class wives.

Murray Straus is a sociologist who has devoted much attention and exploratory study to the issue of violence in marriage. In one study, 385 university students filled out questionnaires indicating whether or not their parents were known to have used or threatened physical force during the last year in which the student lived at home. Sixteen percent of the students indicated that one or the other parent had *threatened* to hit or throw something at the spouse, or had actually done so, or had pushed, grabbed, or shoved the other during a disagreement.[76] However, as Straus cautions, "An obvious limitation of this data is that it describes only unbroken families with a child in college, which is far from representative of the population as a whole. . . . Consequently, a description of the amount of violence between family members based on this data is likely to be an underestimate." Also, the information tells us only about a single year of a couple's married life, and it may be incomplete inasmuch as parents might be hesitant to engage in violence in the presence of their children—even though they might resort to it in private.

Another sociologist, Richard Gelles, in a series of depth interviews with eighty couples, found that in more than half of these marriages at least one instance of husband-wife physical force had occurred at some time.[77] Furthermore, he and other researchers make the point that it is erroneous to consider physical violence (whether between spouses or parents and children) as simply "an abnormality—something which involves sick families."

However, as Murray Straus and his colleague Suzanne Steinmetz write, "The fact that almost all family violence, including everyday beating, slapping, kicking and throwing things, is carried out by normal everyday Americans rather than deranged persons should not lead us to think of violence as being desirable or even acceptable."[78] Rather, they suggest asking *why* so many families resort to violence. Gelles emphasizes that psychological explanations in which "mental illness" is viewed as the major reason for physical abuse are inadequate in themselves. There needs also to be an examination of social situational factors such as childhood socialization patterns, socioeconomic status, community or subcultural values regarding violence, structural stress (unemployment, excess children, and so on), and an awareness of immediate precipitating situations that bring on acts of violence in some families.[79]

Why violence occurs   To understand violence, we may want to recall our definition of conflict as a struggle over limited resources and/or incompatible goals in which it appears that one person or group will have its way at the expense of the other party or group. Conflict need not and often does not result in violence. However, in some situations persons may resort to violence because it may seem there is no other way out. Sociologist William Goode points out that when persons begin to feel a continuing imbalance between investments and payoffs in the daily exchanges of family life they may engage in conflict over this imbalance. For various reasons, they may feel they cannot take one of the other roads usually open in such a situation—escape, submission, or righting the balance. As a result, the conflict "can escalate to the point of violence because no simpler or easier resolution emerges."[80]

In some marriage and family situations, one of the other routes may be chosen. Some persons decide that escape is the answer; thus, the child runs away from home or a spouse deserts the family or files for divorce. In other cases, submission (though given grudgingly and with resentment) might appear to be the only way to "keep the peace." Yielding to the demands of a domineering spouse, for example, may seem easier to the other spouse than bringing injustices out into the open and engaging in conflict. Goode's third alternative, righting the balance, would seem the most desirable way to handle what one or the other spouse feels are imbalances in the husband-wife exchange. This is the renegotiation process we spoke of earlier as exemplified in the way Bob and Julie handled their conflict over the new car. Articles and books have been written to help couples approach the problem of conflict in this way and to fight "creatively," "fairly," and "properly"—in other words, to fight constructively rather than destructively.[81] As sociologist Jetse Sprey has written, "The successful management of conflict requires the ability to negotiate, bargain, and cooperate: a range of behavioral skills."[82] However, some persons fail to develop such behavioral skills and seek a solution to dissension by either escaping or submitting to the wishes and demands of the other person even if they seem unfair. Or out of desperation, either party in a conflict may resort to the fourth alternative mentioned by Goode—actual violence.

It should not be assumed that the *absence* of conflict as we have defined it (in the sense of struggle) suggests a more satisfactory or solidary husband-wife relationship. Seething resentments and hostilities may underlie an outwardly calm marital life. In the example of our hypothetical couple, suppose that neither had expressed feelings of injustice. Julie might have kept to herself (or shared with some relatives or women friends) her feelings that Bob was acting unfairly by not doing the cooking. Resentments could have piled up, but to avoid conflict she would not have voiced her complaints to Bob. Instead, she might have acted increasingly distant and cool toward him. As it was, she was able to bring up the matter and work with Bob toward a constructive solution though negotiation—even before an actual conflict emerged in which each would have struggled for his or her own way. The couple did engage in actual conflict over the car Bob wanted, but again they were able to resolve it since they didn't try to bury the problem but instead were willing to renegotiate after Bob pressed for what he felt was fairness.

Why the family may be a setting for violence Suppression of perceived injustice in order "not to rock the boat" or to be "selfless" or "altruistic" can generate strong feelings which could explode at some unexpected time. Several observations of sociologist Lewis Coser are worth noting in this regard. He points out that "there is more occasion for the rise of hostile feelings in primary than in secondary groups."[83] Primary groups are composed of persons having a close relationship to one another in which, as much as possible, the total range of roles and the complete personality of each is known to the other. The family is probably the most obvious example of such a group. Secondary relationships, on the other hand, involve persons who know and relate to one another segmentally; they share only certain aspects of their lives and see one another only in specific roles. A patient may know a doctor only in the role of physician and know nothing of the physician's role as spouse, parent, church or club member, friend, and so on. The patient and physician are involved in one another's lives only on a secondary level; the physician's relationship with his or her spouse, children, and closest friends, however, is on a primary level. Areas of one's personality and interests which are not disclosed in a secondary relationship are revealed and out in the open in a primary one, such as the family. "If you could see him at home, you'd know what he's really like," is a common bit of folk wisdom.

Coser emphasizes that since primary relations tend to involve the total personality, feelings of intimacy are strengthened. Sharing all aspects of life makes people feel close to each other. Paradoxically, however, such intimacy has the potential of breeding hate as well as love. This happens because persons in close contact are bound to "rub one another the wrong way" on occasion. But since conflict is usually considered "bad" and disruptive for primary relationships, deliberate efforts are made to avoid it. The desire to engage in conflict is suppressed out of concern for affectionate sentiments, peace, and group cohesiveness. However, suppression of conflicts often means that an accumulation of hostilities is occurring, and any eruption of these feelings is likely to have great intensity both because persons in primary relations are so totally involved in one another's lives and also because the hostile feelings have grown to huge proportions by not having been allowed expression earlier.[84]

An outburst in which spouses furiously unleash their gathering storms of hostilities is not likely to solve problems or help their situation. Hostilities and conflict are not one and the same. In the words of Coser, "Whereas conflict necessarily changes the previous terms of the relationship of the participants, mere hostility has no such necessary effects and may leave the terms of the relationship unchanged."[85] To renegotiate, bargain, or engage in actual conflict is like the safety valve on a boiler.[86] "Letting off steam" keeps the entire mechanism from exploding.

When husbands and wives keep hostilities and resentments to themselves, sudden convulsions might occur at any time in the form of devastating, heated verbal exchanges or actual physical violence. Often *both* verbal aggression and physical violence take place. Straus conducted a study to test the hypothesis that verbal aggression is a substitute for physical aggression. The results showed just the opposite: "The more verbal expression of aggression, the more physical aggression."[87] In using the term *verbal aggression,* Straus is not referring to settling an argument through rational discussion, negotiating, and talking over and working through disagreements. Rather, he focused on such aggressive tactics as yelling and insulting the spouse, calling the spouse derogative names, sulking and refusing to talk (the "silent treatment" can be very aggressive), and angrily stomping out of the room.

Types of violence   John O'Brien, a social researcher who has given attention to violence in divorce-prone families, defines violence as "any behavior which threatens or causes physical damage to an object or person." Examples of family violence in the divorce records he examined included wife beating, child beating, threats with a gun, extreme sadomasochism in sex relations, and the starving of the spouse's pet cats.[88] Some sociologists suggest that a distinction should be made between two types of violence. Steinmetz and Straus, for example, speak of violence in which physical force is used to cause pain or injury as an end in itself in contrast to violence in which "pain or injury or physical restraint" is used "as a punishment to induce the other person to carry out some act."[89]

Perhaps we could think of the distinction in terms of what we might call "explosive" violence and "coercive" violence. The child who throws a temper tantrum, the wife who suddenly begins pounding her husband's chest when he tries to smoothe over a disagreement by making sexual overtures when she wants to talk, the husband who kicks over a chair in a fit of rage all may be expressing *explosive* violence. They feel angry and frustrated and feel some need to "get it out of their system" through striking out. *Coercive* violence, in contrast, is goal-oriented and is directed toward accomplishing a task, namely to persuade someone to do or not to do something, or to punish the person, or in some other way to exercise control through physical force. The parent who shakes the child in order to extract the truth when lying is suspected is an example of coercive physical force. "You'd better tell me the truth or I'm just going to shake it out of you!" The husband who reacts to finding his wife in bed with another man by beating them both black and blue is another example of coercive violence (though no doubt combining "explosive" elements as well). "There, that'll show you both! That'll teach you never to do anything like that again, you no-good whore!"

Physical violence is not likely to be conducive to satisfactory social relationships of any sort. Persons in marital situations where violence occurs frequently or where it is intense are likely to want to leave those situations. Since violence may occur because of pent-up hostilities and through *suppressing* desires to struggle for change through renegotiation attempts, it is possible that marital dissolution may come about even though a social conflict situation has not occurred. In fact, social conflict satisfactorily handled might even strengthen the relationship and prevent dissolution or violence.

On the other hand, social conflict may also lead to violence—particularly when nonlegitimate power is used in an attempt to resolve the conflict. One or the other partner may try to force the other into doing something against the person's wishes. The coercion may be verbal and involve threats of rewards withheld or certain nonphysical punishments, or it may be actual physical aggression on the part of the person trying to control the other. The husband blocks the door and snatches away the car keys, yelling at his wife, "I said I don't want you to go!" Conversely, the person who is attempting to resist the coercion may resort to violence. The wife kicks her husband, scratches his arm with her fingernails in an attempt to get back the car keys, and tries to push him away from the doorway as she shouts, "Let me go, you bully!"

Socioeconomic status and violence   We have already seen that husbands who are blocked from success in the economic-opportunity system are likely to attempt to resolve disagreements through exercising power that their wives consider nonlegitimate. There is also some evidence that violence is one of the ways this nonlegitimate power may be exercised in marriage.

A husband might turn to brute force as a means of dominating his wife if it seems the only way he can persuade her to comply with his wishes. As one blue-collar wife told Komarovsky, "Women got to figure men out, on account of men are stronger and when they sock you, they could hurt you." Another wife told of a time her husband pulled off a banister and ripped up three steps in a fit of anger toward her—which caused her to stop and think of what might happen if that physical strength were applied *directly* toward her.[90] Thus, according to Komarovsky, "the threat of violence is another ground of masculine power," particularly at lower socioeconomic levels. In her sample of blue-collar marriages, Komarovsky found that 27 percent of husbands with less than twelve years of education and 33 percent of wives with less than twelve years of education reported that conflicts were handled through violent quarreling, with occasional beating and breaking things. Among the high school graduates in her sample, 17 percent of the husbands and 4 percent of the wives reported such violence in marital quarreling.[91]

O'Brien likewise reports evidence of a connection between violence and a family's relationship to the economic-opportunity structure.[92] O'Brien's sample of 150 divorce applicants included 24 percent upper middle class, 29 percent lower middle class, and 47 percent working class. In one out of six families, violence had occurred to such an extent that it was considered a major reason for initiating divorce.

O'Brien separated the 25 cases of families spontaneously reporting violence from the 125 cases where violence had not been reported as a reason for divorce. He found evidence that physical force on the part of the husband-father was commonly linked with underachievement in the breadwinner role. (See Table 8-B.) Since his sample did not include families with husbands chronically unemployed, the lower class was not represented. Otherwise even more evidence of violence would likely have shown up. The greater incidence of violence characterizing underclass families in ghetto areas says O'Brien, "reflects, not a subcultural disposition toward violence, but rather a greater incidence of men in the father/husband role who fail to have the achievement capacities normally associated with this role."

But why should men become violent with their wives and children because they as husbands and fathers haven't been achievers in the economic-opportunity system? Some men may react aggressively out of a sense of frustration at being blocked from the rewards which achievement in that system would have brought them. Unable to attack the system directly or the forces which they feel hold them back from its benefits, such men turn their attacks upon their families. Their reaction is what we have described as explosive violence.

On the other hand, it is quite possible that coercive violence takes place as well as explosive violence in homes where the husband has not achieved at a high level. Lacking legitimate authority earned by his accomplishments in the realm of work, such a husband may nonetheless feel that he has the right to domineer over his wife. He accepts an ideology of male supremacy, even if his wife views his power as nonlegitimate and does not submit to it unquestioningly or happily. If there is no other means of getting his way, such a husband may try physical force. One behavioral scientist says that the husband's perception of a failure to be in control underlies his violent outbursts.[93] In the thinking of such a husband, not to be "in control" of his wife and children is not to be fully a man.

Goode points out that social systems contain four major elements by which persons may move others to carry out their wishes: (1) money or other material resources, (2) prestige or respect (such as commanded by a person in a position to which others look up), (3) winsomeness (likeability, attractiveness, friendship, love), and (4) force or the threat of force.[94] In other words, we are back to the "carrot and stick" analogy. Persons may get their way either through rewards or

TABLE 8-B COMPARISON OF ACHIEVEMENT STATUS OF HUSBANDS IN VIOLENCE AND NONVIOLENCE SUBGROUPS OF UNSTABLE FAMILIES

Achievement Status of Husband	Prevalence in:	
	Violence Subgroup (Number = 25)	Nonviolence Subgroup (Number = 125)
Husband was seriously dissatisfied with his job	44%	27%
Husband started but failed to complete either high school or college	44	18
Husband's income was the source of serious and constant conflict	84	24
Husband's educational achievement was less than his wife's	56	14
Husband's occupational status was lower than that of his father-in-law (wife's marital mobility downward)	37	28

Source: O'Brien, 1971, p. 695.

punishments meted out to those whom they wish to control. Husbands who lack positive resources with which to reward their wives are likely to find it more difficult to extract submission or compliance from them. Thus, they turn to the one resource that appears to remain to them—physical force.

O'Brien has taken ideas from conflict theory as it applies to the larger society and has shown how these same ideas may be applied to the family. He points out that those in a superior position in a social system may hold such a position because of an *ascribed* status—a status they have not earned but have been granted by virtue of their membership in some social category (whites in a white-dominant society, males over females, feudal lords over peasants, and so on). In such a social system, those in an inferior position may accept and support the arrangement, believing that the group in the superior position has the right to rule because of its advantaged skills and resources. However, says O'Brien, "One of the most common situations leading to a rejection of the legitimacy of those in high status is when their achieved status fails to measure up to their ascribed status."[95] If the superior group is not able to back up its privileged position with a display of adequate resources, or if it fails to distribute such resources fairly to those over whom it holds power, a conflict situation emerges which may erupt in violence.[96] Perceiving a threat to the legitimacy of its superior position, the dominant group may resort to coercive action (violence) against the subordinate group that has dared to challenge its supremacy. Applying these ideas to the family, O'Brien concludes that "one should find that violence is most common in those families where the classically 'dominant' member (male-adult-husband) fails to possess the superior skills, talents or resources on which his preferred superior status is supposed to be legitimately based."

Another reason for more violence at lower socioeconomic levels may relate to childhood gender-role socialization in which boys are encouraged to develop what Jackson Toby has termed "*compulsive* masculinity," with an exaggerated emphasis on roughness and toughness as a sign of manhood. Toby suggests that boys at such levels, having grown up with little opportunity to understand, appreciate, and wield *symbolic* power (such as the power of a physician or business executive), may look on violence as "the most appropriate way to protect one's honor, to show courage, or to conceal fear, especially fear of revealing weakness."[97]

Types of Conflict

Although, as we have seen, violence is one way to resolve conflicts, it is by no means the only way. In order to understand other directions in which conflict may move, it helps to look at three ways of categorizing conflict.

Zero-sum and mixed-motive conflict In a bullfighting contest, either the matador or the bull will win—not both. The goal of the game is to conquer the opponent. Social conflict may also be of this type and is sometimes called zero-sum; the contesting parties expect to have either all or nothing. An assassin stalks and kills his victim; the United States Congress impeaches the President and removes him from office; one nation gains a military victory and forces another nation to surrender unconditionally. Persons or groups on the losing end gain no apparent benefits. The winning party or group takes home "all the marbles," and the game is over. Zero-sum conflict is resolved in the majority of instances by extraordinary coercion or else actual violence.

However, there is another type of conflict insofar as objectives are concerned. Rather than a "winner take all" approach, there occurs a "mixed-motive situation." This kind of conflict is far more frequent in social interaction than is the zero-sum type. In mixed-motive conflict, the contesting parties also want to gain benefits at the other's expense, but they do not wish to totally crush or destroy the other. It is in the interests of both, their maximum joint profit, to continue the relationship—if they are able. The term *mixed motive* is used, writes social psychologist Philip Brickman, "since each party may be partly motivated by a desire to cooperate around the common interests in the relationship and partly motivated by a desire to compete for the more favorable share of those resources which must be divided up."[98]

In the past several decades, wars have come to be fought in ways that suggest mixed-motive rather than zero-sum conflict. The Korean war and the Vietnam war are both examples of no-win struggles. Thus, they are sometimes spoken of as "police actions," "limited warfare," or efforts at "containment," rather than as calls to conquer and divide the spoils. In such conflicts, a nation desires to gain its objectives without destroying the other nation. Being unwilling for the total destruction that atomic warfare would bring, world powers since World War II have contended with one another in mixed-motive fashion.

In our story of Bob and Julie's negotiations over the new car, the conflict was mixed-motive. Each wanted to gain at the expense of the other, but neither wanted to wipe the other out in zero-sum fashion. Each saw value in maintaining their relationship and wanted to cooperate on the basis of all they held in common, even though their competing interests were pulling in different directions. Bob was not ready to insist on a new car to the point of breaking up the marriage, nor was Julie ready to resist to this point. Thus, they had to deal with mixed motives: competition and cooperation.

Personality-based and situational conflict   Another hypothetical couple, the Wilsons, sought a counselor's help because of severe conflicts in their marriage. Ted Wilson complained that his wife neglected household chores to read or watch television. "And she's always nagging me to give her time off from taking care of the kids. What kind of woman is she if she can't stand taking care of her own children and can't keep the house decently clean? Something's wrong with her!" At this point, Betty Wilson broke in: "He's always saying something's wrong with me! Why doesn't he ever look at himself? The first thing he says when he comes in the door each evening is, 'What's for dinner?' or 'Don't you have anything cooked *yet*?' He's only affectionate if he wants sex. He only cares about himself. He won't even baby-sit so that I can take some evening-school courses."

Viewing the Wilsons' problem solely as a *personality-based* conflict, the counselor told Betty she should accept her wife-mother role and "adjust to her womanhood" rather than fight against it. She should stop rebelling against her responsibilities as a homemaker and should leave her husband free to pursue his occupational interests. Her interests should be secondary to those of Ted and the children. Ted, for his part, must learn to be more understanding. "Show Betty more affection and consideration," the counselor advised.

The Wilsons went home, tried out the counselor's advice, and found it didn't work. After a few more months of conflict, they visited a different counselor.

To the second counselor, the Wilsons' case was one of *situational* conflict.

The resolution of situational conflict lies in renegotiation rather than adjustment.

Resolution of such conflict lies in changing the situation rather than trying to change the people to fit the situation. The Wilsons were helped first to see what lay at the root of their problem. Betty felt frustrated in her homemaker role not out of malice or laziness but because she felt blocked from finishing college. She watched programs on public television and read books constantly to keep stretching her mind beyond what she felt housekeeping would allow. The counselor helped the couple see that trying to force Betty to "adjust" or "adapt" wasn't the answer. What they needed to do was to negotiate and find ways to make it possible for her to continue her education.

The Wilsons worked out a plan for sharing household chores and child care, and both the negotiation process and the sharing has strengthened their relationship. Watching his wife's accomplishments and happiness, Ted has a new appreciation and respect for her and finds himself being much more affectionate now that the old hostilities are gone. Betty is so grateful for Ted's willingness to finance her education as well as his sharing child care and home responsibilities that she feels a new love for him. And even housework isn't the same old drudgery that it was in the days of her sulking and resentment. The Wilsons are finding that the changed situation is removing their old complaints about each other.

When sociologists speak of social conflict, they are primarily concerned with conflict of the situational type. There is no denying that personality-based conflicts exist, and there is no denying that personality factors may play a part in certain aspects of situational conflict. However, it helps to make a distinction between fighting that is an end in itself (such as giving vent to tensions and aggressions) and fighting that has a goal in view (settling a disagreement, coming to a decision, changing a structural situation).

Coser refers to persons who act belligerently out of an apparent "need" to fight, hate, and release hostilities. They are always ready to battle, and the "enemy" is not so important to them as is the act of fighting. This is conflict for its own sake. However, it is a serious but common error to try to explain social conflict solely in terms of tension release. *Structural* factors account for much if not most social conflict. Coser cites the example of a worker engaged in strike activity in order to effect changes, such as higher wages, fringe benefits, better working conditions, and so on, and shows how such a man's conflict differs from that of another worker who simply hates the boss because he is an authority figure and reminds him of his father. The first worker's conflict with management is situational; the second man's is personality-based.[99]

Similarly, marital conflicts may have either a situational or personality base; but perhaps far more than is generally realized, such conflicts stem from factors relating to situations which spouses could seek to remedy, instead of simply complaining about one or the other's "unpleasant personality" or how hard it is to get along with him or her. Resolving social conflict over incompatible goals or limited resources is not a matter of "adapting" or "adjustment;" rather it calls for *change.*

Basic and nonbasic conflict It is one thing to engage in conflict within agreed-upon rules of a game; it is quite another to have a conflict about the rules. The first kind of conflict is *nonbasic.* When the rules themselves are called into question and contested, the conflict is clearly *basic.*

When Congress passes a bill and the President vetoes it, Congress may or may not override the veto. But the whole sequence of events is a struggle within the rules set down by the Constitution. That sort of conflict is routine nonbasic conflict. However, what happens when Congress overrides a President's veto and instructs the executive branch to spend money for sewers and roads, only to have the President impound the funds? When that actually happened during the Nixon administration, the conflicts were resolved by court decisions ordering Nixon to use the funds. Again, the rules provided by the Constitution were able to resolve the resistance and struggle.

But at another point in the Nixon administration, journalists were talking about a "constitutional crisis" in which the President was ordered by the courts to release certain papers and tapes which be claimed were covered by "executive privilege." A "crisis" could occur if Nixon did not back down. Would the court use physical coercion to enforce its will? Yet, how could it proceed against the head of the Armed Forces and of the Justice Department? As it turned out, Nixon complied with the basic rule of political conflict that the courts have ultimate legitimate authority in such matters and thus the last word. Had he acted in any other way, it would have been seen as a gross use of raw nonlegitimate power.

Principles involved in conflict-resolution processes at the macro level also may be applied at the micro level. In other words, the same principles that apply to struggles between executive, courts, and Congress apply as well to marital conflict. To illustrate, let's return once again to our story of Bob and Julie. We saw how they resolved their conflict over a new car by renegotiating within the existing rules or role norms which characterize their kind of marriage arrangement. However, at another point, Bob is offered a job in another locale—a position he considers much more challenging and financially rewarding than his current job. But an exciting opportunity has also come up for Julie in their present location. She has been invited to develop and direct a special-education program in the local schools, while at the same time pursuing a master's degree at a nearby university. The stage is set for conflict over their different goals.

Under the rules or norms of a senior partner–junior partner marriage, Bob would expect Julie to forgo her opportunities in special education and move with him, since his role has been defined as chief provider. As such, his occupational demands necessarily take precedence over most other family demands. Another norm characterizing traditional marriage arrangements has been the expectation that marriage will mean children. It is virtually taken for granted that the union of a husband and wife should produce children at some point in order that the gratifications of the father and mother roles may be experienced.

To complicate Bob and Julie's situation further, Bob has started to talk about having a child soon. He feels that his new position will make it possible to manage the economic costs of a baby and suggests that it's time to have one. Julie need not continue working, Bob says, since he will be able to support a family totally if he takes the new job. Thus, still acting under the "rules of the game" for the kind of marriage Bob and Julie have been maintaining, Bob begins to negotiate a new exchange with his wife. He believes that the rules furnish him with legitimate authority to ask her to move with him and to undertake motherhood soon after.

Julie, however, has other ideas. Having always leaned toward modern, equalitarian sex-role norms, she is now beginning to ask questions about the senior partner–junior partner arrangement. The opportunity of a career in developing and administering special-education programs seems challenging. Bob's requests therefore strike her as unjust. She feels that her costs will rise and her rewards drop substantially if she goes along with her husband. She begins to struggle and resist. Conflict has emerged.

Julie bargains, saying she is willing for Bob to move and for them to commute alternately on weekends. Through her conflict and in her specific negotiating process, she is in effect beginning to challenge the norms that govern the senior partner–junior partner arrangement. Open communication was established as negotiations began, but as the conflict progresses certain deep issues begin to move to the fore. Should Julie have children or should she remain voluntarily childless? Should their marriage continue to be based on role specialization, or should they shift patterns to one based on role inter-changeability so that Julie would be considered an equal partner in a dual-career arrangement?

These conflicts are clearly basic in that they involve contention over what the rules of the game should be. The game (marriage) will be very different if fundamental rules are changed. Rules governing American football are very different from those governing European football—a game which is more like soccer than football. In politics, the rules in the United States say that the President shall not use force to resist the courts or Congress. But in many countries today generals and presidents openly use military force to get their way when parliaments or courts cross them. These are two very different political games.

The earlier conflict of Bob and Julie over the purchase of a new automobile was nonbasic. We saw that even nonbasic conflict is likely to bring about situational changes. This is doubly so for basic conflict. But in addition, basic conflict has the potential for serious system disruption. For any social system, basic conflict can mean instability or even total collapse. For instance, if an American President could persuade a general to mobilize troops to resist a congressional order to remove him from office, there would occur the most serious and devastating disruption of American democracy in two centuries. Or if two companies were to experience basic conflict over the rules of their buyer-seller relationship, they might simply terminate the association. Such a breaking off of the relationship would not be so likely to occur over nonbasic conflict, which is more easily negotiable.

In marriage, basic conflict may take place over several core issues. Earlier, we saw that marriage has both an expressive side (love, empathy, companion-ship, displaying affection) and an instrumental side (economic functions, household tasks, and so on). Both in the personal realm and the practical realm of marriage, basic conflict may occur. Marriage was defined as a relationship in which there is both sexual and economic interdependence between two persons, and thus social norms for the marital relationship include the expectation that the husband and wife will have sexual intercourse with one another and will share their material wealth. Basic conflict may occur over either of these norms.

For example, a distressed middle-aged woman wrote to a newspaper advice columnist with the following story: She and her husband were both in their second marriages, and for six years they had found together what she described as a happiness neither had dreamed possible. Almost nightly, they had sexual relations which both enjoyed immensely. Then the husband joined a religious cult and changed his attitudes entirely. The wife wrote: "He said he could no longer kiss me, or touch me, or sleep in the same bed with me because if he did he could not enter the kingdom of heaven because he would be committing adultery since we had both been married before!" After eight months of living this way, the wife was seeking help[100] because the conflict was of the most basic sort.

How basic conflict may occur over economic sharing is illustrated in the later life of novelist Leo Tolstoy and his wife the Countess Tolstoy. Tolstoy had become obsessed with a concern for nonmaterialistic values and a desire to share his royalties and other wealth with those who were poor. His wife considered him selfish and neglectful of his own family. Why should he give away *their* money to strangers? Didn't she deserve some reward for all her years of hard work in caring for their home and rearing the children? For Tolstoy to give away his royalties appeared to his wife as a breaking of the fundamental rules of the game as they applied to economic provision and sharing. The *consumption* of resources for survival and for status is a basic issue in marriage just as is economic *production*.

As we have seen, each of the four ways marriage may be structured also has rules about which partner is the unique or chief provider. The issue of whether or not to have children is also basic—particularly where marriage has been viewed in traditional terms. At the same time, there may occur *nonbasic* conflicts within the same general areas that have been discussed (sex, the provider role, the consumption of resources, and the issue of children). Such secondary conflicts may center around the hours the husband or wife is working, how to discipline the children, how often and with what techniques should sex relations take place, or how to keep expenditures within the budget. But underlying each of these secondary conflicts is an assumption that there is agreement as to the four basic core issues (i.e., that there will be sexual intercourse, that the provider role has been acknowledged to be the primary responsibility of one or both partners, that parenthood will be undertaken or avoided voluntarily, and that consumption and life-style will be of a certain kind). To the degree that such basic consensus exists, struggles which are less central can more satisfactorily be resolved.

In the case of Bob and Julie, Julie's objective is to resolve their basic conflict in such a way that she will become an equal partner with her husband, with her career and interests considered just as important as his. She is also increasingly open to the possibility of remaining childless and avoiding the mother role entirely. This is a very different "game" or arrangement than the couple had before when Julie seemed content to be a junior partner and planned to work only a few years before settling down to have a family. Yet it is precisely those former rules and that earlier game which Bob wants. Since each spouse wants to play a different game with a different set of rules, how can they resolve their mutual struggles and resistances? How can they hold their relationship together and avoid separation or divorce?

Some persons might argue that if the husband could somehow retain final authority, as was traditionally the case, then basic conflicts such as these could be resolved. The husband could simply declare, "This is what we will do," and the issue would be settled. However, that argument overlooks the twin questions of justice and accountability. Husbands have generally tended to resolve conflicts in ways they thought best, with "best" meaning ways that seemed favorable to themselves simply because they were considered to have the final authority. Again it seems appropriate to echo John Stuart Mill's argument of a century ago that there is no inherent structural reason that one partner in a voluntary association such as a business partnership should allow the other to be the final authority.

Moreover, traditionally husbands had authority but no accountability, much as did preparliamentary monarchs. But today even a President who says the "buck stops here" is accountable for the exercise of nonlegitimate power. He is accountable to Congress who can impeach him, the courts who can reverse him, or to voters who can turn him out of office. Thus, in marriage, an appeal to some ultimate authority based on gender whose decisions cannot be disputed, modified, or rejected, or who could not be removed from his position of authority is simply not considered fair or wise in modern society. What Lord Acton said about political power applies as well to the notion of the male (or female) as absolute final arbiter in marriage. "Power corrupts, but absolute power corrupts absolutely."

There are several alternative modes of conflict resolution that Bob and Julie can pursue. Assuming reasonable communication and willingness to negotiate, Bob can agree to a bargain in which the rules are indeed changed. Julie would then become an equal partner with her husband in the sense that each would be equally committed to a career, with the career interests of each given equal priority. As for the matter of starting a family, neither having children nor childlessness is requisite to the equal-partner marriage arrangement; decisions about children are somewhat more optional here than in the other marital patterns (owner-property, head-complement, and senior partner–junior partner). Thus, Bob may try to negotiate with Julie about having a child. If they do decide to have one, issues such as timing and child care become additional matters for negotiation. How extensively should they rely on nursery and day-care facilities? How responsible will Bob be for child care?

Besides bargaining for a child, Bob may also aim negotiation toward persuading Julie to move with him. Let us assume she can find educational and career opportunities in the new locale comparable to those in the old. When Julie agrees to pursue these opportunities rather than her original plans, a new exchange is established in which both spouses experience maximum joint profit. Julie has a new game; she is now an equal partner. At the same time, she has conceded to move and also to have a child—both however under conditions that she does not consider excessively costly or punishing. Bob, for his part, has gained the benefits he wanted (the move and the child), but he agrees to a new game based on role interchangeability in which he is now merely a co-provider and in which Julie possesses as much authority and autonomy as he does.

However, the story could have a different ending. Upon facing their basic conflict, Bob and Julie may simply decide on another mode of resolution— ending the marriage. The key is whether or not Bob is willing for the basic changes in the rules for which Julie is pressing. In other words, is he willing for a new game? If he is not, it is difficult to see what meaningful concessions Julie can make, given her objectives. They are resisting each other over very basic issues; and since both perceive that so much is at stake, no significant negotiations or bargaining can take place. The couple may therefore decide that it is in the best interests of both of them simply to separate and file for divorce. (See Figure 8-4.) Each compares the level of alternatives (rewards and costs) within the marriage with alternatives outside it. Each concludes that the latter alternatives are more desirable or "profitable" (fewer costs, greater rewards) than those in their present situation. And so they leave it.

Collective Conflict

The conflict of Bob and Julie may at first appear to be simply a case of two individuals in conflict, and indeed that is possible. On the other hand, what is happening in the lives of Bob and Julie may reflect on the micro level what is also going on at the macro level of society. Throughout this book, we have focused on processes of social organization at the closeup or individual level *within the context of larger social forces.* Perhaps a better understanding of the individual conflict of Bob and Julie will be gained if we look at what is undoubtedly the most significant of these larger social forces affecting male-female relationships today, namely, the revival of feminism.

A high-priority objective of the women's movement is to raise the consciousness of women as a whole as to their interests vis-à-vis those of men. Feminist leaders encourage collective legal, political, and economic action (in other words, struggle or conflict) in order to enhance women's interests. Sociologist Peter Blau's description of the formation of any protest movement seems fitting. He writes:

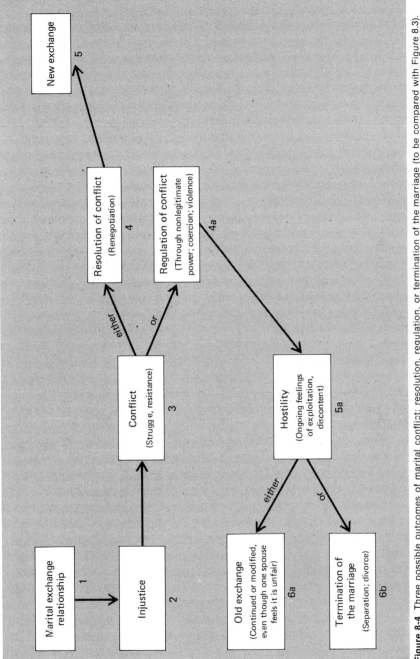

Figure 8-4 Three possible outcomes of marital conflict: resolution, regulation, or termination of the marriage (to be compared with Figure 8.3).

Collective disapproval of power engenders opposition. People who share the experience of being exploited by the unfair demands of those in positions of power, and by the insufficient rewards they receive for their contributions, are likely to communicate their feelings of anger, frustration, and aggression to each other. . . . The social support the oppressed give each other in the course of discussing their common grievances and feelings of hostility justifies and reinforces their aggressive opposition against those in power. It is out of such shared discontent that opposition ideologies and movements develop. . . .[101]

The collective opposition embodied in the women's movement does not mean that every individual female is in actual conflict with every individual male. But it does mean that in the future we may expect that increasing numbers of married women will become more aware of and sensitive to the issue of distributive justice in terms of male-female interests. Consequently, it is possible that increasing numbers of wives who began marriage in the status of either complement or junior partner may later define those situations as not sufficiently rewarding. Through bargaining, negotiation, and basic conflict, they may seek to change the rules of their marital relationship after having been married for a certain time period.

Thus, even though certain bargains may be struck at the outset of marriage, causing the husband to perceive that he is entering a relatively traditional arrangement, current and future conditions of modern society are such that even the basic rules of the relationship may subsequently be challenged. In some instances, husbands may be willing for and may even encourage these kinds of "radical" shifts in the game. In other instances, husbands may be unwilling to make the basic changes for which their wives are pressing; and for a while such situations might contribute to continuing increases in rates of divorce. In time, however, as more males grow up learning less traditional roles for both sexes, divorces resulting from such basic clashes should begin to taper off.

NOTES

1 Bloomington-Bedford Sunday Herald Times, "Dear Abby," June 9, 1974.
2 Aristotle, "The Nicomachean Ethics," quoted in Blau, 1964, p. 199.
3 Seidenberg, 1970, p. 304; see also Niebuhr, 1957.
4 Winter, 1973, p. 4.
5 Winter, 1973, p. 5.
6 Rodman, 1967, Buric and Zecevic, 1967; Safilios-Rothschild, 1967; Michel, 1967; Hallenbeck, 1966; Safilios-Rothschild, 1970; Herr, 1963; Centers, Raven, and Rodrigues, 1971; Liu, Hutchison, and Hong, 1973; Turk and Bell, 1972; Rodman, 1972; Olson and Rabunsky, 1972; Sprey, 1972; Bahr, 1972.
7 Safilios-Rothschild, 1970.
8 Ryder, 1970; Komarovsky, 1962; Safilios-Rothschild, 1969, 1970.
9 Safilios-Rothschild, 1970, p. 540.

10 Blood and Wolfe, 1960.
11 Safilios-Rothschild, 1970.
12 See Turk and Bell, 1972; Scanzoni, 1965; Safilios-Rothschild, 1969; Brown and Rutter, 1966; Hess and Torney, 1962.
13 Olson and Rabunsky, 1972.
14 Greenblat, Stein, and Washburne, 1974.
15 See summaries in Turk and Bell, 1972; Liu, Hutchison, and Hong, 1973.
16 Turk and Bell, 1972, p. 220.
17 Heer, 1963
18 Safilios-Rothschild, 1970; Rodman, 1967, 1972.
19 Safilios-Rothschild, 1970, p. 548.
20 Benston, 1969, pp. 3–4.
21 Gillespie, 1971, p. 457.
22 Blood and Wolfe, 1960.
23 Safilios-Rothschild, 1969, 1970; Centers, Raven, and Rodrigues, 1971; Rodman, 1967, 1972.
24 Centers, Raven and Rodrigues, 1971.
25 Heer, 1963.
26 Waller, 1951, pp. 190–192.
27 Rodman, 1967, 1972.
28 Buric and Zecevic, 1967.
29 Safilios-Rothschild, 1967.
30 Homans, 1961, p. 287.
31 Buckley, 1967, p. 186.
32 Goode, 1964, p. 75.
33 Blood and Wolfe, 1960, pp. 30–33.
34 Komarovsky, 1962, pp. 225–229.
35 Scanzoni, 1970, p. 151.
36 See summary in Winter, 1973, p. 157.
37 Scanzoni, 1970, pp. 159–162; Heer, 1958; Blood and Wolfe, 1960.
38 Davis, 1973, chap. 5; also Lederer and Jackson, 1968, for their concept of *quid pro quo* or "something for something."
39 Goode, 1963, pp. 21–22.
40 Siegel and Fouraker, 1960, pp. 1, 9.
41 Homans, 1961, p. 74.
42 Brickman, 1974, pp. 27, 228.
43 Alexander and Simpson, 1971.
44 Durkheim, 1893.
45 Blau, 1964; Fox, 1974; for a somewhat different perspective on personal marriage contracts, see Weitzman, 1974, pp. 1249–1258.
46 Kelley and Schenitzki, 1972, pp. 304, 306; Siegel and Fouraker, 1960, p. 20.
47 Blau, 1964, p. 99.
48 This definition is based on a combination of Coser, 1956, p. 8; Kriesberg, 1973, p. 17; and Brickman, 1974, p. 1.
49 Kriesberg, 1973, p. 4.
50 As quoted in *Time,* Vol. 103, No. 13 (April 1, 1974), p. 26.
51 Deutsch, 1971, p. 54.
52 Kelley and Stahelski, 1970; White, 1966.
53 Klineberg, 1964, p. 153, as quoted in Brickman, 1974, p. 153.
54 Schelling and Halperin, 1961, p. 8, as quoted in Brickman, 1974, p. 153.
55 Blau, 1964, p. 22.
56 Quoted in Al Stump, "Another Oppressed Minority Is Heard From," *TV Guide,* vol. 22, no. 30 (July 27, 1974), pp. 32–35.
57 Thibaut and Kelley, 1959, pp. 21–23.
58 Blau, 1964; Coser, 1956.
59 Blau, 1964, p. 301.
60 Coser, 1956, p. 73.

61 Scanzoni, 1970, pp. 157–158.
62 Blood and Wolfe, 1960, pp. 243–244.
63 Scanzoni, 1975b.
64 Scanzoni, 1975b.
65 O'Brien, 1971, p. 692.
66 Mulvihill, Tumin, and Curtis, 1969, app. 10.
67 Steinmetz and Straus, 1974, pp. 39 and 93.
68 FBI Uniform Crime Reports, 1973.
69 Gil, 1971.
70 Calvert, 1974.
71 Stark and McEvoy, 1970.
72 Parnas, 1967.
73 FBI Uniform Crime Reports, 1973.
74 O'Brien, 1971.
75 Levinger, 1966.
76 Straus, 1974.
77 Gelles, 1973a.
78 Steinmetz and Straus, 1973.
79 Gelles, 1973b.
80 Goode, 1971.
81 See for example Bach and Wyden, 1968.
82 Sprey, 1971.
83 Coser, 1956, p. 62.
84 Coser, 1956, pp. 63–63. 79.
85 Coser, 1956, p. 40.
86 Blau, 1964, p. 304.
87 Straus, 1974.
88 O'Brien, 1971.
89 Steinmetz and Straus, 1974, p. 4.
90 Komarovsky, 1962, p. 227.
91 Komarovsky, 1962, p. 363.
92 O'Brien, 1971.
93 Whitehurst, 1974, p. 76.
94 Goode, 1971, p. 624.
95 O'Brien, 1971.
96 Grimshaw, 1970.
97 Toby, 1966.
98 Brickman, 1974.
99 Coser, 1956, p. 50.
100 Bloomington (Ind.) Heráld-Telephone, "Dear Abby," Mar. 16, 1973.
101 Blau, 1964, p. 23.

UNIT 4
CHILDREN

9

REPRODUCTION

Ellen and Bill Peck decided not to have children. Soon the pressure was on! People reacted to their childless state with varying degrees of curiosity and hostility. Ellen points out that the question, "Are you going to have any children?" was never asked. Instead it was, "When are you going to have children?"[1]

According to a popular (but scientifically unsupported) folk belief, nature has programmed women so that their life's purpose is to have and rear children. Women are thought to possess some sort of mysterious quality deep within, a "maternal instinct" that produces yearnings for offspring. The folk belief is reinforced by a network of formal and informal societal pressures urging couples to become parents, and those who don't are stigmatized or pitied. These attitudes and societal pressures collectively are sometimes labeled *pronatalism* (from the Latin, "in favor of birth").

Attempting to counteract subtle and not-so-subtle pronatalist influences, Ellen Peck wrote a book entitled *The Baby Trap,* and in addition, she and her husband helped found an organization called the National Organization for Non-Parents (NON), which doesn't hesitate to proclaim that "None is fun!" Such antinatalist groups have arisen in recent years in an effort to call attention to the advantages of remaining childless (or *child-free,* to use their preferred term).

But is it true, as antinatalist groups claim, that couples have babies merely because of societal pressures (since societies cannot continue without replacement of their members)? Or is having babies simply a matter of nature's trickery—a kind of cosmic con game in which persons are carried away in the ecstasy of sexual pleasure only to be rudely awakened by a squirming, squealing, demanding infant who emerges to mock the lovers with an attitude of "Aha! You thought you were just having fun, but look what you got instead—me!" Or might it be that people have children because they want them or value them? No doubt all three explanations contain elements of truth.

REWARDS, COSTS, AND THE MOTIVATION TO HAVE CHILDREN

Throughout this book, we have utilized a model based on an exchange theory of human relationships. That is, persons are attracted to one another and sustain that attraction on the basis of rewards offered to one another. The kinds of rewards may vary from economic security to a sense of being understood, appreciated, and made to feel important by someone else. In other words, both material and emotional rewards may enter the picture in social relationships. At the same time, the bonds formed between persons also involve costs. It takes time and energy and often financial expenditures to keep a relationship going and growing. If costs appear to outweigh benefits, or if the margin of profit (rewards less costs) is extremely minimal, the value of the relationship may be called into question by the person on the losing end.

Already we have seen how this theory operates in the husband-wife relationship, beginning even before marriage in the mate-selection process and continuing through the negotiation and renegotiation process after the marriage takes place. Now we want to see how a theory of rewards and costs helps to explain how couples make decisions concerning reproduction. Assuming they are physically able to have children, will a particular husband and wife *want* to have them? If so, how many and when? Much depends on the perception of costs and rewards, as well as the consideration of alternatives to the parenthood role.

In ancient Hebrew society, no one would have thought to ask if married couples should have children. Had not the Creator commanded, "Be fruitful and multiply"? Children were considered God's gifts, "the fruit of the womb . . . his reward." The scriptures declared that a man needed a quiver full of children as an archer needed arrows. A barren woman was to be pitied. "Give me children or I die!" cried Rachel, the wife of the patriarch Jacob. Married couples desired children to help at home and in the fields and to support them in old age. Sons were needed to carry on the family name and inherit the land. Such an attitude toward children has been common throughout history in traditional, patriarchal, agricultural societies.

A sociological study of *why* people have children would have seemed out of place in biblical times. But such studies are of great interest in today's world. All too little research has been carried out in this area, and what has been done has often been faulty on methodological grounds. Increasingly, however, in dealing with questions of population growth (on the macro level), or "Why are John and Jane Doe going to have another baby?" (on the micro level), social scientists see the need to give attention to the matter of motivation. The birthrate at a given time in history cannot be explained simply and solely in terms of effective contraceptive technology or the lack of it. Although some persons are inclined to explain recent declines in the birthrate by pointing to "the pill," it should be noted that there was also a low birthrate before and during the Great Depression in the United States several decades before the advent of the pill. And even in the early days of the Roman Empire, the emperor Augustus was concerned about low birthrates and therefore devised various incentives to encourage Roman citizens to have large families. By the time of the late Roman Empire, the problem had grown even more acute, because crushing tax burdens and unpaid forced public service made it difficult to support a family of any size.[2]

Clearly, the perceived rewards and costs of having children play their part in family planning. In ancient Hebrew society, the *rewards* were uppermost in mind, and large families resulted. In Imperial Rome, the *costs* were of prime concern, and population replenishment was insufficient. But what about today? Why do some couples want children while others do not?

REWARDS OF PARENTHOOD

Psychologists Lois Wladis Hoffman and Martin L. Hoffman have examined research studies and theoretical literature focusing on reasons why children are valued.[3] Drawing upon their findings, we might group incentives for having children into four main categories according to the rewards children may provide parents.

Rewards of Self-Enhancement

Embarking on parenthood brings a new social identity and a sense of arriving at adult status. "More than finishing school, going to work, or even getting married," Hoffman and Hoffman claim, "parenthood establishes a person as a truly mature, stable, and acceptable member of the community. . . . This is especially true for women, for whom motherhood is also defined as their major role in life."[4] Since few alternative roles are available for uneducated, lower-status women in particular, having a baby is looked upon as perhaps the most important way of gaining identity at this class level.

Closely related to the new sense of self and adult status may be a sense of achievement through parenthood. It might be thought of as *personal* achievement either through having physically produced a child (or several children in social or religious circles where large families are highly esteemed), or through meeting creatively the challenges of rearing children and gaining a sense of pride in a job well done.

On the other hand, parents may experience *vicarious* achievement, a sense of sharing in their children's accomplishments as though these accomplishments were happening to the parents themselves. The mother who never had a chance to take music lessons basks in the reflected glory of her child's performance at a piano recital. The football-loving father swells with pride when his son is chosen high school player of the year. Later, as grown children do well in the occupational sphere, parents feel that their own prestige is enhanced as well. "My son, the doctor" is more than an old joke.

Hoffman and Hoffman also call attention to the reward of power and influence that parenthood brings people, along with a sense of making an impact on one's own life and the lives of others through bringing a child into the world. They suggest that particularly for persons who feel powerless in other areas of life, producing and molding a human being can provide a sense of having an effect on the world that is not otherwise possible.[5] Studies have shown that persons who feel powerless are less likely to use contraceptives,[6] and the Hoffman and Hoffman explanation may fit. On the other hand, of course, the overall sense of powerlessness might *contribute* to the nonuse of contraceptives because the couples involved may feel that contraceptives would do little good anyway—that getting along in life is a matter of fate and "breaks" rather than self-mastery and rational control.

Power and influence over others' lives can provide persons with feelings of importance. Contacts with social agencies and on the job usually put lower-status persons in positions where others have power over them, while they have little if any power over others. But at home they can experience a sense of power denied elsewhere. Social customs and laws allow parents to exercise tremendous control over children. Parents can issue commands; they can insist on having their wishes followed and can, within reasonable bounds, force children to comply. Parents can experience that power which stems from being the chief or only source of material and emotional benefits to others who need them (their children). Such "power benefits" in parenthood may play a part in explaining why lower-status couples tend to have larger families.

Socioeconomic status and fertility Demographers have long noted the inverse relationship between social class and fertility. That is, fertility (the number of children born) goes *up* as socioeconomic status goes *down*. In the words of a 1920s song, "The rich get richer and the poor get children." These statements do not tell the whole story, because much more is involved than social status alone in explaining fertility rates, but in general we may say that lower-status families have more children on the average than do higher-status families.

This point becomes clear in government studies, based upon the 1970

TABLE 9-A AVERAGE NUMBER OF CHILDREN BORN TO EVER-MARRIED WOMEN THIRTY-FIVE TO FORTY-FOUR YEARS OLD, BY SOCIOECONOMIC STATUS AND AGE AT MARRIAGE, UNITED STATES, 1970.

Category	White Wives		Black Wives	
	Not in Labor Force	In Labor Force	Not in Labor Force	In Labor Force
Lower status and early marriage	3.9	3.3	5.6	5.0
Higher status and late marriage	2.9	2.4	2.5	2.0

Source: Adapted from U.S. Bureau of the Census, 1974, *Current Population Reports,* P-23, no. 49, p. 38.

United States census, which separated families (with wives aged thirty-five to forty-four years) into two groups: those with *lower status and early marriage* and those with *higher status and late marriage.* Lower-status families in this case were defined as those in which neither husband nor wife were high school graduates, the husband was a blue-collar or service worker, and the wife was between fourteen and twenty-one years of age at first marriage. The higher-status group contained couples who had one or more years of college (both husband and wife), with the husband's occupation being white-collar and the wife's age at first marriage twenty-two or over. Among white families, the lower-status group had on the average one child more per family than did the upper-status group. Among black families, the lower-status group had on the average three more children per family than did the higher-status blacks.[7] (See Table 9-A.)

The answer to the question "Why do lower-status couples have more children?" may simply be that they want more. They are not so motivated as higher-status couples to prevent births. True, the costs of having children (particularly in the financial realm) are great for lower-status couples, but apparently they feel these costs are more than compensated for by the rewards. As we have seen, for women with few outlets or opportunities for achievement outside the home, the bearing and rearing of children can be extremely gratifying. And for lower-status men, large families can be a source of pride and an opportunity for exercising power not possible elsewhere. Various studies have shown that lower-status men tend to be more authoritarian in their families than are higher-status men,[8] underscoring a point made by Blau and Duncan: "Whereas successful achievers have their status as adult men supported by their superior occupational roles and authority, the unsuccessful find a substitute in the authority they exercise in their role as fathers over a number of

Why do lower-status couples have more children?

children."[9] In addition, children may be looked upon as a form of wealth. In a report for the Population Council, Bernard Berelson has written that childbearing is one of the few ways the poor can compete with the rich. "Life cannot make the poor man prosperous in material goods and services but it can easily make him rich with children."[10]

Rewards of Self-Preservation

The nineteenth-century poet, Thomas Campbell, wrote: "To live in hearts we leave behind/Is not to die."[11] One way to make sure there are hearts left behind in which to "live on" is to have children. Offspring assure the continuation of the family line, the carrying on of the family name, uninterrupted control of a family farm or business, perpetual ownership of family property, and other benefits associated with permanence.

It has long been common folk knowledge that persons desire children as a way of achieving a kind of immortality, and sociological studies provide verification. Men, more than women, tend to mention the survival of the family name as a reason for wanting offspring.[12] In India, for example, demographic research showed that when men were asked to state the benefits of having a wife, a common response was "so our descent will continue." Such an elevation of a wife's benefits was second only to the wife's value in looking after the husband's needs and performing services for him.[13]

Self-preservation benefits in having children not only relate to continuing the family line. In traditional societies, children have been valued for their economic utility. Particularly in agricultural societies, children have been considered assets because they provide families with a supply of workers. In the household, children can help with domestic chores; and older children can care for younger children, freeing mothers for other work (in the fields, for example). Children themselves can assist in agricultural tasks from a very early age.

In societies lacking adequate government plans for old age, children are expected to take responsibility for aging parents, often providing them with a home and nursing care as well as with financial support. Especially in underdeveloped and developing nations, a prime motivation for having large numbers of children is to assure that some will be living to provide for the parents in the parents' old age.[14] Interestingly, this holds true even in rural areas of the People's Republic of China. The Communist government provides old-age assistance only for childless couples. Under the 1950 marriage law, children are required to support elderly parents. Thus, particularly among Chinese peasants, large families are desired. Even though the farms are collectivized, people are paid according to their work. "Families with more able-bodied laborers are more highly rewarded," reports sociologist William L. Parish, Jr., "and the goal of many peasants is to have as many able-bodied males as possible."[15]

Rewards of Pleasure, Affection, and Belonging

Children may be desired because of widely held sentiments about the enrichment they bring to a couple's lives. Youngsters can mean fun, excitement, and laughter in the home. They are persons adults can relax with and play with, enjoying jokes, riddles, teasing, and roughhousing. Sparkle and zest are brought into adult lives. The novelty of a new baby ends the old, dull routine. Such an ideal picture is in the minds of many in anticipating children as pleasure sources for parents.

Furthermore, by having a baby, parents feel they have brought into being someone to love and be loved by. Children provide the promise of warm affection, a sense of belonging. A strong primary group is formed. Even if it seems that no one else in the whole world cares, having children is considered to mean that there is always someone who does care, thereby banishing feelings of aloneness. Parents expect that a loving relationship with their children will

Blue-collar fathers, like this Welsh coal miner, may feel free to openly express affectionate feelings toward children.

continue even if the husband-wife relationship itself comes to an end through death or divorce.

There is some evidence that, especially in blue-collar homes, the companionship and affection provided by children compensates for a lack between the spouses in these expressive areas. Rainwater found in his studies of blue-collar homes that wives especially tended to form intense relationships with their children, because the children seemed to provide a sense of worthwhileness that they did not receive from their husbands. Rainwater reports: "The children (at least when young) seem easier to manage and arouse fewer conflicts than does the difficult task of relating to grown men whom they do not understand too well and of whom they are often a little afraid."[16]

As far as the men themselves are concerned, they too may find that children provide opportunities for physically demonstrating affection in a way that is discouraged elsewhere. In Chapter 7, we discussed the effects of the socialization of men which may inhibit open expressions of affection toward their wives—particularly in blue-collar homes where greater sex-role differences are emphasized. However, with children, such men may feel more comfortable about giving open demonstrations of feelings. They can feel free to touch, cuddle, hug, kiss, tousle children's hair, hold them on their laps, and so on. "It is possible . . . that children provide for men one of the few relationships where they can express warmth and tenderness," write Hoffman and Hoffman.[17]

Altruistic and Religious Satisfactions in Having Children

In a study sponsored by the Planned Parenthood Federation of America, sociologist Lee Rainwater interviewed 409 husbands and wives at various socioeconomic levels in an effort to find out why couples want and have particular numbers of children. In examining his respondents' rationales for large and small families, Rainwater found that he could abstract one central norm, namely the belief that "one should not have more children than one can support, but one should have as many children as one can afford."[18]

Altruistic considerations Rainwater found a widespread belief that parents who didn't have as many children as they could afford were "selfish." Such an opinion was especially prevalent among men who wanted large families. It was less true of women who wanted large families for themselves but at the same time could understand that other couples might choose to limit family size in order to provide more benefits for children already born rather than for reasons of self-indulgence. Yet, the notion has persisted that persons who have large families are somehow more virtuous, self-sacrificing, altruistic, less materialistic, and less apt to spoil their children than are persons with small families. However, in recent years, concerns about a worldwide "population explosion" have challenged this way of thinking to a considerable extent, and the opinion is frequently voiced that the truly altruistic couple may be the one willing to forgo the pleasures of an additional child, whereas "selfish" people are those who insist on adding new persons to an already crowded planet.

Hoffman and Hoffman call attention to another aspect of altruism, namely the concerns of various minority groups for an increase in their numbers and power. They refer to a study of black and Chicano college students in which there was support for the idea of having large families, with typical responses being, "We should double the actual number of Chicanos as soon as possible," and "Black people need more power and you can't have power without people; birth control for blacks is legalized genocide."[19] Among these politically conscious college students, having children is viewed as a service performed in the interests of bettering the conditions of an oppressed people.

Religious considerations Religious satisfactions in having children provide another kind of reward for parents. For some couples, having children is looked upon as a sacred duty. Parenthood provides these husbands and wives with a sense of fulfilling a divine command to "be fruitful and multiply," or brings an assurance that "God has blessed the union," or gives couples an opportunity for outwardly demonstrating compliance with church teachings against contraceptives.

A major difficulty in studying the relationship between religion and fertility springs from the successful efforts of various pressure groups in the late 1950s to eliminate a question on religious affiliation that was considered for inclusion in the United States census. However, enough other research exists to show that religion definitely has an effect on the number of children couples are likely to have.

Roman Catholicism   Numerous studies have shown that Catholics, as a result of their religious ideology, both *have* more children and *intend* to have more children than do couples of other religious groups. In the 1965 National Fertility Study, married women under forty-five years of age who were Protestant had an average of 2.3 children and expected a total of 3.0. Catholic women had an average of 2.8 and expected a total of 3.9 children. Jewish women had 2.1 children and expected to have a total of 2.9.[20]

Our own data from a large regional sample indicate that although the gap in family size between Catholics and non-Catholics is narrowing, it is still there. In 1971, among white married women eighteen to forty-four years of age, Catholics had an average of 2.5 children and intended to have a total of 3.3. Non-Catholics had an average of 2.2 children and intended to have a total of 2.8.[21]

At the heart of Catholic teachings on marital sexuality has been an emphasis on a special mission assigned to husband and wives: "to collaborate with God in the generation and education of new lives." Marriage is considered to be ordained toward begetting children.[22] As we have seen, this teaching has influenced both the actual number of children and the intended number of children among the general population of Catholics. But do church teachings on procreation make any difference among university students as they think about their *future* families? Or does higher education somehow "neutralize" the impact of church teachings? We sought to find answers to such questions by researching family-size preference among systematic random samples of white, never-married undergraduates at a large Midwestern state university at two different times. Again, it was found that Catholics desired more children than non-Catholics. Both in 1971 and 1974, Catholic men and women in this student population reported their intentions to have an average of 2.5 children. Non-Catholics intended to have an average of 2.0 children.[23]

Judaism   Studies have consistently shown the fertility of Jewish women to be the lowest of the three major religious groups. Such a finding again emerged in the 1965 National Fertility Study as we have seen, but Ryder and Westoff make no attempt at explanation, saying only that the number of Jewish respondents in the study was small and that this "precludes any detailed analysis of their behavior."[24]

Jewish teachings have not emphasized procreation as a religious duty in the way that Catholicism has. Methods of birth control were known even in Bible times,[25] although large families were strongly encouraged. But with changing conditions over time—exile, movement to cities, dispersion, and so on—the older laws were modified. A man's duty in preserving the human race was considered fulfilled if he had fathered two children.[26] The Talmud includes passages permitting contraception and even sterilization for women under certain circumstances (such as health problems or out of concern for her other children). These liberal views of birth control were challenged during the Middle Ages, however, when Jewish leaders began opposing contraception and urging couples to have as many children as possible to enlarge the Jewish population which had suffered great losses through persecution, massacre, disease, and malnutrition. But times have changed. Rabbi Robert Gordis, a seminary professor, writes that today Judaism recognizes "that family planning is a necessity of modern life, in view of complex moral, hygienic, and economic factors."[27]

Westoff reports that fertility among Jews in Israel is considerably higher than that of the Jewish population of the United States and probably higher than the Jewish populations of other developed nations as well. Nevertheless, some concern has been expressed in Israel because the average number of births per Jewish woman is 3.2, while among Arabs in that nation it is 7.3. In the early 1950s, Jewish fertility reached a high of slightly more than 4.0 births per woman on the average, but since then the trend has been downward. Westoff refers to one "demographic cynic" who calculates that "if current trends continue, the Jewish population will be a minority in Israel within three generations."[28]

Protestantism Only during this present century have Protestant churches moved away from a position on birth control that in many respects was like that of the Roman Catholic Church. Most major Protestant denominations today, however, would agree with this 1952 statement by a commission of the American Lutheran Church: "Married couples have the freedom so to plan and order their sexual relations that each child born to their union will be wanted both for itself and in relation to the time of its birth. How the couple uses this freedom can properly be judged not by man but only by God. The means which a married pair uses . . . are matters for them to decide with their own consciences."[29]

Some research has indicated that, among non-Catholic groups, members of certain fundamentalist sects and Mormons are likely to have more children than do other non-Catholics.[30]

COSTS OF PARENTHOOD

In an effort to alert children to the problems of an overcrowded world, a book for elementary children contains this exercise in imagination: Youngsters are told to picture the life-styles of two different families. One family has two children, and these children have bikes and skates, nice clothes, music lessons, and a chance to go to summer camp. The parents take vacations, enjoy good food (including steaks), and occasionally take the whole family to restaurants. Plans are already being made for the children to go to college.

The other family in this exercise of the imagination has ten children. They have to share two bicycles among them. There isn't enough money for these children to take music lessons or go to summer camp. The younger children seldom wear anything but hand-me-downs. This family almost never has steak or goes to restaurants or even has very much meat or other nourishing foods—at least not in the way the two-child family does. The children in the large family therefore have colds more often. They also don't do as well in school and can't study quietly at home because of the lack of privacy. Their parents don't feel the family can afford to send the children to college.[31]

Readers of this children's book are being confronted with a traditionally unpopular and underrated fact: There are *costs* as well as rewards involved in having children.

Material Costs in Having Children

From prenatal care through delivery, from childrearing days through college, children are expensive. Economists point out that the financial costs of children are twofold: direct costs (money spent for children's needs) and indirect or "opportunity loss" costs (alternatives which have to be passed by or given up for the sake of the children).

Direct costs of having children are quite obvious: food, clothing, shelter, medical and dental care, toys and recreation, vacation trips, education, and much more. Exactly what such costs add up to varies according to social class, the ages of the children, the number of children (the more children in a family, the less spent per child, but the more spent altogether), and the family's life-style (for example, are they rural or urban?). One sociologist, Thomas J. Espenshade, used data from the 1960–61 Consumer Expenditure Survey to calculate the monetary costs of rearing children to the age of eighteen. Although present-day costs have risen, Espenshade's estimates are illuminating. For example, he found that a lower-income family with one child will spend 40 percent of its income in childrearing over the eighteen-year period. An upper-income family, in contrast, spends only 26 percent of its income in rearing one child to age eighteen. Costs rise as the child grows older, and of course costs rise as more children are added to the family. However, the cost of the first child is approximately twice as much as the cost of a second child in a two-child family. In actual dollars (based on 1960–61 prices), Espenshade estimates that over an eighteen-year period, families spend the following amounts in rearing one child: lower-income families, $38,789; middle-income families, $42,565; upper-income families, $49,145.[32]

Indirect costs of having children may not appear so obvious. They include such losses as doing without that extra room planned for a den, because the new baby needs a bedroom. Or parents may have to forgo savings and investment plans because children make it necessary to spend most of the income immediately. The family's standard of living might be lower because caring for children's essential needs means less money left over for consumption items desired by parents.[33]

One indirect or "opportunity cost" of having children is the loss of potential family income which often results from a mother's being kept from labor-force participation. If a mother does work, some of the family's income will likely be used to pay for child care during the hours she is employed. Such consequences of having a child (or an additional child) are included when economists compute estimated material costs of parenthood. According to the 1972 report of the Commission on Population Growth and the American Future, when a mother forgoes occupational opportunities, it costs the average family over $58,000 in potential income. The *direct* costs of rearing the first child from birth through college were estimated to be $39,924; but when the opportunity costs for the average woman are added, the total costs of rearing a first child are $98,361.[34]

Costs of Children to the Husband-Wife Relationship

According to popular folklore, having children is supposed to draw a husband and wife closer together. It doesn't always work that way. Social psychologist Jum C. Nunnally points out that for years psychologists have given attention to the effects of parents on children, but only in recent years has some attention been given to the other side of the coin, the effects of children on parents.

Nunnally became impressed with this aspect of parent-child relations while working with a colleague on studies of schizophrenic children. "Although it could not be firmly established from the research results," Nunnally writes, "I developed the definite impression that the disrupted home from which the schizophrenic child frequently came was more a product of the child's disrupting the rest of the family than the cause of the child's schizophrenia." He explains further: "The child was a constant source of strain for the other family members—causing embarrassment before neighbors and continual trouble in school, indifferent to affection, requiring many forms of expensive care, and a source of shame to parents and contention between them." Nunnally found that in a number of case studies there appeared to be a gradual deterioration of the families as time went on.[35]

Traditionally, marriage has been viewed as a step in which "two become one." Parenthood means that two become three—or four or even more. And this can spell difficulties even in homes that do not face the kinds of problems Nunnally studied.

On the basis of research among a probability sample of more than five thousand adults, sociologist Karen Renne has reported that "people currently raising children were more likely to be dissatisfied with their marriages than people who had never had children, or whose children had left home, regardless of race, age or income level."[36] She offers several explanations for this finding. First, there is the possibility that couples are less apt to file for divorce if there are children at home. Thus, couples with children may continue in unsatisfactory marriages while childless couples would feel more free to separate. Although she did not test this assumption, Renne suggests that "presumably the unhappiest marriages among childless couples and those whose children have grown up have already been dissolved."

A second possible explanation has to do with the demands parenthood makes on a woman and man, since it means an abrupt role transition—one for which many couples are not prepared.[37] It is one thing to be a wife or husband; it is quite another to be a mother or father as well. The relationship between the spouses may be altered drastically by the baby's arrival. Robert Ryder's research analysis of a study conducted by the National Institute of Mental Health indicates that having a child may result in a wife's feeling dissatisfied with the amount of attention her husband pays to her—either because husbands are less attentive after a baby arrives or else because wives simply desire more attention and assistance at this time.[38]

Sociologist Harold Feldman's research among couples both before and after having their first baby likewise produced the finding that marital satisfaction declined with parenthood.[39] Feldman also found that husbands and wives who had a close relationship with one another during pregnancy were not brought closer together by the child's birth but rather felt their marital satisfaction dropped. He postulates that to such closely knit couples, a baby may be an "interference factor," producing a decline in husband-wife companionship, with the husband in particular feeling cheated of his wife's attention. Where an *increase* in marital satisfaction occurred after becoming parents, the couples were less likely to have had a closely knit husband-wife relationship beforehand. It may be that such couples expect to be drawn closer together as they find in the baby a common interest, a conversation piece, and a reason to work together in joint tasks.

Feldman and other researchers have found evidence that the sexual relationship of a husband and wife may be negatively affected by parenthood.[40] Infants mean interruptions and require parents to be constantly "on duty." Time and energy demands required in parenting may mean less time and energy for the kind of sex life a couple had enjoyed previously. As children grow older, privacy increasingly becomes a problem. Spontaneous moments of romance at unusual times become difficult, and plans and strategies for uninterrupted lovemaking may have to be arranged.

In considering the overall impact of children on a marriage relationship, factors such as family income, race, and wife employment may enter in. Much more research needs to be done taking these and other variables into account. For example, Renne's research cited earlier showed that couples with children present were more likely to be dissatisfied than those couples with no children present at this particular point in their marriage—regardless of whether the family income in 1965 was more than $10,000 or less than that amount. However, among black couples, an interesting finding emerged. Forty-three percent of black husbands and wives reported dissatisfaction with their marriages when children were present and family income was less than $10,000. However, in black families where the family income was over $10,000, only 16 percent of husbands reported dissatisfaction in marriages where children were present. Evidently for black men, the *economic* pressures involved with parenthood are what determine feelings of dissatisfaction or satisfaction rather than parenthood itself.

For women, another factor may enter in. Black wives with children present did not show greater satisfaction with their marriages when family income was over $10,000. Forty-three percent continued to indicate marital dissatisfaction. However, less than half that percentage (20 percent) reported such dissatisfaction if there were no children present and income was over $10,000.[41] One possible explanation is that black wives are likely to be contributing to the family income, and the presence of children makes employment much more difficult. Our own research indicates that among both black women and white women, having children negatively affects marital satisfactions only where wives are employed—no doubt because of the time and energy demands of full-time employment added to the time and energy demands of children, which may crowd out time for expressive interaction between the spouses.[42]

Another way that having children may affect the husband-wife relationship is in the area of disagreements. In the preceding chapter, we saw that more husbands and wives disagree over money and children than over other concerns of marriage. One cost of having children is the necessity of spreading family income over a wider range of persons and needs. Disagreements over childrearing practices may also be costly to the husband-wife relationship, causing dissension that would have been avoided had the couple not had children.

Costs of Children in Terms of Freedom

Even if husbands and wives agree on childrearing practices, the actual carrying out of all the day-to-day responsibilities involved may seem costly in terms of freedom. Parents are expected to be concerned about their children's mental, emotional, physical, spiritual, and social development. Such a task means an investment of enormous amounts of time and energy which the parents might otherwise have put into individualistic pursuits.

Children complicate life, not only in terms of the sheer physical work they occasion, but also in the way they can upset schedules, interfere with plans, and make exceedingly complex what were once simple procedures—things like going on a trip ("We'll have to take the playpen." "Did you get Cindy's diaper bag and baby food, honey?" "Where is Michael's medicine for car sickness?") or planning a night at the movies ("But, Darling, I've tried every baby-sitter I know of! It's not *my* fault Judy called us at the last minute to cancel out.") or even a trip to the grocery store ("Peter! Where are your boots? Oh, why must it always rain on shopping day?" "No, the baby gets to ride in the shopping cart; there isn't room for you." "Jennifer! Don't stand on the shelf like that—watch out for those jelly jars! Oh, no!" CRASH).

Other costs of children include being inconvenienced, making adjustments in living conditions (such as growing accustomed to noise, messes, less privacy, and crowding), emotional stress (worrying over a sick child, fearing the worst when a teenager is late getting home with the car), and feeling tied down and unable to carry out travel and recreation plans freely.

Hoffman found in one study that some university students felt their own parents had been failures at childrearing and were afraid they might not be any more successful themselves in bringing up children. To these students, the difficulty of rearing a child and the fear of failure meant viewing childrearing as costly. But for those students who expected success in parenthood, childrearing and all its difficulties were thought of in terms of a challenge—a value, not a cost.[43]

GENDER ROLES AND FERTILITY CONTROL

Bob and Julie, the hypothetical couple we followed in Chapter 8, found that attitudes toward sex roles and attitudes toward having children are closely linked. When their outlook on marriage was more traditional, they both considered Bob to occupy the chief provider role even though Julie worked too. During the early months of marriage, Julie was not committed to a career but fully expected to drift in and out of the labor market, depending on the needs of her family. Both she and Bob planned that she would quit work when they had a baby and would probably remain at home while the children were small.

Then things began to change. As Julie became interested in commitment to a career, her conception of her role moved from *traditional* (being a wife and mother is a woman's most important calling, and a woman must subordinate her interests to those of her family) to *egalitarian* or *modern* (a woman should strive to use all her talents and abilities to achieve in the economic-opportunity sphere, just as a man is expected to do). No longer was Julie so willing to give up her work in order to bear and rear children. She began wondering if she even wanted any children. A large part in the ongoing negotiations of this couple centered on decisions about children.

Increasingly, social scientists have begun giving attention to how fertility control relates to gender roles. Do choices to bear or not to bear children have anything to do with how men and women conceive of the "proper" or "desirable" roles for males and females? How does employment affect a woman's fertility? Working wives have fewer children than nonworking wives, but does this mean that they deliberately choose to have fewer children because they want or have to work? Or do they work because they have no or few children and therefore fill up their time with a job?

"To beget or not to beget; that is the question." One writer reports first hearing this play on Shakespeare's words in Moscow—"and in Russian!" he adds.[44] Journalist George St. George points out that the birthrate in the Soviet Union has been declining, and the state needs children. Yet women are reluctant to give up their roles as productive workers in the economic sphere and are not eager to exchange "the fruits of advanced civilization for the glory of motherhood." The rewards of working are viewed as being greater than the gratifications of large families. To encourage women to have more children, various authorities have suggested government policies such as cash subsidies for families having a second and third child, or even a practice of paying wages to women who are willing to quit working in order to stay home to bear and rear children. Many educated Soviet women consider such suggestions insulting, writes St. George, "a vicious attempt to push women back into nurseries and kitchen."

Valentina Tereshkova-Nikolaeva, the world's first and only woman cosmonaut, delivered an address at the World Women's Congress in Helsinki on June 15, 1969, in which she criticized attempts to curtail women's economic opportunities in order to allow them more time for child care and domestic concerns. She drew attention to three suggestions by social scientists, sharply disagreeing with each. To urge citizens to return to the old division of labor in which men worked and supported families while women stayed home with children was simply unrealistic. Second, to tell women to break up their lives into various parts, rearing children at one stage and concentrating on careers at another stage, would also be unrealistic since a professional woman would lose her qualifications by being out of her field for so long. The third suggestion, that women work part-time so that the rest of their time could be given to children, was also rejected by Tereshkova-Nikolaeva on the grounds that "such part-time workers cannot count on any solid professional careers, and would be used mostly as supplementary and temporary labor."[45] Her own proposed solution lies in more child-care facilities, communal dining rooms and the like, with the adjustments being made not in a woman's professional life but in her home life, thereby giving her maximum release from tasks that would hinder economic productivity.

One way of securing such maximum release is to limit fertility—that is, to cut down on the number of children a woman has. And this is exactly what Russian women have been doing, along with women in many other industrialized countries. There are many studies, for example, which show that employed mothers in the United States have fewer children than nonworking mothers and also that unmarried females who plan to work desire smaller families.[46]

On the other hand, this pattern of wife employment and lower fertility is not so clean cut in nonindustrialized societies. Sociologist Paula Hass has examined the proposition that the crucial variable in determining the relationship between wife employment and family size is the extent to which the mother role and the worker role are viewed as incompatible. In developing nations, women have often had a tradition of combining work and motherhood, and working has not meant a lowering of fertility. Women could easily be workers and mothers for at least two reasons. First, the home is the center of economic activity, with women often working in simple cottage industries (such as weaving or pottery making) or in agricultural tasks, with children close by. Second, child care is readily available in the form of the extended family, with a number of relatives usually willing to serve as substitute mothers.

However, the changes involved as societies move toward urbanization and industrialization make the worker and mother roles less compatible. Extended families are not so close by, and child care arrangements become more difficult. Employment normally takes place away from the home in developed societies, geographically separating mothers and children. In such cases, it becomes exceedingly difficult for a woman to be employed and at the same time to be the mother of many children. We may expect her to have fewer children if she wants to continue working. But even more crucial, according to Hass, are the woman's attitudes. If she is highly educated and does not think in terms of traditional sex-role stereotypes, and if she is motivated to achieve occupationally and views the role of worker as an alternative to motherhood, she is likely to limit her family size to avoid role incompatibility as much as possible.[47]

Hoffman and Hoffman make a distinction between viewing employment as an alternative to fertility and as a barrier to fertility. A woman who chooses the gratifications of occupational achievement as an *alternative* to the gratifications of children will have lower fertility not because employment prevents her having more children but because she wants fewer children in order to devote herself more fully to her occupation. In contrast, the woman who views employment as a *barrier* to higher fertility will have fewer children because working makes motherhood more difficult; she might prefer to have a larger family but knows that as long as she must work or wants to work, it would be hard to have additional children.

Hoffman and Hoffman suggest if employment operates as only a barrier and not as an alternative to motherhood, child-care facilities could have the effect of increasing rather than decreasing fertility by removing the obstacles that cause much of the mother-worker role incompatibility.[48] Social policy planners sometimes overlook these distinctions between employment-as-barrier and employment-as-alternative by simply stating that providing job opportunities for women will bring about declines in birthrates. The attitudes, motivations, and

As alternative rewards such as educational and employment opportunities become available, women in developing countries may choose to have fewer children.

gender-role norms held by women are more crucial than is the fact of employment in itself.

Our own large-scale study which investigated whether and how sex-role norms affect fertility provided data which clearly show that *the sex-role norms women hold affect both the number of children they intend to have and the number of children they actually do have.*[49] Let's take four hypothetical case studies to see how this association between norms and fertility works.

HYPOTHETICAL CASE ONE

Dorothy is twenty-eight years old, black, and has a master's degree in social work. Her father is a high school teacher and her mother is a librarian. Dorothy's husband is a gynecologist. The couple have been married for three years and have no children at this time, although they would like to have children later. Dorothy has been employed as a social worker since before her marriage, and she plans to take off only a couple months when they have a baby and then return to work.

HYPOTHETICAL CASE TWO

Ginny is twenty-two years old. In answer to the question "Occupation?" she replies, "Housewife—or better yet, homemaker." Ginny is white, Catholic, and married her high school boyfriend at age eighteen, the same month they graduated. Ginny comes from a family that is religiously devout, participating in the Mass regularly; and she and her husband also devoutly practice their religious faith. During Ginny's growing-up years, her father was an auto mechanic and her mother was a full-time housewife. Ginny's husband presently sells appliances in a large department store. The couple have two children and are expecting a third in two months. "This one wasn't planned for," Ginny laughs, "but we'll be glad to welcome him to the family anyway—especially if it's a boy! Our first two are girls." She reports that they had their first daughter in the first year of marriage, and thus she has never held a job.

HYPOTHETICAL CASE THREE

Twenty-year-old Debra is black and the mother of three children. The first child was conceived before her marriage, and the last two were born ten months apart. "We tried to keep from having the babies so close together," she says. "But things just didn't work out. It's just too easy to get pregnant. We couldn't keep it from happening, and I expect it'll happen again." Debra's mother works as a cook in a school cafeteria, and her father is a service station attendant. Debra did not complete high school and works part-time as a housekeeper whenever her husband's mother can come over to take care of the children. Debra's husband is employed as a taxicab driver and is seldom home, a point of contention between them.

HYPOTHETICAL CASE FOUR

Linda—thirty-two years old, white, non-Catholic—is a lawyer with a busy practice. She and her husband (also an attorney) have been married seven years and have two children carefully spaced three years apart. Their son is four years old; their daughter is one. Both are cared for by a live-in housekeeper who loves them as though they were her own grandchildren.

If a sociologist were to interview these same women twenty years from now, which women would be likely to have the most children and which would be likely to have the least? Based upon data from our research project as well as from other studies, it is likely that Dorothy (case 1) and Linda (case 4) would have the fewest number of children. Both Ginny (case 2) and Debra (case 3) would be likely to have larger families than either of the other two women. Gender-role norms play a large part in explaining these differences. (It should be kept in mind that these hypothetical case studies are used for purposes of illustration only. Sociologists are not concerned with predicting the behavior of *individuals* but rather give attention to patterns of behavior and trends among groups of persons who have certain characteristics in common. These hypothetical cases are presented in an effort to illuminate some of our findings from a large probability sample.)

Traditional sex-role norms prescribe that the wife's interests should be subordinate to those of her husband and any children they may have. Her greatest fulfillment is considered to lie in homemaking, motherhood, encouraging her husband in his occupational pursuits, and so on. In contrast, egalitarian sex-role norms prescribe that a woman should have autonomy and should find her fulfillment in her own achievement endeavors rather than through second-hand enjoyment of her husband's success. Under these egalitarian sex-role norms, a woman should be free to pursue her own interests without subordination to those of her husband and any children. Her individual aspirations are considered equally significant to theirs.

However, certain changes have to take place in the traditional structuring of the family in order for the wife to have the freedom to pursue achievement in the economic-opportunity system. Some couples hold sex-role norms that do not encourage such changes but rather encourage family arrangements built around traditional sex roles (men are breadwinners; women are homemakers), and these couples are likely to have more children than couples who hold egalitarian sex-role norms. Many couples are, of course, in between. "Traditional" and "egalitarian" are two ends of a continuum, with some couples leaning one direction and other couples leaning the other direction at various points along the line.

How Gender-Role Norms Affect Decisions about Having Children

Earlier in this chapter, we looked at United States census figures that showed higher-status black families to have an average of two children when the mother worked—a lower average than among either black or white higher-status families with nonemployed mothers and also lower than higher-status white families where the mother worked. Why do higher-status black women have fewer children than all other women? The answer appears to lie in the greater career commitment and more egalitarian sex-role norms held by higher-status black couples. We saw earlier that the tradition of labor-force participation for black wives has encouraged more egalitarian sex roles at all status levels than has been true of comparable whites.[50] But at higher status levels, additional factors enter in to reinforce this traditional bent toward greater egalitarianism. Take Dorothy's case, for example.

Dorothy's case Dorothy comes from a family in which both parents had a college education and both held professional positions. Their higher socio-economic status indicates that they were likely to socialize their children toward more egalitarian sex roles than is true in families of lower socioeconomic status. Furthermore, Dorothy herself is highly educated and committed to a career, and at age twenty-five married a man whose education, occupation, and income indicate high social status. All of these factors fit well with the following statements that were shown to be true of both black and white women in our research project.[51]

1   The higher the *background status,* the greater the egalitarianism in sex-role norms.
2   The higher the *education,* the greater the egalitarianism in sex-role norms.
3   The greater the egalitarianism in sex-role norms and the higher the education, the higher is the *age at marriage.*
4   The greater the egalitarianism in sex-role norms, the more likely married women are to be currently *employed full-time.*
5   The greater the *egalitarianism* in sex-role norms and the fact of *full-time employment,* and the greater the *education* and the *later the age at marriage,* the lower the total number of births intended by younger married women.

Ginny's case   Moving on to the second hypothetical case study, we find that Ginny illustrates some other patterns that showed up in our research. Unlike Dorothy, Ginny grew up in a blue-collar home where the parents held traditional sex-role norms and socialized their children accordingly. Ginny herself holds traditional sex-role norms, which are reinforced by her religious faith, which she adheres to devoutly. She married young, did not go on for further education after high school, had children early in marriage, and has experienced one timing failure in child spacing. Some propositional statements from our research that would fit with Ginny's situation are these:

1   The lower the background status and the lower the education, the more traditional are sex-role norms.
2   The more traditional are sex-role norms and the lower the education, the lower is the age at marriage.
3   The more traditional are sex-role norms, the lower is the likelihood that married women are currently employed full-time.
4   Timing failures and number of children tend to be positively related. In other words, couples who report having children when unintended also tend to report having more children overall.
5   Among Catholics, however, reported past timing failures were found to be positively associated with more egalitarian sex-role norms in the present. It is not clear whether this means that displeasure with contraceptive failures caused women to become more individualistic later on, or whether there had been individualistic tendencies which were put aside for the sake of family-centered interests during the earlier years of marriage.

Egalitarianism in sex-role norms is associated with smaller families.

6 The more traditional the sex-role norms, the greater is the religious devoutness of Catholics.

7 The greater the religious devoutness, the less is the likelihood that their
fertility-control patterns will resemble those of white non-Catholics in
comparable situational contexts.

8 Nonemployed Catholic wives tend to show positive relationships between
husband's income and both birth intentions and number of children at
present. In other words, Catholics seem to accept more than non-Catholics
the idea that "good persons should have as many children as they can
afford." If the earnings of Ginny's husband increase, the couple is likely to
have more children.

There is another way in which gender may enter into the number of children
Ginny will have. Recall her statement that the first two children were girls and
they were now hoping for a boy. Several studies have indicated that couples like
to have children of both sexes. If a husband and wife have two or more girls and
no boys or two or more boys and no girls, they are more likely to "try again" for
another child than are couples who have a child of each sex. The Princeton
Fertility Study, a longitudinal study in which the same couples were studied over

a sixteen-year period, provided data which indicate that the sex composition of the family does affect family size. Couples who fail to achieve the desired sex composition within the number of children originally intended are likely to change their plans and have additional children in an effort to have the sex composition they want.[52] Couples are more likely to have a third, fourth, or even fifth child if all the preceding offspring were of the same sex; and this is especially true if the preceding offspring were girls. The final report of the Princeton Fertility Study, published in 1970, showed that "couples whose first two children are boys are 11 percent more likely to have another child than are couples whose first two children included a child of each sex." But "if the first two children were girls the probability of a third birth is 24 percent higher than if there was a child of each sex."[53]

Other social scientists have pointed out a continued preference for boys, not only in traditionally patriarchal societies such as among Chinese families in Taiwan,[54] but also in modern industrial societies. A study conducted in 1954 among men and women of marriageable age was duplicated nearly twenty years later among university students by different researchers. Similar findings emerged: when asked which sex these men and women would prefer their first child to be or when asked which sex they would like an only child to be, they overwhelmingly chose a boy.[55] There was, however, a slight increase in the percentage of persons to whom the sex of their firstborn didn't matter; and when it came to the sex of an only child, the percentage of men who wanted a boy decreased from 92 percent in 1954 to 81 percent in 1973. There was little change among women when it came to the preferred sex for an only child; about two-thirds indicated a preference for a boy in both surveys. Since the shift in attitudes occurred only among the men, psychologists Candida Peterson and James Peterson felt that the explanation lay in economics rather than the ideology of the feminist movement. Girls are no longer considered a financial liability as they were in the days when they were considered extra mouths to feed until the day they were married off. Now daughters grow up and support themselves just as sons traditionally did—which may in itself be more indicative of feminism (in the sense of changes toward egalitarian sex roles) than these researchers are ready to admit.[56]

Sociologist Gerald E. Markle found that among university students one-third had no preference regarding the sex of their first child; but among those who did indicate a preference, the choice was 12 to 1 in favor of a boy. And in a general sample of persons living in Tallahassee, Florida, Markle found that the preference for a boy was 19 to 1. Markle's studies showed that respondents holding *traditional* sex-role ideologies were much more likely to state that they preferred their first child to be a boy than were respondents holding *egalitarian* sex-role ideologies. This research demonstrated what Markle had hypothesized from a survey of literature showing that in virtually all cultures around the world male babies are preferred; namely, that "an ideology of male superiority" affects first-child sex preference.[57]

But what if there were a movement away from notions of male superiority and male privilege? Our own research indicates that such a change would make a difference in preferences as to the sex of one's child. If men and women are considered of equal worth and equally able to achieve, why should it be more special to have a male child? Evidently this was the reasoning of many respondents in our 1974 sample of university students,[58] who were asked to state the preferred sex of their future child in the event they would choose to have only one child. Interestingly, how students viewed sex-role norms attached to the *husband* position (not the position of the wife) was what influenced only-child sex preferences. Both male and female students who viewed the husband position in egalitarian terms were more likely to indicate a willingness for a child of either sex or a preference for a female than was true of students with more traditional views of sex-role norms for the husband.

The reduction in male rights and privileges that is a part of an egalitarian ideology tends to abolish ideas about the unique character of boys, thus lowering their "market value" and reducing desires for them. As a result, the overall number of children desired by couples should be lowered, because the pressure to "keep trying for a boy" would be eliminated. But in our hypothetical case study of Ginny, the desire for a boy is strong and is reinforced by the traditional sex-role norms held by her and her husband. Chances are that they will have more children in an effort to make sure they have one or more sons.

Debra's case Moving on to hypothetical case 3, we find that Debra's lower social status (both in terms of the present and her parental background), lower education, early age at marriage, premarital pregnancy, and past timing failures are all factors calling for predictions of high fertility over the course of her married life. A return visit by an interviewer twenty years after the first interview would likely turn up information that Debra has become the mother of a large family. Some propositions gleaned from our research that fit Debra's situation are these (in addition to statements 1 through 4 which described Ginny in case 2):

1 The shorter the interval between marriage and the first child's birth, the higher is the number of children likely to be born.
2 The greater the number of children, the lower are perceived satisfactions in the economic and expressive dimensions of marriage.
3 The greater the traditionalism in sex-role norms (related to socialization in childhood, socioeconomic status, education, age at marriage, and so on), the less likely are wives to be currently using efficient and effective means of contraception, and the lower is their confidence that they will be able to prevent unintended births and "spacing and number failures."

Linda's case   The remaining hypothetical case study focuses on Linda. The propositions that describe Dorothy in the first case study also apply to case 4. Linda's egalitarian sex-role norms, high education, high socioeconomic status, later age of marriage, full-time employment before her children were born, as well as full-time employment at present, all combine to indicate the likelihood that her family will remain small. In fact, her family may already be completed in that she has two children, a boy and a girl (although given her egalitarian sex-role views, this one-of-each-sex composition shouldn't matter), and she has confidence that unintended births will be prevented because she has had no timing failures in the past, having effectively used efficient methods of contraception. Two final propositions from our research fit Linda's case:

1 Among working wives, the greater the job status and income, the lower the number of children.
2 Among white non-Catholic wives who are employed or who are well-educated, the greater the egalitarianism in sex-role norms, the less likelihood there is of past contraceptive timing failures. Thus the lower the fertility overall, since among all groupings (black, white, Catholic, and non-Catholic) timing failures and number of children are positively related. (In other words, the more "slipups" or accidental conceptions, the larger will be the family.)

The one reason that Linda might possibly choose to have an additional child relates to her having found satisfactory child-care arrangements with the result that her mother role and career role are not incompatible at this time. But given all the other information we have on Linda, it is unlikely that she will have further children.

Summary statement on gender-role norms and fertility   In summarizing these hypothetical cases illustrating our research on how gender-role norms affect fertility, we may state the following: The greater the *individualism* (a woman's desire for personal and occupational achievement and for freedom to pursue her own interests), the less will be the *familism* (a woman's desire to center her life around husband and children). And the lower the familism, the lower will be the number of children intended and the number of children actually born.

Similarly, we found that among unmarried university students, the more egalitarian were the sex-role norms held, the fewer were the number of children intended.[59] Comparing our 1974 student study with one we conducted three years earlier, we found that the degree of gender-role egalitarianism had increased significantly for both sexes—but especially for women. The trend seems to be for more and more younger women to hold egalitarian norms and individualistic aspirations, and associated with these norms and aspirations is a desire to have smaller families. Women seeking individualistic rewards feel compelled (whether consciously or unconsciously) to cut down familistic costs.

What about men? It appears that men who hold egalitarian views and are open to achievement aspirations in women are also willing to have fewer children. But men have a relatively lower sense of compulsion in the matter. In marital negotiations, we may expect that more egalitarian husbands will simply go along with their wives' limited birth intentions rather than actively taking a part or assuming a leadership role in formulating such plans. On the other hand, husbands who are more traditional might actively attempt to influence their wives' thinking, particularly if the husbands desire more children than do their wives. Or such husbands might simply be less cooperative with respect to contraception. ("Ah, come on, Joanie, don't be a spoilsport! Nothing's going to happen just this one time! And so what if it does? It might be kinda nice to have a new baby.") However, a great deal more research needs to be done on marital decision making about having or not having more children.

CONTRACEPTION, STERILIZATION, AND ABORTION

A century ago, a federal statute known as the "Comstock Law" (named for a self-appointed vice hunter named Anthony Comstock) made it illegal to distribute birth-control information and materials through the mails. Druggists who sold contraceptive devices were arrested. Various states had their own legislation which made it a crime to distribute contraceptive literature, illegal for physicians to prescribe contraceptive devices, or even (as in Connecticut) against the law for couples—single or married—to use contraceptive devices.

Many of these anticontraceptive measures continued into this present century, some until recently. Clergymen denounced birth control as sinful, and Theodore Roosevelt warned of "race suicide." Condoms were referred to as "rubber articles for immoral use." In the 1920s, when the birth-control-movement leader Margaret Sanger needed diaphragms to distribute to women who came to her birth-control clinic, she was unable to obtain such contraceptives in the United States and had to purchase them from abroad. American manufacturers were by then permitted to manufacture contraceptive devices but refused to make the reliable Mensinga diaphragm and instead made unsatisfactory cervical caps. However, it was illegal to import contraceptives. Margaret Sanger's clinic therefore obtained them through illegal channels, importing them from Germany by way of Canada from where they were smuggled across the border in oil drums.[60]

Times have changed. Birth control is a fact of life in modern industrial societies, having gained widespread public acceptance and support. How successfully couples practice the limitation of their families depends on a combination of motivation and methods.

Contraceptive Practices

The 1970 National Fertility Study showed a large drop in the rate of unwanted births between two different time periods (1961 through 1965 and 1966 through

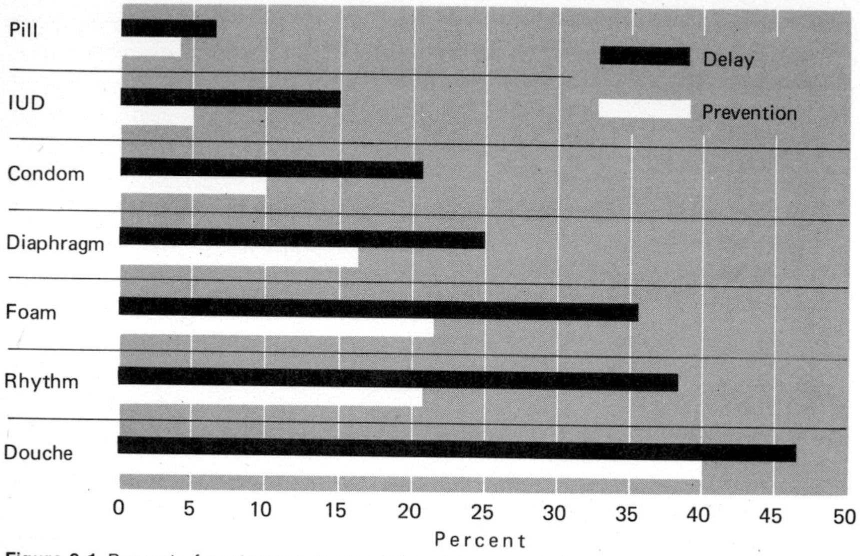

Figure 9-1 Percent of contraceptors who fail to delay a wanted pregnancy or to prevent an unwanted pregnancy in the first year of exposure to risk of unwanted conception, by selected contraceptive method. Source: N. Ryder, 1973, p. 141.

1970). Westoff attributes this decline to improvements in controlling unwanted births, improvements resulting from using contraceptives earlier and more extensively, more usage (or more consistent usage) of the more efficient methods, and greater motivation to avoid pregnancy.[61]

However, even though there has been a drop in unwanted births, studies indicate that about one-third of all married couples who are attempting to prevent a pregnancy will nevertheless have an unwanted conception within five years.[62] Norman B. Ryder, a sociologist who specializes in population research, illustrates in Figure 9-1 how both *methods* and *motivation* enter into the matter of contraceptive failure. The information again comes from the 1970 National Fertility Study.

Ryder defines contraceptive failure as "an unplanned pregnancy which occurs in an interval during which use of contraception is reported." Respondents who reported using contraception prior to a pregnancy and who replied that conception was accidental rather than intentional were asked whether they were attempting to *delay* the next pregnancy or to *prevent* it altogether. It was found that, regardless of the method used, more failures occurred when couples planned only to delay a pregnancy. Evidently, if there are plans to have another baby sometime anyway, more chances are taken.

However, efforts at contraception are more rigorous if the desire is to prevent an *unwanted* pregnancy. Ryder compared couples from the 1961–65 time period with those from ten years earlier (1951–55) and found a considerable decline in contraceptive failures even among couples who use methods other than the reliable pill. This says something about the care with which couples are using even the older conventional birth-control methods. Ryder notes: "This would seem to constitute a small piece of evidence that there has been an increase in the motivation to prevent an unwanted birth, manifested in some users by a shift to the pill, and in others by more diligence in traditional methods."[63]

Charles Westoff, codirector with Norman Ryder of the National Fertility Study, calls attention to some dramatic changes in contraceptive methods chosen by couples in 1970 as compared to methods used in 1965. Among couples practicing contraception in 1965, 23.9 percent were using the pill; but by 1970, the percentage had risen to 34.2. Also significant is the growing acceptance of voluntary sterilization for contraceptive purposes—particularly among older couples who have had all of the children they would like to have. By 1970, such contraceptive surgery had become the most popular method of birth control for couples in which the wife was aged thirty to forty-four. Westoff writes: "One-quarter of all older couples who were currently practicing contraception had been surgically sterilized; the operations were almost equally divided between men and women."[64] Table 9-B shows other changes in the use of contraceptive methods during the period between 1965 and 1970. Usage of some methods declined (for example, condom, diaphragm, rhythm), while usage of other methods increased (the pill, IUD, sterilization).

It is possible to place current contraceptive behavior on a continuum of risk taking (Figure 9-2). At the "extremely high risk" end of the continuum would be the couple who use no contraception whatsoever. If the wife were physically able to conceive, the probability of her becoming pregnant would be high indeed. But moving down and into the "high risk" section of the continuum, we would find couples who use such methods as husband-withdrawal before ejaculation, or the wife's douching immediately after intercourse, or rhythm (having sexual relations only at the time of the month when the wife is considered to be infertile, the one method officially endorsed by the Roman Catholic Church).

At the "extremely low risk" end of the continuum would be husbands who have had vasectomies (the severing of the sperm-carrying tubes from the testicles) and wives who have undergone surgery in which the Fallopian tubes were cut and tied so that the ovum could not be reached by sperm cells. This operation is called a tubal ligation. Women who have had hysterectomies (the removal of the uterus) or total oophorectomies (the removal of both ovaries) are also sterile—although such surgery is ordinarily performed for purposes other than contraception. The next lowest risk method of contraception is the pill, followed on the continuum by the IUD, condom, and diaphragm with contraceptive jelly or cream.

TABLE 9-B METHODS OF CONTRACEPTION USED CURRENTLY BY MARRIED COUPLES, PERCENTS, BY AGE AND COLOR[a] 1965 AND 1970

Current Method	All Couples (Wife < 45) Total[b] 1965 (N= 3,032)	1970 (N= 3,810)	White 1965 (N= 2,441)	1970 (N= 3,273)	Black 1965 (N= 554)	1970 (N= 462)	Younger Couples (Wife < 30) Total[b] 1965 (N= 1,215)	1970 (N= 1,800)	White 1965 (N= 922)	1970 (N= 1,540)	Black 1965 (N= 276)	1970 (N= 222)	Older Couples (Wife 30–44) Total[b] 1965 (N= 1,817)	1970 (N= 2,010)	White 1965 (N= 1,519)	1970 (N= 1,733)	Black 1965 (N= 278)	1970 (N= 240)
Wife sterilized[c]	7.0	8.5	6.3	7.5	14.4	19.3	3.2	3.2	2.8	2.9	6.9	5.0	9.5	13.1	8.4	11.6	21.9	32.5
Husband sterilized[c]	5.1	7.8	5.4	8.3	0.5	1.1	2.9	3.0	3.1	3.2	0.4	0.5	6.5	12.1	6.8	12.9	0.7	1.7
Pill[d]	23.9	34.2	24.0	34.0	21.7	37.4	41.4	49.4	42.5	49.4	30.8	54.1	12.8	20.6	12.8	20.4	12.6	22.1
IUD[e]	1.2	7.4	1.0	7.3	2.9	7.6	1.7	9.2	1.4	8.8	4.7	9.9	0.8	5.9	0.8	5.9	1.1	5.4
Diaphragm[f]	9.9	5.7	10.4	5.7	5.1	5.2	6.2	3.5	6.5	3.5	3.3	3.6	12.3	7.6	12.8	7.7	6.8	6.7
Condom[g]	21.9	14.2	22.4	14.8	17.0	6.7	19.2	11.4	19.2	11.9	18.1	6.3	23.7	16.6	24.4	17.3	15.8	7.1
Withdrawal	4.0	2.1	4.1	2.2	2.2	0.6	2.3	1.7	2.3	1.8	1.8	0.5	5.1	2.5	5.3	2.7	2.5	0.8
Foam	3.3	6.1	3.1	6.1	6.1	6.1	4.8	8.0	4.4	8.2	8.0	6.8	2.3	4.3	2.2	4.3	4.3	5.4
Rhythm	10.9	6.4	11.6	6.7	2.5	1.7	7.5	4.2	7.9	4.4	2.9	0.9	13.0	8.3	13.8	8.8	2.2	2.5
Douche	5.2	3.2	4.2	2.9	17.5	8.0	4.8	2.3	3.8	1.9	15.2	5.9	5.5	4.1	4.4	3.7	19.8	10.0
Other[h]	7.5	4.6	7.3	4.4	10.2	6.2	6.1	4.0	6.0	4.0	8.0	6.8	8.4	4.8	8.1	4.6	12.2	5.8
Percent Total	100	100	100	100	100	100	100	100	100	100	100	100	100	100	100	100	100	100

[a] Who were living together currently.

[b] Includes nonwhites other than blacks.

[c] Surgical procedures undertaken at least partly for contraceptive reasons.

[d] Includes combination with any other method.

[e] Includes combination with any other method except pill.

[f] Includes combination with any method except pill or IUD.

[g] Includes combination with any method except pill, IUD or diaphragm.

[h] Includes other multiple as well as single methods and a small percentage of unreported methods.

Source: Westoff, 1972, p. 11.

Extremely high risk	No contraception at all
Very high risk	Postintercourse douching
High risk	Rhythm, foam, withdrawal, contraceptive jellies (without use of diaphragm), suppositories
Low risk	IUD, diaphragm with jelly or cream, condom
Very low risk	The pill
Extremely low or no risk	Sterilization (tubal ligation, vasectomy, hysterectomy)

Figure 9-2 Continuum of risk-taking in contraceptive practice.

In analyzing our research on how fertility relates to gender-role norms, we found that women who sought individualistic rewards more than familistic rewards were low-risk takers when it came to contraceptive techniques.[65] They tended to use the most efficient methods—the pill or intrauterine devices (IUD), or else very diligent use of the diaphragm with jelly, or their husbands carefully used condoms. Women who ranked higher on familism than individualism, on the other hand, were using methods that placed them on the high-risk section (top half) of the continuum.

It became apparent that the risk-taking level in contraception indicates the degree to which women are indifferent to the *costs* of children or even actually desirous of the *rewards* of children. Women who hold more traditional sex-role norms may think of an unplanned pregnancy as a "surprise" perhaps, but they are not likely to think of such an event as a "disaster" as might be the case with women holding egalitarian sex-role norms and individualistic aspirations. Women who strongly believe in pursuing their own interests (such as career achievement) cannot afford to be indifferent to the costs of children. Any children to be born to them must be carefully planned both as to numbers and timing. Egalitarian wives are therefore more motivated than traditional wives to choose the most efficient birth-control methods and then to use those methods with great care to avoid failures.

This finding is one more piece of evidence that motivation plays a highly significant role in fertility control. Improved methods made possible by advances in research and technology are of great importance but are not in themselves enough. No matter how *theoretically* effective a particular contraceptive technique is, its *actual* effectiveness will in large measure depend upon the user. Women who forget to take their birth-control pills or couples who occa-

sionally neglect to insert diaphragms or to use condoms can expect contraceptive failures, not because the perfect birth-control method is as yet un-
discovered, but rather because their motivation in using presently available
methods is not strong enough.

When persons are sufficiently motivated, unplanned pregnancies seem to
be prevented to a large degree even without the availability of such modern
contraceptives as the IUD or the pill. Earlier we referred to the fact that the
birthrate was declining prior to and during the Great Depression in the 1930s.
Similarly, the current decline in births began before the pill was introduced in
1960. In both instances, perceptions of the costs of children no doubt entered
into the decisions of couples to have smaller families. Such costs, as we have
seen, may be related to actual financial costs or they may involve opportunity
costs—particularly on the part of women who hold egalitarian sex-role norms
and are interested in individualistic rather than familistic rewards. To the degree
that couples are motivated to avoid such costs, they will chose low-risk
contraceptive techniques and use them with diligence.

One problem pointed out by some feminists is that while some of the most
efficient contraceptives may carry low pregnancy risks, they carry other kinds of
risks. And for the most part, these risks must be taken by women, not men. For
example, certain dangers and serious side effects have been associated with
use of the IUD or the pill by some women. Barbara Seaman writes: "If you doubt
that there has been sex discrimination in the development of the pill, try to
answer this question: Why *isn't* there a pill for men?"[66] Male biomedical
researchers counter with claims that the greater availability of female contraceptive methods is not part of a "male chauvinist plot," nor are scientists
"proceeding to research and test contraceptives in order to provide more fun
for men, while ignoring the health needs of women." Rather, they assert, "the
broad areas of attack" or vulnerable physiological targets where contraceptive
measures could be applied in the reproductive process of males are far more
limited than in females.[67]

But for the present time at least, side effects of oral contraceptives for
women have kept some individualistic, egalitarian wives from using or continuing to use them—even though the pill is generally considered to be the most
reliable means (apart from sterilization) of cutting down the risks of unwanted
conceptions. Data from our research indicate that while women with egalitarian
sex-role norms do tend to gravitate toward pill usage, women who are equally
committed to individualism and egalitarianism may avoid the pill because of
concern about physiological effects, choosing instead other reliable, low-risk
methods, and making them work because of strong motivation.[68]

Sterilization

Since sterilization is considered to be the lowest-risk method of contraception
of all, the question may arise: do couples with egalitarian sex-role norms

choose tubal ligations or vasectomies to a greater degree than do couples holding traditional sex-role norms? Much more research needs to be done to answer this question as well as other questions about why couples choose contraceptive surgery, how they feel about it afterward, and so on. In our own research, our findings were similar to those of the National Fertility Study (Table 9-B) in that 23 percent of our older respondents (wife aged thirty to forty-four) who were currently practicing contraception reported having had a contraceptive operation (11 percent of husbands; 12 percent of wives).[69] But we were unable to find any meaningful pattern of variables (not even education) to account for the choice of this "radical" means of birth control by either younger or older couples in our sample.

As of 1970, women with limited education were more likely to have experienced a tubal ligation than were women with more schooling. Although this finding held for both blacks and whites with less than a high school education, Westoff points out that "contraceptive sterilization was utilized especially by black women with less than a high school education, among whom it was the leading method (31.6 percent) along with the pill (31.1 percent)." Among white women with less than a high school education, 14.5 percent reported having been sterilized, a figure that is more than double the percentage of sterilized white women with high school or college education (5.8 and 5.6 percent respectively).[70] Lower-educated women may have turned to contraceptive surgery in a desperate attempt to control fertility after several children and unsuccessful attempts to use other contraceptive techniques. Sometimes pressures for such surgery have come from outside, for example from social agencies.

It should be noted that lower-educated women have traditionally had more children than higher-educated women and therefore have been more apt to meet contraceptive surgery eligibility requirements set up by the medical profession. Restrictive policies of physicians, hospitals, and health insurance companies have in the past meant that more than free choice was involved if a couple chose sterilization. For example, up until 1969, the official manual of the American College of Obstetricians and Gynecologists (ACOG) recommended that contraceptive operations be performed on women only if they were at least twenty-five years old and had five living children. A thirty-year-old woman could not be sterilized unless she had four living children, and a woman thirty-five years old had to have at least three living children before she could have a tubal ligation. These suggestions were adopted by most hospitals, some of which had even more restrictive requirements for sterilization. However, many of these restrictions were dropped after 1969 when the ACOG manual discontinued mentioning the old recommendations. Although vasectomies have generally been performed in physicians' offices rather than in hospitals, they too have been subject to restrictions—often the doctors' own ideas about the desired age of a man and number of children he must have before being sterilized.[71]

With the growing acceptability of sterilization, it is quite possible that more and more younger couples will elect to have such operations when they want either no children at all or no additional children. Authorities in population research such as Harriet Presser and Larry Bumpass point out the growth in popularity of the male contraceptive surgery (vasectomy) which began to take place between 1965 and 1970. They also speculate that new techniques for tubal ligations may make female sterilization more appealing as well. Of special interest is the statement of Presser and Bumpass that "as of 1970, more than one in six couples [who desire no more children] had already been sterilized and nearly 50 percent more indicated that they would 'seriously consider' a sterilization operation to prevent future unwanted pregnancies." By 1975, there were indications that more than one-fifth of married couples in the United States were relying on contraceptive sterilization.[72]

These social scientists also call attention to data from the National Fertility Study which indicate that most couples choosing this permanent method of contraception had previously been using the pill or other efficient methods, and two-thirds of couples sterilized had never had an unwanted birth. More than half of the couples who had undergone contraceptive surgery had three or fewer children. And although it was true that women who had already experienced tubal ligations were more apt to be among the lower educated than the higher educated, there was no association with education among nonsterilized couples who indicated serious interest in such an operation in the future. When asked whether they would *seriously consider* contraceptive sterilization as a way of preventing unwanted children, between one-third and two-fifths of wives in the National Fertility Study sample replied that they would so consider such surgery for themselves, with the percentage of college-educated wives so inclined slightly higher than the percentage of wives with high school or less.

Similarly, the percentage of women who believed their husbands would be willing to consider vasectomies was higher with increasing education. It is quite likely that couples who have higher education and who hold egalitarian sex-role norms and individualistic rather than familistic orientations, who are concerned about avoiding the costs of children, and who desire to minimize the risks of unplanned conceptions will increasingly be open to the idea of achieving permanent contraception through surgery.

Abortion

But what if an unplanned pregnancy occurs among nonsterilized couples holding egalitarian sex-role norms and pursuing individualistic interests? Are such couples more apt to think of abortion as a backup measure than are more traditionally minded couples? This would be an interesting question for future research. However, up until the historic Supreme Court decision in 1973 which swept aside antiabortion laws, abortion was illegal in most states except in certain situations (such as rape, incest, or danger to the mother's life). Although illegal abortions occurred in great numbers, it was difficult to study who had them and why. After July 1970, New York was one state that permitted abortion on request; and what we can learn from the situation in that state may shed some light on expected consequences of the Supreme Court decision after a few years have passed.

Christopher Tietze, M.D., of the Population Council, reports that 70 to 80 percent of the abortions performed on New York City residents since abortion became legal in that state would have been performed illegally if the law had not been changed.[73] He has arrived at these figures through detailed analyses of demographic statistics. For example, he has shown that the increase in legal abortions from about 5,000 per year before the New York law to 75,000 in the 1971–72 period was *not* accompanied by a corresponding decrease in births reported. In other words, the change in the abortion law did not mean that 70,000 infants were not born who would otherwise have entered this world. The relatively small drop in births indicated that only 20 to 30 percent of the legal abortions performed since 1970 in New York City are abortions that took place because the law has made it permissible. The other 70 to 80 percent of abortions would have taken place anyway—but illegally.

What about the 20 to 30 percent of abortions which *do* represent a true increase? Phillips Cutright, a sociologist, and Karen Cutright, a lawyer, write: "It is the modest increase in the number of abortions that accounts for a reduction of illegitimate births in New York in 1971–1972, the first decline observed since New York's illegitimate births were first reported (1954) separately from legitimate births." Furthermore, "the groups most likely to abort are poor, unmarried and nonwhite—the same groups with low levels of effective contraceptive practice."[74] Cutright and Cutright refer to Tietze's estimate that there are 1,500 legal abortions per 1,000 live births among unmarried women in contrast to a ratio of 100 legal abortions per 1,000 live births among married women. This estimate along with other statistical evidence leads them to conclude that "the bulk of the decline in marital fertility is coming from contraception—not legal abortion."

However, among married couples who feel that children would be costly and in conflict with individualistic interests, abortion may seem a viable option in the event of an "accidental" conception. Sociologist J. E. Veevers, for example, found in a sample of fifty-two voluntarily childless couples that although most of the wives had never been pregnant, they reported that if pregnancy should occur they would seek an abortion. One-fifth of these women had already had at least one induced abortion.[75]

VOLUNTARY CHILDLESSNESS

In the children's story "The Gingerbread Man," we are presented with the sad spectacle of a lonely old couple so desperate for a child that they set out to make one out of cookie dough. In Edward Albee's play *Who's Afraid of Virginia Woolf?* childless George and Martha, constantly at odds with one another, railing with insults and hostilities, nevertheless drew solace from a shared secret—the illusion of the imaginary son they had dreamed up together.

According to popular folk belief, married couples without children are to be pitied. Their lives are considered by outsiders to be incomplete. Surely, the reasoning goes, no couple would remain childless unless it couldn't be helped. Perhaps the husband or wife is infertile, physically unable to reproduce. But even then, adoption is always a possibility. That some couples would deliberately choose not to have offspring would strike many persons as absurd.

There is evidence that most people do want children, but there are others who do not.[76] According to both United States and Canadian census data, about 5 percent of couples prefer voluntary childlessness. What is of special interest is the rise in the percentage of wives who express a desire to have no children. In a 1967 census survey, 3.1 wives in the eighteen-to-thirty-nine-year age range had expressed a desire to have no children at all, in comparison to the 5 percent figure for 1974. Especially significant are the changes in the thinking of younger women. Among married women aged eighteen to twenty-four, only 1.3 percent in 1967 expressed a desire not to have children; but by 1973, more than three times as many reported that they wished to remain voluntarily childless (4.2 percent). Education also makes a difference. Of wives in this younger age group who had one or more years of college, 7.5 percent reported that they do not want any children.[77]

If it is true that 1 out of 20 married women deliberately wants to avoid motherhood despite all the pronatalist pressures of relatives, friends, the media, and even the government (such as income-tax laws), the question becomes Why? The little research that has been done thus far on voluntarily childless couples indicates that the answer lies once again in perceived rewards and costs. Veevers points out that some couples who choose not to have children think chiefly in terms of cost avoidance, but other couples look at the reverse side of the coin and emphasize the rewards of an adult-centered life-style.[78]

It is possible to think of the rewards of *not* having children in much the same way that we earlier considered the rewards of having children. Couples who desire the child-free life-style might think in terms of the following:

Rewards of Self-Enhancement and Self-Preservation

Social identity and a sense of adult status can come through means other than parenthood—most notably through individual achievement in a career or public service. Whereas some couples may look upon having children as a way of gaining a sense of self (particularly for women, since motherhood has traditionally been viewed as a woman's major life goal) and as a means of vicarious accomplishments (by "living through" their children and taking pride in children's achievements), other couples feel that children could hinder self-enhancement and block a husband and wife from being all that they could otherwise be. Such voluntarily childless couples feel that children would drain away time and energy that could otherwise be devoted to pursuing individualistic interests and making their own name for themselves. They want to be remembered for their own contributions to the world rather than the contributions of their children.

Rewards of Affection, Belonging, and Pleasure

Whereas couples who want children speak of the expressive rewards expected in parenthood, couples who don't want children may view children in a "three's a crowd" fashion and fear that commitment to parenthood would detract from commitment to the marriage itself. Veevers reports that some of her respondents made such comments as, "A child would come between us. I wouldn't be able to be as close to my husband if I had a child. . . ." or "If you have children, then not all of your emotional involvement would be with each other anymore and you would have lost something." Couples who opt for the child-free life-style are willing to "put all their emotional eggs into one basket" as one respondent told Veevers. Affection and belonging are important for such women and men, but they want to find such affection and belonging in the husband-wife relationship alone rather than seeking these rewards through children. As Veevers has expressed it: "A dominant component [of the child-free life-style] is commitment to the ideal that a married couple should be a self-sufficient unit, who look to each other for the satisfaction of most (and perhaps all) of their social and psychological needs. . . . They relate to each other not only as man and wife, but also as lover and mistress and as 'best friends.' The presence of children makes such dyadic withdrawal difficult if not impossible."[79]

If a sense of affection and belonging is found through the spouse in the child-free life-style, a sense of pleasure, excitement, and adventure is found in the freedom to pursue individualistic and couple interests in a way that would be difficult if not impossible if there were children to consider. Veevers reports that a recurrent theme among her respondents was the search for novelty, the avoidance of routine, the quest for new experiences, new situations, new tasks, a desire to travel, the freedom to just "pick up and go" at a moment's notice. Childless couples also reported that they enjoyed being able to pursue adult activities and adult entertainments without having to be concerned about family recreational activities, child-centered play, and constant consideration of "what is good for the children." They liked, for example, being able to attend movies with adult themes rather than being limited to Disney-type films in the interest of family togetherness.

Altruistic and Religious Satisfactions in Not Having Children

"People who don't want to have children are simply selfish! They think only of themselves and their own convenience." Such has been the familiar accusation hurled at couples who voluntarily choose to remain childless. But with growing concern about population pressures, food and energy shortages, crowding, and all the related problems of too many people on too small a planet, the accusation of selfishness has been aimed toward a different target. Couples who want the rewards of children in great abundance are the ones who are now likely to be labeled self-indulgent and unconcerned about the good of humanity. Couples who forgo the experience of parenthood may be considered by others to be altruistic.

And indeed altruistic motives may very well figure into the decisions of some couples to remain childless. In our own student sample, although no question was asked about preferred childlessness per se, we did find that a prime motivation for limiting family size was a deep concern about population pressures.[80] Two researchers, Susan Gustavus and James R. Henley, Jr., who studied seventy-two childless couples applying for sterilization, found that concern over population growth was one of several reasons these men and women gave for not wanting any children.[81]

Veevers reports that concern with population problems "does provide a supportive rationale indicating that one is not necessarily being socially irresponsible and neglectful of one's civic obligations if one does not reproduce," but that among her sample, such concern was not a motivating force for not having children but was "an *ex post facto* consideration." It was something a childless couple could latch onto after making their decision, but primarily "their satisfaction with being childless is related to concerns other than to their contribution to the population crisis."[82]

Hoffman makes a similar point. Referring to the report of a psychiatrist working with couples having marital difficulties, she states that a recurring theme that emerged during therapy was that of the husband who didn't want children but *pretended* to want them in order not to appear harsh and unloving. "With the socially negative view so prevalent," writes Hoffman, "it has probably been unacceptable to admit the desire for childlessness even to oneself." Such individuals may be the ones most open to concerns about not adding to the world's population since these concerns provide an altruistic rationale for their personal preferences.[83] At the same time, there is no denying that among some socially conscious couples, consideration of population pressures may be a very real motivation in their initial decision not to have children rather than simply a rationale to justify their decision later.

When it comes to the question of *religious* satisfactions in not having children, the issue may seem harder to determine. To some persons, the very notion of religious satisfactions in childlessness would seem absurd, since religious beliefs have traditionally been bound up with notions that children are "blessings from heaven" and that parenthood is a sacred duty. Indeed, in both the Veevers and the Gustavus-Henley samples of childless couples there is an indication that rejection of such notions includes rejection of the religious beliefs and institutions from which they derive. Veevers writes of her sample of fifty-two voluntarily childless wives: "Most individuals are either atheists or agnostics from Protestant backgrounds, and of the minority who do express some religious preference, almost all are inactive."[84] Respondents in the study by Gustavus and Henley were also likely to report that they had no religion.[85]

On the other hand, at least one Protestant scholar sees in voluntary childlessness the possibility of a church-sanctioned commitment somewhat like that of celibacy for reasons of religious service. Just as a person might renounce marriage in order to devote himself or herself to serving God and others with a maximum of freedom, mobility, and time available for one's mission, so might a married couple choose not to have children in order to give full concentration to their ministry. So writes Mennonite theologian John Howard Yoder as he suggests that church mission and service agencies could benefit by encouraging voluntarily childless couples who embrace this life-style in order to dedicate themselves to religious ministries. Similar thinking is taking place among some Roman Catholics.[86]

Choosing the Child-Free Life-Style

J. E. Veevers has given much study and consideration to factors related to the decision of couples not to have children. Several of her findings are of special interest because of what they tell us about how and why the decision not to have children is made.

Many of Veevers' respondents reported having come from unhappy homes in which their parents remained together rather than getting a divorce. The children learned not only that having children doesn't necessarily mean either personal or marital happiness, but also they learned that children can even be the cause of strife in marriage. Furthermore, parents who endure miserable situations "for the sake of the children" may be teaching children that parenthood is entrapping, preventing the option of divorce. Women in the sample who grew up in such homes had negative impressions of motherhood, which were made all the stronger by the fact that their mothers had been "basically dissatisfied with their housework and child-care roles."[87]

Some voluntarily childless wives in Veevers' sample had been "only" children. Thus it may be that the absence of role models and the lack of opportunities to interact with siblings caused some of these women to feel incompetent for or uninterested in the mother role for themselves.

On the other hand, some of the wives in the sample came from large families in which they were the oldest of the children and had responsibility for all the younger brothers and sisters. Being cast in the "little mother" role, these women learned early that children limit one's activities. Often during girlhood, these women had to baby-sit when they would rather have pursued their own interests or attended school events. Taking care of real children provided an experience quite different from that known to little girls who play only with dolls. "The dolls never misbehave in unmanageable ways," writes Veevers, "they never preempt or preclude other activities, and when they become burdensome or boring they can be readily but temporarily abandoned." Not so with real babies. And girls who grow up in the oldest-daughter position in the family often learn that early. They may thus have little desire for taking on the mother role in adulthood.

Egalitarian gender roles and wife employment may also enter into the choice not to have children. Earlier we saw that these factors were related to limiting family size; but for some couples they are also related to avoiding parenthood altogether. Veevers writes: "Most of the childless wives interviewed report that their marriages are characterized by very egalitarian sex roles, with an orientation in which the husband and wife are considered to be of equal value to the relationship, with equal levels of authority and equal levels of competence." Furthermore, "egalitarian role relationships may be both a consequence and a cause of childlessness."[88]

With one exception, all of the childless wives in Veevers' sample work and plan to work indefinitely. About half of the women reported a deep commitment to their work and derive a sense of identity from it, and many have high professional aspirations. "The remaining half work mainly for extrinsic rewards, such as money and the satisfactions of interacting with others in job situations," Veevers reports.[89]

How the choice is made   Veevers found that nearly a third of childless couples decide before marriage that childlessness will be a part of an informal marriage "contract." From the very beginning there is no intention to have children. In most cases, these women in Veevers' sample had made the decision during adolescence and later sought future mates who agreed; although in some cases, the women had not considered a childless marriage until meeting their future husbands.

Among the other two-thirds, childlessness comes about as the result of continually postponing having children until a future time. But the "right time" never comes. For most couples, this postponement seems to come about through a series of four stages—first, a definite period of waiting; second (when the agreed-upon time is up), an indefinite period of postponement when the time to have a baby becomes increasingly vague; third, a critical stage in which the possibility of permanent childlessness is openly acknowledged for the first time; and fourth, an explicit decision (or the recognition of the implicit decision that has been gradually made) that they will never have children.[90]

Interestingly, adoption is often held out as a possibility for voluntarily childless wives. Veevers points out that the importance of the option of adoption lies in the twofold symbolic importance: "the reaffirmation of normalcy" [because of the societal view that "normal, well-adjusted" people will want and like children] and the avoidance of irreversible decisions."[91]

Many voluntarily childless women report a deep commitment to work and high achievement goals.

MACRO VIEW OF REPRODUCTION

If the nursery-tale introduction to childlessness is "The Gingerbread Man," the equivalent introduction to a macro view of the world population situation could be the story of the old woman who lived in a shoe and had so many children she didn't know what to do.

Ansley J. Coale, for many years director of the Office of Population Research at Princeton University, vividly describes what is taking place as world population increases at a rate more rapid than at any time in history.[92] He points out that the *growth rate* (the number of persons added per year per 1,000 population, taking into account both births and deaths) was up until 10,000 years ago about .02, and it took at least 35,000 years for the population to double. Between A.D. 1 and 1750 (the year when the modern accelerated growth phenomenon began), the growth rate was .56 per 1,000, which meant the world population doubled every 1,200 years. However, according to United Nations studies, the growth rate is expected to be about 20 per 1,000 over the next several decades—which would mean a doubling of the world population this time in just under thirty-five years!

Coale illustrates the cumulative effect of even a small number of doublings by referring to an old legend in which a king offered his daughter in marriage to any man who could supply one grain of wheat for the first square on a chessboard, two grains for the second square, double that amount for the third square, and so on. "To comply with this request for all 64 squares," writes Coale, "would require a mountain of grain many times larger than today's worldwide wheat production."

In 1973, the world population was 3.9 billion. According to United Nations projections, there will be 6.4 billion people in the world by the year 2000. Coale points out that if the present growth rate of 20 per 1,000 were to continue so that the population would double every thirty-five years, the earth would be in a similar situation to the legendary king's chessboard. "The consequences of sustained growth at this pace are clearly impossible," says Coale. He explains why. "In less than 700 years there would be one person for every square foot on the surface of the earth; in less than 1,200 years the human population would outweigh the earth; in less than 6,000 years the mass of humanity would form a sphere expanding at the speed of light."

Where Population Growth Is Occurring

It should be kept in mind that not all parts of the world are growing equally. In some nations, there is even governmental concern that not enough people are being born. In other nations, the annual population increase seems staggering and is associated with poverty, inadequate food supplies, extremely crowded living conditions, and other social problems. To understand this imbalance, it helps to think in terms of the United Nations' classifications for areas of the world. "Less developed" societies are those which are "largely rural, agrarian, and at least partly illiterate." "More developed" societies are those "primarily urban, industrial, and literate."[93] Particular populations may be at various points along a continuum of change from being "less developed" to being "more developed."

The less-developed nations are growing in population at a very high rate of increase at the same time that population growth in the rest of the world is more moderate or even low. (See Figure 9-3.) In fact, according to United Nations projections, 90 percent of the anticipated population increase by the year 2000 will have been contributed by the less-developed nations. However, we must be careful in interpreting what this projection means. Demographer Paul Demeny of the Population Council warns: "The frequent references to 'soaring' birth rates in popular interpretations of contemporary demographic changes in the underdeveloped world have little factual basis and in many instances no basis at all. Rapid population growth is mainly a result of falling death rates unaccompanied by adjustments in birth rates."[94]

Demographers speak of this lag between death rates and birthrates as the

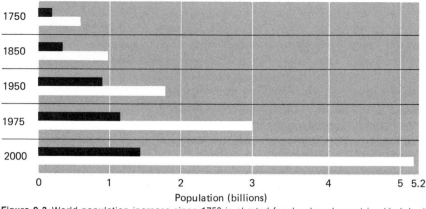

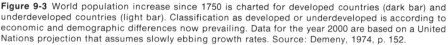

Population (billions)

Figure 9-3 World population increase since 1750 is charted for developed countries (dark bar) and underdeveloped countries (light bar). Classification as developed or underdeveloped is according to economic and demographic differences now prevailing. Data for the year 2000 are based on a United Nations projection that assumes slowly ebbing growth rates. Source: Demeny, 1974, p. 152.

"demographic transition." During the transition, as less-developed countries undergo changes through which they move toward urbanization and industrialization, death rates decline because of medical advances, improvements in sanitation, nutrition, and the like. At the same time, the birthrate in these countries continues as before for a considerable period of time. Population then grows because of this difference in birth and death rates. After the transition to urbanization and industrialization is completed, the birthrate also declines. The wide gap between numbers of deaths per 1,000 population and numbers of births per 1,000 becomes much smaller. (See Figure 9-4.)

At the same time that less-developed nations are growing so rapidly (with growth rates of 2.5 percent per year), the population growth rate in developed nations is now less than 1 percent and falling. In fact, observes sociologist Charles Westoff, in the twenty countries that have 80 percent of the world's "developed" population, "the fertility rate is at, near or below the replacement level."[95] The fertility rate (the average number of offspring per woman over a lifetime of childbearing) is at replacement level when it reaches an average of 2.1 births per woman.

Trends and Government Policies

Throughout most of the developed world, there appears to be a trend toward the two-child family. Fertility studies conducted in a number of developed countries between 1966 and 1972 showed a decrease in the number of children women expected to have. By 1972, recently married women indicated a preference for the following average numbers of children: Belgium, 2.2; Finland, 2.0; Czechoslovakia, 2.2; Poland, 2.2; France, 2.1; Yugoslavia, 2.1; Hungary, 1.9; and

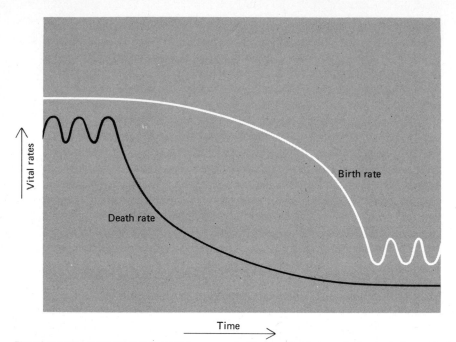

Figure 9-4 The *demographic transition*, represented schematically here, is the central event in the recent history of the human population. It begins with a decline in the death rate, precipitated by advances in medicine (particularly in public health), nutrition, or both. Some years later the birth rate also declines, primarily because of changes in the perceived value of having children. Before the transition the birth rate is constant but the death rate varies; afterward the death rate is constant but the birth rate fluctuates. The demographic transition usually accompanies the modernization of nations; it began in Europe and the United States late in the eighteenth century and early in the nineteenth, but in the underdeveloped nations it began only much later, often in the twentieth century. In the developed countries the transition is now substantially complete, but in much of the rest of the world only mortality has been reduced; the fertility rate remains high. In the interim between the drop in mortality and fertility population has increased rapidly. Source: From Coale, 1974, p. 49.

England and Wales, 1.8.[96] Figure 9-5 shows the trend in the United States toward smaller families as well, with younger wives in all three categories (white, black, and Spanish origin) indicating a greater preference for a two-child family than for any other size.

Governments are aware of the consequences of population growth or the lack of it, and they may utilize various measures to either cut down growth or encourage greater fertility. Where there is a concern about too rapid growth and the problems of crowding, housing, pollution, limited resources, burdens placed on community services, and similar matters related to the well-being of a country and its citizens, governments may seek to encourage birth control through varied programs.

On the other hand, if a government becomes alarmed that a decline in

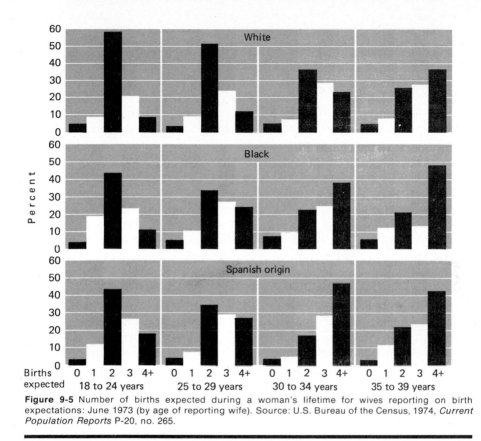

Figure 9-5 Number of births expected during a woman's lifetime for wives reporting on birth expectations: June 1973 (by age of reporting wife). Source: U.S. Bureau of the Census, 1974, *Current Population Reports* P-20, no. 265.

fertility may mean military, economic, and political disadvantages, and may cause such problems as a labor shortage in future years, policies and programs and changes in laws may be instituted in an effort to raise the fertility rate. For example, Romania's fertility rate in 1955 was 3.1 births per woman, but by 1966 it had reached a low of 1.9. Disturbed by this decline, the government repealed its permissive abortion law. By the next year, the fertility rate had doubled to 3.7. This large upsurge in births in 1967 is now causing severe overcrowding in the Romanian school system. Westoff predicts that by 1984 when this group of children enters the labor force, there will be very high unemployment or an out-migration of surplus labor.[97] At the present time, Romanian fertility is once again declining despite the restrictions on legal abortion, as couples rely on diligent usage of contraception and, when necessary, illegal abortion. Another government which became concerned over a low population growth rate was that of President Peron of Argentina. Before his death in 1973 he told the women of Argentina that they had maternal responsibilities to fulfill—and promptly made oral contraceptives illegal.[98]

Costs, Rewards, and Population

It seems clear that on the macro level, no less than on the micro level, reproduction is a matter of costs and rewards. Too many people can be costly, but so can too few. Governments around the world are increasingly aware of population concerns and have set up various commissions to study demographic trends and to suggest policies.[99] Where there is concern about too much population growth, as is occurring in the less-developed nations, attention must be given to the rewards and costs of children on the micro level in order to affect trends at the macro level. Especially is there a need to present alternative rewards, for (in the words of Hoffman and Hoffman), "as long as children satisfy an important value for which there is no alternative, people will climb over a great many barriers and put up with a great many costs before they will diminish fertility. As long as children satisfy important values, even very trivial reasons for another child will seem valid."[100]

To reproduce or not to reproduce, that is the question. In the more-developed nations, we may expect the question to be asked with increasing frequency as modern couples take a new look at parenthood, viewing it as neither an inevitable fate nor a necessary duty but as an *option*. And like any other option, it will be considered in terms of projected costs and rewards. Increasingly, we may expect that rationality will enter into decisions to have children as couples become aware of the responsibilities and consequences entailed. Alice Rossi has pointed out the irrevocability of the parenthood role. One may leave an unsatisfactory job or marriage, but there is no turning back from parenthood once undertaken. "We can have ex-spouses and ex-jobs," writes Rossi, "but not ex-children."[101] Couples cannot afford to take the reproductive aspect of marriage lightly, and indications seem to be that they realize this as perhaps never before.

NOTES

1 Barbara J. Katy, "Cooling Motherhood," *National Observer,* Dec. 20, 1972; Peck, 1971.
2 Boak, 1955.
3 Hoffman and Hoffman, 1973; see also Berelson, 1972.
4 Hoffman and Hoffman, 1973, p. 47.
5 Hoffman and Hoffman, 1973, p. 56.
6 Kar, 1971; Groat and Neal, 1967.
7 *Current Population Reports* 1974, P-23, no. 49, pp. 37–38.
8 Sears, Maccoby, and Levin, 1957; Hoffman, 1963.
9 Blau and Duncan, 1967, p. 428.

10 Berelson, 1972.
11 From "Hallowed Ground," stanza 6.
12 Rainwater, 1965, pp. 147–148; Hoffman and Hoffman, 1973, p. 48.
13 Poffenberger, 1969.
14 Hoffman and Hoffman, 1973, pp. 57–58.
15 Parish, 1974.
16 Rainwater, 1960, p. 87.
17 Hoffman and Hoffman, 1973, p. 53.
18 Rainwater, 1965, pp. 181–182.
19 Buckhout et. al., 1971; Hoffman and Hoffman, 1973, pp. 50–51.
20 Westoff and Westoff, 1971, pp. 164–161, 227; Ryder and Westoff, 1971, p. 68.
21 Scanzoni, 1975b.
22 Humanae Vitae, 1968 (Encyclical on Birth Control given by Pope Paul VI).
23 Scanzoni, 1975c.
24 Ryder and Westoff, 1971, p. 70.
25 Gen. 38:9.
26 Himes, 1936, p. 69 ff. in 1970 edition.
27 Gordis, 1967, pp. 36–41.
28 Westoff, 1974b, pp. 111–112.
29 Quoted in Rehwinkel, 1959, pp. 41–42.
30 Ryder and Westoff, 1971, pp. 70–71; Westoff and Potvin, 1967, p. 130 ff.
31 Frankel, 1970, p. 48.
32 Espenshade, 1973.
33 Mueller, 1972.
34 Reed and McIntosh, 1972.
35 Nunnally, 1972.
36 Renne, 1970.
37 Rossi, 1968.
38 R. Ryder, 1973.
39 Feldman, 1971.
40 Feldman, 1971; Christensen, 1968.
41 Renne, 1970.
42 Scanzoni, 1975b.
43 Hoffman, 1972a.
44 St. George, 1973, p. 155.
45 St. George, 1973, p. 172.
46 See summary in Hoffman and Hoffman, 1973, p. 64.
47 Hass, 1972.
48 Hoffman and Hoffman, 1973, pp. 65–67.
49 Scanzoni, 1975b.
50 Scanzoni, 1971.
51 Scanzoni, 1975b.
52 Westoff, Potter, and Sagi, 1963, pp. 205–207.
53 Bumpass and Westoff, 1970, pp. 93–94.
54 Wu, 1972.
55 "Sexism on the Stork Market," *Human Behavior,* January 1974, pp. 45–46 (comparison of Dinitz, Dynes, and Clark, 1954, with Peterson and Peterson, 1973).
56 Peterson and Peterson, 1973.
57 Markle, 1973, 1974.
58 Scanzoni, 1975c.
59 Scanzoni, 1975c.
60 Kennedy, 1970, pp. 42, 183, 218.
61 Westoff, 1972, p. 9.
62 N. Ryder, 1973; Jaffe, 1973.
63 N. Ryder, 1973, pp. 141–142.
64 Westoff, 1972, p. 11.
65 Scanzoni, 1975b.

66 Seaman, 1972, p. 219.
67 Segal, 1972.
68 Scanzoni, 1975*b*.
69 Scanzoni, 1975*b*.
70 Westoff, 1972, pp. 11–12.
71 Presser and Bumpass, 1972, p. 20.
72 Presser and Bumpass, 1972, p. 18; also news item, *Family Planning Perspectives,* 7 (May/June 1975): 113.
73 Reported in Cutright and Cutright, 1973 p. 8; see also Tietze, 1973, 1975; Sklar and Berkov, 1974.
74 Cutright and Cutright, 1973, pp. 9–10, 15.
75 Veevers, 1973a, p. 358.
76 Hoffman and Hoffman, 1973, p. 22.
77 Veevers, 1972; *Current Population Reports* 1972, P-20, no. 240, p. 6; 1974, P-20, no. 265, p. 3; 1974, P-20, no. 269, p. 5.
78 Veevers, 1974.
79 Veevers, 1974.
80 Scanzoni, 1975c.
81 Gustavus and Henley, 1971.
82 Veevers, 1973a, pp. 363–364.
83 Hoffman, 1972a.
84 Veevers, 1973a, p. 357.
85 Gustavus and Henley, 1971.
86 Yoder, 1974; Everett and Everett, 1975.
87 Veevers, 1973*b*.
88 Veevers, 1974.
89 Veevers, 1974.
90 Veevers, 1973a, pp. 359–360.
91 Veevers, 1973a, pp. 362–363.
92 Coale, 1974.
93 Coale, 1974, p. 48.
94 Demeny, 1974, p. 152.
95 Westoff, 1974b, p. 109.
96 Westoff, 1974b, p. 113.
97 Westoff, 1974b, pp. 112–115.
98 Westoff, 1974b, p. 118.
99 Berelson, 1973.
100 Hoffman and Hoffman, 1973, p. 69.
101 Rossi, 1968.

10
SOCIALIZING CHILDREN FOR ACHIEVEMENT

"I will begin teaching Robyn how to light the candles [for the ritual Sabbath ceremony] and what it is to be a Jewish mother." These were the words of the adoptive mother of three-year-old Nguyen Thi My, one of thousands of Vietnamese orphans brought to the United States in the spring of 1975. Transported from the culture of her birth, the child received a new name and a new cultural environment.[1] Children don't come into the world programmed for life in a particular society. They must learn the ways of a preexisting and ongoing society in order to function within it. They must become social—or in other words, be *socialized.* Children reared in Vietnam learn to speak and write Vietnamese, to eat with chopsticks, and to clap their hands and bow politely in greeting others. Children reared in the United States learn to speak and write English, eat with a fork, and to shake hands. Sociologists Frederick Elkin and Gerald Handel point out that such overt, visible behaviors are only one part of the socialization process. Children also develop "a sense of propriety," a generalized awareness of appropriate behavior in various situations. And they learn to experience certain emotions suited to the occasion. Children *learn,* for example, "to feel proud at winning a fist fight or ashamed for having gotten into one." Socialization includes learning moral values, political orientations, and much more.[2]

Many persons, organizations, and institutions are involved in socializing children (schools, churches, peers, and the mass media, for example). However, the part parents play is extremely important. In earlier chapters, we examined some aspects of parental influence. We saw in Chapter 2 that exchange theory helps explain gender-role socialization as an interchange of rewards and costs between the *socializers* (parents in particular) and the *socializees* (the children). And under "Kin Influence and Marital Choice" in Chapter 4, we looked at parental power in mate selection. We saw that the resource level provided by parents as compared to alternative sources of rewards determines the degree of influence parents are likely to have over a young person's marriage decisions.

In other words, parents socialize their children for adult life both with respect to the gender roles they are expected to fulfill and the relationships they are expected to enter—especially marriage. But another area of socialization is of deep concern to parents as well: socialization for participation in the economic-opportunity system.

IMPORTANCE OF ONE'S OCCUPATION

In a television drama, a middle-aged widow asked her new friend what he did. "I'm a mailman," he said. The woman seemed surprised and commented that he didn't look like a mailman, whereupon he replied in essence: "A mailman isn't what I *am;* it's what I *do.*"

Most persons would agree that there is much more to their lives than the way they earn their livelihood. Yet, in a very real sense, "what I do" and "what I am" are closely intertwined. One's employment becomes an important element in self-identification. Several decades ago, sociologist Willard Waller wrote of "occupational molding"—the way in which persons tend to think of them-selves in terms of their occupational roles. "The lawyer and the chorus girl soon come to be recognizable social types," wrote Waller. "One can tell a politician when one meets him on the street. . . . The doctor is always the doctor, and never quite can quit his role. . . . And what preaching most accomplishes is upon the preacher himself. Perhaps no occupation that is followed long fails to leave its stamp upon the person."[3]

Work is a crucial part of adult life. It provides subsistence and determines a family's living standard. Occupational prestige (or the lack of it) is a main factor determining social status. One's employment regulates time and activities, affects choices of friendship, engages one's thoughts and emotional energies for a large part of the day, and is generally a pervasive influence on a person's entire life.[4] For such reasons as these, parents are usually interested in and concerned about their children's job and career futures.

THE INEQUALITY CONTROVERSY

Even though occupational achievement is a sought-after goal, not all children will grow up with equal chances for success. In spite of ideals expressed in such statements as "equal opportunity for all," "all men are created equal," and "equal before the law," a great deal of inequality exists in American society. Some parents are simply unable to provide their children with the levels of resources that other parents are able to provide. Traditionally, government policy makers have looked to the schools to overcome inequities. The idea has been that if all children are given equal educational opportunities, they will have equal chances for achievement and equal access to the material, power, and prestige rewards of the economic structure.

In recent years, some social critics have challenged such notions. Two books published in 1972 contained similar outlooks and proposals. Murray Milner, Jr., wrote that a dilemma exists because Americans value both equality and achievement. *Equality* suggests that everyone should be treated and rewarded alike. But *achievement* suggests that rewards should go to persons on the basis of accomplishment or at least effort. The mechanism Americans have tried to use to reconcile these contradictory values, says Milner, is the concept of "equality of opportunity." Nevertheless, inequality remains; and in Milner's thinking the solution lies in redistributing wealth so that there would first be *economic* equality, and then there could follow "meaningful educational equality of opportunity."[5]

In a hotly debated book entitled *Inequality,* Christopher Jencks and his colleagues at the Harvard Center for Educational Policy Research made a similar proposal. Educational reform (better schools, compensatory learning programs, assuring that poor children attend school with middle-class children, and so on) is not the key to breaking the cycle of poverty said these writers after examining a wide range of studies from a variety of sources which had been conducted since 1960. Jencks and his associates concluded that genetic differences, test scores, disadvantages passed on to children from parents, and the quality of schools persons attended were not to bear the blame for economic inequality and differences in achievement. "Economic success," they write, "seems to depend on varieties of luck and on-the-job competence that are only moderately related to family background, schooling, and scores on standardized tests." "Competence" is said to be difficult to define since it varies from job to job, "but it seems in most cases to depend more on personality than on technical skills."[6] Jencks and his colleagues suggest that inequality could be reduced by spreading out wealth and eliminating wide differences in income through such means as steeply progressive taxation, income-sharing plans, and constraining employers to reduce wage differences between their worst-paid and best-paid workers.[7] According to this view, society shouldn't be concerned about preparing people to gain the prize; rather, prizes should be given to everyone. The rules of the game should be changed "so as to reduce the rewards of competitive success and the costs of failure."

The Jencks book has had its critics. Sociologist James Coleman distinguishes between "inequality of opportunity" (unequal access to the economic-opportunity system and its rewards) and "inequality of result" (differences in income and other rewards received by different persons). In their concerns over *income* inequality, Jencks and his associates glossed over the realities of *access* inequality. "By minimizing the importance of family background for educational attainment, for occupational status, and for income," writes Coleman, "the authors obscure the inequality of opportunity that does exist in American society."[8]

Many sociological studies have shown the important part family background plays in a person's later occupational achievement. Jencks acknowledges the discrepancies between his conclusions and those of other social scientists who have examined the same data but attributes the divergent interpretations to his focus on differences between *individuals* whereas the main focus of other social scientists has been on differences between *groups*.

Jencks and his colleagues don't deny the existence of inequality between social groupings (blacks, Chicanos, women, and so on) but consider this "relatively unimportant" when compared to the degree of inequality between individuals. They report that the wide gap in earnings between black and white workers seems shocking but claim that they "are even more disturbed by the fact that the best-paid fifth of all white workers earns 600 percent more than the worst-paid fifth." These researchers conclude that "from this viewpoint, racial inequality looks almost insignificant."[9]

Not surprisingly, there has been strong reaction from black social scientists and educators, ten of whom prepared a statement charging that the Jencks study is one of several which "seem to point to the conclusion that blacks and lower-class people are about where they ought to be in the society—at the bottom—and that all efforts to move them, or let them move themselves, are futile."[10] These critics were particularly disturbed by the way the book *Inequality* "serves to take school systems and officials responsible for public education 'off the hook,'" when instead schools should be challenged to change and improve in ways specifically designed to meet the needs of "culturally different children." To these black educators and social scientists, the issue is one of basic human dignity rather than income alone. They write: "Income is valuable insofar as it buys individual choices. Income cannot buy societal appreciation of individual worth, or group cohesion, or community, in a society that is characterized by racism, materialism, and inhumanity. Jencks's repudiation of schooling as an instrument of social improvement is valid only if one accepts income as the end toward which we strive."[11]

The controversy over the Jencks study has generated a great deal of thought and discussion about governmental responsibility in equalizing opportunities for all. Coleman makes the point that all persons start out in life with private resources (both genetic and environmental) provided chiefly by their families. These private resources are *not* equally distributed; and therefore, unless public resources (such as through education) can make up for the lack, children will have unequal chances for achievement. Yet the influence of parents remains crucial. "The most important environmental resources for the development of the young are those expended through enormous investments of time and effort and attention by parents," Coleman emphasizes. "It seems highly unlikely that another, more equal, social arrangement than the family could stimulate this level of personal investment in children."[12]

FAMILY BACKGROUND AND STATUS ATTAINMENT

In modern, industrial societies, families seldom directly control the careers their children will enter or the job rewards they will receive. Occupational achievement depends on merit—on how well persons are equipped to fulfill the demands of a particular job. Nevertheless, parents substantially influence their children's chances for achievement.

American society is open or fluid in that it permits movement between social statuses. It is not a classless society; we have already noted that there is general agreement about the prestige rankings of various occupations, and persons are ranked according to their standing in the economic-opportunity structure. Groups of persons with a particular level of attainment educationally and occupationally are considered to share a certain social position; other groups occupy a higher or lower position on the status continuum. In certain respects, there is an invisible line between nonmanual (white-collar) occupations and those that are manual (blue-collar).[13]

However, the American class structure is not rigid, and children are not trapped in the social positions of their parents. The factory worker's son may become a schoolteacher. The bus driver's daughter may become an accountant or may marry a dentist. Or the reverse may occur; a business executive's son may become a garage mechanic, or the judge's daughter might marry a carpenter.

When persons remain at the same status levels as their parents, sociologists speak of *intergenerational status continuity*. When adult social status differs from that of parents, the situation is one of *intergenerational mobility*. Such mobility may go in either of two directions: upward or downward. The schoolteacher (son of the factory worker) is an example of upward mobility. The judge's daughter who became a carpenter's wife and the executive's son who repairs cars for a living are examples of downward mobility.

Intergenerational Occupational Mobility

Sociologists Peter Blau and Otis Dudley Duncan have published one of the most extensive studies of mobility in the American occupational structure. As with most studies in the past, the focus was only on fathers and sons. These researchers found that class origins influenced a male's attainments in both education and occupation. They wrote: "The family into which a man is born exerts a significant influence on his occupational life, ascribing a status to him at birth that influences his chances for achieving any other status later in his career."[14]

However, since the United States does not have a caste system, it is a man's *achieved* status (the position he earns through his own accomplishments in the opportunity structure) that counts rather than his *ascribed* status (the social status assigned him through his parents). Blau and Duncan were interested in finding out the extent to which ascribed and achieved status remained the same. And if there was change, in what direction did the movement occur?

Blau and Duncan discovered a great deal of *status continuity;* that is, sons remain at the same socioeconomic levels as their fathers to a greater extent than would be likely if one's social destination were not related to one's social origin. At the same time, considerable upward mobility (and a smaller amount of downward mobility) occurs in American society. (See Table 10-A.)

Education and Mobility

Education is a key factor in mobility. We've seen throughout this book that the more schooling persons have, the higher their achieved socioeconomic status is likely to be. However, the likelihood of attending college is directly related to family income. According to the census data listed in Table 10-B, 59 percent of families in 1971 who had college-age young persons and a family income of $15,000 or over had a family member in college full-time. As income went down, so did the percentage of families in each income group who had full-time students. Families with eighteen-to-twenty-four-year-old members and a family income of under $3,000 were sparsely represented in the college population. Only 14 percent of such families had a member attending college full-time.

Even when persons from lower status levels do attend college, they are much more likely than those from higher-status homes to drop out without completing their education. And they are less likely to return to college later.[15] Similarly, at the high school level, there is a higher dropout rate among blue-collar adolescents than among white-collar adolescents.[16] Taken overall, the evidence from a variety of studies suggests a clear linkage between level of social origin and eventual educational attainment which, in turn, may be expected to influence achievement in the economic-opportunity system.

At the same time, a statement of Blau and Duncan should be kept in mind:

TABLE 10-A MOBILITY FROM FATHER'S OCCUPATION TO SON'S FIRST OCCUPA-
TION FOR U.S. MALES 25 TO 64 YEARS OLD (PERCENTAGES)*

Father's Occupation	Son's First Occupation					
	Higher White Collar	Lower White Collar	Higher Manual	Mid Manual	Lower Manual	Farm
Higher white-collar (professionals, managers, proprietors)	28.6	28.2	9.8	22.6	8.5	2.4
Lower white-collar (sales and clerical)	21.1	33.3	7.9	25.1	9.6	3.0
Higher manual (craftsmen and foremen)	7.4	20.5	17.4	36.0	14.0	4.6
Mid manual (operatives and service workers)	6.6	17.3	9.6	47.5	14.8	4.1
Low manual (laborers)	4.6	13.6	6.8	37.2	30.3	7.6
Farm	4.1	6.7	5.8	21.0	12.0	50.3

*The entry in each cell is the percentage of sons whose fathers were in the occupational category listed at the left whose first job was in the category listed at the top. For instance, 28.2 percent of the sons whose fathers were in higher white-collar occupations were first employed in lower white-collar occupations.

Source: Reprinted from Kerckhoff, 1972, p. 9, based upon data from Blau and Duncan, 1967, Table J2.2.

"A man's social origins exert a considerable influence on his chances of occupational success, but his own training and early experience exert a more pronounced influence on his success chances."[17] Through sophisticated mathematical techniques, these researchers and others have been able to determine just *how much* certain factors (such as father's occupation or education) affect a son's future achievement.[18]

One of the most ambitious of such studies has been that of William Sewell and his associates at the University of Wisconsin who in 1957 drew a large random sample of Wisconsin high school seniors for the purpose of learning their socioeconomic origins, educational experience, and educational and occupational plans and aspirations. In 1964, these students were followed up in order to determine their achievements after high school; and still later, information on the earnings of males in the sample was examined. The findings of Sewell and his colleagues are especially important because they help us understand *how* socioeconomic status origins influence educational and occu-

TABLE 10-B FAMILIES WITH MEMBERS 18 TO 24 YEARS OLD, BY FULL-TIME COLLEGE ATTENDANCE AND FAMILY INCOME: OCTOBER 1971 (NUMBERS IN THOUSANDS. CIVILIAN NON-INSTITUTIONAL POPULATION)

Family Income*	Total Families with Members 18 to 24 Years Old†	With Members in College Full-Time	
		Number	Percent
Total	9,644	3,692	38.3
Under $3,000	731	102	14.0
$3,000 to $4,999	935	202	21.6
$5,000 to $7,499	1,310	379	28.9
$7,500 to $9,999	1,448	485	33.5
$10,000 to $14,999	2,382	1,004	42.1
$15,000 and over	2,129	1,255	58.9
Not reported	709	261	36.8

*Income for preceding 12 months.
†Excludes family members who are married, spouse present.

Source: U.S. Bureau of the Census, 1973, *Current Population Reports.* P-23, no. 44, p. 20.

pational attainment in adult life. The process is a complex one and should make us aware of the many different factors involved in socialization for achievement.[19]

Just as a chemist distinguishes between the effects of each of several chemicals on another substance and also observes how various chemicals work in combination, Sewell's concern was to determine the extent to which socioeconomic variables (parents' education and income, and father's occupation) *directly* influenced a person's educational attainment and the extent to which other social-psychological processes entered in and somehow mediated the effects of social status.

For example, a hypothetical student named Jim might come from a family in which both parents had only a grade school education. Taking no other factor than this into account, according to the calculations of Sewell and associates, Jim might be expected on the average to obtain one and one-half years less of education than would be true of Eric whose parents both graduated from college—even if the two boys' fathers had similar jobs and incomes. Or to take another example, a child from a family below the poverty level would be likely to receive on the average one quarter of a year more of schooling if the family income could be raised to the median income level.[20]

These examples show what might be found if we took nothing else into account except social origin measured in terms of four socioeconomic variables, singly or in combination (father's education, mother's education, parents' income, and father's occupation). Yet, this leaves much of the story untold. Other factors enter in, factors which sociologists call *intervening variables* because they intervene between one variable (say family income) and the end result (in this case, educational achievement). In the Wisconsin study, three such intervening variables were taken into account, and they made a great deal of difference, as Table 10-C indicates.

Educational attainment after high school was greatly influenced by such social-psychological factors as a student's academic abilities and high school performance, the degree to which significant others (parents, teachers, friends) encouraged the student, the educational plans of the student's friends, and the student's own educational and occupational aspirations. Of particular interest from the standpoint of parental socialization is Sewell's finding that "the influence of parents on educational and occupational aspirations and ultimately on attainment of higher education is about twice that of teachers, and the influence of friends only slightly less than that of parents."

With regard to policy recommendations, Sewell points out that evidence from the study "raises doubt that programs based on family income supplementation alone will result in any rapid and marked reduction in inequality in higher education." He suggests a "more targeted economic approach" which would make it possible for all young persons to continue their education. If needy families could be assured a college education was possible for their children, parents and teachers might be more prone to encourage the student's academic growth and performance, aiding and enhancing the student's self-esteem and ambitions. Sewell also suggests that programs should be designed to influence the significant others in a student's life (parents, peers, and teachers) since these persons have been shown to have such important effects on a student's educational and occupational aspirations. While not altogether optimistic that such programs would result in disadvantaged parents providing the kind of encouragement "that higher status families give their children in the normal course of their socialization," Sewell writes that, nonetheless, "our research shows that parental influences are so crucial that every effort must be made to utilize this avenue to reduce educational inequalities."[21]

ASPIRATIONS, EXPECTATIONS, AND FAMILY BACKGROUND

A number of studies indicate that less advantaged parents hold as high job aspirations for their children as more advantaged parents—sometimes even higher.[22] They sincerely want their offspring to get ahead and do better than they themselves did in the economic-opportunity system. Parents at lower status levels express beliefs in hard work and may even put pressures on their children to try very hard to succeed. Yet, at the same time, they don't really think their children will achieve the high-level occupational positions they dream about and want.

TABLE 10-C HOW SOCIOECONOMIC ORIGIN INFLUENCES POST-HIGH SCHOOL EDUCATIONAL ATTAINMENT

Variables	Percent of Influence on Educational Attainment
SES variables* (direct influence of each)	12%
SES variables (in association with the other SES variables)	16
Social psychological factors (intervening variables) which mediate influence of SES variables	
Academic ability and high school performance	11
Influence of significant others (parents, peers, and teachers)	23
Educational and occupational aspirations	38

*Socioeconomic status (SES) variables included parental income, father's education, mother's education, and father's occupation.

Source: Based upon findings described in Sewell, 1971, p. 799.

This paradox of great aspirations but low expectations showed up in some of our own research.[23] Parents were asked to agree or disagree with statements designed to measure achievement values. Did parents feel they should try to help children get further ahead than they themselves had done? Did parents believe children should be taught from infancy to do things well, to do better than others, to try to come out on top, to always put the job first even if it would mean giving up fun? These items measured what was termed *mastery,* an attitude toward the economic-opportunity system which emphasized children's learning to manipulate and master skills and opportunities which place persons in a favorable position in that system.

We found that both higher- and lower-status parents believed that their children should be encouraged to work hard and to achieve all that individual capabilities would permit. In fact, although the range of mastery scores was not wide, we were somewhat surprised to find that less advantaged parents seemed even more committed to mastery values than were higher-status parents. It may be that parents who have already achieved know that their children are starting out from a relatively advantaged position and thus do not feel as strongly compelled to pressure their children to try harder to be "number one," since, in a sense, they already "have it made." But persons lower on the social-status ladder may feel they have a longer way to climb and therefore may hope to give their children a push toward success, which (according to the American Dream) comes by diligent effort or "mastery."

However, when it came to other items designed to measure *passivity* (in contrast to mastery), our research showed striking differences between blue-collar and white-collar parents. Even though white-collar parents didn't social-ize their children in mastery values more than blue-collar parents did, white-collar parents made sure that their children got the message that they must *not* be passive toward the economic-opportunity system. Starting out (relatively speaking) as "number one" doesn't guarantee that one will stay in that position. Attitudes of casualness, indifference, or fatalism could mean falling behind in the race toward success. In other words, a passive attitude toward the opportun-ity structure could mean downward mobility, something parents at higher-status levels want to see their children avoid.

Less advantaged parents, on the other hand, scored much higher on the cluster of passivity items. Having themselves failed to achieve the promises of the American Dream, parents at lower status levels seem wary of actual prospects for their children's success. They tend to be guarded and cautious, socializing their children to adjust to the system and "to make the best of things." In other words, what they report *believing* about mastery is undercut by the realities of their own experience. From these realities, passivity attitudes spring.

The lower the social status, the more likely were parents in our sample to believe that children should learn early that there isn't much a person can do about the way things will turn out. Such parents tended to have a fatalistic outlook on life, believing that a person's success or lack of it is "already in the cards" from the time of birth. They considered it desirable to convey to children an attitude of suspiciousness rather than one of trustfulness toward other people. Being less integrated into the economic-opportunity system them-selves, these parents also tended to believe that children should learn that plans seldom work out and are rather futile because planning can only mean disappointment. Persons should learn to live for today and let tomorrow take care of itself. One shouldn't expect too much from life. The neutralizing effect of this passivity outlook on mastery values was like that of an alkali on acid. Robbed of its potency, the mastery belief could do little for children in lower status families—no matter how strongly parents embraced it.

Thus, although most parents see achievement as a goal of socialization, their aspirations and expectations do not always correspond. Therefore, what children learn both from their parents' example and their direct teaching will vary by social class, which means that socialization outcomes are more predictable than would be the case if class factors were not involved.

THE SPECIAL CASE OF FEMALES

As mentioned earlier, sociological studies of intergenerational mobility have usually focused upon the occupational status of father and son. Since the male has traditionally filled the family breadwinner role, serving as the bridge between the economic-opportunity structure and the family, the family's social status has been assigned according to his position in that structure. In past research, not much attention has been given to the social mobility of females except on the basis of their marriages—the hypergamy (marrying up) and hypogamy (marrying down) which was discussed in Chapter 4.

Marriage and Female Social Mobility

"The study of vertical mobility has been highly 'male-centric,'" writes one team of sociologists, noting that female mobility even through marriage has been relatively neglected as an area of research. In an effort toward correcting this lack, Norval Glenn, Adreain Ross, and Judy Tully analyzed data from four United States national surveys and compared female mobility (attained through marriage) with male mobility (attained through occupation).[24] They found that contrary to what has been believed in the past, there is not a pronounced tendency for females to "marry up." Their data, in fact, indicates considerable downward mobility. For instance, there is more downward movement of females across the line between white-collar and blue-collar statuses than is true of males. Of course, a great deal of hypergamy occurs too; but the data showed that women move into a higher social stratum through marriage to no greater extent than men do through occupational achievement. In other words, the class structure is neither more nor less open to a woman's *marrying* her way up the social ladder than to a man's *working* his way up.

Female Educational and Occupational Attainment

Behavioral scientists are beginning to see the need for researching female achievement in much the same way as they research male achievement. In view of issues raised by the feminist movement and with increasing numbers of women entering the labor force, there seems to be good reason to examine women's attainments and social mobility as directly resulting from their own efforts rather than as indirectly resulting from their husbands' achievements.

Earlier, we discussed the massive Wisconsin longitudinal study which traced male educational, occupational, and earning histories over the first ten years after high school, giving attention to any kind of postsecondary school training, military service, and labor-force experience. In 1974, sociologists William Sewell and Robert Hauser stated their intentions not only to continue this study, looking for further light on the how and why of male achievement, but also announced that female educational and occupational achievement would likewise be given attention. "In so doing," they wrote, "we expect to come up with important evidence and interpretations of inequality of opportunity between the sexes as well as between persons of differing socioeconomic origins."[25]

They had good reason for this prediction. Already some data had been collected which showed that even where socioeconomic status and academic

TABLE 10-D EDUCATIONAL OPPORTUNITY ADVANTAGE OF MEN OVER WOMEN AT TOP AND BOTTOM OF SOCIOECONOMIC SCALE

| | *Percent Advantage of Males over Females* | |
	Bottom Socioeconomic Level	*Top Socioeconomic Level*
Chances of obtaining any further schooling	26%	8%
Chances of attending college	58	20
Chances of completing college	86	28
Chances of attending graduate or professional school	250	129

Source: Based upon figures from Sewell, 1971, p. 795.

ability are held constant, "women have lower probabilities of obtaining any further schooling, of attending college, of graduating from college, and of entering graduate or professional school."[26]

Women at lower status levels were especially found to be at a disadvantage, much more so than men at these levels (who are themselves disadvantaged in comparison to persons at higher status levels). Sewell and associates have calculated the extent to which males have a greater chance for education than females at every socioeconomic status level, the extreme ends of which are shown in Table 10-D.

These inequalities by sex occur even though the high school grades of females are better than those of men. Sewell suggests a number of reasons that females are disadvantaged at every level of higher education, but he especially singles out the role of parents in deterring female achievement. "Our data . . . do suggest that parents are less likely to encourage high educational aspirations among their daughters than their sons," he writes, "and that whenever family funds are short parents are more likely to spend them on the sons' education." Furthermore, women themselves have lower educational aspirations than men, "no doubt in part due to their uncertainty about career and marriage opportunities and plans." At the very root seems to lie narrow gender-role socialization which emphasizes domestic roles for females instead of achievement in the educational and occupational spheres.[27]

Horner study In the second half of the 1960s, psychologist Matina Horner conducted a pioneering research effort in hope of discovering *why* educational and occupational attainments are lower among females and *how* females are discouraged from achievement. She knew that although achievement-motivation studies often did not include females, when females were included sex-related differences showed up. For one, among males a relationship between the strength of the achievement *motive* and their actual *performance* was established; but female performance could not be predicted on the basis of achievement-motive scores. A second difference between the sexes was that women, unlike men, didn't show an increase in achievement testing scores under experimental conditions designed to arouse achievement motivation through stressing intelligence and leadership ability.[28]

Horner also noticed that women scored higher than men on achievement-related anxieties. Although usually anxiety has been associated with a fear of failure, Horner wondered if women might not be worried about success as well. To test her hypothesis, she used standard achievement-motivation testing procedures with University of Michigan undergraduates. Included was a "clue" designed to trigger a story which would show any indication of concern over possible negative consequences of achievement.

Women were asked to write a brief story built around this sentence: "After first-term finals, Anne finds herself at the top of her medical school class." For men, the name "John" and male pronouns were substituted. The differences between the stories men wrote and those women wrote turned out to be enormous. Men viewed John's success with pride. He had worked hard to get where he did and could look forward to a great future. Fewer than 10 percent of the men gave any evidence of what Horner termed "the motive to avoid success."

In contrast, over 65 percent of the women expressed negative imagery in their stories, indicating a fear of achievement. Horner found that reactions fell into three categories: (1) *Fear of social rejection.* These stories depict Anne as lonely and unpopular, perhaps in medical school because she found no one to marry her (which is what she really wants), or else jeopardizing her future chances for dating and marriage because her academic standing is higher than that of the males in her class. (2) *Concerns about normality and femininity.* Women displaying these kinds of success-related anxieties wrote stories in which Anne suddenly begins wondering if she really wants to be a doctor. Maybe such ambitions will mean the loss of her femininity; maybe she should become a social worker and *marry* a doctor instead. (3) *Denial.* Women in this category tended to deny the reality of the situation described (some women considered Anne to be a code name for a fictitious person created by some medical students who took turns writing "her" exams), or they distorted the facts, refusing to believe them. One story, for example, said Anne is happy to be on top but even happier that Tom is higher than she!

Horner concluded that "a bright woman is caught in a double bind. . . . If she fails, she is not living up to her own standards of performance; if she succeeds, she is not living up to societal expectations about the female role." Men do not have to face these struggles and anxieties because societal norms not only permit them to achieve but encourage them to do so.[29] But for many women, the "motive to avoid success" seems to operate in a way that neutralizes or contaminates achievement motivation, much as the "passivity orientation" among lower-status families cancels out the expressed belief in mastery values.

Childhood Experiences of Women Who Achieve

Psychologist Lois Wladis Hoffman has written that "the precursors of the underachieving woman can be seen in the female child."[30] Perhaps it may be just as accurate to say that the childhood experiences of the achieving woman foreshadow her later accomplishments as well. Such would seem to be the case from evidence gathered by Margaret Hennig for her doctoral dissertation in business administration at Harvard University.[31]

Hennig studied female presidents and vice-presidents of male-oriented, nationally recognized, medium-to-large business firms and compared them with a control group of women "who appeared overtly to match the top women executives in all factual data but who had never succeeded in rising beyond middle management." The difference between the two groups' achievements appears to lie in the family dynamics of their respective childhoods. The executives were equipped to overcome the double-bind situation and fear of success described by Horner.

Each high-achieving executive was either an only child or the firstborn in an all-girl family with no more than three siblings. Both parents highly valued in their daughter *both* femaleness and achievement; being a girl and being a success were not viewed as contradictory or mutually exclusive. Although all but one of the mothers represented the traditional feminine role model in homemaking, they actively encouraged their daughter to explore roles that were usually considered masculine. Both parents warmly supported their daughter and delighted in her accomplishments. In addition, they sought to help her internalize achievement values and satisfactions. They seemed to want her to learn early to set her own goals and standards of excellence and to experience the pleasure of rewarding herself through a job well done.

The executives also reported that their parents had had unusually strong relationships with each other and with them, respecting each person as a distinct individual. As one respondent expressed it: "I had the fortune to have two full and complete parents. That is, both my mother and my father were separate real people and I had a separate and real relationship with each. Most girls have such experience of sharing common interests with their mothers; few share common interests with their dads."

Overall, the father and mother in such homes created a supportive climate free from gender-role limitations so that over the years their daughter could try out a wide range of roles and behavioral styles. This "security base" prepared these future executives to overcome any obstacles they might encounter from having been born female. When gender-related conflicts came up, "it was the conflict itself, rather than the achievement, that was perceived as needing to be eliminated," writes Hennig. All during childhood, these women had developed high self-esteem—both from their parents who reinforced and encouraged them and from their own experiences of successful accomplishments. Hennig concludes: "During those early experiences, they accepted such a strong concept of themselves as people that even years of later conflict and pressure to split them into two segments—the feminine affective person and the masculine instrumental person—could not cause them to reduce their achievement drive."[32]

SOCIALIZATION PROCESS

Hennig's study of female executives and the part parents played in helping them develop strong achievement motivation brings us to the more general question: *How* do parents socialize their offspring of either sex? Childrearing, like marriage, is a complex process involving actions, interactions, and reactions; and all parties concerned—father, mother, and each child—play a part in this process. In other words, we're back again to exchange theory.

Exchange Theory and Childhood Socialization

Sociologist Stephen Richer has developed a theoretical model of how social exchange may be expected to work in parent-child relationships.[33] Building upon the premise that power is associated with resources, Richer attributes the high degree of power parents hold over very small children to the fact that in the earliest years children are totally dependent upon parents for both material rewards (food, clothing, shelter) and social rewards (comfort, love, affirmation, approval, and so on). Children have few if any alternative sources of such rewards, nor do they in themselves possess equivalent resources which would permit bargaining from an equal power base.

The relationship is one-sided until somewhere in the toddler stage when children discover a resource of their own—one highly valued by parents and which therefore gives children a measure of power in the bargaining process. That resource, according to Richer, is *compliance*—doing what others want them to do. Children perceive that their compliance means a great deal to parents and can make parents happy or unhappy. ("Melissa, please eat your peas. Come on now, be a good girl. It makes Mommy sad when you won't obey." "Timmy! You know you're supposed to tell me when you have to go to the potty!" "Kim, say 'thank you' to Grandma. Kim! Come back here this minute! Say thank you for the present. Oh, that child makes me furious!")

Richer points out that the child's growing awareness of the ability to produce effects on others (the parents' pleasure or displeasure) is a crucial occurrence. "For, though still dependent for basic material and social rewards

Children learn that their compliance is highly valued by adults. By giving or withholding this resource, children gain bargaining power in the parent-child exchange.

on his parents, the child begins to experience feelings of autonomy, a necessary prerequisite for later involvement in self-interested exchange."[34]

When the child starts school, compliance is found to be valued by other adults as well. Now the teacher's praise and approval can be obtained in exchange for the child's conformity to the teacher's wishes. Schoolmates also increasingly become sources of social rewards. No longer is the child quite so dependent upon parents, and with the availability of alternative rewards for the child comes a diminishing of parental power. The child may now place a higher price tag on compliance; hugs, smiles of approval, and expressions of pleasure may not always be enough any more. Thus the parent may suggest material rewards (a dollar for a good report card or a gift for cooperation in something the child doesn't want to do) or may bargain for the child's compliance in a spirit of quid pro quo: you do this for me and I'll do that for you. The early dependence stage has given way to a reciprocity stage.

During adolescence, the child's power increases even more because the resources offered by the peer group take on such importance. One way parents may try to obtain and maintain compliance is through offering new kinds of rewards which will bring greater peer group approval for the adolescent (the keys to the car, opening the home for parties, and the like). However, if the young person has alternative material rewards (money from a part-time job) as well as alternative social rewards (peer approval), dependency on parents is all the more decreased—as is parental power.

Richer acknowledges that the picture just presented may seem a bit overdrawn, but it is intended simply to provide a basic illustration of how social exchange theory may be applied in parent-child relationships. Of special importance is the part socioeconomic status plays in the exchange. For example, parents may view a child's increasing realization that compliance can be granted or withheld as a situation calling for reasoning and reciprocity or as a situation posing a threat to order and therefore calling for coercion (the stick instead of the carrot). Social class has a great deal to do with which of the two approaches parents will take. Studies have shown that parents at lower socioeconomic levels are more likely to use coercion and parents at higher levels are more likely to employ reasoning and bargaining. "The middle-class home is thus more conducive to the development of an exchange system," says Richer, "whereas the cultural patterns at lower status levels inhibit such a system."[35] And when a child reaches adolescence and physical force and coercion are more difficult to utilize, lower-status parents may find themselves relatively powerless because they have few rewards to offer in comparison to alternate sources of benefits now open to their offspring (as was shown in Figure 4-4 in Chapter 4).

Sociologist Robert Winch has tested exchange theory in a study comparing the influence on college males of two social systems: the family and the fraternity. *Identification* was the term he used to denote the lasting influence of one person or social system on another person. (We have already seen in Chapter 2 how important parents consider the reward of such identification on the part of a child who models his or her life after the parent's example and values.) Winch found that since upper-status families (fathers in particular) are better able than lower-status families to reward their sons with such resources as material goods, time, and expertise, sons from families at higher socioeconomic levels are more likely to identify with their fathers than with the fraternity peer group. But when a family lacks resources and expert power, the son looks to another social system for rewards; therefore, the fraternity's influence increases as socioeconomic status decreases.[36]

Class Differences in Socializing for Achievement

"Members of different social classes, by virtue of enjoying (or suffering) different conditions of life, come to see the world differently—to develop different conceptions of social reality, different aspirations and hopes and fears, different 'conceptions of the desirable,'" writes sociologist Melvin Kohn.[37] Another way of saying that persons hold differing "conceptions of the desirable" is to say they hold different values.

Kohn has done extensive research which shows that parental values differ by class, and consequently parents at different status levels socialize their children in dissimilar ways. "Parents tend to impart to their children lessons derived from the conditions of life of their own social class—and thus help prepare their children for a similar class position."[38] For example, in a study of men and work, Kohn found that at higher socioeconomic levels more than at lower levels there was great value placed upon self-direction characteristics—curiosity about how and why things happen as they do, interest in making sound judgments, self-reliance, taking responsibility, facing facts squarely, being able to work under pressure, and so on. At higher status levels, the men tended to evaluate jobs in terms of *intrinsic* qualities (characteristics inherent in the occupation, such as how much freedom it offered, how interesting it was, the opportunities it afforded to use talents or help other people). But at lower status levels, the men tended to judge jobs according to *extrinsic* characteristics (externals such as pay, job security, fringe benefits, work hours, supervisors and co-workers, and so on).[39]

Not only was the conception of the world of work found to differ by socioeconomic status, the conception of the social world was also found to differ. The lower the social status, the more likely were the men to emphasize a rigid conservatism which opposed questioning old, established ways. They were more likely to resist innovation and change and were unable to tolerate nonconformity to the dictates of authority. "The most important thing to teach children is absolute obedience to their parents," was the kind of statement which received much greater agreement among lower-status men. The lower the social position, the more likely were men to view personal morality in terms of conforming to the letter of the law (again emphasizing the external over the internal), and also the less trustful they were of other people.

These outlooks carry over to the socialization of children. Kohn found that the higher the socioeconomic position of fathers, the more highly they valued self-direction in their children and the less likely they were to value conformity to standards imposed from the outside.[40] The contrasting values of higher-status self-direction and lower-status conformity also showed up in a study of mothers. Although Kohn found that mothers at all status levels considered it important that their children be happy, considerate, honest, dependable, obedient, and respectful of others' rights, the higher the social status of mothers, the more likely they were to emphasize curiosity and self-control as desirable qualities for their children. And the lower the status, the more likely were mothers to select obedience, neatness, and cleanliness as desirable. Of particular interest is Kohn's finding that a mother's own educational and occupational attainments (rather than her ascribed status based on her husband's attainments) are related to the values she holds for her children. Kohn found also that those working-class mothers who held high aspirations and wanted their children to attend college tended to be women who themselves had had some educational advantages but who had married down. "One gets the impression," writes Kohn, "that, for many of them, the child's upward mobility represents an opportunity to recoup the status that they, themselves, have lost."[41]

Kohn's findings on different parental values largely held for both blacks and whites. Socioeconomic status, not race, was the key factor in determining whether parents emphasized in their children either self-determination or conformity to external controls.[42] As a further test of his findings, we included in our Indianapolis study of black families some of Kohn's items for measuring parental values. Our results were similar: The lower the status of black parents, the more likely they were to respond that *obedience* was the most important thing a child should learn. The higher the status, the more likely they were to indicate that *autonomy* was the most desired value for their children. We also found, as Kohn did, that the greater the wife's own occupational status, the more likely she was to transmit autonomy values to her children.[43]

Resources Provided by Parents

When Gertrude Hunter entered high school, she enrolled in the college-preparatory program without so much as a second thought. "What happened next," she says, "is, tragically even today, all too familiar to blacks." A faculty adviser called her in and handed her back the form that had contained her carefully worked-out class schedule. But all the college-prep courses had been crossed out! Home economics courses had been substituted. The dazed young woman took the paper home, whereupon her outraged mother promptly marched to school to confront the adviser. Gertrude Hunter describes the scene in her own words: "The adviser attempted to placate my mother. 'Mrs. Teixeira,' she pleaded, 'what is a colored girl going to do with college? If she learns cooking and sewing, she can always get a good job.' But when we left the office, I was enrolled in the college course."

Today, a pediatrician in a high administrative position with the United States Department of Health, Education and Welfare, Dr. Gertrude Hunter looks back with gratitude to her parents' influence on her life. Knowing they expected her to do well in school, she endeavored to fulfill those expectations. Her father and mother helped her see that who and what she was was good. "As a woman," she says, "I was told I would be able to do whatever I wanted. I was taught that my skin had a beautiful color. This constant, implicit reinforcement of positive self-image was my parents' most valuable gift to me."[44]

Self-esteem In the ongoing exchange between parents and children, the resources passed on by parents may be tangible (music lessons, summer camps, college or trade school tuition, and the like) or they may be intangible in the form of attitudes conveyed and aptitudes developed. The building of a

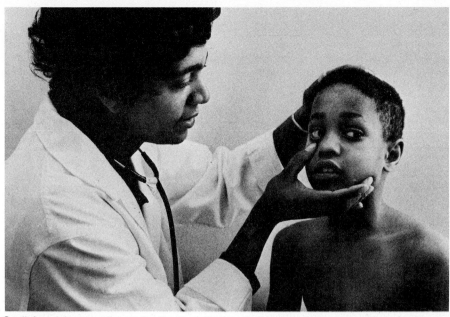

Credit for adult accomplishments often lies with parents who years earlier provided their children with valuable resources for achievement.

child's self-esteem, as in the case of Gertrude Hunter or the executives mentioned earlier, is one example of such an intangible resource.

Sociologist Alan Kerckhoff calls attention to the way children's interactions with their parents' profoundly affect their definition of the world around them so that they come to view it as "friendly or threatening, as a source of opportunity or danger, as controllable or chaotic." In that interaction, a child's self-image begins to evolve; and the world and the self will seem quite different to someone who believes, "I can do anything I set out to do," and someone who believes, "People like me don't have much of a chance in life." Kerckhoff writes: "The self-image is thus a view of oneself in relation to one's environment. Part of that environment is the opportunity structure—how much access to rewards different kinds of people have."[45]

Persons at lower socioeconomic levels tend to see the social stratification system in much the same way as higher-status persons; that is, they rank certain occupations as being more prestigious than others. They generally consider *themselves* to be in lower-status positions in addition to being defined by others in this way, which means, says Kerckhoff, that these attitudes will be conveyed to lower-status children who then follow their parents in developing a "sense of impotence in society." Since such parents have little faith that the American Dream will actualize for them or their children, they emphasize security and risk avoidance rather than looking for opportunities to seize. The child develops the attitude of passivity described earlier rather than a sense of mastery. In a home where there are low expectations for achievement and great pressures for compliance, a child is likely to develop low self-esteem.[46]

However, where parents endeavor to build a strong self-image in children, encouraging them to be upwardly mobile, they provide them with a valuable resource for achievement. Some comments of respondents from our study of black families illustrate how parental encouragement and confidence serve as resources that benefit children. "He has given me the incentive to get ahead," said one male respondent of his father. And these comments were made about mothers: "She had a value system that was a middle-class standard, not like poor people." "She always taught me to save money—what little I could get hold of—and take advantage of every opportunity that would help me to get ahead."[47]

Education and work attitudes Since occupational achievement is so bound up with education, a family that values education provides children with a particularly valuable resource in that children will be encouraged and aided in obtaining as much schooling as possible. Table 10-E indicates that considerable educational and occupational mobility had occurred among our sample of Indianapolis black families, and there is little doubt that parental attitudes aided in such upward mobility in a great many cases.

Numerous respondents made comments such as these: "She saw that I went to school." "Lots of times I didn't plan on going and he saw to it I got there." "He kept telling me I needed an education." "She wanted me to be very smart." "He helped me by financing the things I needed for school." Several spoke of parental sacrifices which made it possible to finish school instead of having to drop out to get a job. "He went without clothes so I could go to school," said one respondent. "She washed and ironed for white folks and helped out so I could go to school," said another. Others spoke of parents making it possible to attend college, art school, or trade school. Respondents reported emotional support, aid with homework, and other forms of help and encouragement parents had given as well.

Attitudes toward work were also conveyed to them by parents. "I used to jump from job to job," said one respondent. "He told me I couldn't get ahead like that—to stay on the job until I could get to know whether I liked it or not." Some told of fathers who had spoken of hardships they themselves had faced so that their children would know what to expect in the job market. Overall, although these parents were aware of the relative deprivation of blacks, they nevertheless endeavored to encourage their offspring to accept the dominant value system of American society with its emphasis on achievement.

However, not all parents had conveyed such positive attitudes. Some respondents spoke of being taught to expect disappointment, and some were

TABLE 10-E EDUCATIONAL AND OCCUPATIONAL MOBILITY AMONG INDIANAPOLIS BLACKS, 1968

Part I. Educational Attainments

Years of School Completed	Male Respondents' Fathers	Male Respondents	Female Respondents' Fathers	Female Respondents
None	12.1%	1.5%	2.5%	1.0%
1–4	14.1	13.1	17.8	3.0
5–8	25.2	29.3	34.7	28.2
9–11	6.6	21.7	6.9	32.1
High school graduate	5.2	18.3	5.0	25.7
Some college or beyond	4.0	16.1	3.4	10.0
No answer	32.8		29.7	
Total	100%	100%	100%	100%
Number	198	198	202	202

Part II. Occupational Distribution of Male Heads of Households

	Fathers of Respondents	Respondents
Middle class	19.6%	33.8%
Upper working class	17.5	34.0
Lower working class	48.9	31.2
No answer	14.0	1.0
Total	100%	100%
Number	400	400

Source: Adapted from Scanzoni, 1971, pp. 156, 160.

actually hindered from movement toward achievement. Some parents were indifferent, offering no advice about getting ahead and doing nothing to encourage educational attainments. One male respondent said of his father: "He hindered us because he wanted us to quit school and go to work; he did not allow us to participate in school activities." A woman said of her mother: "Because I had to do all the housework, she didn't care if I went to school or not."[48]

Among both blacks and whites, a family's position in the economic-opportunity system has a great deal to do with attitudes conveyed to children.

Kohn suggests that the values parents emphasize in their children are generated and maintained by the parents' own occupational experiences. Lower-status jobs are more constricting and seldom provide opportunities for self-direction, emphasizing instead conformity to authority; hence, the lower the status, the more likely does the conformity discussed earlier come to be regarded as a value in its own right on or off the job. In contrast, higher-status occupations permit self-direction and encourage flexibility, creativity, and making one's own analyses and decisions rather than simply obeying orders. Persons with opportunities for self-direction on the job place high value on self-direction in other areas of life as well and seek to convey such attitudes to their children. According to Kohn's studies, children at higher status levels are thus better equipped to get ahead in a society that stresses achievement. They are more likely to have learned to think for themselves, handle responsibility, meet new and problematic situations, and to initiate change instead of merely reacting to it. Lower-status children are less prepared for achievement because their parents have placed primary emphasis on externals and consequences.[49]

Other studies have shown that even the way parents talk in the home affects a child's thinking and speaking abilities and that language patterns vary according to socioeconomic class. As a result, children at higher status levels become better able to label, classify, analyze, conceptualize, and communicate than children at lower socioeconomic levels.[50]

Achievement motivation   There is some evidence that high achievement motivation is associated with certain childrearing patterns, namely, early independence training, encouragement of self-reliance, fewer restrictions, and holding high aspirations.[51] Such patterns would seem to be the opposite of the value orientations of lower-status families (passivity and conformity) and suggest rather the mastery and autonomy more likely to be found at higher status levels.

However, not only are differences in achievement socialization related to class; they are also related to gender. Female socialization at all class levels seems to reflect value orientations generally associated with lower-status levels; that is, girls more than boys are pointed in the direction of passivity and conformity, and boys more than girls are encouraged toward mastery and autonomy. The actual degree of gender typing varies by class, as we saw in Chapter 2, but elements of it are there at all status levels.

Sociologist Alice Rossi has shown that the qualities that have been shown to be characteristic of great scientists are the very qualities that have traditionally been discouraged in the childhood socialization of females: high intellectual ability, intense channeling of energy in the pursuit of work tasks, extreme independence, and apartness from others.[52] On a similar note, psychologist Lois Hoffman points out that socialization practices have usually encouraged females from earliest childhood to want to please others and to work for approval and love. Achievement in tasks is motivated by these learned *affiliative* needs, and "if achievement threatens affiliation, performance may be sacrificed or anxiety may result" (as we saw in Horner's studies). Boys, on the other hand, learn to value achievement much more for its own sake and to become involved in work for the sheer joy of mastering a challenging task.

In view of studies which show that gifted girls are less likely than gifted boys to fulfill their intellectual potential in adulthood, Hoffman's thesis is that females are not given adequate parental encouragement in early strivings toward independence.[53] Parents tend to worry over and protect girls more than boys, fostering dependence and discouraging feelings of confidence and competence. If one is female, there is also less pressure to develop one's own self-identity. "Separation of the self is facilitated when the child is the opposite sex of the primary caretaker," writes Hoffman. Since the mother is usually the primary caretaker, both male and female children form their first attachment to her. However, a boy is encouraged to identify with his father, which prompts an earlier and more complete separation from the primary caretaker and fosters the building of a sense of selfhood. "The girl, on the other hand, is encouraged to maintain her identification with the mother," Hoffman explains; "therefore she is not as likely to establish an early and independent sense of self." She also points out that boys more than girls engage in conflict with their mothers, another way in which the formation of a separate self is facilitated.

But perhaps more than building a sense of selfhood through *separation from* the mother, it is the male child's *identification with* the achiever role of the father that encourages greater autonomy. Hoffman is not unaware of that possibility and refers to studies which show that high-achieving females have also identified with their fathers. Changing attitudes and more egalitarian gender-role norms might show that a female's identification with the mother doesn't in itself hinder self-direction. "The significant factor may be identifying with a mother who is herself passive and dependent," Hoffman states. "If the mother were a mathematician, would the daughter's close identification be dysfunctional to top achievement?" Research is needed to answer that question, but already there is some evidence that the answer is no. Rather, close identification with such a mother might be likely to encourage the daughter to follow the mother's example and become an achiever herself. Other conditions conducive to female achievement are also more likely to be found in those families where the mother is professionally employed, namely, early independence training and a close relationship with a father "who encourages the girl's independence and achievement while accepting her as a female."[54]

Social Status and Child Discipline

The word *discipline* may be defined as training to act in accordance with certain standards, or it may be defined as chastisement or correction for failure to conform to such standards. Sociologist Leonard Pearlin refers to the

Identification with an achieving mother may encourage a daughter to become an achiever herself.

second sense of the word in speaking of discipline as "a systematic reaction to the behavior of children that parents judge to be either a direct threat to parental values and aspirations or an insufficient effort by children to attain these distant ideals."[55]

Pearlin's use of the word *systematic* is deliberate; he is making the point that although parents differ in disciplinary practices, these differences are patterned and cannot be explained simply as the result of personality variations or as momentary reactions to situations in which parents give vent to certain feelings. Pearlin's study of families in Turin, Italy, produced findings that correspond to Kohn's findings in the United States. According to their evidence, disciplinary practices in the home are tied to parental values; and parental values, as we have seen, are linked with social status.

Both middle-class and working-class parents emphasize control in the lives of children; but for middle-class parents the emphasis is on control from within (self-direction), whereas working-class parents stress control from without (obedience to rules and authority). Both social status and the sex of the misbehaving child enter into the reaction of parents with regard to discipline.

Kohn, for example, found that working-class mothers in his sample were more likely than middle-class mothers to employ physical punishment when children (particularly sons) engaged in wild play (boisterousness, aggressive behavior, belligerent and destructive actions) or when children fought with brothers and sisters. The focus was on "the direct and immediate consequences of the disobedient acts" rather than on perception of the child's motivations. From the mother's point of view, what has occurred in such a case is a violation of good order; such nonconformity to acceptable standards of behavior calls for punishment according to working-class values.

Middle-class mothers, on the other hand, were able to tolerate wild play even in its extreme forms. But they could *not* tolerate violent outbursts of temper. The overt behavior in the two instances might be exactly the same ("shouting, wrestling, slamming doors, stamping feet, running"), but what these mothers were concerned about was the child's intent rather than the situation itself. Children's rowdiness and excitement in play weren't viewed as alarming as long as their actions were perceived as "letting off steam." However, if the same actions were viewed as violent outbursts—temper tantrums resulting from a child's feeling frustrated at not getting his or her own way—middle-class mothers tended to resort to physical punishment. Why? Again, parental values seem to have been involved—in this case, the middle-class value of self-control. Parents refused to put up with behavior that indicated the loss of such control.[56]

Gender-based differences   Misbehavior in children may be thought of either in terms of their doing what they shouldn't do (as in the above illustrations) or in their *not* doing what they *should* do (refusing to carry out parents' requests). Kohn found that working-class mothers tended to punish sons for the first kind of misbehavior but not for the second kind. When boys defiantly refused to comply with their mothers' wishes, the mothers tended to refrain from any form of punishment and instead simply did nothing at all. But when daughters refused to do as they were told, they were swiftly punished. At this social-status level, "more is expected of girls than of boys," writes Kohn. "Girls must not only refrain from unacceptable behavior; they must also fulfill positive expectations."[57]

Working-class girls were more likely than boys at this level to be punished for such activities as smoking, swiping something, or fighting with friends. Once again we see the part class differences play in gender-role norms. Kohn points out that for working-class parents, "what may be taken as acceptable behavior (perhaps even as an assertion of manliness) in a preadolescent boy may be thought thoroughly unladylike in a young girl." Middle-class parents, in contrast, tend not to make such distinctions based on gender. Their main concern in matters of discipline is that children of either sex will act according to internalized principles.[58]

Types of discipline   In 1958, social psychologist Urie Bronfenbrenner published a comprehensive review of socialization studies from the 1930s onward. Bronfenbrenner was especially interested in class differences in childrearing, and one of his conclusions was this: "In matters of discipline, working-class parents are consistently more likely to employ physical punishment, while middle-class families rely more on reasoning, isolation, appeals to guilt, and other methods involving the threat of loss of love. . . ."[59]

However, in recent years a number of studies have caused sociologists to raise questions about alleged class differences in the usage of physical punishment, and inconsistencies in earlier studies are being reexamined as well.[60] Pearlin wrote of his Italian study: "By itself, class bears only a modest relationship to physical punishment: Only 8 percent more middle- than working-class parents reported that they had not resorted to any physical punishment in the past six months."[61]

Another sociologist, Murray Straus, found that 52 percent of a sample of university students had experienced actual or threatened physical punishment from their parents during the last year of high school; but there was no relationship between physical punishment and socioeconomic status. Straus was surprised that such class differences didn't show up—especially since the study showed that the highest frequency of physical punishment took place among students who reported their parents emphasized obedience as the most important characteristic of children, and the lowest frequency took place where parents considered self-control and thinking for oneself to be the most desired traits in children. Straus suggested that the explanation for the lack of differences according to class may lie in the fact that working-class students in the sample were from homes where upward mobility was emphasized and where parents had identified with higher-status values and socialization practices. Thus the incidence of physical punishment was no greater among them than among middle-class students.[62]

Kohn's research showed that mothers responded to children's misbehavior in numerous ways—ignoring it, scolding and admonishing, removing the child from the situation or diverting attention, restricting activities, isolating the child temporarily, or punishing the child physically ("everything from a slap to a spanking"). Both working-class and middle-class mothers reported that they generally ignored misbehavior or else admonished their children at this stage (Kohn's sample included only mothers of fifth-graders). Few reported using isolation or restriction, and even fewer punished physically under usual circumstances. Although there was a slight tendency for working-class mothers to be more likely than middle-class mothers to use physical punishment, coercion was not quickly resorted to in either class. Only *persistent* misbehavior was seen to call for punishment. "It would seem, then," says Kohn, "that the difference between middle- and working-class mothers' use of physical punishment is not in the frequency with which they use it, but in the conditions under which they use it"[63]—conditions which we have already examined.

There appears to be no direct relationship between the occasional use of physical discipline (slapping or spanking) and actual child abuse (injuring through beating, battering, and other cruelties). However, since the two behaviors have in common the use of physical force, they are sometimes confused. Child abuse is most likely to occur at the very lowest socioeconomic levels,[64] especially in the underclass of chronically unemployed and troubled families who lack resources for obtaining help or bettering their condition and may take out their frustrations on their children in outbursts of what we called "explosive violence" in Chapter 8. At the same time, the greater occurrence of child abuse at the lowest status levels does not mean that usage of physical means of child *discipline* necessarily increases to any great degree as socioeconomic status decreases, nor does it mean that lower-status parents in general favor child abuse.[65]

Discipline and achievement values   In the socialization process, parents seek to guide their children in the development of characteristics and behaviors which the parents consider to be important for the future—particularly as sons and daughters prepare to fit into the economic-opportunity system in some way. Evidence from the studies of Kohn and Pearlin suggests that the parents' values come from their own place in the economic structure, and these same values are then passed on so that children will find a place there that will quite often be similar to that of the parents. When children deviate from behavior consistent with the parents' values, discipline is employed. In this sense, discipline is an important part of socializing for achievement.[66]

NOTES

1   *The New York Times,* Apr. 5, 1975.
2   Elkin and Handel, 1972, chap. 1; Hess and Torney, 1967; Langton, 1969.
3   Waller, 1932, pp. 375–376, as quoted in Kohn, 1969, p. 192.
4   Haller and Miller, 1971; Slocum, 1966.
5   Milner, 1972.
6   Jencks et al, 1972, p. 8.
7   Jencks et al, 1972, pp. 8–11.
8   Coleman, 1973, p. 97.
9   Jencks et al, 1972, p. 14.
10   Edmonds et al, 1973, p. 43.
11   Edmonds et al, 1973, p. 47.
12   Coleman, 1973, p. 99.
13   Blau and Duncan, 1967, pp. 58–67.
14   Blau and Duncan, 1967, p. 295.
15   Sewell, 1971, p. 796.
16   See summary in Kerckhoff, 1972, pp. 105–108.
17   Blau and Duncan, 1967, p. 402.
18   Duncan, Featherman, and Duncan, 1972; Scanzoni, 1971; Hauser, 1972; Gasson, Haller, and Sewell, 1972; Kerckhoff, 1974.
19   Sewell and Hauser, 1974, p. 5.
20   Sewell, 1971, pp. 798–799.
21   Sewell, 1971, pp. 800–806.
22   Merton, 1959; Purcell, 1960; Mizruchi, 1964; Scanzoni, 1970, 1971.
23   Scanzoni, 1970, chap. 7.
24   Glenn, Ross, and Tully, 1974.

25 Sewell and Hauser, 1974, p. 253.
26 Sewell, 1971, p. 796.
27 Sewell, 1971, p. 804.
28 Horner, 1969, 1970, 1972.
29 Horner, 1969, p. 38.
30 Hoffman, 1972b.
31 Summarized in Hennig, 1973.
32 Hennig, 1973, p. 80.
33 Richer, 1968.
34 Richer, 1968, p. 463.
35 Richer, 1968, p. 463.
36 Winch, 1962; Winch and Gordon, 1974, chap. 3.
37 Kohn, 1969, p. 7.
38 Kohn, 1969, p. 200.
39 Kohn, 1969, p. 76.
40 Kohn, 1969, chap. 5.
41 Kohn, 1969, p. 34.
42 Kohn, 1969, chap. 4.
43 Scanzoni, 1971.
44 Hunter, 1973.
45 Kerckhoff, 1972, p. 56.
46 Kerckhoff, 1972, p. 57.
47 Scanzoni, 1971, p. 79.
48 Scanzoni, 1971, chap. 3.
49 Kohn, 1969, chap. 11.
50 See summary in Kerckhoff, 1972, pp. 48–52.
51 McClelland, 1961; also see Brown, 1965, chap. 9.
52 Rossi, 1965.
53 Hoffman, 1972b.
54 Hoffman, 1974, pp. 162–163; 1973, p. 213.
55 Pearlin, 1972, chap. 6.
56 Kohn, 1969, chap. 6.
57 Kohn, 1969, p. 101.
58 Kohn, 1969, pp. 105–106.
59 Bronfenbrenner, 1958, as quoted in Kerckhoff, 1972, p. 42.
60 Erlanger, 1974; also Straus, 1971.
61 Pearlin, 1972, p. 103.
62 Straus, 1971.
63 Kohn, 1969, pp. 93–95.
64 Gelles, 1973b; Erlanger, 1974.
65 Erlanger, 1974.
66 Pearlin, 1972, p. 99.

UNIT 5

CONTINUING PROCESSES OF MARITAL RELATIONSHIPS

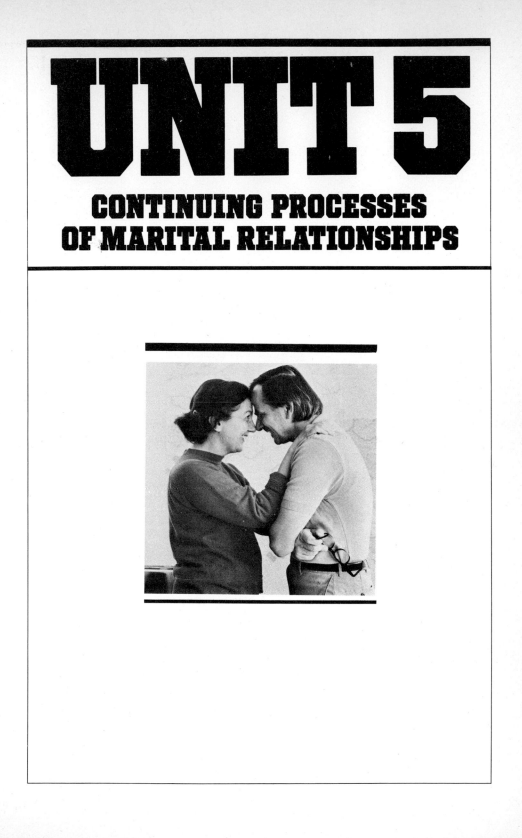

11
THE ONGOING AND UNDOING
OF MARRIAGES

"Wedding memories captured for a lifetime!" Tim announced the photographer's slogan dramatically as he unclasped the envelope and pulled out the white album containing his smiling image "captured for a lifetime" with that of his bride Trudy. He thought about the slogan for a moment: the "wedding part" was over and finished twenty-three years ago, but the "lifetime part" was right now. Somehow it all seemed different from what he had expected.

But Tim kept such thoughts to himself that night, as did others gathered in the apartment of Bob and Julie, the hypothetical couple we met in Chapter 8. It was Valentine's Day, and a group of friends were sharing wedding pictures and swapping stories of how each husband and wife had met. Bob's real estate co-worker Tim recounted the hilarious tale of how he had pursued Trudy even though she was engaged to another man. A younger couple, Larry and Sue, told of their unusual summer-long honeymoon in a Pacific Northwest fire tower, which provided the ultimate in privacy and pay besides! Rounding out the group were Julie's parents, combining a visit with a business trip. At Julie's request, they had brought their wedding photos from thirty-five years earlier.

On the surface, each couple appeared to have what popular magazines would describe as the "ideal" marriage. Each husband and wife seemed happy, they had pleasant memories of their weddings and afterwards, and their marriages were all still intact. Yet if we were to follow each one home, we would see beyond the surface picture to the realities of marriage as a process. Each couple's situation can help us understand more of what happens over the years as marriages go on—and off.

MID-MARRIAGE STAGE

When Tim and Trudy arrived home from the party that night, Tim startled his wife by saying, "I wish we were coming home from a swingers' party! Have you ever thought about that, Trudy—about what it would be like to get together with some couples for . . . well, *you* know?" Trudy replied that she certainly had not ever thought of such a thing, and she couldn't imagine what possessed her husband to make such a suggestion. "I've never been unfaithful to you in all our years of marriage!" she said emphatically. "And I hope your record is just as clear! I can't understand what's got into you. Isn't our marriage good enough? *I* think we have a pretty good relationship, don't you?" Her husband sighed. "Yeh, I guess so. But somehow something seems to be missing."

Disenchantment or "The Best Years of Our Lives"?

According to folk wisdom, as the years of marriage go on, the fires of love burn down. The theme is a familiar one in novels, plays, and films. "You just bite the nail and hang on," was the advice given by an elderly father to his middle-aged son in view of the son's marital discontent in Robert Anderson's drama *Double Solitaire.* A public-television presentation of 1975, the play took its title from the mother-in-law's counsel to the daughter-in-law. While the disenchanted husband heard his father's advice to "just remember, bite on the nail," the middle-aged wife was listening to the older woman's recipe for ongoing marital happiness: playing double solitaire. Most people of course play the card game alone, but, emphasized the mother-in-law, in marriage the spouses can play alone while together. A "double solitaire" marriage was exactly the kind of marriage the younger woman didn't want.

Descriptive literature by writers, family counselors, and a certain number of studies by behavioral scientists have also reinforced the belief that marriages deteriorate in the middle years. "By and large such observations are based on clinical experiences with persons who have so much difficulty in making the transition that they must seek outside help," writes researcher Irwin Deutscher, whose own findings did not support commonly held notions about the "empty nest" period of life when children are grown and gone and parents allegedly have little to bind them together any longer.

While cautioning that definite conclusions cannot be drawn from the

responses of such a small sample (49 urban, middle-class, postparental couples, forty to sixty-five years of age), Deutscher wrote that the majority of wives
and husbands viewed this stage of the family life cycle "as a time of new
freedoms." In particular, his respondents spoke of the freedom from economic
responsibility for the children, freedom to travel or move to another location,
freedom from housework and other tasks, "and finally, freedom to be one's self
for the first time since the children came along."[1]

At the same time, while many early reports of diminished marital satisfaction over time were based on little more than impressions and clinical findings, a
certain amount of data from more rigorous studies have supported such
findings.[2] For example, Blood and Wolfe's widely cited Detroit study produced
the finding that wives became less satisfied as the length of marriage increased.[3] And the Burgess/Wallen longitudinal study, begun in 1937 with 1,000
engaged couples and followed up twenty years after their marriages, showed
that among the 153 couples left from the original sample there was widespread
disenchantment, less intimacy, and decreased "marital adjustment."[4]

Our own studies have yielded inconsistent results, again showing the
uncertainty and need for further research in this area. In our large-scale study of
white Indianapolis husbands and wives, we found that, in general, satisfaction
with physical affection and companionship decreases over time, but satisfaction
with empathy (communication and understanding) increases—although there
are certain variations by socioeconomic status and sex that must be taken into
account.[5] In a more recent study, however, we found that the age of a wife or
husband (highly correlated with the stage of marriage in most cases) made
virtually no difference at all in how satisfactory both black and white persons
evaluated their marriages.[6] Marital satisfaction or dissatisfaction was found to
be tied to socioeconomic factors and perceptions of the wife's abilities rather
than to the number of years the couple had lived together.

Some studies have shown a decline in marital satisfaction during the
childbearing and childrearing stages, particularly for wives, but an increase in
satisfaction during the postparental years.[7] Sociologist Norval Glenn analyzed
data from six national surveys and also found that middle-aged wives whose
children had left home reported greater general happiness and greater marital
happiness than middle-aged wives with a child or children still at home.
Although he cautions against the assumption that the results would be the same
in the case of widows left entirely alone and acknowledges that there are
undoubtedly cases of individuals who experience negative effects from the
postparental stage, he makes the point that in general he did not find evidence
that "the 'empty nest' or postparental stage of the family life cycle is a traumatic
and unhappy period for the typical woman."[8]

Many of the discrepancies in the findings stem from methodological
considerations—sampling, how the studies were conducted, measurements
used, how the data were interpreted, and so on.[9] Until much more research is

conducted, however, we must avoid sweeping generalizations such as the assumption that once the honeymoon is ended, marital satisfaction is "downhill all the way." The middle years of marriage, including the "launching period" (when children are leaving home) and the "empty nest period" (when children are gone), may be very traumatic for some women who experience the period in terms of losing what they consider their most significant role—motherhood. But for other women, this period may be looked upon as bringing both new freedom to explore their own potential and greater opportunities for companionship with their husbands.

Similarly, with regard to the husband-wife relationship itself, some couples may feel that their marital satisfaction remains high or even increases over the years, while other couples experience a decline and may feel that the descriptive terms sometimes used for mid-marriage disappointment are on target. There may be "disenchantment" (a loss of enthusiasm for the partner and the relationship, a cooling of feelings), and there may be "disengagement" (lessened companionship and interaction between the spouses).[10] These are the marriages which sociologists John Cuber and Peggy Harroff have categorized as "devitalized" because of "the clear discrepancy between middle-aged reality and the earlier years." In such cases, the couples report that once they were closely identified with each other, shared many interests, spent a great deal of time together, and thoroughly enjoyed their sex life. Now things have changed, and they do things for and with each other out of duty more than out of the sense of love and delight in one another they once felt. According to Cuber and Harroff, although "the original zest is gone," those couples in their sample who fit into this category tended to "believe that the devitalized mode is the appropriate mode in which a man and a woman should be content to live in the middle years and later."[11]

In attempting to understand the complexities suggested by the various studies on changes in marital satisfaction over the years, perhaps we need to see even *more* complexities rather than trying to boil it all down to a simple truism, such as, "Marital satisfaction does (or doesn't) decline as time goes on." There are structural and situational factors—and not merely personality considerations—to keep in mind. If marital satisfaction is related to socioeconomic status, we need to consider changes in access to the economic-opportunity structure over the family life cycle. How does loss of employment on the one hand, or a sizable promotion on the other, affect satisfaction within marriage? How will the marital relationship be affected by a husband's feelings at middle age that he has not reached the goals of which he had dreamed? How will a wife's decision to seek employment after the children are grown and gone affect her relationship with her husband at this stage of life? Research is needed which takes such situations as these into account. Also, since some studies indicate that marital satisfaction decreases and levels out during the childrearing stages but increases again at the postparental stage,[12] questions need to be raised about the effect of children on a marriage rather than simply the effect of time. Comparative research on marital satisfaction among childless couples over the years would be fruitful in this regard.

The fact of personal growth and change with the passage of time needs also to be taken into consideration. Anthropologist Paul Bohannan, an authority on divorce, suggests that an inability to tolerate change in the spouse often lies at the root of the growing estrangement associated with a marital breakup.[13] As a person changes over the years, the rewards he or she offers to the spouse (and the costs to the spouse) are likely to change as well. This will require renegotiation such as that described in Chapter 8 if the couple is to reach new agreements of expectations so that each spouse experiences maximum joint profit.

Perhaps we might also speculate that a certain amount of disenchantment occurs because of unrealistic expectations stemming from romantic love. When the helplessness of "falling in love" and being swallowed up in a mystery beyond comprehension gives way to the daily routines of living together, a great deal of magic and passion may seem to disappear. In the words of psychoanalyst Erich Fromm: "After the stranger has become an intimately known person there are no more barriers to be overcome, there is no more sudden closeness to be achieved." Thus the exhilaration of falling in love may be sought with someone else, and once again "the stranger is transformed into an 'intimate' person." The intensity again becomes less and ends in the desire for a new adventure in romantic love—"always with the illusion that the new love will be different from the earlier ones."[14]

Subjective Evaluation of Marital Satisfaction

Marital satisfaction is really a subjective matter, depending upon how a marriage lives up to the expectations of the individuals concerned. One couple may consider their marriage deeply satisfying, whereas to an outsider the marriage may seem dull and undesirable. Whether or not wives and husbands are satisfied with their marriage relationship in the middle years depends upon the rewards they expected to receive and felt they deserved and whether or not these rewards materialize. In exchange-theory terms, we can think of Thibaut and Kelley's *comparison level* or CL, an imaginary point on a scale by which persons evaluate costs and rewards in a relationship (just as a certain point on a thermometer serves as the dividing line between temperatures above and below freezing). If the marital rewards minus costs are at a level that meets the expectations of the particular husband or wife, he or she rates the marital relationship above the comparison point (CL)—though the rating is not necessarily conscious. On the other hand, if the outcomes of a particular relationship (the rewards as compared to costs) fall below an individual's personal CL, the relationship will be rated unsatisfactory.[15]

It's possible that in some marriages the level of profit diminishes over the years so that the relationship ceases to be as rewarding as it once was. In other words, to one or both spouses, the marital relationship slides below the CL point. This may explain some cases of disenchantment in the middle years. In other cases, one or both spouses may *raise* their CL point and come to expect *more* from the marriage than they did earlier, with the result that the outcomes of the relationship may be evaluated quite differently than was once the case. A person may not be so easily satisfied as was true earlier in the marriage but may feel that he or she deserves a great deal more at this point in life.

Thibaut and Kelley also speak of another standard of comparison—the *comparison level for alternatives* or CL_{alt} . The CL_{alt} marks the lowest level of outcomes or profit a member of a relationship will accept in the light of available alternatives. Persons consider the reward/cost ratio of the best other situation available to them and weigh the anticipated profit there against their present situation. For example, a husband or wife might have reason to believe that the rewards minus costs in a relationship with a third party would yield greater profit than in the present relationship with the spouse. In some cases, this might mean divorce; in other cases, an extramarital "affair" might result.

Seeking Rewards Outside the Marital Relationship

One of the points made by O'Neill and O'Neill in *Open Marriage* is that the "closed marriage" notion is unrealistic in that it "calls for the two partners to be all things to one another, to fulfill all of one another's needs—emotional, psychological, intellectual, and physical."[16] The authors suggest that women and men need other persons with whom they can share interests, ideas, and activities and can open up certain aspects of their personalities in ways not possible with their mates. Perhaps one partner feels a need for a kindred spirit to share a love of poetry or tennis or music or mechanics—an area in which the spouse has no interest. Why should the "togetherness" of marriage keep a husband or wife from spending time with a third party who shares the particular interest? Many couples today consider the question a valid one and believe that husbands and wives should be free to pursue a variety of outside friendships both with persons of the same sex and persons of the opposite sex. Furthermore, such couples feel they should be able to do so without letting jealousy come into the picture.

The catch comes in the area of sex. If a person feels he or she desires greater variety in sex or simply feels the spouse isn't meeting his or her sexual needs, is the option open to seek sexual rewards with somebody else in the same way that one might seek companionship rewards based on common interests in sports or music?[17]

The definition of marriage utilized in this book includes the publicly acknowledged economic and sexual interdependence of two persons (or more in polygamous societies). Sexual exclusivity and sexual possessiveness have been ideals bound up in the notion of marriage as we know it in our society; the two spouses belong to one another and have unique rights of sexual access to one another. *Adultery* is the legal term for having sexual intercourse with someone other than one's own spouse, and it is negatively sanctioned by public opinion, the law (it is grounds for divorce), and Jewish and Christian religious teachings ("Thou shalt not commit adultery" is one of the Ten Commandments).

According to the 1974 National Opinion Research Center's national survey, 73 percent of adults consider extramarital sex to be "always wrong," as compared to 32 percent who answered that they consider premarital sex to be "always wrong." Sociologist Robert Bell suggests two reasons for the stronger societal disapproval of extramarital sex than of premarital sex: First, since a married person already has a socially approved partner to meet his or her sexual needs, it is assumed that there is no good reason to pursue outside sexual experience. Second, it is believed that sexual involvement outside of marriage will threaten the individual's marriage relationship.[18] Thus, the condemnation of adultery is part of societal concern for the institution of the family.

Nevertheless, it is common knowledge that some married persons do have sexual intercourse with persons other than their spouses. The exact incidence of extramarital sex today is not known, although in the Kinsey studies of the 1940s it was found that by the age of forty, half of the married men in their sample and slightly over a quarter of the married women had experienced extramarital sex. Kinsey and his associates referred to problems of jealousy encountered by many persons who reported extramarital coitus, with divorce as an outcome in a number of cases. The researchers concluded: "These data once again emphasize the fact that the reconciliation of the married individual's desire for coitus with a variety of sexual partners, and the maintenance of a stable marriage, presents a problem which has not been satisfactorily resolved in our culture."[19]

Mate Swapping

"Swing your partner!" is no longer just a square-dance call. The phenomenon of "swinging" (sometimes called "consensual adultery" or "spouse swapping") is being incorporated into the life-style of some married couples today who see it as a way to solve the dilemma posed by Kinsey—a have-your-cake-and-eat-it solution in which a person can enjoy sexual variety, a number of partners, and a stable marriage all at the same time. Some researchers have found that couples involved in swinging claim they have never participated in extramarital sex. To such couples, the term *extra* connotes the idea of something external to the marriage, whereas swinging is defined as a part of the marriage—a mutually agreed upon sexual experience.[20] Two researchers on the subject, James Smith and Lynn Smith, suggest that *co-marital sex* is a more accurate term for situations of consensual adultery in which both spouses participate.[21] (In another form of consensual adultery, either or both may have sexual intercourse outside the marriage but with the spouse's knowledge and consent, even though they do not participate at the same time or place as in swinging. Both forms of consensual adultery are in contrast to what the Smiths call "conventional adultery" which is characterized by concealment and deception.)

Sociologist Mary Lindenstein Walshok emphasizes that co-marital sex involves two distinctive qualities: (1) an agreement between a husband and wife that they will have sexual relationships with others, "but in contexts in which they *both* engage in such behavior at the same time and usually in the same place" (perhaps in different rooms but under the same roof) and (2) that these sexual experiences will take place in an organized framework rather than permitting such experiences to occur spontaneously.[22] Another team of sociologists refers to swinging as an *institutionalized* form of extramarital sex.[23] In other words, swinging is taking on the characteristics of an established, structured form of behavior. Swingers have their own subculture, including rules and norms. (Although there are regional differences, participants are expected to learn and conform to certain behaviors—a kind of swingers' "etiquette," which may include such matters as waiting for the host to give the signal at a party by disrobing first.[24]) The subculture of swinging also has its ideologies, its taboos (against gossip, and usually against emotional involvement and against male homosexuality—although female homosexual practices are encouraged), its communication networks, and its jargon (including code words for various sexual techniques and preferences). A number of swingers' organizations and magazines exist, and their classified ads provide one way interested couples find out about each other. Underground newspapers, clubs, personal referrals, and parties in homes are also ways persons interested in swinging may get together.

At present no valid data is available on the actual incidence of co-marital sex. Crude estimates arrived at by projecting from limited studies, subscriptions to swingers' magazines, and so on, have ranged from half a million couples upward.[25] Most studies have agreed that the types of people who participate in swinging are usually white-collar—and some skilled blue-collar—persons from a variety of occupations. (Physicians, lawyers, dentists, professors, high school teachers, airline pilots, salesmen, owners of small businesses, electricians, plumbers, housewives, and truck drivers have been represented in some studies.) For the most part, researchers have reported the level of education among swingers to be high, and the couples are generally considered to be conventional, somewhat conservative, and "very straight" in areas of life other than their swinging. Ages of swingers have ranged from the late teens to seventy.[26]

According to O'Neill and O'Neill, married couples decide to participate in co-marital sex for a number of reasons: Some spouses feel "they need more sex than their spouse provides." Others may be happy with their marriage relationship but yet feel that marital exclusivity is confining; the structured context of co-marital sex is viewed as a way to explore sex outside of marriage. Others are simply bored with sex with only one person over time and consider swinging as a "stimulant" or "sexual turn-on." And there are some who try group sex in a desperate effort to patch up a failing marital relationship.[27] Sociologist Carolyn Symonds found that swinging sometimes has appeal to persons who feel vague dissatisfaction in marriage or who "have come to a point in their marriage where they feel a desire to expand or experiment."[28]

Most studies have found that swinging was first suggested by husbands and also that men more than women initiate the sexual encounters at swinging parties—though women at swinging parties may covertly express preferences for certain men and provide clues to let them know of their interest and availability.[29] Some researchers point out that many wives are hesitant about swinging at first and participate only to please their husbands, but that eventually they may come to enjoy it as much or more than their husbands.[30] On the other hand, a study of drop-out swingers who later visited marriage counselors revealed that wives are usually the ones who want to discontinue participation in co-marital sex.[31]

Sociologists Michael Gordon and Duane Denfeld suggest that the change in attitudes toward female sexuality, along with improved contraception, "is likely to have greatly increased the incentive for women to seek—as men have always done—sexual variety outside marriage"; and out of all available ways for both spouses to have such variety, "mate swapping is the least threatening and the one most compatible with monogamy." Swinging for recreation is viewed by the spouses as something that is only physical and unlike their marital sex which they view in terms of love and emotional involvement. Swinging involves rules (such as not getting together with sex partners outside designated swinging sessions) so that emotional attachments are discouraged and jealousy kept to a minimum. According to Denfeld and Gordon, swinging is not considered an alternative to monogamous marriage nor intended to disrupt the husband-wife relationship. Rather it may be viewed as "a strategy to revitalize marriage, to bolster a sagging partnership." Hence, the belief among swingers that "the family that swings together clings together."[32] Smith and Smith make a similar point, viewing swinging as an evolutionary development that in the long run could be supportive of marriage by redefining the boundaries of marriage through the incorporation of extramarital sex into the relationship.[33]

Other researchers call for caution. One study indicated that while some couples could incorporate swinging into their life-styles without apparent difficulty, other couples might find their marriage relationship deteriorating as a result.[34] Denfeld's study of reports from marriage counselors on reasons couples drop out of swinging found that in nearly a quarter of the cases, jealousy was the main reason. Some of the other reasons were guilt, threatening the marriage relationship, becoming emotionally involved with other sexual partners, boredom and disappointment when swinging didn't live up to expectations and fantasies, and fear of discovery by the community and by the couple's children.[35]

Denfeld emphasizes that until a probability sample of past, present, and future swingers is used as the basis of a study, there will be many gaps in our knowledge of co-marital sex and its effects on the husband-wife relationship. Thus, while our hypothetical couple, Tim and Trudy, might discuss swinging as a possible way to add zest to a marriage that has become routinized and lost some of its vitality over the years, there is no way at this point to know for certain (on the basis of the limited research evidence available) whether incorporating co-marital sex into their lives would improve or damage their particular relationship.

DIVORCE

In his classic study of divorce and readjustment, sociologist Willard Waller wrote of a couple's teamwork in maintaining "the polite fiction" that all is well in their marriage even though they are moving toward divorce. The societal norm that family matters are private matters usually means that husbands and wives are reluctant to air their grievances or quarrel in front of their mutual friends. During the process of alienation leading toward divorce, the couple may make deliberate attempts to manage their impressions on others—in a sense giving what sociologist Erving Goffman speaks of as "a performance," trying to control how others see their situation. They are likely to act as they think they *should* act because others expect married couples to act in certain ways—even though such actions may be contrary to the realities of their particular case.[36]

Larry and Sue, another of the hypothetical couples at the Valentine's Day party, went home confident that their friends had no idea that they were in the process of breaking up their marriage. When they announced their divorce plans a few months later, their friends were shocked and couldn't believe it. Psychiatrist Arthur Miller points out that such reactions are among a number of feelings friends may experience in such situations. The impending divorce may cause friends to seriously examine their own marriages, and they may feel anxious and threatened. Sometimes there has been an idealization of the marriage of the divorcing couple, and the model with which one identified suddenly seems to be crumbling, bringing a sense of disillusionment as well as emotional loss.[37]

Marital Dissolution as a Process

Just as marriage is a process, so is divorce. Marriage, as we saw in Chapters 7 and 8, is an ongoing exchange of rights and duties, rewards and costs. Marriage involves negotiating and renegotiating again and again. But sometimes the bargaining breaks down. The old pact no longer seems satisfactory to one or both; yet the couple seem unable to strike a new deal on which they can agree. One may try to coerce the other, seeking to get the conflict regulated rather than resolving it. This approach tends only to increase hostility and bitterness, especially when the coercion is viewed by the other spouse as an exercise of nonlegitimate power. The trust element and concern for maximum joint profit is damaged. "If you really wanted what is best for me and for our marriage, you wouldn't be ordering me to do something against my will!" says one spouse. But the other counters: "If you wanted what's best for *me* and cared about what *I* feel is best for our marriage, you wouldn't be resisting me. You'd go along with what I want."

Such was Larry and Sue's situation. Their honeymoon on top of a fire look-out tower in a forest provided an early clue to Larry's love for the outdoors. He hated the city life that meant so much to Sue, but Sue felt things would work out over the years. They could live in the city and vacation in the country. However, Larry became restless and became increasingly determined to move to a well-established, self-supporting rural commune with humanitarian goals and pro-grams. Careful investigation showed that he could use his management skills and perform useful social service while being in an environment he enjoyed. Sue cringed at the notion of living in a farm setting but was even more stunned by Larry's suggestion that she quit her courses in architecture at the university. It would mean an end to her dreams of working in the city where they lived and where there were already indications of a job for her after graduation. But Larry saw nothing out of order about his request, saying wives have always been willing to follow husbands and make sacrifices.

Over the months, Larry and Sue grew increasingly distant from each other. Their interests and life-goals seemed to pull them apart, and they found it harder to talk together about things that really mattered. Certain subjects (careers, life-styles, gender roles) were particularly explosive, didn't lend themselves to discussion and negotiation, and eventually came to be avoided entirely. Where each had once felt reinforced by the other, both now felt that the other was almost like an altogether different person, no longer providing the rewards of emotional support that had meant so much to the other's self-esteem. Instead, there were now psychic punishments—nagging, criticism, smoldering resent-ment, searching for faults to complain about, and a tendency to tear down instead of building each other up as they had once done. These punishments, along with the diminishing rewards, made the relationship seem increasingly costly to maintain. The CL and CL_{alt} of each spouse were affected. Outside alternatives became more and more attractive (for Larry, the prospect of living among like-minded persons and finding encouragement and meaningful activi-ty in the commune; for Sue, the prospect of freedom to pursue her career interests unhindered). The thought of divorce alarmed them at first—they had thought such a thing could never happen to them—but it seemed the only way.

For the couple heading toward divorce, highly valued emotional rewards seem to diminish, and psychic punishments are experienced instead.

Bohannan's "six stations of divorce"   The process Sue and Larry underwent corresponds to what anthropologist Paul Bohannan calls the *emotional divorce*. Divorce may seem perplexing because so many things are taking place at once. Bohannan has isolated six aspects or overlapping experiences involved in each divorce.[38] The emotional divorce centers around the deteriorating marriage relationship. The husband and wife "may continue to work together as a social team, but their attraction and trust for one another have disappeared," writes Bohannan. "The emotional divorce is experienced as an unsavory choice between giving in and hating oneself and domineering and hating oneself. . . . Two people in emotional divorce grate on each other because each is disappointed."

While the emotional divorce is taking place, other aspects of divorce may also be occurring. There is the *legal divorce* (the obtaining of an actual decree), the *economic divorce* (the settlement of money matters and the division of property), the *coparental divorce* (decisions about the custody of any children, visitation rights, each parent's responsibilities, and so on), the *community divorce* (changes in ways friends and others in the community react as the couple's divorce becomes known), and the *psychic divorce* (the sense of becoming uncoupled and regaining a sense of identity as an individual rather than one of a pair).

New life after divorce   Personal adjustment after divorce was a neglected area of study until Waller published his research and theoretical insights on the subject in 1930. A quarter of a century went by before another significant sociological work was published in an effort to understand how persons reorganize their lives after divorce—this time research on divorced women conducted in the Detroit metropolitan area by William Goode. More recently, both behavioral scientists and family counselors have been increasingly focusing attention on post-divorce problems and challenges.[39]

Goode saw the process of readjustment in terms of changes in roles. A person leaves the role of husband or wife and must take on a new role. There are also changes and disruptions in existing social relationships when one is no longer part of a married pair. Post-divorce adjustment, according to Goode, involves incorporating such changes and disruptions into the individual's life in such a way that he or she moves beyond thinking of the prior divorce as the "primary point of reference." In other words, the person ceases to think in terms of "I am an ex-wife (or ex-husband)" but rather in terms of being an individual in one's own right.[40]

Divorce involves a time of transition and grief, which isn't always easy since societal expectations are unclear (people wonder whether to extend sympathy or congratulations after a divorce), and support is often lacking both with regard to the mourning process itself and in terms of helping persons cope with building a new life.[41] Divorce counselor Mel Krantzler speaks of divorce as "the death of a relationship" and suggests that a time of grief is essential for emotional healing just as when an actual person dies. In divorce, the individual is not necessarily mourning the fact that the ex-spouse is gone or wishing that he or she would return—the divorce itself signifies their disinclination to live together satisfactorily. What is happening is grief over the loss of the rewards no longer held out by the relationship, a realization that (in the words of a film title and song, popular in the 1970s) "the way we were" has ended. The enrichment found in the marital partnership has ceased to exist. The net profit is gone.

There is a sense of diminishment of one's very own self in the loss. Waller recognized this when he wrote:

> There is always an element of betrayal when we break with a friend, and our distress is made all the more poignant because we have betrayed not only the friend but the part of us that was in him. . . . The pathos of a marital break attaches . . . to the very essence of the process by which

those who have been one flesh are made separate. Personalities that have been fused by participation in common enterprises and that are held together by their common memories can only be hewn apart at the expense of great psychic travail.[42]

Persons who once learned to live together must now undergo learning to live apart. The interdependence, the daily routines, the regularized sex life, the companionship, the built-in habit systems that have developed over time as the two persons shared a life together—all are changed by divorce.

The adjustment is often difficult. The individual may begin longing for the ex-spouse and the rewards the relationship once held, even though he or she knows this chapter in life is closed and indeed may want it to remain closed. "The memory of a person [may be] dear after the person is dear no more," observed Waller.[43] He writes of a man who reported looking for the mail to arrive at all times of the day, even though he knew there couldn't possibly be any more for him. The man had ambivalent feelings, both longing for and dreading letters from his ex-wife.[44]

At the time of the breakup, the marriage partners may expect the divorce to bring feelings of relief and happiness and may be surprised at the sadness and moments of nostalgia that come up. Part of the reason may lie in what Bohannan sees as a *reversal* of the courtship process and the "rewarding sensation" of knowing one has been selected out of the whole world. Divorce means being de-selected, and "it punishes almost as much as the engagement and the wedding are rewarding."[45]

Yet for many couples, an unsatisfactory marriage can be more punishing than divorce. Krantzler quotes poet-novelist Herman Hesse, himself twice divorced, to show that divorce may open the way for some persons to experience a new exchange of rewards and a creative, fulfilling life that would have been impossible otherwise. "Be ready bravely and without remorse," wrote Hesse, "to find new light that old ties cannot give."[46]

Total Picture

Questions sometimes arise as to how widespread divorce is. One common way demographers measure marital dissolution is through the *crude divorce rate:* the number of divorces per 1,000 persons in the population. Figure 11-1 shows trends in marriage and divorce rates over a hundred-year-period.

In 1867, when divorce statistics first began to be collected, there were about 0.5 divorces per 1,000 population. For the next sixty years, the divorce rate increased consistently, rising about 75 percent every twenty years. Had this pattern continued, the divorce rate in 1947 would have been 2.8. Instead, a very steep rise occurred in the 1940s. Most observers attribute the sharp increase to the high number of "quickie marriages" that took place amidst the uncertainties and upheavals of that period. If G.I. Joe wouldn't be back "till it's over, over

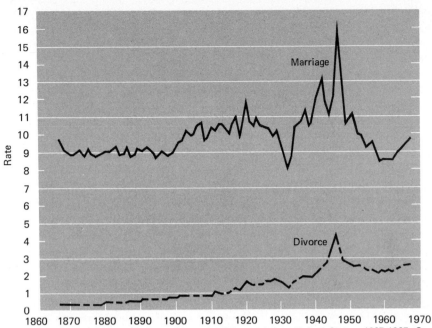

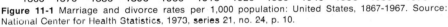

Figure 11-1 Marriage and divorce rates per 1,000 population: United States, 1867-1967. Source: National Center for Health Statistics, 1973, series 21, no. 24, p. 10.

there," why postpone the wedding any longer? But as World War II came to an end, so did many of the hastily entered marriages it had spawned. The divorce rate in 1946 shot up to an all-time high—4.3 divorces per 1,000 population.

Then, just as suddenly, the rate fell again and leveled off during the 1950s, remaining at about 2.1 to 2.3 until 1963. That year the plateau ended and another climb began.[47] Within ten years the rate had nearly doubled, even exceeding the 1946 figure. For every thousand persons in 1973, there were 4.4 divorces; and by 1974, the divorce rate was 4.6.[48]

Using *all* persons in the population as a base on which to calculate divorces presents a problem since many persons aren't "at risk" when it comes to divorce (children and unmarried adults). Demographers therefore sometimes use a more refined way of measuring divorces, taking only married women as the base. This pattern, however, turns out to show the same trends as the crude measure. In 1946, there were 17.9 divorces per 1,000 married women; but by 1963, that figure had dropped to 9.6. In 1973 (latest available figures), 18.2 divorces took place for every thousand married women.[49]

We must keep in mind, of course, that the word "every" shouldn't be taken too literally. By presenting global divorce rates, we are simply trying to bring the divorce picture into perspective in order to gain an overall view. But other

factors enter in, making the likelihood of divorce greater within some populations than others. For example, if we were to look at a group of a thousand
married women who had married very young, had little education, and whose
family income was low, the number of divorces would be much higher than the
number of divorces among another thousand women who had married later and
who had more education and higher family incomes.

Cross-national comparisons   Thinking in terms of "global" divorce rates may
raise the question: How does the United States compare with other parts of the
globe in terms of divorce trends? A glance at crude divorce rates collected by
the United Nations (Table 11-A) will dispel any notion that the United States is
unique in its rising divorce rate.

　　Almost all countries shown in the table report increases in divorce rates—
especially Scotland and the Soviet Union where rates doubled. Sociologists, in
pointing out that trends toward higher divorce rates are "practically worldwide,"
tend to view the phenomenon as an inevitable feature of modern societies.
Rising divorce rates seem to be a by-product of industrialization and urbanization.[50] Why? Because modernization cuts across ideological, cultural, and
national boundaries, making nations highly interdependent and structurally
similar. Consequences of these interdependencies and similarities may be seen
not only in matters of energy distribution, inflation, raw-material allocations,
and the like, but also in marriage, family, and divorce patterns. Especially
noteworthy in this regard are the demands of women throughout the world for
greater autonomy, rights, privileges, and rewards.[51]

What divorce statistics tell us   Sometimes sensationalized reporting of divorce figures in the mass media has given the impression that the family is
"falling apart" and that marriage as an institution is more costly than rewarding
and is therefore "on its way out." However, if that were true, remarriage would
not be so popular. "According to the latest information available," writes Paul C.
Glick of the Bureau of the Census, "about four out of every five of those who
obtain a divorce will eventually remarry." At the very time that divorce rates were
rising in the 1960s, the tendency for divorced persons to remarry also increased.
Evidently, men and women who decided on divorce weren't so much interested
in getting out of marriage per se so much as in getting out of a particular
marriage where the costs seemed to exceed the benefits. Government statistics
show that far more divorced persons than widowed persons remarry. In 1969,
for example, 221 out of every thousand divorced men remarried, while only 39
out of every thousand widowers married again. And out of every thousand
divorced women, 135 remarried, whereas the remarriage rate among widows
was 10 per 1,000.[52] Also, as we saw in Table 5-A in Chapter 5, divorced persons
enter marriage at higher rates than do persons entering marriage for the first
time.

TABLE 11-A DIVORCE RATES PER 1,000 TOTAL POPULATION: UNITED STATES AND SELECTED FOREIGN COUNTRIES, 1962–1969 [Countries are listed according to the size of their latest available divorce rate]

Country	1969	1968	1967	1966	1965	1964	1963	1962
United States	3.17	2.93	2.65	2.55	2.47	2.35	2.27	2.22
U.S.S.R.	2.56	2.72	2.74	2.77	1.56	1.47	1.30	1.34
Hungary	2.13[1]	2.08	2.07	2.03	2.01	1.95	1.82	1.73
United Arab Republic (Egypt)[2]	1.94	1.89[1]	1.85	2.10	2.17	2.15	2.11	2.03
Denmark	1.83	1.56	1.43	1.40	1.37	1.37	1.38	1.38
East Germany	1.69[3]	1.68[3]	1.55	1.50	1.44	1.51	1.33	1.36
Czechoslovakia	1.66[1]	1.51	1.39	1.42	1.32	1.20	1.22	1.20
Sweden	1.52	1.42	1.36	1.32	1.24	1.20	1.12	1.17
Austria	1.35	1.32	1.21	1.19	1.16	1.16	1.14	1.12
England and Wales	1.04	0.93	0.88	0.80	0.78	0.72	0.67	0.61
German Federal Republic	---	1.03	1.00	0.92	0.93	0.91	0.84	0.82
Poland	1.01	0.91	0.85	0.77	0.75	0.67	0.64	0.59
Switzerland	0.96	0.91	0.86	0.82	0.84	0.83	0.82	0.83
Japan	0.90	0.87	0.84	0.81	0.79	0.75	0.73	0.75
Australia	0.89	0.89	0.82	0.85	0.75	0.71	0.69	0.68
Israel	0.84	0.87	0.80	0.85	0.90	0.89	0.95	0.92
Scotland	0.81	0.92	0.58	0.68	0.51	0.46	0.43	0.39
France	0.76	0.73	0.75	0.74	0.72	0.69	0.63	0.65
Netherlands	0.71	0.64	0.59	0.55	0.50	0.51	0.49	0.48
Belgium	0.67	0.63	0.63	0.61	0.59	0.58	0.56	0.51
Mexico	0.62	0.54	0.72	0.65	0.58	0.49	0.48	0.45
Canada	---	0.55[1]	0.55	0.51	0.46	0.45	0.41	0.36
Romania	0.35	0.20	0.00[4]	1.35	1.94	1.86	1.92	2.04
Venezuela	---	0.23	0.25	0.25	0.26	0.25	0.25	0.22
Portugal	0.05	0.08	0.08	0.07	0.08	0.07	0.07	0.08

[1]Provisional.
[2]Includes "revocable divorces" among the Moslem population which are similar to legal separations.
[3]Includes data for East Berlin.
[4]0.00 indicates rate greater than 0 but less than 0.005.

Source: United Nations, *Demographic Yearbook,* 1968 and 1971. As presented in National Center for Health Statistics: *Vital and Health Statistics,* series 21, no. 22, "Divorces: Analysis of Changes, United States, 1969," Public Health Service, U.S. Government Printing Office, Washington, D.C., April, 1973, p. 29.

Evidently these second marriages are quite satisfactory to most couples involved, because divorce "repeaters" are fewer than is sometimes assumed in popular thought. For example, in June 1971, there were almost 4.4 million women between twenty and forty-nine years of age who had been married more than once. The great majority (74 percent) were in an *intact* second marriage. Only 9 percent were in a third or subsequent intact marriage. (The remaining 17 percent included wives whose second marriages may have ended in widowhood or divorce, or they may have been separated, but they had not married a third time.)[53]

Census data do not necessarily indicate widespread disenchantment with marriage but rather that persons appear to expect *more* from that institution and are less willing to settle for relationships that do not live up to their expectations. At the same time, we must keep in mind that the statistics also show that most people are *not* getting divorced. For example, government figures for 1971 showed that among couples where the husband was in the age range of forty-five to fifty-one years, 80 percent of white couples and 64 percent of black couples had only ever been married once.[54] Among the remaining percentages, not all the marriages had been dissolved by divorce; some husbands and wives had lost spouses through death.

Not only are many divorced persons remarrying, and not only do the vast majority of first marriages remain intact, but another factor also needs to be remembered in looking at divorce data: *Divorce rates are not randomly distributed among the population.* Divorce occurs mostly among the young (persons in their twenties and below) and among persons who haven't been married very long. Also we must take into consideration race and socioeconomic factors if we are to gain an accurate picture of marital dissolution.

Age, duration of marriage, and divorce   According to the Census Bureau, "persons who marry when they are relatively young are about twice as likely to obtain a divorce as persons who marry when they are older."[55] As Figure 11-2 illustrates, not only do *more* divorces occur among those married in their teens or early twenties, but the biggest *increase* in divorces has been occurring within this segment of the population as well.

Reality is clouded somewhat by speaking of overall divorce rates without taking into account that the rates are much higher among younger than among older persons. The instability of teenage marriages, however, doesn't always show up in teenage divorce statistics because the persons involved may have left their teens by the time the marriage breaks up and the divorce decree is finalized.[56] Table 11-B shows the ages of husbands and wives at the time their divorce decrees were granted. Notice how much higher the rates are at lower age levels.

This table also indicates that the practice of "waiting until the children are grown and gone" may not be as common as is popularly assumed. There are such cases, to be sure; but statistically, such occurrences are not great. The older couples become, the less likely they are to divorce—especially after the early thirties when divorce rates drop sharply. Half the divorces in the United

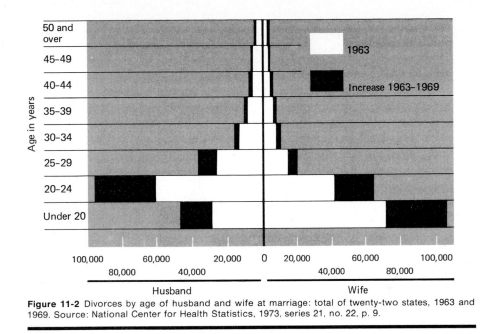

Figure 11-2 Divorces by age of husband and wife at marriage: total of twenty-two states, 1963 and 1969. Source: National Center for Health Statistics, 1973, series 21, no. 22, p. 9.

States take place within the first seven years of marriage; and by the time fourteen years of married life have gone by, three-fourths of those couples who will become divorced will have done so.[57] But age and duration of marriage are not the only considerations to keep in mind in assessing divorce rates.

Race and divorce Census findings indicate that "in 1970, blacks were less likely than whites to have their first marriage intact."[58] Among men who had ever been married, 60 percent of the blacks and 77 percent of the whites were living with their first wives. Among women who had ever been married, almost half of the blacks and nearly two-thirds of the whites were living with their first husbands. Black marriages were found to be dissolved by both divorce and widowhood to a greater extent than white marriages.

In 1974, 62 percent of black families were husband-wife families, but another 34 percent were headed by females (compared to 10 percent of white families). Close to half of the black female heads of families had experienced marital disruption by separation or divorce. (The remainder were single, widowed, or temporary heads during the absence of husbands for military service or other reasons.)[59]

But why should black marriages be less stable than those of whites? A sentence from a census report provides a clue: "Black men . . . with incomes of $10,000 or more in 1969 were more likely than men with lower income—under

TABLE 11-B ESTIMATED NUMBER OF DIVORCES AND DIVORCE RATES, BY AGE OF HUSBAND AND WIFE AT TIME OF DECREE: UNITED STATES, 1969 [Rates computed per 1,000 married population in each age-sex group.]

Age at Time of Decree	Husband		Wife	
	Number of Divorces	Divorce Rate	Number of Divorces	Divorce Rate
Total	639,000	13.8	639,000	13.4
Under 20 years	5,800	19.0	27,900	28.2
20–24 years	102,000	34.0	153,700	30.7
25–29 years	139,800	27.7	136,200	24.3
30–34 years	102,700	21.8	89,800	17.8
35–39 years	81,600	17.0	73,700	14.6
40–44 years	73,300	14.1	63,200	11.7
45–54 years	90,600	9.3	68,800	7.1
55–64 years	32,100	4.3	20,200	3.1
65 years and over	11,200	1.9	5,500	1.4

Source: National Center for Health Statistics: *Vital and Health Statistics,* series 21, no. 22, "Divorces: Analysis of Changes, United States, 1969," Public Health Service, U.S. Government Printing Office, Washington, D.C., April, 1973, p. 8.

$3,000—to have a wife living with them." Similarly, black men who had completed high school were more likely still to be married to their first wives than were blacks who had not completed high school.[60] In other words, educational and economic opportunity have a great deal to do with marital stability. But because of discriminatory practices in a white-dominated society, blacks have not had equal access to such opportunities. While blacks in 1969 had greater chances of having intact marriages if their income reached or exceeded $10,000, their chances were cut by the very fact that only 27 percent of blacks had incomes at this level. But 53 percent of white families that year had incomes of $10,000 or above.[61] And since then, there has been a continuing pattern in which the percentage of $10,000-and-up white families is about 30 percent more than the percentage of black families at this income level.[62]

Socioeconomic status and divorce Over the years, numerous reports from census data both in the United States and in other developed nations has shown that social status and marital stability are positively related: the greater the social status, the greater the marital stability.[63] Table 11-C shows how both higher income and higher levels of education are associated with increased marital stability and lower divorce.

Reasons for the association between socioeconomic status and marital stability were already discussed in Chapters 6 through 8. There we saw the part

TABLE 11-C PERCENTAGE IN EACH EDUCATION AND INCOME CATEGORY IN WHICH BOTH MARITAL PARTNERS HAVE BEEN MARRIED ONLY ONCE, FOR MARRIED COUPLES WITH THE HUSBAND 35 TO 54 YEARS OLD: SURVEY DATE, JUNE 1971

	Both Husband and Wife Married Only Once
Family Income	
Under $5,000	71.7%
$5,000 to $9,999	77.2%
$10,000 to $14,999	80.8%
$15,000 and above	83.0%
Education	
Neither partner high school graduate	75.0%
Both husband and wife high school graduates	83.1%
Husband and wife college graduates	90.4%

Source: U.S. Bureau of the Census, *Current Population Reports,* Series P-20, No. 239 "Marriage, Divorce, and Remarriage by Year of Birth: June 1971," U.S. Government Printing Office, Washington, D.C., 1972, pp. 2, 71-74.

played by an exchange of resources in terms of fulfilling marital rights and duties, and we saw how satisfaction with the instrumental and expressive sides of marriage is closely linked to socioeconomic factors. High marital satisfaction indicates that the partners view the relationship as providing rewards to a greater degree than it exacts costs. Why leave a situation where the profit margin is high? On the other hand, one or both partners may perceive the reward/cost ratio to be so low that the relationship doesn't seem worth maintaining—particularly if alternatives outside the marriage promise greater benefits. Then the question ceases to be "Why leave?" and becomes instead "Why stay?"

Exchange theory also helps us see why particular social groups have higher rates of marital dissolution. For example, the heavy concentration of divorce among young persons cannot be adequately understood until we think in terms of economic factors. Persons with lower education tend to marry earlier. They also tend to hold more traditional gender-role norms and therefore prefer the head-complement form of marriage—or at most, a senior partner–junior partner arrangement. Such wives are socialized to want their husbands to provide for them; yet the lower education and resulting lower incomes of their husbands tend to result in less marital satisfaction and a greater likelihood of divorce. If the wife does go to work, the husband may feel threatened by her independent resources to a far greater extent than would a husband with a higher level of education. Likewise, the lower education of both partners quite likely means that they possess fewer negotiating skills and are less able to work through conflicts.

Or take the matter of higher divorce rates among blacks. Black men have been able to bring relatively fewer resources to their marriages than white men because of economic discrimination by whites and blocked educational and occupational opportunities. In traditional-type marriages, wives may be disappointed that their husbands are not providing them with a desired level of rewards, and the husbands themselves may feel frustrated by their limited access to the opportunity structure. Furthermore, black wives have often entered the work force out of necessity, providing them not only with alternative resources (money earned on their own rather than money provided by their husbands) but also giving them increased power in their marriages. The strong preferences black women have developed for individualism and egalitarianism may result in their being more insistent on justice in terms of opportunities for self-determination and the pursuit of both extrinsic and intrinsic occupational rewards. Thus, the bargaining in black marriages may be "tougher." The willingness of black wives to endure certain kinds of costs (or reduced net profit) may be less than among white wives.

However, a similar situation may be arising in the case of white wives as well. We saw in Chapter 6 that employment rates among married women are increasing, and we have also seen that divorce rates are increasing as well. Historian William O'Neill sees a connection between the two, beginning in the last century.[64] At the present, there is an additional element on the scene—the push toward equal partnership in marriage rather than simply the matter of "working wives" in the junior-partner sense. And this could mean a continuing rise in divorce rates. Educated women may be expected increasingly to desire marriages that are not only satisfying in terms of companionship and affection, but also marriages that provide opportunities to continue growing as a person, sharing the provider role and power in decision making. To the degree that such opportunities are not forthcoming, many women may be willing to end their marriages.

Divorce Trends

Since most divorces occur early in marriage, it appears that unsatisfactory profit and unjust bargains become apparent to one or both spouses before many years have passed. Many such couples are evidently unable to negotiate situations of maximum joint profit, with the result that they have difficulty resolving certain conflicts except through termination of the marital relationship.

At the same time, Chapter 8 made clear that disagreements and conflicts arise in virtually all marriages; and with few exceptions, couples are faced with the challenge of constantly renegotiating, working out modified exchanges, and handling and resolving conflicts. In some cases, situations arise which sociologists term *institutionalized conflict,* particularly in matters of personal habits and preferences. In one marriage, for example, the husband is unhappy with his wife's obesity and has insisted for years that she lose weight. At the same time, the wife has tried for years to persuade her husband to give up smoking. Each resists the other's demands, but neither one is willing to press the issues to the point of divorce. The conflict has been incorporated into their marriage, and they accept it as part of their life together. They avoid *overt* struggles about these matters as much as possible, even though they feel strongly about them. As a taken-for-granted aspect of their relationship, the conflict is thus "institutionalized."

The great majority of couples, black and white, seem able to negotiate in such a way that their marital relationships are maintained. Marital stability is enhanced if the husband has greater socioeconomic resources to contribute. On the other hand, tangible resources contributed by wives may be either beneficial or negative to marital stability. Much depends on how husbands view wives' working.[65] To some husbands, a wife's breadwinning activities are viewed as a threat to the husband's provider role—a role he considers to be uniquely his by virtue of being a male. But to other husbands, a wife's working may be considered her right to fulfillment, bringing positive benefits to the marriage as well. Still other husbands may fall somewhere in between these two categories.

However, in the short run, many men may feel threatened by the increasingly serious occupational commitment of women, and the ensuing conflict may mean a continuation of climbing divorce rates. But in the long run, younger men especially may come to accept the *legitimacy* of a wife's career aspirations and taking on the role of co-provider. Thus, divorce rates may level out and perhaps even decline.

But no one can be sure what course divorce rates will take. We only know that at the present time they are increasing. The Census Bureau has estimated that, *if present increases continue,* one-fourth of women born between 1935 and 1939 will have seen their first marriages end in divorce by the time they reach age fifty in the 1980s. By 1971, when these women were in their thirties, nearly 16 percent were already divorced in comparison to 10.5 percent of women who were in this same age category in 1955.[66]

Changing attitudes toward divorce   In the mid-1970s, a Chicago-area church introduced as part of Sunday worship services the announcement of marital separations. Members of the congregation are encouraged to go up to divorcing couples to express loving concern and acceptance. "We rejoice with Mary and Joe when they get married," the minister is quoted as saying, "but who anguishes with them when their marriage doesn't work?"[67]

An article in a religious periodical suggested a step further—a ceremony of marital dissolution in which the officiant solemnizes the end of one period in a couple's lives and the beginning of another, pointing out that at the time of the wedding the couple needed "the visible bond of marriage" to aid in their growth as persons, but that "now the time has come when that bond is hampering both their growth as individual persons and their common life." An exchange of rings "reconsecrated to freedom" takes place in which the woman and man return these former symbols of marriage, now viewed as tokens of release.[68]

In contrast, around the turn of the century, a writer on Christianity and social issues called divorce the "worst anarchism." Simple anarchy could overthrow the state, Lyman Abbott declared, but the state could be reconstructed. Divorce, however, could destroy the family as an institution and bring about the downfall of civilization. Abbott, like many moral thinkers and writers of his time and since, considered the family (and more specifically, the traditional form of the family in which the husband-father has been the central figure) to be the very foundation of society. Good social order, according to this viewpoint, could not exist side by side with divorce.[69]

Alarmist cries, religious controversies, and legal debates have surrounded the subject of divorce throughout much of history. Changing attitudes today (such as those reflected in the accounts of church-sanctioned divorce ceremonies) and suggestions for reforming divorce laws appear to be rooted in two basic ideals: (1) a concern for individual rights and best interests and (2) a demanding view of marriage in terms of fulfilling high expectations of companionship, empathy, affection, and self-actualization.

Individualism versus familism   The worth, dignity, and freedom of the individual are cherished ideals in our society. But at the same time, there is concern for that which is most beneficial for society as a whole, which sometimes necessitates putting aside individualistic interests. Again we see the old problem first observed in Chapter 5 in connection with communal living: autonomy (self-determination and self-interest) versus community (in which group interests are given primary emphasis, even if individualistic interests are submerged or sacrificed).

During the divorce controversies that accompanied the rising divorce rates from after the Civil War onward, much of the debate centered around opposing perspectives on marriage. There was the traditional view which held up *familistic* ideals, on the one hand, and an emerging view which emphasized *individualistic* ideals on the other. From the standpoint of *familism,* marriage meant subordinating personal prerogatives and interests for the sake of the family (and ultimately, for the sake of one's society, since the family was held to be the basic unit on which society rested). O'Neill writes of moral conservatives who demanded that persons in oppressive marriages remain in them no matter how great the pain. Good would come out of even a bad marriage because of spiritual growth resulting from the "purging, purifying influence of suffering."[70] Providing a way out of an unsatisfactory relationship couldn't be reconciled with the ideals of familism. The availability of divorce was thought to discourage a couple's working at their relationship. Furthermore, according to an article in a religious periodical in 1903: "When people understand that they must live together they learn to soften, by mutual accommodation, that yoke which they know they cannot shake off. They become good husbands and good wives, for necessity is a powerful master in teaching the duties it imposes."[71]

From the familistic viewpoint, marriage was seen in terms of permanence, duty, and fidelity; but from the *individualistic* viewpoint, marriage was seen in terms of pragmatism or practical considerations. What would be best for the individuals involved? If a marriage didn't work out, why force persons to remain in it? Wouldn't it be better for the woman and man and for society in general if such marriages could simply end? These kinds of questions bring us to the second reason that attitudes toward divorce began to change.

High expectations for marriage O'Neill provides historical evidence that the form of family life idealized in the last century (the Victorian patriarchal family) was actually quite recent on the historical scene, having been gradually emerging since the sixteenth and seventeenth centuries. If we view the modern nuclear family as "an essentially new institution rather than as the last gasp of a dying one," it is easier to understand "why divorce became a necessary part of the family system." O'Neill points out that "when families are large and loose, arouse few expectations, and make few demands, there is no need for divorce. But when families become the center of social organization, their intimacy can become suffocating, their demands unbearable, and their expectations too high to be easily realizable." The system is made workable by the "safety valve" of divorce.[72]

He goes on to emphasize that when divorce is viewed in this way, it can be seen as a necessary feature rather than a flaw in the marriage system. Divorce provides persons who are oppressed in their marriages with a way of escape, "and those who fail at what is regarded as the most important human activity can gain a second chance."

Religion and divorce As divorce rates were rising and attitudinal changes were taking place, churches were taking a new look at the divorce question. There was by no means a consensus of opinion. Those who argued according to traditional interpretations of the Bible called for strict opposition to divorce: Had not Jesus taught that man should not put asunder what God has joined together? But as early as the seventeenth century, writer-poet John Milton had argued that this teaching itself legitimates divorce since some persons may not have been "joined by God" even though legally married.[73] During the moral debates over divorce in the late nineteenth century, the same point was made by Carroll Wright, Commissioner of Labor and supervisor of the first United States government statistical report on marriage and divorce. Wright claimed that it was "blasphemous" to call the union of two ill-suited persons "a sacrament on the ground that God hath joined them together." Human beings, not God, were responsible for bad marriages, he argued, and persons who had made a mistake and "missed the divine purpose as well as the civil purpose of marriage" should be provided with a way out.[74]

A modern Jewish position on divorce reflects a similar viewpoint: "Once it becomes clear that the marriage has failed irremediably, Judaism recognizes that the union has lost its sanction and its sanctity. . . . the husband and wife are no longer joined together by God in any meaningful sense, and society stultifies itself by trying to ignore the truth."[75]

Other arguments that have been used in attempting to reconcile divorce with religious teachings center around the ideals of love, mercy, and compassion, the recognition of human frailties, and the suggestion that "Christ saw marriage as an ideal state rather than an institution to be defended at all costs."[76] Even in the Roman Catholic Church, which traditionally has firmly opposed divorce and remarriage, a great deal of rethinking on the subject is taking place today.[77]

Law and divorce   Persons in the legal profession and legislators have also been forced to reexamine the divorce question in view of changing social conditions and attitudes. Will tougher laws preserve marriages? Will families break up at higher rates if divorces are easier to obtain? Some answers are provided by both history and cross-national comparisons.

O'Neill points out that divorces were largely restricted to middle- and upper-class persons when it was both difficult and expensive to obtain a divorce. "But once the legal restraints on divorce were eased, divorce tended to become a lower-class phenomenon."[78] However, this doesn't mean that less restrictive divorce laws *cause* the breakup of lower-status families. We saw earlier that the "glue" that holds a marriage together is not the law but rather the rewards it provides the partners. Spouses who perceive the costs to exceed the rewards may want to leave the relationship; but where the law makes obtaining a divorce difficult, the poor simply leave the relationship *without* divorce. Desertion and separation (sometimes called the "poor man's divorce") do not grant freedom to remarry as divorce does, but they do provide escape from an unsatisfactory marriage. However, when divorces may be obtained more easily, broken marriages among persons with limited opportunities in the economic system are able to take the divorce route rather than the desertion route.

Max Rheinstein, a professor of law, has concluded after thorough research on divorce in the United States and across the world that "a strict statute law of divorce is not an effective means to prevent or even to reduce the incidence of marriage breakdown."[79] Responding to those who blame divorce for "not only broken homes but broken lives," Rheinstein argues that what may harm homes and lives isn't divorce but rather the breakdown of the marriage that precedes divorce. Divorce is only a legal recognition that the marriage has already broken down; it restores the man and woman to freedom to enter new marital relationships. The freedom of remarriage can be good for society, says Rhein-stein, because "it reopens the way for the creation of new homes for the ex-spouses and their children, a home . . . which at least holds the possibility of being more harmonious than that which has broken down.[80]

In his opinion and that of many other concerned persons, society would be better served and marital stability better promoted by helping people to form and maintain satisfactory marriage relationships rather than tightening laws to keep persons locked in unsatisfactory relationships. Even the total banning of divorce wouldn't prevent marital breakups. A number of Latin American coun-tries, for example, permit no divorce whatsoever, but evasive practices have been devised by which persons (especially those with means) do find ways out of unsatisfactory marriages.[81]

Therefore, there is a move today to make laws which will help alleviate some of the pain of divorce rather than adding to that pain through strict and severe legal requirements. One evidence of change is gradual movement away from the *adversary* approach, in which one partner sues the other for divorce (John Doe versus Mary Doe), toward divorce by mutual consent. The concept of "grounds for divorce" (adultery, cruelty, desertion, nonsupport, drunkenness, and so on) is giving way to the simple recognition of a marital breakdown and the partners' desire to separate. The National Conference of Commissioners on Uniform State Laws has proposed a model no-fault divorce law which would make marriage a totally voluntary relationship, "lasting legally only so long as it meets the needs of both partners," emphasizes sociologist Jessie Bernard. Some countries, such as Japan, and a number of states in the United States already have this view of marriage and divorce. Bernard points out that sometimes state legislators hesitate to legitimize divorce by mutual consent because they fear that one partner might force or maneuver an unwilling partner to give consent. "But if one party is adamant in his or her insistence on divorce, the marriage has actually broken down," she writes. Forcing a couple to live together under legal duress wouldn't mean the marriage itself was somehow put together again. "The no-fault divorce recognizes this bitter reality."

At the same time, Bernard is convinced that divorce is not likely ever to become matter-of-fact. "It will probably always be an extremely painful experi-ence for most people, as breaking ties always is, even outside of marriage," she emphasizes. But at the same time, "the idea of forcing people to remain together is repugnant to the present world view."[82]

AGING

We've already followed two couples home from the hypothetical Valentine's Day party, but a third couple in our opening story also deserves attention. Julie's parents, Esther and Fred Blake, are both sixty years old. Although everyone tells Fred that he should be looking forward to his retirement in five years, he rather dreads giving up the work that has meant so much to him for so long. Esther, who has devoted her life to homemaking, has mixed feelings. She looks forward to time for travel and hobbies together, but she also knows from the experience of friends that her own daily routines will be drastically changed with Fred around the house all day. In addition, both are concerned about Fred's eighty-two-year-old mother who lives alone in an apartment near their home. Her health is failing, and they wonder whether they should consider a nursing home for her or invite her to live with them—which would cut down their own freedom.

Neither Fred nor Esther feels "old." As they had shown the group their honeymoon pictures, Fred had said he would like to go back to hike over some of those rugged mountain trails again. "At *your* age?" his wife had teased. "What do you mean, 'At my age'?" countered Fred, "You're only as old as you *think* you are!

The Objective Meaning of Aging

Half-joking remarks like "At *your* age?" or "Act your age!" imply the existence of social norms associated with various stages of life. Since social norms generally guide us throughout life as to how we should or shouldn't act, older people sometimes feel confused and alienated because at this stage behavioral expectations are less clear.

Some sociologists suggest that decreasing social requirements for behavior could actually be viewed as bringing increased freedom for elderly persons.[83] Irving Rosow points out that this freedom results from the fact that, as persons grow older, limitations are placed on their responsibilities and power; therefore their ability to affect others adversely is sharply reduced. "There is less social stake in their behavior," he writes, "and correspondingly little concern with the options that older people exercise and the choices they make." What they do in their private lives is up to them. "So long as they do not become a burden to others or indulge in virtually bizarre behavior, within their means they can do very largely as they want and live as they wish."[84]

It is no doubt true that, for some persons, freedom from normative constraints is considered a reward—as illustrated in the remark of a woman who said, "You have a perfect alibi for everything when you're eighty," since people readily overlook spilled soup, forgotten appointments, "acting silly," and even insisting on one's own way.[85] On the other hand, freedom from social expectations because of decreased power and responsibility to affect the lives of others can be experienced as a punishment or loss. "I'm no longer important to anyone; people don't care what I do any more" could be the feeling.

Not knowing what is expected of oneself is especially hard in cases of what sociologist Leonard Cain calls "asynchronization": the timing of various events in a person's life in a way that doesn't synchronize with other events.[86] According to social expectations, people marry, have children, advance in their occupations, and enter retirement and widowhood at certain taken-for-granted times. Yet the timing of certain events in one area of life doesn't always correspond with what is taking place in another area. Sociologist Vern Bengtson tells of interviewing a fifty-five-year-old steelworker who, having just retired, was considered to have reached *old age* in the economic-occupational sphere of life. But in his family he was relatively *young* in that he was the father of a thirteen-year-old daughter. In a fraternal order, his activities and position caused him to be considered *middle-aged.* This man found it difficult to define himself or know what was expected of him. Friends from work kidded him about being an old man. He didn't know what to do with his time. And his wife was annoyed with his being underfoot all day long.[87]

What is old age?   There is no simple answer to the question, When does a person become old? Surveys in both Great Britain and the United States have shown that the older a person's chronological age, the later he or she tends to think old age begins.[88] Concepts of old age also vary by social status, with lower-status persons tending to believe old age begins earlier (for example, in the fifties), while persons of higher status tend to think old age begins later (about age sixty-five). Bengtson points out that persons of lower status move through their family careers and their work careers more quickly than do higher-status persons.[89] At lower levels, persons tend to marry earlier, have their children sooner, and become grandparents earlier. In addition, because of limited education they usually reach as high as they will ever go occupationally at an earlier age than is true of persons at higher status levels. Not surprisingly then, "old age" seems to arrive sooner.

There are also indications of differing conceptions of old age by race, with blacks tending to define themselves as being older at earlier ages than is true of whites—although we may expect that such differences would disappear to a great degree when factors such as age at marriage and social status are taken into account.[90] We do know from census data, however, that for both men and women, life expectancy is lower and death rates are higher among blacks than among whites. In 1971, the average life expectancy at birth was 61.2 years for black males compared to 69.3 years for white males. Black females could expect to live 68.3 years, while white females had a life expectancy of 75.6 years.[91]

The Census Bureau defines old age as beginning when a person has lived sixty-five years. By this definition, there were 20 million elderly persons at the time of the 1970 census. In other words, 10 out of every 100 persons in the United States have reached old age, whereas in 1900, only 4 out of every 100 persons were sixty-five years or older. The elderly comprise one of the fastest-growing segments of the population, a major reason being the gain in life expectancy due to advances in medical science. Persons born in 1900 could expect to live on the average 47.3 years, but within half a century about twenty years had been added to the average life-span.[92]

The arbitrary setting of age sixty-five as the beginning of old age provides a *social* definition of old age, just as age eighteen or twenty-one socially defines adulthood. However, the change of classification from a minor to that of an adult means that new social and legal privileges and responsibilities, plus a highly regarded status, have been conferred upon a person. In contrast, when one moves from middle age to old age (defined by retirement policies), many privileges and responsibilities are taken away. The status conferred is *not* a highly regarded one, because in an industrial society being old is not esteemed as in other societies where prestige is granted on the basis of accumulated wisdom from many years. In industrial societies, education and innovation rather than past experience are valued keys to the occupational system's rewards. Change is rapid, and new technological skills are required. Practical knowledge of old ways of doing things is considered of limited worth. Thus older persons are expected to move out to make room for the young.

The Subjective Meaning of Aging

To lump together all persons who have passed a certain number of birthdays under the labels "the elderly" or "senior citizens" gives the impression that "the aged" make up a homogeneous category. The word *homogeneous* comes from the Greek and means "of the same kind." But persons at age sixty-five don't suddenly all become alike any more than all persons at twenty-five are alike. Increasingly, social scientists emphasize that much more than age itself must be taken into account. People vary in their outlooks, goals, self-concepts, and social resources. Social status is particularly important because, as sociologist George Maddox stresses, this variable summarizes previous life experience. He goes on to point out that what individuals bring to old age determines to a large extent what old age will mean to them. "Social competence, adaptive flexibility, and a sense of well-being displayed by persons in the middle years of life predict the probable display of these same characteristics in the later years," he writes, adding that in a sense the life cycle is a process in which "success predicts success."[93]

From our earlier discussions of social status, we know that persons with higher education are more likely than those of lower education to possess the social and personal skills mentioned by Maddox. Sociologist Zena Blau provides evidence from various studies showing that the lower the social status level, the more likely persons are to respond to old age with attitudes of *alienation,* "characterized by the feeling that 'there is just no point in living,' by feeling regret over the past, by the idea that 'things just keep getting worse and worse,' and by abandonment of all future plans." Such persons tend to feel they have been failures (having been poor in a society that stresses success) and consider their lives useless. "You know what they ought to do with old men like me?" asked one respondent. "Take us out and shoot us. We're no good for anything."[94]

Old age may also seem difficult for persons at higher status levels, especially when it is accompanied by the loss of significant roles such as that of worker or spouse; but rather than reacting with alienation, the major response is what Blau calls *conformity*—an attitude of adjustment. "Lots of times you don't like the new things," said one respondent referring to the changes brought by the transition to old age, "but there isn't anything you can do about them. You just have to accept them."[95] (However, Blau found another small category which she labeled *innovators,* those persons who—regardless of social status—were able to take old age in stride, enjoy life in the here and now, and continue to develop new interests and friendships. Persons of both sexes who were both socially active and employed were the most likely to be innovators.)

Research has shown that a person's attitude has a great deal to do with aging. "You're only as old as you think you are" has much truth in it. Blau refers to the writer E. B. White, who said at age seventy, "Old age is a special problem for me because I've never been able to shed the mental image I have of myself—a lad of nineteen." Although the years brought changes, he was able to maintain a sense of inner sameness, continuity, and knowing who he was. Such ongoing self-identity and "agelessness" was due in large measure to the fact that he was able to keep up in his craft in spite of the passage of years, a privilege denied most people today. Blau asserts that it is the loss of one's occupational role, "the mainstay of one's identity," that leads people to form a new concept of themselves.[96] In an extensive review of research findings on aging, sociologists Matilda Riley, Anne Foner, and associates emphasize that, "in the main, identification of the self as old is most pronounced among the disadvantaged and those who have experienced sharp discontinuity with the past."[97] Widowhood, retirement, and poor health are cited as examples of such sharp discontinuity. We tend to form a sense of who we are through what we do and through relationships with other people. To find it necessary to leave the most significant role associated with *doing* (occupation) because of ill health or compulsory retirement, or to leave what for the majority of persons is the most significant *relationship* role (spouse), is to leave what seems like a part of one's very self.

Role Exiting

As we've seen, being old is much more than having reached a certain chronological age or of having undergone certain physical changes; it has a social meaning, and it is this social meaning that is most crucial. Zena Blau uses the term *role exiting* to describe the social meaning of aging and to show why persons in our society tend to dread being labeled old: "For it is the sustained experience of being necessary to others that gives meaning and purpose to the life of all human beings. Opportunities to remain useful members of the society are severely undermined by the exits from adult social roles that are typical of old age.''[98] While role exits occur constantly before old age (one leaves the student role to become a wage earner, for example), the role exits most often associated with old age are different, because ''retirement and widowhood terminate a person's participation in the principal institutional structures of society—the nuclear family and the occupational structure.''[99]

Retirement   In 1900, 68 percent of all men aged sixty-five and over were in the labor force; but by 1971, only one out of four men and one out of ten women in this age group were employed.[100] Retirement is a relatively new social institution associated with industrial society and without past precedent.[101] As sociologist Ethel Shanas emphasizes, giving up work at a set age in order to spend the remainder of one's life in retirement ''emerges as a widespread practice only when the level of living within a society is such that persons can be supported by society without themselves being workers.''[102] In simpler societies, the productivity of the elderly is needed, since almost everyone is living near the subsistence level and enforced idleness would be out of the question. But in modern societies, automation, diminishing opportunities for self-employment, and pressures to make room for job-seeking younger workers all combine to make retirement the rule rather than the exception.

The passage of the Social Security Act in 1935 institutionalized retirement and formally defined old age by establishing pension eligibility at age sixty-five. But what this means is that at a certain arbitrarily fixed point in time, a person is suddenly excluded from the occupational structure—the structure that in American society provides such highly valued rewards as prestige, income, and a sense of worth. Blau points out what this role exit means to a male's self-image in particular. Both the material and social rewards associated with the opportunity system are taken away. After having been socialized to consider occupational achievement as the chief aspect of adult identity, males in retirement find themselves not only without a job but without the identity that went with that job. Adding to the strain is the realization that ''retirement is a *social* pattern that implies an invidious judgment about old people's lack of fitness to perform a culturally significant and coveted role.'' It is a form of social banishment and exclusion and is therefore the hardest kind of role exiting one is called upon to bear.[103]

A number of things happen in retirement. No longer can a husband bring home the monetary and status rewards which played such a part in marital power and in the instrumental and expressive exchanges of rights and duties discussed in Chapter 7. Because of the traditional meaning of the breadwinner role, retirement is experienced as much more demoralizing to males than is the case with females who retire from the work force.[104] This might change, however, as more women become committed to careers and take on the equal co-provider role. But for wives who have been full-time homemakers, life goes on much the same as before the retirement period, except that their husbands are now around home all the time.

For men, the changes are many. The daily pattern is disrupted because the once-structured time built around the job is now empty. Social participation is curtailed, since male friendships are usually highly dependent upon their occupational involvement. After a man's retirement, his still-employed, former work associates continue to talk, joke, and gripe about job-related topics, and both he and they begin to realize that he no longer fits in.[105]

Although blue-collar workers tend to report lower job satisfaction than white-collar workers and are more likely to volunteer for retirement, they tend to have greater difficulty in making the transition from worker to retiree. Losing the occupational role means a reduction in feelings of self-worth since blue-collar men are less likely to have other roles to fall back on or tangible evidences of accomplishment that remain (such as college degrees). The occupational role has been their major means of identity. The occupational role has also been highly important to white-collar men, but because of greater resources and role flexibility they have been found to be better able to make the transition to the retired state.[106]

Widowhood   As with retirement, there are differences by socioeconomic status and by sex with regard to the other major role exit associated with old age—widowhood. Of course, a person may lose a spouse before this period of life, but the subject is considered here since it affects such vast numbers at this stage (especially women). The 1970 census showed that more than half the women over age sixty-five had lost a spouse, in contrast to 17 percent of men in this age range. There are more widows than widowers for a combined reason: women tend to marry men older than themselves and men tend to die earlier than women. Among all elderly persons in 1970, there were 722 men for every 1,000 women; and the Census Bureau predicts that the ratio by 1990 will be 675 men over age sixty-five to 1,000 women in this age category.[107]

Since in traditional marriage, a woman's identity and status have stemmed from rewards provided by her husband, the husband's death means not only the loss of a companion with whom one's life was shared but also the loss of the wife role. A new way of looking at life—a reconstruction of reality—takes place during the transition from wife to widow to being one's own person (comparable in a sense to what we saw happens after divorce). At first, many women continue to think in terms of their former wife role and order their lives after their husband's wishes for a time ("Bill wouldn't want me to. . . ." "I think George would expect me to do it this way." "Carl never wanted me to learn to drive."), but many arrive at a point of reaching out and building a new life.[108]

Sociologist Helena Lopata found that widows of lower socioeconomic status (measured by education level) tended to live more isolated lives than did widows at higher status levels. Women with lower education have usually been married to men with low incomes, and husband-wife activities were usually highly segregated by sex which as we saw in Chapter 7, tends to be associated with lower expressive satisfaction. In one sense, widowhood may be less costly to such women in that they do not experience the loss of a companionship they never had. For such a woman, writes Lopata, "isolation is made easy by the fact that she was always marginal to the social system and that she was not socialized into any skills for expanded re-engagement into society."[109] On the other hand, widowhood may be extremely costly in terms of money as such a woman experiences even greater financial restriction than when her husband was alive.

Lopata's research led her to conclude that losing a husband is less disorganizing to the identities of lower-status women than is true of women with higher education because higher-status women have invested more time and energy into constructing a world view built around their husbands. In such homes, there is likely to have been more shared interests, greater communication, empathy and involvement in one another's lives, and less stress on sex-segregated activities. Nevertheless, because of the personal and social resources associated with her educational advantages and other benefits, the higher-status woman is equipped to build a new image of herself and the world if she so chooses. Though the change may be painful, as the process goes on she may come to feel "like a fuller human being, more independent and competent than in the past."[110]

A number of studies indicate that, in general, males have greater difficulty adjusting to widowhood than do females. The loss of a spouse in old age takes its toll on men in many ways: low morale, mental disorders, and high death and suicide rates.[111] Like retirement, widowhood is (in Blau's terms) a role exit. But unlike retirement, widowhood isn't a socially imposed exit but results in most cases from forces beyond human control. Therefore, widowhood doesn't carry with it the sense of having been judged and banished by others as retirement does. But there is still the sense of loss—of being deprived of highly cherished rewards.

The marital rights-duties exchange depicted in the two-story house diagram in Chapter 7 showed that in traditional arrangements, the instrumental side of marriage is characterized by an exchange in which the husband provides the wife with financial and status benefits and the wife rewards the husband by performing the necessary tasks of daily living such as maintaining the home. When death ends the marriage, the surviving spouse is left without these instrumental rewards to a great degree: a wife's husband-based status is gone and often her financial situation is a problem as well, and a husband has lost his means of domestic care. For the first time in his life he may have to cope with laundry, cooking, cleaning, and the like. One result of the traditional gender-linked division of labor in marriage is that an older widow's life goes on much as usual (in terms of housekeeping) while a widower is forced to take on new and often unfamiliar responsibilities. Not only has he lost the role of worker through retirement but now he must take on a different role (homemaker), and so many changes all at once in the later years of life can be difficult.[112]

In addition to the instrumental or practical side of marriage, the expressive or personal side is deeply affected as well. Again, males appear to fare worse in widowhood. Men are more likely than women to have depended entirely on their spouses to serve in the role of confidant, meeting needs for empathy, understanding, affection, communication, and companionship. But women are more likely to have other sources of personal affirmation outside the marriage, not only because they are more likely than husbands to have kept in touch with kin networks over the years, but also because they are more likely to have deep friendships in which they are accepted and appreciated as total persons (and not viewed primarily in terms of a role such as worker) and from which they can draw rich emotional support. Many older women have friends who are already widows and who can serve as role models, providing older women with an opportunity to mentally rehearse for widowhood in advance. When widowhood strikes, the network of widow friends can provide the new widow with companionship in various activities as well as empathy and aid. Blau emphasizes the importance of having at least one intimate friend to bring continuity to life and emotional support in old age. But at the same time, she shows how much more difficult it seems to be for men than women to form such close, long-lasting friendships, since gender-role socialization has traditionally discouraged the development in males of those qualities that are necessary for building deep interpersonal relationships.[113]

We may speculate that adjustments to widowhood may be less difficult and demoralization less common as emerging forms of marriage replace the traditional head-complement model. As women and men come to share equally in breadwinning and domestic roles, they may be better able to cope with losses in the instrumental side of marriage. It also seems likely that the diminished rewards in the expressive side of marriage brought by widowhood will seem less devastating as both sexes become more alike in terms of nurturance qualities and, through having developed the capacity for intimacy, can build and maintain other close relationships to bring meaning to life in old age.

Marriage in the Later Years

Some couples have many years together before death separates them. Research on the later stages of the life cycle is limited at this time, but some of the findings from the relatively few and often small published studies provide the following picture of old age marriage.[114]

Only 3 percent of elderly men and 5 percent of elderly women live in homes for the aged. A growing proportion of widows and widowers are maintaining independent households, and elderly married couples tend to live in separate households from their children as well. In cases of illness, the spouses tend to care for each other, preparing meals, and so on. Gender-role differentiation tends to become lessened, and shared activities tend to increase, since so much

Despite widespread notions about the "sexless older years," many elderly couples continue to enjoy the physical expression of love.

time is available for the husband and wife to spend together in the later years of marriage. Companionship may be enhanced both through greater sharing of household tasks after the husband retires and more joint leisure projects (such as vacations or decorating the home) after all the children have been gone for several years. Close ties between aged parents and adult children based on mutual affection tend to be maintained in spite of geographical separation.

Contrary to many commonly held beliefs and stereotypes about being sexually "over the hill," sexual interest and activity continues among elderly couples. Advancing age usually means a decline in frequency of sexual intercourse, but that doesn't mean that sex will necessarily be eliminated from marital interaction. Findings from the Duke University Longitudinal Study of Aging showed that the majority of husbands and wives were sexually active until over age seventy-five. And close to 15 percent of the couples indicated a pattern in which both sexual activity and interest were increasing rather than decreasing. Among those couples who reported having stopped having sexual intercourse entirely, however, the median age at which intercourse ceased was age

68 for men and age 60 for women. Wives and husbands agreed that husbands were the ones most responsible for stopping sexual intercourse, the main reasons being loss of potency, loss of interest, and illness.[115]

The Sex Information and Education Council of the United States reports that pervasive stereotypes about the alleged "sexless older years" can be destructive in many ways, negatively affecting the older person's sex life, self-image, and the marriages of older people in general. Such stereotypes also cause problems between aged parents and adult children when the parents consider remarriage, can make diagnosing various medical and psychological problems difficult, and may even lead to false accusations and faulty administration of justice in cases of elderly men accused of certain sex offenses. (For example, if elderly women show an interest in small children, they are considered warm and affectionate. But for an elderly man to show such interest brings the risk of being labeled a "dirty old man." It is assumed that his interest in children could only be sexual; and since it's also assumed that old people have no interest in sex, the man's attitudes are thought to indicate a perverted interest which must be watched with fear and suspicion.)[116]

In examining the process of aging, we have seen that many changes may occur over the years as a couple go through life together. Some sorts of exchanges both in the instrumental and expressive realms of marriage continue so long as the marriage lasts. Those couples who have learned to understand and empathize with one another, to enjoy activities together, and to negotiate in times of conflict have the potential of experiencing high rewards and maximum joint profit to the very end.

CONTINUED STORY

After the Valentine's Day party in our opening illustration, Trudy and Tim went home to rethink marriage in the middle years, Larry and Sue continued their movement toward divorce, and Esther and Fred faced the questions and challenges of growing old together. But what about Bob and Julie?

When the group left the apartment, Julie said suddenly, "There's so much involved in being married!" Bob agreed. They started to put away their wedding photos and thought back over all that had taken place in their three years together. They wondered, too, what other kinds of challenges might lie ahead. For one thing they were especially glad: they had learned early in marriage to handle conflict and had developed negotiation skills. And they had learned to allow for change in one another and for the changes in marriage that result. They had learned to work for both individual profit and joint profit. Now they are looking forward to a new life built around the renegotiated exchange of rewards and costs they have worked out together.

Bob is excited about the position he'll be taking in Chicago in the summer, and Julie has already found some excellent opportunities there to continue both her training and her teaching. But they have changed their minds about the baby—at least for the present. They think it might be wise to wait a year or two until they're settled in the new location and until Julie has a chance to complete her master's degree. What lies beyond that, no one really knows. Their life together, like marriage in general, is a continued story—which is really another way of saying *an ongoing process of exchanges and changes.*

NOTES

1   Deutscher, 1962.
2   See summary in Rollins and Feldman, 1970, p. 21.
3   Blood and Wolfe, 1960, p. 264.
4   Pineo, 1961; see summary in Troll, 1971.
5   Scanzoni, 1970.
6   Scanzoni, 1975a.
7   Rollins and Feldman, 1970.
8   Glenn, 1975.
9   Rollins and Cannon, 1974; Troll, 1971.
10   Blood, 1969, pp. 325–333.
11   Cuber and Harroff, 1965.
12   Rollins and Feldman, 1970; Blood and Wolfe, 1960, p. 265.
13   Bohannan, 1970, p. 36.
14   Fromm, 1956, pp. 44–45 in paperback edition.
15   Thibaut and Kelley, 1959, p. 21.
16   O'Neill and O'Neill, 1972, chap. 12.
17   Neubeck, 1969.
18   Bell, 1971, p. 63.
19   Kinsey et. al., 1953, chap. 10.
20   Smith and Smith, 1970.
21   Smith and Smith, 1973.
22   Walshok, 1971.
23   Denfeld and Gordon, 1970.
24   Symonds, 1971, p. 95.
25   Bartell, 1971, p. 20; Smith and Smith, 1974, pp. 78, 85, 263.
26   Smith and Smith, 1974; Bartell, 1971; Denfeld and Gordon, 1970; Walshok, 1971.
27   O'Neill and O'Neill, 1970.
28   Symonds, 1971, p. 86.
29   Henshel, 1973; Symonds, 1971; Varni, 1973.
30   Varni, 1973; Smith and Smith, 1970.
31   Denfeld, 1974.
32   Denfeld and Gordon, 1970.
33   Smith and Smith, 1973.
34   Gilmartin, 1974; see also Gilmartin and Kusisto, 1973.
35   Denfeld, 1974.
36   Waller, 1930, pp. xiv, 107; Goffman, 1959.
37   Miller, 1970.
38   Bohannan, 1970, chap. 2.
39   Waller, 1930; Goode, 1956; Bohannan, 1970; Krantzler, 1973.
40   Goode, 1956, chap. 1.
41   Bohannan, 1970; Krantzler, 1973.
42   Waller, 1930, chap. 5.
43   Waller, 1930, p. 135.
44   Waller, 1930, p. 54.
45   Bohannan, 1970, p. 33.

46 Krantzler, 1973, chap. 8.
47 National Center for Health Statistics, ser. 21, no. 24, p. 9.
48 *Monthly Vital Statistics Report,* 1974, vol. 22, no. 13; 1975, vol. 23, no. 12.
49 National Center for Health Statistics, ser. 21, no. 22, p. 27; *Monthly Vital Statistics Report,* 1975, vol. 24, no. 4.
50 National Center for Health Statistics, ser. 21, no. 22, p. 2; Rheinstein, 1972, p. 120; Rheinstein, 1970, pp. 127–128.
51 Goode, 1963.
52 Glick, 1975, p. 2; National Center for Health Statistics, ser. 21, no. 25, pp. 1–3.
53 *Current Population Reports,* 1974, P-20, no. 263, p. 6.
54 *Current Population Reports,* 1972, P-20, no. 239, p. 70.
55 *Current Population Reports,* 1971, P-20, no. 223, p. 1.
56 National Center for Health Statistics, 1973, ser. 21, no. 23, pp. 15–16.
57 Based on 1969 figures. See National Center for Health Statistics, 1973, ser. 21, no. 22, p. 23.
58 *Current Population Reports,* 1973, P-23, no. 46, p. 70.
59 *Current Population Reports,* 1974, P-20, no. 266; 1973, P-23, no. 46; 1974, P-23, no. 50.
60 *Current Population Reports,* 1973, P-23, no. 46, p. 3.
61 *Current Population Reports,* 1972, P-23, no. 42, p. 31.
62 *Current Population Reports,* 1974, P-23, no. 48, p. 20.
63 Goode, 1962; Cutright, 1971.
64 O'Neill, 1967, chap. 1.
65 Hoffman and Nye, 1974, pp. 189–191.
66 *Current Population Reports,* 1972, P-20, no. 239, p. 5. Using an alternative mathematical technique, demographer Samuel Preston has recently raised questions about these census estimates and suggests that the marital disruption rates of 1973 would mean that 44 percent of marriages could be expected to end in divorce; Preston, 1975.
67 *Chicago Daily News,* Apr. 19, 1975, p. 10.
68 Shideler, 1971.
69 O'Neill, 1967, chap. 2.
70 O'Neill, 1967, chap. 3.
71 Quoted in O'Neill, 1967, chap. 2.
72 O'Neill, 1967, chap. 1.
73 Milton, 1820 edition, pp. 126–128.
74 Quoted in O'Neill, 1967, chap. 7.
75 Gordis, 1967, p. 43.
76 O'Neill, 1967, chap. 3.
77 See *U.S. Catholic,* June 1975.
78 O'Neill, 1967, chap. 1.
79 Rheinstein, 1972, p. 406.
80 Rheinstein, 1972, p. 5.
81 Rheinstein, 1972, chap. 16.
82 Bernard, 1970. States having no-fault divorce provisions are listed in Glick, 1975, pp. 8–9.
83 Bengtson, 1973, pp. 23–26.
84 Rosow, 1973, pp. 36–37.
85 Letter to "Dear Abby," *Bloomington (Ind.) Herald-Telephone,* May 20, 1975.
86 Cain, 1964, p. 289, as quoted in Bengtson, 1973, p. 17.
87 Bengtson, 1973, pp. 17–18.
88 Riley, Foner, and associates, 1968, vol. 1, p. 311.
89 Bengtson, 1973, p. 21.
90 Jackson, 1973, p. 436.
91 *Current Population Reports,* 1974, P-23, no. 48, p. 112.
92 U.S. Bureau of the Census, *We the American Elderly,* 1973, pp. 3–5.

93   Maddox, 1970.
94   Blau, Z., 1973, pp. 156–157.
95   Blau, Z., 1973, pp. 163–166.
96   Blau, Z., 1973, pp. 103–104.
97   Riley, Foner, and associates, 1968, p. 302.
98   Blau, Z., 1973, p. xii.
99   Blau, Z., 1973, pp. 17–18.
100 Shanas, 1972, p. 22; *Current Population Reports,* 1973, P-23, no. 43, p. 28.
101 Loether, 1964, p. 518.
102 Shanas, 1972, p. 222.
103 Blau, Z., 1973, pp. 105, 211–215.
104 Blau, Z., 1973, p. 29.
105 Blau, Z., 1973, p. 89.
106 Loether, 1964, 1967.
107 U.S. Bureau of the Census, *We the American Elderly,* 1973.
108 Silverman, 1972.
109 Lopata, 1973a, p. 270; Blau, Z., 1973, p. 84.
110 Lopata, 1973b, p. 416.
111 Bock and Webber, 1972.
112 Berardo, 1970.
113 Blau, Z., 1973, pp. 72–75; Lowenthall and Haven, 1968.
114 U.S. Bureau of the Census, *We the American Elderly,* 1973; Riley, Foner, and associates, 1968; Smith, 1965; Palmore, 1968; Stinnett, Carter, and Montgomery, 1972.
115 Palmore, 1970, chap. 8.
116 SIECUS, 1970, chap. 8; see also Felstein, 1970.

BIBLIOGRAPHY

Acker, Joan
1973 "Women and social stratification: a case of intellectual sexism." *American Journal of Sociology* 78:936–945.

Adams, Bert N.
1968 *Kinship in an Urban Setting.* Chicago: Markham.

Adorno, T. W., Else Frenkel-Brunswik, D. J. Levinson, and R. N. Sanford
1950 *The Authoritarian Personality.* New York: Harper.

Aird, John S.
1972 "Population policy and demographic prospects in the People's Republic of China." Bethesda, Md.: Center for Population Research, National Institute for Child Health and Human Development.

Alcott, William A.
1837 *The Young Wife.* Boston: G. W. Light.

Aldous, Joan
1970 "Strategies for developing family theory." *Journal of Marriage and the Family* 32:250.

Aldridge, Delores P.
1973 "The changing nature of interracial marriage in Georgia: a research note." *Journal of Marriage and the Family* 35:641–642.

Alexander, C. Norman, Jr., and Richard Simpson
1971 "Balance theory and distributive justice." Pp. 69–80 in Herman Turk and Richard Simpson (eds.), *Institutions and Social Exchange.* Indianapolis: Bobbs-Merrill.

Altman, Dennis
1971 *Homosexual Oppression and Liberation.* New York: Outerbridge and Lizard. Avon Books edition.

Andelin, Helen
1965 *Fascinating Womanhood.* Santa Barbara: Pacific Press. New York: Bantam (revised edition, 1975).

Angrist, Shirley A.
1969 "The study of sex roles." *Journal of Social Issues* 25:215–233.

Arafat, Ibithaj and Betty Yorburg
1973 "On living together without marriage." *Journal of Sex Research* 9.

Bach, G. and P. Wyden
1968 *The Intimate Enemy.* New York: Morrow.

Bahr, Stephen J.
1972 "Comment on 'the study of family power structure: a review 1960–1969.'" *Journal of Marriage and the Family* 34:239–243.

Balswick, Jack O. and Charles W. Peek
1971 "The inexpressive male: a tragedy of American society." *The Family Coordinator* 20:363–368.

Bardwick, Judith M.
1971 *Psychology of Women.* New York: Harper & Row.

1973 "Sex, maternity and self-esteem." Paper read at the National Institute for Child Health and Human Development and the Center for Population Research Conference on Family and Fertility, June 13–16, Belmont, Elkridge, Maryland. Mimeographed.

Barker-Benfield, Ben
1972 "The spermatic economy: a nineteenth-century view of sexuality." *Feminist Studies* 1, (1). Reprinted in Michael Gordon (ed.), *The American Family in Social-Historical Perspective.* New York: St. Martin's, 1972 pp. 336–372.

Barron, Milton L.
1972 *The Blending American.* Chicago: Quadrangle.

Barry, H., III, Margaret K. Bacon, and I. I. Child
1957 "A cross-cultural survey of some sex differences in socialization." *Journal of Abnormal Social Psychology* 55:327–332.

Bartell, Gilbert
1971 *Group Sex.* New York: Wyden.

Becker, Gary S.
1973 "A theory of marriage." *Journal of Political Economy* 81:813–845.

Bell, Robert R.
1966 *Premarital Sex in a Changing Society.* Englewood Cliffs, N.J.: Prentice-Hall.
1971 *Social Deviance.* Homewood, Ill.: Dorsey.
1974 "Married sex: how uninhibited can a woman dare to be?" (with Norman Lobenz). *Redbook* 143 (September):176.

Bell, Robert R. and J. B. Chaskes
1970 "Premarital sexual experience among coeds, 1958–1968." *Journal of Marriage and the Family* 32:81–84.

Bengtson, Vern
1973 *The Social Psychology of Aging.* Indianapolis: Bobbs-Merrill.

Benston, Margaret
1969 "The political economy of women's liberation." *Monthly Rev.* (September):3–4.

Berardo, Felix M.
1970 "Survivorship and social isolation: the case of the aged widower." *The Family Coordinator* 19:11–25.

Berelson, Bernard
1972 "The value of children: a taxonomical essay." *The Population Council Annual Report—1972.* New York: The Population Council.
1973 "Population growth policy in developed countries." Pp. 145–160 in Charles Westoff and others, *Toward the End of Growth: Population in America.* Englewood Cliffs, N.J.: Prentice-Hall.

Berger, Bennett, Bruce Hackett, and R. Mervyn Millar
1972 "The communal family." *The Family Coordinator* 21:419–427.

Berger, David and Morton Wenger
1973 "The ideology of virginity." *Journal of Marriage and the Family* 35:666–676.
Berger, Miriam E.
1971 "Trial marriage: harnessing the trend constructively." *The Family Coordinator* 20:38–43.
Berger, Peter and Hansfried Kellner
1964 "Marriage and the construction of reality: an exercise in the microsociology of knowledge." *Diogenes* 46:1–25.
Bernard, Jessie
1964 *Academic Women.* University Park, Pa.: Pennsylvania State University Press.
1970 "No news, but new ideas." Pp. 3–25 in Paul Bohannan (ed.), *Divorce and After.* Garden City, N.Y.: Doubleday.
1972 *The Future of Marriage.* New York: World.
Berne, Eric
1964 *Games People Play.* New York: Grove (also Ballantine).
Besanceney, Paul H.
1970 *Interfaith Marriages: Who and Why.* New Haven, Conn.: College and University Press.
Bettelheim, Bruno
1969 *The Children of the Dream.* New York: Macmillan.
Blau, Peter
1964 *Exchange and Power in Social Life.* New York: Wiley.
Blau, Peter and Otis Dudley Duncan
1967 *The American Occupational Structure.* New York: Wiley.
Blau, Zena Smith
1973 *Old Age in a Changing Society.* New York: New Viewpoints.
Block, Jeanne Humphrey
1973 "Conceptions of sex role—some cross-cultural and longitudinal perspectives." *American Psychologist* (June):512–526.
Blood, Robert O., Jr.
1963 "The husband-wife relationship." Pp. 282–305 in Nye and Hoffman, 1963.
1967 *Love Match and Arranged Marriage.* New York: Free Press.
1969 *Marriage.* 2nd ed. New York: Free Press.
Blood, Robert O., Jr., and Donald M. Wolfe
1960 *Husbands and Wives.* New York: Free Press.
Boak, Arthur
1955 *Manpower Shortage and the Fall of the Roman Empire in the West.* Ann Arbor: University of Michigan Press.
Bock, E. Wilbur and Irving Webber
1972 "Suicide among the elderly: isolating widowhood and mitigating alternatives." *Journal of Marriage and the Family* 34:24–31.
Bohannan, Paul (ed.)
1970 *Divorce and After.* Garden City, N.Y.: Doubleday.
Bott, Elizabeth
1957 *Family and Social Network.* London: Tavistock.
Bowen, William and T. Aldrich Finegan
1969 *The Economics of Labor Force Participation.* Princeton, N.J.: Princeton University Press.
Brawley, Benjamin
1921 *A Social History of the American Negro.* New York: Macmillan.
Brickman, Phillip (ed.)
1974 *Social Conflict.* Lexington, Mass.: Heath.
Broderick, Carlfred

1971 "Beyond the five conceptual frameworks: a decade of development in family theory." *Journal of Marriage and the Family* 33:139–159.
Bronfenbrenner, Urie
1958 "Socialization and social class through time and space." Pp. 400–425 in E. E. Maccoby, T. M. Newcomb, and E. L. Hartley (eds.), *Readings in Social Psychology*, 3rd ed. New York: Holt.
Brown, George and Michael Rutter
1966 "The measurement of family activities and relationships." *Human Relations* 19:241–263.
Brown, Roger
1965 *Social Psychology.* New York: Free Press.
Buber, Martin
1958 *I and Thou.* New York: Scribner's.
Buckhout, R. et al
1971 "The war on people: a scenario for population control?" Unpublished manuscript, California State College, Hayward.
Buckley, Walter
1967 *Sociology and Modern Systems Theory.* Englewood Cliffs, N.J.: Prentice-Hall.
Buckley, Walter (ed.)
1968 *Modern Systems Research for the Behavioral Scientist.* Chicago: Aldine.
Bumpass, Larry L. and Charles F. Westoff
1970 *The Later Years of Childbearing.* Princeton, N.J.: Princeton University Press.
Burgess, Ernest W., Harvey Locke, and Mary Thomes
1963 *The Family: From Institution to Companionship.* 3rd ed. New York: American.
Burgess, E. W. and P. Wallin
1953 *Engagement and Marriage.* Philadelphia: Lippincott.
Buric, O. and A. Zelevic
1967 "Family authority, marital satisfaction and the social network in Yugoslavia." *Journal of Marriage and the Family* 29:325–336.
Buxembaum, Alva
1973 "Women's rights and the class struggle." *Political Affairs* 52:22.
Cain, Leonard, Jr.
1964 "Life course and social structure." In R. E. L. Faris (ed.), *Handbook of Modern Sociology.* Chicago: Rand McNally.
Calhoun, Arthur W.
1919 *A Social History of the American Family.* Reprint. New York: Barnes *and* Noble, 1960.
Calvert, Robert
1974 "Criminal and civil liability in husband-wife assault." Pp. 88–91 in Steinmetz and Straus, 1974.
Campbell, Helen
1893 *Women Wage-Earners.* Reprint. New York: Arno Press, 1972.
Carlier, Auguste
1867 *Marriage in the United States.* New York: Leypoldt and Holt. Reprint. New York: Arno Press, 1972.
Carns, Donald E.
1969 "Religiosity, premarital sexuality and the American college student." Unpublished doctoral dissertation, Indiana University, Bloomington.
1973 "Talking about sex: notes on first coitus and the double sexual standard." *Journal of Marriage and the Family* 35:677–688.
Carter, Hugh and Paul C. Glick
1970 *Marriage and Divorce: A Social and Economic Study.* Cambridge, Mass.: Harvard University Press.
Centers, R., B. Raven, and A. Rodrigues

1971 "Conjugal power structure: a re-examination." *American Sociological Review* 36:264–278.

Chafetz, Janet Saltzman
1974 *Masculine/Feminine or Human?* Itasca, Ill.: Peacock.

Chesser, E.
1957 *The Sexual, Marital and Family Relations of English Women.* New York: Ray.

Christensen, Harold T.
1968 "Children in the family: relationship of number and spacing to marital success." *Journal of Marriage and the Family* 30:283–289.
1969 "The impact of culture and values." Pp. 155–169 in Carlfred Broderick and Jessie Bernard (eds.), *The Individual, Sex, and Society.* Baltimore: Johns Hopkins.

Christensen, Harold T. and Christina F. Gregg
1970 "Changing sex norms in America and Scandinavia." *Journal of Marriage and the Family* 32:616–627.

Clark, H.
1968 *The Law of Domestic Relations in the United States.* St. Paul: West.

Clatworthy, Nancy Moore
1975 "Living together." Pp. 67–89 in Nona Glazer-Malbin (ed.), *Old Family/New Family.* New York: D. Van Nostrand.

Coale, Ansley J.
1974 "The history of the human population." *Scientific American* 231 (September):41–51.

Cohen, Malcolm S.
1969 "Married women in the labor force: an analysis of participation rates." *Monthly Labor Review* 92 (October):31–35.

Coleman, James S.
1966 "Female status and premarital sexual codes." *American Journal of Sociology* 72:217.
1973 "Equality of opportunity and equality of results." Pp. 93–101 in *Perspectives on Inequality,* compiled by the editors of the *Harvard Educational Review.* Cambridge, Mass.: Harvard Educational Review.

Collins, Randall
1971 "A conflict theory of sexual stratification." *Social Problems* 19:3–21.

Constantine, Larry and Joan Constantine
1971 "Group and multilateral marriage: definitional notes, glossary, and annotated bibliography." *Family Process* 10:157–176.
1973a *Group Marriage.* New York: Macmillan.
1973b "Sexual aspects of group marriage." Pp. 182–191 in R. W. Libby and R. N. Whitehurst (eds.), *Renovating Marriage.* Danville, Calif.: Consensus Publishers.

Coser, Lewis A.
1956 *The Functions of Social Conflict.* New York: Free Press.

Coser, Rose Laub and Lewis A. Coser
1972 "The principle of legitimacy and its patterned infringement in social revolutions." Pp. 119–130 in Marvin Sussman and Betty Cogswell (eds.), *Cross-National Family Research.* Leiden, Netherlands: E. J. Brill.

Cottrell, Ann Baker
1973 "Cross-national marriage as an extension of an international life style: a study of Indian-Western couples." *Journal of Marriage and the Family* 35:739–741.

Cowing, Cedric
1968 "Sex and preaching in the Great Awakening." *American Quarterly* 20:624–644.

Cox, Frank D.
1972 "Communes: a potpourri of ideas." Pp. 237–245 in Frank D. Cox (ed.), *American Marriage: A Changing Scene?* Dubuque, Iowa: Wm. C. Brown.

Cuber, John and Peggy Harroff
1965 *Sex and the Significant Americans.* Baltimore: Penguin.

Current Population Reports
(See U.S. Bureau of the Census.)

Cutright, Phillips
1971 "Income and family events: marital stability." *Journal of Marriage and the Family* 33:291–306.
1972 "Illegitimacy in the United States: 1920–1968." Commission on Population Growth and the American Future, Vol. 1: Demographic and Social Aspects of Population Growth. Washington, D.C.: U.S. Government Printing Office.

Cutright, Phillips and Karen B. Cutright
1973 "Abortion: the court decision and some consequences of a constitutional amendment." Mimeographed. Bloomington, Ind.: Department of Sociology, Indiana University.

D'Andrade, Roy G.
1966 "Sex differences and cultural institutions." Pp. 174–204 in Eleanor E. Maccoby (ed.), *The Development of Sex Differences.* Stanford, Calif.: Stanford University Press.

Davis, Kingsley
1941 "Intermarriage in caste societies." *American Anthropologist* 43:376–395.

Davis, Murray S.
1973 *Intimate Relations.* New York: Free Press.

Demeny, Paul
1974 "The populations of the under-developed countries." *Scientific American* 231 (September):148–159.

Demos, John
1970 *A Little Commonwealth: Family Life in Plymouth Colony.* New York: Oxford.

Denfeld, Duane
1974 "Dropouts from swinging: the marriage counselor as informant." Pp. 260–267 in Smith and Smith, 1974.

Denfeld, Duane and Michael Gordon
1970 "The sociology of mate swapping: or the family that swings together clings together." *Journal of Sex Research* 6 (May): 85–100.

De Rougemont, Denis
1940 *Love in the Western World.* New York: Harcourt, Brace.

Deutsch, Morton
1971 "Conflict and its resolution." Pp. 36–57 in C. G. Smith (ed.), *Conflict Resolution.* Notre Dame, Ind.: Notre Dame Univ. Press.

Deutscher, Irwin
1962 "Socialization for postparental life." Pp. 508–523 in Arnold Rose (ed.), *Human Behavior and Social Processes.* Boston: Houghton Mifflin.

De Vos, George and Hiroshi Wagatsuma
1970 "Status and role behavior in changing Japan." Pp. 334–370 in Seward and Williamson, 1970.

Dinitz, S., R. Dynes, and A. Clark
1954 "Preference for male or female children: traditional or affectional." *Journal of Marriage and Family Living* 16:128–130.

Dizard, Jan
1968 *Social Change in the Family.* Chicago:

Community and Family Study Center, University of Chicago.

Downing, Joseph
1970 "The tribal family and the society of awakening." Pp. 119–135 in Herbert Otto (ed.), *The Family in Search of a Future*. New York: Appleton-Century-Crofts.

Duberman, Lucille
1974 *Marriage and Its Alternatives*. New York: Praeger.

Duncan, Otis Dudley, David Featherman, and Beverly Duncan
1972 *Socioeconomic Background and Occupational Achievement*. New York: Seminar Press.

Dunne, Finley Peter
1969 *Mr. Dooley at His Best*. Edited by Elmer Ellis. New York: Archon Books.

Durkheim, Emile
1893 *The Division of Labor in Society*. Translated by George Simpson. New York: Free Press edition, 1933.

Edmonds, Ronald, Andrew Billingsley, James Comer, James Dyer, William Hall, Robert Hill, Nan McGehee, Lawrence Reddick, Howard Taylor, and Stephen Wright
1973 "A black response to Christopher Jencks' *Inequality* and certain other issues." Pp. 40–55 in *Perspectives on Inequality*. Compiled by the editors. Cambridge, Mass.: Harvard Educational Review.

Ehrmann, Winston W.
1957 "Some knowns and unknowns in research into human sex behavior." *Marriage and Family Living* 19:16–22.

Elkin, Frederick and Gerald Handel
1972 *The Child and Society*. 2nd ed. New York: Random House.

Ellis, Albert
1970 "Group marriage: a possible alternative?" Pp. 85–97 in Herbert Otto (ed.), *The Family in Search of a Future*. New York: Appleton-Century-Crofts.

Emerson, Richard M.
1962 "Power-dependence relations." *American Sociological Review* 27:31–41.

Engels, Friedrich
1884 *The Origin of the Family, Private Property and the State*. Chicago: Charles H. Kerr, 1902.

Enroth, Ronald M. and Gerald E. Jamison
1973 *The Gay Church*. Grand Rapids, Mich.: Eerdmans.

Erlanger, Howard S.
1974 "Social class differences in parents' use of physical punishment." Pp. 150–158 in Steinmetz and Straus, 1974.

Espenshade, Thomas
1973 *The Cost of Children in Urban United States*. Population Monograph Series, No. 14. Berkeley: University of California Institute of International Studies.

Etzkowitz, Henry
1971 "The male sister: sexual separation of labor in society." *Journal of Marriage and the Family* 33:431–434.

Euripides
Hippolytus. Translated by David Grene. Pp. 231–291 in David Grene and Richmond Lattimore (eds.), *Greek Tragedies*, Vol. 1. Chicago: University of Chicago Press,

Everett, William and Julie Everett
1975 "Childless marriages: a new vocation?" *U.S. Catholic* 40 (May):38–39.

Fasteau, Marc Feigen
1974 *The Male Machine*. New York: McGraw-Hill.

Fawcett, James T. (ed.)
1972 *The Satisfactions and Costs of Children: Theories, Concepts, Methods*. A Summary Report and Proceedings of the Workshop on Assessment of the Satisfactions and Costs of Children, April 27–29. Honolulu: East-West Population Institute.

Federal Bureau of Investigation
1973 *Uniform Crime Reports, 1972*. Washington, D.C.: U.S. Government Printing Office.

Feldman, Harold
1971 "The effects of children on the family." Pp. 107–125 in Andrée Michel (ed.), *Family Issues of Employed Women in Europe and America*. Leiden, Netherlands: E. J. Brill.

Feldman, H. and M. Feldman
1973 "The relationship between the family and occupational functioning in a sample of rural women." Ithaca, N.Y.: Department of Human Development and Family Studies, Cornell University.

Feldman, Saul and Gerald Thielbar
1972 *Deviant Life Styles: Diversity in American Society*. Boston: Little, Brown.

Felstein, Ivor
1970 *Sex in Later Life*. Baltimore: Penguin.

Ferriss, Abbott
1971 *Indicators of Trends in the Status of American Women*. New York: Russell Sage Foundation.

Field, Mark G. and Karin I. Flynn
1970 "Worker, mother, housewife: Soviet woman today." Pp. 257–284 in Seward and Williamson, 1970.

Figes, Eva
1970 *Patriarchal Attitudes*. New York: Stein and Day.

Firestone, Shulamith
1970 *The Dialectic of Sex*. New York: Morrow.

Fogarty, Michael P., Rhona Rapoport, and Robert N. Rapoport
1971 *Sex, Career and Family*. Beverly Hills, Calif.: Sage.

Fong, Stanley L. M.
1970 "Sex roles in the modern fabric of China." Pp. 371–400 in Seward and Williamson, 1970

Foote, Nelson
1954 "Sex as play." *Social Problems* 1:159–163.

Form, William H.
1974 Book review of *Work in America*. *American Journal of Sociology* 79:1550–1552.

Fox, Alan
1974 *Beyond Contract: Work, Power and Trust Relations*. London: Faber and Faber.

Frankel, Lillian B.
1970 *This Crowded World*. Washington, D.C.: Population Reference Bureau.

Franklin, Benjamin
1745 "Advice to a young man on choosing a mistress." In Leonard Labare and Whitfield Bell, Jr. (eds.), *The Papers of Benjamin Franklin, Vol. 3*. New Haven, Conn.: Yale University Press, 1961.

French Institute of Public Opinion
1961 *Patterns of Sex and Love*. New York: Crown.

Fromm, Erich
1956 *The Art of Loving*. New York: Harper & Row. Paperback edition, Bantam Books.

Gaer, Joseph and Ben Siegel
1964 *The Puritan Heritage: America's Roots in the Bible.* New York: Mentor.

Gagnon, John H. and William Simon
1967a "Femininity in the Lesbian community." *Social Problems* 15:212–221.
1967b (eds.), *Sexual Deviance.* New York: Harper & Row.
1970 (eds.), *The Sexual Scene.* Chicago: Aldine.
1973 *Sexual Conduct.* Chicago: Aldine.

Gasson, Ruth, Archibald Haller, and William Sewell
1972 *Attitudes and Facilitation in the Attainment of Status.* Washington, D.C.: American Sociological Association.

Gebhard, Paul
1966 "Factors in marital orgasm." *Journal of Social Issues* 22:89–95.
1971 "Human sexual behavior: a summary statement." Pp. 206–217 in Donald Marshall and Robert Guggs (eds.), *Human Sexual Behavior.* New York: Basic Books.
1972 "Incidence of overt homosexuality in the United States and Western Europe." Pp. 22–29 in Livingood, 1972.
1973 "Sex differences in sexual reponse." *Archives of Sexual Behavior* 2:201–203.

Geiger, H. Kent
1968 *The Family in Soviet Russia.* Cambridge: Harvard University Press.

Gelles, Richard
1973a "An exploratory study of intra-family violence." Unpublished Ph.D. dissertation, University of New Hampshire, Durham, N.H.
1973b "Child abuse as psychopathology: a sociological critique and reformulation." *American Journal of Orthopsychiatry* 43:611–621. (Reprinted in Steinmetz and Straus, 1974.)

Gendell, Murray
1963 *Swedish Working Wives.* Totowa, N.J.: Bedminster Press.

Gil, David G.
1971 "Violence against children." *Journal of Marriage and the Family* 33:637–657.

Gillespie, Dair L.
1971 "Who has the power? The marital struggle." *Journal of Marriage and the Family* 33:445–458.

Gilmartin, Brian
1974 "Sexual deviance and social networks: a study of social, family, and marital interaction patterns among co-marital sex participants." Pp. 291–323 in Smith and Smith, 1974.

Gilmartin, Brian and Dave V. Kusisto
1973 "Some personal and social characteristics of mate-sharing swingers." Pp. 146–165 in Roger W. Libby and Robert N. Whitehurst (eds.), *Renovating Marriage.* Danville, Calif.: Consensus Publishers.

Glenn, Norval D.
1975 "Psychological well-being in the postparental stage: some evidence from national surveys." *Journal of Marriage and the Family,* 37:105–110.

Glenn, Norval D., A. A. Ross, and J. C. Tully
1974 "Patterns of intergenerational mobility of females through marriage." *American Sociological Review* 39:683–689.

Glick, Paul C.
1975 "Some recent changes in American families." *Current Population Reports: Special Studies,* Series P-23, No. 52. U.S. Bureau of the Census.

Glick, Paul C. and Arthur J. Norton
1973 "Perspectives on the recent upturn in divorce and remarriage." *Demography* 10:301–314.

Goffman, Erving
1959 *The Presentation of Self in Everyday Life.* New York: Anchor Books.

Goode, William J.
1956 *After Divorce.* Reissued in 1965 as *Women in Divorce.* New York: Free Press.
1959 "The theoretical importance of love." *American Sociological Review* 24:38–47.
1962 "Marital satisfaction and instability: a cross-cultural class analysis of divorce rates." *International Social Science Journal* 14:507–526.
1963 *World Revolution and Family Patterns.* New York: Free Press.
1964 *The Family.* Englewood Cliffs, N.J.: Prentice-Hall.
1971 "Force and violence in the family." *Journal of Marriage and the Family* 33:624–636.

Gordis, Robert
1967 *Sex and the Family in the Jewish Tradition.* New York: The Burning Bush Press.

Gordon, Albert I.
1964 *Intermarriage: Interfaith, Interracial, Interethnic.* Boston: Beacon.

Gordon, Michael
1971 "From an unfortunate necessity to a cult of mutual orgasm." In James Henslin (ed.), *The Sociology of Sex.* New York: Appleton-Century-Crofts.

Gordon, Michael and Penelope Shankweiler
1971 "Different equals less: female sexuality in recent marriage manuals." *Journal of Marriage and the Family* 33:459–465.

Graham-Murray, James
1966 *A History of Morals.* London: Library 33 Ltd.

Greenblat, Cathy, Peter Stein, and Norman Washburne
1974 *The Marriage Game: Understanding Marital Decision Making.* New York: Random House.

Greenwald, Harold
1970 "Marriage as a non-legal voluntary association." Pp. 51–56 in Herbert Otto (ed.), *The Family in Search of a Future.* New York: Appleton-Century-Crofts.

Grimshaw, Allen D.
1970 "Interpreting collective violence: an argument for the importance of social structure." *Annals* 391 (September):9–20.

Groat, H. T. and A. G. Neal
1967 "Social psychological correlates of urban fertility." *American Sociological Review* 32:945–959.

Gustavus, Susan O. and James R. Henley, Jr.
1971 "Correlates of voluntary childlessness in a select population." *Social Biology* 18:277–284.

Hallenbeck, Phyllis
1966 "An analysis of power dynamics in marriage." *Journal of Marriage and the Family* 28:200–203.

Haller, Archibald and Irwin Miller
1971 *The Occupational Aspiration Scale.* Cambridge, Mass.: Schenkman.

Hammond, Boone and Joyce Ladner
1969 "Socialization into sexual behavior in a

Negro slum ghetto." Pp. 41–51 in Carlfred Broderick and Jessie Bernard (eds.), *The Individual, Sex, and Society*. Baltimore: Johns Hopkins.

Harder, Mary White, James T. Richardson, and Robert B. Simmonds

1972 "Jesus People." *Psychology Today* 6 (December):45–50, 110–113.

Harris, Thomas

1967 *I'm OK—You're OK*. New York: Harper & Row. Avon edition in paperback.

Hass, Paula H.

1972 "Maternal role incompatibility and fertility in Latin America." *Journal of Social Issues* 28(2):111–128.

Haug, Marie R.

1973 "Social class measurement and women's occupational roles." *Social Forces* 52 (September):86–98.

Hauser, Richard

1962 *The Homosexual Society*. London: The Bodley Head.

Hauser, Robert M.

1972 *Socioeconomic Background and Educational Performance*. Washington, D.C.: American Sociological Association.

Havens, Elizabeth

1973 "Women, work, and wedlock: a note on female marital patterns in the United States." *American Journal of Sociology* 78:975–981.

Heer, David

1958 "Dominance and the working wife." *Social Forces* 36:341–347.

1963 "The measurement and bases of family power: an overview." *Journal of Marriage and the Family* 25:133–139.

1974 "The prevalence of black-white marriage in the United States, 1960 and 1970." *Journal of Marriage and the Family* 36:246–258.

Hennig, Margaret

1973 "Family dynamics for developing positive achievement motivation in women: the successful woman executive." *Annals of the New York Academy of Sciences* 208 (March):76–81.

Henshel, Anne-Marie

1973 "Swinging: a study of decision making in marriage." *American Journal of Sociology* 78:885–891.

Henslin, James M. (ed.)

1971 *Studies in the Sociology of Sex*. New York: Appleton-Century-Crofts.

Herzog, Elizabeth

1967 *About the Poor: Some Facts and Some Fictions*. Children's Bureau Publication No. 451. Washington, D.C.: U.S. Department of Health, Education and Welfare.

Hess, Robert and Judith Torney

1962 "Religion, age and sex in children's perceptions of family authority." *Child Development* 33:781–789.

1967 *The Development of Political Attitudes in Children*. Chicago: Aldine.

Hill, Reuben

1971 "Modern systems theory and the family: a confrontation." *Social Science Information* 10 (5):7–26.

Himes, Norman

1936 *Medical History of Contraception*. Reprint. New York: Schocken, 1970.

Hoffman, Lois Wladis

1972a "A psychological perspective on the value of children to parents: concepts and measures." In Fawcett, 1972.

1972b "Early childhood experiences and women's achievement motives." *Journal of Social Issues* 28 (2):129–155.

1973 "The professional woman as mother." *Annals of the New York Academy of Sciences* 208 (March):211–217.

1974 "Effects on child." Pp. 126–166 in Hoffman and Nye, 1974.

Hoffman, Lois Wladis and Martin L. Hoffman

1973 "The value of children to parents." Pp. 19–76 in James T. Fawcett (ed.), *Psychological Perspectives on Population*. New York: Basic Books.

Hoffman, Lois Wladis and F. Ivan Nye

1974 *Working Mothers*. San Francisco: Jossey-Bass.

Hoffman, Martin

1968 *The Gay World*. New York: Basic Books.

Hoffman, Martin L.

1963 "Personality, family structure, and social class as antecedents of parental power assertion." *Child Development* 34:869–884.

Hole, Judith and Ellen Levine

1971 *Rebirth of Feminism*. New York: Quadrangle/The New York Times Book Co.

Holmstrom, Lynda Lytle

1972 *The Two-Career Family*. Cambridge, Mass.: Schenkman.

Holter, Harriet

1970 *Sex Roles and Social Structure*. Oslo: Universitetsforlaget.

Homans, George C.

1961 *Social Behavior: Its Elementary Forms*. New York: Harcourt, Brace, and World.

Hooker, Evelyn

1965 "The homosexual community." In *Perspectives in Psychopathology*. New York: Oxford. (Reprinted in Gagnon and Simon, 1967b).

1968 "Homosexuality." Pp. 222–233 in David L. Sills (ed.), *International Encyclopedia of the Social Sciences*, Vol. 14. New York: Crowell Collier and Macmillan. (Reprinted in Livingood, 1972.)

Horner, Matina S.

1969 "Fail: bright women." *Psychology Today* 3 (6):36–38, 62.

1970 "Femininity and successful achievement: a basic inconsistency." Pp. 45–74 in J. Bardwick, E. Douvan, M. Horner, and D. Gutmann (eds.), *Feminine Personality and Conflict*. Belmont, Calif.: Brooks/Cole.

1972 "Toward an understanding of achievement-related conflicts in women." *Journal of Social Issues* 28(2):157–175.

Hunter, Gertrude

1973 "Pediatrician." In *Successful Women in the Sciences: An Analysis of Determinants*. Special issue of the *Annals of the New York Academy of Sciences* 208 (March):37–40.

Jackson, Jacquelyne Johnson

1973 "Family organization and technology." Pp. 408–445 in Kent Miller and Ralph Dreger (eds.), *Comparative Studies of Blacks and Whites in the United States*. New York: Seminar.

Jaffe, Frederick S.

1973 "Commentary: some policy and program implications of 'Contraceptive Failure in the United States.'" *Family Planning Perspectives* 5 (Summer):143–144.

Jencks, Christopher, Marshall Smith, Henry Ackland, Mary Jo Bane, David Cohen, Herbert Gintis, Barbara Heyns, and Stephen Michelson

1972 *Inequality—A Reassessment of the Effect of Family and Schooling in America.* New York: Basic Books.

Jensen, Mehri Samandari
1974 "Role differentiation in female homosexual quasi-marital unions." *Journal of Marriage and the Family* 36:360–367.

Johnston, Jill
1973 *Lesbian Nation.* New York: Simon and Schuster.

Kaberry, Phyllis M.
1953 *Women of the Grassfields.* London: Her Majesty's Stationery Office.

Kadushin, Alfred
1970 "Single parent adoptions: an overview and some relevant research." *Social Service Review* 44 (3).

Kagan, Jerome
1964 "Acquisition and significance of sex typing and sex role identity." In Martin L. Hoffman and Lois W. Hoffman (eds.), *Review of Child Development Research*, Vol. 1. New York: Russell Sage.

Kanowitz, Leo
1973 *Sex Roles in Law and Society.* Albuquerque: University of New Mexico Press.

Kanter, Rosabeth Moss
1968 "Commitment and social organization: a study of commitment mechanisms in utopian communities." *American Sociological Review* 33:499–517.
1972 "'Getting it all together': communes past, present, future." Pp. 311–325 in Louise Kapp Howe (ed.), *The Future of the Family.* New York: Simon and Schuster.
1973 *Communes: Creating and Managing the Collective Life.* New York: Harper & Row.
1974 "Communes for all reasons." *Ms.* 3 (August):62–67.

Kantner, John F. and Melvin Zelnik
1972 "Sexual experience of young unmarried women in the United States." *Family Planning Perspectives* 4 (October):9–17.
1973 "Contraception and pregnancy: Experience of young unmarried women in the United States." *Family Planning Perspectives* 5 (Winter):21–35.

Kar, S. B.
1971 "Individual aspirations as related to early and late acceptance of contraception." *The Journal of Social Psychology* 83:235–245.

Kassel, Victor
1970 "Polygny after sixty." Pp. 137–143 in Herbert Otto (ed.), *The Family in Search of a Future.* New York: Appleton-Century-Crofts.

Katzenstein, Alfred
1970 "Male and female in the German Democratic Republic." Pp. 240–256 in Seward and Williamson, 1970.

Kelley, Harold and Anthony Stahelski
1970 "Social interaction basis of cooperators' and competitors' beliefs about others." *Journal of Personality and Social Psychology* 16:66–91.

Kelley, H. H. and D. P. Schenitzki
1972 "Bargaining." In C. G. McClintock (ed.), *Experimental Social Psychology.* New York: Holt.

Kelly, Janis
1972 "Sister love: an exploration of the need for homosexual experience." *Family Coordinator* 21:473–475.

Kennedy, David M.
1970 *Birth Control in America: The Career of Margaret Sanger.* New Haven, Conn.: Yale University Press.

Kephart, William
1964 "Legal and procedural aspects of marriage and divorce." Pp. 944–968 in Harold T. Christensen (ed.), *Handbook of Marriage and the Family.* Chicago: Rand McNally.

Kerckhoff, Alan C.
1972 *Socialization and Social Class.* Englewood Cliffs, N.J.: Prentice-Hall.
1974 *Ambition and Attainment.* Washington, D.C.: American Sociological Association.

Kinkade, Kathleen
1973 *A Walden Two Experiment.* New York: Morrow.

Kinsey, Alfred C., W. B. Pomeroy, and C. E. Martin
1948 *Sexual Behavior in the Human Male.* Philadelphia: Saunders.

Kinsey, A. C., W. B. Pomeroy, C. E. Martin, and P. H. Gebhard
1953 *Sexual Behavior in the Human Female.* Philadelphia: Saunders. New York: Pocket Books paperback edition.

Kirkendall, Lester
1968 "Understanding the problems of the male virgin." Pp. 123–129 in Isadore Rubin and Lester Kirkendall (eds.), *Sex in the Adolescent Years.* New York: Association.

Klein, Carole
1973 *The Single Parent Experience.* New York: Walker.

Klineberg, O.
1964 *The Human Dimension in International Relations.* New York: Holt.

Kohn, Melvin L.
1969 *Class and Conformity: A Study in Values.* Homewood, Ill.: Dorsey.

Komarovsky, Mirra
1962 *Blue-Collar Marriage.* New York: Random House.

Kraditor, Aileen S.
1968 *Up from the Pedestal.* Chicago: Quadrangle.

Krantzler, Mel
1973 *Creative Divorce.* New York: Evans. New American Library Signet paperback edition.

Krause, Harry D.
1971 *Illegitimacy: Law and Social Policy.* Indianapolis: Bobbs-Merrill.

Kreps, Juanita
1971 *Sex in the Market Place.* Baltimore: Johns Hopkins.

Kriesberg, Louis
1973 *The Sociology of Social Conflicts.* Englewood Cliffs, N.J.: Prentice-Hall.

Kutner, Nancy and Donna Brogan
1974 "An investigation of sex-related slang vocabulary and sex-role orientation among male and female university students." *Journal of Marriage and the Family* 36:474–484.

LaFree, Gary
1974 "Independence among the Igbo women of West Africa." Unpublished paper, Department of Sociology, Indiana University, Bloomington, Ind.

Lamson, Peggy
1968 *Few Are Chosen: American Women in Political Life Today.* Boston: Houghton Mifflin.

Langton, Kenneth
1969 *Political Socialization.* New York: Oxford.

Lasch, Christopher
1973 "Marriage in the Middle Ages." *The Columbia Forum* 2 (Fall).
Learner, Gerda (ed.)
1972 *Black Women in White America*. New York: Random House.
Lederer, W. J. and D. D. Jackson
1968 *The Mirages of Marriage*. New York: Norton.
Lehr, Ursula and Hellgard Rauh
1970 "Male and female in the German Federal Republic." Pp. 220–239 in G. H. Seward and R. C. Williamson (eds.), *Sex Roles in Changing Society*. New York: Random House.
Levinger, George
1966 "Physical abuse among applicants for divorce," an excerpt from "Source of marital satisfaction among applicants for divorce," *American Journal of Orthopsychiatry* 36 (October). as reprinted in Steinmetz and Straus, 1974, pp. 85–88.
Levinson, Daniel J. and Phyllis E. Huffman
1955 "Traditional family ideology and its relation to personality." *Journal of Personality* (March):251–273.
Levi-Strauss, Claude
1949 "The Principle of Reciprocity." Chapter 5 of *Les Structures Elementaires de la Parente*. Presses Universitaires de France. Abridged and translated by Rose L. Coser and Grace Frazer. Pp. 74–84 in Lewis Coser and Bernard Rosenberg (eds.), *Sociological Theory*. 2nd ed. New York: Macmillan.
1956 "The family." Pp. 261–285 in Harry L. Shapiro (ed.), *Man, Culture, and Society*. New York: Oxford.
Lewis, Lionel and Dennis Brissett
1967 "Sex as work: a study of avocational counseling." *Social Problems* 15 (Summer): 8–18.
Lewis, Oscar
1951 *Life in a Mexican Village: Tepoztlan Restudied*. Urbana: University of Illinois Press.
1968 *A Study of Slum Culture*. New York: Random House.
Libby, Roger W. and John E. Carlson
1973 "A theoretical framework for premarital sexual decisions in the dyad." *Archives of Sexual Behavior* 2:365–378.
Liebow, Elliot
1967 *Tally's Corner: A Study of Negro Streetcorner Men*. Boston: Little, Brown.
Liljestrom, Rita
1966 "Sex roles in literature for adolescents and in mass media." In *Talent or Sex*? Stockholm. (Cited in Holter, 1970.)
1970 "The Swedish model." Pp. 200–219 in Seward and Williamson, 1970.
Lindsey, Ben B.
1926 "The companionate marriage." *Redbook* (October).
1927 "The companionate marriage." *Redbook* (March).
Linner, Birgitta
1966 "Sexual morality and sexual reality—the Scandinavian approach." *American Journal of Orthopsychiatry* 36:686–693.
1967 *Sex and Society in Sweden*. New York: Pantheon.
Liu, William T., I. W. Hutchinson, and L. K. Hong
1973 "Conjugal power and decision making: a methodological note on cross-cultural study of the family." *American Journal of Sociology* 79:84–98.
Livingood, John M.
1972 *National Institute of Mental Health Task Force on Homosexuality: Final Report and Background Papers*. Rockville, Md.: National Institute of Mental Health.
Locke, Harvey J.
1968 *Predicting Adjustment in Marriage: A Comparison of a Divorced and a Happily Married Group*. New York: Greenwood.
Loether, Herman
1964 "The meaning of work and adjustment to retirement." Pp. 517–525 in A. B. Shostak and W. Gomberg (eds.), *Blue-Collar World*. Englewood Cliffs, N.J.: Prentice-Hall.
1967 *Problems of Aging*. Belmont, Calif.: Dickenson.
Lopata, Helen Znaniecki
1973a *Widowhood in an American City*. Cambridge, Mass.: Schenkman.
1973b "Self-identity in marriage and widowhood." *The Sociological Quarterly* 14 (Summer):407–418.
Lord, Edith
1970 "Emergent Africa." Pp. 44–66 in Seward and Williamson, 1970.
Lott, J. and B. E. Lott
1963 *Negro and White Youth*. New York: Holt.
Lowenthall, Marjorie Fiske and Clayton Haven
1968 "Interaction and adaptation: intimacy as a critical variable." *American Sociological Review* 33:20–30.
Luckey, Eleanore and Gilbert Nass
1969 "A comparison of sexual attitudes and behavior in an international sample." *Journal of Marriage and the Family* 31:364–379.
Lyness, Judith, Milton Lipetz, and Keith Davis
1972 "Living together: an alternative to marriage." *Journal of Marriage and the Family* 34:305–311.
Macciocchi, Maria
1972 *Daily Life in Revolutionary China*. New York: Monthly Review Press.
McClelland, David C.
1961 *The Achieving Society*. Princeton, N.J.: D. Van Nostrand.
McKinley, Donald Gilbert
1964 *Social Class and Family Life*. New York: Free Press.
Maddox, George
1970 "Themes and issues in sociological theories of human aging." *Human Development* 13.17–27.
Mainardi, Pat
1970 "The politics of housework." Pp. 447–454 in Robin Morgan (ed.), *Sisterhood Is Powerful*. New York: Vintage.
Malcolm X
1964 *The Autobiography of Malcolm X*. New York: Grove.
Malinowski, Bronislaw
1930 "Parenthood, the basis of social structure." In V. F. Calverton and S. D. Schmalhausen (eds.), *The New Generation*. New York: Macauley. Reprinted in Rose L. Coser (ed.), *The Family: Its Structures and Functions*. 2nd ed. New York: St. Martin's, 1974.
Markle, Gerald E.
1973 "Sexism and the sex ratio." Paper read at the annual meeting of the American Sociological Association, New York, August 1973.

1974 "Sex ratio at birth: values, variance, and some determinants." *Demography* 11:131–142.

Martin, Del and Paul Mariah
1972 "Homosexual Love—Woman to Woman, Man to Man." Pp. 120–134 in Herbert Otto, *Love Today*. New York: Association.

Martin, Del and Phyllis Lyon
1972 *Lesbian/Woman.* New York: Bantam Books.

Martin, Ralph G.
1969 *Jennie: The Life of Lady Randolph Churchill.* Englewood Cliffs, N.J.: Prentice-Hall.

Maslow, A. H.
1954 *Motivation and Personality.* New York: Harper & Row.

Masters, William and Virginia Johnson
1966 *Human Sexual Response.* Boston: Little, Brown.
1973 "Why 'working at' sex doesn't work." *Redbook* 140 (April):87.

Mead, Margaret
1935 *Sex and Temperament.* New York: Morrow.
1966 "Marriage in two steps." *Redbook* 127 (July):48–49.
1968 "A continuing dialogue on marriage." *Redbook* 130 (April):44.

Merton, Robert K.
1941 "Intermarriage and the social structure: fact and theory." *Psychiatry* 4:361–374.
1959 "Social structure and anomie: revisions and extensions." In Ruth Nanda Anshen (ed.), *The Family: Its Function and Destiny.* New York: Harper & Row.

Michel, Andree
1967 "Comparative data concerning the interaction in French and American families." *Journal of Marriage and the Family* 29:337–344.

Middleton, Russell
1962 "A deviant case: brother-sister and father-daughter marriage in ancient Egypt." *American Sociological Review* 27:603–611.

Mileski, Maureen and Donald Black
1972 "The social organization of homosexuality." *Urban Life and Culture* 1 (July):187–199.

Mill, John Stuart
1869 "The subjection of women." Reprinted in John Stuart Mill and Harriet Taylor Mill, *Essays on Sex Equality*, edited by Alice Rossi. Chicago: University of Chicago Press, 1970, pp. 125–242.

Miller, Arthur A.
1970 "Reactions of friends to divorce." Pp. 56–77 in Paul Bohannan (ed.), *Divorce and After.* Garden City, N.Y.: Doubleday.

Miller, Daniel and Guy Swanson
1958 *The Changing American Parent: A Study in the Detroit Area.* New York: Wiley.

Miller, Howard L. and Paul S. Siegel
1972 *Loving: A Psychological Approach.* New York: Wiley.

Milner, Murray, Jr.
1972 *The Illusion of Equality: The Effect of Education on Opportunity, Inequality, and Social Conflict.* San Francisco: Jossey-Bass.

Milton, John
1820 *The Doctrine and Discipline of Divorce.* London: Sherwood, Neely, and Jones.

Mitchell, Juliet
1971 *Woman's Estate.* New York: Pantheon.

Mizruchi, Ephraim
1964 *Success and Opportunity.* New York: Free Press.

Monahan, Thomas P.
1973 "Marriage across racial lines in Indiana." *Journal of Marriage and the Family* 35:632–640.

Money, John
1970 "Sexual dimorphism and homosexual gender identity." *Psychological Bulletin* 74:425–440. (Reprinted in Livingood, 1972.)

Money, John and Anke A. Ehrhardt
1972 *Man and Woman, Boy and Girl.* Baltimore: Johns Hopkins.

Monthly Vital Statistics Reports (See U.S. Department of Health, Education and Welfare.)

Morgan, Edmund S.
1956 *The Puritan Family.* Boston: Trustees of the Public Library.

Mueller, Eva
1972 "Economic cost and value of children: conceptualization and measurement." In Fawcett, 1972.

Mueller, Samuel A.
1971 "The new triple melting pot: Herberg revisited." *Review of Religious Research* 13:18–33.

Mulvihill, J. J., M. M. Tumin, and L. A. Curtis
1969 *Crimes of Violence.* Staff Report to the National Commission on the Causes and Prevention of Violence. Washington, D.C.: U.S. Government Printing Office.

Murdock, George P.
1949 *Social Structure.* New York: Macmillan.

Murillo, Nathan
1971 "The Mexican American family." Pp. 97–108 in N. N. Wagner and M. J. Haug (eds.), *Chicanos: Social and Psychological Perspectives.* St. Louis: Mosby.

National Center for Health Statistics (See U.S. Department of Health, Education and Welfare.)

Neubeck, Gerhard (ed.)
1969 *Extramarital Relations.* Englewood Cliffs, N.J.: Prentice-Hall.

Niebuhr, Reinhold
1957 *Love and Justice.* Edited by D. B. Robertson. Cleveland: World.

Nimkoff, M. F. (ed.)
1965 *Comparative Family Systems.* Boston: Houghton Mifflin.

Nisbet, Robert A.
1970 *The Social Bond.* New York: Knopf.

Noble, Jeanne L.
1966 "The American Negro Woman." In John P. Davis (ed.), *The American Negro Reference Book.* Englewood Cliffs, N.J.: Prentice-Hall.

Nunnally, Jum C.
1972 "Major issues, measurement methods, and research strategies for investigating the effects of children on parents." In Fawcett, 1972.

Nye, F. Ivan
1963 "Marital interaction." Pp. 263–281 in Nye and Hoffman, 1963.
1974a "Sociocultural context." Pp. 1–31 in Hoffman and Nye, 1974.
1974b "Husband-wife relationship." Pp. 186–206 in Hoffman and Nye, 1974.

Nye, F. Ivan and Lois W. Hoffman
1963 *The Employed Mother in America.* Chicago: Rand McNally.

Oakley, Ann
1974 *Woman's Work: Housewife Past and Present.* New York: Pantheon.

O'Brien, John
1971 "Violence in divorce-prone families." *Journal of Marriage and the Family* 33:692–698.

Ogilvy, Jay and Heather Ogilvy
1972 "Communes and the reconstruction of reality." Pp. 83–99 in Sallie Teselle (ed.), *The Family, Communes and Utopian Societies.* New York: Harper Torchbooks.

Olson, D. and C. Rabunsky
1972 "Validity of four measures of family power." *Journal of Marriage and the Family* 34:224–234.

O'Neill, Nena and George O'Neill
1970 "Patterns in group sexual activity." *Journal of Sex Research* 6 (2):101–112.
1972 *Open Marriage.* New York: Evans. Avon paperback edition.

O'Neill, William L.
1967 *Divorce in the Progressive Era.* New Haven, Conn.: Yale University Press.

Orden, Susan and Norman Bradburn
1969 "Working wives and marriage happiness." *American Journal of Sociology* 74:392–407.

Ovid
Metamorphoses. Translated by Mary M. Innes. Baltimore: Penguin,

Palmore, Erdman
1968 "The effects of aging on activities and attitudes." *The Gerontologist* 8 (Winter): 259–263.
1970 (ed.), *Normal Aging: Reports from the Duke Longitudinal Study, 1955–1969.* Durham, N.C.: Duke University Press.

Parish, William L., Jr.
1974 "Socialism and the Chinese peasant family." Paper read at the annual meeting of the American Sociological Association, Montreal, Quebec, August 1974.

Parnas, Raymond
1967 "The police response to the domestic disturbance." *Wisconsin Law Review* 914 (Fall):914–960.

Parsons, Talcott
1942 "Age and sex in the social structure." *American Sociological Review* 7:604–606.
1943 "The kinship system of the contemporary United States." *American Anthropologist* 45:22–38.
1955 "The American family: its relation to personality and to social structure." In T. Parsons and R. F. Bales, *Family Socialization, and Interaction Process.* New York: Free Press.

Pearlin, Leonard
1972 *Class Context and Family Relations: A Cross-National Study.* Boston: Little, Brown.

Peck, Ellen
1971 *The Baby Trap.* New York: Bernard Geis.

Peterson, Candida C. and James L. Peterson
1973 "Preference for sex of offspring as a measure of change in sex attitudes." *Psychology* 10 (August):3–5.

Pettigrew, Thomas
1964 *A Profile of the Negro American.* Princeton, N.J.: D. Van Nostrand.

Piddington, Ralph
1965 "A study of French Canadian kinship." *International Journal of Comparative Sociology* 12 (1). Reprinted in C. C. Harris (ed.), *Readings in Kinship in Urban Society.* New York: Pergamon, 1970, pp. 71–98.

Pineo, Peter C.
1961 "Disenchantment in the later years of marriage." *Marriage and Family Living* 23:3–11.

Pitts, Jesse R.
1964 "The structural-functional approach." Pp. 51–124 in Harold T. Christensen (ed.), *Handbook of Marriage and the Family.* Chicago: Rand McNally.

Plato
1945 *The Republic of Plato.* Translated by Francis M. Conford. New York: Oxford University Press.

Pleck, Joseph and Jack Sawyer (eds.)
1974 *Men and Masculinity.* Englewood Cliffs, N.J.: Prentice-Hall Spectrum Books.

Poffenberger, T.
1969 "Husband-wife communication and motivational aspects of population control in an Indian village." Monograph Series No. 10 (December). New Delhi: Central Family Planning Institute.

Polk, Barbara Bovee, Robert Stein, and Lon Polk
1973 "The potential of the urban commune for changing sex roles." Paper read at the annual meeting of the American Sociological Association, New York, August.

Pomeroy, Wardell B.
1972 *Dr. Kinsey and the Institute for Sex Research.* New York: Harper & Row.

Presser, Harriet B. and Larry L. Bumpass
1972 "The acceptability of contraceptive sterilization among U.S. couples: 1970." *Family Planning Perspectives* 4 (October):18–26.

Preston, Samuel H.
1975 "Estimating the proportion of American marriages that end in divorce." *Sociological Methods & Research* 3 (May):435–460.

Purcell, Theodore
1960 *Blue Collar Man.* Cambridge, Mass.: Harvard University Press

Rabin, Albert I.
1970 "The sexes: ideology and reality in the Israeli kibbutz." Pp. 285–307 in Seward and Williamson, 1970

Rabkin, Leslie and Melford Spiro
1970 "Postscript: The kibbutz in 1970." Chapter 9 in Melford Spiro, *Kibbutz: Venture in Utopia.* New York: Schocken.

Rainwater, Lee
1960 *And the Poor Get Children.* Chicago: Quadrangle.
1964 "Marital sexuality in four 'cultures of poverty.'" *Journal of Marriage and the Family* 26 (November):457–466.
1965 *Family Design: Marital Sexuality, Family Size, and Contraception.* Chicago: Aldine.
1966a "Sex in the Culture of Poverty." *Journal of Social Issues* 22 (April) as reprinted in a later version in Carlfred Broderick and Jessie Bernard (eds.), *The Individual, Sex, and Society.* Baltimore: Johns Hopkins, 1969, pp. 129–140.
1966b "Crucible of identity: the Negro lower-class family." *Daedalus* 95 (Winter):172–216.
1970 *Behind Ghetto Walls.* Chicago: Aldine.

Ramey, James
1972a "Communes, group marriage, and the upper-middle class." *Journal of Marriage and the Family* 34:647–655.
1972b "Emerging patterns of innovative behavior in marriage." *Family Coordinator* (October). Reprinted in Smith and Smith, 1974.

Reed, R. H. and S. McIntosh
1972 "Costs of children." In E. R. Morss and R. H. Reed (eds.), *Economic Aspects of Popula-*

tion Change, Vol. 2, Washington, D.C.: U.S. Commission on Population Growth and the American Future.

Rehwinkel, Alfred M.

1959 *Planned Parenthood.* St. Louis: Concordia.

Reiss, Ira L.

1960a *Premarital Sexual Standards in America.* New York: Free Press.

1960b "Toward a sociology of the heterosexual relationship." *Journal of Marriage and Family Living* 22(May):139–155.

1967a "Some comments on premarital sexual permissiveness." *American Journal of Sociology,* 72:558–559.

1967b *The Social Context of Premarital Sexual Permissiveness.* New York: Holt.

1972 "Premarital sexuality: past, present, and future." Pp. 167–188 in Ira L. Reiss (ed.), *Readings on the Family System,* New York: Holt.

1973 "The role of sexuality in the study of family and fertility." Paper read at the conference on "Family and Fertility," sponsored by the Center for Population Research and the National Institute for Child Health and Human Development, June 13–16, Belmont, Elkridge, Maryland. Mimeographed.

Renne, Karen

1970 "Correlates of dissatisfaction in marriage." *Journal of Marriage and the Family* 32:54–67.

Rheinstein, Max

1970 "Divorce law in Sweden." Pp. 127–151 in Paul Bohannan (ed.), *Divorce and After.* Garden City, N.Y.: Doubleday.

1972 *Marriage Stability, Divorce, and the Law.* Chicago: University of Chicago Press.

Richer, Stephen

1968 "The economics of child rearing." *Journal of Marriage and the Family* 30:462–466.

Riegel, Robert E.

1970 *American Women: A Story of Social Change.* Cranbury, N.J.: Associated University Presses, Fairleigh Dickinson University Press.

Riley, Matilda White and Anne Foner, in association with M. Moore, B. Hess, and B. Roth

1968 *Aging and Society*, Vol. 1. New York: Russell Sage.

Robertson, Constance Noyes (ed.)

1970 *Oneida Community: An Autobiography, 1851–1876.* Syracuse, N.Y.: Syracuse University Press.

Rodman, Hyman

1967 "Marital power in France, Greece, Yugoslavia, and the United States: a cross-national discussion." *Journal of Marriage and the Family* 29:320–324.

1972 "Marital power and the theory of resources in cultural context." *Journal of Comparative Family Studies* 3:50–67.

Rollins, Boyd and Harold Feldman

1970 "Marital satisfaction over the family life cycle." *Journal of Marriage and the Family* 26:20–28.

Rollins, Boyd and Kenneth L. Cannon

1974 "Marital satisfaction over the family life cycle: a reevaluation." *Journal of Marriage and the Family* 36:271–282.

Rosenberg, Bernard and Joseph Bensman

1968 "Sexual patterns in three ethnic subcultures of an American underclass." *Annals of the American Academy of Political and Social Science* 376:61–75.

Rosow, Irving

1973 *Socialization to Old Age.* Berkeley: University of California Press.

Rossi, Alice

1964 "Equality between the sexes: an immodest proposal." Pp. 98–143 in R. J. Lifton (ed.), *The Woman in America.* Boston: Beacon Press Daedalus Library.

1965 "Barriers to the career choice of engineering, medicine, or science among American women." Pp. 51–127 in Jacquelyn Mattfeld and Carol Van Aken (eds.), *Women and the Scientific Professions.* Cambridge, Mass.: M.I.T. Press.

1968 "Transition to parenthood." *Journal of Marriage and the Family* 30:26–39.

1973 "Sexuality and gender roles." Lecture given in the Human Sexuality unit of the Year II Program in Psychiatry and Behavioral Sciences, The Johns Hopkins University School of Medicine, February 2. Revised version. Mimeographed.

Rowbotham, Sheila

1972 *Women, Resistance and Revolution.* New York: Pantheon.

Rubin, Zick

1973 *Liking and Loving.* New York: Holt.

Rugoff, Milton

1971 *Prudery and Passion.* New York: Putnam's.

Ryder, Norman

1973 "Contraceptive failure in the United States." *Family Planning Perspectives* 5 (Summer):133–142.

Ryder, Norman and Charles Westoff

1971 *Reproduction in the United States, 1965.* Princeton, N.J.: Princeton University Press.

Ryder, Robert G.

1970 "Dimensions of early marriage." *Family Process* 9 (March):51–68.

1973 "Longitudinal data relating marriage satisfaction and having a child." *Journal of Marriage and the Family* 35:604–606.

Safa, Helen I.

1971 "The matrifocal family in the black ghetto: sign of pathology or pattern of survival?" Pp. 35–59 in Charles O. Crawford (ed.), *Health and the Family: A Medical-Sociological Analysis.* New York: Macmillan.

Safilios-Rothschild, Constantina

1967 "A comparison of power structure and marital satisfaction in urban Greek and French families." *Journal of Marriage and the Family* 29:345–352.

1969 "Family sociology or wives' family sociology? A cross-cultural examination of decision making." *Journal of Marriage and the Family* 31:290–301.

1970 "The study of family power structure: a review 1960–1969." *Journal of Marriage and the Family* 32:539–552.

St. George, George

1973 *Our Soviet Sister.* Washington, D.C.: Luce.

Sandford, Mrs. John

1834 *Woman in Her Social and Domestic Character.* London: Longman, Rees, Orme, Brown, Green, & Longman.

Sandlund, Majbritt

1968 *The Status of Women in Sweden.* Report

to the United Nations. Stockholm: The Swedish Institute.

Satir, Virginia
1967 "Marriage as a statutory five year renewable contract." Paper presented at the annual convention of the American Psychological Association, Washington, D.C., September 1.

Scanzoni, John
1965 "A note on the sufficiency of wife responses in family research." *Pacific Sociological Review* (Fall):109–115.
1970 *Opportunity and the Family.* New York: Free Press.
1971 *The Black Family in Modern Society.* Boston: Allyn and Bacon.
1972 *Sexual Bargaining: Power Politics in the American Marriage.* Englewood Cliffs, N.J.: Prentice-Hall.
1975a "Sex roles, economic factors, and marital solidarity in black and white marriages." *Journal of Marriage and the Family* 37:130–145.
1975b *Sex Roles, Life Styles, and Childbearing: Changing Patterns in Marriage and Family.* New York: Free Press.
1975c "Changes in gender roles." Unpublished student study.

Schelling, T. C. and M. H. Halperin
1961 *Strategy and Arms Control.* New York: Twentieth Century Fund.

Schmidt, Gunter and Volkmar Sigusch
1970 "Sex differences in responses to psychosexual stimulation by films and slides." *The Journal of Sex Research* 6:268–283.
1972 "Changes in sexual behavior among young males and females between 1960–1970." *Archives of Sexual Behavior* 2:27–45.
1973 "Women's sexual arousal." Pp. 117–143 in Joseph Zubin and John Money (eds.), *Contemporary Sexual Behavior: Critical Issues in the 1970s.* Baltimore: Johns Hopkins.

Schmidt, G., V. Sigusch, and S. Schafer
1973 "Responses to reading erotic stories: male-female differences." *Archives of Sexual Behavior* 2:181–199.

Schneider, David M. and Raymond T. Smith
1973 *Class Differences and Sex Roles in American Kinship and Family Structure.* Englewood Cliffs, N.J.: Prentice-Hall.

Schulz, David A.
1969 *Coming Up Black.* Englewood Cliffs, N.J.: Prentice-Hall.

Scott, John Finley
1965 "The American college sorority: its role in class and ethnic endogamy." *American Sociological Review* 30:514–527.

Seaman, Barbara
1972 *Free and Female.* New York: Coward, McCann & Geoghegan.

Sears, Robert, Eleanor E. Maccoby, and Harry Levin
1957 *Patterns of Child Rearing.* Evanston, Ill.: Row, Peterson.

Seeley, John R., R. Alexander Sim, and Elizabeth W. Loosley
1956 *Crestwood Heights.* New York: Basic Books.

Segal, Sheldon J.
1972 "Contraceptive research: a male chauvinist plot?" *Family Planning Perspectives* 4 (July):21–25.

Seidenberg, Robert
1970 *Marriage Between Equals.* First published as *Marriage in Life and Literature.* New York: Philosophical Library. Doubleday, Anchor Press edition, 1973.

Seltman, Charles
1956 *Women in Antiquity.* London: Thames & Hudson.

Seward, Georgene H. and Robert C. Williamson (eds.)
1970 *Sex Roles in Changing Society.* New York: Random House.

Sewell, William H.
1971 "Inequality of opportunity for higher education." *American Sociological Review* 36:793–809.

Sewell, William H. and R. M. Hauser
1974 *Education, Occupation, and Earnings: Achievement in the Early Years.* Department of Sociology, University of Wisconsin, Madison.

Shanas, Ethel
1972 "Adjustment to retirement: substitution or accommodation?" Pp. 219–243 in Frances M. Carp (ed.), *Retirement.* New York: Behavioral Publications.

Shannon, T. W.
1917 *Eugenics: the Laws of Sex Life and Heredity.* Marietta, Ohio: Mullikin. Replica edition. Garden City, N.Y.: Doubleday, 1970.

Shedd, Charlie W.
1968 *The Stork Is Dead.* Waco, Tex.: Word.

Shelly, Martha
1969 "Notes of a radical lesbian." *Come Out: A Liberation Forum for the Gay Community.* Reprinted in Robin Morgan (ed.), *Sisterhood is Powerful.* New York: Vintage, 1970, pp. 306–311.

Sheppard, Harold and Neal Herrick
1972 *Where Have All the Robots Gone? Worker Dissatisfaction in the '70s.* New York: Free Press.

Shideler, Mary McDermott
1971 "An Amicable Divorce." *The Christian Century* (May 5).

Sickels, Robert J.
1972 *Race, Marriage and the Law.* Albuquerque: University of New Mexico Press.

Sidel, Ruth
1972 *Women and Child Care in China.* New York: Hill and Wang. Baltimore: Penguin.

Siecus
1970 *Sexuality and Man.* New York: Scribner's Sons.

Siegel, Sidney and Lawrence Fouraker
1960 *Bargaining and Group Decision Making.* New York: McGraw-Hill.

Silverman, Phyllis
1972 "Widowhood and preventive intervention." *The Family Coordinator* 21 (January):95–102.

Simon, William and John Gagnon
1969 "On psychosexual development." Pp. 733–752 in D. A. Goslin (ed.), *Handbook of Socialization Theory and Research.* Chicago: Rand McNally.

Simon, W., A. S. Berger, and J. H. Gagnon
1972 "Beyond anxiety and fantasy: the coital experiences of college youth." *Journal of Youth and Adolescence* 1:203–222.

Simpson, Joanne
1973 "Meteorologist." *Annals of the New York Academy of Sciences* 208 (March 15):41–46. (Special issue on "Successful Women in the Sciences: An Analysis of Determinants.")

Sklar, J. and B. Berkov
1974 "Abortion, illegitimacy and the American Birth Rate." *Science* 185:909. Also see summary, "Legal abortion reduces out-of-wedlock births." Research news report. *Family Planning Perspectives* 7 (January–February,) 1975: 11–12.

Slocum, Walter L.
1966 *Occupational Careers*, Chicago: Aldine.

Smith, Daniel Scott
1973 "The dating of the American sexual revolution: evidence and interpretation." Pp. 321–335 in Michael Gordon (ed.). *The American Family in Social-Historical Perspective*. New York: St. Martin's.

Smith Harold E.
1965 "Family interaction patterns of the aged: a review." Pp. 143–161 in Arnold Rose and Warren Peterson (eds.), *Older People and Their Social World*. Philadelphia: Davis.

Smith, James and Lynn Smith
1970 "Co-marital sex and the sexual freedom movement." *Journal of Sex Research* 6 (2):131–142.
1974 (eds.), *Beyond Monogamy*. Baltimore: Johns Hopkins.

Smith, Lynn and James Smith
1973 "Co-marital sex: the incorporation of extramarital sex into the marriage relationship." In J. Zubin and J. Money (eds.), *Critical Issues in Contemporary Sexual Behavior*. Baltimore: Johns Hopkins. (Reprinted in Smith and Smith, 1974.)

Sobol, Marion Gross
1974 "Commitment to work." Pp. 63–80 in Hoffman and Nye, 1974.

Sonenschein, David
1973 "The ethnography of male homosexual relationships." Pp. 83–96 in Henrik Ruitenbeek (ed.), *Homosexuality: A Changing Picture*. London: Souvenir Press.

Spiro, Melford E.
1965 *Children of the Kibbutz*. New York: Schocken.
1970 *Kibbutz: Venture in Utopia*. New York: Schocken.

Spreitzer, Elmer and Lawrence Riley
1974 "Factors associated with singlehood." *Journal of Marriage and the Family* 36:533–542.

Sprey, Jetse
1971 "On the management of conflict in families." *Journal of Marriage and the Family* 33:722–732.
1972 "Family power structure: a critical comment." *Journal of Marriage and the Family* 34:235–238.

Stark, Rodney and James McEvoy
1970 "Middle class violence." *Psychology Today* 4 (November):52–65.

Steinmann, Ann, D. Fox, and R. Farkas
1968 "Male and female perceptions of male sex roles." Pp. 421–422 in *Proceedings of the American Psychological Association*.

Steinmetz, Suzanne and Murray Straus
1973 "The family as a cradle of violence." *Society* 10 (September–October.):50–58.
1974 (eds.), *Violence in the Family*. New York: Dodd, Mead.

Stember, Charles H.
1966 *Jews in the Mind of America*, New York: Basic Books.

Stephens, William
1963 *The Family in Cross-Cultural Perspective*. New York: Holt.

Stevens, Evelyn P.
1973 "Marianismo: the other face of machismo in Latin America." In A. Pescatello (ed.), *Female and Male in Latin America*. Pittsburgh, Pa.: University of Pittsburgh Press.

Stinnett, Nick, Linda M. Carter, and James Montgomery
1972 "Older persons' perception of their marriages." *Journal of Marriage and the Family* 34:665–670.

Stoller, Frederick
1970 "The intimate network of families as a new structure." Pp. 145–159 in Herbert Otto (ed.), *The Family in Search of A Future*. New York: Appleton-Century-Crofts.

Straus, Murray
1971 "Some social antecedents of physical punishment: a linkage theory interpretation." *Journal of Marriage and the Family* 33:658–663.
1973 "A general systems theory approach to a theory of violence between family members." *Social Science Information* 12:105–125.
1974 "Leveling, civility, and violence in the family." *Journal of Marriage and the Family* 36:13–29.

Sussman, Marvin B.
1966 "Theoretical bases for an urban kinship network system." Cleveland: Case-Western Reserve University. Mimeographed.

Sussman, Marvin B. and Lee Burchinal
1962 "Kin family network, unheralded structure in current conceptualization of family functioning." *Marriage and Family Living* 24:231–240.

Sussman, Marvin B., Judith N. Cates, and David T. Smith
1970 *The Family and Inheritance*. New York: Russell Sage.

Symonds, Carolyn
1971 "Sexual mate-swapping: violation of norms and reconciliation of guilt." Pp. 81–109 in James Henslin (ed.), *Studies in the Sociology of Sex*. New York: Appleton-Century-Crofts.

Talmon, Yonina
1972 *Family and Community in the Kibbutz*. Cambridge, Mass.: Harvard University Press.

Taylor, Dalmas A.
1968 "The development of interpersonal relationships: social penetration processes." *The Journal of Social Psychology* 75:79–90.

Taylor, Dalmas, Irwin Altman, and Richard Sorrentino
1969 "Interpersonal exchange as a function of rewards and costs and situational factors: expectancy confirmation-disconfirmation." *Journal of Experimental Social Psychology* 5:324–339.

Taylor, Jeremy
1650 *The Rule and Exercises of Holy Living*.

Terman, L. M.
1938 *Psychological Factors in Marital Happiness*. New York: McGraw-Hill.

Thibaut, J. W. and H. H. Kelley
1959 *The Social Psychology of Groups*. New York: Wiley.

Tietze, Christopher
1973 "Two years' experience with a liberal abortion law: its impact on fertility trends in New York City." *Family Planning Perspectives* 5 (Winter):36–41.

1975 "The effect of legalization of abortion on population growth and public health." *Family Planning Perspectives* 7 (May/June):123–127.

Toby, Jackson
1966 "Violence and the masculine ideal: some qualitative data." Pp. 20–27 in Marvin Wolfgang (ed.), *Patterns of Violence: The Annals of the American Academy of Political and Social Science* 364 (March).

Tomasson, R. F.
1970 *Sweden: Prototype of Modern Society.* New York: Random House.

Troll, Lillian
1971 "The family of later life: a decade review." *Journal of Marriage and the Family* 33 (May):263–290.

Turk, J. L. and N. W. Bell
1972 "Measuring power in families." *Journal of Marriage and the Family* 34:215–223.

Turner, Ralph H.
1970 *Family Interaction.* New York: Wiley.

Tyler, Alice Felt
1944 *Freedom's Ferment.* New York: Harper Torchbooks, 1962.

U.S. Bureau of the Census
1972 *Census of Population, 1970: Marital Status.* Final Report PC(2)-4C.
1973 *Census of Population, 1970: Age at First Marriage.* Final Report PC(2)-4D.
1971 *Current Population Reports*, Series P-20, No. 223, October.
1972 *Current Population Reports*, Series P-20, No. 239, September.
1972 *Current Population Reports*, Series P-20, No. 240, September.
1974 *Current Population Reports*, Series P-20, No. 263, April.
1974 *Current Population Reports*, Series P-20, No. 265, June.
1974 *Current Population Reports*, Series P-20, No. 266, July.
1974 *Current Population Reports*, Series P-20, No. 267, July.
1974 *Current Population Reports*, Series P-20, No. 269, September.
1974 *Current Population Reports*, Series P-20, No. 271, March.
1971 *Current Population Reports*, Series P-23, No. 36, April.
1972 *Current Population Reports*, Series P-23, No. 42, July.
1973 *Current Population Reports*, Series P-23, No. 43, February.
1973 *Current Population Reports*, Series P-23, No. 44, March.
1973 *Current Population Reports*, Series P-23, No. 46, July.
1974 *Current Population Reports*, Series P-23, No. 48, July.
1974 *Current Population Reports*, Series P-23, No. 49, May.
1974 *Current Population Reports*, Series P-23, No. 50, July.
1975 *Current Population Reports*, Series P-23, No. 51, April.
1969 *Current Population Reports*, Series P-60, No. 64, October.
1970 *Current Population Reports*, Series P-60, No. 75, December.
1972 *Current Population Reports*, Series P-60, No. 86, December.
1973 *We the American Elderly.* June.
1973 *We the American Women.* March.

U.S. Department of Health, Education and Welfare
1970 *Monthly Vital Statistics Report*, Vol. 18, No. 12, March 27.
1974 *Monthly Vital Statistics Report*, Vol. 22, No. 13, June 27. "Annual Summary for the United States, 1973: Births, Deaths, Marriages, and Divorces."
1975 *Monthly Vital Statistics Report*, Vol. 23, No. 11, January 28.
1975 *Monthly Vital Statistics Report*, Vol. 23, No. 12, February 28.
1975 *Monthly Vital Statistics Report*, Vol. 24, No. 3, May 27.
1975 *Monthly Vital Statistics Report*, Vol. 24, No. 4, July 7.
1971 National Center for Health Statistics Series 21, No. 21, September. *Marriages: Trends and Characteristics.*
1973 National Center for Health Statistics Series 21, No. 22, April. *Divorces: Analysis of Change, United States, 1969.*
1973 National Center for Health Statistics Series 21, No. 23, August. *Teenagers: Marriages, and Divorces, Parenthood, and Mortality.*
1973 National Center for Health Statistics, Series 21, No. 24, December. *100 Years of Marriage and Divorce Statistics 1867–1967.*
1973 National Center for Health Statistics, Series 21, No. 25, December. *Remarriages: United States.*

U.S. Department of Labor
1970 *Dual Careers: A Longitudinal Study of the Labor Market Experience of Women*, Vol. 1. Manpower Research Monograph No. 21.
1973 *Dual Careers*, Vol. 2. Manpower Research Monograph No. 21
1973 *Manpower Report of the President.*

Varni, Charles A.
1973 "Contexts of conversion: the case of swinging." Pp. 166–181 in Roger W. Libby and Robert N. Whitehurst (eds.), *Renovating Marriage.* Danville, Calif.: Consensus.

Veevers, J. E.
1972 "Factors in the incidence of childlessness in Canada: an analysis of census data." *Social Biology* 19:266–274.
1973a "Voluntarily childless wives: an exploratory study." *Sociology and Social Research* 57 (April):356–366.
1973b "The child-free alternative: rejection of the motherhood mystique." Pp. 183–199 in Maryles Stephenson (ed.), *Women in Canada.* Toronto: New Press.
1974 "The life style of voluntarily childless couples." In Lyle Larson (ed.), *The Canadian Family in Comparative Perspective.* Toronto: Prentice-Hall.

Vogel, Ezra F.
1963 *Japan's New Middle Class.* Berkeley: University of California Press.

Waller, Willard
1930 *The Old Love and the New.* Reprint edition. Carbondale: Southern Illinois University Press, 1967.
1932 *The Sociology of Teaching.* New York: Russell and Russell.
1951 *The Family.* Revised by Reuben Hill. New York: Dryden Press. (Original edition published in 1938.)

Wallin, Paul

1949 "An appraisal of some methodological aspects of the Kinsey report." *American Sociological Review* 14:197–210.

Walshok, Mary Lindenstein
1969 "The social correlates and sexual consequences of variations in gender role orientation: a national study of college students." Unpublished Ph.D. dissertation, Indiana University, Bloomington.
1971 "The emergence of middle-class deviant subcultures: the case of swingers." *Social Problems* 18:488–495.
1973 "Sex role typing and feminine sexuality." Paper presented at the annual meetings of the American Sociological Association, New York, August 30.

Washington, Joseph R.
1970 *Marriage in Black and White*. Boston: Beacon.

Weinberg, George
1972 *Society and the Healthy Homosexual*. New York: St. Martin's. Doubleday Anchor Press edition, 1973.

Weinberg, Martin and Colin Williams
1974 *Male Homosexuals*. New York: Oxford.

Weitzman, Lenore
1974 "Legal regulation of marriage: tradition and change." *California Law Review* 62 (July–September):1169–1288.

Weitzman, L. J., D. Eifler, E. Hokada, and C. Ross
1972 "Sex-role socialization in picture books for preschool children." *American Journal of Sociology* 77:1125–1150.

Welter, Barbara
1966 "The cult of true womanhood: 1820–1860." *American Quarterly* 18:151–174.

West, Donald
1968 *Homosexuality*. Harmondsworth: Penguin.

Westoff, Charles F.
1972 "The modernization of U.S. contraceptive practice." *Family Planning Perspectives* 4 (July):9–12.
1974a "Coital frequency and contraception." *Family Planning Perspectives* 6 (Summer):136–141.
1974b "The populations of the developed countries." *Scientific American* 231 (September):109–120.

Westoff, Charles F. and others
1973 *Toward the End of Growth: Population in America*. Englewood Cliffs, N.J.: Prentice-Hall.

Westoff, C. F., R. G. Potter, and P. C. Sagi
1963 *The Third Child*. Princeton, N.J.: Princeton University Press.

Westoff, Charles F. and R. H. Potvin
1967 *College Women and Fertility Values*. Princeton, N.J.: Princeton University Press.

Westoff, Leslie Aldridge and Charles F. Westoff
1971 *From Now to Zero: Fertility, Contraception, and Abortion in America*. Boston: Little, Brown.

Whelpton, P. K., A. A. Campbell, and J. E. Patterson
1966 *Fertility and Family Planning in the United States*. Princeton, N.J.: Princeton University Press.

White, Mervin and Carolyn Wells
1973 "Student attitudes toward alternate marriage forms." Pp. 280–295 in Roger Libby and Robert Whitehurst (eds.), *Renovating Marriage*. Danville, Calif.: Consensus Publishers.

White, Ralph
1966 "Misperception as a cause of two world wars." *Journal of Social Issues* 22:1–19.

Whitehurst, Robert
1969a "The unmalias on campus." Paper presented at the National Council of Family Relations Annual Meetings.
1969b "The double standard and male dominance in non-marital living arrangements: a preliminary statement." Paper presented at the meetings of the American Orthopsychiatric Association, New York.
1974 "Violence in husband-wife interaction." Pp. 75–82 in Steinmetz and Straus, 1974.

Williamson, Robert C.
1970 "Role themes in Latin America." Pp. 177–199 in Seward and Williamson, 1970.

Winch, Robert
1962 *Identification and Its Familial Determinants*. Indianapolis: Bobbs-Merrill.

Winch, Robert and Margaret Gordon
1974 *Familial Structure and Function as Influence*. Lexington, Mass.: D. C. Heath, Lexington Books.

Winick, Charles
1968 *The New People: Desexualization in American Life*. New York: Pegasus.

Winter, David
1973 *The Power Motive*. New York: Free Press.

Wirth, Louis
1938 "Urbanism as a way of life." *American Journal of Sociology* 44:1–24.

Wise, Daniel
1859 *The Young Lady's Counselor*. Cincinnati: Swormstedt & Poe.

Wollstonecraft, Mary
1792 *A Vindication of the Rights of Woman*. Reprint edition, edited by Charles W. Hagelman, Jr. New York: Norton, 1967.

Worthy, Morgan, Albert Gary, and Gay Kahn
1969 "Self-disclosure as an exchange process." *Journal of Personality and Social Psychology* 13:59–63.

Wu, Tson-Shien
1972 "The value of children or boy preference?" In Fawcett, 1972.

Yankelovich, Daniel
1974 "The meaning of work." Pp. 19–48 in J. M. Rosow (ed.), *The Worker and the Job*. Englewood Cliffs, N.J.: Prentice-Hall.

Yette, Samuel
1971 *Newsweek* Feature Service, June 27.

Yoder, John Howard
1974 "Singleness in ethical and pastoral perspective." Mimeographed. Elkhart, Ind.: Associated Mennonite Biblical Seminaries.

Zablocki, Benjamin
1971 *The Joyful Community*. Baltimore: Penguin.

Zetkin, Clara
1934 *Lenin on the Woman Question*. New York: International.